Essential Sermons

Augustinian Heritage Institute

THE WORKS OF SAINT AUGUSTINE
A Translation for the 21st Century

Part III - Homilies

Essential Sermons

THE WORKS OF SAINT AUGUSTINE

A Translation for the 21st Century

Essential Sermons

introduction and notes by

Daniel E. Doyle, O.S.A.

translation by

Edmund Hill, O.P.

editor

Boniface Ramsey

New City Press

Hyde Park, New York

optimae Lorettae Matri dulcissimae
Loretta Ann Callahan
(1926–2007)

Published in the United States by New City Press
202 Comforter Blvd., Hyde Park, New York 12538
www.newcitypress.com
©2007 Augustinian Heritage Institute, Inc. All rights reserved.

Cover design by Leandro De Leon

Library of Congress Cataloging-in-Publication Data:

Augustine, Saint, Bishop of Hippo.
  [Sermons. English. Selections]
  Essential sermons / Daniel Doyle, editor ; Edmund Hill, translator.
      p. cm. — (The works of Saint Augustine)
  Includes bibliographical references and index.
    ISBN 978-1-56548-276-0 (pbk. : alk. paper) 1. Sermons, Latin—Translations into
English—Early works to 1800. 2. Sermons—Early works to 1800. 3. Catholic Church—
Sermons—Early works to 1800. I. Doyle, Daniel Edward, 1953- II. Hill, Edmund.
III. Title.
BR65.A84E5 2007
252'.014—dc22   2007031830

5th printing: December 2018

Printed in the United States of America

Contents

Foreword

The publication of *The Works of St. Augustine, A Translation for the 21ˢᵗ Century,* sponsored by the Augustinian Heritage Institute, founded by the late Fr. John E. Rotelle, O.S.A., has finally placed into the hands of scholars fresh contemporary translations formerly available only in Latin, the lack of which impeded many from consulting the theological depth and breadth of the brilliant Doctor of Grace. Much English-language scholarship in the past fifty years had focused on the works which were more accessible due to modern-language translations, particularly English and French. Scholars with heavy teaching loads, as well as aspiring scholars, often ignored the texts which were only available in Migne,[1] since the Latin can be daunting and requires much more time to comprehend. Because the corpus of the bishop of Hippo is so extensive, scholars often favored reading the classical texts of Augustine which were more readily available in translations, such as *Free Will, The Confessions, The City of God,* and *The Trinity.* Yet Augustine's full range of ideas and theological insights is best gleaned from his occasional works as a priest and bishop with pressing pastoral responsibilities, namely his letters and sermons. The letters have been widely available for some time in the *Fathers of the Church* series, while the sermons were only available prior to the 1990s in a one- volume work that focused on the bishop's preaching on the more important liturgical feasts such as Christmas and Easter.

The Sermons of St. Augustine (*Sermones ad populum*) have been skillfully captured in fresh and contemporary English with insightful and lively commentary by the capable Dominican, Fr. Edmund Hill, whose first volume appeared in 1990 in the *Works of St. Augustine* series. The sermons in their entirety fill eleven volumes, and they include the Dolbeau Sermons discovered in 1989, a collection of thirty sermons that includes twenty-one that were completely unknown thitherto.[2] The volumes have received considerable praise from scholars with the occasional comment that Fr. Hill sometimes lapses into colloquial phrases that sound a bit odd in contemporary American English[3] or engages in rather long commentary in his notes, where he displays his own theological preferences and convictions. I for one appreciate the spontaneity of his comments and find that they put life into theological questions that otherwise appear rather sterile and irrelevant.

This one-volume anthology was born from a direct request of colleagues[4] in the field who teach Augustine or other courses on early Christian writers and who lament the difficulty of using the sermons on their required reading lists because of the

---

1. J.-P. Migne, *Patrologiae cursus completus, Series Latina* (Paris, 1844-1864).
2. This translation is also available electronically in English for those who have access to "Past Masters," a data base accessible to several university libraries possessing licenses, such as Villanova University.
3. A sampling of awkward sounding phrases in contemporary "American English" might include: "It's plain as a pikestaff" found in S. S. 117, 6, 213 and 137, 9, 378, *Sermons, WSA* III/4. Other examples include S. 164, 34 *WSA* III/5, 195: *in hac angustia* is translated "in this cleft stick" instead of the more familiar "in this tight spot"; S. 302, 2 where *exultans* and *exultatione* are translated as "cock-a-hoop."
4. I should mention Lewis Ayers, Patout Burns, Michael Cameron, David Hunter, Thomas Martin and Jane Merdinger among the many. I owe a particular debt of gratitude to William Harmless and Maureen Tilley for a careful reading of the manuscript in its earliest form. I attempted to incorporate their earnest criticism and suggestions in the final edition without jettisoning my own sense of what was needed in this one-volume anthology.

expense involved in purchasing all eleven volumes. It is envisioned as a handbook for those who cannot afford the entire series, altough it cannot replace the eleven-volume edition. I have been teaching a course on the theology of St. Augustine for ten years and have found the inclusion of several samples of the sermons invaluable in capturing Augustine's theology at its best. I believe that many of the gross simplifications of his theology and his subsequent vilification would be unsustainable if more scholars had access to his sermons and letters. Furthermore, given the frequent complaints about the current banal level of preaching today, which settles for generalities, platitudes and political correctness by dumbing down serious theological and ethical questions, Augustine might serve as a model for contemporary preachers who are charged with the awesome task of explaining and applying the words of Sacred Scripture. It is my sincere hope that direct contact with the best of Augustine's preaching will lead ministers of the Word to a more enlivened and theologically robust style of preaching.

Augustine's preaching has come down to us in various collections, including the *Expositions of the Psalms (Enarrationes in Psalmos), Homilies (Tractatus) on the Gospel of John and Homilies (Tractatus) on the first Letter of John* and the *Sermons (Sermones ad populum)*. Since so many of Augustine's sermons are worthy of inclusion, it was necessary to limit this anthology to the *Sermones ad populum*. Furthermore, a decision had to be made as to whether or not the scholarly notes should be included. That would have significantly reduced the number of homilies that could be put in a single volume. After consultation with a committee composed of Joseph Kelly, Thomas Martin and Jane Merdinger, it was decided that we would direct the reader to the eleven-volume edition for the critical notes. The process of choosing the sermons was ultimately a judgment call. I read through all of them several times and presented a list to the same committee for further consideration. I wanted to make sure that the list showcased Augustine's genius as a preacher and I wanted to include the wide range of important theological concerns that he addressed on a regular basis: his doctrine of God, his Christology, his understanding of grace, sin, freedom and the will as well as his approach to married life, wealth, poverty, justice and the Christian life with all of its ethical demands. A concerted effort was made to include samples of his preaching on Mary, the martyrs and the most important liturgical occasions. In the final analysis, because of pagination requirements, the list had to be filtered to make a one-volume affordable edition available to students of Augustine today. This also required a rewriting of Cardinal Pellegrino's impressive introduction, which was composed for the first volume of the Italian-language edition of the sermons prepared in 1979. The scholarship is impeccable but dated, and space requirements dictated a summary overview of the general consensus of scholarship on the more important aspects of his preaching.

Augustine is numbered among the most outstanding theologians of the western Church not only because of his intellectual genius but especially on account of his deep insight and clarity of expression in responding to the most pressing human questions encountered in every generation. His preaching showcases his passion, originality and conviction that hearing the Word and following its example in Christ by the grace of the Holy Spirit is the surest way to eternal life with God.

Introduction to Augustine's Preaching

Why Augustine?

In North America and Europe today you will find preachers not infrequently preaching in half-empty churches. Who are the successful preachers? What do they do differently? The best gauge may well be to look at the faces of those sitting in the congregation. Are they actively engaged, as signaled by a variety of cues such as listening intently, nodding in agreement from time to time? Or do they have blank expressions that betray a preoccupation with something else? We need to transport ourselves back into Roman Africa in the early fifth century and imagine what would draw crowds to a lengthy church service, for instance, in the blistering heat of summer. There may have been cool air inside Hippo's impressive Basilica of Peace but there were no pews on which to sit comfortably and drift off to sleep from time to time if the readings or homily became monotonous. No doubt, then as now, people attended church for a variety of reasons: to seek strength from God, to give thanks and praise, to pray for loved ones who were hurting, to break the monotony of day-to-day living, to connect with neighbors, to be uplifted by the beauty of the liturgy and, perhaps most importantly, to find meaning, purpose and hope amidst life's challenges. The first part of the liturgy was open to all: the baptized, catechumens, the curious and those searching for answers to life's problems. The men and the women stood in different sections. The catechumens, the penitents, the widows, the virgins each stood in their respective section. Here the pressure was on the preacher to connect with his people and engage their interest. He had to compete with other forms of entertainment that could easily lure the crowds away from church and to the games.

North African congregations in late antiquity were known for the lively interruption of spontaneous applause, comment and exclamation that is still characteristic of many African-American congregations or churches in the evangelical or charismatic tradition. Perhaps many today by comparison look fidgety and restless as they squirm in their pew, anxious to move on. Catholic congregations in the United States love to time sermons and are usually quick to complain if the preacher has exceeded an 8-10 minute maximum. This in turn pressures priests to keep it short and sweet lest they acquire a reputation for being long-winded and pedantic.

Walk into a cathedral church today and you will generally find a larger space and a more formalized style of preaching, with the bishop robed in grandeur and sometimes wearing his miter. The temptation when thinking about Augustine is to impose this medieval and modern image on early fifth-century North Africa. Augustine wore no such vestments despite the fact that art work usually depicts him so arrayed. The congregation remained standing while the bishop preached sitting on his chair (*cathedra*) as a sign of his authority as a teacher. Why were people willing to listen patiently through a homily that lasted between thirty minutes and one hour and in some cases even longer? Why is there little patience today in most Catholic churches in the United States for a sermon that goes beyond ten minutes? Much of the problem associated with the decline in church attendance is partially attributed in various surveys to the poor quality and increasing irrelevance of preaching. It is quite

possible that contemporary Christian preachers have much to learn from Bishop
Augustine, who was deeply involved in pastoral activity throughout his almost forty
years of ordained ministry yet possessed the intellectual depth and rhetorical skills to
reflect on the Word as an indispensable source of wisdom in the human quest for
meaning.

The subject of Augustine's preaching and style of biblical interpretation is
a vast topic and the most important aspects were capably addressed by Cardinal
Pellegrino, who wrote the original introduction that is translated in the first volume of
the eleven-volume series[1] and that was originally published in the Città Nuova
Italian edition in 1979. Readers should consult this comprehensive and erudite
treatment, but rather than duplicate Pellegrino's introduction I shall concentrate on
information which should prove useful for students and readers who have less
specialized interests but nevertheless require some orientation regarding the more
salient aspects of Augustine's preaching. His sermons, of which we possess perhaps
ten percent of all that he preached, have come down to us in history in various
collections that appear under a variety of names — *commentaries, treatises, homilies* and *sermons*. The terms have slightly different connotations depending on
whether they were intended to be preached, were actually preached or were
intended as commentaries to assist preachers. "Sermon" became the preferred term
during the fourth century but Augustine was capable of using the words "sermons,"
"homilies" and even "treatises" at times interchangeably. The modern distinction
that a homily is based primarily on the scriptural texts, whereas a sermon is a
discourse on a particular theme not found in the day's biblical readings, does not
apply to Augustine's time. All of Augustine's homilies are thoroughly based on
scripture and on liturgical texts, including several instances where he reflects on the
meaning of the preface dialogue which introduces the great Eucharistic Prayer:
"The Lord be with you. Lift up your hearts!" We shall confine ourselves in this
anthology to the 559 *Sermons to the People* that contemporary scholarship identifies as authentic.[2]

The Heritage of Augustine's Sermons

Why were Augustine's sermons preserved? How did they come down to us over
1600 years? Augustine generally did not write out his sermons in advance. Rather,
according to his first biographer Possidius, he relied on a group of capable stenogra-
phers, some of whom evidently were recruited from his own monastic community.
We must remember that these homilies were never intended to be read but rather to
be heard. Thus we encounter the bishop thinking out loud, using all of his creativity
as a virtuoso performer to communicate persuasively the power of the Word of God
to change hearts and behavior. The sermons have an improvisational and spontaneous character which is unmistakable from the way Augustine cites scriptural texts

1. For the English translation, see Cardinal Michele Pellegrino, "Introduction" in The Works of Saint
   Augustine: Sermons I (New York: New City Press, 1990) 13-137.
2. See Hubertus Drobner, *Augustinus von Hippo : Sermones ad Populum* (Leiden-Boston: Brill, 2000)
   3. An excellent overview of the sermons containing a convenient table is found in Éric Rebillard's
   article, "Sermones" in *Augustine through the Ages*, editor Allan Fitzgerald (Grand Rapids, MI, 1999)
   773-793.

using various wordings, sometimes conflating multiple texts from many parts of the Bible. Unfortunately much of the vitality is lost on the written page, where we miss his intonation, his cadence and his gesture. Augustine is quick to improvise and depart from what he had prepared if he has received a sudden inspiration while listening to the scripture being read in the liturgical assembly. One would err in mistaking this for unpreparedness. His careful use of scriptural texts and the logical development of his arguments indicate otherwise. One of Augustine's earliest preserved letters was written to his bishop, Valerius, shortly after his ordination as a presbyter, requesting time off to study the Bible to prepare for his new task of preaching. He feared taking on the awesome responsibility of charting a course for a boat that he was not fit to row.[3]

The student interested in more detail should consult the impressive work of Verbraken, who dedicated his scholarly life to studying the sermons.[4] Evidently Augustine published various sermons but never formed any collections. Unlike most of the bishop's other works, he never found the time to review them properly, as indicated in *The Revisions* (2, 26, 23), published toward the end of his life, and we have no way of knowing which ones he might have revised. The sermons were evidently saved because they were recognized as a precious treasure of this uniquely talented preacher. It is likely that collections of his sermons were produced by persons who visited the episcopal library in Hippo to consult them prior to the Vandal invasion. Such collections undoubtedly reached Italy and southern Gaul as the Christian faithful fled the Vandal persecution in Africa. They were organized according to themes, chronology or subject matter that related to the gradual development of the liturgical year (Christmas, Easter, feasts of prominent martyrs). All of these sermons were eventually gathered together in the thirteenth and fourteenth centuries. The invention of the printing press made possible the further organization and dissemination of these texts, beginning with a first collection of fifty sermons at Cologne in 1470.

Summary of Manuscript History

The most important milestone in preserving Augustine's sermons was undoubtedly the collection of Augustinian texts undertaken by the congregation of Benedictine monks known as the Maurists, who lived in many different monasteries in France. The most famous can still be seen in the heart of the Latin Quarter in Paris, an architectural gem known today as St. Germain-des-Prés. Why was such meticulous care taken to copy Augustine's sermons faithfully over the centuries? More than likely they were used for spiritual reading (*lectio divina*) and especially as a homiletical resource by less talented preachers as a substitute for composing their own sermons. Augustine himself recommends in *Teaching Christianity* that a less talented preacher should read the prepared homilies of those more gifted rather than

---

3. *Letter* 21, 1.
4. P.P. Verbraken, *Études critiques sur les Sermons authentiques de Saint Augustin*=Instrumenta Patristica 12 (Steenbrugge-The Hague, 1976) 17 ff.

confuse or bore his listeners.[5] Sometimes the homilies were touched up or amended to make them sound more orthodox, pious or grammatically correct. Thus resulted a proliferation of fragmented and spurious texts attributed to the bishop which later proved to be inauthentic. The Maurists began an enterprise in 1679, which lasted until 1700, of establishing "critical editions," according to the day's standards, of the most important writings of the Fathers, which were later published in a series known as *Patrologiae cursus completus, Series graeca et latina* (Paris 1841-66). Volume 5 of the Maurist edition (1683) contains 394 of Augustine's sermons/homilies, of which 363 were declared authentic beyond any doubt, leaving 31 of questionable or doubtful authenticity.

Discovery of "New" Sermons

New sermons have been discovered since the Maurists' groundbreaking work and are identified by various manuscript names, including entire sermons that were formerly available only in fragments. This can create massive confusion for the novice, since the same sermon sometimes comes down to us under different names. The work of identifying a given manuscript as genuinely belonging to Augustine is no easy task and demands a combination of highly skilled philological training and familiarity with the entire corpus of Augustine's writing. The task is somewhat akin to the detective work of an art historian who must identify a painting as the work of a particular artist or of someone in his school. Sometimes this provokes great discussion over a period of decades before a final consensus is reached. Given Augustine's prolific writing and preaching over nearly a half-century, few scholars have the time to dedicate their entire lives to mastering this impressive collection. Isidore of Seville (ca. 560-636) said that anyone who had claimed to have read all of the works of the doctor of grace was surely a liar! Yet intimate, detailed knowledge of the bishop's writing style and intellectual concerns is necessary before a judgment of authenticity can be reached.

To the Maurists' original attribution of roughly 396 authentic sermons to Augustine we can now confidently add another 175 sermons or fragments of sermons that scholars have identified as genuinely Augustinian. The most recent exciting discovery of sermons was made by François Dolbeau in 1990, who luckily came across 26 long-lost sermons from a 15th century Carthusian manuscript now preserved at a library in Mainz.[6] This great find motivated scholars to reassess the importance of the bishop's preaching in order to understand more fully the development of his thought. The reader who is interested in a highly condensed summary of the most important manuscript findings over the centuries up to the present is directed to the Appendix of this volume.

---

5. See *Teaching Christianity* IV, 62.
6. See François Dolbeau, *Vingt-six sermons au peuple d'Afrique* (Paris: Instituts d'Études augustiniennes, 1996) and the important collection of essays on the significance of the Dolbeau discovery in *Augustin prédicateur* (395-411). Actes du Colloque International de Chantilly (5-7 septembre 1966), édités par Goulven Madec (Paris: Études Augustiniennes, 1998). A convenient summary of the most important findings of this discovery is found in Henry Chadwick, "The New Sermons of St. Augustine," *Journal of Theological Studies* 47 (1996) 69-91.

Augustine's Preaching

Augustine's preaching is profoundly Christocentric. He reflects again and again on the central importance of the Word made flesh, citing John's Prologue more often than any other biblical text (over 1000 times in his surviving works).[7] In fact, "of all the Fathers of the Church Augustine is undoubtedly the one who speaks most often and most extensively of Christ in his sermons."[8] He frequently makes reference to Christ the physician (*Christus medicus*) and exhorts all Christians to follow the self-emptying humility inspired by the Christological hymns of Phil 2:6-11.

Preaching was normally the responsibility of the bishop rather than of priests or deacons. Augustine is insistent that the bishop preaches with the authority of Christ: "They aren't my sermons, anyway; I only speak at the Lord's command."[9]

We only possess a fraction of Augustine's homilies. Presently scholars accept a total of 559 authentic sermons attributed to the bishop of Hippo, including the various subdivisions referred to above.[10] Calculating that Augustine assumed the responsibilities of preaching shortly after his ordination to the priesthood in 391, we can conservatively estimate around 4,000 homilies delivered over a period of almost forty years, based on weekly Saturday and Sunday liturgies. To this must be added, of course, the daily liturgies of Lent and Eastertime, not to mention sermons in honor of the saints and martyrs. Verbraken estimates a total of nearly 8,000 sermons preached.[11] The true figure is probably somewhere in between. Drobner believes we possess 7-14% of the total number.[12] Augustine was generally a "long-winded" preacher whose lengthy sermons would more than likely tax the patience of a contemporary Christian. It should be remembered that in antiquity the bishop preached seated while the congregation remained standing! Scholars have estimated that the average length of his sermons ranged from a half-hour to as long as two hours in some instances. Nevertheless, the bishop seemed to learn through years of experience that congregations preferred briefer homilies, and the length of his sermons generally shortened as he became seasoned in his pastoral experience.

In an age accustomed to sound bytes and quick moving stories with action shots in order to hold the attention of a generation raised on MTV and videogames, we may wonder at the patience of congregations in antiquity who could endure such lengthy speeches. Politicians today have long since adapted their discourse to

---

7. I am indebted to William Harmless for this fact.
8. M. F. Berrouard, "St. Augustine et le ministère de la prèdication. Le thème des anges qui montent et qui descendent, " *Recherche augustiniennes* 2 (1962), 488 as cited in Pellegrino's introduction, *Sermons* III, 1, 60, n. 34.
9. S. 82, 15.
10. See Eligius Dekkers / Aemilius Gaar, *Clavis Patrum Latinorum*, Turnholt-Steenbrugge: In Abbatia Sancti Petri³ 1995, 110-122, as cited by Hubertus Drobner in an unpublished paper delivered at the North American Patristic Society meeting in May 2007.
11. See Pierre-Patrick Verbraken, "Saint Augustine Sermons: Why and How to Read Them Today?" *Augustinian Heritage* 33 (1987) 105-116 ["Les Sermons de saint Augustin. Pourquoi et comment les lire aujourd'hui?"]: Lettre de Maredsous 15 (1986) 130-139. Also see the excellent work of Hubertus R. Drobner, who more than any contemporary scholar has called into question the presumed dating on sermons that scholars too facilely use to draw conclusions: *Augustinus von Hippo: Sermones ad Populum, Überlieferung und Bestand, Bibliographie — Indices* (Leiden-Boston-Köln: Brill, 2000). A convenient summary of his findings can be found in English translation in three different articles entitled "The Chronology of St. Augustine's *Sermones ad populum*" published in *Augustinian Studies* 31:2 (2000) 211-218, 34:1 (2003) 49-66 and 35:1 (2004) 43-53.
12. Drobner, "Chronology of Augustine's Sermons II," *Augustinian Studies* 34 (2003) 55.

accommodate the quick TV spot, thereby increasing the likelihood of inclusion on TV news. But it must be remembered first of all that homilies are not "speeches" in the strict sense, since they imply a dialogue between preacher and people made possible by the Holy Spirit. The hearer's attentive listening and active engagement are essential ingredients in the process. Secondly, people in antiquity were raised in an oral culture that took delight in the virtuoso deliveries of talented performers. The stirring rhetoric of Bishop Ambrose drew Augustine, who was then the imperial orator, into the cathedral in Milan from time to time to observe a master orator in the hope of improving his own technique. This became the watershed event that unlocked for him the obstacles that had prevented him from taking scripture seriously. Bishops had to compete with alternative forms of entertainment that regularly drew crowds looking for excitement and diversion, in particular the games and performances in the stadium. People could listen for hours and take delight in the performances of talented orators. Make no doubt about it, Augustine was a virtuoso performer!

The Burden of Preaching

Augustine considered his preaching ministry as a "debt" he owed the people and as the primary responsibility of a bishop. He often spoke about it as breaking open the Word of God. He experienced the duty of preaching as a serious burden, which he emphasized repeatedly on the anniversaries of his ordination as bishop.[13] On one occasion he shares his trepidation at such an awesome responsibility: "How much safer a place you are standing in by listening than I am by preaching." He began his preaching career as a presbyter at the request of his bishop, Valerius, which was a considerable innovation in Roman Africa when the bishop was presiding. Augustine later continued this practice by delegating some of his own priests to preach in his absence and at times even when he was present, as attested by the two sermons preached by Eraclius, designated as his successor.

Augustine preached primarily at his home basilica in Hippo but often enough in Carthage or as a visitor elsewhere. Pellegrino numbered 146 sermons preached at Hippo and 109 in Carthage before the discovery of the Dolbeau sermons. Dozens of homilies were preached elsewhere.[14] There were usually three readings at Sunday Mass: an Old Testament reading, a New Testament reading generally from Paul (except during Easter time, when Acts was read), and a gospel reading. Augustine rarely attempts to comment on all three readings but he frequently makes reference to the responsorial psalm, which was sung, and weaves a verse or two from it into his homily.[15] On ordinary days, the celebrant selected the readings.[16] Augustine sometimes chose to work through a single book of scripture. There was no fixed lectionary for Sundays, although the readings appear fixed during Holy Week and the Octave of Easter and on important feast days.

---

13. S. 153, 1; S. 339-340A.
14. See O. Perler, *Les voyages de Saint Augustin, Recherches augustiniennes* I (Paris: 1958/1969).
15. S. 23, 5.
16. See G. G. Willis, *St. Augustine's Lectionary* =Alcuin Club Collections 44 (London: SPCK, 1962.)

Augustine usually began his homily with a specific reference to the readings just proclaimed,[17] and he frequently exhorts the assembly to pray briefly for his inspiration.[18] Sermon 49 indicates that the bishop was expected to talk about the gospel at some point in his homily.[19] Augustine generally refrained from citing long passages but rather recalled brief passages as a point of departure for a theme he wished to develop. He tended to conclude the homily with an invitation, "Let us turn toward the Lord" (*Conversi ad dominum*), which may well have been accompanied by a ritual gesture of bishop and people turning together in one direction, most probably toward the East. Evidently the bishop preached from a raised platform, since he makes frequent reference to the "highness of the place" (*de superiore*) from which he spoke.[20] He normally preached seated in his *cathedra* while the assembly remained standing.

It is clear that Augustine never read his homilies from a prepared text. That is not to imply that his sermons were merely spontaneous improvisations. To the contrary, in S. 225, 3 he makes a specific reference to his careful preparation: "Before I came to you here, I gave some thought beforehand to what I am going to say to you." The most important preparation is prayer for himself and his listeners rather than devoting hours to elaborate rhetorical phrasing.[21] Augustine was fully capable of accommodating a text read mistakenly by the lector (usually a young boy) as indicated in S. 353: "You see, it wasn't I who instructed the lector to sing this psalm; but it was the one up there [God or the Holy Spirit] who decided what it would be valuable for you to hear." This proves that Augustine took preparation seriously but was flexible enough to improvise when necessary. His sermons are loaded with evidence of spontaneity and improvisation, most especially the conversational tone and the irregularities of the syntax.

Scriptural Content and Biblical Interpretation

Pellegrino's introduction to the *Sermons* provides a large number of specific references to Augustine's direct citation of the scriptural text.[22] Augustine's preaching can be described as a veritable medley of scriptural citations woven effortlessly throughout his homilies with the frequent and near seamless insertion of psalm verses. In S. 339, 7, preached on the occasion of his anniversary as a bishop, he says: "This sermon I am now preaching comes from Holy Scripture." Similarly, he continues shortly thereafter (8): "Listen to Holy Scripture preaching." Oftentimes he uses the phrase, "Pay attention to the gospel," or "Listen to Paul," or "Listen to the apostle." Augustine stays quite close to the biblical text and usually begins with the literal meaning unless it is untenable because it contradicts either more certain parts of scripture or well-established knowledge. He is well aware that some readings are difficult, obscure and potentially dangerous if wrongly interpreted. This should not be surprising since the

---

17. See S. 48, 66, 174, 233.
18. See. Ep. 29 and S. 153, 1.
19. S. 49, 1.
20. S. 23, 1.
21. *Teaching Christianity* IV, 15, 32.
22. See Pellegrino, Introduction, 28-32.

subject of scripture is God. If we readily understood he would cease to be God. The mystery of God and the difficulty of correct interpretation should motivate us to greater study and instill in us deeper humility. In the final analysis, faith is essential to understand scripture correctly. Augustine loved to cite the Septuagint translation of Isaiah 7:9: "If you do not believe you will not understand." An excellent summary of his biblical hermeneutic is found in *Teaching Christianity*, which was composed in two distinct stages and which took close to thirty years to complete. The second and third books of this four-part work treat the subject of biblical interpretation, emphasizing the application of appropriate factual information and the clarification of more difficult and obscure passages through the correct use of allegory to attain a correct doctrinal interpretation. Only when a literal meaning is not plausible does the bishop search for a more symbolic, figurative meaning. Augustine learned this technique first and foremost from St. Ambrose, who unlocked for him the final door to accepting scripture as the authoritative Word of God. An excellent example of an entire homily based on allegorical interpretation is found in S. 149. Another simple example is seen in S. 205, 1, where Augustine comments on Psalm 119:120 (*Let my flesh be transfixed with nails by fear of you*): "Flesh means the lusts of the flesh; the nails are the commandments of justice." S. 346A, 5 provides a clear example of typology, where the camel passing only with difficulty through the eye of a needle, as cited in Luke, is interpreted as a type of Christ. Yet objects that may sometimes have an allegorical meaning, such as mountains, stones and lions, do not always have it. The interpretation of a particular word or thing is not fixed but depends on the circumstances and the context. Thus a lion can sometimes refer to Christ and sometimes to the devil.

The bishop emphasizes the importance of mastering language, history, mathematics and science in order to fully exploit the meaning of a text. For example, in S. 205 he attempts to interpret the meaning of the forty days of Lent based on the science of his time: "This may be because, as several authorities assert, the human being destined to live this life takes shape in the womb in forty days."[23] Augustine will also emphasize the symbolic significance of numbers in a way that confounds the modern reader as the continuation of the previous citation indicates, where he offers another possible explanation for the number forty — "because the four gospels agree with the tenfold law, and four times ten makes up this number." Similarly, in S. 267, preached on Pentecost, Augustine reflects on why Acts 1:5 specifies a hundred and twenty souls: "This is what his disciples were waiting for, a hundred and twenty souls, as it is written, ten times the number of the apostles; I mean, he chose twelve, and sent the Spirit on a hundred and twenty."[24] Augustine's fascination with numbers will puzzle many contemporary readers. We should not be dismissive, however, as we seek to understand the bishop's appreciation of mathematics and numbers as a pure science intimately connected with truth itself.[25] Although numbers strike us as merely random, they must have some hidden signifi-

23. S. 205, 1.
24. S. 267, 1.
25. See John O'Keefe and Rusty Reno's *Sanctified Vision* for a fuller treatment of patristic hermeneutics. Augustine insists in *Teaching Christianity* that the preacher master all of the various disciplines

cance since they are found repeatedly throughout revelation. Indeed, the bishop's willingness to accept the legitimacy of the Donatist lay theologian Tyconius' seven rules for interpreting scripture (*Liber regularum*) further underscores his commitment to solid scripture interpretation based on the most exacting methods of his time.

Constant Engagement

Augustine's preaching is conversational in tone, with a dialogic repartee. He addresses the community with terms of endearment such as "brothers and sisters" (*fratres*), or "dearly beloved" (*carissimi* or *dilectissimi*) or some combination of the two (*fratres carissimi*.) He frequently poses questions, often addressing the congregation in the second person singular — *tu* or *es* — while other times employing the second person plural — *vos* or *estis*. Augustine constantly had to interrupt the congregation and demand their attention as they became bored or lost in their own thoughts, and he frequently uses the refrain: "Now pay attention to me!"[26] Similarly the bishop can detect his connection with the people when he is interrupted by applause, however much this embarrasses him.[27] He frequently solicits their prayer so that he may be up to the difficult task.[28] He follows up on promises he has made in previous sermons: "I remember what I promised last Sunday.... and the sermon went on so long that no time was left for me to discuss the other points. That's why today I promised that I would speak about justice."[29] He often poses an imaginary dialogue and takes both parts, the part of the interlocutor and that of the congregation, as if the assembly itself were responding to the question.[30] Augustine ocasionally engages in a dialogue with important biblical figures such as Peter, Paul, the apostles, John the Baptist, David, Stephen, the martyrs and others, allowing the congregation to eavesdrop on the conversation as he takes the part of both interlocutors. Similarly, he addresses imaginary persons such as "poor one," "rich one," "greedy one," "Donatist," "Pelagian," "heretic." This is vintage Augustine! As with most conversationalists, there is a spontaneity to Augustine's preaching that is fresh and given to frequent digression.

Augustine not infrequently employs sarcasm and humor to make a point, peppering his comments with witty remarks that would surely elicit bouts of laughter or wake up a sleepy congregation.[31] In one instance Augustine says rhetorically that even though he is the bishop preaching to the laity, he has no way of knowing whether or not there are future bishops sitting out in the congregation.[32] Elsewhere he questions the men as to why they appear to be ashamed to attend church, where widows and little old ladies go (S. 306B, 6). One example of his self-deprecating humor is found in the opening of S. 223A, where the bishop most

---

which might be of value in aiding Christians to understand and interpret the deep meaning of the scriptures.
26. See S. 51, 16, 17, 20; 62, 4; 72A, 2; 101, 2; 112, 6; 117, 6.
27. See S. 61, 13; 96, 4; 179, 6-7.
28. S. 149, 16.
29. S. 49, 1.
30. S. 256, 2.
31. S. 105, 2.
32. S. 101, 34.

assuredly succeeded in arousing the congregation's interest: "We have heard many inspired readings, and I don't have the stamina to give you a sermon to equal them in length, and you couldn't take it even if I did."[33] Certainly after the lengthy readings of the Easter Vigil the congregation's patience must have been tested to the limits! Similarly, the bishop's humor is clearly seen in S. 247, 3, where he reflects on the risen Christ's ability to pass through closed doors:

"How big was that bulk, I ask you? As big, of course, as it is in everyone.
Not as big, surely, as it is in a camel? Of course not as big as that."

Rhetorical Style

Augustine incorporates all of the rhetorical tools available to the Latin speaker in late antiquity that he had learned in his course of studies, which depended heavily on the work of Cicero, in particular *On Invention (De inventione.)* Much of this training focused on the art of discourse necessary to win legal battles or be persuasive in political life. His talent and skills were recognized by the great pagan orator Symmachus, who nominated him for the chair of public rhetoric at Milan. His mature thinking on rhetoric is found in *Teaching Christianity,* which he composed over a thirty-year period: the first part comprises Books I-III,25 written in the early months of 397, shortly after his ordination as bishop of Hippo, and the final section concludes with Book IV, completed in 426 or 428. In Augustine's view it is more important that a Christian orator speak wisely and truthfully than eloquently, a conviction that is often lost in present-day politics and marketing.[34] Augustine embodied the threefold requirement for public speaking that he learned from his classical training based on Cicero: *docere* (to teach), *delectare* (to delight), *flectere* (to persuade.)[35] Although Augustine preserves Cicero's ordering of these terms, the orator must first get the listener's attention, however possible, and maintain active interest (*delectare*) in order to teach (*docere*) important truths so that the listener will be persuaded (*flectere*) to follow and put into practice such teaching. Teaching, of course, is of paramount importance.

Augustine is inclined in his popular preaching to employ a very clear and straightforward discourse which is quite different from the elevated rhetorical style of Latin that is commonplace in his more intellectual works, such as *The Confessions, The City of God*, and *The Trinity*. He employs clever literary devices only to hold and keep people's interest, never forgetting that elaborate rhetoric is not an end in itself but a means to the end of teaching and persuasion. The preacher must not attempt to show off or take excessive delight in winning the accolades of the congregation. This desire for approval and popularity is an occupational hazard for a bishop and was such for Augustine throughout his life.[36] He generally avoids the stylistic ornamentation that is found in his classic writings, which are famous for Latin rhythmic clausulas. The presence of such in an allegedly authentic sermon of Augustine may well indicate the work is spurious. The bishop clearly adjusts his

33. S. 223A, 1.
34. *Teaching Christianity* IV, 5, 7.
35. *Teaching Christianity* IV, 12, 27.
36. See *Confessions* X, 36, 59; S. 179, 2.

rhetoric according to the education of his congregation, using a much more elaborate style, for example, when preaching to the more sophisticated crowds attending the liturgy in Carthage. He is willing to break all the grammatical rules and employ the simplest vocabulary when preaching to the more common folk of Hippo. There are myriad ways to gain the listener's attention and various styles or levels of discourse are appropriate to particular topics, depending on the gravity of the subject matter.[37] Augustine favors clarity, simplicity and humility in preaching (*Teaching Christianity* IV, 23) in order that he be properly understood. Grammatical correctness and fancy ornamentation are secondary to clear communication (ibid. IV, 24). Christ's incarnation is a fitting theological justification for this humility. Nevertheless, the bishop recommends a variety of styles in order to maintain the congregation's interest: the plain or simple style, the intermediate style and the grand style. The three styles should be intermingled to keep the listeners engaged (ibid. IV, 51). The art of rhetoric and the memorization of rules are best learned when a person is young; preachers should concentrate rather on prayerful study of scripture. In the final analysis, the witness of the preacher's own lifestyle is much more important than the eloquence of his discourse (ibid. IV, 59-63). Not all the ordained are gifted speakers. Augustine recommends that they read sermons that have been written by those who are more capable (ibid. IV, 62). Most essential is that the preacher and people turn to the Lord in prayer for inspiration before the sermon begins (ibid. IV, 63).

Augustine loves to play on words, at times using alliteration and frequently employing antithesis, as in his description of the newborn Christ on Christmas day: "unspeakably wise, wisely speechless," "concealing what he was and openly displaying what he had become."[38] Much of the delight found in Augustine's preaching is lost in modern language translations, since Latin is an inflected language where the endings determine the words' function in the sentence, allowing for a wide variety of musical rhythms and rhymes that engage and hold the listener's attention.[39] Augustine will frequently repeat the same phrase, letting it grow into a crescendo as he attempts to drive home a certain point, as in S. 212, where he repeats the same phrase, "through/in this form of a servant," eight times in one single paragraph while commenting on Phil 2:27, the great Pauline Christological hymn. Similarly, he repeats the phrase "nursed by his mother" three times in S. 239, 6. Sometimes he will repeat the same word, employing a variety of intensifying adjectives to drive home his message, as we see on the feast of a particular martyr, where he desires to emphasize the virtue of patience: "true patience, holy patience, right patience; Christian patience is a gift of God."[40]

---

37. See *Teaching Christianity* IV, 33-58 where Augustine gives examples for each of the three styles originally articulated by Cicero: the plain or simple style, the intermediate or moderate style and the grand style.
38. S. 187, 1.4.
39. An exhaustive treatment of the wide range of figures of speech available to the bishop is found in Heinrich Lausberg, *Elemente der literarischen Rhetorik* (München: Max Hueber Verlag, 1967)= *Handbook of Literary Rhetoric : A Foundation for Literary Study*, foreword by George A. Kennedy; translated by Matthew T. Bliss, Annemiek Jansen, David E. Orton; edited by David E. Orton and R. Dean Anderson (Leiden-Boston: Brill, 1998).
40. S. 274.

Size and Makeup of Congregation

Teachers and preachers alike must adjust their approach and style of presentation according to the size of the space, the number of participants and their varying backgrounds. Unlike a university classroom, where one may presume a certain homogeneity in terms of age and level of education, the challenges facing a priest or bishop are more daunting, given the relative diversity of a church congregation. A smaller group in a confined space lends itself to more informal conversation, spontaneity and intimate contact, whereas a conference in a large university lecture hall or auditorium demands formality and even theatrics to maintain successful communication. Just how large was the typical congregation addressed by Bishop Augustine? That depended on a number of circumstances: when, where, and what occasion. We know from architectural studies the approximate size of the *Basilica pacis*, his cathedral church in Hippo, excavated in the 1950s, which occupied an area roughly 50 meters in length and 20 meters wide. Clearly there were mixed crowds of old and young and both sexes present for ordinary Sunday liturgies that swelled in size during the major holydays such as Christmas and Easter. Other times Augustine laments the small turnout, as was the case on one feastday of St. Lawrence, when he compared the renown of the martyr in Rome with the rather sparse number in attendance.[41] Some of his listeners were highly educated; most were not, unless he was preaching in a sophisticated metropolitan city such as Carthage. The majority no doubt were poor and simple folk. Some had a fairly thorough knowledge of sacred scripture. The bishop had to pace himself according to his sense of the congregation's ability to follow him. He often repeated himself in order to emphasize a particular point. After years of teaching experience Augustine was aware of the value of repetition in learning fundamental points.

Challenges and Struggles

In his preaching the bishop faced a number of challenges both of a physical nature and of a more psychological nature. The primary physical challenge was his uncertain health and a problem being heard, which was the result of a weak voice and which became increasingly serious as he aged. He constantly interrupts his sermon with pleas that the congregation listen more attentively. On one occasion, while preaching in Carthage, Augustine pleads with the congregation: "Have pity on me, for as you can hear, my voice is weak; help me by not making any noise."[42] Similarly, on another occasion, while visiting the same city, he begs: "If you keep quiet you will hear me."[43] The psychological challenge was greater, when he was aware that there would be some resistance to his message, particularly moral condemnation. He was regularly fatigued both by the heat and by the difficulty of explaining certain difficult passages of scripture. He regularly resisted the temptation to preach to the gallery in order to receive praise and accolades for his performance.

---

41. S. 303, 1.
42. S. 37, 1.
43. S. 153, 1.

Difficulty of Accurate Dating

Professor Hubertus Drobner has made it abundantly clear that scholars rely much too facilely on the conventional tables for dating Augustine's sermons, as if these recorded indisputable facts. It is far from clear that the majority of the sermons can be dated with absolute certainty. Too many scholars construct elaborate theories of interpretation based on the presumed accuracy of dates which are often tentative. Pierre-Marie Hombert's brilliant monograph, *Nouvelles Recherches de Chronologie Augustinienne*, has demonstrated that this is the case with the entire corpus of Augustinian texts.[44] There are two fundamental approaches to dating based on either internal or external evidence. For example, the bishop in a homily delivered at Carthage recalls the recent earthquakes that had decimated the East and had also struck the city of Sitifis in Mauretania, events which are easily identifiable from the reports of various chroniclers as having occurred in the year 419.[45] Or, in the opening words of S. 214, for example, Augustine makes reference to his age and lack of experience, since he is a "new recruit" in the office entrusted to him.[46] Yet even such internal evidence does not eliminate all debate among scholars, since Verbraken argues this sermon may have been preached 20 years later than the date of 391 assigned by most scholars, based on the fact that he was ordained a presbyter that year. S. 256, 3 provides another clear example of internal evidence, where the bishop makes reference to the following day's liturgical feast: "Tomorrow is the feast of the holy martyrs Marianus and James; but because I'm still rather busy on account of this big assembly of the holy council, I will with the Lord's help give the sermon I owe you for their birthday in two days' time." S. 296 is an example of another sermon with explicit details that allows us to date the homily with certainty to June 29, the feast of Saints Peter and Paul, in the year 411.

More often than not external evidence is lacking, which leads to all kinds of guesswork based on allusions, themes and references to contemporary events. Hill has conveniently provided a chronological table in the appendix of each volume of the eleven-volume collection of his translation of the *Sermons*, identifying the positions of various scholars. I am in no position to break new ground here but will summarize the most reasonable estimate based on current consensus.

Hombert calls attention to the critical work of Adalbero Kunzelmann, who uncovered the widespread influence of conclusions drawn from Verbraken's work on the subject, which are often based on a few lines. The problem with chronology is that many dates are proposed in light of the presumed accuracy of dating in other texts which we can no longer accept as accurate. Even the highly important work of Othmar Perler is nearly forty years old.[47] Fresh thinking and estimates are necessary in light of the new insights derived from the discovery and publication of Augustinian texts heretofore unknown by such experts as La Bonnardière, Divjak and Dolbeau. I direct the interested student on Augustine's preaching to the indispens-

---

44. See Pierre-Marie Hombert, *Nouvelles Recherches de Chronologie Augustinienne*, Collection des Études Augustiniennes Série Antiquité 163, (Paris: Institut d'Études Augustiniennes, 2000), in particular, "La Date des Sermons Mayence-grande-Chartreuse," 203-546.
45. S. 19, 6.
46. S. 214, 1.
47. See O. Perler, *Les voyages de Saint Augustin* (Paris, 1969).

able colloquium which took place in Chantilly in 1996.[48] Hombert identifies his method in reassessing the chronology as based on a careful systematic exploitation of parallel passages including identical themes and scriptural citations.[49] For example, it is reasonable to conclude that sermons which emphasize anti-Pelagian themes such as human weakness, the sin of Adam, and the necessity of grace cannot be dated before Augustine began to respond to the challenges posed by Pelagius' teaching. The problem is the traditional date assigned for this (*terminus post quem*), based on the pioneering work of Kunzelmann in 1931, was during the winter of 411-412. That date has been called into question by Dolbeau and others, which means that sermons presumed to have been preached some time after 412 may in fact have to be moved up as early as 406[50] I defer to the works graciously suggested by Professor Drobner himself for scholars to consult in order to appreciate some of the complexities involved.[51]

48. See the collection of papers collected and edited by Goulven Madec, *Augustin Prédicateur (395-422)* = Actes du Colloque International de Chantilly (5-7 septembre 1996) (Paris: Institut d'Études Augustiniennes, 1998.)
49. Hombert, V.
50. See F. Dolbeau, *Seminator Verborum*, Réflections d'un éditeur de sermons d'Augustin, Augustin Prédicateur, 95-111. The specific argument is based on Duval's redating Pelagius' *De natura* closer to 406 than 411-412.
51. Professor Drobner suggested the following works be consulted regarding the delicate issue of dating. I will cite them in chronological order: Adalbero Wilhelm Kunzelmann, *Die zeitliche Festlegung der Sermones des hl. Augustinus*, Diss. Würzburg 1928 = Die Chronologie der Sermones des hl. Augustinus: MA 2 (1931) 417-520; Anne-Marie La Bonnardière, *Recherches de chronologie augustinienne*, Paris 1965; Pierre-Marie Hombert, *Nouvelles recherches de chronologie augustinienne* (= Collection des Études Augustiniennes, Série Antiquité 163), Paris 2000; Hubertus Drobner, *Augustinus von Hippo : Sermones ad Populum* (Leiden-Boston: Brill, 2000); "The Chronology of St. Augustine's *Sermones ad populum*" published in *Augustinian Studies* 31:2 (2000) 211-218, 34:1 (2003) 49-66 and 35:1 (2004) 43-53. José Anoz, "Cronología de la producción agustiniana," *Augustinus* 47 (2002) 229-312.

Table of Themes

23

Sermon 9

Discourse of Saint Augustine on the Ten Strings of the Harp.
Sermon Preached at Chusa

This sermon demonstrates Augustine's skill as a pastor in spelling out the moral implications of the ten commandments, which make significant demands on believers. Sinners should not take faulty comfort by presuming on God's mercy in the psalm refrain, *The Lord is merciful and compassionate* (Ps 86:15), and neglecting the consequences of the final judgement. The location where the sermon was delivered is unknown, although it is identified in one manuscript as a place called Chusa. Section 4 makes clear that Augustine is a visiting preacher outside of Hippo. Hill believes, notwithstanding its length, that the date is late (sometime after 420) because of the anti-Arian references to Jesus' being equal to the Father. (The bishop was inclined to give shorter homilies as he grew older.) Anoz maintains, on the other hand, that Augustine commented on Ex 20:7a predominantly between 395 and 410, which suggests an earlier date. This earlier date is further supported by Augustine's comparison of the ten commandments to a ten-stringed harp in several *Expositions on the Psalms* datable to 403. Augustine follows the Septuagint numbering of the commandments and plucks repeatedly on the "5th string," *You shall not commit adultery*, which he inverts from the 6th in the usual order of the commandments familiar to today's reader. He precludes a literal reading of the commandments, which might justify acts of fornication with the unmarried. He emphasizes that the primary motive for obedience should be love of justice rather than fear of punishment.

God is merciful and just

1. Our Lord and God is *merciful and compassionate, long-suffering, very merciful and true* (Ps 86:15), and just as he is lavish with his prerogative of mercy in this age, so is he severe with his threat of punishment in the age to come. The words I have just spoken are from scripture, contained in the divine authorities, namely that *The Lord is merciful and compassionate, long-suffering, very merciful and true.* All the sinners and lovers of this world are delighted to hear the *Lord is merciful and compassionate,* that he is *long-suffering* and *very merciful.* But if you love him being so very merciful, be afraid too of the last thing he says there: *and true.* If, you see, he had only told you *The Lord is merciful and compassionate, and very merciful,* it's as though you would already be devoting yourself to your sins with a feeling of security and impunity and freedom. You would do what you like, you would enjoy the world as much as you were allowed to, or as much as your lusts dictated to you. And if anyone tried to scold and frighten you with some good advice into restraining yourself from the intemperate and dissolute pursuit of your

25

own desires and your abandonment of your God, you would stand there among the scolding voices, and as though you had heard the divine judgment with a shameless look of triumph on your face, you would read from the Lord's book: "Why are you trying to scare me about our God? He *is merciful and compassionate* and *very merciful.*" To stop people saying that sort of thing, he added one phrase at the end, which says, *and true.* Thus he ruled out the smugness of misplaced presumption and prompted the anxiety of sorrow for sin. Let us by all means rejoice at the Lord's mercy, but let us also fear the Lord's judgment. He spares — but he doesn't say nothing. Yes, he does say nothing, but he won't always say nothing. Listen to him while he is refraining from saying nothing in words, or you will have no time to listen while he is refraining from saying nothing in judgment.

Make it up with your adversary

2. Now, you see, you still have the right to put your case together. So put your case together before the final judgment of your God. There's nothing you can bank on when he comes, no false witnesses you can call that he will be taken in by, no tricky lawyers getting round the law for you with their clever tongues, nor will there be any way for you to fix it so that you can bribe the judge. So what do you do before a judge like that, whom you can neither bribe nor deceive? And yet there is something you can do. The one who is then going to be the judge in your case is the one who is now the witness to your life. We have been shouting out our praises. Let us put our case together. Just as he sees your deeds, so he also hears your voices. Don't let them be in vain, turn them into sighs.

It's time to agree with the adversary quickly. God is so patient, seeing the wicked things done every day and not punishing them, but this does not mean that judgment is not coming quickly. What seems long drawn out in terms of human life is very short to God. But what consolation is it that it all seems a long way off to the world itself and to the human race? Even if the last day of the whole human race is a long way off, is the last day of each human being a long way off? What I'm saying is this: since Adam many years have rolled by, many years have flowed past and will flow from now on, not quite as many indeed, but still until the end of the world the years will go by as they have gone by in the past. What remains seems long, though it is not as much as has already been gone through. And yet from the passage of past time the end of the remaining time is to be expected. There was a day then which was called "today." And from that one to this "today" everything that was future has become past, hasn't it? It's regarded as if it had never been. So will it be with the last bit of time that is left. But let this too be long, let it be as drawn out as you like to suppose, as you like to say, as you like to imagine; put off the day of judgment as much, not as scripture advises but as your imagination devises, put it off as much as you like; you are not going to defer your own last day very long, are you, that is, the last day of your life on which you are going to make your exit from this body? Be assured of old age, if you can. But who can be? From the moment people begin to be able to live, they are also able to die, aren't they? The beginning of life introduces the possibility of death. On this earth and in the human race the only one who cannot yet die is the one who has not yet either begun to live. So the day is uncertain and must be expected as a possibility every day. But if the day is uncertain and must be expected as a possibility every day, make it up with your adversary while he is with you on the road. This life is called a road, along which everybody travels. And this adversary doesn't go away.

Your adversary is the word of God

3. But who is this adversary? This adversary is not the devil, for scripture would never urge you to come to an agreement with the devil. So there is another adversary, whom man turns into his adversary. If the devil were this adversary, he wouldn't be with you on the road. The reason this one is with you on the road is to come to an agreement with you. He knows that unless you come to an agreement on the road, he will hand you over to the judge, the judge to the officer and the officer to prison. These words are gospel; let those who have read them or heard them remember them as I do.

So who is the adversary? The word of God. The word of God is your adversary. Why is it your adversary? Because it commands things against the grain which you don't do. It tells you: *Your God is one* (Dt 6:4); worship one God. What *you* want is to put away the one God who is like the lawful husband of your soul and go fornicating; and what's much more serious, not openly deserting and repudiating him as apostates do, but remaining in your husband's house and letting in adulterers. That is, as if you were a Christian you don't leave the Church, and you consult astrologers or diviners or augurs or sorcerers. Like an adulterous soul you don't leave your husband's house, and while remaining married to him you go fornicating.

You are told *Do not take the name of the Lord your God in vain* (Ex 20:7); do not regard Christ as a creature because for your sake he put on the creature. And you, you despise him who is equal to the Father and one with the Father. You are told to observe the sabbath spiritually, not in the way the Jews observe the sabbath in worldly idleness. They like the free time to spend on their frivolities and extravagances. The Jew would do better doing some useful work on his land instead of joining in faction fights at the stadium. And their women would do better spinning wool on the sabbath than dancing shamelessly all day on their balconies. But you are told to observe the sabbath in a spiritual way, in hope of the future rest which the Lord has promised you. Whoever does whatever he can for the sake of that future rest, even though what he is doing seems toilsome, nonetheless if he refers it to faith in the promised rest, he already has the sabbath in hope, though he does not yet have it in fact. But you, the reason you want to rest is in order to work, whereas you ought to be working in order to rest.

You are told, *Honor your father and mother* (Ex 20:12). You heap insults on your parents, which you certainly don't want to endure from your children. You are told, *You shall not kill* (Ex 20:13). But *you* want to kill your enemy; and the only reason you don't do it, probably, is that you are afraid of the human judge, not that you are thinking about God. Don't you realize that he is the witness of your thoughts? The man you want dead is alive, and God holds you to be a murderer in your heart.

You are told, *You shall not commit adultery* (Ex 20:14), that is, do not go to any other woman except your wife. But what *you* do is demand this duty *from* your wife, while declining to pay this duty *to* your wife. And while you ought to lead your wife in virtue (chastity is a virtue, you know), you collapse under one assault of lust. You want your wife to conquer; you yourself lie there, conquered. And while you are the head of your wife, she goes ahead of you to God, she whose head you are. Do you want your household to hang its head downward? *The husband is the head of the wife* (Eph 5:23). But where the wife lives better than the husband, the household hangs its head downward. If the husband is the head, the husband ought to live better and go ahead of his wife in all good deeds, so that she may imitate her husband and follow her head. Just as Christ is head of the Church, and the Church is ordered to follow its head and as it were walk in the footsteps of its head, so everyone's household has as its head the man and as its flesh the woman. Where the head leads, there the body ought to follow. So why does the head want to go where it doesn't want the body to follow? Why does the husband want to go where he doesn't want his wife to follow? In making this command the word of God is the adversary, since men don't want to do what the word of God wants.

And what am I saying? Because the word of God is your adversary in giving such commands, I am afraid that I too may be some people's adversary because I am speaking like this. Well, why should that bother me? May he who terrifies me into speaking make me brave enough not to fear the complaints of men. Those who don't want to be faithful in chastity to their wives — and there are thousands of such men — don't want me to say these things. But whether they want me to or not, I'm going to say them. For if I don't urge you to come to an agreement with the adversary, I myself will remain at odds with him. The one who tells you to behave is the same as the one who tells me to speak. If you are his adversaries by not doing what he tells you to do, I shall remain his adversary by not saying what he tells me to say.

Against adultery

4. Did I spend as long on all the other points I was making above? No, because I take it for granted about you, beloved, that you worship the one God. I take it for granted in view of the Catholic faith you have that you believe the Son of God to be equal to the Father. You do not take the name of the Lord your God in vain by supposing that the Son of God is a creature. For every *creature is subject to vanity*

(Rom 8:20). But you believe he is equal to the Father, God from God, the Word with God, God the Word through which all things were made, light from light, co-eternal with the one who begot him, one with the one who begot him. But this Word, you believe, put on the creature, took on mortality from the Virgin Mary, and suffered for us. We read all this, we believe in order to be saved. Nor did I linger on the point that whatever you do, you do it in hope of something to come. I know that the minds of all Christians think about the age to come. Anyone who doesn't think about the age to come, and is not a Christian precisely in order to receive what God promises at the end, is not yet a Christian. Nor did I linger on the word of God saying *Honor your father and your mother* (Ex 20:12). Most people honor their parents, and we rarely find parents complaining about their children neglecting them, though it does happen. But since it happens rarely, it only calls for a brief warning. Nor did I want to linger on the place where it says *You shall not kill* (Ex 20:13). After all, I don't believe there is a mob of murderers here.

What has taken more of my time is that evil which spreads its tentacles so widely, which more keenly exasperates that adversary, who is making such a fuss just because he wants sooner or later to be a friend. Complaints in this matter are a daily occurrence, even though the women themselves don't yet dare to complain about their husbands. A habit that has caught on everywhere like this is taken for a law, so that even wives perhaps are now convinced that husbands are allowed to do this, wives are not. They are used to hearing about wives being taken to court, found perhaps with houseboys. But a man taken to court because he was found with his maid, they have never heard of that — though it's a sin. It is not divine truth that makes the man seem more innocent in what is equally sinful, but human wrongheadedness. And supposing today someone has to put up with rather more sharpness from his wife and more open grumbling because she used to assume that it was all right for her husband and now she has heard in church that it is not all right for her husband; so if he has to endure his wife grumbling more freely and saying to him, "What you are doing is not right. We both heard him saying so. We are Christians. Give me the same as you require of me. I owe you fidelity, you owe me fidelity, we both owe Christ fidelity. Even if you deceive me, you don't deceive him to whom we belong, you don't deceive the one who bought us," when he hears things like this which he is not used to, being unwilling to become upright in himself he becomes uptight against me. He gets angry, he becomes abusive. He may even say, "How come this fellow ever came here, or my wife went to church that day?" I certainly think he will say this to himself, for he won't have the courage to say it aloud, not even in front of his wife in private. Because no doubt if he did say it out loud she could answer him back, "Why are you abusing the man you were just now clapping and cheering? After all we are married. If you can't agree with your own tongue, how can you live in agreement and harmony with me?"

I, brothers, have an eye for the danger you are in. I am not taking any notice of your wishes. If the doctor took any notice of sick people's wishes he would never cure them. Don't do what should not be done. Don't do what God forbids. Oh sure, it would have been better for those who don't want to correct themselves that I should not have come here if I was going to speak like this, or that since I have come I shouldn't have said all this.

On top of the world

5. I remember that I told your holinesses the day before yesterday that if we were a pop group or putting on that kind of popular entertainment for your frivolities' benefit, you would have engaged us to give you a day, and everyone would have contributed what you could afford to our fee. But why should we amble through life, kept amused by idle songs that will never be good for anything, fun at the time, turning sour afterward? People attracted by the base sentiments of such songs grow flabby in character and fall away from virtue and trickle away into a base style of life. And because of their base and sordid habits they afterward suffer pain and grief; they have a terrible hangover for what was such pleasant drinking at the time. So it's better for us to sing you what now sound like sour-puss songs which will afterward make you feel on top of the world. Nor are we requiring any fee from you except that you should do what we say — or rather that you shouldn't do it if it's only we who say it. But if he who is afraid of nobody says it to all of us, through whom it happens that in his name and in the glory of his mercy we aren't afraid of anyone either, then we have all heard, so let us all do it, let us all come to an agreement with our adversary.

First three commandments — God

6. Suppose then I'm a pop singer — what more could I sing to you? Here you are — I have brought a harp; it has ten strings. You were singing this yourselves a little earlier on, before I began to speak. You were my chorus. You were singing, weren't you, earlier on: *O God, I will sing you a new song, on a harp of ten strings I will play to you* (Ps 144:9)? Now I am strumming these ten strings. Why is the sound of God's harp sour? Let us all play on the ten-stringed harp. I am not singing you something that you are not meant to do.

You see, the decalogue of the law has ten commandments. These ten commandments are arranged in such a way that three refer to God and seven refer to men and women. God's three, which I have already mentioned: Our God is one, and you should make no likeness, or fornicate behind God's back, because God, Christ, the Son of God is one with the Father. And that's why he should not be taken by us in vain, in such a way that we imagine him to have been made, that is, some kind of creature, though all things were made through him. But because this one God is Father and Son and Holy Spirit, in the Holy

Spirit, that is, in the gift of God, everlasting rest is promised us. Of that we have already received the pledge. That's what the apostle says: *Who gave us the Spirit as a pledge* (2 Cor 1:22). If we have received a pledge so that we may be at peace in the Lord and in our God, that we may be gentle in our God, may be patient in God, we shall also in him from whom we have received the pledge be at rest forever. That will be the sabbath of sabbaths, on account of the rest that comes as the gift of the Holy Spirit. So the third commandment about the sabbath, which the Jews as I said celebrate in a worldly way, we should acknowledge in a spiritual way. It is because the Spirit is called holy that God hallowed the seventh day when he made all his works, as we read it written in Genesis. You don't have any hallowing mentioned there except on that one day when it says, *God rested from his works* (Gn 2:2-3). It was not because God was tired that it had to say *God rested from his works*, but that word contains a promise of rest for you as you toil away. And it is also because he made everything very good that it says like this, *God rested*, to give you to understand that you too will rest after good works, and rest without end. For everything said earlier on, that is, the earlier days, have an evening. But this seventh day, in which God hallowed rest, does not have an evening. It says there "There was morning," so that the day could begin. But it doesn't say "There was evening" to bring the day to an end; it says "There was morning," to make it a day without end. So our rest begins so to say in the morning, but it does not end, because we shall live forever. Whatever we do with this hope in mind, if we do it, then we are observing the sabbath. That is the third string of this decalogue, that is, of the ten-stringed harp. Commandments on three strings refer to God.

The other seven commandments — neighbor

7. If we were told, *You shall love the Lord your God with your whole heart and with your whole soul and with your whole mind* (Mt 22:37), and nothing was said about our neighbor, it would not be a ten-stringed but a three-stringed instrument. But because the Lord added, *And you shall love your neighbor as yourself*, and joined them together by saying, *On these two commandments hangs the whole law and the prophets* (Mt 22:39), the whole law is contained in two commandments, in love of God and love of neighbor. So the decalogue relates to two commandments, that is, to love of God and neighbor. Three strings relate to the first, because God is three. But to the other commandment, that is, the love of neighbor, seven strings refer, how people should live together. This series of seven, like seven strings, begins with the honoring of parents. *Honor your father and your mother* (Ex 20:12). It's your parents you see when you first open your eyes, and it is their friendship that lays down the first strands of this life. If anyone fails to honor his parents, is there anyone he will spare? *Honor your father and your mother*. And the apostle says, *Honor father and*

mother, which is the first commandment (Eph 6:2). How can it be the first, seeing that it is the fourth commandment, unless you take it as the first in the series of seven? It's the first on the second table dealing with love of neighbor. That's why, you see, two tablets of the law were given. God gave his servant Moses two tablets on the mountain, and on these two stone tablets were inscribed the ten commandments of the law — the harp of ten strings — three referring to God on one tablet, and seven referring to our neighbor on the other tablet. So on the second tablet the first commandment is *Honor your father and your mother*; the second, *You shall not commit adultery*; the third, *You shall not kill*; the fourth, *You shall not steal*; the fifth, *You shall not bear false witness*; the sixth, *You shall not covet your neighbor's wife*; the seventh, *You shall not covet anything of your neighbor's* (Ex 20:12-17). Let us join these to those three that refer to love of God, if we wish to sing the new song to the harp of ten strings.

New life, new song

8. You see, this is where of your charity I ask for your closest attention, if I am somehow or other to express what the Lord suggests to me. The Jewish people received the law. They did not observe what is in the decalogue. And any who did comply did so out of fear of punishment, not out of love of justice. They were carrying the harp, but they weren't singing. If you are singing, it's enjoyable; if you are fearing, it's burdensome. That's why the old man either doesn't do it, or does it out of fear, not out of love of holiness, not out of delight in chastity, not out of the calmness of charity, but out of fear. It's because he is the old man, and the old man can sing the old song but not the new one. In order to sing the new song, he must become the new man. How can you become the new man? Listen, not to me but to the apostle saying, *Put off the old man and put on the new* (Eph 4:22.24). And in case anyone should imagine, when he says *Put off the old man and put on the new*, that something has to be laid aside and something else taken up, where in fact he is giving instructions about changing the man, he goes on to say, *Therefore, putting aside lying, speak the truth* (Eph 4:25). That's what he means by *Put off the old man and put on the new*. What he is saying is: "Change your ways." You used to love the world; love God. You used to love the futilities of wickedness, you used to love passing, temporary pleasures; love your neighbor. If you do it out of love, you are singing the new song. If you do it out of fear but do it all the same, you are indeed carrying the harp but you are not yet singing. But if you don't do it at all, you are throwing the harp away. It's better at least to carry it than to throw it away. But again, it's better to sing with pleasure than to carry the thing as a burden. And you don't get to the new song at all unless you are already singing it with pleasure. If you are carrying the harp with fear, you are still in the old song. And just notice what it is I am saying, brothers. Anyone who is still doing it out of fear has not yet come to an agreement with his adversary. He is afraid of God coming and

condemning him. Chastity has no delights for him yet, justice has no delights for him yet, but it is because he is in dread of God's judgment that he abstains from such deeds. He does not condemn the actual lust that is seething inside him. He does not yet take delight in what is good. He does not yet find there the pleasant inspiration to sing the new song, but out of his old habits he is still fearing punishments. He has not yet come to an agreement with the adversary.

Love God as God is

9. Such people are often tripped by thoughts like this, and they say to themselves, "If it were possible to do this, God would not be threatening us, he would not say all those things through the prophets to discourage people, but he would have come to be indulgent to everybody and pardon everybody, and after he came he wouldn't send anyone to hell." Now because he is unjust he wants to make God unjust too. God wants to make you like him, and you are trying to make God like you. Be satisfied with God as he is, not as you would like him to be. You are all twisted, and you want God to be like what you are, not like what he is. But if you are satisfied with him as he is, then you will correct yourself and align your heart along that straight rule from which you are now all warped and twisted. Be satisfied with God as he is, love him as he is.

He doesn't love you as you are, he hates you as you are. That's why he is sorry for you, because he hates you as you are, and wants to make you as you are not yet. Let him make you, I said, the sort of person you are not yet. What he did not promise you, you know, is to make you what he is. Oh yes, you shall be what he is, after a fashion, that is to say, an imitator of God like an image, but not the kind of image that the son is. After all there are different kinds of images even among men. A man's son bears the image of his father, and is what his father is, because he is a man like his father. But your image in a mirror is not what you are. Your image is in your son in one way, in quite a different way in the mirror. Your image is in your son by way of equality of nature, but in the mirror how far it is from your nature! And yet it is a kind of image of you, though not like the one in your son which is identical in nature.

So too the image of God in the creature is not what it is in the son who is what the Father is, that is, God the Word of God through which all things were made. Therefore receive the likeness of God, which you lost through evil deeds. Just as the emperor's image is in a coin in a different way from the way it is in his son. There are, you see, images and images; they are stamped differently on a coin. The emperor's image is to be found differently in his son, differently on a gold sovereign. So you too are God's coin, and a better one in that you are God's coin with intelligence and life of a sort, so you can know whose image you bear and to whose image you were made; a coin of course doesn't know it carries the king's image.

So, as I was in the middle of saying, God hates you as you are but loves you as he wants you to be, and that is why he urges you to change. Come to an agreement with him, and begin by having a good will and hating yourself as you are. Let this be the first clause of your agreement with the word of God, that you begin by first of all hating yourself as you are. When you too have begun to hate yourself as you are, just as God hates that version of you, then you are already beginning to love God himself as he is.

The sick and the doctor

10. Think of sick people. Sick people hate themselves as they are, being sick, and begin by coming to an agreement with the doctor. Because the doctor too hates them as they are. That's why he wants them to get better, because he hates them being feverish; the doctor persecutes the fever in order to liberate the patient. So too avarice, so lust, so hatred, covetousness, lechery, so the futility of the shows in the amphitheater, are all fevers of your soul. You ought to hate them as the doctor does. In this way you are in agreement with the doctor, you make an effort with the doctor, you listen gladly to what the doctor orders, you gladly do what the doctor orders, and as your health improves you begin even to enjoy his instructions. How irksome food is to sick people when they are beginning to recover! Sick people even reckon the moment of recovery worse than the attack. And yet they force themselves to cooperate with the doctor, and however unwillingly and reluctantly, they conquer themselves and take some food. When they are well again how hungrily they are going to take large helpings of what they can hardly take tiny portions of while they are sick! But how is this done? Because they hated their fever and agreed with the doctor, and doctor and patient persecuted the fever together. So then when I say all this I am only hating your fevers, or rather in me the word of God, with which you should come to an agreement, is hating your fevers. What after all am I, but someone needing to be set free with you, cured with you?

Do not fornicate

11. It's not me you must look at now, but God's word. Do not fornicate. Don't be angry with your treatment; I haven't found any other way to proceed. I have come to the fifth string, I a man strumming the ten-stringed harp. Did you think I was going to leave out the fifth? No indeed, I'm going to pluck it constantly. It's on this note that I see practically the whole human race fallen flat on its face, after all; on this note I see them laboring more than on the others. When I strum it, what do I say? Don't commit adultery behind your wives' backs, because you don't want your wives to commit adultery behind yours. Don't you go where you don't want them to follow. You have no case at all when you try to excuse yourselves by saying, "I don't go with someone else's wife, do I? I go with my own maid." Do you want her to say to you, "I don't go with someone else's husband, do I? I go with my own houseboy." You say, "It's not someone else's wife I go with." You

don't want to be told, do you, "It's not someone else's husband I go with"? God forbid she should say that. It is better for her to grieve for you than to imitate you. She, you see, is a chaste and holy woman and really a Christian, who grieves for her fornicating husband, and does not grieve out of jealousy, but out of charity; the reason she does not want you to behave like that is not that she herself doesn't behave like that, but that it does you no good. If the reason she doesn't is in order that you shouldn't, then if you do, she will. But if she owes to God, if she owes to Christ the faithfulness you demand of her, and gives it to you because he commands it, then even if her husband fornicates she offers her chastity to God.

For Christ speaks in the hearts of good women, he speaks inside where the husband doesn't hear him, because he doesn't deserve to if he is that sort of man. So he speaks inwardly and consoles his daughter with words like this: "Are you distressed about your husband's wrongful behavior, what he has done to you? Grieve, but don't imitate him and behave badly yourself, but let him imitate you in behaving well. Insofar as he behaves badly, don't regard him as your head, but me." After all, if he is the head even insofar as he behaves badly, the body is going to follow its head, and both go head over heels to their ruin. To avoid following her bad head, let her hold fast to the head of the Church, Christ. Owing her faithful chastity to him, deferring to him with honor, then husband present or husband absent she does not sin, because the one to whom she is under an obligation not to sin is never absent.

Equality of women and men

12. So then, my brothers, that is what you must do in order to be able to agree with the adversary. Nor is what I am saying really a bitter pill — or if it is bitter, let it cure you. If this is a bitter pill, swallow it. It's bitter because your insides are dangerously ill, and that's why it must be swallowed. Better a little bitter taste in the mouth than eternal torment in the innards, so change yourselves. Those of you who haven't been practicing the virtue of chastity, start practicing it now. Don't say, "It can't be done." It's vile, my brothers, it's shameful for a man to say that what a woman can do can't be done. It's criminal for a man to say "I can't." Can a man not do what a woman can? Come, come! Isn't she made of flesh and blood too? She was the first to be led astray by the serpent. Your chaste wives show you that what you don't want to do can be done, and you say it can't be done.

But I suppose you are going to say that she can do it much more easily because she is so closely guarded and protected by the commandment of the law, by her husband's diligence, by the terror too of the public laws. There is also the great bulwark of her modesty and sense of shame. So there are many safeguards to make a woman more chaste. Let it be manliness that makes a man so. The reason a woman has more safeguards is that being the weaker sex she has more need of them. She blushes before her husband. Are you not going to blush before Christ? You have more freedom, because more strength. It's because it's easy for you to overcome that you are left to your own devices. Over her there is her husband's watchful eye and the terror of the laws, and force of custom, and a greater modesty. And over you there's God, only God.

You see, you can easily find other men like you, whom you are not afraid of making you feel ashamed, because so many behave like this. And such is the perversity of the human race, that sometimes I'm afraid a chaste man will feel ashamed in lewd company. That's why I never stop plucking this string, because of this crooked custom and blemish, as I said, on the whole human race. If any of you committed murder, which God forbid, you would want to drive him out of the country, and get rid of him immediately if possible. If anyone steals, you hate him and don't wish to see him. If anyone gives false evidence you abominate him and regard him as scarcely human. If anyone covets someone else's property he is considered unjust and rapacious. If anyone has tumbled in the hay with his maids, he is admired, he is given a friendly welcome, the injuries are turned into jokes. But if a man comes along who says he is chaste, does not commit adultery, and is known not to do so, then he is ashamed to join the company of those others who are not like him, in case they insult him and laugh at him and say he is not a man. So this is what human perversity has come to, that someone conquered by lust is considered a man, and someone who has conquered lust is not considered a man. The winners are celebrating and they are not men; the losers lie flat on their faces, and they are men! If you were a spectator in the amphitheater, would you be the sort of spectator who thought the man cowering before the wild animal was braver than the man who killed the wild animal?

The interior battle

13. But because you turn a blind eye to the interior battle and take pleasure in exterior battles, it means you don't want to belong to the new song, in which it says *Who trains my hands for battle, and my fingers for war* (Ps 144:1). There is a war a man wages with himself, engaging evil desires, curbing avarice, crushing pride, stifling ambition, slaughtering lust. You fight these battles in secret, and you don't lose them in public! It's for this that your hands are trained for battle and your fingers for war. You don't get this in your amphitheater show. In those shows the hunter is not the same as the guitarist; the hunter does one thing, the guitarist another. In God's circus show they are one and the same. Touch these same ten strings, and you will be killing wild beasts. You do each simultaneously. You touch the first string by which the one God is worshiped, and the beast of superstition falls dead. You touch the second by which you do not take the name of the Lord your God in vain, and at your feet is fallen the beast of the error of impious heresies which had that in mind. You touch the third string, where whatever you do, you do in hope of resting in peace in the age to come, and something more cruel

than the other beasts is slain, love of this world. It is for love of this world, after all, that people slave away at all their affairs. But as for you, see you slave away at all your good works, not for love of this world but for the sake of the eternal rest that God promises you. Notice how you do each thing simultaneously. You touch the strings and you kill the beasts. That is, you are both a guitarist and a hunter. Aren't you delighted with such performances, where it is not the attention of the presidential box we attract, but the attention and favor of the redeemer?

Honor your father and your mother (Ex 20:12). You touch the fourth string by showing your parents honor, the beast of ingratitude has fallen dead. *You shall not commit adultery* (Ex 20:14); you touch the fifth string, the beast of lust has fallen dead. *You shall not kill* (Ex 20:13); you touch the sixth string, the beast of cruelty has fallen dead. *You shall not commit theft* (Ex 20:15); you touch the seventh string, the beast of rapacity has fallen dead. *You shall not utter false testimony* (Ex 20:16); you touch the eighth string, fallen dead is the beast of falsehood. *You shall not covet your neighbor's wife*; you touch the ninth string, dead at your feet is the beast of adulterous thoughts. It's one thing, you see, not to do anything like that apart from your wife, and another not to desire someone else's wife. That's why there are two commandments: *You shall not commit adultery*; and *You shall not covet your neighbor's wife*. *You shall not covet your neighbor's property* (Ex 20:17). Touch the tenth string, dead at your feet lies the beast of greed. Thus with all the wild beasts fallen dead, you can live carefree and innocent in the love of God and in human companionship. Just by touching ten strings, how many beasts you kill! For there are many other heads under these headings. With each single string it isn't a single beast but whole herds of beasts that you slay. In this way then you will sing the new song with love and not with fear.

Do good to others

14. Now don't say to yourself, when perhaps you would like to indulge in a little lechery, "I haven't got a wife, I can do what I like; after all, I'm not sinning behind my wife's back." You know very well what price was paid for you, you know very well what you are approaching, what you are about to eat, what you are about to drink, or rather whom you are about to eat, whom you are about to drink. Restrain yourself from acts of fornication. And don't try me on with this one, either: "Yes, I visit the brothel, I go along to a harlot, I go with a prostitute, but even so I'm not breaking that commandment which says *You shall not commit adultery*, because I haven't yet got a wife so I'm not doing anything against her. Nor am I breaking the commandment which says *You shall not covet your neighbor's wife*. Seeing that I visit the common stew, what commandment am I infringing?" Can't we find a string to twang in this case? Can't we find a string, some catgut to tie up this runaway with? He won't escape,

there's something he can be tied up with. But let him only love, and he will find himself not trussed up but dressed up. We can find it in these very ten strings. The ten commandments are reducible, as we have heard, to those two commandments, that we should love God and our neighbor, and these two to the one we are looking for. There is one: *What you do not want done to you, do not do to another* (Tb 4:15). There the ten are contained, and there also are contained the two.

Temple of God

15. "That's all very well," you say; "if I commit a theft I do something I don't want done to me; if I kill, I do something which I certainly don't want to suffer at someone else's hand; if I don't show respect to my parents while I want it shown me by my children, I am doing what I don't want to put up with myself; if I'm an adulterer and attempt anything like that, I am doing what I don't want to put up with myself — ask anyone and he will say 'I don't want my wife to do anything like that'; if I covet my neighbor's wife, I don't want anyone to covet mine, so I'm doing something I don't want to put up with myself; if I covet my neighbor's property, I certainly don't want to be deprived of mine, so I'm doing something I don't want to put up with myself. But when I go with a harlot, to whom am I doing anything that I don't want to suffer myself?" To God himself, that's who; it's much more serious than you think.

Your holinesses, please try and understand. *What you do not want done to you, do not do to another* can be applied to two commandments. How can it be applied to two commandments? If you don't do to a man what you don't want to suffer from a man, it applies to the commandment about your neighbor, to love of neighbor, to the seven strings. But if you want to do to God what you don't want to put up with from man, what's going on now? Aren't you doing to another what you don't want to put up with yourself? Has man become dearer to you than God? "So how am I doing it," he says, "to God himself?" You are disfiguring yourself. "And how do I injure God by disfiguring myself?" In the same way as someone would injure you if he wanted, for example, to throw stones at a painted panel of yours, a panel with your portrait on it hanging uselessly in your house to feed your vanity, feeling nothing, saying nothing, seeing nothing. If somebody throws stones at it, doesn't the insult fall on you? But when you through your fornications and dissolute lusts disfigure in yourself the portrait or image of God, which you are, you observe that you haven't gone in to anybody's wife, you observe that you haven't done anything against your own wife, seeing you haven't got a wife. And don't you observe whose image you have vandalized with your lusts and unlawful fornications?

Finally, God who knows what is good for you, who really does govern his servants for their good and not his own — because he doesn't need servants as if to assist him, but you do need a Lord to aid you — so the Lord himself who knows what is good for you has allowed you a wife, nothing more. This was his order, this his commandment, to prevent his temple, which you have begun to be, from falling into ruin through unlawful pleasures. Is it I who am saying this? Listen to the apostle: *Do you not know that you are God's temple, and the Spirit of God dwells in you?* He is saying this to Christians, he is saying this to the faithful: *Do you not know that you are God's temple, and the Spirit of God dwells in you? If anyone ruins God's temple, God will ruin him* (1 Cor 3:16-17). Do you see the threat he is making? You don't want your house ruined; why do you ruin God's house? Are you really not doing to someone what you don't want to suffer yourself?

So there you are, he has no way of escape. He didn't think he was caught, but he is. All the sins men commit are a matter of the vicious corruption of manners, or of deeds that harm others. It's true you cannot harm God with your evil deeds, but you do offend him with your vices, you do offend him with your corrupt manners, you do him an injury in yourself. For what you are injuring is his grace, his gift.

Serve God

16. If you had a servant you would wish your servant to serve you. You, then, serve your God who is a much better master. You didn't make your servant, he made both your servant and you. Do you want one with whom you were made to serve you, and not want yourself to serve one by whom you were made? So while you want your servant, a man, to serve you and do not want yourself to serve your own master, you are doing to God what you don't want to put up with yourself.

So that one commandment contains two, those two contain ten, those ten contain them all. So *sing a new song to the harp of ten strings* (Ps 144:9). But to sing a new song, become new people. Love justice; it has its own kind of beauty. The reason you don't want to see it is because you love something else. If you didn't love something else, you would in fact see justice. You see it well enough, don't you, when you demand it? You see trust well enough, don't you, when you require it from your servant? What a beautiful thing is trust! When you require it from your servant, that's when it's beautiful; that's when it's seen, when it's demanded of someone else. When it's required of you, you don't see it. You see gold, you don't see trust. But just as gold gleams to the eyes in your head, so trust gleams to the eyes in your mind. You open the eyes of your mind to it when you want your servant to be trustworthy. And if he is, you praise this servant to the skies and say, "I've a splendid servant, I've a great servant, I've a trusty servant." What you praise in your servant you don't show to your master, and it is all the more infamous of you because you expect to have better service from your servant than God has from you. It's God who commands your servant to be good to you. Just as he commands your wife not to commit adultery even if you do, so he commands your servant to serve you well even if you don't serve your God.

Now see to it that all this avails to lead to your amendment, not to your ruin. After all the fact that this servant serves unworthy you worthily, that is, that he serves unworthy you well, serves you faithfully and loves you sincerely, he owes this duty to God, not to you. So it is only right that you too should notice that you are under a master, whom he takes notice of in order to serve you. So carry out the saying, *What you do not wish done to you, do not do to another* (Tb 4:15). But when you say that "to another," think of both of them, both your neighbor and God. Sing to the harp of ten strings, sing a new song, come to an agreement with the word of God, while it is with you on the road. *Come to an agreement with your adversary quickly* (Mt 5:25), or you will come with disagreement before the judge. If you do what you hear, you have come to an agreement with him. But if you don't do it, you are still quarreling with him, and until you do it you haven't settled matters at all.

Tiny sins

17. But in order to come to that agreement, keep yourselves from detestable and corrupting practices, from going with detestable inquiries to astrologers, to soothsayers, to fortune-tellers, to augurs, to sacrilegious rites of divination. Keep yourselves as far as you can from idle shows. If any pleasures of the world creep into your thoughts, school yourselves in works of mercy, school yourselves in almsgiving, in fasting, in prayer. These are the means of purging ourselves of the daily sins which we cannot help creeping into our thoughts because of our human weakness. Don't shrug them aside because they are small; fear them, rather, because they are many. Listen, my brothers. These sins are tiny, they aren't big ones. This is no wild beast like a lion, to tear your throat out with one bite. But it's often the case that many tiny beasts can kill. If someone's thrown into the flea-pit, doesn't he die there? They are not very big, it is true, but human nature is weak and can be destroyed even by the tiniest creatures. So it is with little sins. You notice they are little; take care, because they are many. How tiny are grains of sand! Put too much sand into a boat, it sinks it and you can write it off. How tiny are drops of rain! They fill rivers and wash away houses, don't they? So don't just shrug these sins aside.

You will say, no doubt, "Who can exist without them?" In case you say this — and it's true, nobody can — a merciful God, seeing how fragile we are, has provided remedies against them. What are the remedies? Almsgiving, fasting, prayer: there are three of them. To make sure, though, you are telling the truth in your prayers, your almsgiving must be thorough and complete. What is thorough and complete almsgiving? Out of your abundance to give to anyone who has nothing, and when anyone does you harm, to forgive them.

Almsgiving

18. But don't imagine, brothers, that adultery can be committed every day, and cleaned away by almsgiving every day. A daily giving of alms is not enough to wipe out this and other graver misdeeds. It depends whether you change your mode of life, or whether you keep it up. These things have to be changed; so, if you were an adulterer, stop being an adulterer; if you were a fornicator, stop being a fornicator; if a murderer, stop being a murderer; if you used to haunt astrologers and other such sacrilegious pests, give it up from now on. Or do you really think these things can be wiped off the slate by daily almsgiving unless they cease to be committed?

What I mean by daily sins are those that are easily committed by the tongue, such as an unkind word, or when someone gives way to excessive laughter, or daily trivialities of that sort. Even in things that are allowed there can be sins. For example, if in intercourse with your wife you exceed the measure appropriate for begetting children, that is already a sin. That, after all, is the purpose of marrying a wife; it is even entered in the official contract or register: "for the sake of procreating children." When you wish to enjoy your wife more than the need to have children obliges you to, it's now a sin. And it is such sins as these that daily almsgiving wipes the slate clean of. In the matter of food, which is of course allowed, if you happen to exceed the proper measure and take more than is necessary, you are sinning. These things I've mentioned happen every day, and yet they are sins, and because there are so many of them they are not insignificant. Indeed, because there are so many of them, and every day, we should take care they do not ruin us by their numbers, if not by their size. It is such sins, brothers, that I say can be wiped clean by daily almsgiving. but mind you do give alms, and don't stop. Just think about your everyday life oozing with these sins, I mean these tiny ones.

Be generous in almsgiving

19. And when you give alms, don't do it proudly, and don't pray like that Pharisee there. And yet what did he say there? *I fast twice a week, I give tithes of everything I possess* (Lk 18:12). And the blood of the Lord had not yet been shed! We have received such a stupendous price paid for us, and we don't even pay out as much as that Pharisee. And you have the Lord saying unmistakably in another place, *Unless your justice abounds more than that of the scribes and Pharisees, you shall not enter into the kingdom of heaven* (Mt 5:20). So, they give tithes, that is, ten percent; you, if you give one percent, you boast about having done something terrific. What you pay attention to is what the other person doesn't do, not to what God tells you to do. You measure yourself by comparison with someone worse, not by the instruction of someone better. Just because he does nothing, it doesn't mean you are doing something great. But because you are so pleased with any minimal good works of yours — in fact, because your sterility is so great that

the slightest yield pleases you vastly — you congratulate yourselves, as though you had nothing to worry about, over a few miserable grains of almsgiving, and forget the great heaps of your sins. You have forked up, perhaps, heaven knows what paltry alms, which someone else either didn't have, or didn't fork up when he did have it. Don't look around you at who isn't doing anything, but ahead of you at what God is telling you to do.

Lastly why, in this matter of worldly status, are you not satisfied with being better off than many; why, instead, do you want to be rich, equal to people who are richer than you are? You don't consider how many poorer people you surpass; you want to overtake richer people. But in the matter of almsgiving there is a limit, of course. Here the rule is, "How far can I go?"; and there the rule isn't, "How many rich people am I richer than?" Nobody thinks of the extreme want of countless beggars, nobody looks back at the hordes of the poor trailing behind you, but all eyes are fixed on the smattering of rich people ahead of you. Why, in the matter of doing good, is not notice taken of that man Zacchaeus, who gave half of his goods to the poor? But we are forced to hope that at least some notice will be taken of that Pharisee who gave tithes of all he possessed.

Excuses for almsgiving

20. Don't be sparing of transitory treasures, of vain wealth. Don't increase your money under the guise of family piety. "I'm saving it for my children"; a marvelous excuse! He's saving it for his children. Let's see, shall we? Your father saves it for you, you save it for your children, your children for their children, and so on through all generations, and not one of them is going to carry out the commandments of God. Why don't you rather pay it all over to him who made you out of nothing? The one who made you is the one who feeds you with the things he made; he is the one who also feeds your children. You don't, after all, do better by entrusting your sons to your patrimony for support, than to your creator.

And anyhow, people are just lying. Avarice is evil. They want to cover up and whitewash themselves with a name for family piety, so that they may appear to be saving up for their children what in fact they are saving up for avarice. Just to show you that that is what very often happens: they say about somebody, "Why doesn't he give alms? Because he is saving for his children." It so happens he loses one of them. If he was saving for his children, let him send that one's share after him. Why should he keep it in his money-bags and drop him from his mind? Give him what is due to him, pay him what you were saving for him. "But he's dead," says he. In fact he has gone on ahead to God; his share is now owed to the poor. It's owed to the one he has gone to stay with. It's owed to Christ, since he has gone to stay with him. And he said, *Whoever did it to one of the least of these did it to me, and whoever failed to do it to one of the least of these failed to do it to me* (Mt 25:40.45). But what's that you say? "I'm saving it for his brothers"? If he had lived, he wasn't going to share it with his brothers. Oh dead faith! Your son is dead, isn't he? Whatever you may say, you owe him dead what you were saving for him alive. "Yes, my son is dead, but I am saving my son's share for his brothers." So that's how you believe he's dead, is it? If Christ did not die for him, then he's dead. But if there is any faith in you, your son is alive. He's alive as alive can be. He hasn't passed away, he has passed on, on ahead. How will you have the nerve to face your son who has passed on ahead, if as he passes ahead you don't send his share on to him in heaven? Or can't it be sent on to heaven? It most certainly can. Listen to the Lord himself telling you, *Lay up for yourselves treasure in heaven* (Mt 6:20). So if this treasure is looked after better in heaven, shouldn't it be sent on to your son this very moment, since if it is sent on it won't be lost? Are you going to hold on to it here where it can get lost, and not send it on where Christ keeps an eye on it? Well, since you are holding on to it here and don't want to send it on after your son, to whom do you entrust it? To your brokers and solicitors. You entrust to brokers the share of the one who has passed on ahead, and you won't entrust it to Christ to whom he has passed on ahead? Or does your solicitor suit you, and Christ not suit you?

Be Christians

21. So you see, brothers, it's a lie when people say "I'm saving it for my children." It's a lie, my brothers, it's a lie. People are just greedy. Well, at least here is a way of forcing them to confess what they don't want to, by making them ashamed of being silent about what they are. Let them pour it out, vomit up in confession what they are loaded with. Surfeited with iniquity, you have a bad attack of heartburn. Use confession as an emetic, but don't, like dogs, return to your vomit.

Be Christians. It's little enough being called a Christian. How much do you spend on actors? How much do you spend on hunters? How much on persons of ill repute? You spend money on people who kill you; by the public shows they exhibit they are slaying your souls. And you rave about who can spend most. If you raved about who can save most, no one would put up with you. To rave about who can save most is miserly. To rave about who can save most is miserly. To rave about who can spend most is spendthrift. God doesn't want you a miser, nor does he want you a spendthrift. He wants you to invest what you have, not to throw it away. You compete over who will win at being worse, you don't take pains about who can be better. And if only you just didn't take pains about who can be worse! And you say, "We are Christians"!

You throw away your money to court popularity, you hold on to your money against the commandments. And look, Christ is not commanding you anyway; Christ is asking you, Christ is in need. *I was hungry*, says Christ, *and you did not give me to eat* (Mt 25:42). It's for your sake he was willing to be in need, so that you would have somewhere to sow the earthly things he has given you, and from them reap eternal life. Don't be sluggish about it, taking the line of "I'm all right, Jack." Mend your ways, redeem your sins. And when you do this, give thanks to God, from whom you have received the ability to live good lives. And give him thanks in such a way that you don't crow over those who are not yet living good lives, but encourage them to do so by your behavior. If you do this you will have, as far as it's possible in this life, perfect justice. Spend your time in good works, in prayer, in fasting, in almsgiving because of your tiny sins, and keep yourselves from those big sins, and in this way you will come to an agreement with the adversary, and you will say with confidence when you pray, *Forgive us our debts just as we too forgive our debtors* (Mt 6:12). You have, after all, something to be forgiven every day, just as you have something to forgive every day. Walking confidently along the road in this way, you will not need to fear any holdups by the devil, because Christ has made himself into a broad road and highway which leads us straight home. Complete freedom from care is to be found there, and total rest, since it is a place where even the very works of mercy will have ceased, because there will be no unfortunate in need there. So it will be the sabbath of sabbaths, and there we shall find what here we desire. Amen.

Sermon 14

Sermon Preached One Sunday at Carthage
in the New Market Basilica on the Verse of the Psalm:
*To You Has the Poor Man Abandoned Himself,
You Will Be Guardian for the Orphan*

> Here Augustine dares to preach a sermon that not only indicts the rich for their pride and alleged failure to care for the poor but also challenges the poor for their self-righteous sense of moral superiority over the rich. This sermon was surely preached at Carthage in the New Market Basilica on May 28, probably in 418, on the day after S. 13 was delivered. Augustine identifies the *poor man* and *orphan* in Ps 10:14 as the *poor in spirit* who carefully avoid pride. The truly poor person is not simply destitute but puts his trust in God. The rich have the opportunity to relieve the poor and can also enter the kingdom. Christ represents the ideal poor person. At the end Augustine realizes he is "out of time," and he concludes by identifying the orphan as one who possesses a heavenly Father.

Who are the poor?

1. We have been singing to the Lord and saying: *To you has the poor man abandoned himself, you will be a guardian for the orphan* (Ps 10:14). Let's look

for the poor man, let's look for the orphan. Don't be surprised at my suggesting we should look for what we see and experience so much of. Isn't the whole place full of poor people? Isn't the whole place full of orphans? And yet in the whole place I am looking for the orphan.

But first I must show you, in your charity, that what we are thinking of is not what we are looking for. Those who are poor, toward whom God's mandates are carried out and alms given them, about whom we agree it is written, *Shut up your alms in the poor man's heart, and it will entreat the Lord for you* (Sir 29:12) — there are certainly plenty of people like that, but this poor man has to be understood in a more profound way than that. This poor man is of the kind of which it is said, *Blessed are the poor in spirit, for theirs is the kingdom of heaven* (Mt 5:3). There are poor people who don't have any money, can scarcely find enough to eat every day, are so in need of other people's assistance, of their pity, that they are not even ashamed to beg. If these are the ones meant by *To you has the poor man abandoned himself,* what are we to do who are not like this? Does it mean that we who are Christians have not abandoned ourselves to God? What other hope have we then, if we haven't abandoned ourselves to him who never abandoned us?

Disease of pride

2. So learn to be poor and abandon yourselves to God, O my fellow poor! A man's rich, he's proud. In these riches, which are commonly called riches, which are the opposite of this poverty, commonly so called, in these riches then there is nothing to be so carefully avoided as the disease of pride. Anyone who has no money, doesn't have ample means, has no particular reason to put on airs, while someone who has no reason to put on airs is not praised for not putting on airs. Someone who does have a reason should be praised if he doesn't put on airs. So why should I praise a poor man for being humble, when he has no reason to put on airs? Who could endure a person both needy and proud? Praise the rich man for being humble, praise the rich man for being poor. The one who writes to Timothy wants them to be like that, when he says, *Order the rich of this world not to be haughty in mind* (1 Tm 6:17). I know what I am saying: give them these orders. The riches they have are whispering persuasively to them to be proud, the riches they have make it very hard for them to be humble. Give me Zacchaeus, a man of great wealth, head tax-collector, confessor of sins, short in stature, shorter still in self-esteem, climbing a tree to see as he passed the one who was going to hang for him on a tree; give me this man saying *Half my goods I give to the poor.* But you are very rich, Zacchaeus, you're very rich indeed! There's the half you are going to give away; why are you keeping the other half? Because *if I have robbed anyone of anything, I am paying it back fourfold* (Lk 19:2-8).

The rich and the poor Lazarus

3. But any beggar will say to me, wasted by disease, festooned in rags, faint with hunger, he will answer me and say, "It's me the kingdom of heaven is owed to. I'm like that Lazarus fellow, who lay in front of the rich man's house covered with sores, whose sores the dogs used to lick, and he tried to fill himself with the crumbs that fell from the rich man's table. I'm more like him," he says; "it's our sort to whom the kingdom of heaven properly belongs, not the sort of people who wear purple and fine linen and feast sumptuously every day. That's the kind of man he was, in front of whose house lay the poor man full of sores. And see what happened to both of them. The destitute man came to die, and was carried away by angels to Abraham's bosom. The rich man also died and was buried. The poor man, I suppose, was probably not even buried. And what next? When the rich man was in torment among the dead in the underworld, he lifted up his eyes and saw the poor man he had despised taking his ease in Abraham's lap. He longed for a drop, he from whom the other had longed for a crumb, and because he had loved opulence he found no tolerance. He wanted to help his brothers, thoughtless as ever, thoughtful too late; nothing at all of what he asked for did he get. So let us set apart," he says, "the poor and the rich. Why urge me to perceive other meanings? It's obvious who are poor, it's obvious who are rich."

Example of Abraham

4. So now you listen to me, Mr. Poorman, about what I have suggested. When you identify yourself with that holy sore-infested man, I fear that pride may stop you being what you say you are. Don't despise rich people who are compassionate, rich people who are humble, and to repeat what I said a moment ago, don't despise the rich who are poor. Mind you too are poor, Mr. Poorman — poor meaning humble. If a rich man has become humble, how much more ought a poor man to be humble! The poor man has nothing to be puffed up about, the rich man has something to struggle with. So listen to me. Be truly poor, be gentle, be humble. You see, if you start boasting about that ragged, sore-ridden poverty of yours, because that is what that man was like who used to lie destitute in front of the rich man's house, then you are noticing that he was poor, but there is something else you are failing to notice. "What am I failing to notice?" he says. Read the scriptures and you will discover what I am saying. Lazarus was poor, yes; the one into whose bosom he was carried was rich. *It so happened*, it says, *that the poor man died and was taken away by angels*. Where to? *To Abraham's bosom* (Lk 16:22), that is, to the secret place where Abraham was. Don't take it literally, as though the poor man was raised up into the folds of Abraham's tunic. It was called "bosom" because it was secret or hidden. That's why it says, *Pay back our neighbors in their bosom* (Ps 79:12). Why "in their bosom"? In their secret, hidden places. What does it mean, *Pay back in their bosom?* Wrack their consciences.

So read, or if you can't read listen when it is read aloud, and see that Abraham was one of the richest people on earth, in gold, silver, household, flocks, possessions. And yet this rich man was poor because he was humble. Yes, he was humble: *Abraham believed God*, you see, *and it was reckoned to him for justice* (Gn 15:6). He was justified by the grace of God, not by his own presumption. He was faithful, he was a man of good works. He was ordered to sacrifice his son, and did not hesitate to offer what he had received to the one from whom he had received it. He was tested by God, and set up as an example of faith. He was already known by God, but he had to be shown to us. He wasn't puffed up by what might have seemed his very own good works, because this rich man was poor. And to show you that he wasn't puffed up as though his good works were his own — he knew all right that whatever he had, he had from God, and he never boasted in himself but in the Lord — listen to the apostle Paul: *If Abraham was justified by works, he has something to boast about, but not before God* (Rom 4:2).

Finding a poor person

5. So you see why, although there are plenty of poor people, we are right to look for the poor person. We look in the crowds and we can scarcely find one. A poor man confronts me and I go on looking for a poor man. Meanwhile *you*, mind you stretch out your hand to the poor man whom you do find; it is in your heart that you are looking for the one you are looking for. And *you*, you're saying "I'm poor like Lazarus." This humble rich man of mine isn't saying "I'm rich like Abraham." So you are exalting yourself, he is humbling himself. Why are you getting swollen-headed, and not copying him? "I, the poor man," he says, "have been lifted up to Abraham's bosom." Don't you see that it was a rich man who received the poor man? Don't you see that it is rich people who relieve the poor? If you are arrogant toward those who have money and deny that they belong to the kingdom of heaven, when perhaps there is a humility found in them that is not found in you, aren't you afraid that when you die Abraham may say to you, "Depart from me, because you have spoken ill of me"?

Worries of the rich and the carefree unconcern of the poor

6. So let me remind our rich people of what the apostle reminded us all. We were reminded *not to be haughty in mind, nor to set our hopes on the uncertainty of riches* (1 Tm 6:17). Those riches, which you think are full of delights, are full of dangers. A man was poor, and he used to sleep more soundly; sleep came more easily to the hard earth than to the silver-plated bedstead. Think of the worries of the rich, and compare them with the carefree unconcern of the poor. But this rich man must listen too and not be haughty in mind nor set his hopes on the uncertainty of riches. Let him use the world as though he were not using it. Let him realize he is walking along a road, and has come into his riches as into an inn. He may rest, by all means — he is a traveler. He may rest and go on his way. He doesn't take with

him what he finds in the inn. There will be another traveler, and he will have what's there but will not take it away with him. Everyone is going to leave behind here what they have acquired here. *Naked, he says, I came forth from my mother's womb; naked I shall return to the earth. The Lord has given, the Lord has taken away* — actually, he hasn't taken away, seeing that *to you has the poor man abandoned himself* (Ps 10:14) — *Naked I came forth from my mother's womb, naked I shall return to the earth* (Jb 1:21).

7. Listen to another poor man: *We brought nothing into this world, nor can we take anything out of it. Having food and clothing, with this we are content. For those who would be rich fall into temptation and many desires, foolish and harmful ones, which plunge men into destruction and ruin. The root of all evils is avarice; chasing after this, some people have strayed away from the faith and involved themselves in many sorrows* (1 Tm 6:7-10). Who are the ones who have strayed away from the faith and involved themselves in many sorrows? Those who would be rich.

Now let that ragged man answer me; let's see if he doesn't want to be rich. Let him answer, no lying now. I can hear his tongue, but I am questioning his conscience. Let him say if he doesn't want to be rich. Because if he does, he has already fallen into temptation and many desires, foolish and harmful ones. I said "desires," not "property," mark you. How has he done so? Simply by wanting to be rich. What's the result of that? Many, foolish, harmful desires, which plunge people into destruction and ruin. Do you see where you are at? What's the point of showing me your total lack of means, when I can convict you of such greedy dreams?

So now then, compare the two of them. This man's rich, that one's poor. But this man is already rich, he doesn't want to become so. He is rich, whether from his parents or from gifts and legacies. Let's suppose too, let's make him rich too by unjust means. But he doesn't want any longer to add to his pile; he has set bounds, fixed a limit to his greed; with all his heart he is now fighting on the side of goodness.

Don't be jealous of what you don't have

8. "He's rich," you say. "Yes, he's rich," I reply. Again you continue with the accusation and say, "It is by unjust means that he's rich." Well, what if he makes friends with the mammon of injustice? The Lord knew what he was saying. He certainly wasn't making a mistake when he gave the advice, *Make yourselves friends with the mammon of injustice, that they in turn may receive you into the tents of eternity* (Lk 16:9). Suppose that rich man is doing this? He is finished with greed, he is practicing goodness.

As for you, you have nothing, but you want to get rich. You will fall into temptation. But perhaps what reduced you to the extreme of poverty and indigence was that you had some family property or other to support you, and you were robbed of it by some artful dodger. You moan and groan, I can hear you, you say what evil times they are. What you are moaning and groaning about — you would do it yourself if you had the chance. Well, I ask you, don't we see this sort of thing, are there not examples of it every day and all around us? Yesterday he was moaning because he was losing his own property; today, in a great man's retinue, he seizes someone else's.

Christ, the model of authentic poverty

9. We have found the genuine poor man, we have found him to be kind and humble, not trusting in himself, truly poor, a member of the poor man who became poor for our sake, though he was rich. Look at this rich man of ours, who for our sake *became poor, though he was rich* (2 Cor 8:9); see how rich he is: *All things were made through him, and without him was made nothing* (Jn 1:3). There is more to making gold than to having it. You are rich in gold, silver, flocks, household, farms, produce; you were unable to create these things for yourself, though. See how rich he is: *All things were made through him.* See how poor he is: *The Word became flesh, and dwelt among us* (Jn 1:14). Who can fittingly reflect upon his riches, how he makes and is not made, how he creates and is not created, is not formed but forms, forms changeable things while changelessly abiding, ephemeral things while himself everlasting? Who can fittingly ponder his riches? Let us ponder his poverty instead, in case being poor ourselves we may just be able to grasp it.

He is conceived in a woman's virginal womb, he is enclosed in his mother's belly. What poverty! He is born in a mean lodging, wrapped in baby clothes and laid in a manger; he becomes fodder for poor beasts. And the Lord of heaven and earth, creator of angels, maker and founder of all things visible and invisible, sucks, cries, is reared, grows, puts up with being his age, conceals his ageless majesty, later on is arrested, scorned, scourged, mocked, spat at, slapped, crowned with thorns, hung on a tree, pierced with a lance. What poverty! There is the head of the poor people I am looking for, the poor man of whom we find the genuinely poor person to be a member.

The orphan has God as Father

10. Let's be quick about looking for the orphan, because we are tired out from searching for the poor. Lord Jesus, I'm looking for the orphan, and it's tired I am while I'm looking. Answer me quickly, so that I can find him. *Do not say*, he says, *you have a father on earth* (Mt 23:9). The orphan on earth finds an immortal Father in heaven. *Do not say*, says he, *you have a father on earth.* We have found this orphan. Let him pray, this orphan. Let us hear him praying and imitate him. What is his prayer? *Since my father and my mother have abandoned me. My father*, he says, *and my mother have abandoned me; but the Lord has taken me up* (Ps 27:10). So if *blessed are the poor in spirit, because theirs is the kingdom of heaven* (Mt 5:3), then *to you has the poor man abandoned himself.* And *if my father and my mother have abandoned me, but the Lord has taken me up*, then *you will be a guardian for the orphan* (Ps 10:14).

Sermon 29

A Sermon Preached at Carthage in the Restored Basilica
During the Vigil of Pentecost, on the Verse of Psalm 118:
Confess to the Lord Since He Is Good

This sermon was preached on Psalm 118:1, *Confess to the Lord since he is good*, at the Restored Basilica in Carthage, called such either because the church had been returned after confiscation during the great persecution of 303-313 or because the building had been restored to Catholics after a period of occupation by the Donatists. One editor of the Latin text says that the sermon should be dated to the Vigil of Pentecost on May 24, 397; Hill argues for a date not earlier than 419 because its content is similar to S. 19, also preached at the same basilica, which makes reference to a recent earthquake in the East and another at Sitifis in Mauretania (west of Carthage) datable to 419. Augustine defines confession to include both repentance of sins and praise of God. Even bad people want only good things: a good house, a good wife, a good shirt. What God hates is sin; so too should we, since all sin requires punishment.

God is good of himself

1. We have been admonished to confess to the Lord, and indeed commanded to do so by the Spirit of God. And we have been told the reason for confessing to the Lord: *since he is good.* It is said very briefly; it can be thought about very deeply. *Confess to the Lord*, he says. And as though we asked him "Why?" the answer comes, *since he is good* (Ps 118:1). What more can you ask for, if you ask for anything, than the good? Such is the power of the good, that the good is what is sought even by the bad.

But all the other things that are called good get their being good from some particular good. Now if we examine all good things on what they get their being good from, we should call to mind, *And God made all things, and behold they were very good* (Gn 1:31). So nothing would be good unless it had been made by the good. And by what sort of good? By one that nobody made. So there would be nothing good, unless it had been made by the good which had not itself been made. The heavens are good, but made good; the angels are good, but made good; the stars are good, the sun and the moon, the alternation of night and day, the changes of the seasons, the unrolling of the ages, the course of the years, the germination of trees and plants, the natures of animals, and among all these things the praise-making creature, man.

They are all good, but made good. And it's from God that they get their goodness, not from themselves. The one who made these things is good beyond all of them, because no one made him good, but he is good of himself. So, *Confess to the Lord since he is good.*

Confession can mean either praising or repenting

2. Confession can mean either praising or repenting. You see, there are some less well-informed people who immediately beat their breasts when they hear about confession in the scriptures, as though it can only be about sins, and as if they are being urged now to confess their sins. But to convince your honors that confession doesn't only refer to sins, let us listen to the one about whom we cannot possibly doubt that he had no sin at all, as he cries out and says, *I confess to you, Father, Lord of heaven and earth* (Mt 11:25). Who said this? One *who did no sin, nor was deceit found in his mouth* (1 Pt 2:22); who alone could say with absolute truth, *Behold, the prince of the world is coming, and in me he will find nothing* (Jn 14:30). And yet he confesses. But this confesser is a praiser, not a sinner. Anyway, listen to what he confessed. Listen to words of praise, and what this praise is about is our salvation. For what, precisely, does the Son without sin confess to God the Father? *I confess to you, Father,* he says, *Lord of heaven and earth, because you have hidden these things from the wise and prudent, and have revealed them to little ones* (Mt 11:25). This is what he recited in praise of the Father, that he has hidden these things from the wise and the prudent, that is from the proud and the arrogant, and revealed them to the little ones, that is the weak and the humble.

Confession of sins, not excuses

3. But of course it's also true that the confession of sins is equally salutary. That's why we heard in the psalm that was read first, *Set a guard, Lord, on my mouth, and a door of restraint around my lips, and do not tip my heart into words of malice, to excusing my sins with excuses* (Ps 141:3-4). He asks God to put a guard on his mouth. And he goes on to explain what it is a guard against. There are people, you see, and plenty of them, who as soon as they are blamed for anything rush to make excuses. Now to make excuses is to look for reasons and to adduce pretexts why a sin should not be regarded as belonging to you. One says "The devil did it for me"; another says "My luck did it for me"; another "I was forced to it by fate"; no one blames himself.

Your accuser goes on scoring points off you, as long as you insist on making your own excuses. So do you want to ensure that your accuser — the devil, that is — suffers and groans? Do what you have heard, do what you have learned, and say to your God, *I myself have said it, Lord. Have mercy on me, heal my soul, since I have sinned against you* (Ps 41:4). "I myself," he says, "I myself have said it; not the devil, not luck, not fate. I myself have said it. I'm not making excuses, on the contrary, I accuse myself. I have said it. Have mercy on me, heal my soul." What's he ill with, anyway? "Since I have sinned against you."

4. So, *Confess to the Lord since he is good.* If you want to praise, what can you more safely praise than the Good One? If you want to praise, if you want to make the confession of praise, what can you more safely praise than the Good One? If you want to confess your sins, to whom can you more safely do it than the Good One? You confess to a man, and because he is bad you are condemned. You confess to God, and because he is good you are purged.

If you are thinking of the confession of praise, whatever it is you are going to praise fully and at length, your attention is concentrated on showing that what you are praising is good. Good things, after all, are rightly praised, just as bad things are rightly blamed. The praise of your Lord is put to you very briefly — *he is good.* If you too are good, praise what makes you good; if you are bad, praise what can make you good. If you are good, you see, you get being good from him; if you are bad, you get being bad from yourself. Run away from yourself and come to him who made you, because by running away from yourself you follow yourself up, and by following yourself up you stick fast in him who made you.

Praise what makes you good

5. How many good things there are that you want, bad man! You're certainly bad. Tell me what you want that isn't good. You want a horse, only a good one; you want a farm, only a good one; you want a house, only a good one; you want a wife, only a good one; you want a shirt, only a good one, boots, only good ones. It's only your soul you want bad! Aren't you being a contradiction in terms, by wanting good things while being bad yourself? If you want good things, first be what you want. If being bad you have acquired many good things, what use is it to you, seeing that you yourself have perished?

Love your souls, all of you, if they are good; hate your souls if they are bad. However, by loving him from whom comes everything good, you will be good. Hate your bad points, give preference to the good ones.

6. What does it mean, to hate your bad points? To repent and confess your sins. You see, everyone who repents, and in repenting confesses his sins, is angry with himself, and by repenting he after a fashion punishes in himself what displeases him. What God hates is sin. If you too hate in yourself what God also hates, you are all the same united to God in some part of your will — provided you hate in yourself what God also hates. Be savage against yourself, so that God may intercede for you and not condemn you. Sin, after all, must undoubtedly be punished. That's what sin deserves, punishment, condemnation. Sin must be punished, either by you or by him. If it is punished by you, then it will be punished without you being too; but if it is not punished by you, then it will be punished and so will you.

So, *Confess to the Lord since he is good.* Praise him as much as you can, love him as much as you can. *Pour out your hearts before him, God our helper* (Ps 62:8), *since he is good* (Ps 118:1).

Sermon 39

On the Text in Sirach: *Do Not Delay to Turn to the Lord,*
Nor Put It off from Day to Day

Here Augustine attacks the false allure of money, honors and power. There is nothing wrong per se in wealth and riches as long as they are put to good use. Almsgiving and prayer can help in making up for past sins. The homily focuses on the world's power to seduce us through money, power and honors in order to impress others. Those who possess more should give more. There is no internal evidence to date this sermon but it clearly showcases the bishop at his seasoned best, leading Hill to estimate between 405 and 420.

The last day is hidden from us

1. We have heard God, brothers, saying through the prophet, *Do not delay to turn to the Lord, nor put it off from day to day. For suddenly his wrath will come, and in the time of vengeance he will destroy you* (Sir 5:7). He has promised you that on the day you turn to him and are converted he forgets your past badness. But did he ever promise you life for tomorrow? Or perhaps God didn't promise you that, and some astrologer did, so that God may condemn both you and him? God very beneficially leaves the day of death uncertain; we should all very beneficially think about our own last day. It's by the mercy of God that a man doesn't know when he is going to die. The last day is hidden from us, in order that every day may be taken seriously.

2. But the world retains its hold on us, on all sides its charms decoy us. We like lots of money, we like splendid honors, we like power to overawe others. We like all these things, but let's listen to the apostle: *We brought nothing into this world, neither can we take anything out* (1 Tm 6:7). Honor should be looking for you, not you for it. You, after all, should sit down in the humbler place, so he that invited you may make you go up to a more honored place. But if he doesn't wish to, eat where you are sitting, because you brought nothing into this world. Do you think it's a small matter that you are eating someone else's food? Sit down anywhere and eat. Are you going to say, "It's my food"? Listen to the apostle: *We brought nothing into this world.* You have come to the world, you have found a full table spread for you. But *the Lord's is the earth and its fullness* (Ps 24:1).

3. *For those,* he says, *who wish to get rich* — he didn't say "who are rich," but "who wish to get rich"; he was reproaching greed, not means — *who wish to get rich fall into temptation and desires many and harmful, which plunge people into destruction and ruin* (1 Tm 6:9). You like money. Aren't you afraid of these things? "Money's a good thing, lots of money's a good thing." *They fall into temp-*

tation; aren't you afraid? *They fall into desires many and harmful*; aren't you afraid? What do such desires lead to? *Which plunge people into destruction and ruin*; and are you still deaf: Aren't you afraid of destruction and ruin? God's thundering away like this, and are you snoring?

The worm in the apple of riches is pride

4. However, to those who are already rich the apostle still had some advice to give: *Command,* he says, *the rich of this world not to have proud thoughts.* The worm in the apple of riches is pride. It's difficult for someone who's rich not to be proud. Take away pride, and riches will do no harm. But pay attention to what you should do with them, in case what God has lavished on you should remain idle in your hands. *Not to have proud thoughts*; take that vice away. *Nor set their hopes on the uncertainty of riches* (1 Tm 6:17); take that vice away too. When you've taken these things away, practice the good works you now hear about. *Let them be rich,* he says, *in good works* (1 Tm 6:18). Let them not set their hopes on the uncertainty of riches, but what should they set them on? *On the living God, who provides us abundantly with everything for our enjoyment* (1 Tm 6:17). God bestows the world on the poor, he bestows it on the rich. Does it mean that, just because he's rich, he's got two bellies to fill? Attend to it, all of you, and see that the poor sleep having taken their fill from the gifts of God. The one who feeds you feeds them through you.

With death all riches are lost

5. So, let us not love money. But if you already have it, this is what should be done with it. Be rich, you people who have it. But rich in what way? *In good works. Let them give readily,* he says, *let them share* (1 Tm 6:18). At this, avarice is already pulling in its horns. Listen to what follows: *Let them give readily, let them share …*

It's just as if you'd drenched him with a bucket of cold water; he goes numb, he shivers, he clasps his arms to himself, and he says, "I'm not going to throw away all my work." You poor fish, do you want to throw away your work? You're going to die, see? And just as you brought nothing here, so you can take nothing away from here. Since you've taken nothing away with you, won't you have thrown all your work? So listen to God's advice. Don't panic because he said, *Let them give readily, let them share.* Listen to what follows. Wait for it, don't shut the door in my face, don't bang down the receiver of your mind; wait for it. Do you want to see why *Let them give readily, let them share* doesn't mean you will throw everything away, and in fact is the only way to avoid throwing everything away?

Let them lay down for themselves, he says, *a good foundation for the future, that they may take hold of the true life* (1 Tm 6:19). So this one you take pleasure in is a false life. It's as if you were living here in a dream. If you are living here in a dream, you are going to wake up when you die, and the way you're going, you'll find you've got nothing in your hands. It's like a beggar sleeping, and in a dream he comes into a legacy, and no one could be happier than he before he gets up. He sees himself in his dream handling marvelous clothes, gold and silver plates, strolling into lovely, spacious parks, waited on by a bevy of servants. He wakes up, and he bursts into tears. And just as when he is awake he rails at the man who cleaned him out, so now he rails at the one who woke him up. There's a psalm which has spoken very clearly about this: *They slept their sleep*, it says, *and all the men of wealth found nothing in their hands* (Ps 76:5), after they had finished their sleep.

Christ wanted to be destitute for our sakes

6. So because you brought nothing with you, you are going to take nothing away from here. Send up above what you have acquired, and it won't be thrown away. Give to Christ; you see, Christ wanted to get something from you here. You give something to Christ, and are you throwing it away? You are not throwing it away if you entrust it to your slave, and are you throwing it away if you entrust it to your master? You are not throwing it away if you entrust your slave with what you have earned, and will you be throwing it away if you entrust your master with what you have got from your master in the first place?

Christ wanted to be destitute here — but for our sakes. All the poor people you see — Christ was well able to feed them all, just as he fed Elijah, using the crow. Yet eventually he withdrew the crow even from Elijah. That Elijah should be fed by the widow was a favor he granted the widow, not Elijah. So when God makes people poor, because he doesn't want them to have anything, when he makes people poor he is testing the rich. That's what's written, after all: *The poor man and the rich have met each other* (Prv 22:2). Where have they met each other? In this life. This one was born, that one was born, their lives have crossed, they have met each other. And who made them? The Lord. The rich man, to help the poor; the poor man, to test the rich.

Let everyone do it according to his means. You should not do it to the extent of going broke yourself. That's not what I'm saying. Your extras are someone else's necessities. You heard just now, when the gospel was being read, *Whoever gives a cup of cold water to one of my little ones for my sake shall not lose his reward* (Mt 10:42). He has put the kingdom of heaven up for sale, and fixed the price of it at a cup of cold water. But only when it's a poor person giving alms — then his alms should be a cup of cold water. If you've got more you should give more. That widow did it with two farthings. Zacchaeus gave half his goods, and kept back the other half to pay back the people he had cheated.

Almsgiving is of use to those who have changed their manner of life. You are giving to Christ in need in order to make up for your past sins. After all, if the reason you give is in order to be allowed to sin any time you like with impunity, you are not feeding Christ, but trying to bribe the judge. So give alms with the purpose of getting your prayers heard and getting God to help you change your manner of life for the better. And those of you who are changing your way of life, see that you change it for the better. And by almsgiving and prayers may past evils be blotted out and future good things come that are everlasting.

Sermon 49

Sermon Preached at the Shrine of Saint Cyprian on a Sunday

This sermon focuses on the importance of "doing justice." Hill believes that it reflects the mature preacher because of its relative brevity, and he estimates the year 420. The reference to St. Stephen in section 11 without any mention of Christmas precludes the martyr's feast day on Dec. 26th and points likely to a Sunday during Easter, when the Book of Acts was read. The location is clearly the Celerina Basilica in Carthage. Augustine offers sound advice on the subject of human relations. In the case of a friendship among three, a falling out between two members should not affect the third: "Remain the friend of both."

Preface

1. We heard several holy lessons while they were being recited, and about these it is my duty to say whatever the Lord may be pleased to grant. But every listener to the readings remembers best what has been read last, and expects something to be said about that by the handler of the word. So since the holy gospel was the last thing to be recited, I don't doubt your graces are expecting to hear something about that vineyard, and about the hired laborers, and about the wage of a dollar. I, though, remember what I promised last Sunday. I wanted to explain something that had been read from the holy prophet — what had been was that the man who asked what sacrifices he should appease God with was informed that God required nothing of him but to do judgment and justice, and to love mercy, and to be ready to go with the Lord his God. Well I dealt with the point about judgment to the best of my ability, and the sermon went on so long that no time was left for me to discuss the other points. That's why I promised that today I would speak about justice. But those of you who were expecting me to talk about the gospel mustn't consider yourselves cheated. The work in that vineyard, after all, is precisely justice.

Justice and faith

2. So consider that you yourselves have been hired. Those who came in as children can reckon they were hired at the first hour; if you came in as teenagers, at the third hour; as young people, at the sixth; as mature adults, at the ninth; as decrepit old things, at the eleventh. Don't argue about the time; listen to the work you are to do, wait serenely for your wages. And if you reflect what sort of person your Lord is, don't resent the wages all being the same. You know what the work is, but I will remind you. Listen to what you know, and do what you hear.

I have said that the work of God is justice. But when the Lord Jesus was asked what the work of God is, he replied, *This is the work of God, that you should believe in the one whom he has sent* (Jn 6:29). Our loving Lord could have said, "Justice is the work of God." So have I, a mere hired laborer, had the gall to take up a position against the head of the household? If justice is the work of God, as I said, how can what the Lord said be the work of God, namely to believe in him — unless believing in him is justice? "But look," you say, "we have heard from the Lord that this is the work of God, that you should believe in him; from you we have heard that the work of God is justice. Prove to us that believing in Christ is justice."

Do you think — since I am replying to a just and urgent question — do you think that believing in Christ is not justice? What is it then? Give a name to this work. Undoubtedly, if you consider carefully what you have heard, you are going to answer me, "This is called faith. Believing in Christ is called faith." I accept what you say: believing in Christ is called faith. Now you in your turn listen to another text of scripture: *The just lives by faith* (Hb 2:4). Do justice, believe; *the just lives by faith*. It's hard for someone who believes well to live badly. Believe with your whole heart, believe without wavering, without hesitation, without pitting human skepticism against the faith.

"Faith" comes from the Latin *fides*, and that is so called because it is no sooner said than done. There are two syllables when you say *fides*. The first syllable is from *factum*, what's done, the second from *dictum*, what's said. So, I'm asking you whether you believe. You say, "I believe." Do what you say, and it's faith. I can hear your voice as you reply, I can't see your heart as you believe. But I'm not the one who hired you into the vineyard, am I, I who cannot see your heart? I don't do the hiring, I don't indicate the work to be done, I don't make up the dollar-a-day pay packet. I am your fellow worker. With whatever strength he has been pleased to grant me, I am laboring in the vineyard. But in what kind of spirit I am laboring the one who hired me can see. *For to me*, says the apostle, *it is a very small thing that I should be judged by you* (1 Cor 4:3). You too can hear my voice, you cannot see my heart. Let us all set our hearts before God for him to see, and do our work wholeheartedly. Let us not offend the one who hired us, so that we may receive our wages without effrontery.

We are light and darkness

3. We too, beloved, will be able to see each other's hearts, but only later on. For the time being, however, we are still carrying around with us the darkness of this mortality, and we walk by the lamplight of scripture, as the apostle Peter says: *We have the firmly established prophetic word, to which you would do well to attend, as to a lamp in a dark place, until the day dawns and the morning star rises in your hearts* (2 Pt 1:19). Accordingly, beloved, because of the faith with which we believe in God, we are the day in comparison with unbelievers. In unbelief we were the night together with them, but now light, as the apostle says: *You were once darkness, but now light in the Lord* (Eph 5:8). Darkness in yourselves, light in the Lord. Again in another place: *For you are all sons of light and sons of the day;*

we are not of the night, nor of the dark (1 Thes 5:5). *Let us walk becomingly as in the day* (Rom 13:13). So we are the day in comparison with unbelievers.

But in comparison with that day, when the dead will rise and this perishable thing will put on imperishability and this mortal thing put on immortality, we are still the night. As though we were already in the day, the apostle John says to us, *Dearly beloved, we are children of God.* And yet because it is still night, how does it go on? *And it has not yet appeared what we shall be. We know that when he appears we shall be like him, because we shall see him as he is* (1 Jn 3:2). But that's the wages, not the work. *We shall see him as he is* is the wages. Then it will be a day than which there can be none brighter.

Meanwhile, then, in this already-day let us walk becomingly; in this still-night let us not pass judgment on one another. You can see, I hope, that the apostle Paul saying, *Let us walk becomingly as in the day*, is not at odds nor out of tune with his fellow apostle Peter saying, *To which you would do well to attend*, namely to the divine word, *as to a lamp in a dark place, until the day dawns and the morning star rises in your hearts.*

Impossible to read the heart

4. Now observe the apostle Paul also saying the same thing: *Therefore do not make any judgment before the time.* And when will the time be? *Until the Lord comes and lights up things hidden in darkness and reveals the thoughts of the heart, and then everyone shall have praise from God* (1 Cor 4:5). What does *before the time* mean, if not "before you see each other's hearts"? Just see if this is what I have been saying. Listen bit by bit to all the words of that sentence. *Do not make any judgment before the time.* And when will the time be? *Until the Lord comes and lights up things hidden in darkness, and he will reveal the thoughts of the heart, and then everyone shall have praise from God.* How will the darkness find fault with you, when you are being praised by the light?

Then hearts will be out in the open, but now they are lying low. Someone or other is looked at askance as an enemy, and perhaps he's a friend. Someone else rather looks like a friend, and is possibly a hidden enemy. Oh what darkness! This one roars, and he loves; that one coos, and he hates. If I judge by their words, I avoid calm waters and run on the reef; I flee from a friend and cling to an enemy. That's all the result of the heart lying low. And that's where believing is to be done, there inside where it's lying low, where it's hidden. It was to cultivate this that you were hired. That's where you must work together by believing, where your fellow worker can't see you but your Lord can. *The just lives by faith* (Hb 2:4). Do just that.

Judge yourself, don't spare yourself

5. I have already discussed judgment, last Sunday, pointing out that you should judge yourself, and when you find yourself to be crooked or perverse you shouldn't coddle yourself, but correct yourself and become straight or upright, and so take pleasure in the upright God. The upright God, you see, cannot be pleasing to the crooked man. Do you want to take pleasure in the upright God? Be upright yourself. Judge yourself, don't spare yourself. Whatever there is about you that displeases you, clean it up, mend it, put it straight. Use the holy scriptures like a mirror. This mirror has a reflective sheen that doesn't lie, a sheen that doesn't flatter, that doesn't respect the person of anyone. You're beautiful, you see yourself beautiful; you're ugly, you see yourself ugly. But when you come in front of it in your ugliness and see yourself ugly, don't blame the mirror. Go back to yourself, the mirror isn't deceiving you, take care you don't deceive yourself. Pass judgment on yourself, be sorry about your ugliness, and so as you turn away and go off sorry and ugly, you may be able to correct yourself and come back beautiful.

So when you have judged yourself without flattery, go on to judge your neighbor. The fact is, you see, that you judge by what you see. Because it can happen that while you see the badness that is defiling you, it can happen that your neighbor comes and confesses his badness to you, and discloses to a friend what he had concealed even from himself. Judge according as you see; what you don't see, leave to God. And when you judge, love the person, hate the vice. Don't love the vice for the person's sake, nor hate the person for the vice's sake. Your neighbor is the person; the vice is your neighbor's enemy. You show that you love your friend if you hate what harms your friend. If you believe, you act accordingly, because *the just lives by faith* (Hb 2:4).

Love the person, hate the vice

6. There are plenty of instances in human affairs of what I am saying. Sometimes your dearest friend has an enemy who was a friend of you both. Of three friends two begin to be enemies of each other; what is the one to do who remains in the middle? He desires, insists, implores you to hate with him the one he has begun to hate, and he says to you like this: "You are not my friend, since you are my enemy's friend." The words you get from this one, you also get from that one. You see, there were three of you. There were the three of you, two began to fall out, the one left was you. If you join this one, you will have that one as your enemy; if that one, this one; if both, both will complain. There's a trial and a testing for you; there you have the thorns in the vineyard we have been hired to work in.

Perhaps you are expecting to hear from me what you should do. Remain the friend of both of them. They have fallen out with each other; let them fall in with you and with each other through your good offices. If you hear nasty things about each of them from the other, don't betray them to the other — or else though they are enemies now, they may perhaps become friends later and betray to each other their betrayers. But that's an all too human reason I have given, and it's not for the eyes and ears of the one who has hired us. Look, no one is betraying you. It's God who sees, God who judges you. You have heard a word from an angry man, from someone who's been deeply hurt, who has flared up in a temper. Let it die in you. Why disclose it, why pass it on? After all, if it stays in you, it won't burst you.

So, of course, say to your friend, who wants to make you the enemy of your friend — speak to him and so to say massage his aching spirit with a soothing liniment — say to him: "Why do you want me to be his enemy?" "Because he's my enemy," he answers. "So you want me to be your enemy's enemy? What I ought to be the enemy of is your vice. This one you want to make me the enemy of is a human being. You have another enemy, whose enemy I ought to be if I am your friend." "Who is this other enemy of mine?" he answers. "Your vice." "What's my vice?" he asks. "The hatred you hate your friend with." So be like a doctor. A doctor doesn't love the sick person if he doesn't hate the sickness. To set the sick free, he persecutes the fever. Don't love the vices of your friends if you love your friends.

A speck and beam in the eye

7. But who's talking? Do you suppose I do what I say myself? My brothers, I do do it, if I do it first on myself. And I do it on myself, if I receive the ability to from the Lord, then I do it. I hate my vices, I offer my heart for healing to my doctor. I persecute them as best I can, I sigh about them, I confess that they are in me, and finally, I blame myself. You that were finding fault with me, first put yourself right. That's justice, which saves us from being told, *You see the speck in your brother's eye, and do not see the beam in your own eye? Hypocrite, first pull the beam out of your own eye, and then you will be able to see to draw the speck out of your brother's eye* (Mt 7:3-4).

Anger is a speck, hatred is a beam. But nurse a speck, and it becomes a beam. Anger grown chronic becomes hatred, the speck that is nursed becomes a beam. So to prevent the speck becoming a beam, *do not let the sun go down upon your wrath* (Eph 4:26). You can see, you know perfectly well that you are riddled with hate, and you find fault with someone for being angry? Eliminate the hatred, and you are quite right to reproach anger. There's a speck in his eye, a beam in yours. After all, if you are busy hating, how can you see what you are to pull out? There's a beam in your eye. Why is there a beam in your eye? Because you made light of the speck that was planted there. You went to sleep with it, you got up with it. You cultivated it in yourself, you watered it with groundless suspicions; by believing the words of flatterers and people telling you nasty tales about your friend you nursed the speck instead of whipping it out.

Are you getting very frightened, or aren't you? I'm telling you: Don't hate, and you've nothing to worry about. And you answer me and say to me, "What does hating matter? And what's wrong with a man hating his enemy?" You are hating your brother. But if you make light of hatred, listen to something you are failing to take into account: *Whoever hates his brother is a murderer* (1 Jn 3:15). Whoever hates is a murderer. Can you now say, "What do I care about being a murderer?" Whoever hates is a murderer. You haven't prepared any poison, you haven't gone so far as to strike your enemy with a sword, you haven't hired a hit-man for the crime, or worked out a place and a time. Finally, you haven't committed the crime yourself. You have only hated — and you have killed yourself before him.

So learn justice, to hate only vices, and to love people. If you stick to this, and practice this sort of justice, so that you prefer even vicious people to be cured rather than condemned, then you have been doing good work in the vineyard. But mind you work at this, my brothers.

Forgive with all your heart

8. Look — after the sermon there's the dismissal of the catechumens. The faithful will stay behind. We are coming to the place in the service for prayer. You know what it is we are going to draw near to. What are we going to say to God first? *Forgive us our debts, just as we too forgive our debtors* (Mt 6:12). See that you do forgive, see that you do. You are coming to these words in the prayer. How are you going to say them, how are you not going to say them? Finally, I ask you, Are you going to say them, or aren't you? You hate, and you say them? "In that case," you answer, "I'm not saying them." You're praying, and not saying them? You hate, and you say them? You pray, and you don't say them? Come on, come on, answer quickly. So if you do say them you lie; if you don't say them, you don't deserve anything.

Look at yourself, observe yourself. You are shortly going to pray; forgive with all your heart. If you want to quarrel with your enemy, quarrel first with your own heart. Quarrel, I tell you, quarrel with your own heart. Tell your heart, Don't hate. But that heart of yours, those feelings of yours — are still hating. Tell your soul, "Stop hating. How will I pray, how will I be able to say *Forgive us our debts*? Well, I can say this, of course, but how can I say what follows? *Just as we too*." We too what? "*Just as we too forgive*." Where is your faith? Do what you say: *Just as we too.*

9. But your soul doesn't want to forgive, and is made miserable by your saying to it, Stop hating. Answer it, "*Why are you miserable, my soul, and why do you upset me?* (Ps 42:6). Why are you miserable? Stop hating, or you will destroy me. Why do you upset me? *Hope in God.* You are very ill, you are gasping, you're crippled with disease. You're unable to rid yourself of hatred. *Hope in God,* he's the doctor. For your sake he hung on the cross, and he hasn't yet avenged himself. Why do you want to avenge yourself? That's what your hating means, you see, a desire for revenge. Look at your Lord hanging, look at him hanging, and giving you a directive from that kind of judicial bench which is the cross. Look at him hanging there, and concocting a medicine for you in your illness from his own blood. Look at him hanging there. You want revenge? You want to get even? Look at him hanging there, and listen to him praying, *Father, forgive them, because they do not know what they are doing* (Lk 23:34).

Cast your eye on Stephen

10. "But he could do that," you say to me, "I can't. I, after all, am just a man, he's God. I'm a man, that man is the God-man." So why is God man, if man is not to correct himself? But anyway look, it's just me talking to you. It's too much for you, man, to imitate your Lord; cast your eye on Stephen, your fellow servant. Saint Stephen, certainly, was a man. Or was he God and man? He was simply a man. He was what you are. As for what he did, it was only with a grant in aid from the one whom you too are asking for help. However, just see what it was he did.

He was speaking to the Jews, he was being harsh and he was being loving. I have got to show you both, because I said he was being harsh, and I also said he was being loving. I'm bound to demonstrate both, Stephen harsh and Stephen loving. Listen to him being harsh: *Stiffnecked* — they are Saint Stephen's words when he was addressing the Jews — *Stiff-necked and uncircumcised of heart and ears, you people have always resisted the Holy Spirit. Which of the prophets did your fathers not kill?* (Acts 7:51-52).

You have heard him being harsh; now I owe you the other Stephen; listen to him being loving. That made them very angry, and growing hotter and more violent they returned evil for good, they rushed to pick up stones, and began stoning the servant of God. Now, Saint Stephen, prove your love. Now, now let's see you, now let us watch, now let us observe you conquering and triumphing over the devil. We heard you raging against them while they kept silent; let's see if you love them when they are raging. You were raging against them while they kept silent; let's see if you love them while they are stoning you. After all, if you hate and have ever been able to hate, now is the time for it, when you are being stoned. Then, surely, if ever, you ought to hate. Let's see if you pay back hardness of heart to the hard stones, to the stones who are stoning you. It's stones, you see, who are throwing stones, rock-hard men throwing rocks. They received the law on stone, and they throw stones.

11. Let's go and see, beloved, let's go and see, let's watch this great spectacle. Let's watch the show that is also to be presented tomorrow. Let's go and see. Here's Stephen being stoned. Suppose him to be set there in front of our very eyes. Ho there, member of Christ, ho there, athlete of Christ; look upon him who for your sake hung upon the cross. He was being crucified, you are being stoned. He said, *Father, forgive them, because they do not know what they are doing* (Lk 23:34). What do you say? Let me hear. Let me see whether I may at least be able to imitate you.

First the blessed Stephen stood and prayed for himself, and said, *Lord Jesus, receive my spirit.* When he had said that he knelt down, and on his knees he said, *Lord, do not hold this crime against them. Saying this, he fell asleep* (Acts 7:59-60). Oh what blissful sleep, what true and perfect rest! There you are, that's what resting really is — praying for enemies.

But I have a little question, please, to ask you, Saint Stephen. Please explain to me, I don't know what it means, why you prayed for yourself standing, and knelt for your enemies. Perhaps he will give us an answer we can understand: "I prayed for myself standing, because I had no difficulty in praying and obtaining a favor for myself, as one who served God faithfully." There's no difficulty in praying for the just. That's why he prayed for himself standing.

Then it came to having to pray for the Jews, for the slayers of Christ, for the slayers of the saints, for his own executioners who were stoning him; he thought of their colossal, their extreme disloyalty, which it would be very hard to pardon — and he knelt down.

Kneel down in this vineyard, doughty worker. Kneel down, I say, for the work of this vineyard, doughtiest of workers. You have done great work, quite outstanding, quite beyond praise. You have dug very deep to pull up hatred of your enemies from your heart.

Turning to the Lord etc.

Sermon 51

The Harmony Between the Evangelists Matthew and Luke
Concerning the Lord's Genealogy

This sermon is rather avant garde in its treatment of the equality of the sexes in an era known for patriarchy. It was preached on the Octave of Christmas (Jan. 1st) or the Feast of the Epiphany (Jan. 6th), 418, ostensibly to explain the discrepancies in the genealogies of Matthew and Luke, but Augustine is primarily concerned with the subject of sexual morality within marriage. Jesus came as a man to honor the male sex and was born of a woman to honor the female sex. Joseph is a true parent of Jesus even though he was not the biological father. Sexual expression is not necessary for a true marriage (unlike the present Code of Canon Law's requirement.) The bishop maintains that the patriarchs engaged in sexual intercourse with their multiple wives for the purpose of procreation only. Polygamy was permitted them for purposes of procreation in order to build up the population of Israel. Augustine is decidedly negative on assigning any positive role to sexual pleasure.

Fulfillment of a Christian promise

1. Let's hope that the expectations which your graces have will be met by the one who raised them; because while we may safely assume that what I have to say to you is God's word and not mine, nonetheless I can much more properly

say what the apostle says so humbly: *We have this treasure in earthen vessels, that the exceeding greatness of the power may be God's and not come from us* (2 Cor 4:7). So I am sure you remember the promise I made you. I made the promise in God, and through him I now intend to keep it. When I made it, you see, I was asking for his help in keeping it, and now I am receiving his help in keeping it. But your graces will also remember that on Christmas morning I put off solving a question I had raised, because there were many people celebrating that day's feast with us, who usually find explanations of the word of God rather a bore. But now, I assume, it is only people who want to listen that have come together here. So I am not speaking to hearts that are deaf, or to disdainful minds.

These expectations, though, of yours are like prayers for me. More than that; the games on today have blown many people away from here, for whose salvation I am greatly concerned, and I urge you, brothers, to feel as much concern for them yourselves, and to pray earnestly to God for those who are not yet in earnest about the shows truth puts on, but are still given over to shows put on for the flesh. You see, I know, I have no doubt at all that there are now some among you who thought very little of today; but they are breaking the habits that they had stitched together. People do change, after all, both for better and for worse. We are alternately heartened and saddened by experiences of this sort almost every day; heartened by people going straight, saddened by people turning crooked. That's why the Lord did not say that whoever begins will be saved, but *Whoever perseveres*, says he, *to the end, that's the one who will be saved* (Mt 10:22).

Bring home to your friends the delight of your show

2. What more wonderful present could be given us by the Lord Jesus Christ, Son of God who is also son of man because he was even prepared to become *that* — what more magnificent present could he bestow on us, than to add to his sheepfold not only the spectators of these frivolous shows, but also several of those who are used to being themselves the spectacle in them to be gaped at? As well as the fans of the hunters, you see, he has also hunted the hunters themselves into the nets of salvation, because he too once provided a spectacle to be gaped at. Let me tell you how. He told us himself, before he became a spectacle to be gaped at he foretold it himself, and in prophetic language he declared beforehand what was going to happen as if it already had. He said in the psalm, *They dug my hands and my feet, they counted all my bones* (Ps 22:16.17). There you have how he became a spectacle to be stared at, so that they even counted his bones. He goes on to call it a spectacle even more plainly: *They, however, looked at me closely and stared at me* (Ps 22:17). He was stared at in mockery, he was stared at by people who didn't even cheer him on in that show, but raged against him; in much the same way he had his witnesses and martyrs stared at in the beginning, as the apostle says: *We have become a spectacle to the world and to angels and to men* (1 Cor 4:9).

There are, however, two kinds of people who look on at such spectacles, one of materially-minded, the other of spiritually-minded people. The materially-minded look on, and think how wretched and unfortunate those martyrs are, thrown to wild beasts, beheaded, burned with fire, and they are filled with detestation and horror. Others, however, look on, as do the holy angels also, and don't fix their attention on the mangling of bodies, but instead marvel at the completeness of faith. A splendid spectacle offered to the eyes of the mind is a spirit whole and unbroken while the body is torn to pieces. That is what you people gaze on with pleasure when the accounts of such things are read in church. After all, if you didn't form some sort of picture of what happened, it would mean you weren't listening at all.

So you can see that in fact you haven't disdained the show today, but rather have chosen which show you will attend. May God then be with you and help you to bring home to your friends, whom you are so sorry to see running off to the stadium today and refusing to come to church, to bring home to them the delights of your show. This, we hope, will cheapen in their eyes the other shows for love of which they have cheapened themselves, and start them joining you in loving God, whom no one can possibly be shamed by loving, because you are loving one who cannot be beaten; joining you in loving Christ, who by the very fact of seeming to be beaten became the champion who beat the whole world.

Because he did indeed beat the whole world, as we can see, brothers. He has subjected all the powers to himself, he has made kings pass under the yoke, not with a proud army but with the absurdity of the cross, not by hacking away with steel but by hanging on a tree, suffering in body, acting in spirit. In their view his body was hoisted up on the cross; he in fact was subduing their minds to the cross. In short, what jewel in the crown of rulers is more precious than the cross of Christ upon their foreheads?

If you love him, you need never lose countenance, never look foolish. How many people, do you suppose, are coming back from the stadium with their tails between their legs, because the ones they were yelling for were beaten there! In fact, they would have been even more badly beaten if they had won; they would have become a prey to vain rejoicing, a prey to the excitement of a twisted kind of greed. They have been defeated by the very fact of their running off there. How many do you suppose there were, brothers, who were in two minds today whether to come here or go there. Those who made up their minds by thinking about Christ and came along to the church defeated not any mere human being but the devil himself, the most dreadful hunter of the whole world. But those who eventually decided to run along instead to the stadium were of course beaten by the very one the others had defeated; defeated in him who said, *Rejoice, because I have overcome the world* (Jn 16:33). The reason the commander-in-chief allowed himself to be tested and tried was to teach his soldiers how to fight.

Nobody should belittle Christ for being born of a woman

3. So then in order to do this, our Lord Jesus Christ became a son of man, by being born of course of a woman. But supposing he hadn't been born of the virgin Mary, would he have been any the less so? Someone may say, "He wanted to be a man; he would have been a man, even though he hadn't been born of a woman; after all, the first man he made he didn't make from a woman." Let's see how to answer this one. You say, "Why should he choose a woman in order to get born?" The answer you get is, "Why should he avoid a woman in order to get born?" Suppose I am not able to show why he should choose to be born of a woman; you must still show me what he ought to avoid in a woman. But really we have been through it all before; if he had avoided a woman's womb, it would rather have indicated that he could be defiled by it. But in fact, the more undefiled he was in his own proper being, the less reason he had to shrink from a bodily womb, as though he could be defiled by it. But instead, by being born of a woman, he would bring home to us a point of great significance.

After all, brothers, I too am perfectly ready to admit that if the Lord had wanted to become man without being born of woman, it would have been something quite easy for his sovereign majesty to achieve. Just as he was able to be born of a woman without a man, so he could have been born without even a woman. But what he is showing us here is that in neither of its sexes need humanity despair of itself. Human beings, of course, are divided by sex into males and females. So if, while appearing as a man — and I agree he had to be that — he had not been born of a woman, women would have despaired of themselves, remembering their first sin, how it was through a woman that the first man was ensnared, and would have thought that there was absolutely no hope for them in Christ. So he came as a man to show his preference for the male sex, and he was born of a woman to comfort the female sex. It's as though he made them a little speech and said, "To show you that it's not any creature of God's that is bad, but that it's crooked pleasures that distort them, in the beginning when I made man, I made them male and female. I don't reject and condemn any creature that I have made. Here I am, born a man, born of a woman. So I don't reject any creature I have made, but I reject and condemn sins, which I didn't make. Let each sex take note of its proper honor, and each confess its iniquity, and each hope for salvation."

Man was ensnared through a woman administering poison; let man be restored through a woman administering salvation. Let woman compensate for the sin of the man ensnared through her by giving birth to the Christ. That too is why women were the first to tell the apostles about God rising from the dead. A woman brought the news of death to her man in paradise; and women too brought the news of salvation to men in the Church. The apostles were to carry the news of Christ's resurrection to the nations; the news was brought to the apostles by women. Nobody, therefore, should belittle Christ for being born of a woman, the sex that could not defile him as liberator, the sex to which he owed a testimonial as creator.

(...)

Faith in the scriptures

6. Some people bring up their pettifogging objections, and say, "Matthew, of course, is an evangelist, isn't he?" "Yes," we reply, with pious lips, with devout hearts, without the slightest hesitation; that's our straight answer: "Matthew is an evangelist." "Do you believe him?" they ask. Does anyone fail to answer, "I do" — as your pious murmurs indicate? Yes, brothers; if you have no qualms about believing, there's nothing you need be ashamed of. I am speaking to you as one who was myself caught out once upon a time, when as a lad I wanted to tackle the divine scriptures with the techniques of clever disputation before bringing to them the spirit of earnest inquiry. In this way I was shutting the door of my Lord against myself by my misplaced attitude; I should have been knocking at it for it to be opened, but instead I was adding my weight to keep it shut. I was presuming to seek in my pride what can only be found by humility.

How much more fortunate are you people now! How serenely you learn, how safely, those of you who are still little ones in the nest of faith, being fed with spiritual food. But I, poor wretch, fondly imagining I was ready to fly, left the nest and fell to the ground before I could fly. The Lord, though, in his mercy, to save me from being trampled to death by the passers-by, picked me up and put me back in the nest. You see, I was seriously put out by these very problems which I am about to state and solve for you now, without the slightest qualm, in the name of the Lord.

How is Christ son of Abraham and son of David

7. So, as I was saying, this is how these people bring their quibbling charges: "Matthew," they say, "is an evangelist, and you believe him?" Certainly it follows; we admit he is an evangelist, we are bound to believe him. "Now look at the genealogy of Christ as set out by Matthew: *The book of the genealogy of Jesus Christ, son of David, son of Abraham* (Mt 1:1). How is he the son of David, how is he the son of Abraham?" "Well, you can only show how by listing the generations." "We all agree, surely, that when the Lord was born of the Virgin Mary, neither Abraham nor David was still around in the ordinary human way. And you are saying he is the son of David, you are saying he's the son of Abraham, both at the same time?" Suppose we now turn to Matthew and say, "So prove your assertion. What I'm hoping for is a list of Christ's ancestors." *Abraham*, he says, *begot Isaac. Isaac begot Jacob. Jacob begot Judah and his brothers. Judah begot Perez and Zerah by Tamar. Perez begot Hezron. Hezron begot Ram. Ram begot Amminadab. Amminadab begot Nahshon. Nahshon begot Salmon. Salmon begot Boaz by Rahab. Boaz begot Obed by Ruth. Obed begot Jesse. Jesse begot David the king.*

Now observe how from here on we come from David to Christ, who is called the son of Abraham and the son of David. *David*, he continues, *begot Solomon by her who had been Uriah's wife. Solomon begot Rehoboam. Rehoboam begot Abijah. Abijah begot Asa. Asa begot Jehoshaphat, Jehoshaphat begot Joram.*

*Joram begot Uzziah. Uzziah begot Jotham. Jotham begot Ahaz. Ahaz begot
Hezekiah. Hezekiah begot Manasseh. Manasseh begot Amon. Amon begot
Josiah. Josiah begot Jechoniah and his brothers at the time of the migration
to Babylon. And after the migration to Babylon Jechoniah begot Shealtiel.
Shealtiel begot Zerubbabel. Zerubbabel begot Abiud. Abiud begot Eliakim.
Eliakim begot Azor. Azor begot Zadok. Zadok begot Achim. Achim begot Eliud.
Eliud begot Eleazar. Eleazar begot Matthan, Matthan begot Jacob. Jacob begot
Joseph, the husband of Mary, of whom was born Jesus, who is called the Christ*
(Mt 1:2-16). So in this way, by a chain of successive parents and ancestors, we
find how Christ is the son of David and the son of Abraham.

(...)

Christ's ancestry through Joseph

16. Here's another of their niggling objections. Christ's ancestry, they say, is
traced through Joseph and not through Mary. May I have your holinesses' attention for a moment? They say it ought not to have been traced through Joseph.
Why oughtn't it? Wasn't Joseph Mary's husband? "No," they reply, "who says
he is?" Well, scripture says he was her husband, on the angel's authority: *Do not
be afraid*, it says, *to take Mary as your wife. For what is conceived in her is of the
Holy Spirit* (Mt 1:20-21). He is also told to give the child a name, even though it
was not born of his own seed. *She will bear a son*, it says, *and you shall call his
name Jesus*. Scripture does, of course deliberately state that he was not born of
Joseph's seed, when Joseph, anxious about how Mary came to be pregnant, is
told, *It is of the Holy Spirit*. And yet he is not deprived of his paternal authority,
since he is told to give the child a name. And in any case, the Virgin Mary
herself, perfectly well aware that she had not conceived Christ by Joseph's
conjugal embrace, still calls him Christ's father.

Joseph, the father of Christ

17. Let me tell you on what occasion. When the Lord Jesus Christ was twelve
years old — as a human being, since as God he is before all times and apart from
time — he stayed behind in the temple when they left, and went on engaging his
elders in discussion, and winning their admiration at his teaching. They were
returning from Jerusalem, and looked for him in their company, that is among those
they were traveling with. When they didn't find him they went back, very worried,
to Jerusalem, and found him discussing things in the temple with the old men, when
he was — as I said — twelve years old. But why be surprised? The Word of God is
never silent, though he is not always heard. So he is found in the temple, and his
mother says to him, *Why have you treated us like this? Your father and I have been
very worried, looking for you. And he said, Did you not know that I have to be about*

my Father's business? (Lk 2:48-49). He said this because he was the Son of God in the temple of God. That temple, after all, wasn't Joseph's but God's.

"So there you are," somebody says; "he didn't agree that he was Joseph's son." Now just a little more patience, please, brothers, because we haven't much time and we want it to last the sermon. When Mary said *Your father and I have been very worried looking for you,* he answered, *Did you not know that I have to be about my Father's business?* because he was not willing to be their son in such a way that they didn't realize he was the Son of God. The Son of God is always the Son of God, the one who created them, after all. But as son of man, born in time of the virgin without seed of her husband, he still had each of them as a parent. How do we prove this? Mary has already said, *Your father and I have been very worried, looking for you.*

Mary's modesty

18. In the first place, brothers, we should not pass over in silence such saintly modesty as Mary's, especially for the lesson it offers for the ladies, our sisters. She had given birth to Christ, the angel had come to her and told her, *Behold, you shall conceive in the womb, and you shall bear a son, and you shall call his name Jesus. He will be great, and will be called Son of the Most High* (Lk 1:31-32). She had been found worthy to bear the Son of the Most High, and she was so humble. She didn't put herself before her husband even in the order she mentioned them in, and say "I and your father," but "Your father and I" is what she said. She took no notice of the dignity of her womb, but she paid attention to the right order of marriage. The humble Christ, after all, would never have taught his mother to be proud. *Your father and I have been very worried, looking for you.* "Your father," she says, "and I"; because the head of the woman is the man. How much less reason, then, for other women to be proud!

Mary too, you see, was called "a woman," not suggesting any loss of virginity, but simply using the word proper to her sex. The apostle says of the Lord Jesus Christ, *Made of a woman*; but for all that, he did not cancel the article of our faith in which we confess that he was born of the Holy Spirit and the virgin Mary. For it was as a virgin that she conceived, as a virgin that she gave birth, and a virgin that she remained. But they called all females "women," according to the usage of the Hebrew language. Here is the clearest example. The first female, whom God made of the rib taken from the man's side, was already called "woman" even before she slept with the man, which happened, we are told, after they had departed from paradise; scripture says, *He fashioned it into a woman* (Gn 2:22).

Christ does not deny Joseph as father

19. So when the Lord Jesus Christ answers *I had to be about my Father's business,* while he is indicating that God is his Father, he is not thereby denying that Joseph is his father too. How can we prove this? By the scripture, which puts it like

this: *And he said to them, Did you not know that I had to be about my Father's business? But they did not understand what it was he said to them. And when he had gone down with them, he came to Nazareth and was subject to them* (Lk 2:49-51). It doesn't say, "He was subject to his mother," or "He was subject to her," but it says "He was subject to them." Who was he subject to? To his parents, surely. They were both his parents, and he was subject to them, seeing fit to be so just as he saw fit to be the son of man.

Just now it was the ladies receiving instructions; now it's the children's turn, to accept the example of respecting their parents and being subject to them. The whole world is subject to Christ; Christ is subject to his parents.

Son and Lord of David

20. So you see, brothers, when he said *I have to be about my Father's business,* he did not mean us to take him as saying "You are not my parents." They, though, are his parents in time, that Father is so eternally. They are the parents of the son of man. He is the Father of the Word and of his Wisdom, the Father of his power, through which he formed everything. If everything is formed through that which reaches mightily from end to end and disposes all things sweetly, then they too were formed through the Son of God, they to whom he himself would later on be subject as son of man.

And the apostle calls him the son of David: *whom he had,* he says, *from the seed of David, according to the flesh* (Rom 1:3). As a matter of fact, the Lord himself put this problem to the Jews, and the apostle solves it here in these very words. After saying *whom he had from the seed of David,* he adds *according to the flesh* in order precisely to have us understand that according to the divinity he is not the son of David, but the Son of God, the Lord of David. This is how the apostle speaks somewhere else, when he wanted to speak in favor of the Jewish stock: *whose are the fathers,* he says, *of whom is Christ according to the flesh, who is God above all things, blessed for ever* (Rom 9:5). *According to the flesh* means "son of David"; *God above all things, blessed for ever* means "Lord of David."

So the Lord says to the Jews, *Whose son do you say the Christ is? They answered, David's.* They knew that perfectly well, they could gather it easily enough from the preaching of the prophets. And indeed he was *from the seed of David,* but *according to the flesh,* through the virgin Mary, married to Joseph. So when they answered that Christ was the son of David, Jesus said to them, *So how does David in the spirit call him Lord, saying: The Lord said to my lord, Sit at my right hand until I place your enemies under your feet? So if David in the spirit calls him Lord, how is he his son?* (Mt 22:42-46; Ps 110:1) And the Jews couldn't answer. That's what we have in the gospel. He did not deny he was the son of David, even though they were unaware that he was the Lord of David. What they held to about the Christ was that he came to be in time; what they did not understand about him was that he *is* in eternity. So therefore, wishing to teach them about his divinity, he put a problem to them about his humanity, as though to say, "You know that the Christ is the son of David; answer and tell me how he can also be the Lord of David." But to prevent them saying "He isn't David's Lord," he quoted David himself as a witness. And what does *he* say? He says the truth, of course. On the one hand you have that place in the psalms where he says to David, *I will place of the fruit of your body upon your throne* (Ps 132:11). There you have "son of David." And how is the one who is the son of David also "Lord of David"? *The Lord said to my lord*, he says, *Sit at my right* (Ps 110:1). Are you surprised at David having his son as his Lord, when you see Mary has given birth to her Lord? David's Lord, because he's God; David's Lord, because he's everyone's; but David's son, on the other hand, because he's the son of man. One and the same person who's Lord and who's son: David's Lord, because *since he was in the form of God, he did not think it robbery to be equal to God*; David's son, because *he emptied himself, taking the form of a slave* (Phil 2:6-7).

Married love

21. So we can't say that Joseph wasn't a father, just because he never slept with the mother of the Lord — as though it were lust that made someone into a wife, and not married love. Would your holinesses please pay attention. Some time later Christ's apostle in the Church was going to say, *It remains that these who have wives should be as though they had none* (1 Cor 7:29). And we know many brothers and sisters bearing much fruit in grace, who by mutual consent withhold from each other in the name of Christ the desire of the flesh, but do not withhold from each other their mutual married love. The more the former is held in check, the stronger grows the latter. Aren't there couples who live like that, not looking for the joys of the flesh from each other, not demanding from each other the debt of desire? And yet she is subject to her husband, as is only proper. And the more truly so, the more chaste she is; and he genuinely loves his wife, as it is written, *in honor and sanctification* (1 Thess 4:4), as a fellow heir of grace, *just as Christ*, it says, *loved the Church* (Eph 5:25). So if the bond exists, if there is a marriage, if you can't say there isn't a marriage just because that act is not performed which can also be performed, but unlawfully, outside marriage (and if only all couples could live like that, but many can't), then these people should not unjoin couples who can so live, and not deny that he is a husband or she is a wife, just because they don't come together in the flesh, but are tied together in their hearts.

The procreation of children

22. From this, my brothers, you should get some idea of what scripture thought about those ancestors of ours who were married with the sole intention of obtaining offspring from their wives. So chaste were they in their relations with

their wives, even though according to the popular custom of the time they had several, that they never went in to them for carnal intercourse except for the sake of procreation, thus really and truly holding them in honor.

But anyone who desires his wife's body for more than is prescribed by this limit (the purpose of procreating children) is going against the very contract with which he married her. The contract is recited, it's read out in the presence of all the witnesses, and what's read out is: "for the sake of procreating children"; and it's called the matrimonial contract. Unless this were what wives are given away and taken for, who with any sense of shame would give away his daughter to another's lust? But to save parents from being ashamed when they give away their daughters, the contract is read out, to make them fathers-in-law, not whoremongers. So what's read out in the contract? "For the sake of procreating children." The father's brow clears, his face is saved when he hears the words of the contract. Let's consider the face of the man who is taking a wife. The husband too should be ashamed to take her on any other terms, if her father is ashamed to give her away on any other terms.

But if they can't manage it (I mentioned this a moment ago), let them demand the debt, but don't let them go beyond their debtors. Both the woman and the man may relieve their weakness with each other. Don't let him go to another woman, don't let her go to another man (that's where adultery gets its name from, as much as to say *ad alterum*, to another). Even if they go beyond the limits of the matrimonial bargain, don't let them go beyond the limits of the matrimonial bed. Is it really not a sin, to demand the debt from your marriage partner more than is required for the procreation of children? It is indeed a sin, though a venial one. The apostle says *But I say this as a permission* (1 Cor 7:6). When he was talking about this whole matter he said, *Do not deprive one another, except by consent for a time in order to be free for prayer; and come together again, lest Satan should tempt you through your lack of moderation* (1 Cor 7:5). What does that mean? Don't impose upon yourselves beyond your strength, lest by refraining from each other you lapse into adulterous liaisons. *Lest Satan should tempt you through your lack of moderation.* And in case he should appear to be ordering what he was allowing (it's one thing to give orders to strength, another to make allowances for weakness), he immediately added, *But I say this as a permission, not as a command. For I would like all men to be like me* (1 Cor 7:6-7); as though to say, "I'm not telling you to do this, but I'm pardoning you if you do."

Sustaining the human

23. So, my brothers, think hard about this. Take these great men who only have wives for the sake of getting children, and such we learn the patriarchs were according to the indisputable evidence of so many pages of holy scripture; so if men who only have wives for the purpose of getting children, if they could be shown a way of having children without sexual intercourse, wouldn't they

embrace such a blessing with unspeakable joy? Wouldn't they be tremendously happy to receive it?

You see, there are two works of the flesh which keep the human race going; holy and prudent people lower themselves to these works out of duty, the foolish plunge into them through greed. It's one thing to lower oneself to something out of duty, quite another to fall into it through greed. What are these things that keep the human race going? The first, for each one of us individually, which pertains to the taking of nourishment (which cannot be taken, of course, without a certain amount of sensual pleasure), is eating and drinking; if you don't do it, you die. So this is one of the props which sustain the human race in existence, in accordance with its own proper nature — eating and drinking.

But this prop sustains people in existence simply as individuals. They don't provide for a succession of generations by eating and drinking, but by marrying wives. So that's how the human race keeps going — first, so that people may just keep alive. But because, of course, they can't live for ever, however much care they bestow on the body, provision is therefore made for those who are dying to be succeeded by those who are being born. In this respect the human race, as it says somewhere, is rather like the leaves of a tree; of an olive tree, though, or bay tree, or any other evergreen, which is never without foliage, but yet doesn't always have the same leaves. As it says in that place, the tree sheds some while it produces others; the ones that are opening succeed the ones that are falling. It's always shedding leaves, it's always clothed with leaves. So with the human race: it doesn't feel the loss of those who die every day, because they are being made up for by those who are being born. Thus the whole species of the human race continues in its proper manner, and just as there are always leaves to be seen on a tree of that sort, so the earth is always evidently full of human beings. If however they only died and weren't born, then the earth would be stripped of all people, as some kinds of trees are stripped of all their leaves.

Duty and lust

24. So then, since the human race carries on like this, necessarily relying on these two props, about which enough has been said, the wise and prudent and faithful person lowers himself to each out of duty, and doesn't dive in out of lust. How many people plunge ravenously into the business of eating and drinking, staking their whole lives on it as though it were the very reason for living! While in fact the reason they eat is to live, they think the reason they live is to eat. Every wise and sensible person finds fault with such people, and so especially does the divine scripture, as gluttons and drunkards and guzzlers, *whose god is their belly* (Phil 3:19). What brings them to the table is the lust of the flesh, not the need of restoring the tissues. And thus these people fall upon their food and drink. But those who sit down to their victuals out of the duty of staying alive do not live in order to eat, but eat in order to live. And so if these sensible and moderate people were offered the chance of staying alive without food and drink, how joyfully they would embrace this blessing, being

no longer obliged to lower themselves to what they had never been in the habit of plunging into! Instead they would always be hanging upon the Lord, their attention to him never flagging because of the need to shore up the ruins of the body.

How do you imagine the holy Elijah took it, when he received a cup of water and a bread roll, to last him as nourishment for forty days? Surely, with great pleasure and relief, since he was in the habit of eating and drinking because it was his duty to stay alive, not because he was the slave of greed. Now try offering the same benefit if you could — to someone who has set the whole of his happiness and good fortune in feasting, like a pig in the feeding trough. He loathes your so-called benefit, he refuses it utterly, he regards it as a punishment. So too in this other conjugal duty, sensual men don't look for wives for any other reason, and that's why in the long run they are hardly satisfied even with their wives. Well if they can't or won't eliminate this sensual lust, if only they wouldn't allow it to go beyond the debt they and their wives owe each other, or even beyond what is conceded to human weakness! But obviously if you asked such a man "Why are you marrying a wife?" he would no doubt answer, out of a sense of shame, "For the sake of children." Then if someone he could have no hesitation in trusting were to tell him, "God is able to give you children, and most certainly will give them to you, even if you don't perform that act with your wife," that would certainly have him cornered, and he would have to confess that it isn't for the sake of children that he was looking for a wife. So let him admit his weakness, and accept that he was only pretending to accept a wife out of a sense of duty.

Polygamy in the Old Testament

25. In this way those saints of old, men of God, looked for children, wanted to have children. This was the one purpose for which they united themselves with women, they had intercourse with women — in order to beget children. This was the reason they were allowed to have several. After all, if unrestrained sensuality were pleasing to God, one woman in those days would have been allowed to have several husbands, just as one man was allowed several wives. Why did none of those chaste women ever have more than one husband, while a man had several wives, if not because one man having several wives can result in a numerous progeny, whereas one woman will not be able to bear more children just by having more husbands? It follows then, brothers, that if our ancestors coupled with women and had intercourse with them for no other purpose than the begetting of children, they would have been absolutely delighted if they could have had children without that act of the flesh, seeing that it was for the sake of having them that they condescended to it out of duty, and did not plunge into it out of lust.

Can it mean then that Joseph wasn't a father, just because he had a son without any act of carnal desire? Far be it from Christian chastity to think so, seeing that Judaism didn't think so either. Love your wives, but love them chastely. Make use of the sexual act to the extent of begetting children. And because there is no other way in which you can have children, bring yourselves down to it with regret. It is, after all, the punishment of that Adam from whom we all trace our origin. Don't let's congratulate ourselves about our punishment. It was a fitting punishment for one who deserved to reproduce mortal offspring, because he had made himself mortal by his sin. God has not removed that punishment, because he wants man to remember what he is being recalled from and what he is being called to; and he wants him to seek that ultimate embrace in which there cannot be any corruption.

Adoption

26. So a high birth rate was a necessity in that people up to the coming of Christ, to secure a numerous population in which could be prefigured all the models and examples of the Church that had to be prefigured. That's why they had the duty to marry wives, through whom the population could increase, and in that population the Church of the future could be prefigured.

But when the king of all the nations was born, the special honor of virginity started with the mother of the Lord, who was not only found worthy to have a son, but also found worthy not to lose her virginity. Such then was the style of that marriage, a marriage without any carnal corruption; so why should not the husband in this marriage chastely receive as his own what his wife chastely gave birth to? Just as she was chastely a wife, so was he chastely a husband; and just as she was chastely a mother, so was he chastely a father. So anyone who says, "He oughtn't to be called a father, because he didn't beget his son," is more interested in satisfying lust in the procreation of children than in repressing the sentiment of love. Joseph achieved much more satisfactorily in spirit what another man desires to achieve in the flesh. After all, people who adopt children beget them chastely in the heart, though they cannot do so in the flesh.

Just look, brothers, just look at the rights conferred by adoption, how a man becomes the son of someone whose seed he was not born from, and as a result the one who adopts him has by this act of will more rights over him than the one who begot him has by nature. That being the case, then, not only did Joseph have every right to be called a father, he had the greatest possible right. After all, men also beget children of women who are not their wives, and they are called natural children, and children born in wedlock are given preference over them. As far as the carnal act goes, they are conceived and born in exactly the same way. So why are these given preference, if it isn't because the love of the wife of whom the lawful children are born is the more chaste? The distinction is not based on carnal intercourse, which is the same in the case of both women. How is the wife superior, except in her sense of fidelity, her sense of the marriage bond, her sense of a more genuine and a chaster love? So if anyone could get children of his wife without intercourse, should he not do so all the more joyfully, the more pure she is whom he loves the more dearly?

(...)

Sermon 53A

The Eight Beatitudes in the Gospel

Who are the poor in spirit? The rich, ironically, worry more than the poor but can indeed be poor in spirit. This is a masterful treatment of the eight beatitudes in Matthew's Gospel, beginning with the meaning of *poor in spirit*. This sermon does not appear in the Maurist edition and there is no certainty about the dating or location, although two scholars suggest anytime between 405 and 411, while another dates it toward the end of Augustine's preaching career, between 425 and 430. I believe the classic anti-Donatist refrain in section 13, "It's not the penalty that makes the martyr, but the cause," indicates the earlier dating.

Putting into practice God's word

1. Your graces have heard the holy gospel together with me. May the Lord assist me as I talk to you about the passage that has been recited, so that what I say may be suitable for you, and bring forth fruit in your habits and conduct. Every hearer of God's word, you see, should reflect that he ought to order his life in accordance with what he hears; he shouldn't be content with praising God's word with his lips and treating it with contempt by the way he lives. After all, if what is said is a pleasure to hear, how much greater a pleasure it should be to put it into practice. I, here, am playing the part of the sower, you are God's field; don't let the seed be wasted, let it come to a good harvest.

With me you have just heard how Christ the Lord, when his disciples came to him, *opened his mouth and began to teach them, saying, Blessed are the poor in spirit, for theirs is the kingdom of heaven* (Mt 5:2-3), etc. So the one true master began teaching his disciples when they came to him, and he said what I have briefly reminded you of. You too have come to me, in order that with his help I may speak to you and teach you. Can I do anything better than teach the same things as such a great master set before us in his words?

Who possesses security?

2. So, be poor in spirit, in order that the kingdom of heaven may be yours. Why are you afraid of being poor? Think of the wealth of the kingdom of heaven. People are afraid of poverty; let them be afraid, rather, of iniquity. After the poverty of the just, in any case, will come great prosperity, because there will be complete security; here, on the other hand, the more you increase what are called riches but are really not so, you also increase fear, and you don't put an end to greed. You can find me many rich people; can you find me one who has no

worries? He's in a fever to go on getting, he's in a sweat about losing. When can such a slave ever be free? It's slavery to serve any mistress; and can it be freedom to serve Dame Avarice?

So, *Blessed are the poor in spirit*. What does "poor in spirit" mean? Being poor in wishes, not in means. One who is poor in spirit, you see, is humble; and God hears the groans of the humble, and doesn't despise their prayers. That's why the Lord begins his sermon with humility, that is to say with poverty. You can find someone who's religious, with plenty of this world's goods, and yet not thereby puffed up and proud. And you can find someone in need, who has nothing, and won't settle for anything. This one does not have more grounds for hope than the former; the first is poor in spirit, because humble, while this one is indeed poor, but not in spirit. That's why the Lord Christ, when he said *Blessed are the poor*, added *in spirit*.

The apostle speaks to the poor

3. Any of you then who are listening and are poor, don't seek to become rich. Listen to the apostle, not to me; see what he said: *There is great gain*, he says, *in piety with contentment. For we brought nothing into this world, and we cannot take anything out of it either; if we have food and clothing, let us be content with that. For those who wish to become rich* — he didn't say "who are," but *"who wish to become"* — *those therefore who wish to become rich, fall into temptation*, he says, *and into a snare, and many foolish and harmful desires, which plunge men into ruin and destruction. For avarice is the root of all evils, and some people by craving for it have gone astray from the faith and involved themselves in many sorrows* (1 Tm 6:6-10). When you hear "riches" it sounds such a lovely word. *They fall into temptation*; is that a lovely word? *Many foolish and harmful desires*; is that a lovely word? *Ruin and destruction*; is that a lovely word? To be involved in many sorrows; is that a lovely word?

Don't let one unreal good lead you astray, and get you stuck with so many real evils. Because, however, the apostle was not addressing those who are rich with these words, but those who are not, to warn them off wanting to be what they are not, let's also see with what sort of words he accosts those he already finds to be rich. I have told you what had to be said, and you that are poor have heard me; now it's the turn of any of you here that are rich to listen to the same blessed apostle.

Paul exhorts the rich

4. Writing to his disciple Timothy, with the rest of the advice he gave him he also said this: *Command the rich of this world*. The word of God has already found them to be rich; if it had found them to be poor, it would have told them the things I have already mentioned. So, *command the rich of this world not to be haughty in*

their ideas, nor to set their hopes on the uncertainty of riches, but on the living God, who bestows all things on us abundantly for our enjoyment. Let them be rich in good works, let them be ready to give, to share, let them store up for themselves a good foundation for the future, so that they may lay hold of true life (1 Tm 6:17-19).

Let's consider these few words for a few moments. Above all, he says, *command the rich not to be haughty in their ideas.* Nothing so easily generates pride as riches. Anyone who's rich and not proud has trampled on riches and become dependent solely on God; being both rich and proud means not possessing, but being possessed. Being rich and proud means being like the devil; what have you got when you are rich and proud, when you haven't got God?

He also added: *nor to set their hopes on the uncertainty of riches.* Having riches ought also to mean knowing that what you have can be lost; so try and have what cannot be lost. So after saying *nor to set their hopes on the uncertainty of riches,* he added: *but on the living God.* Riches indeed can be lost; and I only hope they get lost without getting you lost too. The psalm mockingly addresses the rich who set their hopes on riches: *Although man walks in the image* of God. Man of course was certainly made after the image of God (Gn 1:27), but he should recognize himself as something that has been made, lose what he himself has made, and remain what God made him. So, *although man walks in the image* of God, *yet will he be troubled in vain.* Why's that, *he will be troubled in vain? He stores up, and does not know for whom he has collected them* (Ps 39:6). The living can observe the truth of this about the dead; they can see the property of many dead people not being owned by their children, but they either squander it by riotous living or get cheated of it by sharp practice; and what's much more serious, while all this effort is being put into gaining possession, the one who gains possession also loses possession of himself. Many people are killed for the sake of their wealth, so there you are; they left behind them here what they used to own; since they never did with it what he told them to, how were they able to face him when they went to meet him? So mind that your riches are the real ones: God himself, *who bestows all things on us abundantly for our enjoyment.*

The example of the sower

5. *Let them be rich,* he says, *in good works.* Let that be where their wealth becomes apparent, that be where they sow. It's about works such as these, you see, that the same apostle was speaking when he said, *But in doing good let us not falter; for in time we shall reap* (Gal 6:9). Let them sow; he can't yet see what he is going to gain; he must trust, and scatter the seed. Can the farmer who is sowing already see the crop harvested? He flings and chucks around grain that has been garnered with so much care and toil. He entrusts his seed to the earth; won't you entrust your works to the one who made heaven and earth? So, *let them be rich —* but *in good works.*

Let them be ready to give, to share. Why *to share?* Don't let them be the only ones to have. You've spoken, my dear apostle, you have taught us about sowing; now show us the harvest. He does so. Now hear about the harvest. Don't be idle about sowing, greedy-guts; hear, I repeat, about the harvest. After saying, you see, *Let them be rich in good works, let them be ready to give, to share,* because he has only told them so far to scatter the seed, he has to tell them what they may expect to harvest, so he goes on. *Let them,* he says, *store up for themselves a good foundation for the future, so that they may lay hold of true life.* The bogus life, which delights in riches, is going to pass away. So after this life we have to come to the true life.

You are very fond of what you own; put it in a safer place, or you may lose it. Certainly your whole anxious preoccupation, whoever you are who are so fond of riches, is not to lose what you own. Listen to the advice of your Lord: there is no safe place for it on earth; transfer it to heaven. You were always ready to entrust what you had accumulated to the most faithful of your slaves; well, entrust it to your faithful Lord. However faithful your slave may be to you, he can still lose it without wishing to. Your God can't lose anything; whatever you entrust to him, you will possess at his place, when you also possess him.

The rich and poor have met each other

6. Because I said "Transfer it and put it in heaven," don't let a materialistic thought creep into your mind and say to you, "And when am I to dig up, or take what I own from the earth and place it in heaven? How am I to climb up there? What kind of cranes am I to use to lift everything I own up there?" Look at the hungry, look at the naked, look at the needy, look at the immigrants, look at the captives; they shall be your porters as you transfer your property to heaven. No doubt the same thought occurs to you here, and you say to me, "How shall these people be my porters? Just as I was wondering how I could lift up my property to heaven, and was unable to find an answer, so I wonder now how people I give it to are to lift it up there, and again I can't find an answer."

So listen to what Christ says to you: "Make out a letter of credit; give to me there, and I will pay you back here." Christ says, "Give to me there on earth where you have plenty, and I will pay it back to you here." Here too you are going to say, "How shall I give to Christ? Christ is in heaven, seated at the right hand of the Father. When he was here in the flesh he was prepared to be hungry for our sakes, and thirsty, to be in need of hospitality; all these kindnesses were shown him by religious people who were found worthy to receive their Lord into their houses. Now, though, Christ doesn't need anything, he has established his incorruptible flesh at the right hand of the Father. How am I to give him anything here, when he doesn't need anything?"

It has evidently escaped you, what he said, *What you have done for one of the least of mine, you have done for me* (Mt 25:40). The head is in heaven, but he's got members on earth; let the member of Christ give to the member of Christ, let the one who has give to the one who lacks. You are a member of Christ, and you have something to give; he's a member of Christ, and he is in need in order that you may give it. You are both walking along the same road, you are companions together. The poor man's shoulders are free, you the rich man are weighed down with packages. Give away some of what you are staggering under, give some of your heavy load to the needy; in this way lighten your own burden, and your companion's lot.

Holy scripture says, *The rich and the poor have met each other; and the Lord made them both* (Prv 22:2). A lovely, lovely saying, *the rich and the poor have met each other*. Where have they met each other, but in this life? This one's well dressed, that one's in rags — but only when they met each other. They were both born naked — even the rich one was born poor. He shouldn't fix his attention on what he found here, but cast a glance back at what he brought with him. What did the wretched creature bring with him when he was born, but nakedness and tears? That's why the apostle says, *We brought nothing into this world, nor, what's more, can we take anything out of it* (1 Tm 6:7). So he should send ahead of him something he can find when he leaves it. So there is the poor man and there's the rich, and they have met each other, and the Lord made them both; the rich to help this one, the poor to test that one. So, *blessed are the poor in spirit, for theirs is the kingdom of heaven* (Mt 5:4). They may possess wealth, they may not possess wealth; let them only be poor, and theirs is the kingdom of heaven.

Who are the meek?

7. *Blessed are the meek, for they shall inherit possession of the earth* (Mt 5:5). Meek. Those who don't oppose the will of God, they are the meek. Who are the meek? Those who, when it goes well with them, praise God, and when it goes badly don't blame God; who glorify God in their good works, and blame themselves for their sins. *They shall inherit possession of the earth*. Which earth, which land, if not the one of which the psalmist says, *My hope are you, my portion in the land of the living* (Ps 142:5).

The mourning of the penitent

8. *Blessed are the mourners, for they shall be consoled* (Mt 5:4). My brothers, mourning is really mourning when it is the mourning of the penitent. Every sinner, surely, ought to be a mourner. Who do we mourn for, but the dead? And what is quite so dead as the wicked? Here's a great thing; they only have to mourn for themselves, and they come to life again. Let them mourn by repentance, they shall be consoled by remission of sentence.

Hungry now, satisfied later

9. *Blessed are those who are hungry and thirsty for justice, because they shall be satisfied* (Mt 5:6). Being hungry for justice is proper to this earth of ours. Being satis-

fied will come in another place where nobody will sin; it will be repletion with justice such as the angels enjoy. We meanwhile, who are hungry and thirsty for justice, should be saying to God, *Your will be done on earth as it is in heaven* (Mt 6:10).

A beggar to God

10. *Blessed are the merciful, for they shall obtain mercy* (Mt 5:7). The best possible order: after saying *Blessed are those who are hungry and thirsty for justice, because they shall be satisfied*, he added, *Blessed are the merciful, for God will show them mercy*. You are hungry, you see, and thirsty for justice. If you are hungry and thirsty, you are a beggar to God. So you are standing as a beggar at God's door; and there's another beggar standing at your door. The way you treat your beggar is the way God treats his.

Where God sees is where he gives the prize

11. *Blessed are the pure in heart, for they shall see God* (Mt 5:8). Do everything mentioned already, and your heart is purified. You have a pure heart, because you don't pretend to be friendly, and nurse unfriendly feelings in your heart. Where God sees is where he gives the prize. Anything there in your heart that gives you pleasure, don't give it your approval or your praise; and if an evil desire tickles you, don't consent to it; and if it grows very keen, you must pray to God against it, that something may be done inside about purifying the heart, where God is being prayed to. Clearly, when you want to invite God to answer to prayer, clean out your inner room. Sometimes the tongue is silent and the soul is sighing, that means God is being prayed to inside in the room of your heart; there should be nothing there to offend God's eyes, nothing to cause him displeasure.

But perhaps you may find difficulty in cleaning out your heart; call him in, he won't refuse to clean out a place for himself, and he will agree to stay with you. Or are you afraid of receiving such a great potentate, and being turned upside down by him, as people of modest and slender means are usually afraid of being forced to receive in their houses great folk who are passing through? I agree, there's nothing greater than God; don't worry, all the same, about not having enough room; receive him, and he enlarges your living space. You have nothing to set before him? Receive him, and he feeds you; and, what is even more marvelous to hear, he feeds you on himself. He will be your food, because he said so himself: *I am the living bread who came down from heaven* (Jn 6:41). Bread of this sort invigorates, and never deteriorates. So, *blessed are the pure of heart, for they shall see God*.

Be a promoter of peace

12. *Blessed are the peacemakers, for they shall be called sons of God* (Mt 5:9). Who are the peacemakers? Those who make peace. Do you see two people quarreling? Be a promoter of peace between them. Say nice things about this one to that

one, and about that one to this one. Do you hear one of them, apparently in anger, saying nasty things about the other? Don't repeat them; suppress the abuse uttered by an angry individual, give honest thought to the business of reconciliation. What's more, if you want to be a peacemaker between two quarreling friends of yours, begin the work of making peace with yourself; you should first pacify yourself inside, where perhaps you are wrangling and brawling with yourself every day. That person had some internal wrangling going on in himself, didn't he, who said, *The flesh lusts against the spirit, and the spirit against the flesh; for these are opposed to each other, so that you cannot do whatever you will* (Gal 5:17)? They are the words of the holy apostle. *For I delight in the law of God according to the inner self, but I see another law in my members fighting against the law of my mind, and taking me captive in the law of sin which is in my members* (Rom 7:22-23). So if there is a kind of daily battle going on in the inner self, and the good fight is being fought to save the higher powers from being overcome by the lower, to stop lust conquering the mind, covetousness conquering wisdom, then that's the right kind of peace you should be making in yourself, to ensure that the better part of you controls the lower.

Now the better part of you is the one where the image of God is to be found. This is called mind, it's called intelligence; that's where faith glows, hope takes courage, charity is kindled. Does your mind want to be capable of conquering your lusts? Let it submit to one greater than itself, and it will conquer one lower than itself, and you will have in yourself a peace that is genuine, stable, and supremely well ordered. What is the order of this peace? God controls the mind, the mind controls the flesh; nothing could be better ordered.

But the flesh still has its weaknesses. It wasn't like that in paradise; it became like that through sin, it's because of sin that it is chained to this clashing with our own selves. One who is without sin has come to harmonize our soul with our flesh, and he has been good enough to give us the pledge of the Spirit. *For as many as are led by the Spirit of God, these are the sons of God* (Rom 8:14). *Blessed are the peacemakers, for they shall be called the sons of God.*

All this fighting, though, which tires us out in our weakness — even when we don't give in to evil desires, we are still somehow or other engrossed in the combat, we are not yet safe — all this fighting will be over then, when death is swallowed up in victory. Listen how it will be over and done with: *The perishable body* — this is what the apostle says — *has to put on imperishability, and this mortal thing put on immortality. But when this mortal thing has put on immortality, then shall come about the saying that is written: Death has been swallowed up in victory* (1 Cor 15:53-54). War is at an end, and eliminated by peace. Listen to the victory celebrations: *Where, O death, is your striving? Where, O death, is your sting?* (1 Cor 15:55). That's now the tone of victory celebrations. No enemies at all will be left, no contender within, no tempter without. So, *blessed are the peacemakers, for they shall be called the sons of God.*

It's not the penalty that makes the martyr, but the cause

13. *Blessed are those who suffer persecution for the sake of justice* (Mt 5:10). The addition of these last words distinguishes the martyr from the bandit; the bandit too, after all, suffers persecution for his evil deeds, and he is not competing for a prize, but paying the penalty that is his due. It's not the penalty that makes the martyr, but the cause; you must first choose your cause, and then you can suffer the penalty without a qualm. There were three crosses in one place when Christ suffered; himself in the middle, on this side and that two robbers. Just look at the punishment, it's all exactly the same; and yet one of the robbers found paradise on the cross. He in the middle delivers judgment, and while condemning the proud he comes to the relief of the humble. That cross was for Christ his judicial bench. What will he do when he comes to judge, if he could do that while he was being judged? To the robber who confessed he said, *Amen, I tell you, today you shall be with me in paradise* (Lk 23:43). This one, you see, acknowledged his case was different. What had he said, anyway? *Remember me, Lord, when you come into your kingdom* (Lk 23:42). "I'm well aware," he says, "of my evil deeds; certainly, let me go on being crucified, until you come." And because everyone who humbles himself shall be exalted, he immediately delivered his verdict and granted a pardon: *Today*, he said, *you shall be with me in paradise*.

But the Lord, all of him, was buried on that very day, wasn't he? Well, as regards the flesh he would be in the tomb; as regards the soul he would be among the shades of the underworld, not to be chained there, but to release others from their chains. So if on that selfsame day he would be among the shades as regards the soul, in the tomb as regards the flesh, how could he say, *Today you shall be with me in paradise*? But is Christ, all of him, just soul and flesh? Has it slipped your mind that *In the beginning was the Word, and the Word was with God, and the Word was God* (Jn 1:1)? Has it slipped your mind that *Christ is the power of God and the wisdom of God* (1 Cor 1:24)? So it's in the person of the Word that he said, *Today you shall be with me in paradise*. "Today," he says, "as regards the soul I am going down to the shades, but as regards the godhead I am not departing from paradise."

Chew the cud on what you have received

14. To the best of my ability I have expounded all the beatitudes of Christ to your graces. Indeed, you are all so keen, I see, that you still want to hear more. Your graces have challenged me to say much, and no doubt there are other things I could say. But it's better that you should chew the cud on what you have received, and inwardly digest it to your profit.

Sermon 56

On the Gospel of Matthew 6:7-13: On the Lord's Prayer to Those Seeking Baptism

This sermon was most likely preached during the scrutinies of candidates for Baptism (who were known as *competentes*), since it involves the *traditio* and *redditio* of the Apostles' Creed and the Lord's Prayer. It can be dated to a Lent sometime between 410 and 416. Augustine fails to comment on the Creed and moves directly to a commentary on the Lord's Prayer, so more than likely this sermon was preached closer to Easter. "Give us this day our daily bread" refers not only to human sustenance but also to the Word of God. All the faithful including bishops must pray daily for forgiveness of the sins which occur after baptism. Almsgiving and prayer purify a person from daily sins, provided they are not serious enough to exclude him from receiving the Eucharist. Augustine affirms the value of petitionary prayer in contrast to the contemporary tendency to emphasize the superiority of thanksgiving and praise.

The creed and the prayer

1. The blessed apostle showed that these times, in which it was going to happen that all the nations believed in God, were foretold by the prophets, by quoting this evidence from scripture: *And it shall come to pass, that everyone who calls upon the name of the Lord shall be saved* (Rom 10:13; Jl 2:32). Previously, you see, it was only among the Israelites that the name of the Lord, who made heaven and earth, had been called upon; the other nations used to call upon deaf and dumb idols, by which they were not heard, or upon demons, by whom they were heard to their own harm. But when the fullness of time had come, what had been foretold was fulfilled: *And it shall come to pass, that everyone who calls upon the name of the Lord shall be saved.*

Well, then the Jews, even those who believed in Christ, started begrudging the gospel to the Gentiles, and saying that the gospel of Christ should only be preached to people who had been circumcised. So it was against these that the apostle Paul brought this documentary evidence: *And it shall come to pass, that everyone at all who calls upon the name of the Lord shall be saved.* Then to convince those who didn't want the Gentiles to be evangelized, he added immediately, *But how are they to call upon one in whom they have not believed? Or how are they to believe in one of whom they have not heard? Or how are they to hear without someone preaching? Or how are they to preach, if they are not sent?* (Rom 10:14-15).

So it's because he said, *How are they to call upon one in whom they have not believed,* that you didn't first receive the prayer and afterward the creed; but it was first the creed, where you would learn what you were to believe, and afterward the prayer, in which you would come to know whom you were to call upon. So the creed is a matter of faith, the prayer, of course, is a matter of praying, because it's the one who believes whose appeals are heard.

What you should avoid in asking

2. Now many people ask for what they shouldn't, being ignorant of what's good for them. So when you make your appeal, there are two things to beware of: asking for what you shouldn't ask and asking for it from someone you shouldn't ask it from. From the devil, from idols, from demons you mustn't ask for anything that is properly asked for. From the Lord our God, from the Lord Jesus Christ, from God the Father of the prophets, apostles, and martyrs, from the Father of our Lord Jesus Christ, from the God who made heaven and earth and the sea and all that is in them, it's from him that you must ask for anything that it is right to ask for. But you must take care not to ask for anything, even from him, that we ought not to ask for.

It's true, human life is something we are right to ask for, but if you ask deaf and dumb idols for it, what good does it do you? Again, if you demand the death of your enemies from God the Father who is in heaven, what good does it do you? Haven't you heard or read in the psalm, in which the damnable traitor Judas is foretold, how the prophet said about him, *May his prayer become a sin for him* (Ps 109:7)? So if you stand up and start praying for harm to befall your enemies, your prayer will become a sin.

The prophetic utterances of the psalms

3. In the holy psalms, though, you have read how the one who is speaking in the psalms appears to call down many evils upon the heads of his enemies. "And of course," someone will say, "the one who speaks in the psalms is just; why does he demand such dreadful things for his enemies?" He's not demanding them, he's foreseeing them; it's the prophetic utterance of a seer, not the malignant curse of ill-will. In the spirit, you see, they knew to whom evil had to come and to whom good; and they prophesied it, as though they were demanding what they foresaw.

But how do *you* know that the one you are wishing and praying evil upon today is not going to be better than you in the future? "But I know his evil disposition." And you know *your* evil disposition. You may, if you like, have the nerve to judge the disposition of the other person, which in fact you don't know; but you actually *know* your own evil disposition. Don't you hear the apostle saying, *I was previously a blasphemer and persecutor and a doer of injuries; but I obtained mercy, because I acted ignorantly in unbelief* (1 Tm 1:13)? When the apostle Paul was persecuting Christians, binding them wherever he found them, and dragging them off to the high priests for trial and punishment, what do you think, brothers: was the Church praying against him or for him? Surely, surely, the Church of God had learned the lesson from its Lord who said as he hung on the cross, *Father, forgive them, for they do not know what they are doing* (Lk 23:34). So it was praying like that for Paul, or rather for Saul as he still was, that something might happen with him like what did in fact happen. He says, you remember, *But I was not known by sight to the Churches of Judaea which are in Christ; they were only being told that the one who used to persecute us once upon a time is now preaching the faith he was once ravaging; and they began glorifying God through me* (Gal 1:22-24). Why should they be glorifying God about it, unless they had been praying to God about it before it happened?

When you pray, it's devotedness you need, not wordiness

4. So the first thing our Lord did was to cut out long-windedness, to stop you presenting God with a flood of words, as though you were keen on teaching God something with your flood of words. So when you pray, it's devotedness you need, not wordiness. *But your Father knows what is necessary for you, before you ask him for it* (Mt 6:7-8). So don't talk much, because he knows what is necessary for you. Here though, I suppose, someone may say, "If he knows what is necessary for us, why should we say even a few words? Why pray at all? He knows; let him give us what he knows we need." Yes, but the reason he wanted you to pray is so that he can give to an eager recipient, not to one who is bored with what he has given. This eager desire, you see, is something he himself has slipped into our bosoms. So then, the words our Lord Jesus Christ has taught us in his prayer give us the framework of true desires. You are not allowed to ask for anything else, but what is written here.

Attention from the one who prays will bring action from the one who listens

5. *You therefore*, he says, *must say, Our Father who art in heaven* (Mt 6:9). With these words, you, as you can see, have begun to have God as your Father. You certainly will have him as such, when you have been born — although even now, before you are born, you have already been conceived by his seed, to be duly brought forth from the womb of the Church, so to say, in the font. *Our Father, who art in heaven*. Remember that you have a Father in heaven. Remember that you were born from your father Adam for death, that you are to be reborn from your Father God for life. When you say this, make sure that you also say it from the heart. Affection from the one who prays will bring action from the one who listens.

Hallowed be thy name (Mt 6:9). The name of God, which you are asking to be hallowed, is holy anyway. Why ask, seeing it's already holy? And then, when you ask for his name to be hallowed, isn't it as if you were asking him to do himself a favor, not you? Understand it correctly, and you are indeed asking for a favor for yourself. What you are asking for, you see, is that what is always holy in itself should be hallowed by you. What does "hallowed be" mean? May it be treated as holy, not disdained. So you can see that when you ask for this, you are asking for something good for yourself. It's bad for *you*, after all, if you treat God's name with disdain, not for *God*.

May we belong to your kingdom

6. *Thy kingdom come* (Mt 6:10). Who are we saying this for? Even if we didn't ask, God's kingdom is going to come, isn't it? The kingdom, or reign, it's talking about, after all, is the one that will come about after the end of the world. I mean, God always has a kingdom, and he's never without a kingdom, served as he is by the whole of creation. But what kingdom are you asking for? The one about which it is written in the gospel, *Come, blessed of my Father, receive the kingdom which has been prepared for you from the beginning of the world* (Mt 25:34). There you are, then, that's the one we mean when we say, *Thy kingdom come*. We are requesting it to come in us; we are requesting to be found in it. I mean, look — it's going to come; but what good will it do you, if it finds you on the left hand?

So in this case too you are requesting something good for yourself, you are praying for yourself. What you are longing for, what you are setting your heart on by this prayer, is that you may live in such a way as to belong to the kingdom of God, which is to be given to all the saints. So you are praying for yourself, that you may live a good life, when you say, *Thy kingdom come*. May we belong to your kingdom; may it also come to us, the kingdom that is going to come to your holy ones and just ones.

May your will be done in me, so that I don't resist your will

7. *Thy will be done* (Mt 6:10). And won't God do his will if you, my friend, don't happen to say this? Remember what you gave back in the creed: "I believe in God the Father almighty." If he's almighty, who are you to pray that his will should be done? So what does it mean, *Thy will be done*? May it be done in me, so that I don't resist your will. So here too you are praying for yourself and not for God. God's will, after all, will certainly be done in you, even if it isn't done by you. Yes, God's will is going to be done, both in those to whom he will be saying, *Come, blessed of my Father, receive the kingdom which has been prepared for you from the beginning of the world*, by their receiving the kingdom for their holiness and justice; and also in those to whom he will be saying, *Go into the everlasting fire, which has been prepared for the devil and his angels* (Mt 25:41); in them too the will of God will be done by the wicked being condemned to everlasting fire.

It's another matter, that it should be done by you. So you have good reason to pray that it may be done in you — it's so that it may be for your good. In any case, whether it's for your good or for your undoing, it will be done in you; but let it also be done *by* you. So why do I say, *Thy will be done in heaven and on earth*, instead of saying, "Thy will be done by heaven and by earth." Because whatever is done by you, he does in you. Nothing is ever done by you which he doesn't do in you. But sometimes he does in you what isn't being done by you; never, though, is anything done by you if he doesn't do it in you.

May our enemies become heaven

8. What does it mean, though, *in heaven and on earth*, or *as in heaven, so also on earth?* The angels do your will, may we do it too. *Thy will be done, as in heaven, also on earth.* Heaven is the mind, earth is the flesh. When you say, if of course you ever do say, what the apostle said, *With the mind I serve the law of God, but with the flesh the law of sin* (Rom 7:25), God's will is being done in heaven, but not yet on earth. But when flesh has given its consent to mind, and death is swallowed up in victory, so that no fleshly desires remain with which the mind can be in conflict, when wrangling on earth has ceased, when the war in the heart has ceased, when the situation has ceased of which it is written, *The flesh lusts against the spirit, and the spirit against the flesh; for these are opposed to each other, so that you are unable to do what you would* (Gal 5:17); so when this war has ceased, and all lust has been changed into love, nothing will remain in the body to resist, nothing needing to be tamed, nothing to be curbed, nothing to be kicked, but everything will contribute harmoniously to justice — then is done *thy will in heaven and on earth*. We are demanding perfection when we make this prayer.

Again, *thy will be done in heaven and on earth*. In the Church heaven is spiritual people, earth worldly people. So, *thy will be done in heaven and on earth*: just as the spiritual people serve you, so too may the worldly people change for the better and serve you. *Thy will be done in heaven and in earth.* There is yet another meaning, a very, very gracious one. We have been urged, you see, to pray for our enemies. Heaven is the Church, earth the Church's enemies. So what is *Thy will be done in heaven and on earth?* May our enemies believe as we too believe in you; may they become friends, and put a stop to hostilities. They are earth, that's why they are opposed to us; may they become heaven, and they will be with us.

We are all beggars of God

9. *Give us this day our daily bread* (Mt 6:11). Here it's now obvious that we are praying for ourselves. When you say, *Hallowed be thy name*, it has to be explained to you that you are praying for yourself, not for God. When you say, *Thy will be done*, this too has to be explained to you, in case you should suppose you are requesting a favor for God that his will may be done, and not rather praying for yourself. When you say, *Thy kingdom come*, this too has to be explained, in case you should suppose you are requesting a favor for God, that he may reign. But from this place on, until the end of the prayer, it's clear that we are asking God for things for ourselves.

When you say, *Give us this day our daily bread*, you are admitting that you are begging from God. But don't be ashamed about it; however rich anyone may be on earth, he has to beg from God. The beggar stands at the rich man's door; but the rich man himself is standing at the door of the great millionaire. People beg from him, and he begs himself. If he had no needs, he wouldn't be dinning his prayers into God's ears. And what does the rich man stand in need of? I make bold to say, the rich man stands in need of his daily bread. After all, why has he got all this plenty? Where does it come from, if God hasn't given it? What will he still have, if God withdraws his hand? Haven't many people gone to bed rich and got up poor? And that he doesn't feel the pinch is the result of God's forbearance, not of his own power.

Our daily food on this earth is the word of God

10. But now this bread, dearly beloved, which fills our bellies and every day restores our tissues; you can see that God gives this bread not only to those who praise him but also to people who blaspheme him, just as he makes his sun rise on the good and the bad, and sends rain on the just and the unjust. You praise him, he feeds you; you blaspheme him, he feeds you. He is waiting for you to repent, but if you don't change your ways, he condemns you.

So because both good and bad people receive this bread from God, do you assume there isn't any other kind of bread, which the children ask for, about which the Lord said in the gospel, *It is not good to take the children's bread away, and throw it to the dogs* (Mt 15:26)? Well, there certainly is. What is this other kind of bread, and why is it too said to be daily? It's absolutely necessary, you see; we can't live without it, not without bread. It's just shameless to beg for riches from God; it isn't shameless to beg for your daily bread. The one provides you with the stuff of pride, the other provides you with the staff of life. And yet, because this visible, tangible bread is given to both good and bad alike, there is also a daily bread which the children ask for; the very word of God, which is doled out to us every day. That's our daily bread; it's not our bellies, gents, that live on it, but our intelligence.

It's absolutely necessary for us right now, as workers in the vineyard; it's our food, not our wages. Whoever hires a worker for his vineyard, you see, owes him two things: both food so that he doesn't faint, and wages for him to enjoy. Our daily food on this earth is the word of God, which is always being served up in the Churches; our wages when the work is finished is called eternal life. Again, by this daily bread of ours you can understand what the faithful receive, what you are going to receive when you have been baptized; for this too we do well to ask, and say, *Give us this day our daily bread*, that we may live in such a way as not to be excluded from the altar.

We are in debt not over money but over sins

11. *And forgive us our debts, as we forgive our debtors* (Mt 6:12). Neither about this petition do I have to explain that we are making it for ourselves. It's our own debts we are requesting the forgiveness of. We are in debt, you see, not over money, but over sins. Now you say, perhaps, "You too?" We answer, "We too." "You too, holy bishops, you're in debt?" We too are in debt. "Really, you too? No, no, my lord, don't do yourself an injustice." I'm not doing myself an injustice, I'm telling the truth; we too are in debt. *If we say that we have no sin, we deceive ourselves, and the truth is not in us* (1 Jn 1:8). Yes, we've been baptized, and yes, we are in debt.

Not that anything was left over that wasn't forgiven us in baptism; but that by going on living we have contracted debts that need to be forgiven every day. Those who are baptized and depart this life come up from the font without any debts and go off on their way without any debts. But those who are baptized and held in this life pick up something through the weakness of their mortal flesh, which even if it doesn't lead to their being shipwrecked, still needs to be pumped out; because if it isn't pumped out, the level in the bilges gradually rises until the whole ship is swamped. Well, praying this prayer is pumping out the bilgewater.

Not only ought we to pray, but also to give in charity, because when the ship's bilges are being pumped out to stop its being swamped, hands as well as voices are engaged. We engage our voices in the work when we say, *Forgive us our debts, as we too forgive our debtors*; we engage our hands when we carry out, *Break your bread to the hungry, and bring into your house the destitute without shelter* (Is 58:7); *Lock up an almsdeed in the heart of a poor man, and it will pray for you to the Lord* (Sir 29:12).

Daily purification of the Lord's Prayer

12. So with all our sins forgiven *through the bath of regeneration* (Tit 3:5), we would have been thrust into a very awkward corner, if we hadn't been given the daily purification of this holy prayer. Almsgiving and prayer clean out sins — provided such ones are not committed as require us to be excluded from the daily bread, provided we avoid the sort of debts that deserve sure and severe condemnation. Don't call yourselves just, as though you had no cause to say, *Forgive us our debts, as we too forgive our debtors*. Keep yourselves, of course, from idolatry, from consulting astrologers, from relying on spells for cures; avoid heretical errors and schismatical divisions; refrain, naturally, from murder, from adultery and fornication, from theft and robbery, from bearing false witness, and any other sins I don't actually mention, which have fatal results, so that you have to be cut off from the altar, and to be bound on earth so as to be bound in heaven — all very dangerous and deadly, unless it's loosed on earth so as to be loosed in heaven.

But quite apart from sins like that, there's no lack of opportunity for people to sin. By seeing with pleasure what you ought not to see, you sin. And who can check the eye's swift glance? Can anyone check ears or eyes? Yes, yes, you can shut them when you like, and they are shut very quickly. You have to make an effort to shut your ears. You lift up your hands and put them over your ears; and if someone snatches your hands away, your ears remain open, and you can't shut them against accursed words of impurity, of seduction, of deception. When you hear something you ought not, even if you don't do it, aren't you sinning? You take a certain pleasure in hearing something bad. And the death-dealing tongue — how many sins it commits! Sometimes they are such as exclude a person from the altar. The whole business of blasphemy is its province; and we say so many silly, idle things to no purpose.

Fine: let's suppose your hands do nothing bad; your feet don't run off to anything bad; your eyes don't stray to any lewdness; your ears are not willingly open to any dirtiness; your tongue doesn't wag in any way that's improper. Tell me: can you control your thoughts?

My brothers, we are often praying and thinking of something else, as though we had forgotten in whose presence we are standing, or indeed in whose presence we are lying prostrate. If all these things are piled up on top of us, are we to say they don't weigh us down, just because they are so tiny? What's the difference, whether lead is pressing down on you, or sand? The lead is one big lump, the sand is tiny grains, but there are plenty of them to weigh you down. These sins are tiny; have you never seen rivers filled with tiny drops, and farms swept away? They are tiny, but they are many.

A bargain with God

13. So let's say it every day, and let's mean what we say, and let's do what we say: *Forgive us our debts, as we too forgive our debtors.* We are making a bargain with God, an agreement and a contract. This is what the Lord your God says to you: "Forgive, and I will forgive. You haven't forgiven? It's you, in that case, who are holding your sins against yourself, not me." Really and truly, my dearest children, believe me, I know what you can get out of the Lord's Prayer, and above all from this sentence in the whole prayer, *Forgive us our debts, as we too forgive our debtors;* so listen to me. You are due to be baptized, so forgive everything; and any of you who have anything against anyone in your heart, forgive it with all your heart. Enter the baptismal font in that frame of mind, and you can be quite certain that absolutely all your sins are forgiven, both what you have contracted by being born of your parents in line from Adam with original sin (that's the sin that has you running with your baby to the grace of the Savior), and what you have added in your life in thought, word, and deed — they are all forgiven, and you will come up out from there, as from the presence of your Lord, with the assurance that all your debts have been cancelled.

Love your enemies

14. So now then, about these daily sins, for which I have told you that you have to say, as a kind of daily wash and brush up, *Forgive us our debts, as we too forgive our debtors* — what are you going to do about them? You've got enemies; is there anyone living on this earth who doesn't have an enemy? Watch yourselves; love them. In no way at all can your raving enemy do you more harm than you do to yourself, if you don't love your enemy. He, after all, can do damage to your house in the country, or your cattle, or your household, or your manservant or maidservant, or your son or your wife, or at most, if he's given that much authority, to your person; can he, as you yourself can, do any damage to your soul?

Exert yourselves, my dearest friends, to attain this perfection, I implore you. But is it I who have given you the capacity to do so? *He* has given it to you, the one to whom you say, *Thy will be done, as in heaven, so also on earth.* However, you mustn't assume it's impossible; I know, I have learned, I have satisfied myself that there are Christian people who love their enemies. If it seemed impossible to you, you would never do it. First of all believe that it can be done, and pray, that God's will may be done in you.

After all, what good do you get from things going wrong with your enemy? If he had nothing wrong with him, he wouldn't be your enemy. Wish him well, he stops being wrong, and he won't be an enemy. I mean, it's not the human nature in him that is hostile to you, is it, but the fault in it. Is the reason for his hostility to you the fact that he has a soul and flesh? In this he's the same as you; you have a soul, he has a soul; you have flesh, he has flesh. He's of the same stuff as you are; you were both made together from earth by the Lord, both quickened by him. He is exactly what you are too; look on him as your brother. In the beginning our two parents were Adam and Eve, he our father, she our mother; so we are brothers. Forget about the original beginning: God is our father, the Church our mother; so we are brothers.

"But my enemy's a pagan, he's a Jew, he's a heretic." And why do you suppose I just said a moment ago, *Thy will be done, as in heaven, so also on earth*? Oh, Church! Your enemy is a pagan, a Jew, a heretic; he's earth. If you are heaven, call upon the Father who is in heaven, and pray for your enemies. Because Saul too was an enemy of the Church; they prayed for him to such effect that he became a friend. Not only did he stop being a persecutor, but he worked hard to be a cooperator.

Actually, if you want to know the truth, they did pray against him — but against his ill-nature, not against his real nature. You, too, pray against your enemy's ill-nature; may that die, and he live. You see, if your enemy dies, you are going without an enemy, I suppose, but you haven't found a friend, but if it's his ill-nature that dies, then you have both lost an enemy and found a friend.

Pray that you may love your enemies

15. All right; go on saying, "Who is able to? Who ever did it?" May God do it in your hearts. I too know this: spiritual people do it. Are all the faithful in the Church like that, as they approach the altar, and receive the body and blood of Christ? And yet they all say, *Forgive us our debts as we too forgive our debtors*. Suppose God answers them, "Why are you asking me to do what I promised, when you people don't do what I told you to? What did I promise? To forgive your debts. What were my orders? That you too should forgive your debtors. How can you do that, if you don't love your enemies?"

So what are we to do, brothers? Is Christ's flock reduced to such a small number? If only those who love their enemies are in a position to say, *Forgive us our debts as we too forgive our debtors*, I don't know what to do, I don't know what to say. I mean, am I to tell you, "If you don't love your enemies, don't pray"? I daren't do that; on the contrary, pray that you may love them. But what am I going to tell you? "If you don't love your enemies, don't say the Lord's prayer, *Forgive us our debts, as we too forgive our debtors*"? Suppose I do tell you, "Don't say it." If you don't say it, they are not forgiven. If you do say it and don't do it, they are not forgiven. So it has to be said, and it has to be done, for them to be forgiven.

You must forgive straightaway

16. I see a way, though, by which I can give comfort, not to a small number but to the vast mass of Christians, and I know that you are longing to hear this. *Forgive, that you may be forgiven* (Lk 6:37), said Christ. And what do you all say in the prayer we are dealing with now? Forgive, Lord, in the same way as we forgive. That's what you are saying: "Forgive our debts, Father who art in heaven, in the same way as we too forgive our debtors." That's what you've got to do, and if you don't do it, you will perish.

So now, what? When you are told, "Your enemy is asking your pardon," you must forgive straightaway. Is that also asking too much of you? It seemed too much to ask you to love your enemy while he was raving against you; is it too much to ask you to forgive a man on his knees before you? What do you say to that? He was raging against you, and you hated him. I'd rather you didn't hate him even then; I'd rather you remembered, even then as you endured his ravings, the Lord saying, *Father, forgive them for they do not know what they are doing* (Lk 23:34). So that's what I would really like, that even at the moment when your enemy was raging against you, you should turn eyes to the Lord your God uttering such words.

But perhaps you will say, "*He* did that, but as the Lord, because he's the Christ, because he's the Son of God, because he's the Only begotten one, because he's the Word made flesh; how can *I* do it, a mere human being, warped and sickly into the bargain?" Well, if you think it's too much for you to set your sights on your Lord, turn your thoughts to your fellow servant. Saint Stephen was being stoned; and under the hail of stones he knelt down and started praying for his enemies and said, *Lord, do not hold this crime against them* (Acts 7:60). They were hurling stones, not asking pardon, and he was praying for them. That's what I want you to be like. Exert yourself, stretch yourself a little. Why always drag your heart along the ground? Listen; lift up your heart, stretch it; love your enemies. If you can't love him while he's raging, love him at least while he's begging. Love the man who says to you, "Brother, I have done you wrong; forgive me." If you don't forgive him then, I don't say, "You are deleting the Lord's Prayer from your heart," but "You are deleting yourself from God's book."

Get rid of the hate from your heart

17. But if you do forgive him then at any rate, then at any rate get rid of the hate from your heart; get rid of the hate, I say, from your heart, not the severity. "What if the one who is asking pardon has to be punished by me?" Do what you will; I imagine, after all, that you love your son even when you are beating him. You pay no attention to his tears under the strokes of the cane, because you are keeping an inheritance for him. All I'm saying is, you must rid your heart of hatred when your enemy begs you to pardon him. But you will say, perhaps, "He's lying, he's pretending." O Mr. Judge-of-the-heart, tell me your father's thoughts, tell me your own thoughts of yesterday. He's begging, he's imploring your pardon; forgive him, forgive him totally. If you don't forgive him, you harm yourself, not him. Because he knows what he is going to do.

Are you, a fellow servant, unwilling to forgive your fellow servant? He will go to the Lord of you both and say to him, "Lord, I asked my fellow servant to forgive me, and he wouldn't; please forgive me yourself." Is a master not allowed to discharge his servant's debts? So that one gets his pardon and leaves the Lord's presence absolved; you, however, remain bound. How are you bound? The time for prayer is going to come, the time for you to say, *Forgive us our debts, as we too forgive our debtors.* The Lord will answer you, "Not on your life! When you owed me such a huge amount, you begged for mercy and I forgave you the lot. Oughtn't you also to have mercy on your fellow servant, as I for my part had mercy on you?" These words come from the gospel, not from my imagination. If, however, when you are asked for pardon, you forgive the suppliant, then you can say this prayer. And even if you are not yet capable of loving someone who is raging against you, you can say this prayer all the same: *Forgive us our debts, as we too forgive our debtors.* Let's pass on to the rest.

Deliver us from temptation

18. *Bring us not into temptation* (Mt 6:13). We say *Forgive us our debts, as we too forgive our debtors,* on account of our past sins, which we can't undo. You can so act as not to do what you have done; how can you act so that what you have done

hasn't been done? So it's because of the things that have already been done that this passage of the Lord's Prayer comes to your help: *Forgive us our debts, as we too forgive our debtors.* What will you do about those that you can still fall into? *Bring us not into temptation, but deliver us from evil. Bring us not into temptation, but deliver us from evil* — that is, from temptation.

Three petitions

19. There will always be those three petitions, *Hallowed be thy name; thy kingdom come; thy will be done in heaven and on earth.* These last three petitions are about human life now. God's name, after all, ought always to be hallowed in us, we ought always to be in his kingdom, we ought to do his will; this will last forever. But daily bread is needed now; from this article onward, the other things we pray for belong to the needs of this present life. Daily bread is needed in this life, having debts forgiven is needed in this life, because when we come to that life we shall have finished with debts. Temptation occurs on this earth, it's on this earth that we are sailing on a dangerous voyage, on this earth that stuff seeps in through the seams of our weakness which has to be pumped out.

But when we have become the equals of the angels of God, heaven forbid we should say, heaven forbid we should ask God to forgive our debts, which will be non-existent. So here it's a matter of daily bread, here a matter of debts being forgiven, here a matter of our not entering into temptation, because in that life temptation cannot enter; here a matter of our being delivered from evil, because in that life there will be no evil, but good will abide for ever and ever.

Sermon 61

On the Words of the Gospel of Matthew 7:7-11:
Ask And You Will Be Given, etc.; An Exhortation to Almsgiving

Scholars ascertain that this sermon was preached at Hippo between 412 and 416, based on the oblique reference to Pelagian ideas, which began to circulate in North Africa in 411 or 412. This sermon showcases Augustine's preaching at its best in his ability to employ images and categories of trading that come from everyday life. God delays in responding to our prayer in order to increase our appreciation for these gifts once received. Human beings should not presume to ask God for gifts as beggars unless they are willing to help their fellow beggars. Rich and poor alike are all born naked, feeble and crying. The danger in riches is pride. Our superfluities should provide the poor with their necessities. Bishops are ambassadors on behalf of the poor. God alone can make human beings good.

God is our Father

1. In the reading from the holy gospel the Lord urged us to pray: *Ask*, he said, *and you shall be given; seek, and you shall find; knock, and it shall be opened to you. For everyone who asks receives; and the seeker finds, and to the one who knocks it shall be opened. Or who is the man among you of whom his son asks for a loaf, will he hand him a stone? Or if he asks for a fish, will he hand him a snake? Or when he asks for an egg, will he hand him a scorpion? If you therefore*, he says, *bad though you are, know how to give good gifts to your children, how much more will your Father who is in heaven give good things to those who ask him?* (Mt 7:7-11). *Bad though you are*, he says, *you know how to give good gifts to your children.* It's a wonderful thing, brothers; we are bad, and we have a good Father. What could be clearer? We have heard ourselves mentioned: *Bad*, he says, *though you are, you know how to give good gifts to your children.* And after calling them bad, see what sort of Father he shows them. *How much more will your Father ... ? Whose Father? Bad people's*, of course. *And what kind of Father? No one is good but God alone* (Lk 18:19).

God makes people good

2. So, brothers, the reason that we, being bad, have a good Father is in order that we may not always remain bad. No bad person can make a good one. If no bad person can make a good one, how can a bad man make himself good? The only one who can make a good person out of a bad one is the one who is always good. *Heal me, Lord*, he says, *and I shall be healed; save me, and I shall be saved* (Jer 17:14). Why do they say to me, silly people saying silly things, "You can save yourself if you want to"? *Heal me, Lord, and I shall be healed.* We were created good by the good God, seeing that *God made man upright* (Eccl 7:29); but by our own decision we became bad. We were able to change from good to bad, and we shall be able to change from bad to good. But it's the one who is always good that can change bad to good, because man, by his own will, cannot heal himself. You don't look for a doctor to wound you; but when you have wounded yourself, you look for one to heal you.

So things that are good for a time, temporal goods, bodily, material goods, these we know how to give to our children, even though we are bad. That such things too are good, after all, who can deny? Fishes, eggs, bread, apples, corn, this light, this air we breathe, they are all good. The very riches which make people so proud, so that they don't recognize other people as their equals; which make people proud, I repeat, more in love with their splendid clothes than aware of their common skin — these very riches, then, are good. But all these good things I have mentioned can be possessed by good and bad alike, and while indeed they are good, yet they cannot for all that make people good.

Increase your justice

3. So there is a good that can make good, and there's a good with which you can do good. The good that makes good is God, for only the one who is always good can make man good. In order that you, therefore, may be good, call upon God. There is, however, another good with which you can do good, anything, that is, that you may have. It's gold, it's silver, it's good, not such that can make you good, but such that you can do good with it.

You've got gold, you've got silver, and you are lusting for gold and you are lusting for silver. You've got it, and you are lusting for it; you are full, and you are still thirsty. It's a disease you've got, not prosperity. There are people with a disease which makes them full of moisture and yet always thirsty; they are full of moisture, and they are thirsting for moisture! So how can you enjoy your prosperity, when your lust for money suggests a bad case of dropsy?

So you've got gold, it's good; you've got something to do good with, but not something to be good with. "What good," you ask, "am I going to do with gold?" Haven't you heard the psalm, *He has distributed*, it says, *he has given to the poor; his justice abides for ever and ever* (Ps 112:9)? This is the good, this is the good you are good with, justice. If you have the good you can be good with, do good with the good you are not good with. You've got some money, disburse it. By disbursing your money you increase your justice. *He has distributed*, you see, he has disbursed, *he has given to the poor; his justice abides for ever and ever*. Notice what gets less, and what increases; what gets less is money, what increases is justice. It's what you are going to say goodbye to that gets less, what you are going to leave behind that gets less; what increases is what you are going to possess for ever.

Disburse money in order to get justice

4. I'm advising you how to make a profit; learn the tricks of trading. After all, you admire a trader who sells lead and acquires gold; won't you admire a trader who disburses money and acquires justice? "But I," you say, "don't disburse money because I haven't got any justice. Let the fellow who has got some justice disburse money. I haven't got any justice. At least let me have some money." So it's because you haven't got any justice that you don't wish to disburse any money? Rather, I'm telling you, disburse money in order to get justice. After all, whom will you get justice from if not from God the fountain of justice? So if you want to get some justice, be a beggar to God, who a little while ago was advising you in the gospel to ask, to seek, to knock. He knew his beggar, and here he is, a great householder and rich, rich, that is, in spiritual and eternal riches, and he's urging you and telling you, "Ask, seek, knock. *Whoever asks receives; the seeker finds; to the one who knocks it is opened* (Mt 7:7)." He urges you to ask; will he refuse you what you ask?

The unjust judge

5. Now by way of contrast look at a parable or comparison, like the one about that unjust judge, designed to urge us on to prayer, when the Lord said, *There was a certain judge in a city who neither feared God nor respected man. A certain widow used to plead with him every day and say, Give me justice. For a time, he wouldn't do so* (Lk 18:1-8). She never stopped pleading, and he did out of weariness what he wouldn't do out of kindness. Thus by way of contrast he has urged us in this parable to ask.

Importunity

6. *He came to his friend*, he said — someone a guest had just landed on — *and he began to knock and say, A guest has come to me, lend me three loaves. The other answered, I am already taking my rest, and my servants are at rest with me.* The other one doesn't give up, he stands his ground, he insists, he goes on knocking, and like a friend goes on begging from a friend. And what does he say? *I tell you that he gets up, and not because of friendship but because of his importunity he gives him as much as he wanted* (Lk 11:5-8). Not for friendship's sake, though he is a friend, but on account of his importunity. What does importunity mean? Because he didn't give up knocking; because even when he was refused, he didn't turn away. The one who was reluctant to give did what he was asked to, because the other didn't falter in asking.

How much more readily will the good God give to us, seeing that he is urging us to ask, seeing that it annoys him if we don't ask. But when he is sometimes rather slow in giving, he is upping the value of his gifts, not refusing them. Things long desired are obtained with greater pleasure; if they are given at once, they lose their value. Ask, seek, insist. By asking and seeking you grow in your capacity to receive. God is keeping for you what he doesn't wish to give you straightaway, so that you for your part may learn to have a great desire for great things. That's why *it is necessary always to pray and not to falter* (Lk 18:1).

We ask the good God

7. So then, my brothers, if God has made us his beggars by advising us and urging and ordering us to ask, to seek, to knock, we too should take some notice of those who ask us for things. We do some asking ourselves. Who are we, asking for things? Who are we, that are doing the asking? What are we asking for? We are asking the good God for things; we that are doing the asking are bad people, but we are asking for justice, by which we may become good. So we are asking for something we can keep forever; something, once we are sated with it, that will put an end to all further needs.

But in order to be sated with it, we must be hungry and thirsty; by being hungry and thirsty we must ask, we must seek, we must knock. *Blessed*, you see, *are those who are hungry and thirsty for justice.* Why blessed? Hungry and thirsty, and they are blessed? Can dire want ever be blessed? It's not because they are hungry and thirsty that they are blessed, but *because they shall be satisfied* (Mt 5:6). Over there, bliss will be found in satisfaction, not in hunger. But hunger must precede satisfaction, or else by being too persnickety you may not get to the refection.

We are God's beggars

8. So we have said who we must ask for things from, who we are that must do the asking, what we must ask for. But we too are asked for things. We are God's beggars, remember; for him to take notice of his beggars, we in our turn must take notice of ours. In this case too we should consider, when we are asked for something, who they are that are doing the asking, from whom they are asking for it, what they are asking for. Who are doing the asking? Human beings. From whom are they asking for it? From human beings. Who are doing the asking? Mortals. From whom are they asking for it? From mortals. Who are doing the asking? Fragile creatures. From whom are they asking for it? From fragile creatures. Who are doing the asking? Poor wretches. From whom are they asking for it? From poor wretches.

Apart from the extent of their assets, those who are doing the asking are exactly like those who are being asked. How can you have the face to ask your God for something, if you don't take any notice of your equal? "I'm not like him," he says; "heaven preserve me from being like him!" Some puffed-up poodle swathed in silk speaks like that about the fellow in rags. But *I'm* asking questions about you both when you are naked. I'm not asking what you are like in your clothes, but what you were like when you were born. You were both naked, both feeble, both beginning a miserable life, and so both crying.

Poor and rich alike at birth and death

9. Come on, then, rich man, call to mind your beginnings; see whether you brought anything here. Now that you have come, you have found so much here. But tell me, please, what did you bring with you? Tell me what you brought. Or if you are ashamed to say, listen to the apostle: *We brought nothing into this world.* Nothing, he says, did we bring into this world. But perhaps because you brought nothing, and found much when you were here, you are going to take something away with you from here? This too, perhaps, so fond you are of riches, you are frightened to admit; so listen to this as well. Let the apostle say this also, since he is in no mind to flatter you: *We brought nothing into this world,* when we were born, of course, *but neither can we take anything out* (1 Tm 6:7), of course, when we leave the world. You brought nothing, you will take nothing away from here, why preen yourself against the poor?

When babies are born, put aside the parents, the slaves, the hangers-on; put aside the press of servile flatterers, and just take note of the rich babies crying. Let a rich woman and a poor woman give birth together; let's suppose they don't observe what they have given birth to; let them withdraw for a while and then come back, and see if they can tell which is whose. So there you are, rich man, you brought nothing into this world, but neither can you take anything out. What I have just said about newborn babies, I can say equally about the dead. Sure, when by some chance ancient tombs are broken open, tell the rich man's bones apart, if you can. So, rich man, listen to the apostle: *We brought nothing into this world*; admit it, it's true. *But neither can we take anything out*; admit it, this too is the truth.

It's one thing to be rich, another to wish to become rich.

10. So how does it go on? *If we have food and clothing, let us be content with that. For those who wish to become rich fall into temptation and many desires, harmful ones too, which plunge a man into ruin and destruction. For avarice is the root of all evils, and some people by chasing after it have gone completely astray from the faith.* Notice what they have let go. You are sorry that they have let it go; now see what they have involved themselves in: *they have gone completely astray from the faith, and involved themselves in many sorrows* (1 Tm 6:8-10).

But who? *Those who wish to become rich.* It's one thing to be rich, another to wish to become rich. A person is rich who was born of rich parents; he's not rich because he wished to be, but because he is the heir of many generations. I note his possessions, I don't ask questions about his wishes. In this text it's greed that is being rebuked, not gold, not silver, not riches, but greed. As for those who don't wish to be rich, or who don't care, or who aren't burnt up with greedy desires, not catching fire from the matches of avarice, but who are rich all the same, they should listen to the apostle. It was read today. *Command the rich of this world.* Command them. What? Command them, above all, *not to be haughty in their ideas.* You see, there is nothing riches are so likely to breed as pride. Every fruit, every grain, every kind of corn, every tree, has its own proper worm. There's one worm for apples, another for pears, another for beans, another for wheat. The worm in riches is pride.

True riches, eternal life

11. So, *command the rich of this world not to be haughty in their ideas.* He has cut out the vice, let him indicate now the use. *Not to be haughty in their ideas.* Not to be haughty about what in their ideas? About what follows: *not to set their hopes on the uncertainty of riches.* Those who don't set their hopes on the uncertainty of riches are not haughty in their ideas. If they haven't got big ideas, let them be afraid. If they are afraid, they don't have big ideas. How many people, rich yesterday, are poor today? How many people go to sleep rich, and with bandits coming and taking everything away, wake up poor? So, *not to set their hopes on the uncertainty of riches, but on the living God, who bestows all things on us abundantly for our enjoyment* (1 Tm 6:17); things both temporal and eternal, but for enjoyment rather

eternal things, and for use, temporal ones. Temporal things for our use as travelers, eternal ones for our enjoyment as settled at home. Temporal things with which we may do good, eternal ones with which we may be made good.

So this is what the rich should do: not be haughty in their ideas, nor set their hopes on the uncertainty of riches, but on the living God, who bestows all things on us abundantly for our enjoyment; that's what they must do. But what are they to do with what they have? Let me tell you what: *Let them be rich in good works, let them be easy givers.* After all, they've got the wherewithal. Poverty is difficult and grim. *Let them be easy givers*; they've got the wherewithal. *Let them share*, that is, take some notice of their fellow mortals. *Let them share, let them store up for themselves a good foundation for the future.* "You see," he says, "just because I say *Let them be easy givers, let them share*, it doesn't mean I want them looted, want them stripped naked, want them left empty. I am teaching them how to make a profit, when I point out, *Let them store up for themselves.* I'm not telling them to do this so that they can lose it; I'm showing them where to transfer the account. *Let them store up for themselves a good foundation for the future, so that they lay hold of true life* (1 Tm 6:18-19)." So this one is a false life; let them lay hold of true life. After all, *Vanity of vanitators, and all is vanity. What is this great abundance for man in all his toil, at which he toils under the sun?* (Eccl 1:2-3). So true life is to be laid hold of, our investments are to be transferred to the place of true life, so that we may find there what we give here. The one who transforms us also transforms those investments.

Let your superfluities provide the poor with their necessities

12. So give to the poor, my brothers. *If we have food and clothing, let us be content with that* (1 Tm 6:8). The rich man gets nothing more with his riches than what the poor man is pleading for from him, food and clothing. What more do you get from all the things you have? You've got your food, you've got your necessary clothing; necessary, I say, not vain, not superfluous. What else can you get from your riches? Tell me. For sure, it will all be your superfluities. Well, let your superfluities provide the poor with their necessities.

"But I," you say, "have expensive meals, I eat expensive food." What about the poor man? "Cheap stuff; the poor eat cheap food. I," he says, "eat expensive food." I've a question for you both, when you have both had your fill: the expensive food goes into you; what happens when it's gone in? If we had mirrors in our stomachs, wouldn't we be disgusted by all the expensive foods you have stuffed yourself with? The poor man's hungry, the rich man's hungry; the poor man wants to eat his fill, the rich man wants to eat his fill. The poor man eats his fill of cheap food, the rich man eats his fill of expensive food. Repletion is the same in each case; it's the same goal they both want to reach, but one gets there directly, the other in a roundabout way.

"But my expensive dishes," you say, "taste nicer." You're so nice, so persnickety, you can scarcely eat your fill. You don't know what food tastes like when real hunger drives you on. But I haven't been speaking like this in order to force the rich to eat the meals and food of the poor. Let the rich keep to the habits their delicacy requires, but let them be sad that they cannot do otherwise. They would do better, surely, if they could do otherwise. So if the poor man isn't proud of his beggary, why should you be proud of your delicacy? Go on making use of your special, expensive foods, because you have got into the habit of them, because you cannot do otherwise, because if you change your habits you get sick. Go on making use of your superfluities, but give the poor their necessities. Go on using expensive things, but give the poor their cheap things.

He looks to you, you look to God. he looks to a hand that was made as he was, you look to a hand that made you. But it didn't only make you, it also made the poor man with you. He gave you both this life as a single road to travel along. You have found yourselves companions, walking along the same road; he's carrying nothing, you have an excessive load; he's carrying nothing with him, you are carrying more with you than you need. You are overloaded; give him some of what you've got; at a stroke, you feed him and lessen your own load.

Looking for fruit

13. So give to the poor; I'm begging you, I'm warning you, I'm commanding you, I'm ordering you. Give to the poor whatever you like. You see, I won't conceal from your graces why I thought it necessary to preach this sermon to you. Ever since I got back here, every time I come to the church and go back again, the poor plead with me and tell me to tell you that they need to get something from you. They have urged me to speak to you; and when they see they are not getting anything from you, they come to the conclusion that I am laboring among you to no purpose.

They also expect to get something from me. I give as much as I have, I give what I can, but I'm hardly in a position, am I, to meet all their needs. So because I am not in a position to meet all their needs, I am at least their ambassador to you.

You have heard me, you have applauded; thanks be to God. You have received the seed, you have given back words. I find your applause more of a burden than a gratification, it's putting me in danger. I put up with it, and I tremble at it. All the same, my brothers, these plaudits of yours are no more than the leaves of trees; what we are looking for is fruit.

Sermon 63

On the Words of the Gospel of Matthew 8:23-27:
And As He Went Aboard a Boat, etc.

This is one of Augustine's shortest sermons and there are few clues about its dating. Hill suggests it has the characteristics of the older Augustine, who had a propensity for shorter homilies. The Maurists note that they found it in earlier printed editions and that the sermon does not survive in any manuscripts. The homily is a beautiful illustration of Augustine's skill as an interpreter in his explanation of the significance of Jesus' calming the sea.

The sleep of Christ is a sign

1. I have something to say to you, if the Lord enables me to do so, about the reading from the holy gospel which we have this moment heard, and in it I want to urge you not to let the faith sleep in your hearts against the storms and waves of this world. After all, it can scarcely be true that Christ the Lord had power over death, and did not have power over sleep, and that sleep possibly overtook the Almighty against his will, as he was out sailing. If you do believe this, he is asleep in you, but if Christ is awake in you, your faith is awake too.

The apostle says, *That Christ may dwell through faith in your hearts* (Eph 3:17). So even the sleep of Christ is a sign and a sacred symbol. The people sailing in the boat are souls crossing the present age *on a paltry piece of wood* (Wis 10:4). The boat was also a figure of the Church. We are all of us temples of God, and every one of us is sailing a boat in his heart, and we don't suffer shipwreck if we think good thoughts.

Let Christ stay awake in you

2. You have heard an insult — it's a high wind; you've got angry — it's a wave. So as the wind blows and the waves break, the boat is in peril, your heart is in peril, your heart is tossed about. When you hear the insult, you are eager to avenge it; you do avenge it, and by giving way to someone else's evil, you suffer shipwreck. And why is that? Because Christ is asleep in you. What does it mean, that Christ is asleep in you? That you have forgotten Christ. So wake Christ up, remember Christ; let Christ stay awake in you, think about him.

What were you wanting? Revenge. It has escaped your memory that he, when he was being crucified, said, *Father, forgive them, because they do not know what they are doing* (Lk 23:34). The one who was asleep there in your heart did not want revenge. Wake him up, call him to mind. The memory of him is his word;

the memory of him is his command. And if Christ is awake in you, you will say to yourself, "What sort of person am I, wanting to get my own back? Who am I, brandishing menaces against another human being? I may well die before I get my own back. And when I depart from the body in a rage, breathing out fire and slaughter, thirsting for revenge, that one who did not wish to be avenged won't receive me. No, he won't receive me, the one who said, *Give, and it will be given you, forgive, and you will be forgiven* (Lk 6:38.37). So I will restrain my anger, and return to calmness of heart." Christ has commanded the sea, and there has come a great calm.

Wake up Christ and so sail on a calm sea

3. What I have said about anger, you should hold onto as a rule to be followed in all your temptations. A temptation arises, it's a wind; you are troubled by it, it's a wave. Wake Christ up, let him talk to you. *Who is this, when even the winds and the sea obey him?* (Mt 8:27). Who is this, whom the sea obeys? *His is the sea, and he made it* (Ps 95:5). *All things were made through him* (Jn 1:13). Imitate the winds and the sea instead; submit to the creator. At Christ's command the sea hears, and will you be deaf? The sea hears, and the wind drops, and are you still blowing? "What do you mean?" I say things, I do things, I think things up — what else is that but blowing, and not dropping at the word of Christ?

Don't let the waves overwhelm you when your heart is upset by a temptation. And yet because we are human, if the wind has driven us on and shaken our souls with passion, don't let's despair; let's wake up Christ, and so sail on in a calm sea, and reach our home country.

Turning to the Lord, etc.

Sermon 70A

Again from the Same Chapter of the Gospel on Humility

This sermon follows S. 68 in the manuscript collection edited by Mai and thus was most likely preached at Hippo in the last years of Augustine's life, between 425 and 430. The rich and the poor alike labor: "The poor man labors in work, the rich man labors in thought." Christ is looking for a humble Christian.

We all labor in this world

1. The mouth of the Lord, that trumpet of justice and truth, as though he were standing up in the general meeting of the whole human race, calls out and says, *Come to me, all you who labor and are overburdened, and I will refresh you.*

Take my yoke upon you, and learn from me, because I am meek and humble of heart, and you shall find rest for your souls. For my yoke is comfortable, and my burden is light (Mt 11:28-30). If you don't labor, you needn't heed, but if you do labor, you should pay heed to the words, *Come to me, all you who labor and are overburdened.* If you are not overburdened, you needn't heed; but if you are overburdened, you should pay heed to the invitation, *Come to me, all you who labor and are overburdened.* What for? *And I will refresh you.* Everybody who labors and is overburdened seeks refreshment, longs for rest.

And who doesn't labor in this world? I would like to be told, who doesn't labor, either by working or by thinking? The poor man labors in work, the rich man labors in thought. The poor man wants to get what he hasn't got, and labors; the rich man, afraid of losing what he has got and wishing to add to it what he hasn't got, labors even more. But anyway, all of us carry our burdens of whatever sins they may be, and these press down on our proud necks, and yet for all that, under such a top-heavy pile, pride heaves itself up; though weighed down by sins, pride continues to swell up.

That's why the Lord says — well, what? *I*, he says, *will refresh you. Take my yoke upon you and learn from me.* What, Lord, are we to learn from you? We know that in the beginning you were the Word, and the Word with God, and the Word who was God; we know that all things were made through you, visible and invisible. What are we to learn from you? How to hang up the sky, fix the earth solid, pour out the sea, spread the air around, fill all the elements with the appropriate animals, arrange the ages, rotate the seasons? What are we to learn from you? Or do you perhaps want us to learn how to do the works you did on earth? Is that what you want to teach us? So we are to learn from you how to cleanse lepers, how to drive out demons, put fevers to flight, command the sea and the waves, raise the dead? Not things like that either, he says. Tell us, then, what? *Because I am meek and humble of heart.* Let God put you to shame, human pride. The Word of God says it, God says it, the Only-begotten says it, Such high majesty came down to humility, and is man going to stretch himself up? Pull in your horns, O man, and reduce yourself to the humble Christ, or you may stretch yourself so far that you burst.

God is humble, and are you proud?

2. Just now the psalm was being sung, just now the alleluia was being recited: *Who is like the Lord our God, who dwells on high and observes humble things?* (Ps 113:5-6). When he observes you, may he find you humble, and not condemn you. He's the one who said it, his was the keynote address, he was the one inviting the human race to this salvation: *Learn from me*, he says, not how to create the creation; learn *that I am meek and humble of heart*. He was in the

beginning; what could be more sublime? *The Word was made flesh* (Jn 1:1, 14); what could be more lowly? He rules the world; what could be more sublime? He hangs on the cross; what could be more lowly? When he did all this for you, why do you still rear up, still swell up, you inflated balloon? God is humble, and are you proud?

Perhaps because it said *The Lord is sublime and observes lowly things,* (Ps 138:6) you say to yourself, "Then he doesn't observe me." What could be more unfortunate than you, if he doesn't observe you, but ignores you? Observing indicates compassion, ignoring indicates contempt. But no doubt, because the Lord observes lowly things, you imagine you escape his notice, because you are not humble or lowly, you are high and mighty, you are proud. That's not the way to be missed by the eyes of God. I mean, just see what it says there: *The Lord is sublime.* Sublime indeed. How are you going to get to him? Will you look for a ladder? Look for the wood of humility, and you have already got to him. The Lord is sublime, he observes lowly things, but high and mighty things (don't imagine you escape notice, you that are so proud) *but high and mighty things he knows from afar* (Ps 138:6). He knows them, all right, but from afar. *Salvation is far from sinners* (Ps 119:155).

What about lowly things? Them he knows from close at hand. Marvelous, the ingenuity of the Almighty! He is sublime, and he observes lowly things from close at hand; the proud are high, he the sublime knows them from afar. *The Lord is near to those who have crushed their hearts, and the humble in spirit he will save* (Ps 34:18).

So, brothers, don't let pride swell in you, let it shrivel instead and rot. Be disgusted by it, throw it out. Christ is looking for a humble Christian. Christ in heaven, Christ with us, Christ in hell — not to be kept there, but to release others from there. That's the kind of leader we have. He is seated at the right hand of the Father, but he is gathering us up together from the earth: one in this way, one in that; by favoring this one, chastising that one, giving this one joy and that one trouble, may he that gathers gather us up; may he gather us up, otherwise we are lost; may he gather us together where we can't get lost, into that land of the living where all deserts are acknowledged and justice is rewarded.

Sermon 72

On the Words of the Gospel of Matthew 12:33:
Either Make the Tree Good and Its Fruit Good

This sermon was preached at Carthage between July 17 and August 10, 397.
The allusion in the final paragraph to the world's undergoing a severe beating
may be a reference to the sack of Rome by the Goths in 410. There is no point to
possessing good things if one's conscience is empty. Honors and promotion
are only good when they are used well. Otherwise they can lead to ruin. The
real good is what you can never lose against your will.

If people persist in being bad, they can't possibly perform good works

1. Our Lord Jesus Christ has been warning us to be good trees, able to
produce good fruit. He said, *Either make the tree good and its fruit good, or
make the tree bad and its fruit bad. For by its fruit the tree is known* (Mt 12:33).
When he says, *Make the tree good and its fruit good*, this is not, of course, a
warning but a salutary command, which has to be obeyed. But his saying, *Make
the tree bad and its fruit bad*, is not commanding you what to do, but warning
you what to avoid.

He was speaking, you see, against the sort of people who thought they could
say good things or perform good works while remaining bad themselves. This,
the Lord Jesus says, is not possible, because the person has to be changed first,
before the works can be changed in quality. I mean, if people persist in being
bad, they can't possibly perform good works; if they persevere in being good,
they can't possibly perform bad works.

He found all the trees bad

2. But was anybody found to be good by the Lord, seeing that Christ died for the
wicked? So he found all the trees bad, but gave all who believe in his name authority to
become children of God. That means that anybody who is a good person today, that is,
a good tree, was found to be a bad one and has been made into a good one. And if,
when he found them to be bad, he had preferred to uproot the trees rather than to let
them remain, would there have been any that did not deserve to be uprooted?

But he came to pay out mercy in advance, so that later on he might pass judgment, according to the terms he was addressed in, *Mercy and judgment I will sing
to you, O Lord* (Ps 101:1). So he granted those who believe the forgiveness of sins,
he didn't want to foreclose on their old mortgages. He granted them forgiveness of
sins; he made them into good trees. He deferred the axe, he provided the security.

Let us be found bearing fruit

3. John has something to say about this axe: *Already the axe is laid to the root of
the trees. Every tree that does not produce good fruit will be cut down and thrown
on the fire* (Mt 3:10, Lk 3:9). This is the axe the householder threatens to use in the
gospel, when he says, *Look, it's now three years I have been coming to this tree
and not finding any fruit on it. Now I really should clear the space; accordingly, let
it be grubbed up,* And the share-cropper pleads for it: *Master, leave it this year too,
I shall dig round it and add a basketful of dung. If it produces fruit, fine; if not, you
will come and grub it up* (Lk 13:7-9).

The Lord visited the human race for a kind of three years, that is to say, through
three particular ages. The first age, before the law; the second age, under the law;
the third is now, which is the age of grace. I mean, if he hadn't visited the human
race before the law, where would Abel have sprung from, or Enoch, or Noah, or
Abraham, Isaac, and Jacob? He wanted to be known as the Lord of these, and
while all nations were in fact his, he wanted it to seem as if he were just the God of
three men: *I am*, he said, *the God of Abraham and Isaac and Jacob* (Ex 3:14).

And if he hadn't come visiting in the time of the law, he wouldn't have given
the law. After the law the householder came in person; he suffered, died, and
rose again, he gave the Holy Spirit, he had the gospel preached throughout the
world. And still some tree has remained unfruitful. There is still some part of the
human race, it's still not correcting itself.

The share-cropper pleads; the apostle prays for the people: *I bend my knees*,
he says, *to the Father for you, that rooted and founded in love, you may have the
power to grasp with all the saints what is the length and breadth, the height and
depth; to know also the surpassing knowledge of the love of Christ, that you may
be filled up with all the fullness of God* (Eph 3:14, 17-19). Bending the knees, he
is pleading with the householder for us not to be uprooted.

So then, because there's not the slightest possibility of his not coming, let us
make sure he finds us bearing fruit. Digging round the tree means the humility,
the self-abasement of the penitent; every hole dug is low down, a kind of abase-
ment. The basket of dung is the dirt of repentance. After all, what could be dirtier
than dung? And yet, if you use it well, what could be more productive?

Let everyone of us be a good tree

4. So let every one of us be a good tree. Don't think you will produce good
fruit if you remain a bad tree. There won't be any good fruit, except from a good
tree. Change your heart, and the work will change too. Pull up greed, plant love.
I mean, just as greed is the root of all evils, so love is the root of all good things.

So why do people mutter and argue with each other and say "What does good
mean?" Oh, if only you knew what good meant! What you want isn't very good;
what you don't want to be, that's the real good. For example, you want to enjoy

health of body; that's something good, and yet you shouldn't think it is a particularly great good, seeing that it can be enjoyed also by someone bad. You want to have gold and silver; yes, here too I say, it's something good, but only if you use it well. And you won't use it well if you are bad. And thus gold and silver are a bad thing for the bad, and a good thing for the good. Not that gold and silver makes them good, but that, because it finds them good, it is put to good use. You want to get a promotion; that is a good thing, but here, too, only if you use it well. How many people are there for whom promotion has been the occasion of their ruin? And how many people are there for whom promotion has been a means of doing good?

You want to have good things, and you don't want to be good

5. So let us sort out the differences between these various good things, if we can, because we are talking about good trees. And here the only thing we each have to think about is to turn one's eyes upon oneself, to learn about oneself, to examine oneself, to look at oneself, to seek oneself and find oneself, and then to kill what displeases one and to engraft and plant what pleases one. After all, when you find yourself to be empty of the better goods, what's the point of avidly longing for exterior goods? I mean to say, what's the use of coffers full of good things, if your conscience is empty? You want to have good things, and you don't want to be good!

Don't you see how you ought to blush for your good things, if your house is full of good things, and the only bad thing it has in it is you? I mean, is there anything at all that you would actually like to have bad? Tell me. Well, of course, there's absolutely nothing at all. Not a wife, not a son, not a daughter, not a servant, not a maid, not a country house, not a coat, finally not even a pair of boots, and yet you want to have a bad life! I beg you on my knees, put your life before your boots. Everything around you which your eyes rest upon is elegant and beautiful, it's all precious to you, and you yourself, are you cheap and ugly in your own eyes?

If the good things your house is full of could answer you, these things you have chosen to have and are afraid to lose, wouldn't they cry out to you, "You want to have us good, so we too want to have our master good"? They are silently appealing against you to your master, "Look here, you've given so many good things to this man, and he himself is bad. What good does everything he has do him, when he doesn't have the one who gave him everything?"

The real good

6. So someone is going to ask, admonished by these words of mine, and perhaps pricked in his conscience, he's going to ask what good is, what sort of good, what makes it good. You have rightly understood that that's what you ought to ask. I will answer your inquiry, and say, "The real good is what you cannot lose against your will.

"I mean, you can lose your gold even when you don't want to; you can lose your house, your position, your physical health, but the good by which you are really and truly good, you neither receive against your will nor lose against your will."

So now I ask what sort of thing this good is. The psalm has some important advice for us, perhaps it's the thing we are looking for. It says, *Children of men, how long, dull of heart?* How long that tree in its three years' existence? Children of men, how long, dull of heart? What does "dull of heart" mean? *Why love vanity and go seeking falsehood?* And then giving us the reverse side, he tells us what we should go seeking: *Know that the Lord has magnified his Holy One* (Ps 4:2-3).

Christ has already come, he has already been magnified, he has already risen and ascended into heaven, already his name is being preached throughout the whole world; how long, dull of heart? Let times past be enough; now that this holy one has been magnified, *how long, dull of heart?* After that three-year period, what's left but the axe? *How long, dull of heart? Why love vanity and go seeking falsehood?* And still, yes still, even after Christ the Holy One has been magnified, still vanities and pointless, showy, tawdry things are avidly sought after! Truth is already crying out, and vanity is still sought after! *How long, dull of heart?*

The world is getting a severe beating

7. This world is deservedly being severely scourged, since the world now knows the words of the Lord. *And the servant,* he says, *who does not know his master's will, and does things that deserve a beating, will be beaten lightly* (Lk 12:48). Why? To make him find out his master's will. So, a servant who does not know this will: that was the world, before the Lord magnified his Holy One. It was a servant who did not know his master's will, and so he was beaten lightly. But the servant who already knows his master's will, which is the present situation, ever since the Godhead has magnified his Holy One, and who doesn't do his will, shall be beaten severely.

So why be surprised if the world is getting a severe beating? It's the servant who knows his master's will and still does things that deserve a beating. So it shouldn't rebel against being severely beaten, because if it is unjustly unwilling to listen to God's commands, it will justly have to endure God's revenge. At the very least, it shouldn't complain about his chastising it, when it sees it has earned a beating, if it wants to earn his mercy.

Sermon 72A

On the Words of the Gospel of Matthew 12:41:
And Behold, Something More Than Jonah Here, etc.

There is no clear indication of location but Hill believes this sermon was most likely preached at Hippo sometime in 417 or 418, based on the preacher's familiarity with the congregation. Augustine takes up the role of fear and greed in decision-making and the danger of pride in those who rely solely on free will in living a good life. Christ appears to snub his mother in Mt 12:46-50 (*Who is my mother?*) to teach a lesson that parental love should never be placed before love of God. Christ honors the male sex in being born as a male and the female sex in his mother. This sermon is particularly important for Augustine's Mariology: "It means more for Mary to have been a disciple of Christ than to have been the mother of Christ." Mary is first and foremost a representative figure of the Church.

The Jewish people and the people of Nineveh

1. Even if we were keen to discuss everything in the passage that has been read from the gospel, my dear brothers and sisters, there would hardly be enough time for each particular by itself; much less is there enough for everything. That the prophet Jonah, who was thrown into the sea and lodged in the belly of a sea monster and vomited up alive on the third day, represented the savior who suffered death and rose again on the third day was indicated by the savior himself. He compared the Jewish people to its disadvantage with the people of Nineveh, because the people of Nineveh, whom the prophet Jonah was sent to with a message of doom, appeased the wrath of God by their repentance and earned his mercy: *And behold*, he says, *something more than Jonah here*; the Lord Jesus clearly meaning us to understand himself.

Those people heard the servant and corrected their ways; these people heard the master and not only didn't correct their ways, but even went on to kill him. *The queen of the south*, he went on, *will rise up with this generation in the judgment and condemn it, for she came from the ends of the earth to hear the wisdom of Solomon, and behold, something greater than Solomon here* (Mt 12:40-42). It wasn't anything very much for Christ to be something greater than Jonah, something greater than Solomon; after all, he's the Lord, they were servants. The point is, what sort of people must they have been who took no notice of the Lord in their midst, when gentile foreigners listened to his servants?

The quest for the good

2. Then he continues: *But when the unclean spirit has gone out of a person, he walks about through the dry places looking for rest, and he doesn't find it. Then he says I will return to my house which I came from. And he comes and finds it vacant, swept clean and furnished. Then he goes and takes along with him other seven spirits more wicked than himself, and they go in and dwell in it and the last state of that person turns out worse than the former. So shall it be with this worst of generations* (Mt 12:43-45). If this were to be explained in a way to give you a thorough understanding of it, the sermon would last rather a long time. Still, I will touch upon it briefly, as far as the Lord enables me to, because I don't want to send you away fasting from any understanding of this matter.

When sins are forgiven in the sacraments, the house is cleaned out, but it needs an occupant, the Holy Spirit, and the Holy Spirit only lives in the humble of heart. God, you see, says, *Upon whom shall my Spirit rest?* And he answers the question, *Upon the humble and the quiet and the one who trembles at my words* (Is 66:2). So when he becomes the occupant, he fills and guides and leads the person, restrains from evil and spurs on to good, makes justice delightful, so that the person does good out of love for what is right, not out of fear of punishment. No one is capable on their own of doing what I have said. But if you have the Holy Spirit as the occupant of your house, you will find him also assisting you in everything good.

There are some proud people, however, who, once their sins have been forgiven, rely solely on the free choices of the human will for living a good life, and by that very pride they shut their doors in the Holy Spirit's face, and the house remains apparently cleaned up from the mess of sins, but vacant, with nothing positively good in it. Your sins have been forgiven, you have been cleared of evils, but it is only the Holy Spirit who will fill you with good things. And he is repelled by pride. You are relying on yourself, he leaves you to yourself; you trust in yourself, you are handed over to yourself. But once that greed, which made you bad, has been driven out of a person, that is to say, from your consciousness when your sins were forgiven, it wanders through desert places looking for rest, and not finding any rest, that greed comes back to the house, finds it cleaned up, brings with it other seven spirits more wicked than itself, and the last state of that person will be worse than the first.

He brings seven others with him. What's the meaning, though, of *other seven?* So does it mean that the unclean spirit too is sevenfold? What is all this about? Well, the number seven signifies totality. It had all gone out, it had all come back, and if only it had come back alone! What's the meaning of *He takes along with him other seven?* Ones he didn't have when he was bad, these are the others he will have now that he is spuriously good. Pay attention, as I try to explain what I am saying, if I can, as far as God helps me to. The Holy Spirit is presented to us as sevenfold in his activity, so that he may be in us *The Spirit of wisdom and understanding, of counsel and courage, of knowledge and piety, and of the fear of God* (Is 11:2-3). Now set against this sevenfold good the opposite sevenfold evil: the spirit of folly and error, the spirit of rashness and cowardice, the spirit of ignorance and impiety, and the spirit of pride against the fear of God. These are seven wicked spirits; who are the other seven more wicked still?

Another seven more wicked still are found in hypocrisy: one evil spirit of folly, another worse one of pretended wisdom; an evil spirit is the spirit of error, another worse one is the pretense of truth; an evil spirit is the spirit of rashness, another worse one is the pretense of counsel; an evil spirit is the spirit of cowardice, another worse one is the pretense of courage; an evil spirit is the spirit of ignorance, another worse one is pretended knowledge; an evil spirit is the spirit of impiety, another worse one is the pretense of piety; an evil spirit is the spirit of arrogance, another worse one is pretended reverence. Seven were not to be borne; who could put up with fourteen? So it necessarily follows that when you add to malice the pretense of truth, the last state of a person is worse than the first.

The mother and brothers of Jesus

3. *While he was saying all this to the crowds* — I am carrying on with the gospel — *his mother and his brothers were standing outside, wishing to speak to him. Someone brought him the message, saying, look, your mother and your brothers are outside, they wish to speak to you. And he said, Who is my mother, or who are my brothers? And stretching out his hand over his disciples, he said, These are my mother and my brothers. And whoever does the will of my Father who is in heaven, that one is a brother to me, and a sister and a mother* (Mt 12:46-50). This is all I wanted to talk about; but because I was unwilling to pass over the previous passage in silence, I have a feeling I have taken up rather a lot of time.

You see, the passage I have just recited to you presents us in a very intricate and knotty sort of way with the problem: how could Christ the Lord, with any sense of filial duty, so snub his mother, and not any old mother either, but such a mother as to be a virgin mother, on whom he conferred motherhood without depriving her of her maidenhead; a mother who conceived as a virgin, gave birth as a virgin, remained her whole life long a virgin. It was such a mother as that whom he snubbed, to stop maternal affection from interfering with the work he was doing and obstructing it.

What was he doing, in any case? He was talking to people, pulling down old selves, building up new ones, setting souls free, releasing prisoners, enlightening blind minds, doing a good work, doing it enthusiastically in word and deed. And in the middle of all this along comes a message about family affection! You heard how he answered. Why should I repeat it? I hope you mothers hear it too, and don't obstruct the good works your sons are doing with family affection. I mean, if you want to be obstructive and to barge in on them while they are busy, and in this way at least interrupt some work that ought not to be delayed, then you should be snubbed by your sons. I say it boldly, you should be snubbed, filial duty requires you to be snubbed. And if a son is concentrating his attention on some good work and therefore ignores his mother when she comes bustling in, what right has she, married woman or widow, ever to be angry with him, when Mary the virgin was ignored in this way?

But I suppose you are going to say to me, "So you're comparing my son to Christ, are you?" No, I'm neither comparing him to Christ nor you to Mary. So Christ the Lord did not condemn maternal affection, but he did demonstrate by his own great example that even mothers must be ignored for the sake of God's work. He was teaching by talking, and he was teaching by taking no notice. The reason he was prepared to take no notice of his mother was to teach you, where God's work is concerned, to take no notice even of your father.

Christ born of a woman

4. After all, couldn't Christ the Lord have become man without a mother, seeing that he was able to do so without a father? If it was necessary, indeed because it was necessary, for the one who made man to become man for the sake of man, consider and call to mind what he made the first of men from, the means he was able to adapt to the institution of the human race at the beginning; well, couldn't he afterward adapt to his personal use the same kind of means for the restoration of the human race? Would it have been difficult for the Wisdom of God, the Power of God, the only-begotten Son of God, would it have been difficult for him to make the man whom he was to attach to himself from whatever material he wished? Angels showed themselves to men as men. Abraham provided holy angels with food, he invited them to eat as men, and he didn't only see them, he also touched them, seeing that he washed their feet. So the angels were scarcely producing phantomlike illusions, were they? So if an angel could exhibit a true human appearance when he wished, couldn't the Lord of angels make a true human being to take to himself from whatever he wished?

But he didn't wish to have a human being as father, to avoid coming to mankind by means of sexual desire; he wished however to have a human being as mother, in order, by having a mother among men, to teach men a useful lesson by snubbing her for the sake of God's work. He wished to adopt the male sex in himself, and he was happy to honor the female sex in his mother. You see, right at the beginning the woman too sinned, and gave the man sin to drink; each partner was taken in by the devil's deceit. If Christ, then, had come as a man without any acknowledgment of the female sex, women would have despaired of themselves, particularly because it was through that woman that the human race fell. In fact he honored both sexes, he acknowledged both, he took both to himself. He was born of a woman; don't despair, men; Christ was happy to be a man. Don't despair, women; Christ was happy to be born of a woman.

Let both sexes come running together to the salvation Christ brings; let the male come, let the female; in faith there is neither male nor female.

So Christ is teaching you to ignore your parents, to love your parents. You see, you only love your parents properly and devotedly when you do not put your parents before God. *Whoever loves* — they are the Lord's own words — *Whoever loves father or mother more than me is not worthy of me* (Mt 10:37). It seems as though by these words he was advising you not to love; in fact, if you pay careful attention, he was advising you to love. After all, he could have said, "Whoever loves father or mother is not worthy of me." But he didn't say that, or he would have been speaking against the law he gave himself. I mean, he himself gave that law through Moses his servant, where it is written, *Honor your father and your mother* (Ex 20:12). He didn't promulgate a contrary law, but he reinforced that one. He taught you to get the order right, without undermining your filial obligations. *Whoever loves father or mother* — yes, but *more than me*. So they should love, but not more than me. God is God, man is man. Love your parents, oblige your parents, honor your parents, but if God calls you to something greater, which could be obstructed by parental affection, get things in the right order, do not turn love upside down.

Did Christ have a mother?

5. Given the obvious truth of this teaching of our Lord and Savior Jesus Christ, would you believe it, but the Manichees actually worked out a ridiculous argument with which they tried to prove that the Lord Jesus Christ didn't have any mother. This, you see, is their sense, or rather their nonsense, that the Lord Jesus didn't have a human mother, and they maintain it against the gospel, against the light of Truth himself. And just see how they argue their case. "Look," they say, "he says so himself." What does he say? *"Who is my mother, who are my brothers?* He himself," they say, "denies it, and you want to impose on him something he denies; he says 'Who is my mother or who are my brothers,' and you say, 'He has a mother.' "

You fool, you stubborn, argumentative, rightly hated mule! Tell me, how do you know the Lord said *Who is my mother or who are my brothers?* You deny Christ had a mother, and you attempt to prove your point from his having said *Who is my mother or my brothers?* If someone else got up and said that Christ the Lord said nothing of the kind, how would you prove him wrong? Answer, if you can, the person who denies that Christ said this. The way you prove him wrong will prove you wrong yourself. I mean, Christ himself didn't whisper in your ear, did he, that he actually said this? Answer me, so you can be proved wrong by your own mouth, answer, so you can prove that Christ said this.

I know what he's going to say: "I will take the book, open the gospel, recite his words, written in the holy gospel." Fine, fine; I will grab you with the gospel, I will tie you up with the gospel, I will gag you with the gospel. Recite from the gospel whatever you think supports your case. Open it, read, *Who is my mother?* A bit higher up you will read why he said this: *Someone brought him a message: Look, your mother and your brothers are standing outside.* I'm not yet pressing you, I'm not yet gripping you, not yet gagging you, you can still say, "He was of course a false messenger, he was suggesting untruths. That's why the Lord contradicted the false messenger. I mean, after getting the message, he replied, *Who is my mother?* This was as much as to say, 'You say, Your mother's standing outside'; I say, 'Who is my mother?' Whom do you want us to believe," he says, "the messenger's insinuation, or Christ's rejection of the message he brought?"

So listen, I still have some questions to ask you. Keep hold of the gospel, don't toss me the volume aside. Hold on to it, allow the gospel its authority. If you don't allow it, you will have no means of proving that the Lord said, *Who is my mother?* Since, however, you will attribute a proper authority to the gospel, observe what I am going to ask you. A little earlier on I had asked you how you knew whether Christ really said, *Who is my mother?* What came before that? "A messenger had said to Christ, *Your mother's standing outside.*" Before the messenger said this, or rather to provide him the occasion for saying it, what came before that? I insist you read it. I see you are now afraid to read it.

The Lord answered and said, Who said that? I don't mean, who said *Who is my mother?* You will answer, of course, that the Lord said it. Who said, *The Lord answered?* You will be answering, no doubt, "The evangelist said it." Was what this evangelist said true or false? You will say, I suppose, "Was what true or false?" *The Lord answered and said to him* is what the evangelist said; was that true or false? If you say it's not true, what the evangelist said, that the Lord answered, then how do you know that the Lord said, *Who is my mother?* If, however, it's because the evangelist said he said it, that you claim to prove that the Lord said *Who is my mother?* then you can't prove that the Lord said this unless you believe the evangelist. Now then, if you believe the evangelist (because you are not saying anything to me if you don't believe the evangelist), read what this same evangelist said just above.

Authority of the gospels

6. How long I'm taking over you! How long I'm keeping you on tenterhooks! It will be a kindness to finish you off quickly. Attend closely, look at it, read it. I see you don't want to. Here, give me the book, I'll read it. *While he was saying all this to the crowds.* Who's saying this? The evangelist, and if you don't believe what he says, then Christ said nothing either. But if Christ did say *Who is my mother?* then what the evangelist wrote is true. Just see what he said earlier on: *While he was saying all this to the crowds, his mother and his brothers were standing outside, wishing to speak to him.* That messenger hasn't yet brought him any message, the one you can say was lying. Notice what the message is he

was going to bring, observe what the evangelist said first: *While the Lord was saying all this to the crowd, his mother and his brothers were standing outside.* Who is saying this? The evangelist, on whose word you believe that the Lord said *Who is my mother?*

But if you don't believe this statement like the other one, then the Lord did not say *Who is my mother?* But in fact the Lord did say *Who is my mother?* So trust and believe the one who said that the Lord said *Who is my mother?* You see, the one who said that the Lord said *Who is my mother?* is the same person as the one who said, *While he was saying all this, his mother was standing outside.* "So why did he deny he had a mother?" He didn't do that at all. Understand it correctly; he didn't deny he had a mother, but he put the work he was doing before her.

When all is said and done, the only point here is to find out why the Lord said, *Who is my mother?* The first point to notice is that he did have one, about whom he could say, *Who is my mother?* He had one, she was standing outside, wishing to talk to him. "Tell me how you know this." The evangelist says so, and if I don't believe him, then the Lord doesn't say anything. So he had a mother. "But what's the meaning of *Who is my mother?*" It means, "Compared with this work I'm doing, who is my mother?" If you see someone who has a father in danger, and say to him, "Let your father get you out of it," and he knows his father is not in a position to get his son out of that jam, won't he answer you, without the slightest disrespect to his father, and with simple truth, "Who is my father? For what I'm wanting, for what I am aware of needing right now, what is my father?" So compared with what Christ was doing, releasing those in chains, giving light to blind minds, building up inner selves, constructing a spiritual temple for himself, what and who is his mother?

But if you insist on thinking that Christ didn't have a mother on earth, just because he said, *Who is my mother?* then his disciples didn't have fathers on earth either, because the same Lord said to them, *Do not call anyone your father on earth.* They are the Lord's own words: *Do not call anyone your father; for you have one Father, God* (Mt 23:9). It's not that they didn't have fathers, but when it comes to being born again, you must look for the Father of rebirth. You are not being asked to condemn the father of your first birth, but to put the Father of rebirth before him.

It means more for Mary to have been a disciple of Christ than to have been the mother of Christ

7. But look here, my brothers and sisters, concentrate more, I beg you, on what follows, concentrate your attention more on what Christ the Lord said as he stretched out his hand over his disciples: *This is my mother and my brothers; and*

whoever does the will of my Father who sent me, that person is a brother to me and a sister and a mother (Mt 12:40-50). Didn't the Virgin Mary do the will of the Father? I mean, she believed by faith, she conceived by faith, she was chosen to be the one from whom salvation in the very midst of the human race would be born for us, she was created by Christ before Christ was created in her. She did, yes of course holy Mary did the will of the Father. And therefore it means more for Mary to have been a disciple of Christ than to have been the mother of Christ. It means more for her, an altogether greater blessing, to have been Christ's disciple than to have been Christ's mother. That's why Mary was blessed, because even before she gave him birth, she bore her teacher in her womb.

Just see if it isn't as I say. While the Lord was passing by, performing divine miracles, with the crowds following him, a woman said, *Fortunate is the womb that bore you.* And how did the Lord answer, to show that good fortune is not really to be sought in mere family ties? *Rather, blessed are those who hear the word of God and keep it* (Lk 11:27-28). So that's why Mary too is blessed, because she heard the word of God and kept it. She kept truth safe in her mind even better than she kept flesh safe in her womb. Christ is truth, Christ is flesh; Christ as truth was in Mary's mind, Christ as flesh in Mary's womb; that which is in the mind is greater than what is carried in the womb.

Mary is holy, Mary is blessed, but the Church is something better than the Virgin Mary. Why? Because Mary is part of the Church, a holy member, a quite exceptional member, the supremely wonderful member, but still a member of the whole body. That being so, it follows that the body is something greater than the member. The Lord is the head, and the whole Christ is head and body. How shall I put it? We have a divine head, we have God as our head.

Be the mother of Christ

8. So then, my dearest friends, look to yourselves; you too are members of Christ, you too are the body of Christ. Take thought to how you can be what he said: *Look, there are my mother and my brothers.* How are you to be Christ's mother? *And whoever hears, and whoever does the will of my Father who is in heaven, that person is a brother, a sister and a mother to me.* For example, I can understand brothers, I can understand sisters; it's because there is one inheritance, and therefore Christ in his mercy, while being the only Son, did not wish to be alone as the Son, but wished us to be heirs of the Father, his own fellow heirs. That inheritance, you see, is such that it cannot be reduced in value by any number of co-heirs.

So I can understand how we are the brothers of Christ, how holy and faithful women are Christ's sisters. But how can we understand being the mothers of Christ? What now? Have we the nerve to call ourselves the mothers of Christ?

Indeed we do have the nerve to call ourselves the mothers of Christ. I mean, I have called you all his brothers and sisters, so why shouldn't I dare call you his mother too? But what I certainly haven't got the nerve to do is to deny what Christ said.

Come on now, friends, think of how the Church, which is plain enough, is the bride of Christ; what's more difficult to understand, but is true all the same, is that she is the mother of Christ. The Virgin Mary came first as a representative figure of the Church. How, I ask you, can Mary be the mother of Christ except by giving birth to the limbs and organs of Christ? You people, to whom I'm speaking, you are the limbs and organs, the members, of Christ. Who gave you birth? I hear you answering to yourselves, "Mother Church." This holy and honorable mother is like Mary in that she both gives birth and is a virgin. That she gives birth I can prove by pointing to you; you were born of her; she gives birth to Christ, because you are the members of Christ.

I have proved she gives birth; now let me prove she is a virgin. The divine evidence does not let me down; no, it certainly doesn't. Come out and stand before the people, blessed Paul. Be a witness on behalf of my assertion; cry out, and say what I want to say: *I have betrothed you to one husband to present you as a chaste virgin to Christ.* What does this virginity consist in, how is he afraid it may be corrupted? Let the one who has mentioned the virgin tell us. *I have betrothed you to one husband to present you as a chaste virgin to Christ, but I am afraid, he says, that as the serpent led Eve astray with its cunning, so too your minds*, he says, *may be corrupted from the chastity which is in Christ* (2 Cor 11:2-3).

Preserve that virginity in your minds; virginity of the mind is the integrity of Catholic faith. In the same way as Eve was corrupted by the serpent's talk, so must the Church remain a virgin by the gift of the Almighty. And so, just as Mary gave birth in her womb as a virgin to Christ, so let the members of Christ give birth in their minds, and in this way you will be the mothers of Christ. It isn't something out of your reach, not something beyond your powers, not something incompatible with what you are. You became children, become mothers too. You were the mother's children when you were baptized, then you were born as members of Christ. Bring whomever you can along to the bath of baptism, so that just as you became children when you were born, you may likewise be able, by bringing others along to be born, to become mothers of Christ as well.

Sermon 75

On the Words of the Gospel of Matthew 14:24-33: *But the Boat
in the Middle of the Sea Was Being Tossed about by the Waves,* etc.

Augustine views the Church as the surest way of staying close to Christ. Christians should remain in the boat of the Church in order to navigate the storms and temptations of life and thus to reach a safe destination. All human beings are foreign travelers in this world. Each detail of the gospel means something; for example, the mountain where Jesus retreats to be alone in prayer represents the heights of heaven and the wood of the boat is the Lord's cross. This sermon was most likely preached before 400 at an unknown location.

Jesus in the boat

1. The reading of the gospel which we have just heard appeals to the humility of us all, to see and acknowledge where we are, and to what destination we should be hurrying. You see, that vessel carrying the disciples, battling in the waves against the wind, must mean something. Nor was it for no reason at all that the Lord left the crowds and went up the mountain to pray by himself; and then coming to his disciples found them in distress, as he himself was walking on the sea, and reassured them by getting into the vessel, and calmed the waves.

Why, though, should it be surprising if the one who established everything in existence can also calm everything down? All the same, after he had got into the boat, its passengers came and said, *Truly, you are the Son of God* (Mt 14:33). But before they had this evidence of who he was, they had been troubled when they saw him on the sea; they said, you see, *It's a specter!* (Mt 14:26). But he, by getting into the boat, allayed the mental turmoil in their hearts, where doubt was putting their minds in greater danger than their bodies were in from the waves.

We should stay in the boat

2. In everything, though, that the Lord did, he was advising us how we should live here. It's clear that in this world every single person is a foreign traveller, though not everybody is very keen to return to the home country. Now by the very nature of the voyage we are bound to endure turbulence and storms, but it's essential that at least we should stay in the boat. I mean to say, if there's danger in the boat, without the boat there's certain destruction. However powerful the shoulders of the swimmer in the ocean, sooner or later the vastness of the sea will defeat him, and he will be swallowed up and drowned.

So it's essential we should stay in the boat, that is, that we should be carried on the wood, to be enabled to cross this sea. Now this wood, on which our feebleness is carried, is the Lord's cross, with which we are stamped and reclaimed from submersion in this world. We suffer from seasickness, but the one who will come to our aid is God.

The prayer of Christ on the mountain

3. As for the Lord leaving the crowds and going up to pray alone on the mountain, that mountain represents the heights of heaven. Leaving the crowds, you see, the Lord alone ascended into heaven after his resurrection, and there he *intercedes for us* (Rom 8:34) as the apostle says. So there is some meaning in his leaving the crowds and going up the mountain to pray alone. I mean, so far he alone is the firstborn from the dead, at the Father's right hand after the resurrection of the body, our high priest and advocate of our prayers. The head of the Church is up above, so that the rest of the body may follow at the end. So if he is interceding for us, on the top of the mountain so to say, way above the highest peak of all creation, he is praying alone by himself.

Keep yourself in the ship, and turn to God with your requests

4. Meanwhile the vessel carrying the disciples, that is, the Church, is being tossed about and battered by the storms of temptations and trials; and there's no easing up of the contrary wind, that is, of the devil's opposition to her, but he goes on making every effort to prevent her from reaching calm waters. But the one who is interceding for us is greater than he is. For in this turbulent situation in which we find ourselves struggling, he gives us confidence by coming to us and reassuring us. The one thing he has to do is stop us from shaking ourselves loose in our agitation in the boat, and hurling ourselves into the sea. Because even if the boat is being agitated and tossed about, still it is a boat. It alone carries the disciples, and receives Christ on board. Sure, it's in distress and danger in the sea, but without it we all perish immediately.

So keep yourself in the ship, and turn to God with your requests. With sailors, you see, when every other plan fails, when the vessel doesn't answer the helm, and cramming on more sail is more dangerous than useful, when all human efforts and endeavors have been tried and found unavailing, then all that's left to them is the urgent pouring out of their voices to God in prayer. Well now, if God enables seafarers to come safely to port, is he going to leave his Church to her fate, and not bring her through to the final haven of rest?

Absence of the Lord

5. And yet, my dear brothers and sisters, the only thing that causes really serious trouble and agitation in this ship is the absence of the Lord. When you are firmly settled in the Church, can you experience the absence of the Lord? When can you find the Lord absent? When you are overcome by some strong desire.

Take, for example, what is said somewhere in a symbolical sense: *Do not let the sun go down upon your anger, or give the devil any room* (Eph 4:26-27). It should not be understood of this sun which is the most sublime of the heavenly bodies visible to us, and which we share the sight of with the animals, but of that light which can only be seen by the pure hearts of the faithful, according to the text, *That was the true light which enlightens every man who comes into this world* (Jn 1:9). This light of the visible sun, after all, enlightens even the tiniest and most short-lived insects. So the true light is justice and wisdom, which the mind ceases to see when it is overcome by the turmoil of anger, as by a cloud; and then it's as though the sun is going down upon a person's anger.

So it is that when in this ship too Christ is absent, we are each of us being tossed about by our own storms and iniquitous desires. The law says to you, for example, *You shall not bear false witness* (Ex 20:16; Dt 5:20). If you know what the truth of the evidence is, you have light in your mind; but if you are overcome by greed for sordid gain, and decide in your heart of hearts to bear false witness for the sake of it, then you are already beginning to be tossed about by the storm in the absence of Christ. You are being heaved up and down by the waves of your avarice, you are being endangered by the storm of your desires, and with Christ apparently absent, you are on the verge of sinking.

Turning back

6. What really has to be guarded against is the ship going off course and turning back. This happens when people give up hope of heavenly rewards, and turn under the distorting pull of greed to things that can be seen but pass away. You see, people who are being troubled and tempted by their passions, and yet keep their sights on the realities of the inner life, do not despair like that, but pray for their offenses to be forgiven and remain determined to win through and sail across the rage and fury of the sea. But those who allow themselves to be so deflected from their true selves that they say to themselves, "God doesn't see, because after all he doesn't think about me, or care whether I sin," they are turning the bows right around, running before the squall, and being driven back where they came from. There are, after all, a great many ideas that can occur to human hearts; and when Christ is absent the ship is beset by the dangerous currents of this world and its many storms.

Fourth watch of the night

7. The fourth watch of the night, though, is the end of the night, seeing that a watch consists of three hours. So it means that it's already the end of the world, with the Lord coming to help us and being seen to walk upon the waters. For although this vessel is still being beset by squalls of trials and temptations, it can for all that see God glorified walking over all the surges of the sea, that is, over all the sovereign powers of this world.

Previously, you see, when he was showing us an example of humility in the flesh, it was said with reference to his passion that the waves of the sea rose mightily against him, to which he yielded voluntarily for our sakes, so fulfilling the prophecy, *I came into the depth of the sea, and the tempest overwhelmed me* (Ps 69:2). Thus he didn't rebut the false witnesses, nor the savage roar of the crowd, *Have him crucified!* (Mt 27:21). He didn't use his power to quell the raging hearts and stop the mouths of the furious mob, but he bore it all with patience. They did to him whatever they wanted, because *he became obedient unto death, even death on a cross* (Phil 2:8).

Afterward, though, when he had risen from the dead, in order to pray alone for his disciples gathered in the Church as in a ship, and borne up by faith in his cross, as by wood, and threatened by the trials and temptations of this world as by the waves of the sea, his name began to be honored in this same world, in which he had been discarded, accused, and put to death. Thus the one who, by his sufferings in the flesh, had come into the depth of the sea, and the tempest had overwhelmed him, was now trampling on the necks of the proud by the honor given his name, as on the spray and froth of the waves. So it is that we now see the Lord walking over the sea, and behold all the rage and savagery of this world cast down beneath his feet.

Errors of the heretics

8. But in addition to the dangers of the storm we also have the errors of the heretics. People are never lacking who will try to seduce the minds of those in the boat, by saying that Christ was not born of the virgin, and that he didn't have a real body, but only seemed to other people's eyes to be what he really wasn't. And these heretical opinions have sprung up when the name of Christ was already being glorified among all nations, with Christ, so to say, already walking on the sea. The disciples said, *It's a spectre!* But he steadied them against these pestilential ideas with his own words, saying, *Have faith; it's really me, don't be afraid* (Mt 14:26-27).

It's out of a kind of pointless fear, you see, that people have formed these ideas about Christ, when they observed the honor shown him and his greatness; and they don't consider that if he could rightly be glorified like that, he could be born like that; it's as though they were frightened out of their wits at seeing him walking on the sea. This action illustrated and symbolized his surpassing dignity; and they treat it as the appearance of a spectre. But when he says *It's really me*, what else is he saying but that what is not real is not in him? And so if he showed flesh, flesh it really was; if bones, they were real bones; if wounds, they were real wounds. After all, *In him it was not a case of "Yes and No"; in him it was just "Yes"* (2 Cor 1:19), as the apostle says. That's where these words come from, *Have faith; it's really me, don't be afraid.*

What it amounts to is, "Don't be so awestruck by my dignity that you wish to deprive me of any reality. Even if I walk on the sea, even if I have the haughty surges of the world, like furious waves, under my feet, still I have appeared as a real human being, still it is true what my gospel tells about me, that I was born of the Virgin, that being the Word I became flesh, that I was telling the truth when I said, *Feel me and see, that a spirit does not have any bones, as you can see that I have* (Lk 24-39); that the hands of the doubter touched the real traces of my wounds. Therefore, *It's really me; don't be afraid."*

It's really me; don't be afraid

9. But this business of the disciples thinking he was a spectre doesn't only point to these people; it doesn't only indicate those who deny that the Lord really had human flesh and who sometimes even upset the passengers in the ship with their blind and twisted reasoning. It also points a finger at those who think that the Lord told lies about some things, and who don't believe that what he threatened the wicked with will ever come about. As though he were truthful in parts and a liar in parts, like a spectre showing in his words, like something that is and it isn't. But those who rightly understand his meaning when he says, *It's really me, don't be afraid*, from now on believe all the Lord's words, and dread the punishments he threatens just as much as they hope for the rewards he promises. Just as it's true what he is going to say to those placed at his right hand: *Come, blessed of my Father, receive the kingdom which has been prepared for you from the beginning of the world*, so it's equally true what those put on the left are going to hear: *Go into the eternal fire, which has been prepared for the devil and his angels* (Mt 25:34, 41).

This opinion too, you see, which people entertain, that what Christ threatened the wicked and the rakes with isn't really true, arises from their seeing many nations and countless multitudes subject to the authority of his name. As a result, Christ seems to them to be a spectre, because he was walking on the sea. That is to say, the reason they assume he was lying when he threatened such punishments is that it hardly seems possible he could let such countless peoples perish, who have submitted to the supreme authority of his name. But they should listen to him saying, *It's really me*.

So the ones who needn't be afraid are those who believe that Christ always spoke the truth, and who not only set their hearts on what he has promised, but also take care to avoid what he has threatened. Because even if he does walk over the sea, which means that all the races of humanity established in this world have submitted to him, all the same he is not a spectre, and therefore he is not lying when he says, *Not everyone who says to me, Lord, Lord, will enter into the kingdom of heaven* (Mt 7:21).

Peter walking on the water

10. So what now is the significance of Peter being so bold as to come to him over the water? Peter, you see, often represents the Church. So what else are we to suppose is meant by *Lord, if it is you, order me to come to you over the water* (Mt 14:28), but, "Lord, if you are truthful and never lie at all, let your Church too be glorified in this world, because prophecy foretold this about you? So let her walk

over the water, and in this way may she come to you, she to whom it was said, *The rich among the people will sue for your favor* (Ps 45:12)."

But the Lord is not subject to the temptations of human praise, while human beings in the Church are often thrown off balance by human praise and fame, and are on the verge of going under. That's the meaning of Peter shaking with alarm in the sea, aghast at the tremendous force of the storm. I mean, who wouldn't be alarmed by the words, *Those who call you happy lead you astray, and disturb the paths of your feet* (Is 3:12)? And because the conscience struggles against the desire for human praise, it is a good thing in such a plight to turn to prayer and supplication; or else it could happen that after being lulled by praise, you are overturned and sunk by being reprimanded. Cry out, Peter, as you stagger in the waves, and say, *Lord, save me.* The Lord, you see, is stretching out his hand. He does indeed rebuke you and say, "*Little faith, why did you doubt?* (Mt 14:30-31). Why didn't you keep your eyes on the one you were aiming at and make straight for him, and in this way boast only in the Lord?" And yet he does snatch you from a watery grave, and because you are admitting your weakness and imploring him to help you, he doesn't allow you to perish.

When the Lord was taken aboard the boat, their faith was made fast and all doubts and hesitations laid to rest; the stormy sea was stilled, and thus they came to the safety of *terra firma*. Then they all worship him, saying, *Truly, it's the Son of God you are* (Mt 14:33). This, you see, is what everlasting joy consists of: recognizing and loving transparent Truth, and the Word of God, and the Wisdom through which all things were made, and his extraordinary loving kindness.

Sermon 80

On the Words of the Gospel of Matthew 17:18-20: *Why Could We Not Cast Him Out*, etc.: On Prayer

This sermon on prayer was likely preached in 410 but the location remains unknown. The purpose of prayer is not to inform God what we need, since God already knows what we need before we ask. God sometimes appears to resist our prayers as a form of hard love. All human beings are sick and require the expert care of the divine physician. Human beings tire of prayer only when desire grows cold. Temporal benefits are worth praying for, but only to an extent, since some people profit from such while others are harmed.

The apostles' unbelief

1. Our Lord Jesus Christ rebuked even his disciples for unbelief, as we heard when the gospel was read just now. When they said, *Why could* we *not cast him out?* he replied, *Because of your unbelief* (Mt 17:19-20). If the apostles were unbelievers, who is a believer? What are the lambs to do if the rams stumble? However, the mercy of the Lord was not denied them for their lack of faith; instead he rebuked them, nursed them along, perfected them, decorated them.

After all, they were themselves aware of their weakness, and so as we read somewhere in the gospel, they said to him, *Lord, give us more faith* (Lk 17:5). *Lord,* they say, *give us more faith.* The first thing that stood them in good stead was knowledge, knowing what they had too little of; they were even more fortunate in knowing where to look for it. *Lord,* they say, *give us more faith.* See how they were carrying their hearts, so to say, to the wellhead, and knocking to get it opened up, so that they may fill them up there. He wanted to make them knock at his door in order to exercise them in desiring, not to rebuff them in their knocking.

Keep on asking

2. After all, dear brothers and sisters, do you imagine that God doesn't know what your needs are? And as he knows what we lack, he knows in advance what our desires are. In any case, when he was teaching his disciples the Lord's Prayer, he warned them not to be garrulous in prayer, and said, *Do not be garrulous; for your Father knows what you need before you ask him for it* (Mt 6:78). Now the Lord is saying something else.

So what's the situation? Because he didn't want us to talk a lot in prayer, he told us, *Do not talk much when you pray; for your Father knows what you need before you ask him for it.* Well, if our Father knows what we need before we ask him for it, why should we talk even a little? What's the point of any prayer, if our Father already knows what we need? He says to someone, "Don't go on and on asking me; after all, I know what you need." "If you know, Lord, why should I ask at all? You don't want me to make a longwinded request, in fact you are telling me practically to make none at all."

And what about that other place? The one who says *Don't talk a lot in prayer* says somewhere else, *Ask and you will be given.* And in case you should suppose that it was only casually and by the way that you were advised to ask, he added, *Seek and you will find*; and in case you should reckon that this too was just said in passing, notice what he threw in next, notice how he clinched the matter: *Knock and it will be opened to you* (Mt 7:7). Yes, notice how he kept on adding things; in order for you to receive he wanted you to ask; for you to find, he wanted you to seek; for you to enter in, he wanted you to knock.

So how can this be? Since our Father already knows what we need, why are we to ask? Why are we to seek, why are we to knock? Why should we tire ourselves out asking and seeking and knocking, just to inform someone who already knows it all? In another place we have the Lord's words that we *ought always to pray, and not grow weary* (Lk 18:1). If we ought always to pray, how can he say *Do not be garrulous*? How can I be praying always if I've got to finish quickly? Here you tell me to finish quickly, here you tell me *to pray always and not to grow weary*. What can it mean?

Well, in order to sort this one out too, you must ask, seek, knock. You see, the reason the door is shut is not to rebuff you, but to exercise your wits. So, my friends, I'm obliged to urge on both you and myself to prayer. What I mean is that in all the many evils of this present life the only hope we have is in knocking by prayer, and in believing and being firmly convinced that your Father doesn't give you what he knows is not good for you. I mean you know, of course, what you desire; but he knows what's good for you. Think of yourself as being under a doctor, and as being sick which is in fact the case; this whole life of ours is, after all, a sickness; and a long life is nothing but one long sickness. So think of yourself as being ill under a doctor. You have suddenly had the lovely idea, the lovely idea of asking the doctor to let you have a glass of wine. There is no reason you shouldn't ask, because it may possibly do you no harm, and it may be good for you to get it. Don't hesitate to ask; ask, don't think twice about it. But if you don't get it, don't feel bad about it. If this holds good when you are under the care of a human doctor, concerned with your body, how much more so under the care of the divine doctor, the creator and restorer of both your body and your soul?

Go to the heavenly doctor

3. So then, seeing that in this chapter of the gospel the Lord exhorts us to prayer after saying *It was because of your unbelief that you could not cast out this demon*, he exhorted them to prayer, you see, by concluding like this: *This kind is only cast out by fasting and prayers* (Mt 17:19.21; Mk 9:29). If a person is to pray in order to cast out someone else's demon, how much more to cast out his own avarice? How much more to cast out his own habit of drunkenness? How much more to cast out his own loose living? How much more to cast out his own uncleanness?

How many things there are in us which, if they persist, bar our entry into the kingdom of heaven! Just think, brothers and sisters, how urgently people beg doctors for merely temporary health, how if someone is desperately ill he's neither slow nor shy about clinging to the man's feet, about washing the expert surgeon's feet with his tears. And what if the doctor tells him, "The only way you can be cured is if I tie you down, cauterize, wield the knife"? He will answer, "Do what you like, only cure me." How keenly he must long for a few days' volatile health, as fleeting as the morning mist, if for its sake he is willing to be tied down, and cut open, and burnt, and kept from eating what he likes and drinking what he likes and when he likes! He endures all this, just to die a little later; and he is reluctant to put up with a little suffering in order not to die ever! If God, the heavenly doctor in charge of us, said to you, "Do you want to be cured?" wouldn't you say, "Yes, I do"? Or perhaps you wouldn't say it, because you think you are perfectly well, and that means your illness is worse than ever.

Christ came to the sick, he found all of us sick

4. Take, for instance, two sick people; one pleads with the doctor in tears, the other, delirious in his sickness, pours scorn on the doctor. The doctor can hold out hope to the one who is crying, but can only wring his hands over the one who is laughing at him. Why? Because the more certainly he imagines himself to be well, the more dangerously ill he is shown to be.

That was the case with the Jews. Christ came to the sick, he found all of us sick. We should none of us flatter ourselves on our health, or we won't present ourselves to this doctor. *For all have sinned, and are in need of the glory of God* (Rom 3:23). So since he found all of us sick, there have been two kinds of sick people. Some have come to the doctor, clung to Christ, listened to him, honored him, followed him, been converted. He has received them all, without any revulsion, to treat them, and has treated them free, curing them by his divine omnipotence. So when he has taken them in and joined them to himself for treatment, they have been jubilant.

But the other kind of sick people, who were already delirious in their wickedness illness and didn't know they were ill, were insolent toward him because he took in the sick, and they said to his disciples, *Look what sort of man your teacher is, eating with sinners and tax-collectors.* He, of course, knew what they were and what he was, so he answered them, *It's not people who are well that need a doctor, but people who are sick.* And he goes on to show them whom he means by those who are well and those who are sick. *I did not come,* he says, *to call the just, but sinners* (Mt 9:11-13). "If sinners don't approach me", he is saying, "what was the point of my coming? Who did I come for?" If all are fit and well, why should such a doctor ever come down from heaven? Why should he make us up a remedy, not from his medicine chest, but from his own blood?

So that kind of sick people who were less seriously ill, who were aware of being ill, clung to the doctor in order to be cured. But those who were dangerously ill were insulting toward the doctor and dismissive of the sick. And in the end, how far did their frenzy carry them? To seizing the doctor, binding him, scourging him, crowning him with thorns, hanging him up on a tree, killing him on a cross. Why be surprised? The sick slew the doctor, but the doctor, once slain, cured them of their frenzied delirium.

The words of the doctor hanging on a cross

5. From the start, you see, on the cross itself he did not forget his role, but demonstrated his patience to us, and gave us the example of loving our enemies. He saw them seething round him, and being the doctor he knew what their disease was,

knew they had lost their wits in a delirium or frenzy, and so he immediately said to the Father, *Father, forgive them, for they do not know what they are doing* (Lk 23:34). Do you imagine those Jews weren't really an evil-minded, bloodthirsty, cruel mob, hostile to the Son of God? And do you imagine that those words were just empty and ineffective, *Father, forgive them, for they do not know what they are doing*? He saw them all, but he recognized there those who would later be his own.

Finally, he died because it was appropriate that by his death he should slay death. God died, to strike a balance in a kind of celestial bargain, to prevent humanity seeing death. Christ, you see, is God, but he didn't die in that aspect in which he was God. It's the same person who is God and who is man, since Christ is one person, God and man. The human was taken on that we might be changed for the better, it didn't drag God down to an inferior mode of being. I mean, he took on what he was not, he did not lose what he was. So since he was both God and man, wishing us to live by what was his own, he died by what was ours. In himself, you see, he had nothing to die with; but then we had nothing to live by.

What was he then, this one who had nothing to die with? *In the beginning was the Word, and the Word was with God, and the Word was God* (Jn 1:1). Look for something that God can die with, and you won't find it. We, however, die, being flesh; humanity carrying sinful flesh. Look for something that sin can live by, and it doesn't have anything. So he couldn't have death by what was his very own, nor could we have life by what was our very own. But we have life from what is his, he has death from what is ours.

What an extraordinary tradeoff. What did he give, and what did he get? When human traders go trading it is to exchange goods. Trading in olden days, you see, was barter or exchanging goods. A person gave what he had, and got what he didn't have. For example, he had wheat and didn't have barley; someone else had barley and not wheat; the first one traded some wheat which he had for some barley which he didn't have. How much would it be worth for a greater quantity of one commodity to make up for its lesser value? So here you have one trader offering barley to get wheat; and at the other end of the scale, one offering lead in order to acquire silver. But he has to give a lot of lead against a little silver. Another offers wool, to acquire cloth. We can't possibly list them all. But no one, surely, offers life to acquire death.

So the words of the doctor hanging on the cross were not in vain. You see, in order to die for us, because the Word couldn't die, *The Word became flesh and dwelt amongst us* (Jn 1:14). He hung on the cross, but in the flesh. There's the cheapness which the Jews despised; there's the dear love by which the Jews were set free. It was for them, after all, that he said, *Father, forgive them, for they do not know what they are doing*. And those words were not ineffective. He died, he was buried, he rose again. After spending forty days with his disciples, he ascended into heaven, he sent the Holy Spirit he had promised on those who were expecting him. They were filled with the Holy Spirit they received, and began to speak with the tongues of all nations. Then the Jews who were present, thunderstruck at simple, uneducated men, whom they knew to have been brought up among them in one language, speaking in Christ's name all languages, well they were shaken to the core. Then when Peter spoke they learned where this gift came from. That man bestowed it, who had hung on the cross. That man bestowed it, who had been laughed at as he hung on the cross so that seated in heaven he might give the Holy Spirit. They heard, they believed, those about whom he had said, *Father, forgive them, for they do not know what they are doing.* They believed, they were baptized, and they underwent conversion. What sort of conversion? The blood of Christ, which they had shed in fury, they drank in faith.

Call upon the Lord when we stumble and stagger in this life

6. So, to conclude this sermon where we began it, let us pray, and put all our trust in God; let us live as he commands us, and when we stumble and stagger in this life, let us call upon him as the disciples called upon him, when they said, *Lord, increase our faith* (Lk 17:5). Peter too was full of confidence, and staggered; yet he wasn't ignored and allowed to drown, but given a helping hand and set on his feet. Just what, after all did he place his confidence in? It wasn't in himself, it was in the Lord. How's that? *Lord, if it is you, bid me come to you over the water.* The Lord, you remember, was walking over the waters. *If it is you, bid me come to you over the water.* I know, you see, that if it is you, you have only to command, and it will happen. And he said, *Come.* He got down from the boat at his command, he began to tremble at his own weakness. And yet when he grew afraid he cried out to him: *Lord, deliver me,* he said. Then the Lord took him by the hand and said, *Little faith, why did you doubt?* (Mt 14:28.30.31). It was he that invited him, he that delivered him when he tottered and staggered. This fulfilled what was said in the psalm, *If I said, My foot has slipped, your mercy, Lord, would come to my help* (Ps 94:18).

Two sorts of benefits: temporal and eternal

7. So then, there are two sorts of benefits, temporal ones and eternal ones. Temporal ones are such things as health, wealth, honor, friends, house, children, wife and the other things of this life through which we are traveling as foreigners. So let us place ourselves in the wayside hotel of this life, like travelers who are going to pass on, not like owners who are going to stay.

Eternal benefits, on the other hand, are first and foremost eternal life itself, the imperishability and immortality of flesh and soul, the company of angels, the heavenly city, unfailing titles of nobility, a Father and a fatherland, the one beyond death, the other beyond enemies. We should be longing for these benefits with infinite desire, pray for them with tireless perseverance, not with long speeches but with the evidence of our sighs. Desire is praying always, even if the tongue is silent. If you desire always, you are praying always. When does prayer nod off to sleep? When desire grows cold.

So let us beg for these everlasting benefits with insatiable eagerness, let us seek those good things with a singleminded determination, let us ask for those good things without a scruple of anxiety. Those good things, after all, benefit those who have them, and cannot possibly do them harm. But these temporal things are sometimes of benefit, and sometimes harmful. Many people have profited from poverty and been harmed by riches; many have profited from the obscurity of private life, and been harmed by the honors of high public office. And again, money has been good for some people, and so has high position: good for those who use them well, but for those who use them badly they have harmed them more than ever, if they have not been deprived of them.

And therefore, dear brothers and sisters, let us ask for these temporal benefits too, but in moderation, safe in the knowledge that if we receive them, the one who gives them knows what is suitable for us. You've asked, have you, and haven't been given what you asked for? Trust the Father, who would give it to you if it suited you. Look, you can work it out from a comparison with yourself. Your small son, ignorant of the ways of the world, stands in the same relation to you as you, ignorant of the divine world, stand in to the Lord. So there's your little boy, crying at you all day long to give him a pruning knife, to play with as a sword. You refuse to give it to him, you don't give it, you ignore his tears in order not to lament his death. Let him cry, let him torment himself in a tantrum for you to lift him up on a horse; you don't do it because he can't control it; it will throw him and kill him. You are denying him a part, because you are keeping the whole for him. But so that he may grow up and possess the whole safely, you don't give him a dangerous little part.

Whatever we are like, that's what the times are like

8. So that's why I'm saying, dear brothers and sisters, pray as much as you can. Evils abound, and God has willed that evils should abound. If only evil people didn't abound, then evils wouldn't abound. The times are evil, the times are troubled, that's what people say. Let us live good lives, and the times are good. We ourselves are the times. Whatever we are like, that's what the times are like.

But what are we to do? We can't convert the vast majority to a good life, can we? Let the few people who are listening live good lives; let the few who are living good lives bear with the many living bad ones. They are grains of wheat, they are on the threshing floor; they can have chaff with them on the threshing floor, they won't have it with them in the barn. Let them put up with what they don't want, in order to come to what they do.

Why should we be vexed, and find fault with God? Evils abound in the world to stop us loving the world. Great are the people, real saints are the faithful, who have made light of the beautiful world; we here can't even make light of the ugly one. The world is evil, yes it's evil, and yet it is loved as if it were good. And what precisely is this evil world? It isn't the sky and earth and the waters and all that is in them, fishes, birds, trees. All these things are good. The evil world is the one made by evil people.

But because, as I have said, as long as we live we cannot be without evil people, let us moan and groan to the Lord our God, and put up with evils in order to attain to things that are truly good. Don't let's find fault with the Father of the family; after all, he cares for us dearly. He is supporting us, not we him. He knows how to manage what he has made. Do what he has told you, and hope for what he has promised.

Sermon 82

On the Words of the Gospel of Matthew 18:15-18: *If Your Brother Has Sinned Against You, Reprove Him Between Him And Yourself Alone;* and on the Words of Solomon (Prv 10:10): *One Who Winks Deceitfully With the Eyes Heaps Up Grief for Men,* etc.

Augustine observes that fraternal correction is a difficult but necessary expression of hard love. Christians must be on guard that such correction is not motivated by hidden anger, hatred or envy. We should not minimize or make light of any sins committed against another. Fraternal correction should be based on love and never on hate. Sins committed less publicly should be rebuked less publicly. Bishops are sometimes criticized for their failure to reprove sinners publicly, but they may have good reasons to rebuke privately, even though some find fault with their perceived negligence. No Christian should risk putting off moral reform. This sermon demonstrates how Augustine views Christ as the proper hermaneutical key to interpreting the Old Testament. Although certain passages of scripture may appear at times contradictory, "scripture is never at war with itself and each point is true." Based on the heading in one 10th-century manuscript, scholars believe this sermon was preached at Milev (Milevis), a town in the western part of Numidia, 40 miles inward from the coast. Augustine's friend Severus was bishop there and the sermon is datable by comparison with Letter 95, written in August 409 to Paulinus of Nola, based on similar content.

(...)

Follow the scriptures

9. So, brothers and sisters, let us listen to these two instructions in order to understand them, and set ourselves in a calm frame of mind between them both. Let us make peace with our own hearts, and we shall find that holy scripture is never and nowhere at war with itself. It is all absolutely true; each point is true. But we have to distinguish; sometimes this is to be done, and sometimes that. Sometimes your brother should be reproved between yourself and him alone, sometimes your brother is to be reproved in front of everybody, that the rest too may learn to fear. If we sometimes do the one and sometimes the other, we shall be maintaining the harmony of the scriptures, and in acting in compliance with them, we shall not be going astray. But someone's going to say to me: "When am I to do this, and when that? How am I to avoid rebuking him between myself and him alone, when I ought to rebuke him in front of everyone, or rebuking him in front of everyone when I ought to be rebuking him privately?"

Public or private reprove

10. Your graces will see soon enough which we ought to do when, but if only we aren't sluggishly reluctant to do it. Notice carefully: *If your brother*, he says, *has sinned against you, reprove him between yourself and him alone.* Why? Because he has sinned against you. What's the meaning, precisely, of "against you"? It means you know he has sinned, because it was something private, not known to other people, when he sinned against you. Look for a chance to do it privately, when you correct him for sinning. After all, if you are the only one who knows that he has sinned against you, and you want to censure him for it in front of everybody, you won't be reproving him, but betraying him.

Look how that just man, Joseph, showed such goodness in sparing the shameful wrong of which he suspected his wife, before he knew how she had conceived. He saw she was pregnant, and he knew he had not known her intimately himself. So there was a suspicion, amounting to a certainty, of adultery. And yet because he was the only one who had noticed it, the only one who knew it, what does the gospel say about him? *But Joseph, being a just man, and unwilling to disgrace her publicly.* A husband's sense of injury did not look for revenge; he wanted to help the sinner, not punish her. *Being unwilling*, it says, *to disgrace her publicly, wished to divorce her privately.* While he was thinking about this, *behold, the angel of the Lord appeared to him in a dream* (Mt 1:19-20), and pointed out the truth of the matter, that she had not dishonored her husband's bed, because she had conceived the Lord of them both by the Holy Spirit.

So, your brother has sinned against you. If you are the only one who knows it, then in fact he has only sinned against you. I mean if he affronted you in the hearing of several other people, then he also sinned against them, making them witnesses of his wickedness. I'm only saying, my dearest brothers and sisters, what you too can easily recognize for yourselves. When someone, in my presence, insults my brother, God forbid I should reckon that insult has nothing to do with me. Of course, he insulted me too; indeed he did me the greater injury, imagining I would be pleased with what he did. Those sins, then, are to be rebuked in front of everybody which are committed in front of everybody. Those which are committed less publicly are to be rebuked less publicly. Distinguish between the occasions, and scripture is at peace with itself.

Private reprove

11. Let's act like that, because that's how we should act, not only when someone sins against us, but also when anybody's sin is unknown to someone else. We should rebuke privately, censure privately, and not betray people by wishing to censure them publicly. What we are wanting to do is to rebuke and correct; what if some enemy of theirs wants to hear about something he can punish? A bishop, for example, knows someone or other is a murderer, and nobody else knows he is. I want to rebuke him publicly, while you are looking for a chance to bring an indict-

ment. Well of course, I will neither give him away, nor ignore his sin. I will rebuke him privately, set God's judgment before his eyes, terrify his bloodstained conscience, try to persuade him to repent. That is the kind of Christian charity with which we should all be equipped.

That's why people sometimes find fault with us bishops, because we seem not to reprove sinners. They either suppose that we know what in fact we don't, or they suppose that we say nothing about what we do know. But perhaps I too know what you know; and yet I don't reprove it in your presence, because what I want to do is to cure, not accuse. There are people who commit adultery in their own homes; they sin privately. Sometimes they are reported to me by their wives out of extreme jealously, sometimes out of a real concern for their husbands' salvation. I don't give them away publicly, but censure them in private. Let the evil terminate where the evil happens. I don't however neglect that wound; I try above all to show a man set in the habit of that sort of sin, and carrying a wounded conscience around with him, that the wound is in itself deadly.

Sometimes people who commit this sin treat it lightly out of heaven knows what kind of perversity. They hunt about for heaven knows what null and worthless proofs in their support, and they say, "God doesn't mind the sins of the flesh." Well, what about what we have heard today, *Fornicators and adulterers God will judge* (Heb 13:4)? So there you are, pay attention, any of you afflicted with this sort of disease. Listen to what God is saying, not to what your own prejudice is saying in favor of your sins, or your friend, perhaps, chained with the same shackles of wickedness as yourself — though in fact he is more your enemy and his own. So listen to what the apostle says: *Let marriage be held in honor among all, and the marriage bed be undefiled. But fornicators and adulterers God will judge.*

The rebuke is public, but the correction is private

12. So come now, brother, let yourself be corrected. You're afraid your enemy may bring an indictment against you, and aren't you afraid God may judge you? Where's your faith? Be afraid while there is time for being afraid. Sure, the day of judgment's a long way off. But the last day of each and every one of us cannot be a long way off, because life is short. And because it is always uncertain just how short, you don't know when your last day is going to be. Correct yourself today, ready for tomorrow. Let private rebuke avail you right now. I am speaking publicly, and I'm censuring privately. I'm knocking at the ears of all of you, but I meet the consciences of some of you only. If I said, "You there, adulterer, mend your ways," I might in the first place be asserting something I didn't know; I might perhaps be giving too much credit to something I had heard quite casually. So I don't say, "You there, adulterer, mend your ways," but, "Whoever you are, adulterer, in this congregation, mend your ways." The rebuke is public, but the correction is private. I know that the one who fears God is mending his ways.

You are God's temple

13. What he mustn't do is say to himself, "God doesn't mind sins of the flesh." *Do you not know*, says the apostle, *that you are the temple of God, and the Spirit of God dwells in you? Whoever violates God's temple, God will destroy him* (1 Cor 3:16-17). Don't deceive yourselves, any of you, But someone will say, perhaps, "God's temple is my mind, not my body," adding the proof text, *All flesh is grass, and all the splendor of the flesh as the flower of grass* (Is 40:6). Miserable interpretation, punishable thought! Flesh is called grass because it dies, but take care that what dies for a time doesn't rise stained by crime. Do you want to have a completely clear judgment on the point? *Do you not know*, says the same apostle, *that your bodies are the temple of the Holy Spirit in you, which you have from God?* Now you can't make light of bodily sins; here you have it that even *your bodies are the temple of the Holy Spirit in you, which you have from God.* You were making light of bodily sins, were you, you make light of sinning against a temple? Your very body is the temple of God's Spirit in you. Now see what you are doing to God's temple.

If you chose to commit adultery in church, within these four walls, could anything be more infamous than you? But now you yourself are God's temple. A temple you come in, a temple you go out, a temple you stay at home, a temple you get up. Mind what you do, mind you don't offend the inhabitant of the temple, or he may abandon you and you will fall into ruin. *Do you not know*, he says, *that your bodies* (and here the apostle was talking about fornication, in case they should make light of bodily sins) *is the temple of the Holy Spirit in you, which you have from God, and you are not your own? For you have been bought for a great price.* If you make light of your body, just reflect on your price.

Let yourself be corrected now

14. I myself know, and so does anyone who stops to reflect a little, that nobody who fears God will fail to correct himself at his words, unless he assumes that he has longer to live. This is the thing that kills many people, when they say, "Tomorrow, tomorrow," and suddenly the door is shut. He remained outside, croaking like a crow, because he didn't know how to moan like a dove. "Tomorrow, tomorrow"; it's the caw of the crow. Moan like a dove and beat your breast; but when you give yourself blows on the breast, take care you emerge from the beating corrected. Otherwise what you may appear to be doing is not beating your conscience, but ramming down a bad conscience into concrete with your fists, making it harder and more solid than ever, not correcting it.

Moan and groan, but not with meaningless moans and groans. Someone will perhaps say to you, "God promised me pardon when I have corrected myself; I'm safe, I read the divine scripture, *On the day the wicked man turns away from his wickedness and does justice, I will forget all his wickedness* (Ez 18:21-22). I'm safe; when I correct myself, God grants me a pardon for my bad deeds." And what am I going to say? Am I going to protest against God? Am I going to say to God,

"Don't grant him pardon"? Am I going to say this wasn't written, God didn't make this promise? If I say any of this, what I say is all untrue. What you say is right, what you say is true. God did promise pardon for your correcting yourself; I can't deny it. But tell me this, please — look, I agree, I know, I grant you, God did promise you pardon. I mean, did anyone promise you tomorrow? That place you are reading to me from, about how you are going to receive pardon if you correct yourself: read to me from it how long you are going to live. "I don't read that," you say. So you don't know how long you are going to live.

Let yourself be corrected now, and so always ready. Don't be afraid of the last day, like a thief who digs through the wall while you're asleep, but wake up and correct yourself today. Why put it off till tomorrow? "Life will be long." This long life of yours, let it be a good one. No one puts off a good long dinner, and are you willing to have a bad long life? Surely if it's long, it will be all the better for being good; if it's short, you do well to extend it into eternity as a good one. It's really very odd, I must say, how people neglect their lives, so that the only things they are quite agreeable to having bad are their lives. You are buying a country cottage, you look for a good one; you want to marry a wife, you'd rather have a good one; you want children to be born to you, you hope they'll be good ones; you hire a pair of boots, and you don't want bad ones; and you love a bad life! What has annoyed you about your life so much, that it's the only thing you like being bad, with the result that among all your good things, you alone are bad?

The ministry of rebuking

15. So, my brothers and sisters, if I wanted to rebuke any of you, taking you aside to do so, no doubt you would listen to me. But I'm now rebuking many of you publicly. Everyone applauds me; I hope someone is listening. I don't like someone applauding me with his words, and ignoring me in his heart. You see, when you applaud and don't correct yourself, you are a witness against yourself. If you are bad, and yet like what I say, then don't like yourself; because if you don't like yourself when you're bad, you will like yourself when you have put yourself right, as I told you a couple of days ago, if I'm not mistaken.

In all my sermons I am presenting you with a mirror. They aren't my sermons, anyway; I only speak at the Lord's command, it's only dread of him that stops me keeping quiet. I mean to say, who wouldn't much rather keep quiet, and not have to give an account of you? But it's quite a time since I accepted this burden, and now I neither can nor should shrug it off my shoulders. You heard, my brothers and sisters, when the Letter to the Hebrews was being read, *Obey your leaders and submit to them; because they keep watch over your souls, as having to render account for you; that they may do this with joy and not with sadness; for that would not be for your profit* (Heb 13:17).

When do we do this with joy? When we see people making progress in the words of God. When does the workman labor with joy in the fields? When he looks at the tree and sees the fruit; when he looks at the crop, and looks forward to plenty of grain on the threshing floor. He hasn't labored in vain, he hasn't bent his back in vain, he hasn't worn down his fingers to the bone in vain, he hasn't endured cold and heat in vain. That's what he means when he says *that they may do this with joy and not with sadness; for that would not be for your profit.* He didn't say, "it would not be for their profit." No; but he said *it would not be for your profit.* You see, when those leaders are saddened by your bad deeds, this is for their profit; their very sadness does them good, but it is not for your profit. But I don't want anything to be for my profit, which is not also for your profit. So, brothers and sisters, let us work at doing good together in the field of the Lord, that together we may enjoy the reward.

Sermon 94A

On the Martyrdom of John the Baptist and on the Persecution Which Christians Have to Endure Even in the Time of Peace

Hill proposes August 29, 405 as the most likely date for this sermon, based on the recurring phrase, "It isn't the punishment that makes the martyr, but the cause," and particularly in view of the decision of a council of Catholic bishops in Carthage to be more aggressive toward the Donatists through imperial laws. Since Christ is the way and the truth and the life, John the Baptist died for the truth and as such is a true martyr. Christians should fight to the death for truth and justice, never giving false witness.

Why do we say that John was a martyr?

1. The Church of Christ, dearly beloved brothers and sisters, certainly has no doubt about what the Lord wished to teach us from this chapter of the holy gospel, namely that John is a martyr. He even earned his martyrdom before the Lord himself had suffered. He was born first and suffered first, not however as the author of salvation but as the judge's precursor. He went ahead of the Lord, you see, taking a humble supporting role himself, giving the title of majesty to the heavenly Master.

Why do we say John was a martyr? Was he arrested by the persecutors of Christians, brought to court and interrogated? Did he then confess Christ, and suffer? That, after all, is what the other martyrs can be said to have experienced after Christ's passion. So what makes this man a martyr? His having his head cut off?

I mean, it isn't the punishment that makes the martyr, but the cause. Is it because he offended a powerful woman? How did he offend her? On what point did he give offense? By telling the truth to the king who had become her husband, telling him it was not lawful for him to have his brother's wife. It was truth that earned him her hatred, and by earning her hatred he came eventually to his passion and his prize. These are the fruits of the age to come. In a word, lasciviousness dances, innocence is damned; but damned by men, awarded the prize by almighty God.

He died for Christ who is truth

2. So nobody should say "I can't be a martyr, because Christians aren't being persecuted." You have heard that John underwent martyrdom; and if you consider the matter truly, he died for Christ. "How," you ask, "did he die for Christ, seeing that he wasn't interrogated about Christ or forced to deny Christ?" Listen to Christ himself saying, *I am the way and the truth and the life* (Jn 14:6). If Christ is the truth, anyone who is condemned to death for the truth suffers for Christ, and is correctly awarded the prize.

So we should none of us make excuses. All times are open season for martyrs. Nor should anyone say that Christians aren't persecuted. The judgment of the apostle Paul cannot be annulled, because it is true; Christ spoke through him, he wasn't lying. He said, you see, *All who wish to live loyally in Christ Jesus will suffer persecution* (2 Tm 3:12). "All," he says; he makes no exceptions for anyone, he leaves nobody aside. If you want to prove the truth of what he said, start living loyally in Christ, and you'll soon see that what he says is true.

Just because persecution by earthly kings has quieted down, does that mean the devil is not on the prowl? That ancient enemy is always on the watch against us; don't let us go to sleep. He sets lures and traps, he insinuates evil thoughts; to goad people to an ever worse kind of fall, he sets out advantages and gains, he threatens disadvantages and losses. When it comes to the crunch with him, it is painful to reject his evil suggestions and willingly accept death as we know it. Understand me, brothers and sisters. If someone compels you — for instance, some aristocrat who holds your life in his grasp compels you to give false evidence (and he doesn't say to you "Deny Christ") — what do you think of doing: choosing the falsehood or dying for the truth?

And yet in fact "Deny Christ" is precisely what the persecutor does say to you. After all, if Christ is the truth, as we have already said, obviously if you deny the truth you deny Christ. Now everyone who tells a lie is denying the truth. What about the one who gives false evidence — why does he do it? Because he's afraid, of course. Don't we call it a persecution of all Christians when they are struggling for the truth? Well, now they are being tested one by one; each one is subjected to trial in his or her own particular case.

John refused to keep quiet about the truth

3. But let's come back to you: what was your enemy going to do to you, forcing you to perjure yourself with false evidence? There he was, threatening you with slaughter, thirsting for your blood, puffed up with his power like billowing smoke — what was he going to do? Feebleness answers, "He would have killed me." "He wouldn't have killed you." "I'm telling you, *I know* he would have killed me." If that's the case, I too will have an answer for you: "You, brother, are also a killer, by giving false evidence. He would have killed you, yes — but your body. What would he do to your soul? The house would have been pulled down, its inhabitant would have been awarded the prize. There you have what your enemy would have done to you, if you had stood firm in the truth, and not given false evidence. He would have killed all right, but the body, not the soul.

"Listen to your Lord, anxious to reassure you: *Do not be afraid,* he says, *of those who kill the body, and afterward have nothing they can do. But fear him who has the power to kill body and soul and cast into hell. Yes, I tell you, fear that one*" (Lk 12:5). That's the one John feared. He refused to keep quiet about the truth, and endured the wickedness of an evil couple; through a shameless woman he earned the hatred of a king, and so attained to martyrdom.

True martyrs contend for the truth which is Christ

4. All, you see, who wish to live loyally in Christ are battered by that sort of persecution. After all, people suffer persecution for the sake of worldly gain, or for fear of loss; either for this present life, or under the threat of death, because this world in this age is not without persecution.

But we have to discriminate, and see who suffers for what. And they will be true martyrs if they contend for the truth which is Christ, and are legitimately awarded the prize. I mean, people who suffer persecution for the sake of this world, which is in a bad way, can be subjected to temporal punishment.

Fight to the death for truth

5. So then, brothers and sisters, what we have learned from today's reading is that we should fight to the death for truth, and never give false evidence, never perjure ourselves, but stick to the path of justice even when it is dangerous — there's nothing very remarkable, after all, in sticking to the path of justice when it's perfectly safe and enjoyable to do so. That being the case, let us always bear in mind that the devil is on the watch against us, our tempter and our persecutor; and in the name and with the help of the Lord our God, let us be more ardently on the watch against him, to prevent his overcoming us in any matter through greed, which is his usual means of temptation; because who is not defeated by greed and fear, which are the enemy's weapons from which human beings who place their hope in this world end up tied up in knots and thus are quite powerless to attain the truth?

In a word, there are two doors available to the devil to knock at and enter by; the front door is greed, the back door is fear. If he finds both shut among the faithful, he passes on. "And what," you ask, "is this greed, what this fear?" Listen to what it is: that you shouldn't ardently desire what passes, and neither should you fear what fades away and perishes with time. And then, you may be sure, the enemy won't find a niche to lodge in. Because we are faced with a struggle against him right to the end. I don't only mean us bishops who stand or speak in this higher place and speak to you from here, but all the members of Christ are faced with this struggle.

Stand fast in the Lord

6. On this point, it's the custom in Numidia to adjure the servants of God like this: "If you overcome." You can see that such a mode of address has some point with someone who is fighting. Here too where we are talking, in Carthage, and in the whole proconsular province and Bizacena, not to mention Tripoli, the customary way for the servants of God to adjure each other is "By your crown."

And I now adjure you, by your crown, to fight against the devil with all your hearts, and if we all overcome together, we shall all be awarded the prize and be crowned together. Why, why do you say to us bishops, "By your crown," and behave badly, lead bad lives? Live good lives, do good, both inwardly and outwardly conduct yourselves well, and you yourselves will be our crown. The apostle was addressing the people of God, which is what you are, when he says *My joy and my crown, stand fast in the Lord* (Phil 4:1). So if temporal prosperity smiles on you, stand fast in the Lord; if temporal adversity frowns on you, be steady in the Lord. Don't fall away from him, who always stands fast, and standing waits for the warrior, and helps you to win by standing and fighting, and so finally you come to him to be awarded the prize of your crown.

Sermon 96

On the Words of the Gospel, Mark 8:34: *If Anyone Wishes to Follow Me,
Let Him Deny Himself,* etc., and on the Words of 1 John 2:15:
Whoever Loves the World, the Love of the Father Is Not in Him

Augustine preached this sermon was between Ascension Thursday and Pentecost, but there is no hint of the year. People must be willing to deny themselves
in order to follow Christ regardless of their particular state in life. The way to
advance to the heights is humility. Virginity is clearly superior to marriage. All
the baptized are called to holiness.

Whatever is hard in the commandment is made easy by charity

1. What the Lord has commanded seems hard and harsh, that any who wish to follow him should deny themselves. But nothing can be hard and harsh which is commanded by one who helps us to do what he commands. You see, both these things are true, both what is said to him in the psalm: *Because of the words of your lips I have kept to hard ways* (Ps 17:4); and what he himself said, *My yoke is easy, and my burden light* (Mt 11:30). The fact is, whatever is hard in the commandments is made easy by charity.

We know what wonderful things love can do. Often enough, the very love itself is base and licentious; but how many hard things people have endured, how many indignities and intolerable pains they have put up with in order to obtain what they loved — whether the lover of money whom we call a miser, or the lover of prestige and power whom we call ambitious, or the lover of beautiful bodies whom we call licentious! And could anyone list all the different sorts of love? Reflect, though, for a minute on what labors all lovers undertake, without even noticing that they are labors; and try to stop them from such painful exertions, and they exert themselves all the more strenuously.

So since most people are somehow like the loves that drive them, and since their one concern in determining how they ought to live should only be to choose what they should love, why be surprised if those who love Christ and want to follow Christ should deny themselves in loving him? If you get lost, I mean, through loving yourself, then of course you get found through denying yourself.

Put God's will before all

2. Man's first ruin was caused by love of self. I mean, if he hadn't loved himself, and had put God before himself, he would have wanted always to be subject to God, and he wouldn't have turned away to disregarding God's will and doing his own. That, after all, is what loving oneself means, wanting to do one's own will. Put God's will before all that; learn to love yourself by not loving yourself. Just to show that loving yourself is a vice, this is what the apostle says: *For people will be lovers of self* (2 Tm 3:2).

And do those who love themselves really have confidence in themselves? They begin, you see, by forsaking God to love themselves, and then are driven out of themselves to love what is outside themselves; so that this same apostle, after saying, *People will be lovers of self*, very precisely goes on immediately to add, *lovers of money*. Now, you can see that you are outside yourself. Stay in yourself, if you can. Why go outside? Has money really made you rich, you lover of money? As soon as you began to love things outside yourself, you lost yourself.

So when a person's love also reaches out from himself to what is outside, he begins to disintegrate with dissipation, and to squander his powers somehow or other like the spendthrift prodigal son. He empties himself, he pours himself out, he ends up penniless, he herds pigs. And finding it wearisome in the extreme, herding pigs, he eventually recollects himself, and says, *How many hired servants of my father are eating bread, and here am I, perishing from hunger?*

But when he says this, what are we told about this son, who threw away all his money on whores, who wanted to have under his own control all the property that was being kept very well for him with his father — he wanted to have it all entirely at his own disposal, he poured it all out like water, he ended up penniless? What are we told about him? *And he returned to himself.* If he returned to himself, it means he had gone away from himself. Because he had fallen from himself and gone away from himself, he first returns to himself in order to return to the one from whom he had fallen, in falling from himself. You see, by falling from himself he had remained in himself. So in the same way, when he returns to himself he must not remain in himself, in case he again goes away from himself. On returning to himself, what did he say in order not to remain in himself? *I will arise and go to my father* (Lk 15:17-18). That's the place from which he had fallen from himself; he had fallen from his father, he had fallen from himself. He had gone away from himself to things outside. He comes back to himself and sets off to his father, where he can keep himself in the utmost security.

So if he had gone away from himself and from the one he had gone away from, then by coming back to himself to go to his father, he must deny himself. What does denying himself mean? He mustn't rely on himself, must realize he is merely human, and pay attention to the prophetic dictum, *Cursed be everyone who places his hope in man* (Jer 17:5). He must disengage himself from himself, but not in a downward direction. Let him disengage himself from himself, in order to stick to God. Whatever good there is in him, let him attribute it to the one who made him; whatever about him is bad, he has made himself. God did not make what is bad about him. Let him jettison everything of his own doing, seeing that he has been his own undoing. *Let him deny himself,* he said, *and take up his cross, and follow me* (Mk 8:34).

Follow the Lord

3. Follow the Lord where to? Where he went, we know perfectly well; we solemnly celebrated that occasion only a very few days ago. He rose from the dead, he ascended into heaven; that's where we are to follow him to. Obviously we mustn't despair about getting there — but because he made us the promise, not because we mere human beings can manage it on our own. Heaven was a long, long way away from us before our head had gone up to heaven. Now, though, what reason have we to despair, if we are the body and limbs of that head? So that's where we have to follow him. And who wouldn't want to follow him to such a residence? Especially because we are beset with so many fears and griefs on earth. Who wouldn't want to follow Christ there, where total happiness reigns, total peace, perpetual security? It's good to follow him there; but we have to see by what road.

After all, the Lord Jesus didn't speak these words after he had risen from the dead. He hadn't yet suffered; the cross was still to come, still to come also was the dishonor, the abuse, the scourging, the thorns, the wounds, the insults, the taunts, death. The road is exceedingly rough, it makes you very reluctant, you don't want to follow. Follow, all the same. The roughness is what we human beings have made for ourselves, but Christ by coming back has trampled it down till it is rubbed smooth.

I mean, who wouldn't want to advance to the heights? Everyone delights in being at the top. But the step up to it is humility. Why stretch your foot out to what is beyond you? That way, you want to fall, not climb higher. Begin with the step, and you have already climbed higher. Those two disciples didn't want to bother with this step of humility when they said, *Lord, give orders that one of us in your kingdom should sit on your right, the other on your left.* They were after a place at the top, they didn't see the step. The Lord, however, pointed out the step. How did he reply? *Can you drink the cup which I am going to drink?* (Mk 10:37-38). You are after a place of supremacy, can you drain to the dregs the cup of humility? That's why he didn't simply say, *Let him deny himself and follow me,* but added, *Let him take up his cross and follow me* (Mk 8:34).

Taking up the cross means renunciation

4. What does "take up his cross" mean? Let him bear with whatever is troublesome; let him follow me like that. You see, when he begins to follow me in his manner of life and by keeping my commands, he will find many people speaking against him, many telling him to stop, many trying to dissuade him — and among them apparent companions of Christ. They were walking with Christ, those people who tried to stop the blind men crying out. So whether it's threats or enticements, or any kind of attempts to stop you, if you want to follow him, turn them into your cross; endure it, carry it, don't collapse under it.

These words of the Lord's look like an exhortation to martyrdom. If a persecution breaks out, ought not everything to be despised for Christ's sake? We love the world, but we should put the one who made the world before it. The world is great, but greater is the one who made the world. The world is beautiful, but more beautiful still the one who made the world. The world is alluring, but much more pleasing is the one who made the world. The world is bad, and the one who made the world is good.

How shall I be able to unravel and explain what I have said? May God help me. What have I said, after all? Why have you applauded? Look, I've raised a question, and yet you've already applauded. How can the world be bad if the one it was made by is good? Didn't God make everything, *and behold, it was very good?* Doesn't scripture bear witness in every single case that God made things good, by saying *And God saw that it was good?* And it rounded out the whole at the end by saying how God created everything, *and behold it was very good* (Gn 1:3, 31).

Good and bad in the world

5. So how is the world bad, and the one who made the world good? How? Because *the world was made through him, and the world did not know him* (Jn 1:10). The world was made through him, heaven and earth, and all things that are in them; the world did not know him, lovers of the world. Lovers of the world and despisers of God, that's the world that did not know him. So that's the way the world is bad, because there are bad people who prefer the world to God. And he is good, the one who made the world, made heaven and earth and sea, *and* the people who love the world. The only thing, you see, he didn't make in them is the fact that they love the world and don't love God. The people themselves, though, as far as their nature is concerned, he did make; as far as their fault is concerned, he did not make them. Let man but erase what he has made, and he will be pleasing to the one by whom he was made.

Another world was made

6. Because there is also a good world consisting of people, but made so out of a bad one. The whole world, you see, if you take world as meaning people, leaving aside world in the sense of heaven and earth and all things that are in them; if you mean people by world, then the whole world was made bad by the one who first sinned. The whole mass is vitiated in its root. God made man good; that's what scripture says: *God made man upright, and they themselves have sought out many devices* (Eccl 7:30).

From the many run to the one, collect what has been scattered together into one, flow together, secure yourself, stay with the one; don't go after the many. That's where true happiness lies. But we have flowed away, we have wandered out into dissolution; we were all born with sin, and to what we were born with we ourselves have also added by leading bad lives, and the whole world has become bad. Christ, however, came, and chose what he had made, not what he found; he found all bad, you see, and by his grace he made the good. And so another world was made, and world persecutes world.

The persecuting world

7. Which is the world that persecutes? The one about which we are told, *Do not love the world, and the things in the world. Whoever loves the world, the charity of the Father is not in him. Because all the things in the world are the lust of the flesh, and the lust of the eyes, and the ambition of the world, which is not from the Father, but is from the world. And the world passes, and its lust; but whoever accomplishes the will of God abides for ever, just as God also abides for ever* (1 Jn 2:15-17). There you have both worlds I mentioned, both the persecuting one, and the one it persecutes. Which is the persecuting world? *All the things in the world are the lust of the flesh, and the lust of the eyes, and the ambition of the world, which is not from*

the Father but is from the world; and the world passes. There you are, that's the persecuting world. Which is the world it persecutes? *Whoever accomplishes the will of God abides for ever, just as God also abides for ever.*

The world condemned persecutes; the world reconciled suffers persecution

8. But look here, the one which persecutes is called the world; let's find out whether the one which suffers persecution is also called the world. Or are you completely deaf to the voice of Christ saying — or rather of holy scripture testifying: *God was in Christ reconciling the world to himself* (2 Cor 5:19)? *If the world hates you,* he said, *know that it first hated me* (Jn 15:18). There you are, the world hates. Whom but the world? Which world? *God was in Christ reconciling the world to himself.* The world condemned persecutes; the world reconciled suffers persecution. The world condemned: whatever is outside and apart from the Church; the world reconciled: the Church. *For the Son of man,* he says, *did not come to judge the world, but that the world might be saved through him* (Jn 3:17).

All members must follow Christ

9. But in this holy world, good, reconciled, saved — or rather to be saved but now saved in hope, *for in hope we have been saved* (Rom 8:24); so in this world, that is the Church, all of which is following Christ, he says universally, *Whoever wishes to follow me, let him deny himself.* I mean this is not something for virgins to pay heed to, which married women don't have to; or which widows ought to and wedded women not; or which monks ought to, and married men not; or which clergy ought to and lay people not. On the contrary, the universal Church, the whole body, all its members distinguished from each other by the various offices they have been properly allotted, they all ought to follow Christ. The whole of that only one must follow, the dove must follow, the bride must follow, redeemed and dowered by the bridegroom's blood she must follow.

The integrity of virgins has its place there; the continence of widows has its place there; the modesty of the married has its place there; adultery has no place there; no forms of unlawful and punishable licentiousness have a place there. Those members, though, which do have their place there in their own way, their own place, their own sort, let them follow Christ; let them deny themselves, which means let them not rely on themselves; let them take up their cross, which means let them put up in the world with whatever the world inflicts on them for Christ's sake. Let them love him who alone does not let us down, alone is not deceived, alone does not deceive; let them love him, because what he promises is true. But because he doesn't give it now, faith staggers. Hang on, persevere, tolerate, bear the delay, and you have taken up your cross.

We should march on along the road, following Christ

10. The virgin mustn't say, "I shall be alone there." After all, Mary won't be alone there, but the widow Anna will be there too. The married woman mustn't say, "The widow will be there, not me." After all, it's not the case that Anna will be there and Susanna won't be there. But of course, those who are going to be there should test themselves on this point, that those who have a lower status here should not envy, but should love those who have a better one. Look, for example, my dear brothers and sisters, to show you what I mean: one person has chosen the married life, one the celibate life. If the one who has chosen married life starts hankering for some adultery, he has looked back; he has been hankering for something unlawful. But the one who from a commitment to celibacy wishes later on to return to marriage, has also looked back; he has chosen something lawful, and has also looked back.

So is marriage to be condemned? No, marriage is not to be condemned; but as for the one who has chosen it in this case, see where he has got to. He had already gone on ahead. When he had been living as a licentious young man, marriage lay ahead of him; he was tending in its direction. But once he has chosen celibacy, marriage is behind him. *Remember Lot's wife*, said the Lord (Lk 17:32). Lot's wife, by looking back, stayed where she was. So everyone of us, wherever we have got to, should be afraid of looking back, and should march on along the road, following Christ. Forgetting what lies behind, stretching out to what lies ahead, let us follow according to our inner intention toward the palm of God's calling in Christ Jesus. Let married people put the unmarried above themselves; let them acknowledge that they are better; let them respect in them what they do not have themselves; and in them let them love Christ.

Sermon 98

On the Words of the Gospel, Luke 7:11-15, and on the
Three Dead Persons Whom the Lord Raised

There is no evidence where this sermon was preached but it is generally dated before 418. Augustine reflects on the three dead people Jesus restored to life during his public ministry and he assigns an allegorical meaning to each. He interprets the four days Lazarus lies dead as four stages which lead to the habit or addiction of sinning: the tingle of pleasure, consent, the deed itself and finally the addiction or habit. The sermon is important for understanding Augustine's theology of sin and reconciliation.

The raising of the dead

1. All who hear about them and believe are moved by the miracles of our Lord and savior Christ Jesus; but some in one way, others in another. Some, you see, are amazed at his bodily miracles, and have no idea of observing a greater kind. Others, though, hear about the miracles performed on bodies, and now have a greater admiration for those performed on souls. The Lord himself says, *For just as the Father raises the dead and gives them life, so too the Son gives life to whom he will* (Jn 5:21). Not, of course, that the Son gives life to some, the Father to others; but the Father and the Son give it to the same people, because the Father does everything through the Son.

So no one who is a Christian should doubt that even today the dead are raised. But all of us have eyes with which we can see the dead rise in the way the son of this widow rose, as we have just been told in the gospel. Not all, however, have the wherewithal to see those who are dead in the heart rise again; to see that, you need to have already risen in the heart yourself. There is more to raising up someone to live for ever, than to raising up someone who will only die again.

Two kinds of death

2. His widowed mother rejoiced over that young man brought back to life. About people daily restored to life in the spirit their mother the Church rejoices. He was dead in the body, they in the mind. His death was visible, and visibly lamented; theirs being invisible was neither investigated, nor even noticed. The one who knew the dead investigated; he alone knew the dead who was able to make them come alive.

After all, unless the Lord had come to raise the dead, the apostle would not have said, *Awake, you that sleep, and arise from the dead, and Christ shall shed his light upon you* (Eph 5:14). You hear about someone asleep when he says *Awake, you that sleep*, but you understand someone dead when you hear *and arise from the dead*. Those who are dead in the visible sense are often said to be asleep. And obviously, for him who can rouse them they *are* all asleep. I mean, for you or me, someone dead is dead, and they don't wake up however much you punch or pinch them, or even pull them to pieces. But for Christ, that young man to whom he said *Arise* (Lk 7:14) was only asleep; and so he arose straightaway. No one rouses a person asleep in bed as easily as Christ does someone asleep in a tomb.

We should learn from miracles

3. Now we find that three dead people were visibly brought back to life by the Lord, thousands invisibly. In fact, who knows how many he visibly brought back to life? I mean, not everything he did was written down. That's what John says: *Many other things Jesus did, which if they were written down, I think the whole world would not be able to contain the books* (Jn 21:25). So then, many others

were almost certainly restored to life; but it is not without point that three were recorded. Our Lord Jesus Christ, you see, wanted the things he did materially to be also understood spiritually. I mean, he wasn't just performing miracles for the sake of miracles; he did them so that what he did should be marvelous to those who saw them, true to those who understood them.

It's like people seeing the letters in a beautifully written codex, and unable to read; they are indeed full of praise for the copyist's hand and the beauty of the letters; but they haven't the slightest idea what those letters mean, what they have to say; they are admiring with their eyes, ignorant in their minds. Others, though, both praise the scribe's artistry and grasp the meaning — namely those who are able not only to see what is available to all, but also to read, which those who haven't learned how to can't do. In the same way those who saw Christ's miracles, and didn't understand what they meant, and what they suggested somehow or other to those who did understand, were only astonished that such things could happen. But others were both astonished at the things that happened and enriched by understanding what they meant. That's the group we should belong to in the school of Christ.

I mean, if you say that the only reason Christ performed miracles was simply in order that there should be miracles, then you are capable of saying that he didn't even know it wasn't the right season for fruit, when he went looking for figs on that tree. You see, it wasn't the season for fruit, as the evangelist says in so many words; and yet Jesus, feeling hungry, went looking for fruit on the tree. Was Christ ignorant of what any country bumpkin knew? Did the tree's creator not know what the gardener of the tree knew perfectly well? So when he felt hungry and went looking for fruit on the tree, he indicated that he was hungry for one thing and looking for something else; and he found the tree with no fruit and full of leaves; and he cursed it and it withered. What had the tree done in not providing fruit? How was the tree to blame for its unfruitfulness? But there are people who are unable, by their own will, to bear fruit. Their sterility is a fault, seeing that their fruitfulness is a matter of their will. So there were the Jews, who had the words of the law and didn't have its deeds — full of leaves and bearing no fruit.

I've said this simply to persuade you that the reason our Lord Jesus Christ performed miracles was to signify something by these miracles, so that in addition to the fact that they were wonderful, and tremendous, and divine, we should also learn something from them.

Three dead people restored to life

4. So let's see what he wanted us to learn from the three dead people he restored to life. He restored to life the dead daughter of the ruler of the synagogue, who was very ill when he was sent for to come and deliver her from that illness. And as he was on the way, the news came she had died; and as if there were no further reason why he should be put to trouble, the father was told, *The girl is dead; why still*

trouble the Master? He carried on all the same, and said to the girl's father, *Do not be afraid, only believe.* He comes to the house, and finds preparations for the normal funeral obsequies already under way, and says to them, *Do not weep, for the girl is not dead, but asleep* (Mk 5:35-39). He was telling the truth; she was asleep — but for him by whom she could be woken up. He did wake her up, and restored her alive to her parents.

He also woke up this young man, the widow's son, about whom I have just now been reminded I must speak to your graces whatever he is pleased to inspire me with. You have just heard how he was woken up. The Lord was approaching a town, and here was a dead man being carried out of the gate. He was moved with pity because the widowed mother, now deprived of her only son, was weeping, and he did what you heard, saying, *Young man, I say to you, get up. The dead man got up, began to speak; and he restored him to his mother* (Lk 7:12-15).

He also roused Lazarus from the tomb. There too, when the disciples he was talking to heard Lazarus was sick (and he loved him), he said, *Our friend Lazarus is asleep.* They thought he meant the wholesome sleep of a sick man. *If he's asleep, Lord,* they said, *he is out of danger.* He answered, *I tell you,* now speaking plainly, *our friend Lazarus is dead* (Jn 11:11-14). Both things he said were true: "For you he's dead, for me he's asleep."

Three sorts of sinners

5. These three sorts of dead persons are three sorts of sinners, whom today too Christ is still restoring to life. You see, that daughter of the ruler of the synagogue was dead inside the house; she hadn't yet been carried out in public from the privacy of the house's four walls. It was there inside that she was woken up and restored alive to her parents. This young man, though, was no longer in the house, but all the same he was not yet in the grave; he had been carried out of doors, but not yet committed to the ground. Just as the Lord roused the dead girl who hadn't yet been carried out, so he roused the dead man who had been carried out but not yet buried. There remained a third thing for him to do: to raise up also one who had been buried; and this he did with Lazarus.

So then, there are some people who have sin inside in their hearts, but don't yet have it in actual deed. Someone or other is moved by some lust. After all, the Lord himself says, *whoever sees a woman to lust after her has already committed adultery with her in his heart* (Mt 5:28). He hasn't yet approached her physically, he has consented in his heart. He has a dead man inside, he hasn't yet carried him out. And as often happens, as we know, people experience this sort of thing in themselves every day; sometimes when they've heard the word of God, as though the Lord were saying, "Arise," they condemn their having consented to some wickedness, they breathe again to salvation and justice. The dead person rises again inside the house, the heart revives in the privacy of its own thoughts. This resurrection of a dead soul takes place inside, within the recesses of conscience, as though within the four walls of the house.

Others, after consenting to the wicked thought, proceed to put it into practice, like people carrying out the dead man, with the result that what was previously kept private now appears in public. But we don't, surely, have to despair of these people who have proceeded to some sinful act. Wasn't that young man too told, *I say to you, get up*? Wasn't he too given back to his mother? So in the same way those too who have already committed the sin, if they happen to have been admonished and stirred by a word of truth, can rise again at the voice of Christ, and be restored alive to their mother. They have been able to step out into a sinful action, they have not been able to perish forever.

But people, who by doing what is wrong also tie themselves up in evil habits, become defenders of their own evil deeds. They get angry when they are reproved to the extent that the men of Sodom, for example, once said to the just man who was reproving them for their depraved and wicked intentions, *You came here to live, not to give us laws* (Gn 19:9). So habituated were they to their unspeakable vileness, that now wickedness set the standard of justice, and it was the person who forbade it rather than the one who perpetrated it that was reproved. Such people, weighed down by malignant habit, are as it were not only dead but buried. But what must I say, brothers and sisters? Not only buried, but as was said about Lazarus, *He's already stinking*. That massive stone placed against the tomb, that is the hard force of habit which weighs on the soul and doesn't allow it either to rise or even to breathe.

Four stages of sin

6. It also says, *He is four days dead* (Jn 11:39). And indeed, to this state of habit or addiction I am speaking of, the soul comes by four stages. First, you see, there is the tingle of pleasure in the heart; second, consent; third, the deed; and fourth, addiction, habit. There are some people, to be sure, who so firmly push unlawful things away from their thoughts, they don't even find any pleasure in them. There are others who find them pleasant, but don't consent; here death is not finalized, but somehow or other initiated. Add consent to pleasure; that is already a death sentence. From consent they proceed to action, action turns into habitual addiction, and the case looks so desperate that one says, *He is four days dead, he is already stinking*.

So the Lord came, and for him of course everything is easy; and yet he showed you a certain sense of difficulty. He groaned in spirit, he showed that loud shouts of censure and disapproval are required for people who have become hardened in bad habits. And yet at the voice of the Lord raised in a shout, the bonds of necessity were ruptured. The Lord, you see, can even set the four days' dead free from their evil habits, because even this four days dead man was only sleeping for Christ who wished to revive him.

But what did he say? Notice the special way of reviving employed here; he came forth from the tomb alive — and was unable to walk. And the Lord said to the disciples, *Unbind him and let him go* (Jn 11:44). He himself raised the dead man, they released the bound man. Notice that there is something which belongs exclusively to the sovereignty of God raising the dead. Somebody addicted to an evil habit is rebuked by being told a home truth. How many there are who are rebuked and don't listen! So who's acting inside with the person who does listen? Who is it breathing in the breath of life inwardly? Who is it driving out the hidden death, bestowing the hidden life? Isn't it the case that after the expressions of disapproval and the tongue-lashings people are left to their own thoughts, and begin to think over what a bad life they are leading, and what an appalling addiction they are held down by? Then, being thoroughly displeased with themselves, they decide to change their manner of life. Such people have risen again; being displeased with what they used to be, they have come back to life. But while reviving like this, they still can't walk. These are the bonds of the guilt they have incurred. So there is a need for the person who has come back to life to be unbound, absolved, and allowed to walk. This is the office he gave to the disciples when he told them, *What you unbind on earth has been unbound also in heaven* (Mt 18:18).

May those who are dead come back to life

7. So then, dearly beloved, let us listen to all this in such a way that those who are alive may go on living, those who are dead may come back to life. If it's a case of the sin still being harbored in the heart and not having emerged into actual deed, let it be repented of, let the thought and intention be corrected, let the dead person arise privately inside the house of conscience. If it's a case of actually having committed what you intended, even so there is no need to despair. As a dead person you didn't rise indoors, so rise then when you have been carried out. Repent of what you have done, come to life straightaway; don't go down into the depths of the grave, don't receive on top of you the dead weight of a habit or addiction. But perhaps I am already speaking to some who are already weighed down by the hard stone of their habits, already hard pressed by the dead weight of custom, already four days dead and stinking. These mustn't despair either; the dead are buried deep, but Christ is high up. He knows how to heave aside the huge loads of earth with a shout, he knows how to restore inwardly to life through his own presence, how to hand over to his disciples for unbinding. Let such people too repent. I mean, when Lazarus had been revived after being four days dead, no stench of death remained in him once he was alive again.

So then, those who are alive, let them stay alive. But any who are dead, in whichever of these three kinds of death they find themselves, let them take steps, now, to rise again with all speed.

Sermon 101

Sermon Preached at Carthage in the Faustus Basilica on the Harvest and the Sower and the Preaching of the Gospel

This sermon was preached between May 14th and May 24th, namely between the feast of the Ascension and Pentecost, 397, since Augustine, as bishop of Hippo, had come to Carthage to attend his first all-Africa council, which was being held then. This sermon can be dated so precisely because it is listed in Possidius' Index, which at least two scholars maintain lists in chronological order 32 sermons preached in Carthage that summer. The sermon is a masterful exemple of Augustine's ability to interpret scripture to promote vocations for the ministry. He insists that it is more important to listen to the content of preaching than to focus on the preacher's sinfulness and imperfections.

Reapers to the Jews, sowers to the nations

1. In the passage of the gospel which has just been read I am being urged to investigate, and as best I can to say, what harvest it is about which the Lord says *The harvest is plentiful, but laborers few. Ask the Lord of the harvest to send laborers into his harvest* (Lk 10:2). Then to the twelve disciples whom he also called apostles he added seventy-two others, and sent them all, as is clear from his own words, into the harvest that was ready and waiting. So what was that harvest? I mean, that harvest cannot have been among those nations where nothing had been sown. So it remains for us to understand that this harvest was to be found among the Jewish people. This was the harvest which the Lord of the harvest came to. To this harvest he sent reapers; to the nations, on the other hand, he sent not reapers but sowers. So we can take it that this harvest was gathered among the Jewish people. That was the harvest, you see, from which the apostles themselves were chosen. That was where it was ripe for the reaping, because that was where the prophets had sown.

It is a pleasure to contemplate God's husbandry, and to be delighted by his gifts, and to work in his fields. It was at this husbandry, you see, that that man worked who said, *I labored more than all of them.* But wasn't the strength to work given him by the Lord of the harvest? That's why he added, *Not I, though, but the grace of God with me* (1 Cor 15:10). That he was engaged in husbandry he shows clearly enough when he says, *I planted, Apollo watered* (1 Cor 3:6).

Now this apostle, who had turned from Saul into Paul, that is from Proudman into Small — he's called Saul after King Saul, Paul from littleness; *Paulum*, you see, means "a little," so he was, in a way, interpreting his own name when he said *I, you see, am the smallest of all the apostles* (1 Cor 15:9); so this Paul, that is, Little and Small, was sent to the nations. He himself says that he was sent above all to the nations. That's what he writes; we read it, we believe it, we preach it.

So he himself says in his letter to the Galatians, that after he had already been called by the Lord Jesus he went to Jerusalem and discussed the gospel with the apostles, that they shook his hand as a sign of harmony, a sign of agreement that in no way at all did his gospel differ from what they themselves had learned. Then he says that it was agreed between him and them that he should go to the nations, they to the circumcision; he as a sower, they as reapers. Quite rightly did the Athenians, although unwittingly, also bestow on him this title; on hearing the word from him, you see, they said, *Who is this sower of words?* (Acts 17:18).

Two harvests: one complete, one yet to come

2. So, your attention, please. Let it be your pleasure too to contemplate with me in God's agricultural policy two harvests, one complete, one yet to come; complete in the Jewish people, yet to come in the peoples of the nations. Let me prove this; and how else, but from the scriptures of the Lord of the harvest? Why, we have it right here, stated in this very passage: *The harvest is plentiful, the laborers few. So ask the Lord of the harvest to send laborers into his harvest.* But in that harvest there were going to be Jews, contradicting and persecuting: *Behold*, he says, *I am sending you like lambs in the midst of wolves* (Lk 10:2-3). Let me show you something even clearer about this harvest. In the gospel according to John, when the Lord sat down tired at a well, great symbolic mysteries were enacted, but time is too short to run through them all. But what time does allow me to say on this point, please listen to me attentively.

I have undertaken, you see, to show you the harvest among the peoples among whom the prophets had preached; the reason, after all, why they had been sowers was in order that the apostles might be able to be reapers. The Samaritan woman is talking to the Lord, and among other things, after the Lord has told her how God ought to be worshiped, she says, *We know that the Messiah will come, who is called Christ, and he will teach us everything*; and the Lord answers her, *I, the one talking to you, am he* (Jn 4:25-26). Believe what you hear, what you can see: *I, the one speaking to you, am he.* What had she said, though? *We know that the Messiah will come*, whom Moses and the prophets proclaimed, *who is called Christ.* So the harvest was already a dense crop. To spring up it had had Moses and the prophets as its sowers; now ripe, it was waiting for the apostles as its reapers. As soon as she heard this, she believed; she left her water pot there, and ran off in a hurry, and began to proclaim the Lord. The disciples had gone to buy food. On their return they found the Lord talking to the woman, and they were surprised, but didn't dare to say, *What or why are you talking to her?* (Jn 4:27). They kept their surprise to themselves, suppressing the impulses of their hearts.

So then, the name of Christ was nothing new to this Samaritan woman. She was already expecting him to come; she had already believed that he would come. How had she come to believe, if nobody had sown? But now listen to this stated more explicitly still: The Lord said to the disciples, *You say that summer is still a long way off. Lift up your eyes and see the lands white for the harvest*; and he added, *Others labored, and you have entered into their labors* (Jn 4:35, 38). Abraham labored, and Isaac, Jacob and Moses, the prophets. They labored at sowing. On the coming of the Lord, the harvest was found to be ripe. Reapers were sent in with the sickle of the gospel, and carried their sheaves to the Lord's threshing floor, where Stephen would be threshed.

The sowers go to the nations

3. Now that's where Paul got his seeds from. He is sent to the nations, and he doesn't keep quiet about it in highlighting the grace which he in particular had specially received. I mean, he says in his writings that he had been sent to preach the gospel where Christ had not been well known. So now, because that harvest has been gathered, and all the Jews who remained were chaff, let us take a look at the harvest which we are. It was sown by apostles and prophets. The Lord himself sowed — he was, after all, in the apostles, because he himself also reaped; I mean, they were nothing without him; he is complete without them; he says himself, you see, *Because without me you can do nothing* (Jn 15:4).

So Christ is already sowing among the nations, and what does he say? *Behold, a sower went out to sow* (Lk 8:5; Mk 4:3; Mt 13:3). In that other text reapers are sent to reap. Here a sower went out to sow tirelessly. What concern was it of his, after all, that some fell on the path, some on rocky places, some among thorns? If he had been anxious about these difficult soils, he would never have reached the good soil. What concern is it of ours, what business of ours is it still to argue about the Jews, and talk about chaff? What we only have eyes for is not to fall on the path, nor on the rock, nor in the thorns, but in good soil, *My heart is ready, O God* (Ps 57:7), from which to produce thirtyfold, sixtyfold, one thousand one hundred-fold; one is less and one is more, but all of it is wheat.

Don't let it be on the path, where the seed gets trodden on by the passersby, and like a bird the enemy can snatch it away. Don't let it be on rock, where shallow soil makes it sprout immediately, and unable to bear the sun. Don't let it be among thorns, worldly cravings, the anxieties of a vicious life. What, after all, could be worse than anxiety about a life that does not allow one to attain life? What more wretched than losing life by worrying about life? What more unfortunate than to lapse into death by being afraid of death? Let the thorns be weeded out, the field prepared, the seed received, the harvest reached; long for the barn, and you needn't fear the fire.

Stewards share what they receive

4. So it's our business, those of us, whatever sort of people we are, whom the Lord has appointed laborers in his field, to say these things to you: to sow, to plant, to water, even to dig round some trees and put on a basket or two of manure. It's our business to do all this faithfully, yours to receive it faithfully, the Lord's to help us in our work, you in your faith, all of us in battling away, but overcoming the world in him.

So I've told you what your business is; now I want to say what ours is. Perhaps some of you may think, now that I've said that, that I'm wanting to say something quite unnecessary; and you may start saying to yourselves in your private thoughts, "Oh, if only he'd let us go now! He's already told us what our business is; what's his business got to do with us?" I think it's better that with mutual tit-for-tat charity we should all be each other's business. In some sense you all belong to one family or household. We are the stewards within the same household, of course. We all belong to the one Master. What I give out I don't give out from my own property, but from his, from whom I too receive. I mean, if I do give out from what is my own, I shall be giving out a lie. *Whoever speaks a lie*, you see, *speaks from what is his own* (Jn 8:44).

So you ought to listen to what also concerns the stewards, so that you may rejoice with us, if you find us to be up to the mark, or even so that you may be instructed in this matter yourselves. How many future stewards, after all, are present in this congregation? We too were once where you are now. We are to be seen now distributing their rations to our fellow servants from a higher place; but not so many years ago we were receiving our rations with our fellow servants in the lower place. I'm speaking as a bishop to lay people; but how can I tell how many future bishops I'm talking to?

The qualities of a preacher should not be taken literally

5. So let's see how we up here should understand what the Lord commanded those he was sending out to preach the gospel, and to reap the harvest. Let's see. *Do not*, he says, *take purse or bag or shoes, and greet nobody on the road. And whatever house you enter, say: Peace be to this house. If a son of peace is there, your peace will rest upon him; if not, it will return to you* (Lk 10:4-6). We must briefly run through each item.

Do not, he says, *carry a purse*. What do we do in fact? I carry a purse, I admit it, when I go on a journey; I carry expenses for the road. *Nor a bag*. Perhaps I don't carry a bag. *Nor shoes*. What? Did he tell us to walk about barefoot? You can see for yourselves; we all wear shoes. I mean, we don't publish our words and hide our feet; we walk about wearing shoes before your eyes. And now the next item; if anyone greets us on the road and we don't greet them back, we are judged and condemned as proud; we are spoken ill of, and this leads to speaking ill of the Lord. So we do also salute people on the road. The next thing after all that is quite easy, to say on entering a house, *Peace be to this house*. But how thoroughly we are caught red-handed with purse and shoes!

Let's take a look at the Lord himself, and see if he can comfort us, and grant us some understanding of these words. Because as a matter of fact, even what I said was easy, namely saying on entering a house *Peace be to this house* (and surely nothing could be easier) — well, what immediately follows can also put us in a spot if we take it literally, What does he say, after all? *Say, Peace be to this house.*

Nothing easier. But how does it go on? *If there is a son of peace in that house, your peace will rest on him; otherwise, it will return to you.* What is all this? How will peace come back to me? Shall I only have it if it comes back to me? If it rests on him, does it mean I have lost it? An impossible thought for sane minds.

So not even this is to be taken literally; and therefore, presumably, neither is the purse, nor the shoes, nor the bag; and particularly not that bit that appears to oblige us to a show of pride, if we take it in its obvious sense without qualification, the bit about not greeting anyone on the road.

The meaning of the purse

6. Let us observe our Lord, our true example and help. Can we prove he's our help? *Without me you can do nothing* (Jn 15:5). Can we prove he's our example? *Christ suffered for us,* Peter says, *leaving us an example, to follow in his steps* (1 Pt 2:21). This Lord of ours had funds on the road, he entrusted these funds to Judas; indeed in him he put up with a thief. Now I, with my Lord's gracious permission, eager only to learn, have this to say to my Lord: "Lord, you put up with a thief in Judas; how did you come to have anything to be pilfered? You've instructed me, a poor weak man, not to carry a purse. You yourself carried funds, and that was where you put up with a thief. If you hadn't carried them around with you, he wouldn't have found anything to make away with."

How can he get out of that one? Surely, only by saying to me, "You must understand it rightly when you hear, *Do not carry a purse.* What is a purse, anyway? Money shut up; wisdom hidden away." What's the meaning then of *Do not carry a purse*? Do not keep your wisdom to yourselves. Receive the spirit; it ought to be a spring in you, not a purse; something to be spent and splashed around, not something to be shut up tight. It's the same for the bag as for the purse.

The meaning of the shoes

7. What are the shoes? Well, what *are* the shoes we wear? Leather from dead animals. The hides of dead animals are what we protect our feet with. So what are we being ordered to do? To give up dead works. This is symbolically what he instructs Moses to do in his honor, when the Lord says to him, *Take off your shoes. For the place you are standing in is holy ground* (Ex 3:5). There's no holier ground than the Church of God, is there? So as we stand in her let us take off our shoes, let us give up dead works. As for these shoes I walk around in, this same Lord of mine tells me not to worry. If he hadn't worn shoes, John would not have said about him, *I am not worthy to undo his shoelaces* (Lk 3:16).

So let there be intelligent obedience in considering this matter, not proud obstinacy creeping into it. "I," says he, "fulfill the gospel, because I go barefoot." "Fine; you're able to do it. I'm not. Let us hold onto what we have received *together.* Let us be ablaze with charity, let us love each other. And in this way it will turn out that I love your strength, and you bear with my weakness."

The meaning of greeting no one on the road

8. What's your opinion, though, you there, who refused to understand the way in which all this was said, and were thus obliged by your perverse understanding to bring a false accusation against the Lord himself in the matter of funds and shoes? What's your opinion? Do you think it's right that when we meet our nearest and dearest on the road, we shouldn't greet our elders, nor return the greeting of our juniors? Is that how you fulfill the gospel — by keeping mum when someone greets you? That will mean that you are more like a milestone or a signpost than a traveler.

So let's be done with stupidity, let's understand the Lord's words sensibly — and greet nobody on the road. There must be a reason, after all, why we are told to do this; or do you think he wouldn't want us to do what he told us to? So what does it mean, *Greet nobody on the road*? It can, I suppose, be taken fairly straightforwardly in the sense that he told us to look sharp about carrying out his orders, and that he said *Greet no one on the road* as though to say, "Put everything else aside while you carry out your orders." This would be a use of that figure of speech, by which people are in the habit of exaggerating what they say.

We needn't look very far for another example. A little later in the same discourse he says, *And you, Capernaum, who have been exalted right up to heaven, will be thrust down to hell* (Lk 10:15). What's the meaning of *you have been exalted right up to heaven*? The walls of that town didn't touch the clouds, did they, didn't reach the stars? Then what does it mean, *you have been exalted to heaven*? You thought yourself excessively blessed and fortunate; you are excessively powerful, excessively proud. So just as here it was by way of exaggeration that he said *you are being exalted to heaven* to a town which was not in fact climbing up or being exalted to heaven, it was also to heighten our sense of urgency that he said, "So run, so carry out what I have told you, that you don't let even the slightest thing hold you back from your business; on the contrary, ignore everything else, and hurry along to the end set before you."

Another interpretation

9. But there is something else which I prefer to think here. I won't deny I see a meaning that more directly concerns me and all of us stewards; but it is also relevant to you listeners. When you greet, you wish a person well, saying good morning, goodbye, farewell. So greeting is about welfare. So what's the meaning of *Greet nobody on the road*? People who greet others on the road bid them "fare well" casually or by the way. (I see you have caught on quickly. However, I mustn't stop there just for that reason. I mean, you haven't all got the point so quickly. By their exclamations I see some have understood; by their silence I see rather more of you still looking for the point. But because we are talking about a road, let's go on walking as on a road. Quick walkers, wait for those who are slower, and walk together.) So what did I say? When you bid someone fare well on

the road, you do it casually, by the way. You weren't actually going to see the person you greet. You were doing one thing, another thing cropped up. You were aiming at one thing, and coincidentally found something else to do.

So what does greeting, or bidding "fare well," casually and by the way stand for? For proclaiming eternal welfare, salvation, casually and by the way. And proclaiming welfare or salvation is simply preaching the gospel, isn't it? So if you preach, do it deliberately, out of love, not casually and by the way. There are people, you see, who in proclaiming the gospel are really seeking something else; the apostle bemoans such people when he says, *For all are seeking their own advantage, not that of Jesus Christ* (Phil 2:21). These too were saying "Fare well," that is proclaiming the welfare of salvation, they were preaching the gospel. But they were really intent on some other goal, and that's why they were greeting, or bidding people "fare well," casually, by the way. And what does this mean? If you are like that, whoever you are, you are doing something good, it seems; but in fact, if you are like that when you do it, you are not actually doing it, but it is being done through you.

Learn from the preachers what is good

10. The apostle, it seems, allowed even for ministers like that; but this doesn't mean he told them to be like that. They too actually do something, and people profit by it. They are aiming at something else, and they happen to proclaim Christ. Don't you worry about what the preacher is aiming at; hold onto what he is proclaiming. Don't you bother about what he wants, it's not your business. Learn how to fare well, learn about salvation from his mouth; hold on to faring well and salvation as learned from his mouth; don't be the judge of his heart.

But you see him aiming at something else, do you? What has that got to do with you? Learn from him how to fare well. *Do what they say.* That stopped you from worrying. "What did?" *Do what they say.* "But they do bad things." *Do not do what they do* (Mt 23:3). They do good things, they don't greet along the road, they don't proclaim the gospel casually, by the way. Be imitators of them, as they are of Christ. A good man preaches to you; pick the grapes from the vine. A bad man preaches to you; pick the grapes hanging in the hedge. The cluster has ripened on a vineshoot twined among the thorns; it hasn't sprung from the thorns. Naturally when you see something like that and your mouth waters, you must be careful how you pick it, in case you are scratched by the thorns when you stretch out your hand to the grapes.

That's what I'm saying: learn from him what's good, taking care not to fall into his bad habits. Let him preach casually, by the way; let him bid you "fare well" on the road. It won't do him any good that he didn't listen to Christ's order, *Do not greet anyone on the road.* But it won't do you any harm; whether it's from someone passing by or from someone coming to visit you, that you learn how to fare well, you are in possession of that welfare, that salvation. Listen to the apostle allowing for these things, as I mentioned earlier: *So what, provided that in every way, whether casually or with sincerity, Christ is proclaimed? Over this also I rejoice, and what is more I will go on rejoicing. For I know that this will be to my advantage for salvation, through your supplication* (Phil 1:18.19).

They preach peace, and they have peace

11. Such then should Christ's apostles be, preachers of the gospel, not greeting on the road; that is, not looking for something else, but proclaiming the gospel out of genuine brotherly love, let them come to the house and say, *Peace be to this house.* They don't only say it with their lips; they pour out what they are full of. They preach peace, and they have peace. They are not like those of whom it is said, *Peace, peace, and there is no peace* (Jer 8:11). What's the meaning of *Peace, peace, and there is no peace?* They preach it and don't have it; they praise and don't love it; *they say and they don't do* (Mt 23:3). As for you, though, be sure you accept peace, whether Christ is being proclaimed casually or with sincerity.

So then, if someone is full of peace and gives the greeting, *Peace be to this house, if there is a son of peace there,* his peace will rest on that man; *otherwise* — I mean, there may possibly be no son of peace there, but the one who has given the greeting hasn't lost by it at all — *it will return,* he says, *to you* (Lk 10:5-6). It returns to you, never having left you.

What he intended to say, you see, was this: "That you have proclaimed it is to your advantage; it was no use to the person who didn't receive it. Because he remained empty, though, it doesn't mean that you lost your reward. Recompense is made to you for your intention; it is made to you for the charity you have spent generously. You will be rewarded by the one who rid you of all anxiety through the angels' words, *Peace on earth to men of good will* (Lk 2:14)."

Sermon 104

Discourse on Martha and Mary, as Representing Two Kinds of Life

There is no indication of date or place, although Anoz cites Hombert's estimate of around 415. This sermon constitutes a powerful meditation on Martha and Mary. Augustine's interpretation is flavored by the Neoplatonic predilection for "the one" over "the many." Martha is not reprimanded for her service and hospitality. Mary, rather, is praised for her attention to the one, namely, Christ. Service will no longer be needed at the end time, but praise and love will abide forever. Martha represents the present life with its toil; Mary represents the eternal life of happiness and rest.

Martha and Mary

1. When the holy gospel was read, we heard how the Lord was welcomed as a guest by a devout woman, and that she was called Martha. And while she was busy seeing to all the serving, her sister Mary was sitting at the Lord's feet, and listening to his words. One was working hard, the other sitting still, doing nothing. One was dishing out, the other was being filled. Martha, though, slogging away and rushed off her feet with all the business of serving, interrupted the Lord with an appeal, and complained about her sister because she wouldn't help her with the work. But the Lord answered Martha on Mary's behalf; he had been appealed to as judge, and he made himself counsel for the defense. *Martha*, he said, *you are busy about many things, when there is one thing necessary. Mary has chosen the better part, which shall not be taken away from her* (Lk 10:41-42).

We have heard both the appeal to the judge, and the judgment; a judgment that answers the plaintiff, and defends the client he had taken under his wing. Mary, you see, was absorbed in the sweetness of the Lord's words. Martha was absorbed in the matter of how to feed the Lord; Mary was absorbed in the matter of how to be fed by the Lord. Martha was preparing a banquet for the Lord, Mary was already reveling in the banquet of the Lord. So while Mary was listening with such plea-sure to his wonderful words, and her avidly eager mind was being fed by them, just imagine how afraid she must have been, when her sister appealed to the Lord, that he would say to her, "Get up and help your sister." She was held there, you see, riveted to the spot by the wonderful delights of the mind, so much greater, surely, than those of the belly. He excused her, she went on sitting there, more serene than ever. But how did he excuse her? Let us turn our attention to the point, let's take a look, let's investigate as minutely as we can; let us too join in the feast ourselves.

Was Martha reprimanded?

2. What about it, after all? Are we to suppose that Martha was reprimanded for her service, for busying herself with the cares of hospitality, for welcoming the Lord himself as a guest? How could she possibly be reprimanded for that, seeing that she rejoiced in welcoming such a guest?

If that's really the case, let people all give up ministering to the needy; let them all choose the better part, which shall not be taken away from them. Let them devote their time to the word, let them pant for the sweetness of doctrine, let them busy themselves with theology, the science of salvation; don't let them bother at all about what stranger there may be in the neighborhood, who may be in need of bread or who of clothing, who needs to be visited, who to be redeemed, who to be buried. Let the works of mercy be laid aside, everything be concentrated on the one science. If it is the better part, why don't we all grab it, when in this case we have the Lord himself as our attorney? After all, we are not afraid of offending against his justice in this matter, when we are indemnified by his judgment.

One has precedence over many

3. And yet it's not like that; but what it is like is what the Lord said. It's not like the way you understand it; it is, however, like the way you ought to understand it. *You are busy about many things, when there is one thing necessary. Mary has chosen the better part.* You didn't choose a bad one, but she chose a better. What makes it better? Because you are concerned with many things, she with one. One has precedence over many, because one doesn't come from the many, but the many come from the one. Things that were made are many; he that made them is one. Heaven, earth, sea, and all that is within them, how many they all are! Who could count them all, who could conceive their multiplicity? Who made them? God, all of them, and behold they are very good. Very good, everything he made; how much better the one who did the making?

Let us consider, then, our busy involvement with many things. Service is needed by those who wish to restore their tissues. Why is this? Because people get hungry, because they get thirsty. Distress calls for compassion. You break your bread to the hungry, because you have found him hungry. Abolish hunger; whom will you break your bread to? Abolish traveling; to whom will you offer hospitality? Abolish nakedness; for whom will you find clothes? Let sickness be no more; whom will you visit? No more captivity; whom will you redeem? No more quarreling; whom will you reconcile? No more death; whom will you bury? In that age, that world that is to come none of these evils will exist, and therefore none of these services.

So Martha did well to minister to the Lord in his mortal flesh and his bodily — I don't know what I should call it — his bodily needs, or bodily will, or his willed needs? But who was it in this mortal flesh? *In the beginning was the Word, and the Word was with God, and the Word was God.* There you have what Mary was listening to. *The Word became flesh and dwelt amongst us* (Jn 1:1, 14). There you have what Martha was serving.

So, *Mary has chosen the better part, and it shall not be taken away from her,* what she chose, you see, will abide for ever, and that's why it shall not be taken away from her. She wished to busy herself with the one thing; she was already in possession of it: *For me it is good to cleave to God* (Ps 73:28). She was sitting at the feet of our head; the more lowly her position, the more ample her gains. Water, after all, flows down into the lowliness of the valley; it runs off the swelling highness of the hill.

So the Lord did not find fault with work, but made a distinction between functions. *"You are busy,"* he said, *"about many things; for all that, there is one thing necessary.* Mary has already chosen this for herself; the multiplicity of toil passes away, the single unity of charity remains. So what she has chosen shall not be taken away from her. What you have chosen, though — this follows, of course, this is, of course, implied — what you have chosen will be taken away from you. But it will be taken away for your benefit, so that the better part may be given you. Toil, you see, will be taken away from you, so that rest may be given you. You, my dear, are still on the high seas; she is already in port."

Two kinds of life in two women

4. So you see, beloved, and as far as I can tell you now understand, that in these two women who were both dear to the Lord, both lovely people, both disciples of his; so you see, and understand something of great importance, those of you who do understand, something even those who don't understand ought to hear and to know; that in these two women two kinds of life are represented: present life and future life, toilsome and restful, miserable and beatific, temporal and eternal life. Two sorts of life, which I have briefly described to the best of my ability: now it's up to you to think about them more fully.

To the best of your ability take a look at what this life holds — I'm not talking about a bad life, not a wicked one, nor a criminal nor a self-indulgent nor an impious one; rather, about a laborious life, full of hardship, chastened by fears, tried by anxieties; I'm talking about the kind of innocent life one may expect Martha to have led — so take a look at that sort of life, as best you can, and think about it, as I said, in greater detail than I can talk about it. As for a wicked kind of life, it was entirely wanting in that household, to be found neither with Martha nor with Mary. If such ever had been there, it fled when the Lord came in.

So there remained in that house, which welcomed the Lord, two kinds of life in two women; both innocent, both praiseworthy; one laborious, the other leisurely; neither criminally active, neither merely idle. Both innocent, both, I repeat, praiseworthy; but one laborious, as I said, the other leisurely; neither criminally active, which the laborious kind has to beware of; neither merely idle, which the leisurely kind has to avoid. So there were in that house these two kinds of life, and the very fountain of life himself.

In Martha was to be found the image of things present, in Mary that of things to come. The kind Martha was leading, that's where we are; the kind Mary was leading, that's what we are hoping for; let us lead this one well, in order to have that one to the full. But now, what share have we got of that one, insofar as we have any at all, as long as we are here? How much is it that we already have from that one? What is it that we have from there? Even now, you see, we do enjoy something of that sort. You've left your shops and offices, you've laid aside your family matters, you've gathered here, you are standing still and listening; insofar as you are doing this, you are like Mary. And it's easier for you to do what Mary does, than for me to do what Christ does. However, if I do say anything that is Christ's, that's why it nourishes you, because it is Christ's, because it's our common bread, which I too live on, if in fact I live. But *now we live, if you for your part stand fast in the Lord* (1 Thes 3:8); not in us, but in the Lord; because *neither the one who plants is anything, nor the one who waters, but the one who gives the increase, God* (1 Cor 3:7).

The life that Mary represents

5. But how much really is it, that by listening and understanding you derive and grasp of that life which Mary represented; how much really is it? *In the morning I*

will stand before you and gaze (Ps 5:3). *To my hearing you will give joy and gladness, and bones that have been humbled will exult* (Ps 51:8). Bones that have been humbled, like the limbs of one rooted to the spot. That was the case with Mary; she humbled herself, she was filled.

She was sitting down; so what's this I've just said, *In the morning I will stand up and gaze*? How can sitting down be like standing up, if morning stands for the age to come? When the night of the present age has gone, *I will stand up*, he says, *and see; I will stand up and gaze*. He didn't say, "I will sit down." So how can Mary, by sitting down, provide the image of this tremendous reality, if, *I will stand up and gaze*? Well, don't let all this bother you; it's a matter of physical limitations; both things cannot be demanded of the human body, that it should simultaneously both stand and sit. I mean, if it's sitting it's not standing; if it's standing it's not sitting; the body can't be doing both at once. But if I prove to you that the mind *can* do both at once, will there be any grounds left for hesitation? Because if it can do such a thing now, it will be much easier to do it then, when all difficulties will be at an end.

Here you are, then, with an example to help you get the point. Paul himself says, *Now we live, if you for your part stand fast in the Lord*. This great apostle, indeed Christ through the apostle, is commanding us to stand. So how can the same apostle, indeed Christ himself through the apostle, say to us, *Only as for what we have reached, let us walk in it* (Phil 3:16)? Standing in this place, walking in that; never mind walking, *so run that you may obtain* (1 Cor 9:24). And so, dearly beloved, just notice and understand: he's both bidding us walk and bidding us stand; not in such a way that when we stand we must stop walking, or when we walk we must give up standing; but both at once, we must both stand and run. What does that mean, we must both stand and run? We must both remain true, and make progress.

Lord, make your ways known to me (Ps 25:4). What else are we being told to do along the ways of the Lord made known to us, except walk? *Lead me, Lord, along your way* (Ps 86:11). What else are we asking for, but to walk? And again, as though asking to be fixed in one spot: *Do not allow my feet to be moved* (Ps 121:3). And elsewhere expressing his relief and giving thanks, *And he did not allow my feet to be moved* (Ps 66:9). If you were to ask him, "How could you desire the ways of the Lord to be made known to you, how could you wish to be led by him along his way, while at the same time you are desiring that your feet shouldn't be moved, and being thankful that he hasn't allowed your feet to be moved? How did you walk, if you didn't move your feet?" — he would answer you, "I both walked, because I acted, and I stood still, because I did not fall back."

So don't be too surprised, brothers and sisters; there you are; what the body can't do, the mind can. As far as the body is concerned, when you walk you don't stand; when you stand you don't walk. As far as the mind is concerned, as far as faith, as far as your intention is concerned, both stand and walk, both remain true and make progress, because *Now we live, if you for your part stand fast in the Lord*, and *so run that you may obtain*. So in this way, beloved, you will both sit and stand. We shall sit down, because we shall behold the creator from a lowly position; we shall stand up, because we shall remain forever.

The Lord will make us recline, and passing along will wait on us

6. As a matter of fact, I can go a step further: we are also going to recline, which of course is neither sitting nor standing. We shall recline. I wouldn't dare suggest it, unless the Lord had promised it. *He will make them recline*. He is promising his servants a great reward, and says, *He will make them recline, and passing along he will wait on them* (Lk 12:37). This is the life promised us, that the Lord will make us recline, and passing along will wait on us. The same thing was said when he marveled at that centurion's faith and praised it: *Amen I tell you, that many shall come from east and west, and shall recline with Abraham, Isaac, and Jacob in the kingdom of heaven* (Mt 8:11).

A tremendous promise, a most felicitous return on investments. Let us behave so as to deserve it; may we be helped by God so as to be able to reach the place where the Lord will serve us as we recline at his table. After all, what will reclining be, but resting? And what will serving be, but providing food? What is that food and what is that drink? It's truth, of course. That is a food that refreshes, and doesn't fail; it feeds, and by feeding makes people whole; nor is it consumed into the one it feeds, but it remains whole and restores to wholeness.

Don't you believe that God can feed in that way, when even now your eyes are fed in that way by this material light? Your eyes feed on light. Let many people see, the light is as much as ever; let few people see, it is as much as ever; the eyes are refreshed, and the light doesn't fail or run out. You draw from it, and don't diminish it; you take your pick from it, and don't break it off. If this light can do this for the eyes, can't God do it for man transformed? He can, most certainly he can; why don't you yet profit by it? Because you are busy with many things; Martha's business has kept you fully occupied, kept all of us so in fact. I mean, who can abstain from this kind of service? Who can take a breather from this kind of concern? Let us do these things in all innocence, let us do them in all charity.

That thing about us reclining will come too in its own good time, and he will pass along and wait upon us. He wouldn't wait upon us then, you see, unless he had passed from here to the Father, because he was still here when he made that promise. And he didn't want us to think that he would be presenting us with anything like the form of a servant which we were familiar with here; so,

Passing along, he said, *he will wait upon them* (Lk 12:37). And the evangelist has this to say about this passing: *But when the hour had come for Jesus to pass from this world to the Father* (Jn 13:1). *Have I been with you*, he said, *so long a time, and you have not come to know me?* (Jn 14:9). If Philip had known what he would later hear, he might have answered, "I haven't come to know you, because you haven't yet passed along, passed over." Which is why Mary too is told after the resurrection, *Do not touch me, for I have not yet ascended to the Father* (Jn 20:17).

Toil passes, and rest will come; but rest only through toil

7. So, beloved, I beg you, I urge you, I warn, command, implore you, let us desire that life together, let us run together toward it as we go, so that we may stop in it as a reward for our perseverance. The moment is coming, and that moment will have no end, when the Lord will make us recline, and will wait on us. What will he serve us with but himself? Why ask what you are going to eat? You will have the Lord himself. What will it be, I mean, that we feed on, what but *In the beginning was the Word, and the Word was with God, and the Word was God* (Jn 1:1)? What will reclining be, but resting? What will feeding be, but the inexpressible delight of contemplating him? *In your right hand is delight* (Ps 16:11).

One thing have I begged from the Lord, this will I seek; not the many things I'm busy with, but *one thing have I begged from the Lord, this will I seek; that I may dwell in the house of the Lord through all the days of my life, that I may gaze upon the delight of the Lord* (Ps 27:4). That is not the bliss of people working themselves to the bone. *Be still and see* — what? — *that I am the Lord* (Ps 46:10). A tremendous vision, inexhaustibly satisfying contemplation. And what else is "Recline and eat," but "Be still and see"? So don't let's entertain crude material ideas, nor think, if I may so put it, of a jolly wedding feast. These things will pass; they are to be tolerated, not loved. If you want to fill Martha's role in them, let it be with modesty, with compassion; modesty in your behavior, compassion in your generosity. Toil passes, and rest will come; but rest only through toil. The ship passes, and you arrive home; but home only by means of the ship. We are sailing the high seas, after all, if we take account of the surges and storms of this world. The reason, I am convinced, that we are not drowned is that we are being carried on the wood of the cross.

Sermon 105A

On the Words of the Gospel, Luke 11:5-13:
Which of You Will Have a Friend? etc.: On Prayer

This sermon was preached in the summer of 411 while the sacking of Rome
was still fresh in everyone's mind. Augustine parts company with those who
see the Church's destiny as tied to Rome's past glory and present power. It simply is not true that Rome's decline coincided with its adoption of Christianity.
Augustine develops here his theology of prayer and asks what is it that we are
to ask, seek, knock for.

The giver is all ready to give, but the petitioner needs to be put right

1. The holy gospel, which we heard when it was read just now, encourages us to
pray. It gives us firm hope that no one who asks, seeks and knocks leaves the
Lord's presence empty-handed. He didn't say, you see, that there are some who
ask and don't receive, but *Everyone*, he says, *who asks shall receive, and who
seeks shall find, and who knocks shall be opened to* (Lk 11:10). And he illustrated
the point with a comparison by way of contrast; if a friend comes to a friend, and
asks for three loaves because of a guest who has just arrived at his place, and asks at
a time when it is a great nuisance to get up and give it to him; and the other answers
that he can't give it to him, because he's already gone to bed, and his boys are with
him in the bedroom; for all that he doesn't stop asking; *I tell you*, he says, *that not
out of friendship but out of the nuisance he is enduring from him, he will get up and
give him as many as he has need of* (Lk 11:8). If the one who is overcome by the
nuisance you make of yourself doesn't refuse, how can the one who urges you to
ask refuse? That's the point of this comparison.

If he doesn't deny, when the man asks for three loaves, that he is his friend, and
yet doesn't give it to him out of friendship, but in order not to go on being
disturbed, will God who is Three, when we ask him for himself, not give us
himself? Well, I don't think that that friend would give his friend three loaves such
that one would be white, one brown, one barley.

So because Jesus Christ our God, the only begotten Son of God, has given us
the firm hope of obtaining what we ask for by encouraging us to pray, we have to
know what we ought to pray for. Is there anyone, after all, who doesn't beg God for
things? But you have to take care what you beg him for. The giver is all ready to
give, but the petitioner needs to be put right. You get up in the morning and request
God that you may get rich. Is that something really important, that God's children
ought to ask God for? The reason God has chosen to grant riches even to the worst
of men is so that his children might not ask for them from their Father as something
very important. In fact, by his very deeds God is addressing us after a fashion, and

saying to us, "Why ask me for riches? Is that all there is of importance or value that I will give you? Just take a look at the people I do give them to, and be ashamed of asking for them; the believer asking for what the actor's got, even the Christian housewife asking for what the call girl's got." Don't ask for such things in your prayers. Let him give them if he wants, not give them if he wants. We ought to trust him, surely, when he says, *For it is not in a person's abundance that life consists* (Lk 12:15). Why? Because riches have been bad for many people; I don't know whether you could find anybody they have been good for. Perhaps you could find somebody they haven't been bad for; I don't know whether you could find anybody they've been good for.

You may say, I suppose, "So were riches no good to the person who used them well by feeding the hungry, clothing the naked, welcoming strangers, redeeming captives?" People who do all that are acting in such a way that riches won't be bad for them. I mean, what if they didn't have that amount of wealth to do all this with, and yet were the sort of people who would do it if they had? God doesn't pay any attention to the vast extent of people's means, but to the kind intent of people's wills. The apostles weren't rich, were they? All they left was their nets and boat to follow the Lord. You have given up a great deal when you have given up your hopes in the world, like that widow and her two farthings, which she put in the treasury. No one, he said, gave more than she did; and many people who were rich gave much; they didn't give more than this widow into the gifts of God, that is into the treasury. Many rich people were putting in large amounts, and he was observing — not the amounts they were putting in, though. Then she came in with her two farthings. Who would bother to give her so much as a glance? Well, he gave her a glance, the one who observed the fullness of the heart, not the hand. He not only observed her, he pointed her out; in pointing her out he said nobody put in as much as she did. Nobody, after all, put in as much as she who left herself absolutely nothing.

So if you only have a little, you will give a little; if you have more, you will give more. And yet, when you give a little from the little you have, does this mean you will get less or receive less, because you have given less? If we are going to examine what is given, there will be large amounts and small amounts, big sums and little sums. But if we examine the hearts of the people it's given by, we will sometimes find a meager, needy little heart in the big sums, a big, wealthy, lavish heart in the little ones. Yes, you observe the large amounts given, and you don't observe how much the person who has given much has left for himself, how much, finally, he has spent on charity, how much he has grabbed of other people's property, and then gives some of that to the poor, as though he would grease the palm of the divine judge's hand.

So then, what you are doing by giving is making sure that riches won't be bad for you, not that they will be good for you. I mean, even if you were poor, and gave a little from the little you had, just as much would be put down to your account as to the rich man's for giving a lot, or even more, as with that widow woman.

Let's suppose, you see, that the kingdom of heaven is up for sale, for the price of almsgiving. A most fertile and valuable estate has been put up for us to buy; one which, after we have acquired it and come into possession of it, we won't leave to some successors on our decease, but will always remain in possession of, never to leave it, never to move out of at all. A splendid estate, an estate worth buying indeed! It remains for you to inquire how much it's worth, in case you aren't worth what it's worth, and are not able to buy it, though you are most eager to get it. You may not think you can make it, so I'll tell you its price: it's worth whatever you have.

I'll add something else to make you even happier, if you are not the jealous type. When God has put you in possession of this estate you are to buy, don't keep out any other buyer. The patriarchs bought it; did they keep out the blessed prophets? The prophets bought it; did they not permit the apostles to buy it? The apostles bought it, and still yet other buyers joined them, the martyrs. In a word, so many people have bought it, and it's still up for sale.

So let's see if the rich have been able to buy it, and the poor haven't been able to buy it. Let's look at more recent examples, let's leave aside the most ancient buyers of this estate. Having given half his goods to the poor, since he was very rich, Zacchaeus bought it, a leading publican, who had accumulated great wealth. They were called publicans, not as being public-spirited, but as men who contracted to collect the tolls. The holy gospel makes this clear to you, when a certain apostle was called, about whom it is written, *He saw a certain man sitting in the customs house, Matthew by name* (Mt 9:9). This man whom he called from the customs house is elsewhere called Matthew the publican.

So that man Zacchaeus, after the Lord had gone in to his house and been welcomed by him most unexpectedly — he had longed with all his heart to see him; being small in stature he couldn't do so in the crowd; he climbed a tree and saw him passing by from there; in order to see the one who for his sake was going to hang on a piece of timber, he hung himself on a piece of timber, so when the Lord had come into his house, he was overjoyed (because he had already come into his heart beforehand): *I give away half my goods.* But he kept a lot for himself. Notice why he kept the other half: *And if I have robbed anyone*, he says, *by fraud, I am repaying fourfold* (Lk 19:8). A lot was kept, not to be possessed, but to make restitution with for robbery. A great buyer gave a great deal. Rich a moment before, all of a sudden poor.

Because he bought at such a high price, does that mean that the poor man Peter didn't buy with his nets and his boat? The estate was worth to each just as much as each of them had. After them that widow also bought it. She gave two farthings and bought it. Could there be anything cheaper? Yes. I find there is an even cheaper price for this vast estate than were those two farthings. Listen to the seller himself, the Lord Jesus. *If anyone*, he says, *gives a cup of cold water to one of these littlest ones of mine, amen I tell you, he will not lose his reward* (Mt 10:42). What could be cheaper than a cup of water, and cold at that, so that you aren't even forced to buy firewood?

I don't know whether you think that anything cheaper could be found than this tiny little price. And yet, there is something. You don't have as much as Peter had, much less do you have as much as Zacchaeus had, you can't even find two farthings. Is a cup of cold water not available at the moment? *Peace on earth to men of good will* (Lk 2:14). There's no point in discussing this difference in prices any further. If we really understand, if our thinking is sound, a good will is the price of that estate. That is what bought it for Peter, that is what bought it for Zacchaeus, that is what bought it for the widow, that is what bought it for whoever offers a cup of cold water. That alone is enough to buy it, if you have nothing else besides.

We ought to know what we ought to ask for

2. Why have I said all this? What had I proposed? That we ought to learn what to ask for from the passage of the gospel in which the Lord has given us great hope, by saying, *Ask and you shall receive, seek and you shall find, knock and it shall be opened to you; for everyone who asks receives, and who seeks shall find, and whoever knocks, it shall be opened to him* (Lk 11:9-10). Because he has given us this great hope, we ought to know what we ought to ask for. Thus it came about that I was warning you not to regard riches, when you pray, as something very important to ask, seek, knock for. When you knock, you want to go in. The way to go in by is narrow. Why carry a lot with you? So you ought first to send on ahead what you are carrying, so that without a load you can enter easily by the narrow door. So don't request riches from the Lord God as though they were worth very much. Why be afraid you won't have enough and won't be able to buy that estate? Didn't I tell you that it's worth just as much as you have? And if you haven't got anything, you yourself will be its price, because even if you have a great deal, you may not buy it unless you also give yourself.

You will answer me, no doubt, "So what ought we to ask for from God?" Oh, here's another thing not to ask for — the death of your enemies. Such prayers as that are positively malevolent. I really don't know whether it's for your own good you have been heard, when you rejoice over your enemy's death. Who isn't going to die, anyway? Who knows when he's going to die? You're delighted because someone else has died; how do you know you won't be the next to breathe your last, in the very act of celebrating? Learn to pray that your enemy, that is enmity itself, may die. Your enemy is a person. There are two words there: "person" and "enemy." May the person live, the enemy die.

Don't you recall how Christ the Lord struck down his enemy Saul, a most enthusiastic persecutor of his members, how he laid him low, slew him? Certainly he slew him; because the persecutor died, the preacher was raised up. If you don't believe me that he died, ask the man himself; let the man himself be heard, the man himself be read. Listen to his own words in a letter of his: *But I live, now not I. I live*, he says, *not I.* So he's dead. So how could he speak? *But Christ lives in me* (Gal 2:20). So pray then, as best you can, that your enemy may die — but look how he is to die. If he dies, you see, and doesn't depart from the body, you've not only lost an enemy, you've also acquired a friend. So don't pray and ask God too for the visible deaths of your enemies.

"What," you will say, "are we to ask for? Worldly honors?" Smoke that blows away. You were safer lower down the scale. Are you disposed to face the dangers of the heights? Honors too, in any case, are only given by God, just like riches; but to make you think lightly of riches, he reminded you of the sort of people they are also given to. They are given to good people, so that you shouldn't think they are something bad; they are given also to bad people, so that you shouldn't think they are a particularly great good. It's the same too with honors; worthy people receive them, unworthy people receive them also, to save worthy people from regarding them as important.

"So come on," you say, "tell us now what we ought to ask for." Well, I won't have you on tenterhooks with many surprises, since I have already mentioned the gospel text, *Peace on earth to men of good will* (Lk 2:14). Ask for a good will. Riches, honors, all that sort of thing, do they ever make you good? Even if they are good in themselves, they are very minor goods, which good people use well and bad people badly. A good will makes you good.

Do you mean to tell me you are not ashamed, if you want to have good things and to be bad yourself? You've got many good things: gold, silver, jewels, farms, household staffs, flocks of cattle and sheep. Be ashamed in the presence of your good things. Be good yourself as well. After all, what could be more unfortunate than you are, if your country seat is good, your clothes are good, your sheep good, finally your galoshes are good, and your soul is bad? So learn, friends, to ask for a good that is, if I may so put it, good-making; that is, a good that makes people good. A good will makes you good. I mean, all those things are good, but they don't make you good.

To show you that they are good, they include those things the Lord mentioned, bread, a fish, an egg. To show you they are good, he said himself, *If you, though you are bad, know how to give good gifts to your children* (Lk 11:11-13). You are bad, and you give good things. Ask that you may be good. That, you see, is what he was advising them, when he said, *If you, though you are bad*; it was to advise them what they should ask for, that is, to stop being bad and be good.

So let him teach us what we ought to ask for. There, in the same passage of the gospel, listen to his words as he continues. *If you*, he says, *though you are bad, know how to give good gifts to your children*, and yet are going to remain bad; so in order not to remain bad, listen to what follows: *how much more will your Father from heaven give the good Spirit to those who ask him* (Lk 11:13). There you have the good thing by which you can become good. The good Spirit of God produces good will in men and women. The price of that estate, possession of which is called eternal life, is God himself. Eternal life, will there be anything more valuable for us? Will anything, I repeat, be able to make us richer, when God is the estate we possess? Or have I uttered an insult in saying that God is going to be our property? I haven't. I learned what I have just said. I found a holy man praying and saying, *O Lord, my share of the inheritance* (Ps 116:5).

Stretch wide the net of your insatiable desires, greedy, and find something greater than God, find something more precious than God, find something better than God. What won't you possess, when you possess him? But all right, rake in to yourself gold, silver, as much as you can. Cut out the neighbors; keep a tight grip on your estate by enlarging it, till you reach the ends of the earth. Having bought up the whole earth, add the seven seas. Let everything you can see be yours; let everything under the water which you can't see be yours. When you've got all this, what will you have in fact, if you haven't got God?

So if by having God a poor man is rich, and by not having God a rich man is a beggar, don't ask him for anything except himself. What won't he give you, when he gives you himself? What will he give you, if he doesn't give you himself? So then, ask for the good Spirit; let him dwell in you, and then you will be good. *For as many as are led by the Spirit of God, these are the sons of God.* And what comes next? *But if sons, also heirs, heirs indeed of God, but fellow heirs of Christ* (Rom 8:14, 17). Why is it you were so keen on riches? So, will God's heir be a pauper? As the heir of some extremely wealthy senator you would be rich; and as God's heir will you be poor? As Christ's fellow heir, will you be poor? When the Father himself is your inheritance, will you be poor?

Ask for the good Spirit, since it is already at the inspiration of the good Spirit that you are asking for the good Spirit. You must have something of that Spirit, you see, in order to ask for that Spirit. If you had nothing of it, I mean, you wouldn't ask for anything of it. However, because you haven't got as much as will satisfy you, you both have it and ask for it, until what's written comes about, *Who satisfies your desire with good things* (Ps 103:5); until what's written somewhere else comes about: *I will be satisfied, when your glory is revealed* (Ps 17:15). So, *blessed are those who are hungry and thirsty for justice*, not for this earthly bread, not for earthly water, not for earthly wine, but for justice: *for they shall be filled* (Mt 5:6).

Sermon 107

On the Words of the Gospel, Luke 12:13-21:
I Tell You, Refrain from All Avarice

Here Augustine addresses the salutary role that the fear of God should play in the life of a Christian. He emphasizes that each and every word is important in scripture: "He [Christ] could have put it like this: 'Beware of avarice.' He made it his business to add *all*, and to say, *Beware of all avarice.*" Even the virtuous have a tendency toward self-righteousness and avarice, being susceptible to sin in order to hold onto their possessions. This sermon was preached sometime in Carthage between 411 and 420.

Refrain from all avarice

1. You who fear God, I'm sure you listen to his word with fear and carry it out with cheerfulness, so that in the end you may receive what he has promised, after hoping for it in the meanwhile. We have this minute heard the Lord giving us a command, Christ Jesus the Son of God. Truth has given us a command, Truth who can neither deceive nor be deceived; let us listen, let us fear, let us beware.

So what did he command us? *I tell you*, he said, *refrain from all avarice* (Lk 12:15). What's *from all avarice*? What's the meaning of *from all*? Why did he add *from all*? I mean, he could have put it like this: "Beware of avarice." He made it his business to add *all*, and to say, *Beware of all avarice.*

The inheritance

2. The reason he said this becomes apparent to us in the holy gospel; it's the very occasion for his making these remarks at all. A man, you see, appealed to him against his brother, who had gone off with the whole of their father's estate, and not given his brother his share. You will observe what a good case this appellant had. After all, he wasn't trying to grab what belonged to someone else, but to get what was left him by his parents. He was asking for it from the Lord, to whom he had appealed as a judge. He had an unfair brother, but had found a just judge against his unfair brother.

So, ought he to let this chance slip in such a good cause? Or who was there that would say to his brother, "Pay your brother his share," if Christ wouldn't say it? Was that judge going to say it, whom the brother, being perhaps richer and much much rougher, was corrupting with a fat bribe? So the wretched man, deprived of his paternal means of support, having found such a perfect judge, approaches him, makes his appeal, asks his help, very briefly states his case. After all, what need was there to plead the case at length, when he was speaking to one who could also see into his heart? *Lord*, he said, *tell my brother to divide the inheritance with me* (Lk 12:13).

The Lord didn't say to him, "Let your brother come." Nor, for that matter, did he send for him to be present, or when he was present say to the complainant, "Prove what you were saying." He was asking for half the inheritance, asking him for half of it on earth; the Lord was offering him the whole of it in heaven. The Lord was giving him much more than he was asking for.

Christ did not want to divide the inheritance

3. *Tell my brother to divide the inheritance with me*. A just case, and a short case. But let's listen to both his judgment and his teaching. *Man*, he said. *"Man*; after all, seeing that you attach such importance to this inheritance, what are you but a man?" He wanted to make him more than a man is. What more did he want to make him, in wanting to remove avarice from him? What more did he want to make him? *I said, You are gods, and sons of the Most High, all of you* (Ps 82:6). There you have what he wanted to make him; he wanted to count him among the gods, who are without avarice.

Man, who set me up as a divider between you? (Lk 12:14). And there was his servant Paul, who also didn't want to be a divider, when he said, *I beseech you, brothers, all to say the same thing, and that there should not be schisms among you*. Then he went on to warn those who were rallying to his own name, and dividing Christ, *Each one of you says, I am Paul's man, I am Apollo's, I am for Cephas, I am for Christ. Has Christ been divided up? Was Paul crucified for you? Or were you baptized in Paul's name?* (1 Cor 1:10-13). So just note how bad the people must be, who want him to be divided who refused to be a divider. *Who set me up*, he said, *as a divider between you?*

A person's life is not to be found in the abundance of what he possesses in it

4. You have asked for a favor, listen to some advice. *I tell you, beware of all avarice* (Lk 12:15). "Perhaps you," he is saying, "would call someone grasping and greedy, if he was after other people's property; I, though, am telling you not to set your heart in a grasping, greedy manner, even on your own." That's the point of *all*. *Beware, he says, of all avarice*. It's heavy, that weight. If by any chance those this weight is laid on are weak, they should ask the one who laid it on them to be good enough to give them the necessary strength.

After all, my dear brothers and sisters, it's not something to be treated lightly, when our Lord, our redeemer, our savior who died for us, who gave his blood as the price to redeem us with, our advocate and judge; it's no light matter when he says, *Beware*. He's the one who knows how bad it is; we don't know; let us believe him. *Beware*, he says. "What of? Why?" *Of all avarice*. "I look after my own, I don't take what belongs to others." *Beware of all avarice*. It's not only the grabber of other people's property who is avaricious, but the one who greedily looks after his own. But if the person who greedily looks after his own is to be blamed like that, how must the one be condemned who grabs other people's property?

Beware, he says, *of all avarice; because a person's life is not to be found in the abundance of what he possesses in it* (Lk 12:15). Someone who stashes away vast quantities — how much does he take from it all to live on? When he's taken that, and somehow or other has set aside in his mind what's enough to live on, let him consider who will have the rest that's left over; or perhaps, while you are saving what to live on, you may be storing up what to die from. Here's Christ, here's Truth, here's Severity. *Beware*, says Truth; *Beware*, says Severity. Even if you don't love Truth, fear Severity. *A person's life is not to be found in the abundance of what he possesses.* Believe him, he's not deceiving you. Are you, there, maintaining the opposite: "On the contrary, a person's life *is* to be found in the abundance of what he possesses"? He is not deceiving you; you are deceiving yourself.

Abundance comes along

5. So this chance incident of that complainant seeking his share, not desiring to usurp someone else's, produced this judgment of the Lord, so that he did not say "*Beware* of avarice," but added, *of all avarice*. That wasn't enough, either; he gives the example of a rich man whose territory had succeeded. *There was*, he says, *a rich man whose territory had succeeded*. What does it mean, *had succeeded*? The territory he possessed had produced huge crops. How big were the crops? So that he couldn't find room to store them. Abundance suddenly put him in a tight spot, this ancient greedy-guts. I mean, how many years had already gone by, and yet those barns of his had been sufficient? So much, then, was produced, that the usual store places were no longer sufficient. And the wretched man looked around for a plan, not how to be generous in distributing the surplus, but how to store it, and by thinking hard he came up with a plan.

He gave the matter prudent thought, he saw a wise solution. What was his wise solution? *I will pull down the old barns*, he said, *and put up new, more spacious ones, and I will fill them; and then I will say to my soul* — what do you say to your soul? — *Soul, you have many good things laid up for very many years; sit back, eat, drink, have a good time* (Lk 12:18-19). That's what this wise discoverer of a plan said to his soul.

You don't deserve to have, if you don't want to be what you want to have

6. *And God said to him*; God isn't too grand to talk even to fools. Some of you may say, perhaps, "And how did God talk to a fool?" O my brothers and sisters, how many fools is he talking to here, when the gospel is chanted? When it was read, those who hear, and don't do, aren't they fools? So what did the Lord say? Because that man for his part thought how wise he was in working out a plan, *Fool*, he said; *Fool*, because you think you're clever; *Fool*, because you have said to your soul, *You have many good things laid up for very many years, today is your soul being required of you* (Lk 12:20).

The soul to which you said, *You have many good things,* is being required today, and doesn't have any good thing. Let it think lightly of these good things, and be good itself; and then when it is required, let it depart in peace without anxiety. I mean, I ask you, what could be more crooked than a man who wants to have many good things, and doesn't want to be good himself? You don't deserve to have, if you don't want to be what you want to have. I mean, do you want to have a bad country cottage? Of course not, but a good one. A bad wife? No, but a good one. Then a bad poncho perhaps, or even a bad pair of boots? Why only a bad soul?

He didn't here say to this fool, with his empty thoughts and his building of barns, and his unawareness of the bellies of the poor; he didn't say to him, "Today your soul will be whisked off to hell." he said nothing of that sort, but only *will be required of you.* "I'm not telling you where your soul is going to go; only that, whether you like it or not, it's going to do a flit from here, where you are saving up so much for it. Look, you fool; you have only thought of filling your new, bigger, barns, as though there were nothing else that could be done with it all."

The forehead of the inner self

7. But maybe that man wasn't yet a Christian. We at least, brothers and sisters, should listen; we to whom as believers the gospel is chanted, we by whom the one who said all this is worshiped, whose sign is worn by us on our foreheads, and held in our hearts. It makes a great deal of difference, you see, where a person keeps the sign of Christ, whether on the forehead, or both on the forehead and in the heart. You heard, when the holy prophet Ezekiel was speaking, how before God sent an exterminator of a wicked people, he first sent a marker, and said to him, *Go, and mark with a sign the foreheads of those who groan and grieve over the sins of my people, which are committed among them* (Ez 9:4). He didn't say "which are committed outside them," but "among them." Yet for all that they groan and grieve; and that's why they have been marked with a sign on the forehead — the forehead of the inner self, not the outer one. There's a forehead of the face, you see, and a forehead of the conscience. In fact, sometimes the inner forehead gets a knock, and the outer one blushes; it either blushes for shame, or turns pale with fright.

So there is a forehead of the inner self. That's where those people were marked, to save them from being wiped out. Because even if they didn't put right the sins that were committed among them, at least they were pained by them, and by their very pain they set themselves apart; while set apart for God, they were mixed together in the eyes of men. They are marked with a sign in secret, they escape harm in public. The destroyer is sent next, and is told, *Go, destroy, do not spare young, old, male, female; but do not go near those who have the sign on their foreheads* (Ez 9:6). What a sure guarantee has been given you, my brothers and sisters, you among this people who are groaning and grieving over the wicked deeds committed in your midst, and are not committing them!

Beware of all avarice

8. In order, though, not to commit wicked deeds, *Beware of all avarice.* I'm now giving you a wider definition of what is meant by *all avarice.* That man is greedy and avaricious in lust, who is not satisfied with his wife. And idolatry too is

called avarice, because you can be greedy in the sphere of the divine, when you are not satisfied with the one, true God. What, but a greedy, grasping soul, could make itself many gods? What but a greedy, grasping soul could make itself many martyrs?

Beware of all avarice. Fine, you only love what is your own, and boast that you don't go after other people's property; consider what evil you do by not listening to Christ when he says, *Beware of all avarice.* Fine, you only love what is your own, you don't make off with what belongs to others. You've acquired it by your labor, you've acquired it justly; you are a legitimate heir, someone you've deserved well of has made you an endowment; you've sailed the seven seas, you've put yourself at risk, you haven't committed fraud, you haven't sworn to a lie, you've acquired what God willed; and you keep a tight and greedy grip on it, with a perfectly good conscience, just because you haven't come by it in a wrongful way, and you are not after someone else's property.

If you won't listen to him when he says, *Beware of all avarice,* at least listen to how much evil you are going to do because of what is your very own. Here then, for example, it so happens you are made a judge. You are not corruptible, because you are not after someone else's property; nobody gives you a bribe and says, "Give judgment against my adversary." What an idea, a man who doesn't have his eye on someone else's property, like you — when could you ever be persuaded to do such a thing? Now see what evil you are going to do on account of your own property. That person who wants you to judge the case wrongly, and give judgment for him against his adversary — perhaps he's an influential man, and can ensure by a malicious accusation that you lose your own property. You notice what influence he has, you think about it, you think about your property which you take such care of, which you are so fond of — not that you have wrongfully acquired it, but that you have wrongfully clung to it. You are noticing the sticky birdlime, which ensures that you lack the free wings of virtue, and you say to yourself, "I offend this man, he's very powerful at the moment, he will insinuate bad things about me — and I'm outlawed, I lose everything I have." You are going to judge wrongfully, not with an eye on someone else's property, but to save your own.

Beware of all avarice, even in your own things

9. Give me a person who has listened to Christ, give me a person who has listened in fear and trembling to the words, *Beware of all avarice.* And don't start telling me, "As for me, I'm a poor man, working class, very ordinary, one of the masses; when can I ever hope to be a judge? I'm not afraid of that temptation, the danger of which you have just set before our eyes." Look, I'm telling the poor man too what he ought to be afraid of. A rich and powerful man sends for you, to give some false evidence on his behalf. What are you going to do now? Tell me. You've a nice little property; you've worked hard, you've built it up, you've saved. That man is insistent; "Give false evidence on my behalf, and I will give you so much

this and so much that." You, not being the sort to have your eyes on what belongs to others, say, "I couldn't dream of it; I'm not after what God hasn't wished to give me, I don't accept it. Leave me alone." "You don't want to accept what I can give? I'll take away what you have."

So there you are; now prove yourself, now question yourself. Why look at me? Look at yourself inside, see what's inside you, examine what's inside you. Take your seat in judgment on yourself, set yourself before yourself, and stretch yourself on the rack of God's commandment, and torture yourself with fear, and don't be soft on yourself; answer yourself. Well, there you are; what will you do, if someone threatens you like this: "I will strip you of what you have acquired with such hard work, unless you give false evidence on my behalf"? Give him back, *Beware of all avarice.*

"O my servant," he will say to you, "whom I have redeemed and set free, whom from being a servant I have adopted as a brother, whom I have placed in my body as a part of it, listen to me: let him strip you of what you have acquired, don't let him strip you of me. You are holding onto what is yours in case you perish? Haven't I told you, *Beware of all avarice?*"

Let us beware of all avarice if we want to enjoy eternal wisdom

10. There you are, all upset, there you are, being tossed to and fro, your heart battered by storms like a ship. Christ is asleep; wake him up as he dozes, and you won't suffer from the storm as it rages. Wake him up, the very one who wished to have nothing here, who arrived at the cross for your sake, whose bones were counted by scoffers as he hung there naked; and beware of all avarice. Not merely avaricious love of money; beware of the avaricious love of life. A horrific sort of avarice, this, a fearsome sort of avarice.

Sometimes a person will make light of what he possesses, and say, "I won't give false evidence." "I won't give it, you tell me? I'll strip you of all you own." "Strip me of all I own, you won't strip me of what I own inside." After all, that man didn't remain poor, who said, *The Lord has given, the Lord has taken away; as it pleased the Lord, so has it happened; therefore may the Lord's name be blessed. Naked I came forth from my mother's womb, naked shall I return to the earth* (Job 1:21). Naked outwardly, clothed inwardly. Naked outwardly in rags, and rotting rags at that; clothed inwardly. How? *May your priests be clothed with justice* (Ps 132:9).

But what if he says, when you have shrugged off whatever you possess, what if he says, "I'll kill you"? Give him this answer, if you have listened to Christ: "You'll kill me? Better you should kill my flesh, than that I with a false tongue should kill my soul. What are you going to do to me? You are going to kill the flesh; out goes the soul, free, due at the end of the world to receive back even the flesh which it has thought lightly of. So what are you going to do to me? But if I give false evidence on your behalf, I will be killing myself with my tongue. And it won't be in the flesh that I kill myself, because *The mouth that tells a lie kills the soul* (Wis 1:11)."

Perhaps you won't say this, though. Why won't you say it? Because you want to stay alive. Do you want to stay alive longer than God planned for you? Are you really on your guard against all avarice? God wanted you to live up to the point when this man approached you. Perhaps he's going to kill you, and so make a martyr of you. Don't cherish a greediness for living, and you won't have to endure an eternity of dying. Do you see how in every case this avarice, by which we want more of anything than we need, causes us to sin? Let us beware of all avarice if we want to enjoy eternal wisdom.

Sermon 112

Preached in the Restored Basilica, on Those Invited to the Dinner

Most scholars agree this sermon was preached in Carthage some time between 411 and 420; one writer suggests the location was Hippo Diarrhytus (Bizerta), when Augustine was returning to Hippo Regius (his own town) from Carthage after the dedication there of a rebuilt basilica. This homily is a meditation on the sacrificial character of the Eucharistic banquet through reflection on the Lucan text (Lk 14:16-24) about the three groups that excused themselves from a dinner. The homily concludes in an aggressive tone, as Augustine insists that heretics and schismatics return to Catholic unity.

1. Readings from holy scripture have been set before us, which are both for all of us to listen to, and for me, with the Lord's help, to offer some comments on in a sermon. In the reading from the apostle God is being thanked for the faith of the nations, for the reason of course that it was he who brought it about. In the psalm we said, *God of power, convert us, and show us your face, and we shall be saved* (Ps 80:7). In the gospel we were invited to the dinner. Or rather, others were invited, we weren't invited, but just brought; not only brought but even compelled. That, I mean, is what we heard, that *A certain man made a great dinner* (Lk 14:16). Who can this man be but *the mediator of God and men, the man Christ Jesus* (1 Tm 2:5)?

He had sent for those invited to come, because now the time had come for them to come. Who can those invited have been, but the ones called by the prophets, sent beforehand? What a long time ago it was that the prophets were sent, and issued the invitation to Christ's dinner! Now they were sent to the people of Israel. They were sent often enough, often enough they issued the invitation, so that when it was time for the dinner people should come. They, however, received the invitation, disdained the dinner. What does that mean, received the invitation, disdained the dinner? They read the prophets, and slew Christ.

But when they killed Christ, they then unwittingly prepared a dinner for us. The dinner now being ready once Christ had been sacrificed, after Christ's resurrection the dinner, or supper of the Lord which the faithful know about, was entrusted to us, instituted by his own hands and words, and then the apostles, to whom the prophets had previously been sent, were sent themselves. "Come to the dinner" — this was the way, you see, in which it had been ordained that Christ should be sacrificed — said the apostles. "Come to the dinner."

The three excuses

2. They excused themselves, those who refused to come. How did they excuse themselves, brothers and sisters? There were three excuses. One said, *I have bought a manor, I am going to inspect it; please excuse me.* Another said, *I have bought five yoke of oxen, I want to try them out; please excuse me.* A third said, *I have married a wife; please excuse me, I cannot come* (Lk 14:18-20). We may assume, may we not, that these are the excuses which hinder all those who decline to come to the dinner. Let us take a look at them, analyze them, find out what they really amount to, in order to beware of them.

The buying of the manor marks the tendency to domineer. So here pride is being castigated. I mean it's most enjoyable to have a manor, to hold it, to possess it, to subject the people on it to oneself, to domineer, to lord it over them. It's a bad vice, that, the first of all vices; you see, the first man wanted to lord it, in not being willing to have a Lord. What is lording it, or domineering, anyway, but rejoicing in one's own authority? There's a greater authority; let us submit to that, in order to make sure we are safe. *I have bought a manor; please excuse me.* Pride, being invited, refused to come.

Five yoke of oxen

3. Another said, *I have bought five yoke of oxen.* Wouldn't "I have bought some oxen" have been enough? Undoubtedly there's something here that challenges us by its very obscurity to inquire and understand, and prompts us, just by being shut, to knock. *Five yoke of oxen*; the senses of the body. We count five senses of the body, as everyone knows; and if perhaps you hadn't realized it, you will undoubtedly recognize it when you are reminded of it. So we find five senses of the body: sight in the eyes, hearing in the ears, the sense of smell in the nostrils, taste in the gullet, touch in all parts. White and black and any kind of color, light and shade, we perceive by seeing. Harsh noises and melodious ones we sense by hearing. Pleasant smells and nasty ones we sense by smelling; sweet and bitter we sense by tasting. Hard and soft, smooth and rough, hot and cold, heavy and light, we sense by touching.

There are five of them, and they are yokes, or each a pair. That they are yokes or pairs can easily be seen with the first three senses: there are two eyes, two ears, two nostrils; there you are, with three yokes. In the gullet, though, that is the sense of taste, you can find a sort of pairing, because nothing will be perceived to have a taste unless it touches tongue and palate. The sensuous pleasure that belongs to the touch is less obviously paired; yet it is both outer and inner; so it too is a pair.

Why are they called yokes of oxen? Because with these senses we seek out earthly things, and oxen have their gaze focused on the earth. Now there are people, far removed from the faith, given to earthly concerns, of a materialistic cast of mind; they refuse to believe anything but what they can perceive with these five senses of the body. Indeed it is in its senses that they posit the standards for all truth. "I," he says, "don't believe anything except what I can see. There you have the sum of my knowledge, there you have my science. It's white, it's black. It's round, it's square, it's this or that color; I perceive it, I know it, I grasp it; nature herself teaches me. It's a voice, my senses tell me it's a voice. It sings well, sings badly, is pleasant, is hoarse. I perceive it, I know it, it has reached me. It smells nice, smells nasty; I sense it, I know it. This is sweet, this is bitter, this salty, this insipid; what more you can tell me, I don't know. I perceive by touch what is hard, what is soft, what is smooth, what is rough, what's hot, what's cold. What more are you going to show me?"

How many eat and drink judgment upon themselves

4. That was the kind of obstacle that held back our apostle, Thomas, who wasn't even prepared to believe his eyes about the Lord Christ, that is about Christ's resurrection. *Unless I put my fingers*, he said, *into the place of the nails and the wounds, and my hand into his side, I will not believe* (Jn 20:25). And the Lord, who could have risen without any trace of his wounds, preserved the scars, to be touched by the doubter, and for the wounds of his mind to be healed. All the same, he is going to issue invitations to the dinner, in spite of the excuse of the five yoke of oxen; and so he said, *Blessed are those who do not see, and yet believe* (Jn 20:29).

We, my brothers and sisters, invited to supper, have not been hindered by these five pairs or yokes. After all, we haven't desired to see the Lord's face in this life, or longed to have his voice proceeding from his own mouth, enter our ears. We haven't sought any temporal odor in him — there was a woman who poured a most precious ointment over him, that house was filled with the fragrance, but we weren't there — there you are, we didn't smell it, and we have believed. He gave the supper, consecrated by his own hands, to the disciples; but we didn't sit down to that banquet, and yet every day we eat of that supper by faith.

And don't imagine it was a great thing to have been present at that supper, which he gave out with his own hands, without faith. Better faith later on than perfidy then and there. Paul wasn't there, but he believed. Judas was there, but he betrayed. And how many people even now, though they never saw that table at that time, nor observed with their eyes what the Lord held in his hands, nor tasted it in their mouths, yet because it's the same supper that is still prepared now — how many there are even now who in this same supper eat and drink judgment upon themselves!

We have believed in Christ and so we receive with faith

5. But how, we may ask, did the occasion arise for the Lord to talk about this dinner? One of the guests — he was at a banquet, you see, to which he had been invited — had said, *Blessed is the one who eats bread in the kingdom of God.* He was sighing for it as though it were a long way off, and there was the bread itself seated in his presence. What, I mean to say, is the bread of the kingdom of God, but the one who says, *I am the living bread, who have come down from heaven* (Jn 6:41)? Don't get your gullet ready to eat, but your mind. That precisely is the beauty of this supper. We have believed in Christ, I mean, and so we receive with faith. We know what to think about as we receive; we receive a tiny portion, and in our minds we take our fill. So it is not what is seen, but what is believed, that feeds us.

So then, we haven't even taken refuge in the last of the senses, we haven't said, "Let those believe who saw the risen Lord — if what is said is true — and felt him with their hands; we haven't touched him; why should we believe?" If we thought like that, we would be hindered by those five yoke of oxen from coming to the dinner. And to show you, brothers, that it wasn't the enjoyment of these five senses, which soothes us and induces pleasurable feelings, that was being noted, but a kind of curiosity, he didn't say *I have bought five yoke of oxen,* I am going to feed them, but *I am going to try them out.* If he wants to try them out, it means he wants to avoid doubt through these pairs, just as Saint Thomas wanted to avoid doubt by these pairs. "Let me see, let me touch, let me put my fingers in." "Here you are," he said. *"Put your fingers into my side, and do not be unbelieving* (Jn 20:27). I was slain for your sake; through the place you want to touch I shed my blood to redeem you; and you still have doubts about me, unless you touch me? Here you are then, I grant you this too, this too I offer you; touch and believe. Find the place of the wound; heal the wound of doubt."

The things of this world — he didn't say "Don't have them," but "Don't love them"

6. The third one said, *I've married a wife.* This represents the pleasures of the flesh. How many people it hinders from coming to the dinner! If only it were just those outside, and not those inside as well. There are people who may say, "It doesn't go well with you unless the delights of the flesh are available." They are the ones the apostle quotes as saying, *Let us eat and drink, for tomorrow we die* (1 Cor 15:32). That's the sort of thing that rich man said in his pride as he feasted: *"Let us eat and drink, for tomorrow we die.* Who ever rose again from there to come back here? Who has ever told us what goes on there? This is all that we can take with us, that it went well with us in this life." Whoever says this has married a wife; he has

embraced the flesh, he makes merry with the pleasures of the flesh, he excuses himself from the dinner; let him take care he doesn't die of an inner hunger.

Pay attention to John, the holy apostle, the evangelist: *Do not love the world, nor the things that are in the world* (1 Jn 2:15). O you who are coming to the Lord's supper, *do not love the world, nor the things that are in the world*. He didn't say, "Don't have them," but "Don't love them." You've had them, you've possessed them, you've loved them — you've stuck. Love of earthly things is the birdlime for spiritual wings. Look, you have coveted them: you've stuck. Who will give you wings like a dove's? When will you fly to where you may find a true test, when here, where you've got badly stuck, you have perversely wanted to rest? *Do not love the world*; that's the divine clarion call. The assembly the clarion call is directed to is the whole earth. The entire world is being told, *Do not love the world, nor the things that are in the world. Whoever loves the world, the charity of the Father is not in him, since all that is in the world is the lust of the flesh, and the lust of the eyes, and the ambition of the age* (1 Jn 2:15-16). He began from the bottom; where the gospel ended, that's where he began; and where the gospel began is where he put the conclusion: *The lust of the flesh: I have married a wife. The lust of the eyes: I have bought five yoke of oxen. The ambition of the age: I have bought a manor.*

Because he was seeking the inner sense of faith,
he presented himself also to their outer senses

7. The reason, though, that these senses are here presented to us with reference to the eyes alone, the whole represented by the part, is that among the five senses the eyes have first place. That's why, though sight properly belongs to the eyes, we usually talk about "seeing" in connection with all five senses. How? First of all, as regards the eyes themselves, you say, "See how white it is, observe and see how white it is"; this, of course, with reference to the eyes. "Listen, and see how tuneful it is"; can you reverse it and say, "Listen, and see how white it is"?

This use of the word "see" runs through all the senses; but this is not the case with the words that are proper to the other senses. "Look, and see how white it is"; "listen, and see how tuneful it is"; "smell it, and see how pleasant it is"; "taste, and see how sweet it is"; "touch, and see how soft it is." Of course, since all five are *senses*, we could instead say it like this: "Listen, and sense how tuneful it is," or, "Smell it, and sense how pleasant it is"; "taste, and sense how sweet it is"; "touch, and sense how hot it is"; "feel it, and sense how smooth it is"; "feel it, and sense how soft it is." However, we don't usually say anything of the sort.

I mean, take the case of the Lord himself; when he appeared to his disciples after his resurrection, and they still tottered in faith when they saw him, supposing that they were seeing a ghost, he said, *Why do you doubt, and why do thoughts rise in your hearts? See my hands and my feet.* And it isn't just "See"; *Touch*, he goes on, *and feel, and see* (Lk 24:38-39). Look and see; *feel and see*. See with your eyes alone; see with all your senses. Because he was seeking the inner sense of faith, he presented himself also to their outer senses. We for our part have perceived nothing about the Lord at all through these outer senses; we have heard with our hearing, and believed with our hearts; and what we have heard didn't come from his own mouth but from the mouths of his preachers, from the mouths of those who were already dining with him, and inviting us to join them by belching their appreciation.

Let us come to the dinner

8. Let us be done, then, with vain and bad excuses; let us come to the dinner at which we can inwardly take our fill. Let us not be prevented by arrogance or pride; let no unlawful curiosity either lift us high with excitement or cast us down in terror, and in either case turn us away from God; let no sensual voluptuousness divert us from heartfelt willingness. Let us come, let us take our fill.

And who did come, but the beggars, the infirm, the lame, the blind? The ones who didn't come were the rich and the healthy, apparently striding along very well, sharp-sighted and observant; that is to say, supremely self-confident, and thus all the more desperate their cases, the prouder they were. Let the beggars come, because the one issuing the invitation is the one who became poor for our sakes, when he was rich, so that through his poverty we beggars might be enriched. Let the infirm come, because *the doctor is not needed by the healthy, but by the sick* (Mk 2:17; Lk 5:31; Mt 9:12). Let the lame come, those who say to him, *Straighten out my steps according to your word* (Ps 119:133). Let the blind come, those who say to him, *Enlighten my eyes, lest I should ever fall asleep in death* (Ps 13:3).

All such came on time, when those who had earlier been invited were rejected by their own excuses. They came on time, they came in from the squares and alleys of the city. And the servant who had been sent answered, *Lord, what you commanded has been done, and there is still room. Go out*, he said, *into the high roads and hedges, and whomever you find, compel them to come in* (Lk 14:22-23). Whomever you find, don't wait for them to agree; compel them to come in. I have prepared a great dinner, a great house; I won't tolerate any empty places there.

From the squares and alleys came the Gentiles; let the heretics and schismatics come from the highroads and hedges. *Compel them to come in.* Here they can find peace, because those who put up hedges are seeking divisions. Let them be dragged from the hedges, wrenched from the thorns. They are stuck fast in the hedges, and they don't want to be compelled. "Let us come in of our own free will," they say. That wasn't the order the Lord gave: *Compel them*, he said, *to come in.* Let necessity be experienced outwardly, and hence free willingness be born inwardly.

(*End of the sermon on those who were invited to the dinner*)

Sermon 112A

On the Two Sons from the Gospel

There is an indication that this sermon was not preached at Hippo. The date assigned by Hill is 400, while Hombert suggests 403-404. Augustine follows the traditional patristic allegorical interpretation of the parable of the prodigal son: "The man who has two sons is God: the elder son is the people of the Jews, the younger, the people of the Gentiles." The inheritance received from the Father is the whole sum of human gifts, talents and abilities. The younger son who squanders his inheritance made the mistake of feeding himself with the husks of secular doctrines which could never satisfy him. Augustine is somewhat unusual in the sympathy he has for the older son, who represents the Jews, who resent the fact that the Gentiles gained admission to salvation on easy terms, without the burden of circumcision and the law. Likewise, the bishop employs multivalent symbolism by interpreting the younger son as both Christ and the Gentiles.

Finishing the sermon

1. We ought not to linger over matters already dealt with; but while we oughtn't to linger over them, we ought to remind ourselves of them. With your good sense you will remember that last Sunday I undertook in a sermon to discuss the two sons, whose story was also told in the gospel today; and that that sermon could not be brought to a conclusion. But after that bit of trouble, it was the will of the Lord our God that I should also speak to you today. I must pay the debt of a sermon, I must always remain in the debt of love; the Lord will be standing by, to ensure that my lowliness is able to satisfy your expectations.

The two sons

2. The man who has two sons is God who has two peoples; the elder son is the people of the Jews, the younger the people of the Gentiles. The property received from the Father is the mind, intellect, memory, capability, and whatever else God has given us to understand and worship him with. On receiving this patrimony the younger son *set out to a region far away*; far away indeed, to the point of entirely forgetting his creator. *He squandered his property by living extravagantly* (Lk 15:13); spending and not earning; spending what he had, and not acquiring what he didn't have; that is to say, wasting all his capabilities on luxury, on idols, on depraved desires, which Truth called harlots.

Unlawful curiosity represents a pestilential poverty of truth

3. Nor is it surprising that famine followed on this riotous living. *Now there was a dearth in that region*; not a dearth of visible bread, but a dearth of invisible truth. To escape the dearth, *he threw himself on a certain prince of that region* (Lk 15:14-15). This is to be understood as the prince of demons, the devil, on whom all prying, inquisitive people throw themselves; because unlawful curiosity represents a pestilential poverty of truth. He for his part, wrenched away from God by the insistent hunger of his intelligence, was reduced to slavery, and assigned the job of feeding pigs, a form of slavery, that is, which the lowest of the low and unclean demons like to wallow in. It wasn't for nothing, after all, that even the Lord allowed the demons to enter a herd of pigs. This young fellow fed on husks, which couldn't satisfy him. We take the husks to be secular doctrines, which crackle, but don't satisfy, fit food for pigs, not human beings; that is, for demons to take pleasure in, not for the faithful to be justified by.

The meaning of the return

4. At last the time came when he saw where he had got to, what he had lost, whom he had offended, on whom he had thrown himself. *And returning to himself*, first to himself, and so to his father. Perhaps, you see, he had said, *My heart has forsaken me* (Ps 40:12), and so he had first to return to himself, and in this way come to realize that he was a long way away from his father. This is how scripture admonishes some people: *Return, transgressors, to the heart* (Is 46:8). *Returning to himself*, he found himself in a sorry state: *Trouble and pain*, he says, *I found, and I called on the name of the Lord* (Ps 116:3-4). *How many hired servants*, he said, *of my father have bread enough and to spare, but I am perishing here of hunger?* (Lk 15:17). How can this thought have occurred to him, if he wasn't already hearing the name of God preached? Some people did have bread, who didn't indeed keep it well, but were looking for some other advantage, And about them it is said, *Amen I tell you, they have received their reward* (Mt 6:5). They are the sort, I mean, who are to be regarded as hired servants, not as sons, and whom the apostle is referring to when he says, *Whether opportunistically or sincerely, let Christ be proclaimed* (Phil 1:18). He wants us to understand certain people, you see, who in looking for their own advantage are hired servants, while in proclaiming Christ they have bread and to spare.

The son had previously left his heart in pride; he had now returned to his heart in anger

5. He gets up and goes back; if he had just lain down and fallen, he would have stayed where he was. His father sees him from a long way off, and runs to meet him, because it's his voice in the psalm: *You have known my thoughts from afar* (Ps 139:2). What thoughts? Those, in which he said to himself, *I will say to my father: I have sinned against heaven and before you. I am no longer worthy to be called your son; make me like one of your hired servants* (Lk 15:18-19). He hadn't

yet said it, you see, but was only thinking of saying it. His father, though, heard him as though he were saying it.

Sometimes, you see, when you find yourself in trouble or trial of some kind, the thought occurs to you to pray; you mull over what you are going to say to God in your prayer, like a son demanding compassion from his father as a right. And you say to yourself, "I will tell my God this and that; after all, I'm not afraid when I say this, when I cry like this, that my God is not going to listen to me." The moment you say this, as a rule he is already listening to you; after all, when you were thinking these thoughts, you didn't conceal them from the eyes of God. He was right there, while you were disposing yourself to pray, just as he would be right there when you actually began to pray.

That's why it says in another psalm, *I said, I will declare my wrongdoing against myself to the Lord.* Notice how he was still saying something to himself, still getting something read; and immediately he added, *And you have forgiven the impiety of my heart* (Ps 32:5). How close God's mercy is to anyone who confesses! I mean God is not far from the contrite of heart — that's what you find written, after all: *The Lord is near to those who have crushed their hearts* (Ps 34:18).

So this lad had already crushed his heart in the region of dearth; I mean, he had returned to his heart to pound his heart; he had previously left his heart in pride; he had now returned to his heart in anger. He was angry with himself, all set to punish, not himself but his wrongdoing; he had returned, all set to earn his father's right response. He spoke in anger, according to the text, *Be angry, and do not sin* (Ps 4:4). Repentance, you see, always means being angry with yourself, seeing that because you are angry, you punish yourself. That's the source of all those gestures in penitents who are truly repentant, truly sorry; the source of tearing the hair, of wrapping oneself in sackcloth, of beating the breast. Surely these are all indications of being savage with oneself, being angry with oneself. What the hand does outwardly, the conscience does inwardly; it lashes itself in its thoughts, it beats itself, indeed, to speak more truly, it slays itself. It's by slaying itself, you see, that it offers itself *a sacrifice to God, a crushed spirit; a contrite and humbled heart God does not spurn* (Ps 51:17). Just so, then, this lad by pounding, humbling, beating his heart, slew his heart.

How can you be capable of carrying God, unless God, being carried, carries you?

6. Although he was still bracing himself to speak to his father, and saying to himself, *I will arise, and go, and I will say,* his father perceived his thoughts from a long way off, and ran to meet him. What does running to meet him signify, but getting in first with his compassion? *While he was still a long way off,* it says, *his father ran to meet him, moved with pity* (Lk 15:18-20). Why was he moved with pity? Because the boy was in such a pitiful state. *Running to meet him, he pressed on him,* that is, put his arm round his neck. The arm of the Father is the Son; he gave the prodigal son Christ to carry; a load which didn't weigh him down, but lifted

him up. *My yoke*, he said, *is light, and my load is light* (Mt 11:30). He was pressing on him as he stood upright; by pressing on him he was not allowing him to fall again. So light is the load of Christ, that not only does it not weigh down, but it even lifts up, and lightens. This isn't, either, just in the way that loads are said to be light which are less burdensome, but still weigh something; and it's one thing to carry a heavy load, another to carry a light load, another to carry no load at all. The man carrying a heavy load appears to be weighed down; the one carrying a light load is less weighed down, but still he feels some weight; but the man who carries no load at all is evidently walking along with his shoulders completely free.

Well, Christ's load is not like that at all; it's a relief, you see, to carry it, so that you can be lifted up and lightened; if you put it down, you find yourself more weighed down than ever. And don't let this strike you, brothers and sisters, as impossible. Perhaps we can find an example, to help you see what I mean, from the natural world; it too, as a matter of fact, is marvelous, not to say unbelievable. Observe it in the case of birds. Every bird carries its wings; notice and see how they fold their wings when they come down to earth to rest, and how after a certain fashion they place them on their sides. Do you consider they are burdened by them? Let them remove the burden, and they will fall. The less a bird has carried that load, so much the less has it flown. So you come along and remove that load, as though taking pity on it; if you really want to take pity, forbear; or if the feathers have already been plucked out, nurse the bird, so that its burden can grow again, and it can fly from the ground.

That, of course, is the sort of burden which was desired by the one who said, *Who will give me wings like a dove, and I will fly away and take my rest?* (Ps 55:6). So the fact that the father pressed on his son's neck means that he raised him up, not that he weighed him down, he gave him a guerdon, not a burden. I mean, how can you be capable of carrying God, unless God, being carried, carries you?

God works with the ministers of the Church

7. So the father gives instructions for him to be presented with the first robe, which Adam had lost by sinning. Now that he has kissed his son and received him back in peace he gives instructions for him to be presented with the robe, which is the hope of immortality in baptism. He orders him to be given a ring, as a pledge of the Holy Spirit, and shoes for his feet, in readiness for the gospel of peace, so that the feet of one announcing good news might be beautiful.

So God does all this through his servants, that is through the ministers of the Church. Do they give the robe from their own resources, from their own resources the ring or the shoes? They owe a service, they perform a duty; the one who gives is the one from whose secret treasures these things are brought out. He also gave instructions for the fatted calf to be killed; that is, for his son to be admitted to the table at which Christ who was slain is fed upon. You see, for everyone who comes from a long way away and runs to join the Church, he is slain precisely when he is proclaimed as having been slain, when you are admitted to his body. The fatted calf was killed, because the one who had been lost was found.

The Jews and the Gentiles

8. And the elder brother is angry when he returns from the fields, and refuses to go in. He is the people of the Jews, whose spirit appeared even in those who had already come to believe in Christ. The Jews couldn't stomach it that the Gentiles should come on such easy terms, without the imposition of any of the burdens of the law, without the pain of physical circumcision, that they should receive saving baptism in sin; they couldn't stomach their feasting on the fatted calf. At all events, they had already believed, and when the matter was explained to them, they acquiesced.

But even now, when perhaps some Jew, who has cherished the law of God in his mind, and lived according to it without blame, someone such as Saul said he was, who among us became Paul, all the greater for being lesser, all the more exalted for becoming the least — "Paul," after all, means least, which is why we say "I'll speak to you a little later, or a little before." So what is Paul? *For I am the least of the apostles* (1 Cor 15:9): he said it himself. So then any Jew who is like that, knowing himself and having a good conscience, who has worshiped the one God from his earliest youth, the God of Abraham, Isaac and Jacob, the God proclaimed by the law and the prophets, and who has observed the predictions of the law, begins to think about the Church, as he sees the human race running in the name of Christ; when he thinks about the Church, he is approaching the house from the fields.

That's what's written, you see: *When the elder brother was arriving from the fields, and approaching the house* (Lk 15:25). Just as the younger brother, I mean, is growing every day among the heathen who believe, so too the elder brother, although rarely, still all the same does return among the Jews. They think about the Church, they are astonished at what it is; they see that the law is with them, the law is with us; the prophets are with them, the prophets are with us; that with them there is no longer any sacrifice, with us a daily sacrifice; they see that they have been in the Father's fields, and yet are not eating of the fatted calf.

Symphony — a concord of voices

9. There is also to be heard, coming from the house, the sound of a symphony and choir. What does "symphony" mean? A concord of voices. Those who engage in discord are out of tune; those who enjoy concord are in tune with each other. The apostle was teaching the art of symphony when he said, *I beseech you, brothers, all to say the same thing, and not to have schisms among you* (1 Cor 1:10). Who isn't charmed by this holy symphony, that is, the agreement of voices that don't clash, with no one striking a tuneless or jarring note, which would offend the ears of a person of good understanding? And "choir" also suggests this concord; the only thing that gives pleasure in a choir is the voices of many singers, blending as one, achieving a unity out of them all, not breaking out into a discordant variety.

The complaint of the Jews

10. When he heard this sound coming from the house, *he was angry and refused to go in* (Lk 15:28). Just as it has actually happened, in fact, that a Jew of good standing among his own people should say, "Christians can do so much! We hold fast to our ancestral laws; God spoke to Abraham, from whom we are sprung. Moses received the law, after liberating us from the land of Egypt and leading us through the Red Sea. Here are these people, holding our scriptures, singing our psalms throughout the whole world, and they have a daily sacrifice; we, though, have lost both sacrifice and temple."

He also asks a servant what's going on here. Let the Jew ask any servant he likes; let him open the prophets, open the apostle, ask anybody; neither the Old Testament nor the New has kept silent about the calling of the nations. The questioning of the servant we must take as being the searching of the Book; there you will find scripture saying to you, *Your brother has come back, and your father has killed the fatted calf for him, because he has got him back safe* (Lk 15:27). That's all right for the servant to say; but whom, precisely, did the father get back safe? One who was dead and came to life again, that's the one he got back to restore to health and save. And the slaying of the fatted calf was the due of the one who had gone a long way away; by going a long way away from God, after all, he had become godless. That servant, the apostle Paul, answered, *For indeed Christ died for the godless* (Rom 5:6).

Taking umbrage himself, he was angry and wouldn't go in; but when his father spoke to him, he went in; he refused to go in at the reply of a servant. And really and truly, my dear brothers and sisters, this does happen. Often enough we beat the Jews in an argument about the scriptures of God, but it's still the servant speaking, and so the son gets angry; they don't want to come in like that, just to get beaten in an argument. "What's that? The sound of the symphony has moved you, the choir has moved you, the celebration and merrymaking in the house, the feasting on the fatted calf specially slaughtered, all this has moved you; nobody is shutting you out." Who are you talking to? As long as it's merely a servant speaking, he gets angry, refuses to come in.

A superior applies greater force by pleading than by ordering

11. Come back to the Lord, where he says, *Nobody comes to me, except the one whom the Father has drawn to me* (Jn 6:44). So the father goes out and pleads with his son; that is drawing him; a superior applies greater force by pleading than by ordering. And that's what happens, beloved, when such people hear us, people immersed in the scriptures, and having the kind of conscience about good works that enables them to say to their Father, *Father, I have never disregarded your commandment* (Lk 15:29). So then, when they are beaten in argument from the scriptures, and they can't find any way to answer, they get angry, they resist, as

wishing to win the argument themselves. Afterward, you leave him to his thoughts, and God begins to speak to him inwardly; that's the meaning of the Father going out and speaking to his son, "Come in and join the feast."

The complaints of the elder son

12. And he retorted, *Look, here am I, serving you all these years, and I have never disregarded your commandment; and you have never even given me a kid, to eat with my friends. Lo and behold, here comes this son of yours, who swallowed up his inheritance with harlots, and you have killed the fatted calf for him* (Lk 15:29-30). These are inner thoughts, where now the father is speaking in secret ways. He's reacting, you see, and answering, not now a servant who has answered his inquiries, but his father pleading with him somehow or other, and gently admonishing him, and he says, "What is all this? Here are we, holding by the scriptures of God, and we haven't withdrawn from the one God, we haven't stretched out our hands to a foreign god. We have only known that one God, we have always worshiped him, the one who made heaven and earth; and we haven't received a kid."

Where do we find a kid? Among sinners. Why does this elder son complain that he was never given a kid? He was looking for a chance to sin, and to feast on that; obviously that was what he took umbrage about. This is what still grieves the Jews, namely, that they came to their senses and realized that the reason why they weren't given Christ, is that they thought he was a kid. You see, they recognize their own voice in the gospel, in those Jews of an earlier generation who said, *We know that this man is a sinner* (Jn 9:24). He in fact was a calf, but as long as you think he's a kid, you have remained without this feast. *You have never even given me a kid —* because the Father didn't have a kid, knowing the one he did have to be a calf. You are outside, because you haven't even received a kid; come in then now to the calf.

You are with me always

13. What, after all, is the father's reply? *Son, you are with me always* (Lk 15:31). The Father bore witness that the Jews, who have always worshiped the one God, were near to him. We have the testimony of the apostle saying that they were near, while the Gentiles were far away. Speaking to Gentiles he says, *Coming* (that is, Christ) *he preached the good news of peace to you who were far away, and peace to those who were near* (Eph 2:17). Far away, like the younger son; he is showing the Jews that they hadn't gone far away to feed pigs, they hadn't abandoned the one God, they hadn't worshiped idols, they hadn't served demons.

I'm not speaking of all of them, in case you should meet profligate and turbulent Jews. I hope you meet instead the sort who disapprove of these ones, serious people who keep the commandments of the law, who, while not yet coming in to the fatted calf, are still able to say, *I have not disregarded your commandment* (Lk 15:29). The sort to whom, when they are on the point of coming in, the Father says, "*You are with me always.* Indeed you are with me, because you didn't set out to go far away; but still you are wrong to go on staying outside the house. 1 don't want you to miss our feast. Don't be jealous of your younger brother. You are with me always."

God did not indeed underwrite what was said, a little carelessly and boastfully perhaps, *I have never disregarded your commandment*; he said, *You are with me always*, but he did not say, "No, you have never disregarded my commandment." What God said is true, which is not entirely the case with the rather rash boast, though in some of the people he was possibly a transgressor without for all that withdrawing from the one God. So the father could truly say, *You are with me always, and all that is mine is yours* (Lk 15:31). Because it is yours, does it mean it isn't your brother's? In what way is it yours? If you have it jointly, not if you brawl about it separately. *All that I have*, he says, *is yours*.

He made him a present, it would seem, of what he said was his own. Did he subject heaven and earth to him, or the angels in their sublime greatness? We don't have to understand it like that. In fact, the angels are not going to be subjected to us, seeing that the Lord promised us equality with them as a great reward: *They will be*, he said, *equal to the angels of God* (Mt 22:30). There are other angels, though, on whom the saints will pass judgment: *Do you not know*, says the apostle, *that we shall judge angels?* (1 Cor 6:3). You see, there are angels who are always holy, there are angels who are disobedient; we shall be put on an equal footing with the good angels, we shall judge the bad angels.

So how is everything that is mine yours? It's true that all that is God's is ours, but not that all is subjected to us. After all, you don't say "My slave" in the same sense as "My brother." Of whatever you say "It's mine," and you're telling the truth, when you are speaking truly, it's yours; but your brother with the same entitlement as your slave? You say "my house" in one way, "my wife, my husband" in another; "my children" one way, "my father, my mother" in another. I grant you, quite apart from what I think, all things are yours. "My God," you say; but still, do you say "My God" in the same way as "My slave"? Rather, "My God" in the same way as "My master." So then, we have one above us, our Lord and master, whom we are to enjoy; we have things beneath us, which we are to have dominion over. All things are ours, therefore, provided we are his.

All that is mine is yours

14. *All that is mine*, he said, *is yours*. If you're peaceable, if you are readily placated, if you are prepared to rejoice at the return of your brother, if our feasting doesn't vex you, if you don't remain beside the house even though you have already come from the fields, then all that is mine is yours. *But it was right that we should feast and rejoice* (Lk 15:22), because *Christ died for the ungodly* (Rom 5:6), and rose again. That, you see, is the meaning of what was actually said here: *Because your brother was dead, and has come to life again; was lost and is found* (Lk 15:32).

Sermon 114

On the Words of the Gospel, Luke 17:3-4: *If Your Brother Sins Against You, Rebuke Him,* etc.: Preached One Sunday at the Shrine of Saint Cyprian in the Presence of Count Boniface, on Forgiving the Brethren

Perler argues convincingly that this sermon was delivered between April and July 424, when Augustine was visiting Carthage for the last time. All Christians, regardless of their state in the Church, must seek forgiveness since they too seek to be forgiven. The daily recitation of the Lord's Prayer by all Christians proves as much.

The forgiveness of sins

1. The holy gospel, as we heard when it was chanted, was advising us about the forgiveness of sins. That's what I have to remind you of in my sermon. You see, I am a servant of the word, not mine but God's, of course, our Lord's, whom nobody serves without honor, nobody ignores without punishment. So this Lord of ours, Jesus Christ, who abiding with the Father made us, and himself being made for our sakes remade us, this very Lord our God tells us, as we heard, *If your brother sins against you, rebuke him; and if he is sorry, forgive him; and if he sins against you seven times a day, and comes and says, "I am sorry," forgive him* (Lk 17:3-4).

By "seven times a day" he simply wanted you to understand any number of times at all — in case perhaps he should sin eight times, and you refuse to forgive him. So what does "seven times" mean? It means always, as often as he sins and is sorry. You see, *Seven times a day I will praise you* (Ps 119:164) is the same as *His praise always in my mouth* (Ps 34:1) in another psalm. And why seven times should stand for always, there is the plainest possible reason: in the recurring passage of seven days the whole of time rolls by.

Grant pardon to your fellow human being

2. So whoever you are who give a thought to Christ and long to receive what he promised, do not be slow to do what he told you. After all, what did he promise? Eternal life. And what did he tell you to do? Grant your brother pardon. As though he were saying to you, "You, a human being, see you grant pardon to your fellow human being, so that I, God, may come to you." But not to mention — or rather to pass over for the moment — those more sublime divine promises, according to which our creator is going to make us equal to his angels so that we may live without end in him and with him and on him — to pass over this for the time being, don't you want to receive from God this very thing you are told to grant your brother or your sister? This very thing, I repeat, you are told to grant them, don't you want to receive it from your Lord? Tell me if you don't want to, and then in that case don't grant it.

What does this amount to, but that you should forgive anyone who asks you to, if you are asking to be forgiven yourself? Or if you have nothing to be forgiven, then, I make bold to say, by all means don't forgive. Though I shouldn't have said that either. Even if you have nothing to be forgiven, you ought to forgive, because God too forgives, and he really has nothing that needs to be forgiven him.

Forgive others in order to be forgiven yourself

3. Now you are going to say to me, "But I'm not God; I'm a sinful man — or woman." Well, thank God you admit to having sins. So forgive others in order to be forgiven yourself. All the same, it's God himself who urges us to imitate him. First of all it is the Lord Christ, of whom the apostle Peter says, *Christ suffered for us, leaving us an example, that we might follow in his footsteps* (1 Pt 2:21); and of course, he didn't have any sin, and he died for our sins and shed his blood for the forgiveness of sins. For our sake he took upon himself what he did not owe, to set us free from debt. He ought not to have died, we ought not to live. Why not? Because we are sinners. Death was no more his due than life is ours. He accepted what was not his due; he gave us what was not ours.

But as we are discussing the forgiveness of sins, in case you should imagine it's asking too much of you to imitate Christ, listen to the apostle saying, *Forgiving one another, just as God in Christ has forgiven you. Be therefore* — they are the apostle's words, not mine — *be therefore imitators of God.* Of course, it's sheer pride to presume to imitate God. *Imitators of God* — sure, it's pride, pure and simple — *like most dear children* (Eph 4:32-5:1). You are called his child; if you scorn to imitate, why do you seek to inherit?

Don't bear grudges in your heart

4. I would say this, even if you had no sin at all which you desired to be quit of. But as it is, whoever you are, you are human. You may be a just person, you're human; you may be a lay person, you're human; a monk or a nun, you're human; a clergyman, you're human; a bishop, you're human; an apostle, you're human. Listen to the words of an apostle: *If we say we have no sin, we are deceiving ourselves.* Who said it? That one, that one, that John the evangelist whom the Lord Christ loved above the rest, who reclined on his bosom; that's the one who says, *If we say.* Not "if you say that you have no sin," but *if we say that we have no sin, we are deceiving ourselves, and the truth is not in us.* He included himself in the fault, in order to be included in the pardon.

If we say. Observe what he says. *If we say that we have no sin, we are deceiving ourselves, and the truth is not in us. But if we confess our sins, he is faithful and just, to forgive us our sins, and to purify us of all iniquity* (1 Jn 1:8-9). How purify? By pardoning; not as though not finding anything to punish, but as finding something to let us off for. So if we have any sins, brothers and sisters, let us forgive those who ask us to, forgive those who say they're sorry. Don't let's bear grudges in our hearts. The more we bear grudges, you see, the more they rot our hearts.

Forgive as I forgive

5. So I want you to be forgiving, because I've caught you begging for pardon. You are asked, forgive. You are asked, and you will be asking. You are asked, forgive; just as you too will be asking to be forgiven yourself. Look, the time is approaching for prayer; I will get you in the very words you are going to say. You are going to say, *Our Father who art in heaven*; after all, you won't be counted among his children if you are not going to say, *Our Father*. So you're going to say, *Our Father, who art in heaven*. Carry on. *Hallowed be thy name*. Say the next bit. *Thy kingdom come*. Carry on still. *Thy will be done, as in heaven, also on earth*. Notice what you add next: *Give us today our daily bread*. Where are your riches? Why, you're begging!

But the point we are dealing with here: say what comes next after *Give us today our daily bread*, carry on with what follows. *Forgive us our debts*. You have come to my words: *Forgive us*, he says, *our debts*. So do what follows *Forgive us our debts*. On what terms, by what bargain, by what agreement? By what instrument, read out in court? *As we also forgive our debtors* (Mt 6:9-12).

It's little enough that you won't forgive; you go on to lie to God as well. The terms have been stated, the rule fixed. "Forgive, as I forgive." So he won't forgive unless you forgive. "Forgive, as I forgive." You want forgiveness when you seek it; forgive anyone who seeks it from you. These prayers were dictated by the heavenly law officer himself. He is not deceiving you. Ask according to the heavenly law, say, *Forgive, as we also forgive*. And do what you say. If you lie in your prayers, you derive no benefit. If you lie in your prayers, you both lose your case and earn a penalty. If anyone lies to the emperor, he is convicted of lying when he comes to hold court; but when you lie in your prayer, you are convicted in the very act of praying. After all God, to convict you, doesn't require witnesses against you. He dictated the prayers for you to say as your counsel; if you lie, he becomes the witness against you; and if you don't straighten yourself out, he will be your judge.

So both say it and do it; because if you don't say it, you are asking against the rule, and so don't obtain what you ask for; but if you say it and don't do it, you will also be guilty of lying. There is no way to get round this phrase, except by fulfilling what you say. Do you imagine we can cross out this phrase from our prayer? Or would you like *Forgive us our debts* to remain there, while we cross out what follows, *as we also forgive our debtors*? You won't cross it out, or you may be crossed out first yourself.

So in the prayer you say *Give*; you say *Forgive*: to receive what you haven't got, to be let off what is due to your offenses. Do you want to receive? Give. Do you want to be forgiven? Forgive. It's a simple enough combination. Listen to Christ in another place: *Forgive, and you will be forgiven; give, and it will be given you* (Lk 6:37-38). *Forgive, and you will be forgiven*. What will you be forgiving? Sins others have committed against you. What will you in your turn be forgiven? The sins you in your turn have committed. *Give, and it will be given you.* You that are longing for eternal life, give support to poor people's temporal life. Relieve the temporal life of the poor, and in return for such a tiny and earthly seedling as that, you will receive as your harvest eternal life. Amen.

Sermon 117

On the Words of the Gospel of John 1:1-3:
In the Beginning Was the Word, and the Word Was with God,
and the Word Was God, etc.: Against the Arians

This sermon was delivered around 418, or perhaps in 420, according to one scholar. Augustine's preaching here is not his best, but nevertheless he displays his theological acumen on such complex issues as Christology and the mystery of God, as he confronts the Arian heresy. The bishop has a distinctly apophatic approach to the mystery of the Word of God, namely, God can best be understood by emphasizing what he is not: he is not unjust, deceitful, ugly, evil, etc. Augustine employs the analogy of fire and light to tease out the relationship between the Father as the begetter and the Son as the begotten. Which comes first? He also uses the analogy of the mirror and the image, and he insists that humility is central to understanding the mystery of God.

If you want to buy this Word, don't look for something outside yourself to give

1. The passage of the gospel we have just heard, dearly beloved brothers and sisters, calls for purity in the eyes of our hearts. As a result, you see, of John's preaching of the gospel we have come to accept our Lord Jesus Christ as the maker of the entire creation in virtue of his divinity, and as the restorer of the fallen creation in virtue of his humanity. In the gospel itself we can discover what sort of man and how great a man John was, and thus from the merit of the retailer we can form some estimate of the price of the Word which could be uttered by such a man; or rather how that which surpasses all things can have no price. When a thing is put up for sale, it is either equal in value to the price, or it is less than it's worth, or it exceeds its value. When someone buys something for as much as it's worth, the price is equal to the thing bought; when he buys it more cheaply, the price falls beneath its value; when he buys it more dearly, it exceeds it. Now nothing can be equated with the Word of God, nor can anything fall beneath it at exchange, nor can anything exceed it. Well of course, all things can be put beneath the Word of God, because *all things were made through him* (Jn 1:3); however, they are not put beneath it as though they were a good price for the Word, so that anybody could pay something, and receive the Word, cheaply, in exchange.

Still, if one can talk like this, and a certain way or fashion of speaking does allow it, you can say that the price for buying the Word is you, the buyer, when you give yourself in exchange for yourself to this Word. And so when we buy something, we look for something to give, in order to get the thing we want to buy, by paying the price. And what we give in exchange is something outside us; even if we had it with us, it goes out outside us in order that we may have with us the thing we are buying with it. Whatever price people buying things find to pay for them, it has to be such that they pay what they have and receive what they don't have. The people, though, remain, from whom the price departs, and what they are paying the price for arrives instead. But now if you want to buy this Word, if you want to have it, don't look for something outside yourself you can give; give yourself. When you have done that, you don't lose yourself, as you lose the price when you buy something.

If you want to buy it, give yourself

2. So the Word of God is set before us all. Let those buy it who can; all those who devoutly wish to can do so. You see, in that Word there is peace: *And peace on earth to people of good will* (Lk 2:14). So if you want to buy it, give yourself. This is the quasi-price of the Word (if it can be stated at all), when on paying it you do not lose yourself, and you acquire the Word for which you pay over yourself, and you acquire yourself in the Word to whom you pay yourself.

And what do you pay over to the Word? Not something entirely alien to the Word for which you are giving yourself; but something that was made through that Word is given back to him to be refashioned. *All things were made through him.* If all things, then of course humanity too. If heaven, if earth, if sea, if everything that is in them, if the entire creation, then of course, most obviously, that creature who was made to the image of God, man, was made through the Word.

An unchangeable form

3. We are not now discussing, brothers and sisters, possible ways of understanding the text, *In the beginning was the Word, and the Word was with God, and the Word was God* (Jn 1:1). It can only be understood in ways beyond words; human words cannot suffice for understanding the Word of God. What we are discussing and stating is why it is not understood. I am not speaking in order that it may be understood, but telling you what prevents it being understood.

You see, it is a kind of form, a form that has not been formed, but is the form of all things that have been formed; an unchangeable form, that has neither fault nor failing, beyond time, beyond space, standing apart as at once the foundation for all things to stand on, and the ceiling for them to stand under. If you say that all things are in it, you are not lying. The Word itself, you see, is called the

Wisdom of God; but we have it written, *In wisdom you have made them all* (Ps 104:24). Therefore all things are in it. And yet because it is God, all things are under it.

What I am saying is how incomprehensible is the passage that was read to us. But in any case, it wasn't read in order to be understood, but in order to make us mere human beings grieve because we don't understand it, and make us try to discover what prevents our understanding, and so move it out of the way, and hunger to grasp the unchangeable Word, ourselves thereby being changed from worse to better. The Word, after all, does not make progress, or grow, when someone who knows it comes along. But it is whole and entire if you abide in it, whole and entire if you fall away from it; whole and entire when you return to it; abiding in itself and making all things new.

So then it is the form of all things, a form that has not been constructed, beyond time as I said, and beyond space or place. Anything, after all, that is contained in place is circumscribed, as a form is circumscribed by its limits; it has bounds from which and as far as which it extends. And then, anything contained in a place and extended in bulk and space is less in its parts than in its totality. May God enable you to understand.

The Word is not less in his parts than in his totality

4. Now every day we can make judgments about the bodily objects that meet our eyes, which we can see and touch, and among which we find ourselves — make judgments that any such body has its form or shape in a place. But everything that occupies the space of a particular place is less in its parts than as a whole. Take a part of the human body, for example an arm; an arm of course is less than the whole body. And if an arm is less, then it occupies less space. Again, the head, being part of the body, is in a smaller place and is less than the whole body which it is the head of. So everything that is in a place or space is less in its parts than in its totality.

We must have no such ideas, no such thoughts about that Word. We must not form images of spiritual realities in materialistic terms. That Word, that God, is *not* less in his parts than in his totality.

Let us make a devout confession of ignorance,
instead of a brash profession of knowledge

5. But you are quite unable to imagine or think of such a thing. And such ignorance is more religious and devout than any presumption of knowledge. After all, we are talking about God. It says, *and the Word was God* (Jn 1:1). We are talking about God; so why be surprised if you cannot grasp it? I mean, if you can grasp it, it isn't God. Let us rather make a devout confession of ignorance, instead of a brash profession of knowledge, Certainly it is great bliss to have a

little touch or taste of God with the mind; but completely to grasp him, to comprehend him, is altogether impossible.

God belongs to the mind, he is to be understood; material bodies belong to the eyes, they are to be seen. But do you imagine you can completely grasp, or comprehend, a body with your eyes? You most certainly can't. I mean, whatever you look at, you are not looking at the whole of it. When you see someone's face, you don't see their back while you see their face; and when you see their back, you don't at that moment see their face. So then you don't see things in such a way as to grasp or comprehend them whole. But when you are looking at another part of something which you hadn't seen before, you will never say that you have grasped the whole, even of the thing's surface, unless memory acting with you helps you to remember you have already seen the other part which you are moving away from. You handle what you are seeing, turning it this way and that; or else you go round it yourself in order to see the whole of it. So you cannot see the whole of it with one glance. And as long as you are turning it around in order to see it, you are seeing parts of it; and by putting together the other parts you have seen, you seem to be looking at the whole of it. But in fact what is at work here is not eyesight, but a lively memory.

So then, brothers and sisters, what can be said about that Word? Look, here we are, saying about material things staring us in the face, that we cannot take them all in, grasp them totally, by a look. So what mind's eye will be able to grasp God, take all of him in? It is enough to touch his fringes, if the mind's eye is pure. But if it does touch upon him, it does so with a kind of immaterial and spiritual touch, but still does not embrace or comprehend him all; and that too, if the mind is pure.

And we human beings are made blessed by our hearts just brushing against that which abides always blessed; and that is itself eternal blessedness; and that by which we are made alive is eternal life; that by which we are made wise is perfect wisdom; that by which we are enlightened is eternal light. And notice how by brushing against it you are made into what you were not, while that which you brush against is not made into what it was not. What I am saying is: God does not increase thanks to those who know him, but those who know him do, thanks to their knowledge of God.

Don't let us imagine, my dearest brothers and sisters, that we are doing God a good turn, because I said that in some way or other we give a price for him. After all, we are not giving him something which would increase his capital value — he that remains entire when you fall remains entire when you return, who is ready to be seen by those who turn back to him, and so to make them blessed, and to punish with blindness those who turn away from him. You see, he first asserts his rights in the soul that turns away from him, with the primary penalty — that blindness; after all, if you turn away from the true light, that is from God, you are already struck blind. You don't yet feel the penalty — but it's already there within you.

The Arian controversy

6. And so, my dearest brothers and sisters, we must understand the Word of God as being born, immaterially, inviolably, unchangeably, not with any temporal birth, but born all the same of God. May we suppose that we can somehow or other persuade a certain kind of unbeliever not to shrink away from the truth which we are told by the Catholic faith? This is opposed to the Arians, by whom the Church of God has often been sorely tried, when materialistically-minded people find it easier to accept what they have been accustomed to see. Some people, you see, have had the nerve to say, "The Father is greater than the Son, and precedes him in time"; that is, there is one who is greater than the Son, namely the Father, and the Son is less than the Father, and is preceded by the Father in time. And this is how they argue: "If he was born, then obviously the Father was there before the Son was born to him."

Pay attention; may he stand by me, with the help of your prayers, and your desire to receive with attentive devotion whatever he may grant, whatever he may suggest; may he stand by me, so that I may somehow or other complete the explanation I have begun. And yet, brothers and sisters, before I go on, if I am unable to explain the matter, do not imagine that it is reason which has failed; no, it's the person — me. And so I'm urging you and begging you to pray; may God's mercy be present, and thus get the matter stated by me in such a way as is right for you to hear, and for me to state it.

So then, this is what they, those Arians, say: "If he is the Son of God, he was born." We agree — I mean, he wouldn't be the Son if he hadn't been born. It's plain as a pikestaff, faith accepts it, the Catholic Church approves — it's true. Then they go on: "If the Son was born to the Father, then the Father was there before the Son was born to him." This is what faith rejects, what is rejected by Catholic ears. Whoever holds this opinion is anathema, is outside, does not belong to the partnership and company of the saints. "So," they say, "give us a reason, how the Son could be both born to the Father, and also coeval, the same age as the one of whom he was born."

(...)

Coeval things can be compared with coeternal ones

11. I think your holinesses have now understood what I am saying; that temporal things cannot be compared with eternal ones, but that with a slight and tenuous likeness coeval things can be compared with coeternal ones. So let us find some coevals, and be advised concerning these likenesses by the scriptures. We read in the scriptures about Wisdom herself, *For she is the radiance of eternal light.* Again we read *a mirror without spot of the greatness of God.* Wisdom herself is called the radiance of eternal life, is called the image of the Father (Wis 7:26); from this let us see if we can gather a likeness, and find some coevals which may help us to understand coeternals.

You there, you Arian, if I can find a begetter not preceding in time what it begot and find something begotten that is not younger in time than the one it was begotten by, then it is only fair that you should concede to me the possibility of these coeternals being found in the creator, when it has been possible to find coevals in creation. Yes, now I think some of the brethren have got the idea. Some of them, clearly, have leapt ahead from when I said *For she is the radiance of eternal light.* Fire, you see, sheds light, light is shed by fire. If we ask which comes from which, we are reminded every day when we light a lamp of a certain invisible and inexpressible reality, and thus a sort of lamp is lit for our understanding in the dark night of this age.

Notice a person lighting a lamp. Before the lamp is lit, there is no fire yet, nor is there yet any beam of the light which comes from the fire. Now I put a question to you, and say, "Does the beam of light come from the fire, or the fire from the beam?" Every single soul answers me (because God was determined to plant in every single soul the seeds of understanding, the basic elements of wisdom); every single soul answers me, and nobody hesitates, that the brightness comes from the fire, not the fire from the brightness. So let us name the fire the father of that brightness — because I have already given you advance notice that we are looking for coevals, not coeternals. If I wish to light a lamp, there is no fire there yet, nor yet any of that brightness; but as soon as I light it, simultaneously with the fire comes the brightness too. Give me here fire without brightness, and I will believe you that the Father can have existed without the Son.

What coeval is to the time-bound, coeternal is to the eternal

12. So there you are. The matter has been stated, as far as such a tremendous matter could be stated by us; with God assisting your earnest prayer and your open minds, you have taken in as much as you could take in. All the same, these matters remain inexpressible. Don't imagine that anything worthy or adequate has been said; it hasn't, not even in the comparison of coevals with coeternals, which has meant comparing time-bound things with things that abide, extinguishable things with things that are immortal.

But because the Son is also called the image of the Father, let us take a comparison from this idea too, in things that are very, very different, as I have warned you before. From a mirror comes the image of a person looking in the mirror. This can't help us very much to bring clarity into the matter which we are trying, in whatever way we can, to explain. I will be told, after all, "The one looking in the mirror was already there, and had already been born. The image appears as soon as a beholder appears. But the one who is beholding or looking was there even before he approached the mirror. So how are we to find the means of extracting a likeness or comparison here, such as we drew from fire and its brightness?"

Let us take the simplest example. You know perfectly well how water often reflects the images of bodies. What I'm saying is this: when anybody passes or stands over a stretch of water, he sees his image there. So now let us suppose something born over water, like a bush or shrub; isn't it born with its image? As soon as it begins to exist, its image begins to exist with it, it doesn't precede its image in being born; you can't show me that something was born over water, and that afterward its image appeared, while the thing itself appeared first without its image. No, it's born with its image; and yet the image comes from the thing, not the thing from the image. So it's born with its image, and the bush and its image begin to be simultaneously. Don't you agree that the image comes from the bush, that the bush is not begotten of the image?

So you admit the image comes from the bush. And so both generator and what is generated began to be simultaneously. Therefore they are coeval. If the bush were always there, the image derived from the bush would always be there too. Now what derives from another is, of course, born. So it is possible for a generator to exist always, and always with it to exist what is born of it. That's where we were sweating, that's where we were in a bit of trouble, how we could understand an everlasting birth. So the Son of God is so called insofar as the Father also is, insofar as he therefore has one from whom he is; not insofar as the Father was there first, and afterward the Son. The Father is always there, always there the Son from the Father. And because anything that is from another is born, therefore the Son is always born. The Father is always there, always there his image from him; just as that image of the bush is born of the bush, and if the bush were always there, the image too would always be born of the bush. You couldn't find coeternals begotten of eternal begetters, and you have found coevals born of time-bound begetters. I understand the coeternal Son born of an eternal begetter. What coeval is to the time-bound, you see, that coeternal is to the eternal.

(...)

We pass from milk to solid food in the divine mysteries

16. But in order to get there, if we cannot yet see the Word as God, let us listen to the Word as flesh. Because we have become flesh-bound, materialistic, let us listen to the Word who became flesh. The reason he has come, you see, the reason he has taken upon himself our infirmity, is so that you may be able to receive a firm discourse of God's, as he bears your infirmity. And it is very properly called milk, because he is giving milk to the little ones, so that he may give them the solid food of wisdom when they are grown up. Take the milk patiently, in order later on to be able to feed on the solid food avidly. I mean, how is even the milk produced on which babies are breast-fed? Wasn't there some solid food on the table? But the baby is incapable of eating the solid food on the table. So what does the mother do? She incarnates the food and produces milk from it. She produces for us what we are capable of taking.

In the same way the Word became flesh, so that we little ones might be nourished on milk, being babies still with respect to solid food. There is, however, this difference, that when the mother incarnates the food and makes milk, the food is turned into milk; whereas the Word, remaining unchangeably itself, assumed flesh, in order to be somehow or other combined with it. It did not dissolve, not change what it is in order to speak to you through your condition; he wasn't transmuted and changed into a man. Being nonconvertible, you see, and unchangeable, and remaining altogether inviolable, he became what you are in relation to you, remaining what he is in himself in relation to the Father.

Catch hold of God's lowliness

17. What does he say himself, after all, to the weak and infirm, so that they may recover that kind of sight and to some extent at least attain to or brush against the Word through which all things were made? *Come to me, all you who toil and are overburdened, and I will refresh you. Take my yoke upon you and learn of me; because I am meek and humble of heart* (Mt 11:28-29). What is this harangue that the master, the Son of God, the Wisdom of God through whom all things were made, is addressing to us? He is calling the human race, and saying, *Come to me, all you who toil, and learn of me.* You were thinking, no doubt, that the Wisdom of God was going to say, "Learn how I made the heavens and the stars; also, since in me all things, even before they were made, had been numbered how in virtue of their unchangeable ideas even the hairs of your head have been numbered. Is that the sort of thing you were thinking she would say? No; but first this: *that I am meek and humble of heart.*"

There is what you have got to get hold of, brothers and sisters, and it's certainly little enough. We are striving for great things; let us lay hold of little things, and we shall be great. Do you wish to lay hold of the loftiness of God? First catch hold of God's lowliness. Deign to be lowly, to be humble, because God has deigned to be lowly and humble on the same account, yours, not his own. So catch hold of Christ's humility, learn to be humble, don't be proud. Confess your infirmity, lie there patiently in the presence of the doctor. When you have caught hold of his humility, you start rising up with him. Not as though he has to rise, insofar as he is the Word; but it's you, rather, who do so, so that he may be grasped by you more and more.

At first your understanding was very shaky and hesitant; later you come to understand with greater certainty and clarity. It's not he that is growing, but you that are making progress, and it's as though he seems to be rising up with you. That's how it is, brothers and sisters. Trust God's instructions, and carry them out, and he will give muscle to your understanding. Don't be presumptuous, and as it were give knowledge priority over God's instruction, or you will remain full of hot air, instead of solid understanding. Think of a tree; it first seeks out the lowest level, in order to grow upward; it fixes its roots in the lowly soil, in order to stretch out its topmost branches to the sky. Can it reach upward from anywhere except its humble roots? You, though, wish to comprehend the heights without charity; you are challenging the winds without roots. That's the way to come crashing down, not to grow. With Christ dwelling in your hearts through faith, be rooted and grounded in love, that you may be filled with all the fullness of God.

Sermon 132

On the Words of the Gospel of John 6:55-56: *My Flesh Is Food Indeed and*
My Blood Is Drink Indeed, Whoever Eats My Flesh, etc.

Hill argues for a rather late date around 420 most likely during Lent in Hippo
given the direct exhortation: "Look, it's Easter time, put your name down for
baptism." The sermon is catechetical and focuses on sexual ethics for both the
married and the unmarried. Husbands should be as faithful to their wives as
they expect from the so-called "weaker sex." Young men who are not yet married should keep themselves chaste for their wives. Those committed to virginity
must exercise even greater vigilance to avoid any kind of temptation. This sermon features the bishop's preoccupation about the danger of unchastity.

Invitation to the catechumens

1. As we heard when the holy gospel was being read, the Lord Jesus Christ has
encouraged us with the promise of eternal life to eat his flesh and drink his blood.
Some of you who heard this already do it, others not yet. I mean, those of you who
have been baptized and are believers know what he was talking about. But those of
you who are still catechumens, or hearers so-called, could indeed be hearers when
it was read, but hardly also understanders, surely.

So my words are addressed to both sorts. Let those who already eat the flesh
of the Lord and drink his blood reflect about what they eat and what they drink,
in case, as the apostle says, they should be eating and drinking judgment upon
themselves. Those, on the other hand, who are not yet eating and not yet
drinking should be in a hurry to come to such a feast as this that they have been
invited to. During these days the teachers are feeding you; Christ provides food
every day. That's his table there, laid among us in the middle. What can the
reason be, my dear hearers, that you can see the table, and don't come to the
feast?

And perhaps just now, while the gospel was being read, you said to yourselves,
"Can we guess what he means when he says, *My flesh is food indeed, and my blood*
is drink indeed (Jn 6:55)? How can the Lord's flesh be eaten, and the Lord's flesh
be drunk? I can't imagine what he means." Well, who closed the door, to stop you
knowing the answer? It's veiled in secrecy; but if you like it will be unveiled.
Come to the point of professing the faith, and you will have solved the problem.
The faithful, you see, already know what the Lord meant by his words. You,
though, are called a catechumen, you're called a hearer, and yet you're deaf;
because while indeed the ears on your head are open, and you can hear what was
said, you still have the ears of your heart shut tight, and so you don't understand
what was said. I'm just stating the case, not giving any explanations. Look, it's

Easter time, put your name down for baptism. If the festival doesn't get you excited, at least let curiosity lead you on, so that you may learn what is meant by *Whoever eats my flesh and drinks my blood abides in me, and I in him* (Jn 6:56). In order to learn with me what it meant, *knock, and the door will be opened for you* (Lk 11:9). And just as I am telling you, "Knock, and the door will be opened for you," so I too am knocking; open the door for me, I'm shouting in your ears, but I'm knocking at your breast.

Advice to spouses

2. But if the catechumens, my dear brothers and sisters, need to be encouraged not to delay coming to this wonderful grace of being born again, what great pains I should be taking over the instruction of the faithful, so that coming to be born again may really benefit the catechumens, and they may avoid eating and drinking at this wonderful feast to their own condemnation! Now in order not to eat and drink to their condemnation, they must live good lives. It's for you to encourage them in this, not by words but by your behavior; those who haven't yet been baptized should be in a hurry to follow you, in such a way that they don't perish by imitating you.

Those of you who are married, keep yourselves faithful to your wives. Pay them what you require of them. Husband, you require your wife to be chaste; give her an example how to be so, not just a lecture. You're the head, notice the way you are going. The way you should be going, after all, is one on which it won't be dangerous for her to follow you; what I mean is, you yourself should travel the road on which you want her to follow. You are demanding self-discipline from the weaker sex; you both have the promptings of the flesh to deal with; let the one who is the stronger be the first to overcome them.

And yet the sad fact is that many husbands are overcome in this matter by their wives. Wives preserve their chastity, while husbands are not prepared to do so; and in the very fact of not doing so they like to have the reputation of being real men; as though what makes it the stronger sex is that it is so much more easily conquered by the enemy! It's a struggle, it's a battle, there's fighting to be done. The man is stronger, braver than the woman; the man is the head of the woman. The woman fights and wins; and you just give in to the enemy? The body stands up to him, and does the head keel over?

As for those of you who haven't yet got wives, and yet already approach the Lord's table and eat the flesh of Christ and drink his blood, if you intend to marry wives, keep yourselves for your wives. As you want them to come to you, so they in turn should be able to find you. What young man is there who doesn't want the wife he marries to be chaste? And if he is engaged to a virgin, can you imagine him not wanting her undefiled? You are looking for an undefiled wife, be undefiled yourself. You want her to be pure, don't be impure yourself.

I mean, it's just not the case that she can manage it, and you can't. If it couldn't be done, she couldn't manage it either. But because in fact she can, let her teach you that it can be done. She too, in order to manage, has to be governed by God. But you, if you manage to do it, will have all the more to boast about. Why all the more to boast about? Because she is under the pressure of parental custody, held in check by the bashfulness of the weaker sex; finally she has laws to be afraid of, which you don't. That's why you will have more to boast about if you manage it because if you manage it, it will be because you fear God. She has many things to fear besides God; all you have to fear is God.

But the one you fear is greater than all the others. He is to be feared in public, he is to be feared in private. You go out, he sees you; you come in, he sees you. The lamp's lit, he sees you; the lamp's put out, he sees you. You go into your bedroom, he sees you; you turn things over in your mind, he sees you. Fear him, him whose whole concern is to see you, and at least out of fear, be chaste. Or else, if you want to sin, of course, find somewhere he can't see you, and then do what you like.

Advice for those who have taken vows

3. As for those of you who have taken vows, chastise the body more strictly, and don't let the curb on lust be relaxed even for permissible things; which means it's not just a matter of avoiding unlawful copulation, but of refraining even from lawful looks and sights. Remember that whichever sex you belong to, whether male or female, you are leading the life of angels on earth. Angels, you see, don't get married, or take wives. That's what we shall all be like, when we have risen from the dead. How much better you people are, then, who already begin to be before death what everyone will be after the resurrection!

Preserve and respect your different grades, because God is keeping for you your respective honors. The resurrection of the dead has been compared to the stars in the sky. *For star differs from star in glory*, as the apostle says; *so too the resurrection of the dead* (1 Cor 15:41-42). There will be one splendor there for virginity, another for married chastity, another for holy widowhood. They will be variously bright, but they will all be there. Their brightness unequal, the sky they have in common.

Be faithful to your various commitments

4. So then, bearing in mind your various grades, and being faithful to your various commitments, approach the flesh of the Lord, approach the blood of the Lord. Any of you who know yourselves to be otherwise, don't approach. Let your consciences rather be pricked by my words. You may be thankful, those of you who know that they are keeping for their wives what they require from their wives; those of you who know that they are keeping total continence, if this is what they have vowed to God. But those of you who hear me saying, "Any of you who do not keep chaste must not approach to partake of that bread," may well be saddened by this.

And I myself would much rather not say this; but what am I to do? Should I hush up the truth, because I'm afraid of other people? So if these servants do not fear their Lord, am I not to fear him either? As though I didn't know he had said, *You wicked and lazy servant, you should have given, so that I could collect* (Mt 25:26-27). Well look, I have given, O Lord my God; here I am, in the sight of you and your angels, and in the sight of this people of yours I have invested your money, because I am terrified of your judgment. I have given, it's for you to collect. Even if I don't say this, you are going to do it.

So this is what I prefer to say: "I have given, it is for you to convert, for you to spare. Make those people chaste who have been unchaste, so that we may all rejoice together in your presence when the time comes for judgment, both I who have invested your money, and the one in whom I have invested it."

Do you all approve of that? Let it be approved then. Any of you who are unchaste, mend your ways while you are still living. I, after all, can speak the word of God; but to deliver the unchaste who persist in their wickedness from the judgment and condemnation of God, that is something I cannot do.

Sermon 137

On the Gospel of John 10:1-16:
On the Shepherd, the Hireling, and the Thief

Scholars place this sermon between 400 and 405 or between 408 and 411 or before 420. Hill favors the earliest dating. There is no consensus as to where it was preached. It is an excellent compendium on Augustine's *totus Christus* Christology and his anti-Donatist ecclesiology. The Church can tolerate sinful ministers since Christ is the true source of the Church's holiness and the real minister of every sacrament. Pastors who avoid rebuke of their flock are like hired hands. Even bad clergy preach moral truth in the pulpit, and their words should be heeded even when they are not matched by their deeds.

In Christ's body is to be found the unity of
its members and the framework of love

1. Your faith, dearly beloved, is not unaware — and I know that this is what you have learned from the teaching of the Master in heaven, in whom you have placed your hope — that our Lord Jesus Christ, who has already suffered and risen again for us, is the head of the Church; and that the Church is his body, and that in his body, as its very health, is to be found the unity of its members and the framework of love. Anyone who grows cold in love is sick in the body of Christ.

But God, who has already raised our head on high, has the power to heal the sick members too, provided, that is, that they haven't amputated themselves by extreme wickedness, but stick in the body until they are healed. Whatever, you see, remains in the body need not despair of being restored to health; but any part that has been amputated can be neither treated nor healed.

Since then he is the head of the Church, and the Church is his body, the whole Christ is both head and body. He has already risen again. So we have our head in heaven. Our head is interceding for us; our head, sinless and deathless, is already placating God for our sins, so that we too, when we rise again at the end, and are changed into heavenly glory, may follow our head. After all, where the head goes, there too go the other parts of the body. But while we are here, we are still parts of it; we must never despair, because we are going to follow our head.

Christ in heaven; Christ on earth

2. I mean to say, brothers and sisters, observe the loving affection of this head of ours. He is already in heaven, and he is struggling here as long as the Church is struggling here. Christ is hungry here, thirsty here, he's naked, he's a migrant, he's sick, he's in prison. You see, whatever his body suffers here, he said he suffers too; and at the end, as he sets his body apart to the right, and sets apart the rest by whom it is now being kicked around to the left, he is going to say to those on his right, *Come, blessed of my Father, receive the kingdom which has been prepared for you from the origins of the world.* How have they deserved this? *For I was hungry, and you gave me to eat*; and the other things in the same vein, as though he had received it all personally himself; to the point that, quite failing to understand, they answer and say, *Lord, when did we see you hungry, a migrant and in prison?* And he says to them, *When you did it for one of the least of mine, you did it for me* (Mt 25:31-40).

It's the same too with our own bodies; the heads up on top, the feet are on the ground; and yet in a crush of people jammed in a narrow space, when someone treads on your foot, doesn't your head say, "You're treading on me"? Neither your head nor your tongue is being trodden on by anybody; it's up on top, it's perfectly safe, nothing bad has happened to it. And yet because through the binding power of love there is a unity from the head right down to the feet, the tongue didn't detach itself from that unity, but said, "You're treading on me," though nobody had touched it. So just as the tongue which no one has touched says, "You're treading on me," in the same way Christ the head, which no one is treading on, says, *I was hungry, and you gave me to eat.* And to those who did not do this, he said, *I was hungry, and you did not give me anything to eat.* And how did he conclude? Like this: *These will go into eternal burning, but the just into eternal life* (Mt 25:35.42.46).

Christ is the gate in the head, the shepherd in the body

3. So when the Lord was speaking just now, he said he was a shepherd; he also said he was a gate. You've got each thing there; both *I am the gate* and *I am the shepherd* (Jn 10:9.11). He's the gate in the head, the shepherd in the body. You see, he says to Peter, whom he singles out to represent the Church, *Peter, do you love me? He answers, Lord, I do. And then a third time, Peter, do you love me? Peter was upset that he asked him a third time* (Jn 21:15-17); as though the one who could see his conscience when he was going to deny him could not see his faith when he wanted to confess him.

He knew him at all times, he even knew him when Peter didn't know himself. A time, indeed, when he didn't know himself was when he said, *I will be with you to the death* (Lk 22:33), and didn't know how weak he was. As indeed usually happens with sick people; the patient doesn't know what's going on in him, but the doctor knows, while it's the patient who is suffering the disease, not the doctor. The doctor says what's going on in the other person much more accurately than the one who's ill says what's going on in himself.

So at that time Peter was sick, the Lord was the doctor. The one claimed to have a strength of character which he didn't have, while the other felt the pulse of his heart, and said he was going to deny him three times. And it happened just as the doctor had foretold, and not as the sick man had over-confidently assumed. So after his resurrection the Lord questioned him, not because he was unaware of the eagerness with which he would confess his love of Christ, but in order to cancel the threefold denial of fear with a threefold confession of love. (...)

A grape from a thorn

13. My dear brothers and sisters, does a priest or a bishop ever go up and say anything else from this higher place in the pulpit, but not to grab other people's property, not to commit frauds, not to engage in crime? They can't say anything else, because they occupy the chair of Moses, and it is the chair speaking through them, not they themselves. So what about, *Do they gather grapes from thorns, or figs from thistles?* and *Every tree is known by its fruit* (Mt 7:16)? Can a Pharisee say good things? The Pharisee is a thornbush; how can I pick a grape from a thorn? Because you, Lord, said *Whatever they say, do it; but whatever they do, don't do it.* Are you telling me to pick a grape from thorns, even though you have said, *Do they gather grapes from thorns?*

The Lord answers you, "I didn't tell you to pick a grape from thorns; but use your eyes, see if it doesn't sometimes happen, perhaps, that while a vine is creeping across the ground, it gets tangled in a thornbush." Because we do find this, my dear brothers and sisters, a vine planted in sedge grass, because there is a thorny hedge there, it stretches out its tendrils and weaves them into the thorny hedge, and the bunches of grapes hang among the thorns; and anyone who sees the bunch picks it, not however from the thorns but from the vine which is twined around with thorns. So that's how they are thorny; but by their occupying the chair of Moses, the vine has got tangled up with them, and bunches of grapes hang from them, that is to say good words, good commandments.

You then, take care to pick the grapes, and the thorns won't prick you, when you pick this bunch. *Whatever they say, do it; but whatever they do, don't do it.* But the thorn will prick you, if you do what they do. So in order to pick the grapes, and not get stuck in the thorns, *Whatever they say, do it; but whatever they do, don't do it.* Their deeds are thorns, but their words are grapes, from the vine though, that is from the chair of Moses.

Augustine is a shepherd, not a hired hand

14. So these people run away when they see the wolf, when they see the robber. But this is what I had started to say, that the only thing these people can say from their place of eminence in the pulpit is, "Do good, don't perjure yourselves, don't defraud people, don't cheat people by running rings round them." Sometimes, though, they live in such a way that the bishop will be consulted about grabbing someone else's country place, and his advice will be sought about how best to do it. It's sometimes happened to me, I'm speaking from experience; I wouldn't have believed it otherwise. Many people come asking me for evil advice, advice on how to lie effectively, on how to diddle their opponents by getting round the law; and they think I'm pleased and gratified by their doing so. But in the name of Christ, if the Lord is pleased to let me say so, no such person has ever tempted me, or got what he wanted from me.

Because if the one who called us wishes, we are shepherds, not hired hands. But what does the apostle say? *To me it is of no importance to be judged by you, or by any human judgment; but I do not even judge myself. For I have nothing on my conscience, but I am not thereby justified. But the one who judges me is the Lord* (1 Cor 4:3-4). It doesn't mean I have a good conscience, just because you praise it. Why in any case praise what you can't see? Let the one who can see praise it; let him also correct me, if he sees anything there which offends his eyes. Because I too am not saying that I am in perfect good health; but I beat my breast and say to God, "Be gracious to me, and don't let me sin." And yet I think — and after all, I'm speaking in his presence — that I don't look for anything else from you except your welfare and salvation; and I frequently grieve over the sins of our brothers and sisters, and suffer agonies and torments in spirit, and sometimes I reprove them severely, or rather I never fail to reprove them. All those of you who really take in what I am saying, can bear me out how often brothers who sin have been reprimanded by me, and very severely reprimanded.

Augustine's account

15. Now I'm going to set out our policy to your holinesses. In the name of Christ you are the people of God, you are the Catholic people, you are members of Christ. You are not separated from the unity. You are in communion with the members of the apostles, in communion with the memorial shrines of the holy martyrs who are scattered throughout the world, and you are entrusted to our care, so that we have to give a good account of you. Now you know perfectly well everything that is in my account. You, Lord, know that I have spoken, that I have not kept quiet, you know with what urgency I have spoken, you know that I have wept before you, when I spoke and was not listened to. I think that that is the sum total of my account.

You see, I have been reassured by the Holy Spirit speaking through the prophet Ezekiel. You know that reading about the watchman: *Son of man*, he says, *I have set you as a watchman for the house of Israel. If, when I say to the wicked man, Wicked man, you shall die the death, you do not say it* — that is, the reason, after all, I am telling you is that you should tell him; if you do not inform him — *and the sword comes and takes him* — that means the thing I have threatened the sinner with — *that wicked man indeed shall die in his wickedness, but I will require his blood from the hand of the watchman.* Why? Because he didn't say anything. *But if the watchman sees the sword coming, and sounds the trumpet, so that he may escape, and he does not watch himself* — that is, doesn't correct himself so that the punishment which God is threatening him with may not overtake him — *and the sword comes and takes someone, that wicked man indeed has died in his iniquity; you, however*, he says, *have delivered your soul* (Ez 33:7-9).

And in that place in the gospel, what else is he saying to the servant? When he said, *Lord, I knew that you are a difficult or hard man, because you reap where you have not sown and gather where you have not scattered; and I was afraid and went away and hid your talent in the ground; here you are, you have what is yours. And he answered, Wicked and slothful servant, much rather precisely because you knew me to be difficult and hard, reaping where I have not sown and gathering where I have not scattered,* my very avarice ought to have taught you that I look for a profit on my money. *You ought therefore to have given my money to the money-lenders, and I on my return would have demanded what is mine with interest* (Mt 25:24-27).

Did he say, "You should have given and demanded"? So we, brothers and sisters, are the ones who give to the money-lenders; the one who's going to demand it back with interest is still to come. Pray that he may find us all ready.

Sermon 149

On Four Questions: First on Peter's Vision: Acts 10;
Then on Three Questions Arising from the Sermon on the Mount:
Matthew 5:16 and 6:1; 6:3; 5:44

Scholars differ on when this sermon was preached — whether in 400, 404-405, or 412. The homily displays Augustine's creative allegorical skills and high-lights his understanding of the symbolic role of Peter as representative of the whole Church. The bishop is particularly sensitive to not boring his listeners.

Peter's vision

1. I remember that the day before last Sunday I became a debtor to your holi-nesses on the subject of some questions propounded from the scriptures. The time has come to pay, if the Lord is good enough to enable me to do so. I don't like being in debt too long, except for the one debt of charity, which is always being paid and always being owed.

I said then that we would have to inquire about Peter's vision, what the meaning could be of that *receptacle, like a linen sheet let down from heaven by four lines, and in it were all the four-footed beasts of the earth, and creeping things, and birds of the sky*; and of what Peter was told by the divine voice, *Kill and eat* (Acts 10:11-13); and of its being done three times, and then taken up.

Immoderate use of God's gifts is a sin

2. Against those who choose to think that Peter was being ordered by the Lord God to be a glutton, it is easy to argue. First of all, because even if we were to choose to take literally the command, *Kill and eat*, killing and eating is not a sin; what is a sin is immoderate use of God's gifts, which he has allotted to human use.

Eating certain meat — symbolic sign of future realities

3. The Jews, you see, had accepted that there were certain animals which they could eat, and others from which they must abstain. The apostle Paul makes it clear that they received this law as a symbolic sign of future realities, when he says, *Therefore let no one judge you over food or over drink, or over the matter of a festival day or new moon or sabbath, which is all a shadow of things to come* (Col 2:16-17). And so now, in the time of the Church, he says somewhere else, *All things are clean for the clean; but it is bad for the person who eats so as to give cause for offense* (Tit 1:15; Rom 14:20).

At the time the apostle wrote this, you see, there were people who used to eat meat in such a way as to make the weak stumble. You see, the sacrificial flesh of animals the diviners used to sacrifice was then sold in the butchers' shops, and many of the brethren used to abstain from eating any meat at all, in case even in ignorance they should come upon cuts from animals from which sacrifice had been made to idols. That's why the same apostle says elsewhere, in case consciences should be worried stiff with fear, *Anything up for sale at the butcher's, eat without asking any questions for the sake of conscience, for the earth is the Lord's and its fullness* (Ps 24:1). And again, *But if any unbeliever invites you, and you want to go, eat everything that is set before you without making any distinctions because of conscience. But if someone tells you that it is sacrificial meat, do not eat it, for the sake of the one who has pointed it out, and for the sake of conscience* (1 Cor 10:25-28). So in these matters everything is established as being clean or unclean, not in virtue of physical contact, but in virtue of purity of conscience.

The meaning of the forbidden animals

4. That's why a freedom has been granted to Christians that was not granted to Jews. It's because all the animals which the Jews were forbidden to eat are signs of things, and, as it says, *shadows of things to come*. As for example, what was prescribed for them that any animals which chew the cud and have cloven hoofs they could eat; but any which lack one or other of these conditions, or both of them, they should not eat; certain kinds of people are here signified who do not belong to the company of the saints.

The cloven hoof, you see, refers to morals, the chewing of the cud to wisdom. Why does the cloven hoof signify good morals? Because it doesn't slip easily; slipping up, you see, is the sign of sin. And how does chewing the cud refer to the teaching of wisdom? Because scripture says, *A desirable treasure rests in the mouth of the wise man, while the foolish man swallows it* (Prv 21:20 LXX). So those who hear, and out of carelessness forget, so to say swallow what they have heard, so that they no longer have a taste of it in the mouth, but just bury what they hear under forgetfulness. But those who meditate on *the law of the Lord day and night* (Ps 1:2) are chewing the cud, as it were, and enjoying the flavor of the word with a kind of palate of the heart. So the commandment given to the Jews signifies what sort of people do not belong to the Church, that is to the body of Christ, to the grace and company of the saints; those, namely, who are either heedless listeners, or have bad morals, or who are to be censured for both kinds of vice.

Christians not bound by Jewish observances

5. So too all the rest of the commandments given to the Jews in this way are shadowy signs of things to come. After the light of the world, our Lord Jesus Christ, has come, they are read only in order to be understood, not also in order to be observed. So Christians have been given the freedom not to observe this idle custom, but to eat what they like, in moderation, with a blessing, with thanksgiving. So perhaps Peter too was told *Kill and eat* in this sense, that he need

no longer be bound to Jewish observances; he was not, however, being ordered to satisfy an insatiable maw or become a disgusting glutton.

Symbolic meaning of Peter's vision

6. But all the same, to prove to you that all this was a symbolic showing, that vessel contained creeping things; could he possibly eat creeping things? So what does all this symbolism mean? That receptacle signifies the Church; the four lines it was hanging from are the four quarters of the earth, through which the Catholic Church stretches, being spread out everywhere. So all those who wish to go apart into a party, and to cut themselves off from the whole, do not belong to the sacred reality signified by the four lines. But if they don't belong to Peter's vision, neither do they do so to the keys which were given to Peter. You see, God says his holy ones are to be gathered together at the end from the four winds, because now the gospel faith is being spread abroad through all those four cardinal points of the compass. So those animals are the nations. All the Gentile nations, after all, were unclean in their errors and superstitions and lusts before Christ came; but at his coming their sins were forgiven them and they were made clean. Therefore now, after the forgiveness of sins, why should they not be received into the body of Christ, which is the Church of God, which Peter was standing for?

Peter represents the Church

7. It's clear, you see, from many places in scripture that Peter can stand for, or represent, the Church; above all from that place where it says, *To you will I hand over the keys of the kingdom of heaven. Whatever you bind on earth shall also be bound in heaven; and whatever you loose on earth shall also be loosed in heaven* (Mt 16:19). Did Peter receive these keys, and Paul not receive them? Did Peter receive them, and John and James and the other apostles not receive them? Or are these keys not to be found in the Church, where sins are being forgiven every day? But because Peter symbolically stood for the Church, what was given to him alone was given to the whole Church.

So Peter represented the Church; the Church is the body of Christ. Let him then receive the Gentiles now made clean, their sins having been forgiven; that's why the Gentile Cornelius had sent for him, and the Gentiles who were with him. This man's charities had been accepted and had cleansed him after a fashion; it only remained for him, like clean food, to be incorporated into the Church, that is, into the Lord's body. Peter, though, was worried about handing the gospel over to the Gentiles, because those of the circumcision who believed were not allowing the apostles to hand on the Christian faith to the uncircumcised; and they were saying they ought not to be admitted to share in the gospel unless they accepted circumcision, which had been the tradition of their ancestors.

(...)

The left and right hands

15. There are two questions left; but I'm afraid of being a burden to those of you who are easily bored, while again I'm afraid of cheating those of you who are still hungry. Still, I remember what I have answered, and what I am owing. It remains to see what the meaning is of, *Do not let your left hand know what your right hand is doing* (Mt 6:3); and also on the subject of loving one's enemy, why the people of old were apparently authorized to hate the enemies whom we are commanded to love. But what am I to do? If I explain these points briefly, perhaps I won't be understood in the right way; if I take a bit longer, I'm afraid I may weigh you down with the load of my words, rather than lift you up with the results of my explanations. But certainly, if you grasp less than is satisfactory to you, hold me in your debt to talk about these things more fully some other time. All the same we ought not to leave them now with absolutely nothing said about them.

The left hand of the spirit is material greed, the right hand of the spirit is spiritual love. So if, when you give alms, you mix in some greed for temporal advantages, hoping to gain some such thing from that good work, you are mixing the left hand's knowledge with the right hand's works. But if you come to a person's help out of simple charity and with a pure conscience before God, with an eye on nothing else but to please the one who enjoins such acts, then your left hand does not know what your right hand is doing.

The one storeroom

16. The question, though, about loving one's enemy is more difficult, and cannot be answered so shortly. But while you are listening, pray for me; and perhaps God will quickly give us what we imagine to be difficult. We all live, after all, from one and the same storeroom, because we are all in one and the same household. So what you and I imagine to be hidden away somewhere in the furthest corner cupboard, perhaps the one who is dealing out the rations is placing on the doorstep, so that it can be most easily given to those who ask for it.

The Lord Christ himself loved his enemies; didn't he say, hanging on the cross, *Father, forgive them, because they do not know what they are doing* (Lk 23:34)? Stephen followed his example, when stones were being hurled at him, and said, *Lord, do not hold this crime against them* (Acts 7:59). The servant imitated his Lord, so that none of the other servants might be reluctant, and imagine that doing this was something only the Lord could do. So if it's too hard for us to imitate the Lord, let us imitate our fellow servant. After all, we have all been called to the same grace.

So why were the ancients told, *You shall love your neighbor and hate your enemy* (Mt 5:43)? Because, perhaps they were also told the truth; but it has been told us more openly, thanks to the succession of the ages, through the presence in our New Testament age of the one who could see what needed to be concealed and what plainly revealed and for whom. Thus, you see, we do have an enemy whom we are never ordered to love; but it's the devil. *You shall love your neighbor*, a human being; *and hate your enemy*, the devil. But while enmities often arise among men toward us, in the minds of those who by their disbelief give the devil a foothold and become his instruments, enabling him to operate through the children of unbelief; still it can happen that a person relinquishes his ill-will and is converted to the Lord. So even while he is still ranting and roaring, and persecuting, he is to be loved, and prayed for, and done good to. In this way you will both fulfill the old commandment to love your neighbor, a man, and hate your enemy, the devil; and also fulfill the new one to love your enemies, men, and to pray for those who persecute you.

(...)

Sermon 161

On the Words of the Apostle, 1 Corinthians 6:15:
Do You Not Know that Your Bodies Are Members of Christ? Etc.

Hill suggests a date around 415-420 and presumes that this sermon was preached in Hippo, but there is no compelling evidence. The sermon demonstrates the bishop's courage in taking on difficult pastoral issues and boldly confronting the problem of adultery. Augustine does not hesitate to use fear of eternal punishment as an incentive to exhort fellow Christians to avoid immoral behavior. The sermon memorably describes the relationship between the soul and the body: "The life of the body is the soul; the life of the soul is God." Only the just are truly free. At the conclusion Augustine praises virginity as a higher form of loving based on greater beauty of the heart.

Your body is a member of Christ

1. We heard the apostle, when he was read, rebuking and curbing human lusts, and saying, *Do you not know that your bodies are members of Christ? So shall I take the members of Christ, and make them the members of a harlot? Perish the thought!* (1 Cor 6:15). So he said our bodies are the members, or parts, of Christ; since Christ is our head in that he became man for our sakes, the head of which it is said, *He is the savior of our body* (Eph 5:23); his body, though, is the Church. So if our Lord Jesus Christ had only taken on a human soul, only our souls would be his members. But in fact he also took on a body, and thus is a real head for us, who consist of soul and body; and therefore our bodies too are his members.

So if any of you were longing so intensely for a little fornication that you were ready to undervalue yourself, and in yourself to despise yourself, at least don't despise Christ in yourself; don't say, "I'll do it, I'm nothing; *all flesh is grass* (Is 40:6)." But your body is a member of Christ. Where were you off to? Come back. Over what precipice, so to say, were you so keen to throw yourself? Spare a thought for Christ in yourself, recognize Christ in yourself. *So shall I take the members of Christ, and make them the members of a harlot?* The harlot, you see, is the woman who agrees to commit adultery with you; and perhaps she is a Christian, and is also taking the members of Christ and making them the members of an adulterer.

Together you are despising Christ in yourselves, and not recognizing your Lord, or giving a thought to your price, your true value. What sort of Lord is that, do you think, who makes his slaves into his brothers and sisters? Brothers and sisters, though, wasn't enough; he also had to make them into his members. Has such great worth, such tremendous dignity, really grown so cheap? Because it was bestowed so graciously, is it not to be treated with respect? If it hadn't been bestowed, it would be desired; because it has been bestowed, is it to be despised?

Your body is a temple of the Holy Spirit

2. But these bodies of ours, which the apostle says are members of Christ thanks to Christ's body, which he took to himself of the same nature as our bodies; so these bodies of ours the apostle also says are the temple of the Holy Spirit in us, whom we have received from God. Because of Christ's body, our bodies are members of Christ; because of Christ's Spirit dwelling in us, our bodies are the temple of the Holy Spirit. Which of these two within you are you prepared to despise? Christ whose member you are, or the Holy Spirit whose temple you are?

As for that harlot, who agreed to join you in wrongdoing, I don't suppose you will dare to take her into your bedroom, where you have your marriage bed; but you look for some neglected, dirty corner of your house, where you can wallow in your dirty games. So you show respect to your wife's bedroom, and you show no respect to the temple of your God? You don't bring a shameless woman into the place where you sleep with your wife, and you go yourself to a shameless woman, though you are God's temple? I rather think God's temple is something better than your wife's bedroom.

Wherever you go, after all, Jesus can see you; the one who made you, and when you were lost redeemed you, and when you were dead died for you. You don't know who you really are; but he never takes his eyes off you, not to help you this time, but to punish. Yes, *the eyes of the Lord are on the just, and his ears are turned to their prayers*; but he added something immediately, to terrify those who were granting themselves a false security, who were saying to themselves, "I'll do it; after all God doesn't stoop to watching me doing such dirty things." Listen to what comes next, consider who you belong to, since wherever you go Jesus can see you: *But the frown of the Lord is on those who do evil, to destroy their memory from the land* (Ps 34:15-16). From which land? The one of which it says, *My hope are you, my portion in the land of the living* (Ps 142:5).

The immoral person is excluded from the kingdom of God

3. It may well be, after all, that a thoroughly bad man, unjust, an adulterer, quite shameless, a fornicator is glad that he does all this, and he grows old, though lust doesn't grow old in him, and he says to himself, "Is it really true, that *the frown of the Lord is on those who do evil, to destroy their memory from the land*? Here am I, already an old man, who have been doing so many bad things from my first steps right up until today, I've buried many chaste men before myself, have myself led the funeral cortège of many a chaste young man to the grave, and I the old lecher have outlived the chaste and virtuous. What's this that it says here: *The frown of the Lord is on those who do evil, to destroy their memory from the land*?"

There's another land, where there's no lecher, there's another land in the kingdom of God. *Make no mistake; neither fornicators, nor idol-worshippers, nor adulterers, nor the effeminate, nor men who lie with men, nor thieves, nor the grasping, nor the drunken, nor the scurrilous shall possess the kingdom of God* (1 Cor 6:9-10). Which means, he will destroy their memory from the land. Many people, you see, who commit such sins nurse fond hopes for themselves. It's because of people who live abandoned lives, and nurse fond hopes of the kingdom of heaven, where they are not going to get to, that it says, *He will destroy their memory from the earth.* You see, there will be a new heaven and a new earth, where the just shall dwell; there the ungodly, there the evil, there the utterly wicked people are not permitted to dwell. Any of you like that should choose now where you would like to dwell, while there is still time, still the chance for you to change.

Two dwellings: eternal fire and the eternal kingdom

4. There are, in fact, two kinds of dwelling; one in eternal fire, the other in the eternal kingdom. Granted that in the eternal fire this person and that will endure different torments; there they will be, all the same, there they will all be tormented; one less the other more, because it will be more tolerable for Sodom in the day of judgment than for another city; and some people travel round sea and land to make one proselyte, and when they've made one, they make him twice as much a child of gehenna as they are themselves. Granted that some there get double, some single measure; granted that some get more, others less; it's not a district where you would naturally choose yourself a place. Even the milder torments there are worse than any that you dread in this world.

Think how you tremble if someone starts telling tales about you, in case you should be put in prison; and are you yourself going to live a bad life against yourself, to get yourself put in the fire? You quake in your shoes, you're worried to death, you grow pale, you hurry to the church, you beg to see the bishop, you fall at his feet. He asks why.

"Save me," you say.

"What's going on?"

"Look, that man's telling lies about me."

"And what's he going to do to you?"

"My lord, I'm being blackmailed; my lord, I'm about to be put in prison. Take pity on me; save me." That's how much prison is feared by people, how they are afraid of being locked up; and they aren't afraid of being burnt up in gehenna!

Then again, when misfortunes come thick and fast, and affliction strikes more cruelly than ever, and strikes to the point of death, when the one concern is to save the person from dying, from being killed, and everyone starts shouting that first aid must be given, begging for any kind of assistance: "Come and help; quickly, for his life's sake; S.O.S., for his soul's sake." The whole urgency of the disaster lies in the expression "for his life's sake, for his soul's sake." Certainly one must rally round, and not refuse to respond to this fear; what can be done must be done, by whomever it can be done.

The death of the soul is to be feared more than the death of the body

5. But all the same, I myself would like to question this person whose life is in danger, and who is tugging at my heart-strings on that account; because he is saying, "Hurry, for my soul's sake." I've an easy answer to make to this: "Certainly I will hurry for the sake of your flesh; if only you would hurry yourself for the sake of your soul. And you know perfectly well that I'm hurrying for the sake of your body, not for the sake of your soul. I prefer to listen to Christ speaking the truth, than to you muttering out of a false fear. I mean, the Lord himself says, *Do not fear those who kill the body, but cannot kill the soul* (Mt 10:28). Sure, you want me to hurry for the sake of your soul. But look, the one you're afraid of, and at whose threats you turn pale, can't kill your soul; he can strike savagely as far as the body is concerned; just stop striking savagely yourself at your soul. It can't be killed by him, it can be by you; not with a spear, but a tongue. The enemy who stabs you puts an end to this life. *But the mouth that lies kills the soul* (Wis 1:11)."

So from the things people are afraid of in this time, they should work out what they really ought to be afraid of. I mean, they're afraid of prison, and not afraid of gehenna? Afraid of the inquisitor's torturers, and not afraid of hell's angels? Afraid of torment in time, and not afraid of the pains of eternal fire? Afraid, finally, of dying for a moment, and not afraid of dying forever?

God is the life of the soul

6. This fellow who's going to kill you, whom you're afraid of, who gives you the shudders, whom you're running away from, dread of whom won't let you sleep, and if you see him in a dream when you are asleep, you're paralyzed with fright — what's he going to do to you? He is going to exclude your soul from your flesh; consider where your soul goes when it's excluded. You see, the only way he

can kill your flesh is by excluding from it the soul by which your flesh lives. It is, of course, by the presence of your soul that your flesh lives, and as long as your soul is present in your flesh, your flesh is of necessity alive. But the fellow who's seeking your death wants to eject from your flesh your life, by which your flesh lives.

Do you imagine there isn't some life by which your soul itself lives? The soul, you see, is a kind of life, by which your flesh lives. Do you imagine there's no other kind of life, by which your soul itself lives? Or rather, that just as your flesh has life, namely the soul by which your flesh lives, the same also happens with your soul, that it has some kind of life of its own? And that just as the flesh, when it dies, breathes out the soul which is its life, so too the soul, when it dies, breathes out some life of its own? If we can discover what this life is, not of your body, because that is your soul; but the life of the life of your body, that is, the life of your soul; if we can discover it, then I think that, proceeding from this death in which you are afraid of your soul being ejected from the flesh, you ought to be much more afraid of that other death, afraid of the life of your soul being cast out of your soul.

So let me put it very shortly; and indeed, why am I taking so long about it? The life of the body is the soul, the life of the soul is God. The Spirit of God dwells in the soul, and through the soul in the body, so that even our bodies are the temple of the Holy Spirit, whom we have received from God. You see, the Spirit comes to our souls, because *the love of God has been poured forth in our hearts through the Holy Spirit who has been given to us* (Rom 5:5); and the one who possesses the chief part possesses the whole. In you, of course, the chief part is played by what is the better. God, by holding what is the better, which is your heart, your mind, your soul, automatically through the better part possesses the lower, which is your body.

Therefore, let your enemy rage, let him threaten you with death, let him carry out the threat if he is allowed to, and exclude your soul from your flesh; only don't let your soul exclude its life from itself. If you are justified in your lamentations, and imagine yourself saying to that powerful enemy of yours, "Don't strike, spare me the shedding of my blood"; can't God say to you, *Have mercy on your own soul by pleasing God* (Sir 30:24)? Perhaps your soul is saying to you, "Ask him not to strike, because otherwise I'm leaving you. I mean, if he does strike, I can't stay with you. Ask him not to strike, if you don't want me to leave you." Now, who is it, saying to you, "if you don't want me to leave you"? It's you yourself; you, I mean, doing the talking, are your soul. So if that man strikes the flesh, it's you that flee away, you that depart, you that emigrate; what's lying in the dust is dust. Where will that thing be that animated the dust? The thing that was given you by the breath of God, where will that be? If it hasn't breathed out its life, that is its God, it will be in him whom it hasn't lost, in him whom it has not excluded from itself. But if you yield to your soul's weakness when it says to you, "He strikes, and I leave you," aren't you afraid of God when he says to you, "You sin, and I leave you"?

If you are afraid of death, love life

7. From a vain, futile sort of fear, let us move on to grasping a useful sort. It's a vain sort of fear which all people have who are afraid of losing temporal things, people who are going to move on some time or other, and are petrified of moving on, always wanting to put off what they cannot finally avoid. This kind of fear people have is futile; and yet it's there, and it's very strong, and it can't be resisted. It's about this that people have to be rebuked and taken to task, about this they should be mourned and wept over, that they are afraid of dying, and the only thing they ever do about it is to die a bit later. Why don't they do something about not dying? Because whatever they do, they can't manage not to die.

"But they can do something, surely, to ensure that they never die?" No way at all. No matter what you do, however vigilant you are, wherever you run away to, whatever defenses you try out, however much money you spend to ransom yourself, however cunningly you trick your enemy, you can't trick that fever. All you are doing to ensure you don't die promptly at the hand of your enemy, only ensures that you will die sometime later on at the hand of a fever.

You do have something, though, you can do in order not to die ever. If you are afraid of death, love life. Your life is God, your life is Christ, your life is the Holy Spirit. You don't please him by behaving badly. He won't live in a tumbledown temple, he won't enter a filthy temple. But plead with him to clean a place out for himself; plead with him to build himself a temple; to construct himself what you have destroyed; to restore himself what you have defaced; to raise up himself what you have thrown down. Cry out to God, cry out inside, cry out where he is listening; because that's also where you sin, and where he sees you; cry out to him there, where he is listening and can hear you.

It's dread of the bad, not yet love of the good

8. And when you've straightened out your fear, and begun to be afraid in a useful sort of way, not of temporal torments but of the pain of eternal fire, and for that reason avoided being an adulterer; because that's what we were talking about, remember, on account of the apostle's saying, *your bodies are members of Christ* (1 Cor 6:15); so when you have refrained from starting on a course of adultery for the very good reason that you are afraid of burning in everlasting fire, you don't yet deserve to be praised. You don't indeed need to be grieved over as before, but still you are not yet deserving of praise.

After all, what's so splendid about being afraid of punishment? There is something splendid, but that's loving justice. I'm going to question you, and find you out. As for you then, observe my interrogating you out loud, and conduct your own interrogation of yourself in silence. So I say to you:

"When lust overpowers you, and the other party is agreeable, why don't you commit adultery?" And you will answer:

"Because I'm afraid of gehenna, afraid of the punishment of eternal fire, afraid of Christ's judgment, afraid of the devil's company, and of being punished by him and burning with him."

What now? Am I going to say, "You are wrong to be afraid," as I did say to you about that rival of yours because he was aiming at killing your body? In that case, yes, I was right to say, "You're wrong to be afraid; God has reassured you, saying *Do not fear those who can kill the body*." But now when you tell me, "I'm afraid of gehenna, I'm afraid of burning, I'm afraid of being punished forever," what am I to say? "You're wrong to be afraid"? "It's futile to be afraid"? I daren't say that, considering that the Lord himself removed fear only to introduce fear; and he went on, after saying *Do not fear those who can kill the body, and afterward have nothing they can do; but fear the one who has the authority to kill both body and soul in the gehenna of fire; yes, I tell you, fear that one* (Lk 12:4-5; Mt 10:28). So when the Lord instills fear, and instills it very forcefully, and by repeating the word gives double emphasis to the threat, am I going to say, "You are wrong to be afraid"? That I will not say. Certainly be afraid, there's nothing better to be afraid of, there's nothing you should fear more.

But I've a further question for you: "If God didn't see you when you do it, and nobody would convict you of it at his judgment, would you do it?" You take a look at yourself. After all, you can't answer all my words openly. Examine yourself. "Would you do it?" If you would, it means you are afraid of punishment, you don't yet love chastity, you don't yet have charity. You are afraid like a slave; it's dread of the bad, not yet love of the good. But go on being afraid, all the same, so that this dread may keep guard over you, may lead you to love. This fear, you see, with which you are afraid of gehenna, and that's why you don't do wrong, is restraining you; and in this way, though your mind inside wants to sin, it won't let it. Fear, you see, is a kind of warder, it's like the pedagogue of the law; it's the letter threatening, not yet grace assisting. All the same, let this fear keep guard over you, while being afraid stops you doing wrong, and in good time charity will come. It enters your heart, and to the extent that it comes in, fear goes out. Fear, you see, was ensuring that you didn't do it; charity is ensuring that you don't want to do it, even if you could entertain the idea with impunity.

The more charity enters, the less fear becomes

9. I have said what you should be afraid of, I have said what you should be desirous of. Set your sights on charity, let charity come in. Open the door to her by being afraid to sin, open the door to love that doesn't sin, open the door to love that lives uprightly. When she comes in, as I had started to say, fear begins to go out. The more she enters, the less fear becomes. When she has come in completely, there will be no more fear left, because *perfect love casts out fear* (1 Jn 4:18).

So charity comes in and drives out fear. She doesn't come in, however, without a companion of her own. She has her own fear with her, and brings him in herself; but he is a chaste fear, *abiding for ever and ever* (Ps 19:9). Slavish fear is the kind which makes you afraid of burning with the devil; chaste fear is the kind which makes you afraid of displeasing God. Consider, my dearest friends, our ordinary human feelings, and question them. A slave is afraid of offending his master, in case he has him flogged, has him put in chains, has him shut up in a dungeon, has him worn out on the treadmill. It's because he's afraid of these things that the slave doesn't sin; but when he judges the eyes of his master are not on him, and there is no witness he can be convicted by, he does it. Why does he do it? Because he was afraid of the punishment, and didn't love justice.

A good man, though, a just man, a free person—because only the just are really free; *everyone*, you see, *who commits sin is the slave of sin* (Jn 8:34)—a free person takes delight in justice in itself; and if he could sin without anybody seeing and being a witness, he dreads God too as a witness. And if he could hear God saying to him, "I can see you when you sin, I won't sentence you to damnation, but you displease me"; he doesn't want to displease the eyes of a father, not of a fearsome judge, and so he's afraid, not of being damned, not of being punished, not of being tortured, but of spoiling his father's joy, of displeasing the eyes of someone who loves him. You see, if he himself loves, and is aware of his Lord loving him, he doesn't do what would displease the one who loves him.

The power of dishonest love

10. Take a look at the smooth, dishonorable sort of lovers; ask yourselves if any wanton and worthless fellow, out of love for a woman, dresses otherwise than in a fashion that pleases her, dresses differently from the way his beloved likes, or wears any jewelry except what she likes. She only has to say, "I don't want you to wear a coat like that"; he doesn't wear it. If she says to him in winter, "I just love you in shirt-sleeves," he prefers to shiver, rather than displease her. Is she ever going to sentence him to eternal damnation for displeasing her? Is she ever going to send him to prison, ever going to bring along the torturers? The one and only thing he's afraid of is this: "I won't see you"; the one and only thing he trembles at is this: "You shan't see my face." If a shameless hussy can say this and strike terror, does God say it, and not strike terror? Obviously he does, and how! But only if we love him. If we don't love, though, we are not terrified by that. But we are terrified like slaves, are we, of fire, of gehenna, of the horrifically savage threats of hell, of the countless swarms of the devil's angels, and of his punishments? Well, if we don't love that other thing very much, at least let us fear all this.

Visible accessories

11. So let's have no more fornications. *You are God's temple, and the Spirit of God dwells in you. If anyone reduces God's temple to ruins, God will ruin him* (1 Cor 3:16-17). Marriage is lawful, you shouldn't go looking for anything more. After all, it isn't a very big burden that has been imposed on you. A greater love has imposed a greater burden on virgins. Virgins have declined to do what was allowed,

in order to be more pleasing to the one to whom they vowed themselves. They have aimed at that greater beauty of the heart. "What orders are you giving?" It's as though they said, "What orders are you giving? That we shouldn't live in adultery, is that your command? For love of you, we are doing more than you require."

About virgins, says the apostle, *I have no command of the Lord's*. So why are they doing this? *But I have some advice to give* (1 Cor 7:25). These women, then, are so loving that earthly marriage is not worth much to them anymore, earthly embraces no longer attract them, and they have acknowledged the commandment to the extent of not turning down the advice; in order to be more pleasing to the one they love, they have paid more attention to their make-up and their ornaments. You see, the more attention people pay to the ornaments and finery of this body, that is of the outer self, the greater the neglect of the inner self; while the less attention they pay to finery for the outer self, the more the inner self is decked out with the finery of beautiful behavior.

That's why Peter too says, *Not adorning themselves with braided hair*, as soon as he said "adorning themselves," what else should literal-minded, sensual people think of but these visible ornaments, and visible finery? He immediately turned our thoughts away from what greed would be looking for. *Not*, he said, *with braided hair, and not with gold, or pearls, or expensive dresses; but that hidden self of the heart, who is rich in the sight of God* (1 Pt 3:3-4). God, I mean to say, would not give riches to the outer self, and leave the inner self in want; he has given invisible riches to the invisible self, and invisibly adorned the invisible self.

The love of virgins

12. Eager to please with such adornments, God's young ladies, the holy virgins, have neither desired what was allowed them nor consented to what they were being forced into. Many of them, you see, have had to overcome the contrary efforts of their parents with the fire of heavenly love. Father was furious, mother was in tears; she didn't care, because she had before her eyes *one comely of form above the sons of men* (Ps 45:2). It was for him, and him alone that she longed to adorn herself, in order to care only and wholly for him. Because *the woman who is married thinks about the affairs of the world, how to please her husband; but the one who is unmarried thinks about God's affairs, how to please God* (1 Cor 7:34).

Notice what it means to love. He didn't say, "She thinks about how not to be condemned by God." That, after all, is still that slavish fear, the guardian indeed of bad people, to make them refrain from bad behavior, and by refraining become fit to open their doors to charity. But these women are not thinking how to avoid being punished by God, but how to please God with their inner beauty, with the elegance of the hidden self, the elegance of the heart, where they are naked to his eyes — inwardly naked, not outwardly; both inwardly and outwardly pure and untouched.

At least let the virgins teach married men and women not to go in for adultery. They do more, over and above what is lawful; let these at least not do what is not lawful.

Sermon 164

On the Words of the Apostle, Galatians 6:2.5: *Bear Your Burdens for Each Other*,
and on Those Others: *Each One Will Bear His Own Burden*; Against the Donatists,
Preached Shortly After the Conference Held at Carthage

> This sermon was preached at Hippo, shortly after Augustine's return from the
> conference of 411 at Carthage, in September or October of that year. Augustine
> reflects at length on the meaning of *Bear one another's burdens* in Gal 6:2.
> Some burdens, namely personal sins, must be carried alone; others can be
> shared. Augustine cites Mt 11:30: *My yoke is easy and my load is light.*
> Both riches and poverty, namely having too much or not enough, can be
> burdensome. The rich and the poor can reduce each other's load. Ordinary
> Christians should not attempt to judge Donatists and others who receive Com-
> munion unworthily, but bishops do not have the same luxury.

The law of Christ won't be fulfilled, unless we carry our burdens for each other

1. Truth is urging us through the apostle to bear our burdens for each other;
and in so urging us to bear our burdens for each other, he shows how profitable it
is for us to do that, by going on to say: *And in this way you will fulfill the law of
Christ* (Gal 6:2); which won't be fulfilled, unless we carry our burdens for each
other. What these burdens are, and how they are to be carried — since of course
we must all try as best we can to fulfill the law of Christ — I will try with the
Lord's help to show you. Remember to exact to the last farthing what I have
proposed to demonstrate; and when I have paid the debt, don't go on claiming it.
This is what I have proposed to demonstrate, with the Lord assisting both my
intention and your prayers on my behalf: what the burdens are which the apostle
tells us to carry for each other, and how they are to be carried. If we do this, the
value he placed on it, that we would be fulfilling the law of Christ, will accrue
automatically.

We must distinguish between burdens

2. Somebody says, "Well, did the apostle speak all that obscurely, that you
should try to explain what these burdens are, or how they are to be borne for one
another?" There is a problem there, which forces us to distinguish between
burdens. Right in this very same section of the reading you have this statement: *But
each one will bear his own burden* (Gal 6:5). So it's already crossed your minds: if
each one will carry his own burden, how can he say, *Carry your burdens for each
other*? The only answer is that we must distinguish between burdens, or the apostle
will be thought to be contradicting himself. I mean, it isn't in some quite different
place, not in another letter, after all, not after all much earlier or later in this letter,

but in this very same place, so that these same words come next to each other, that he stated both things; both that each one will carry his own burden, and that he urged and exhorted us to carry our burdens for each other.

Two kinds of burdens

3. So there are some burdens of a sort that each carries his own, and one doesn't carry it with another, nor throw it onto another. And there are other burdens of a sort that you quite rightly say to your brother, "I'll carry it with you," or "I'll carry it for you." So if such a distinction has to be made, understanding is not all that easy.

So against those who thought that a person can be contaminated by somebody else's sins, the apostle answered, *Each one will bear his own burden.* Again, against those in whom this could make room for indifference, so that being assured they wouldn't be contaminated by other people's sins, they wouldn't bother to correct anyone: *Carry your burdens for each other.* It's briefly stated, the distinction briefly made; and this, I rather think, hasn't prevented the truth being made plain. I mean, you both heard it briefly, and understood it quickly. I haven't seen into your minds; but I heard your voices bearing witness to your minds. So now, as being sure of what we have understood, let us discuss the matter a little more widely, not to gain understanding, but to appreciate better what has been understood.

The burdens are sins

4. The burdens, of which we all have to carry our own, are sins. To human beings carrying the loads of these detestable burdens, and sweating under them all to no purpose, the Lord says, *Come to me, all you who labor and are overburdened, and I will refresh you* (Mt 11:28). How does he refresh them, burdened with sins, except by pardoning sins? Delivering an address to the whole world from the platform, so to say, of his sublime authority, he cries out, "Listen, human race; listen, children of Adam; listen, race of unproductive toilers! I can see your toil; you just see what I have to give. I know, you are laboring and overburdened; and what is even more pitiable, you are strapping loads of calamity onto your own shoulders; worse still, you are asking for burdens to be added to these, not asking for them to be laid aside."

Avarice and laziness

5. Could any of us in a short time run through the vast number and variety of these loads? However, let us mention a few of them, and from these make an informed guess about the rest. Consider a man burdened with the load of avarice; look at him sweating, gasping, thirsty under this load — and with all his

efforts adding to the load. What are your expectations, money-grubber, as you hug your burden, and harness the evil load to your shoulders with the straps of greed? What are your expectations? Why all the toil? What are you panting for, what are you lusting after? "To satisfy Avarice, of course."

Oh vain hopes, and good-for-nothing business! So you are really expecting to satisfy Avarice? She can weigh you down, you can't satisfy her. Or perhaps she doesn't weigh very much? Under this load have you lost your wits as completely as that? Avarice doesn't weigh very much? So why does she wake you up from sleep, why does she sometimes not even allow you to sleep? And perhaps together with her you have another burden of laziness, and these two absolutely worthless loads, which fight each other into the bargain, weigh you down and tear you apart. After all, they aren't giving you the same orders, they aren't issuing similar commands. Laziness says, "Sleep"; Avarice says, "Get up." Laziness says, "You don't need to endure cold weather." Avarice says, "You must even put up with storms at sea." The first says, "Have a nice long holiday." The other won't let you take a holiday.

Her command is not only, "Carry on," but also, "Sail across the sea, seek out countries you do not know. There is merchandise to be exported to India." You don't know the language of the Indians, but the lingo of Avarice seems universally intelligible. You will come, unknown, to someone unknown to you; you give, you receive, you buy, you bring. You have braved dangers to arrive, you experience more dangers on your return. Tossed about in a storm at sea, you cry out, "God, deliver me!"

Can't you hear him answering, "Why should I? Did I send you? It was Avarice who told you to go and acquire what you didn't have. What I told you to do, was to give what you did have to the poor at your door, without any bother. She sent you to the Indies to bring back gold. I set Christ at your door, from whom you could buy the kingdom of heaven. You work so hard at the bidding of Avarice; at my bidding you don't work at all. We have both issued instructions; you haven't listened to me; you've obeyed her, let her deliver you."

Let charity lay upon you a yoke that will do you good

6. How many people are carrying these loads! How many of you, shouldering such loads, applaud me now as I speak against them! They have come in with their loads, they go out with their loads. They have entered in love with money, they depart in love with money. I, in speaking against these loads, have been working very hard. If you applaud, drop what you are carrying.

Finally, don't listen to me; listen to your emperor as he cries out, "*Come to me, all you who labor and are overburdened.*" You don't really come, you see, unless you stop laboring. You want to run to me, but you can't do it with those heavy loads. "*Come to me,*" he says, "*all you who labor and are overburdened, and I will refresh you* (Mt 11:28). I am pardoning your past sins, I will take away what was blinkering your eyes, I will heal the sores on your shoulders. I will certainly relieve you of your loads, but I won't let you go entirely free of loads. I will relieve you of bad loads and place good ones upon you." After saying, you see, *and I will refresh you*, he added, *Take my yoke upon yourselves* (Mt 11:29). Greed had laid an evil yoke upon your neck, let charity lay upon you a yoke that will do you good.

Carry the feathers of peace, accept the wings of charity

7. *Take my yoke upon you, and learn from me.* If any and every kind of human teaching has lost all value for you, *learn from me.* Christ the teacher, the master, is calling out, the only Son of God who alone is truthful, true, the truth, is calling out, *Learn from me.*

Learn what? That *in the beginning was the Word, and the Word was with God, and the Word was God, and all things were made through him* (Jn 1:1-3)? Shall we ever be able to learn that from him, to manufacture a world, to fill a sky with lights, to arrange the changes of day and night, to instruct the seasons and ages how to run their course, to endow seeds with their energy, to fill the earth with animals? The heavenly master is not telling us to learn any of that. He does all that as God.

But because this God was also willing to be man, insofar as he is God, listen to him for your renewal; insofar as he is man, listen to him so that you can imitate him. *Learn*, he says, *from me*; not how to manufacture the world and create various natures; nor even those other things which he achieved here, hiddenly as God, manifestly as man. He doesn't mean them either: "Learn from me how to drive out fevers, put demons to flight, raise the dead, command the winds and the waves, walk on the waters"; he doesn't mean that either by *Learn from me*. Yes, he did give these powers to some of his disciples, to others he didn't give them. But what he says here, *Learn from me*, he says to everyone; nobody is to be excused from this commandment: *Learn from me, since I am meek and humble of heart* (Mt 11:29).

Why hesitate to pick up this load? This load's heavy, is it, humility and a sense of duty? This load's heavy, is it, faith, hope, charity? These, you see, are the things that make you humble, make you meek. And notice that you won't be overburdened if you listen to him: *for my yoke is easy, and my load is light* (Mt 11:30). What does he mean by light? That if it weighs anything, it's still less? That avarice weighs more, justice less? I don't want you to understand it like that. This load is not a weight to burden you with, it's wings to help you fly. Birds too, after all, have the load of their feathers. And what are we to say? They carry them, and are carried by them. They carry them on the ground, they are carried by them in the sky. If you want to show kindness to a bird, especially in summer, and say, "This poor little bird is burdened with feathers," and start pulling off this burden, the poor little bird you wanted to help will remain grounded. So carry the feathers of peace, accept the wings of charity. That's the load for you, that's how the law of Christ will be fulfilled.

Each one carries a burden

8. There are other kinds of burden. Look now, some money-grubber or other comes in. You know he's a money-grubber, he stands beside you, and you are not a money-grubber. You are even kind-hearted, you give what you have to the poor, you don't pant after what you haven't got; you listen to the apostle saying, *Command the rich of this world not to be haughty, nor to hope in the uncertainty of riches, but in the living God, who provides us abundantly with everything to enjoy; let them be rich in good works, to give readily, to share, to treasure up for themselves a good foundation for the future, that they may lay hold of true life* (1 Tm 6:17-19). You've heard this, acknowledged it, learnt it, held onto it, done it. Go on doing what you are doing, don't slack off, don't stop. *It is the one who perseveres to the end that shall be saved* (Mt 10:22).

You have done a person a good turn, the person's ungrateful; don't be sorry for having done a good turn, don't pour away by being sorry what you have filled up by being kind. Say to yourself, "This one I've done it for doesn't notice; that other one for whose sake I've done it does notice. If this one did notice, if he wasn't ungrateful, it would do him more good than me. Let me hold fast to God, since what I do doesn't escape his notice; not only what I do, but even what I do in my heart. Let me place my hopes in his rewarding me, since he doesn't require a witness for my good deed."

That's the sort of person you are, and perhaps here among the people of God a money-grubbing grabber of other people's property, who always has his eyes on other people's goods, comes and stands next to you. You know what he is, and he's a believer, or rather he's called a believer. You can't drive him out of the church, there's no way you can correct him by punishing or rebuking him; he's going to approach the altar with you. Don't worry. *Each one will bear his own burden* (Gal 6:5). Remember the apostle, and approach the altar yourself without anxiety; *each one will bear his own burden.*

Only don't let him say to you "Carry it with me"; because if you agree to share avarice with him, it won't lessen the burden, but instead the two of you will be weighed down by it. So let him carry his load, and you yours, seeing that when your Lord tossed that sort of load off your shoulders, he placed another one on them; he tossed aside the load of greed, replaced it with the load of love. So each person, according to the nature of his desires, carries his own load, a bad person a bad one, a good person a good one.

The burdens of poverty and riches

9. Now turn again to that other precept: *Carry your burdens for each other* (Gal 6:2). What you have, you see, is Christ's burden, which enables you to carry with someone else his own burden. He's poor, you're rich; his burden is poverty; you haven't got a burden like that. Take care you don't say, when the

poor man pleads with you, *Each one will carry his own burden*. Pay heed in this case to the other precept: *Carry your burdens for each other*.

"Poverty is not my burden, it's my brother's burden." Consider whether riches aren't a greater burden for you. You haven't got poverty as a burden, but you have got riches as a burden. If you look at it in the right way, this is a burden. He's got one burden, you another. Carry his with him, and let him carry yours with you, so that you end up by carrying your burdens for each other. What's the burden of poverty? Not having anything. What's the burden of riches? Having more than is needed. He's overburdened, and you're overburdened too. Carry his having nothing with him, let him carry your having more than enough with you, so that your loads may be spread equally.

You see, if you give to a needy person, who's got nothing, you reduce his load for him, which consisted of having nothing; if you give him something, he starts having something; his burden, that's called not having anything, is reduced. And he in turn is reducing your burden, which is called having more than enough. The two of you are walking along God's road in the journey through this world. You were carrying vast superfluous provisions, while he didn't have any provisions at all. He has attached himself to you, desiring to be your companion; don't ignore him, don't turn him away, don't leave him behind. Can't you see how much you are carrying? Give some of it to him, since having nothing he's carrying nothing, and you will be helping your companion, and he will be relieving you. I rather think that is a sufficient explanation of the apostle's considered judgment.

The Donatists

10. Don't let them sell you smoke, those who say, "We are holy, we don't carry your loads, that's why we don't communicate with you." Those big men carry loads of division, the big men are carrying loads of exclusion, loads of schism, loads of heresy, loads of dissension, loads of animosity, loads of false testimony, loads of trumped up accusations. We have tried and we are continuing our efforts to lift these loads from the shoulders of our brothers. They, I'm afraid, love them and hug them to themselves, they refuse to become a little smaller, because their heads have been swollen by their very loads. It's true, I suppose, a person who puts down a load which he was hoisting on his neck seems to grow smaller; but it's a weight he has put down, not his own stature.

Don't break the Lord's nets

11. "But I," you say, "am not communicating with other people's sins" — as though what I'm saying to you were "Come and communicate with other people's sins!" That's not what I'm saying. I know what the apostle would say, and I say the same. Just because of other people's sins, if they really were such and not rather your own, you shouldn't desert God's flock which is a mixture of sheep and goats;

you shouldn't leave the Lord's threshing-floor, as long as the straw is being threshed; you shouldn't break the Lord's nets, as long as they are hauling both good and bad fish to the shore.

"And how," you say, "am I to put up with someone whom I know to be bad?" Isn't it better you should put up with him than that you should put yourself down outside? Here's how you are to put up with him: you only have to pay attention to the apostle saying *Each one will carry his own burden* (Gal 6:5); that judgment should set you free. It means you wouldn't be communicating with him in avarice, but you would be communicating with him at the table of Christ. And what harm would it do you, if you communicated with him at the table of Christ? The apostle says, *For whoever eats and drinks unworthily is eating and drinking condemnation to himself* (1 Cor 11:29). To himself, not to you. Certainly if you are a judge, if you have received authority to judge according to Church rules, if he is accused before you, and convicted by true documents and witnesses, place restrictions on him, rebuke, excommunicate, degrade him. Tolerance must keep awake in such a way that discipline doesn't go to sleep.

The case of Caecilian

12. "But," they say, "Caecilian was condemned." Condemned? By whom? First in his absence, then though innocent by betrayers. These things have been formally alleged, inserted in the records, proved. They did indeed try to weaken the force of truth, and attempted as best they could to cloud its clear skies over with the clouds of unsubstantial considerations. The Lord stood by us, his clear sky overcame their clouds. And notice how, without meaning to, they absolved the Church of the whole world, in whose communion we rejoice, whatever sort of people we may be in her. It's not ourselves but she that we are protecting, defending, preserving, as we defend the Lord's threshing-floor.

Yes, it's on behalf of the Lord's threshing-floor that I am loudly claiming a hearing. As for who I may be on the floor, you don't have to care about that; I'm waiting for the winnowing. I don't want you, I say, to care about that; or if you insist on caring, don't do it by wrangling, but in a way that will enable you to heal your brothers. Take care of the straw, if you can; but don't abandon the grain if you can't take care of the straw. Sometimes the straw too is pushed off the threshing-floor; occasionally even some grains, but not far off. But there are good workmen who go round the threshing-floor, and with rakes and brooms clean up what has been pushed off the edge, and pull it and summon it back onto the floor, even if it means pulling and compelling.

The rakes and brooms for cleaning up are these secular laws. Call them back, drag back the wheat even with some earth mixed up with it, or the wheat may be lost because of the earth. Caecilian was condemned, they say. He was condemned once in his absence, cleared three times when present. We answered them; and though they are the sort of men you can't teach anything, we reminded them briefly about their own doings, and said, "Why do you bring up against Caecilian the council of seventy bishops which passed judgment on him in his absence? Several judgments were passed by a council of Maximianists against Primian in his absence." We said, "Caecilian was condemned by those people in his absence, Primian was condemned by these in his absence. Just as these aren't prejudicial to the absent Primian, so in the same way those couldn't have been prejudicial to the absent Caecilian."

The Donatists condemned by their own opinions

13. What do you suppose they answered, when caught in this cleft stick? What could they say, after all? How could they avoid being trapped in the nets of truth? In order to break these nets by violence, what do you think they said, very briefly, and absolutely in *our* favor? As a matter of fact much, practically everything they said, worked in our favor, as the Acts will indicate, which your graces are of course going to read as soon as ever they are published. But as regards this particular point, I beg and beseech you by Christ to hold onto it, to repeat it, to have it always on your lips. You see, a briefer, surer, clearer judgment in our favor could not have been given.

So what did he say, when we made this objection: "These cannot be prejudicial to Caecilian, any more than those are to Primian"? Their spokesman replied, "You cannot prejudge one case by another, nor one person by another." What a perfectly short, clear, true reply! You see, he didn't know what he was saying, but like Caiaphas when he was high priest, he prophesied. "You cannot prejudge one case by another, nor one person by another." If you can prejudge neither one case by another, nor one person by another, it follows that each one must bear his own burden.

Now let him go and make his objection about Caecilian to you; not to you, any individual, but to the whole world; let him cast Caecilian in its teeth. When he does that, in fact, he is casting an innocent man in the teeth of innocent people; the records will show this in the clearest possible way. Caecilian was cleared. But suppose he wasn't cleared, suppose he was found guilty; listen to the echo of your own voice coming from the whole world: "You can neither prejudge one case by another nor one person by another." You incurably spiteful, heretical soul, since you are giving judgment against yourself, why do you accuse the judge? If I bribed him to give judgment for me, who bribed you to condemn yourself?

The error of the Donatists

14. If only some time or other they would just think about this, think about it even late in the day, think about it at least when their spite and arrogance is on the wane; if only they would come to their senses, question themselves, examine

themselves, answer themselves, for the sake of the truth not be afraid of the people whom they have so long palmed off with falsehood. They are afraid of shocking them, you see; they blush for shame before human weakness, and they don't blush for shame before the unconquerable truth.

What they are afraid of, of course, is people saying to them, "So why did you deceive us? Why did you lead us astray? Why did you say so many bad and untrue things?"

Their answer should be, if they feared God, "It was human to be mistaken, it's diabolical to remain in the mistake out of spiteful animosity. It would indeed have been better if we had never gone wrong; but at least let us do the next best thing and finally correct our error. We deceived you, because we were deceived ourselves. We preached untruths, because we believed others who preached untruths."

They should say to their people, "We have gone wrong together, let us together withdraw from our error. We were your leaders into the ditch, and you followed us when we led you into the ditch; and now follow us when we lead you back to the Church." They could say that; they would be saying it to indignant people, saying it to angry people; but they too would sooner or later lay aside their indignation, and come, even though late in the day, to love unity.

We must be patient with the Donatists

15. We, however, brothers and sisters, must be patient with them. The eyes we are trying to care for are inflamed and swollen. I am not saying we should stop caring for them, but that we should avoid provoking them to greater bitterness by crowing over them. Let us mildly give a reasonable account of the affair, not proudly brag about victory. *The servant of the Lord*, says the apostle, *should not wrangle, but be gentle with everyone, willing to learn,* patient, correcting those who think differently with modesty, in the hope that God would grant them repentance, and they would recover their wits from the devil's snares, by whom they are being held captive according to his will.

So put up with them patiently if you are sound of mind and body yourselves; put up with them patiently insofar as you are of sound health yourselves. Which of us, after all, is perfectly sound of mind and body? When the just king sits upon his throne, which of us will be able to boast that he has a pure heart, or which of us will be able to boast that he is clean of all sin? So as long as we are such, this is what we owe ourselves, that we should carry our burdens for one another.

Turning to the Lord, etc.

Sermon 172

On the Words of the Apostle, 1 Thessalonians 4;13:
But We Do Not Wish You to Be Ignorant, Brothers, About Those Who Are Asleep,
So that You Should Not Be Saddened, Like the Rest Who Have No Hope
and About the Works of Mercy, by which the Dead Are Helped

There is no indication of its date or location, but this homily was certainly preached in a liturgical setting in which the dead were commemorated, similar to the present All Souls Day in the Latin Church. Augustine accepts the appropriateness of grief even for the believer, given the disruptive nature of death, but we should never lose sight of hope. The sermon provides an interesting glimpse into Christian funeral practices in Roman North Africa: processions, expensive burial arrangements, monuments, prayers, eucharistic sacrifice, alms. These rites serve both to soothe our human grief and to implore God's mercy to forgive the sins of our departed loved ones.

It's nature, not belief, that has a horror of death

1. The blessed apostle warns us not to be saddened about those who are asleep, that is about our dearest dead, like the rest who have no hope, hope namely in the resurrection and eternal imperishability. The reason why scripture usually and most appropriately says that they are asleep, is that when we hear that word "asleep," we need not despair in the least about their one day waking up. That's why we sing in the psalm, *Will the one who is asleep not be sure to rise again* (Ps 41:8)? So about the dead, those who love them naturally feel a certain sadness. It's nature, not belief, that has a horror of death. And death would not have happened to man but for the punishment that had been preceded by a grave fault.

And so if animals, which were so created that they would all die, each kind in due course, run away from death, cling to life, how much more should human beings do so, who would have lived without end if they had been willing to live without sin? And so it is that we cannot help being sad when those we love abandon us by dying. Because even if we know that it is not forever that they are leaving us while we have to stay behind, but that it is only for a short time that they are going ahead of us, and that we are going to follow; still, when death, so abhorrent to nature, overtakes someone we love, our very feeling of love for that person is bound to grieve. That's why the apostle did not advise us not to feel sad, but *not like the rest who have no hope*. So when our dear ones die, we are saddened by the necessity of losing them, but still cherish the hope of receiving them back again. Grief on the one hand, consolation on the other; there we are affected by human weakness, here restored by faith; there we feel pain according to our human condition, here we are healed by the divine promise.

We will only be able to enjoy after this life what we have earned in the course of it

2. So it is that funeral processions, crowds of mourners, expensive arrangements for burial, the construction of splendid monuments, can be some sort of consolation for the living, but not any assistance for the dead. It is not to be doubted, though, that the dead can be helped by the prayers of holy Church, and the eucharistic sacrifice, and alms distributed for the repose of their spirits; so that God may deal with them more mercifully than their sins have deserved. The whole Church, I mean, observes this tradition received from the Fathers, that prayers should be offered for those who have died in the communion of the body and blood of Christ, whenever their names are mentioned at the sacrifice in the usual place, and that it should be announced that the sacrifice is offered for them. When, however, works of mercy are performed for their sakes, who can doubt that this benefits those for whom prayers are not sent up to God in vain?

There can be no doubt at all that these things are of value to the departed; but to such of them as lived in such a way before they died, as would enable them to profit from these things after death. For those, you see, who have departed from their bodies without *the faith that works through love* (Gal 5:6) and its sacraments, acts of piety of this sort are performed in vain. While they were still here they lacked the guarantee of this faith, either because they did not receive God's grace at all, or received it in vain, and so stored up for themselves not mercy but wrath. So no new merits are won for the dead when their good Christian friends do any work on their behalf, but these things are credited to them as a consequence of their preceding merits. It was only while they lived here that they could ensure that such things would be of help to them after they ceased to live here. And so it is that when any of us finish this life, we will only be able to enjoy after it what we have earned in the course of it.

Tears should be quickly dried by the joy of faith

3. And so it is perfectly in order for loving hearts to grieve at the death of their dear ones, but with a sorrow that will let itself be assuaged; and to shed the tears that suit our mortal condition, but that are also prepared to be consoled. These should be quickly dried by the joy of the faith with which we believe that when the faithful die, they depart from us for only a little while, and pass on to better things. Let mourners also be comforted by the good offices of their fellow Christians, whether these consist of helping with the funeral arrangements or comforting the bereaved; or else there would be just cause for people to complain, *I waited for someone to share my grief, and there was none; for people to console me, and I could not find any* (Ps 69:20). Let proper care be taken, according to one's means, over burying the dead and constructing their tombs, because the holy scriptures count these things too among good works. People were praised in them, and held up as an example to us, not only as regards the respect shown to the remains of the patriarchs and other holy men and

women, and to the corpses of any human beings left lying unburied, but also as regards the body of the Lord himself.

By all means let us perform these last offices for our dead, and thereby soothe our natural human grief. But we should be much more punctilious, more pressing and more generous in seeing to those things which can help the spirits of the dead, such as offerings, prayers, and expenditure on good works and almsgiving; that is, if we love those who have died in the flesh, not the spirit, with an affection that is not merely of the flesh, but also spiritual.

Sermon 179

On the Words of the Apostle James 1:19.22: *But Let Each of You Be Quick to Hear, but Slow to Speak*, and on These Others in the Same Place: *But Be Doers of the Word, and Not Hearers Only*

Augustine preached this sermon as a "guest homilist" with an extra warmth and familiarity, which suggests his home town of Thagaste, some time before 409 or perhaps even before 405. Perhaps this explains the packed congregation referred to in section 10. The great danger for a bishop is to seek accolades and popularity, which results in pride. Augustine offers an extended reflection on Martha and Mary: Martha's difficult task of serving will be taken away, whereas Mary's delight in feeding on the bread of life, truth and justice will last forever. The sermon ends abruptly, which suggests that the original was probably lost.

It's a futile preacher outwardly of God's word, who isn't also inwardly a listener

1. The blessed apostle James is summoning us to be earnest hearers of the word of God, when he says, *But be doers of the word, and not hearers only, deceiving yourselves* (Jas 1:22). It isn't, you see, the one whose word it is, nor the one through whom the word is uttered, but your own selves that you deceive. So on the strength of this utterance flowing from the wellspring of truth, through the absolutely truthful mouth of the apostle, I too make bold to add my own exhortation to you; and while I'm exhorting you, to take a look at myself. After all, it's a futile preacher outwardly of God's word, who isn't also inwardly a listener. Nor are we, who have to preach the word of God to his various peoples, such strangers to common humanity and faithful reflection, that we are unaware of our own danger when we do so. However, he gives us the reassurance that while we are put in danger by our ministry, we are aided by your prayers.

Because to show you, brothers and sisters, how much safer a place you are standing in than we are, I need only quote another saying of this same apostle: *But let each of you be quick to hear, but slow to speak* (Jas 1:19). And so first let me speak about this duty and task of ours, because of this saying in which we are urged to be quicker to listen and slower to speak; and then, when I have made my excuses for this duty of ours which has us speaking so often, I will come to the point which I first put before you.

When I hear, that's when I rejoice

2. It is our duty to exhort you not to be hearers only of the word, but also doers. So because we speak to you so often, wouldn't anyone, who disregards our obligations, pass judgment on us when he reads, *But let every person be quick to hear but slow to speak* (Jas 1:19)? Well there you are, your eagerness never permits us to observe this recommendation. So you ought to be praying, to be supporting me whom you are compelling to be in danger.

And yet, my brothers and sisters, let me tell you something I would like you to believe, because you can't see it in my heart. Here I am, speaking to you so assiduously, at the bidding of my lord and brother, your bishop, and at your insistence; and yet I tell you that what gives me really solid satisfaction is listening. I repeat, the time my satisfaction, my joy, is really solid and unalloyed is when I am listening, not when I'm preaching. Then, you see, I can enjoy myself without a qualm. That pleasure has no side to it; where there is only the solid rock of truth, there's no need to fear the precipice of pride. And to show you that that's how it is, listen to what it says here: *To my hearing you will give exultation and gladness.* When I hear, that's when I rejoice. Then he went on to add, *The bones that have been humbled will exult* (Ps 51:8).

So when we are listening, we are humble; but when we are preaching, even if we aren't hurtling down the steep slope of pride, we are certainly at least having to put the brakes on. Even if I don't get a swollen head, I'm in real danger of getting one. But when I'm listening, I can enjoy it without anyone to cheat me of it, I can take pleasure in it without anyone noticing me. Such joy was also known by that friend of the bridegroom, who said, *The one who has the bride is the bridegroom; but the bridegroom's friend stands, and listens to him.* And that precisely is why he stands, because he listens to him. Because even the first man stood by listening to God, and fell by listening to the serpent. So, *the bridegroom's friend stands and listens to him; and with joy,* he says, *he rejoices because of the bridegroom's voice* (Jn 3:29). Not because of his own voice, but because of the bridegroom's. And yet, while he heard the bridegroom's voice inwardly, he did not fail to relay it to the people outwardly.

Mary was listening to the word of Christ

3. This is the part that Mary also chose for herself, who sat at the Lord's feet and listened at leisure to his word, while her sister was serving them and distracted with all the serving. John the Baptist was standing, she was sitting; yet she in her heart

was standing, and he in his humility was sitting. Standing, you see, signifies perseverance; sitting, humility. And to show you that standing signifies perseverance, the devil is said not to have had this perseverance; it's said about him, *He was a murderer from the beginning, and did not stand in the truth* (Jn 8:44). Again that sitting signifies humility is shown by that psalm, where it is reminding us about repentance, and says, *Arise after you have sat down, you who eat the bread of sorrow* (Ps 127:2). What's the meaning of *Arise after you have sat down*? *Whoever humbles himself shall be exalted* (Lk 14:11).

What a good thing, though, it is to listen, the Lord himself attests, when he speaks about Mary who was sitting at his feet and listening to his word. When her sister, you see, distracted with the serving, complained that she had been deserted by her own sister, what she heard from the Lord she had appealed to was: *Martha, Martha, you are busy with many things; for all that, one thing is needed. Mary has chosen the better part, which shall not be taken away from her* (Lk 10:41-42). Was it something bad, then, that Martha was doing? Can any of us find suitable words to express what a wonderfully good thing it is to offer hospitality to the saints? If to any saints at all, how much more to the head and chief members, Christ and the apostles? Don't all of you who practice this excellent virtue of hospitality, when you hear what Martha was doing, don't you all say to yourselves, "O blessed, O lucky woman, to have the honor of receiving the Lord; whose guests turned out to be the apostles, walking about in the flesh!" And you mustn't lose heart either, just because you can't do what Martha did, welcome Christ into your house with his apostles; he himself reassures you: *When you did it for one of these least of mine, you did it for me* (Mt 25:40).

So it's a great work, a really great work, which the apostle enjoins on us when he says, *contributing to the needs of the saints, practicing hospitality* (Rom 12:13). He also praises it in the letter to the Hebrews, when he says, *This way some people have entertained angels unawares* (Heb 13:2). So it's a great service, a great gift. And yet *Mary has chosen the better part*; because while her sister was worrying and slogging away, and taking care of all sorts of things, she was unoccupied, sitting down, listening.

Martha's part passes away, but the reward given for it does not pass away

4. The Lord, however, showed us what made that the better part. Immediately after saying *Mary has chosen the better part*; as though we were to query this, wishing to know what made it better, he added, *which shall not be taken away from her* (Lk 10:42). What are we to make of this, my brothers and sisters? If the reason the part she chose is better, is that it shall not be taken away from her, then undoubtedly Martha chose the part which will be taken away from her. Plainly, it will be taken away from all people who minister to the bodily needs of the saints; what they do will be taken away from them. After all, they are not always going to be ministering to the saints. I mean, what do they minister to, but infirmity? What do they minister to, but mortality? Who do they minister to, but the hungry and the

thirsty? All these things will have ceased to be, when this perishable thing has put on imperishability, and this mortal thing has put on immortality. When the need has disappeared, there will be no ministering to the need.

The hard work will be taken away, but the reward will be paid. Who will there be then to serve food to, when no one is hungry? Or drink, when nobody's thirsty? Or lodging, when nobody's a stranger? So in order to be in a position to pay the reward for this work, the Lord agreed to be in need, together with his disciples. He too was hungry and thirsty, not because he was compelled to be, but because he agreed to be. Yes, it was a good thing that the one through whom all things were made should be hungry; this after all would be a piece of good fortune for whoever might feed him. And when anybody fed the Lord, what was being given, who was it being given by, what was it being given from, who was it being given to?

What was being given? Food was being given to bread. Who was it being given by? Obviously, by those who wished to receive more. What was it being given from? Not from what was their very own, surely? I mean, what did they have that they had not received? To whom was it being given? Wasn't it to the one who had created both what he was receiving and the person he was receiving it from? Yes, this is a great service, a great work, a great gift. And yet *Mary has chosen the better part, which shall not be taken away from her*. So Martha's part passes away; but, as I said, the reward given for it does not pass away.

Mary was eating the one she was listening to

5. Mary's part, though, does not pass away. Notice how it doesn't pass away. What was Mary enjoying while she was listening? What was she eating, what was she drinking? Do you know what she was eating, what she was drinking? Let's ask the Lord, who keeps such a splendid table for his own people, let's ask him. *Blessed*, he says, *are those who are hungry and thirsty for justice, because they shall be satisfied* (Mt 5:6). It was from this wellspring, from this storehouse of justice, that Mary, seated at the Lord's feet, was in her hunger receiving some crumbs. You see, the Lord was giving her then as much as she was able to take. But the whole amount, such as he was going to give at his table of the future, not even the disciples, not even the very apostles, were able to take in at the time when he said to them, *I still have many things to say to you; but you are unable to hear them now* (Jn 16:12).

So what, as I was saying, was Mary enjoying? What was she eating, what was she drinking so avidly with the mouth of her heart? Justice, truth. She was enjoying truth, listening to truth, avid for truth, longing for truth. In her hunger she was eating truth, drinking it in her thirst. She was being refreshed, and what she was being fed from was not diminishing. What was Mary enjoying, what was she eating? I'm lingering on the point, because I'm enjoying it too. I make bold to say that she was eating the one she was listening to. I mean, if she was eating truth, didn't he say himself, *I am the truth* (Jn 14:6)? And what more yet can I say? He was being eaten, because he was bread: *I*, he said, *am the bread who came down from heaven* (Jn 6:41). This is the bread which nourishes and never diminishes.

What Mary chose was growing, not passing along and away

6. And so, would your graces please think hard. Look, we're talking about ministering to the saints, preparing food, serving drink, washing feet, making beds, welcoming under a roof; isn't all this going to pass away? But has anyone the nerve to say that we are now being fed on truth, but won't be fed on it when we attain to immortality? If we are now being fed on crumbs, won't we then have a full table? It was about that spiritual food, you see, that the Lord was talking, when he praised the centurion's faith and said, *Amen, I tell you, I have not found such great faith in Israel. And therefore I tell you, that many shall come from the east and the west, and shall sit at table with Abraham and Isaac and Jacob in the kingdom of heaven* (Mt 8:10-11). Far be it from us to think of that food on the table of that kingdom, as if it were the same sort as that about which the apostle says, *Victuals for the belly, and the belly for victuals; but God will eliminate both it and them* (1 Cor 6:13). Why will he eliminate them? Because there won't be any hunger there. What will be eaten there won't ever come to an end.

This, after all, is the reward he is promising his saints when he says, *Amen I tell you, that he will make them sit down; and he will pass along and wait upon them* (Lk 12:37). What can *he will make them sit down* mean, but he will make them rest, make them take their ease? And what about *he shall pass along* (or he will pass) *and wait upon them*? After this passing along of his he will wait upon them. Here, you see, Christ made a passing along, or a passing over. We will come to him where he has passed over to; there he is no longer passing over. You see, "Pasch" in the Hebrew language means Passover. The Lord indicated this, or rather the evangelist, where he said about the Lord, *But when the hour had come for him to pass over from this world to the Father* (Jn 13:1).

So what Mary chose was growing, not passing along and away. The human heart's delight, you see, in the light of truth, in the wealth of wisdom, the delight of a human heart, a faithful heart, a holy heart — no pleasure can be found to compare with it in any respect at all, not even to be called less than this. I mean, if you call anything less, it can imply that by growing it will become equal. I don't want to say "less"; I'm not making any comparison, it's of a different kind altogether, it's quite, quite different. Why is it, after all, that you are all paying attention, all listening, all excited, and when something true is said you are delighted? What have you seen, what have you grasped? What color has appeared before your eyes, what form, what shape, what figure, what lines and limbs, what beauty of body? None of these things. And yet you love it. I mean, when would you have applauded like that, if you didn't love it? When would you have loved it, if you hadn't seen anything? And so, though I am not showing you any form of a body, any lines, color, beautiful movements, though I'm showing you nothing, you all the same are seeing, loving, applauding. If this delight in the truth is lovely now, it will be much lovelier then. *Mary has chosen the better part, which shall not be taken away from her* (Lk 10:42).

Inwardly, where nobody can see us, we are all hearers

7. I have shown your dearest graces, to the best of my ability, as far as the Lord has been kind enough to help me, how much safer a place you are standing in by listening than I am by preaching. You, in this way, are doing, after all, what we are all going to be doing then. I mean, there won't then be any teacher of the word, but only the Word as teacher. So we come now to the consequence, which it is up to you to put into practice, up to us to remind you about. You, after all, are hearers of the word, we its preachers. Inwardly though, where nobody can see us, we are all hearers; inwardly in the heart, in the mind, where he is teaching you, who prompts you to applaud. I, you see, am speaking outwardly, he is arousing you inwardly. So we are all hearers inwardly, and all of us, both outwardly and inwardly in the sight of God, ought to be doers.

How can we be doers inwardly? *Because whoever looks at a woman to lust after her, has already committed adultery with her in his heart* (Mt 5:28). He can even be an adulterer where no human eye can see, but God can certainly punish. So who is the doer inwardly? The one who does not look lustfully. Who is the doer outwardly? *Break your bread to the hungry* (Is 58:7). When you do that, your neighbor too can see it; but what spirit you do it in, only God can see. So, my dear brothers and sisters, *be doers of the word, and not hearers only, deceiving yourselves* (Jas 1:22), not God, not the one who's preaching. I, after all, or anyone else who preaches the word to you, can't see your hearts; what you are doing inside, in your thoughts, we can't see. Man cannot do it, but God is looking, since the human heart cannot be concealed from him. He can see with what eagerness you listen, what you think, what you grasp, how much you profit from what he supplies you with, how urgently you pray, how you beg God for what you haven't got, how you thank him for what you have; he knows all this, because he is going to demand his due. We bishops can invest the Lord's money in you; the rent-collector is coming, who said, *Wicked servant, you should have given my money to the bankers, and I, when I came, could have collected it with interest* (Mt 25:26-27).

To hear and to do is to build upon rock

8. So, my brothers and sisters, don't deceive yourselves, just because you come eagerly to hear the word, if you fail to do what you hear. Just think; if it's lovely to hear, how much more so to do. If you don't hear it at all, if you neglect the matter of hearing, then you are building nothing. If you hear and don't do, then you're building a ruin. On this matter Christ the Lord gave us an extremely apt comparison: *Whoever hears*, he said, *these words of mine and does them, I will compare him to a sensible man who builds his house upon rock. The rain poured down, the rivers came up, the winds blew, and struck that house, and it did not fall.* Why didn't it fall? *For it was founded upon rock.* So to hear and to do is to build upon rock. Because merely to hear is to build. *But whoever*, he says, *hears these words of mine and does not do them, I will compare him to a foolish man who builds.* He

too builds. What does he build? Here you are; *he builds his house*; but because he doesn't do what he hears, even by hearing *he builds upon sand*. So the one who hears and doesn't do, builds on sand; the one who hears and does, on rock; the one who doesn't hear at all doesn't build either on sand or on rock. But notice what follows: *The rain poured down, the rivers came up, the winds blew, and they struck at that house and it fell; and its ruin was complete* (Mt 7:24-27). What a sad, sad sight!

It's bad to hear and not do

9. So someone says, "What's the point of my hearing what I'm not going to do? Because by hearing," he goes on, "and not doing, I will be building a ruin. Isn't it safer to hear nothing?" That's an alternative, to be sure, that the Lord declined to touch on in the comparison he put forward. But he gave us a clue to the answer. In this world, you see, rain, winds, rivers are never still. You're not building on rock, so that they can come, but not throw you down? You're not building on sand, in case when they come they should tumble your house down? So because you are hearing nothing, you will be left just like that, without any roof at all. The rain comes, the rivers come; does that mean you're safe, because you are carried away naked, stripped of everything? So consider carefully just what part you have chosen for yourself. You won't find security, as you imagine, by not hearing. You will of necessity be overwhelmed, carried off, drowned.

So if it's a bad thing to build on sand, a bad thing to build nothing at all; the only good thing left is to build on rock. So it's bad not to hear; it's bad to hear and not do; the only thing left is to hear and to do. So, *be doers of the word, and not hearers only, deceiving yourselves* (Jas 1:22).

You can't excuse yourself

10. After such an exhortation, I'm afraid that instead of uplifting you with the word, I may crush you with desperation. Possibly, you see, there's someone in this packed congregation, one person perhaps, or two, or even several, who is inclined to pass judgment on me and say, "I would like to know if this guy who's speaking to me does all the things that he hears himself or says to others." My answer to him is, *But to me it is a very small matter to be judged by you or any human court* (1 Cor 4:3); since I too am able to know, partly at least, what I am; what I may be tomorrow I don't know. But to you, whoever you are that are bothered in this way, the Lord has given an assurance about me. You see, if I do what I say or what I hear, *be imitators of me, as I in my turn am of Christ* (1 Cor 4:16). But if I say and don't do, listen to the Lord: *What they say, do; but what they do, don't do* (Mt 23:3).

So if you have a good opinion of me, you can praise me; if a poor opinion you can accuse me; but you can't excuse yourself. I mean to say, how are you going to excuse yourself if you hurl an accusation against an evil preacher of the truth, who tells you God's word and does his own evil works; when your Lord, your redeemer, who shed his blood as your price, who enrolls you in his militia, and makes a brother out of his slave, when he never stops warning you and saying, *What they say, do; but what they do, don't do? For they say*, he goes on, *and do not do.* They say good things, do bad things; you, then, listen to the good things, and don't do the bad things.

Here you will answer, "How can I hear good things from a bad man? *Do they gather grapes from thorns?* (Mt 7:16)."

Sermon 184

On Christmas Day

Augustine's Christmas sermons rank among the finest examples of his preaching. They are imaginative, emotive and theologically rich, but never sentimental. They model Augustine's deep Christology with their accent on the divine humility of the incarnation, and they also show his devotion to the Virgin Mary. He loves to describe the newborn Christ as the speechless Word, playing on the meaning of the Latin, *infans* meaning "without speech." Hill parts company from Kunzelman and others who date this sermon after 412, and he argues for a much earlier date, based on the much more elaborate rhetorical style which Augustine was famous for in the early years following his ordination as a priest and bishop. The concluding section is a *tour de force* that powerfully brings to a climax the Christmas message.

Let the humble hold fast to the humility of God

1. The birthday of our Lord and Savior Jesus Christ, the day on which *Truth sprang from the earth* (Ps 85:11) and Day from Day was born into our day, has dawned once more, brought round again by the cycle of the year to be celebrated by us; *Let us rejoice and make merry on it* (Ps 118:24). For what the humility of such sublime greatness has bestowed upon us is grasped by the faith of Christians, while far from the comprehension of the godless; since God *has hidden these things from the wise and the prudent, and revealed them to the little ones* (Lk 10:21). So let the humble hold fast to the humility of God, in order that, helped by this wonderful conveyance as by a kind of vehicle for their weakness, they may arrive at the heights of God. As for the wise and the prudent there, they aim at the loftiness of God without believing in his humble lowliness; and so, by overstepping this and not reaching that, they have remained, empty and weightless, inflated and elated, at a windy middle level, suspended between heaven and earth.

They are indeed wise and prudent, but in the affairs of this world, not of the one by whom the world was made. Because if they were possessed of the true wisdom, which is from God and is God, they would understand that it was possible for flesh to be taken on by God without his being changed into flesh; they would understand that he took to himself what he was not, while remaining what he was; and that he came to us in a man without ever departing from the Father; and that he continued to be what he is, while appearing to us as what we are; and that his divine power was confined in the body of an infant without being withdrawn from the whole mass of the universe.

The whole universe is his work as he remains with the Father; his work as he comes to us is the virgin's child-bearing. The virgin mother indeed provided a demonstration of his greatness, being found a virgin after giving birth just as she was a virgin before conceiving, being found, not put, with child by her husband; without male intervention carrying a male in her womb; all the more blessed and admirable for receiving the gift of fertility without losing that of integrity. They prefer to regard this stupendous miracle as fiction rather than fact. Thus in Christ, true God and true man, they despise the human because they cannot believe it; they do not believe the divine because they cannot despise it. We, however, find the body of man in the humility of God all the more welcome, the more contemptible it seems to them; and the more they think it is impossible, the more divine it seems to us that a man was born by a virgin bringing forth.

Rejoice, all Christians; it is the birthday of Christ

2. So then, let us celebrate the birthday of the Lord with all due festive gatherings. Let men rejoice, let women rejoice. Christ has been born, a man; he has been born of a woman; and each sex has been honored. Now therefore, let everyone, having been condemned in the first man, pass over to the second. It was a woman who sold us death; a woman who bore us life. *The likeness of the flesh of sin* (Rom 8:3) has been born, so that the flesh of sin might be cleansed and purified. And thus it is not the flesh that is to be faulted, but the fault that must die in order that the nature may live; because one has been born without fault, in whom the other who was at fault may be reborn.

Rejoice, holy brothers, who, choosing above all to follow Christ, have not sought to get married. The one you have found to be so worth following did not come to you by way of marriage, in order to enable you to set aside that by which you came into the world. For you came by way of carnal marriage, without which he came to his spiritual marriage; and he has given you the grace to turn your backs on any thought of weddings, because it is you above all whom he has invited to the wedding. The reason you have not sought the state from which you were born, is that you have loved more than others the one who was not so born.

Rejoice, holy sisters, virgins; for you a virgin gave birth to the one whom you may marry without loss of virginity; neither by conceiving nor by giving birth can you lose what you love.

Rejoice, you just (Ps 33:1); it is the birthday of the Justifier. Rejoice, you who are weak and sick; it is the birthday of the Savior, the Healer. Rejoice, captives; it is the birthday of the Redeemer. Rejoice, slaves; it is the birthday of the one who makes you lords. Rejoice, free people; it is the birthday of the one who makes you free. Rejoice, all Christians; it is the birthday of Christ.

The two births of Christ

3. Born of his mother, he commended this day to the ages, while born of his Father he created all ages. That birth could have no mother, while this one required no man as father. To sum up, Christ was born both of a Father and of a mother; both without a father and without a mother; of a Father as God, of a mother as man; without a mother as God, without a father as man. Therefore, *who will recount his begetting* (Is 53:8), whether that one without time or this one without seed; that one without beginning or this one without precedent; that one which never was not, or this one which never was before or after; that one which has no end, or this one which has its beginning in its end?

Rightly therefore did the prophets foretell that he would be born, while the heavens and the angels announced that he had been. The one who holds the world in being was lying in a manger; he was simultaneously speechless infant and Word. The heavens cannot contain him, a woman carried him in her bosom. She was ruling our ruler, carrying the one in whom we are, suckling our bread. O manifest infirmity and wondrous humility in which was thus concealed total divinity! Omnipotence was ruling the mother on whom infancy was depending; was nourishing on truth the mother whose breasts it was sucking. May he bring his gifts to perfection in us, since he did not shrink from making his own our tiny beginnings; and may he make us into children of God, since for our sake he was willing to be made a child of man.

Sermon 187

On Christmas Day

Augustine's rich Christology is immediately apparent in the opening paragraph where, basing himself on John's prologue, he refers to the Word made flesh "through whom all things were made" as the "creator of His mother." Similarly, in an impressive rhetorical display, the bishop uses antithesis to hold together the human and divine natures in the one person of Christ: "Unspeakably wise, wisely speechless as an infant; filling the world, lying in a manger; directing the course of the stars, sucking his mother's breasts; so great in the form of God, so small in the form of a servant, in such a way that neither the greatness was diminished by the smallness, nor the smallness overwhelmed by the greatness." Hill opts for a date considerably before 411 and perhaps even before 400, based on Augustine's elaborate and laborious style. Hill also believes that the rhetorical sophistication suggests that the sermon was preached in Carthage rather than in Hippo.

The greatness and the humility of Christ

1. *My mouth shall speak the praise of the Lord* (Ps 51:15); of that Lord *through whom all things were made* (Jn 1:3), and who was himself made among all things; who is the revealer of the Father, creator of his mother; the Son of God from the Father without mother, the son of man from his mother without father; great as the day of the angels, little in the day of men; the Word, God before all times, the Word, flesh at the appropriate time; the maker and placer of the sun, made and placed under the sun; marshaling all the ages from the bosom of the Father, consecrating this day from the womb of his mother; remaining there, coming forth from here; producer of heaven and earth, appearing on earth under heaven; unspeakably wise, wisely speechless as an infant; filling the world, lying in a manger; directing the course of the stars, sucking his mother's breasts; so great in the form of God, so small in the form of a servant, in such a way that neither the greatness was diminished by the smallness, nor the smallness overwhelmed by the greatness.

When he took human limbs to himself, after all, he did not abandon his divine works; nor did he stop reaching mightily from end to end, and disposing all things sweetly. When he clothed himself with the weakness of the flesh, he was received, not locked up, in the virgin's womb; thus the food of wisdom was not withdrawn from the angels, while at the same time we were enabled to taste and see how sweet is the Lord.

The human word and the divine Word

2. Why should all this surprise us about the Word of God, seeing that this sermon I am addressing to you flows so freely into your senses, that you hearers both receive it, and don't imprison or corner it? I mean, if you didn't receive it, you wouldn't learn anything; if you cornered it, it wouldn't reach anyone else. And of course this sermon is divided up into words and syllables; and yet for all that, you

don't each take portions and pieces of it, as you would of food for the stomach; but you all hear it all, each of you hears it all. Nor am I afraid, while I'm talking, that one of you by hearing it may swallow it all, so that another would be left with nothing to eat; but I wish you all to be so attentive, cheating nobody's ears and mind, that each of you may hear it all, and leave all of it for the others to hear too. Nor does this happen at successive times, in such a way that the sermon being delivered first comes into you, then has to go out from you if it is to enter someone else; but it comes simultaneously to all of you, and the whole of it to each of you. And if the whole of it could be retained in the memory, just as all of you have come to hear the whole of it, so you could each go away with the whole of it.

How much more, then, could the Word of God, *through which all things were made* (Jn 1:3), and which while abiding in itself *renews all things* (Wis 7:27); which is neither confined in places, nor stretched out through times, nor varied by short and long quantities, nor woven together out of different sounds, nor ended by silence; how much more could this Word, of such a kind as that, make a mother's womb fruitful by assuming a body, while still not departing from the bosom of the Father; come forth from there to be seen by human eyes, from here continue to enlighten angelic minds; go forth from there to all the earth, from here to stretch out the heavens; from there become man, from here make man?

Thought and Word

3. None of you therefore should believe that the Son of God was converted and changed into a son of man; but rather we must believe that while remaining the Son of God he became the son of man, and that the divine substance was not consumed, while the human substance was perfectly assumed. Just because it says, you see, *the Word was God*, and *the Word became flesh* (Jn 1:1.14), it doesn't mean that the Word became flesh in such a way that it ceased to be God; considering that in that very flesh which the Word became Emmanuel was born, *God with us* (Mt 1:23).

Just as the word which we carry in the mind becomes voice when we utter it from the mouth; and yet it isn't changed into this voice, but remains whole in itself, while the voice is assumed to carry it out to others; and in this way what is to be understood can remain inside, and what is to be heard can sound outside. Yet for all that it's the same thing that is uttered in a sound as had previously sounded in silence; and thus when word becomes voice, it isn't changed into voice, but remaining in the light of the mind, it both goes forth to the listener in the voice of flesh it has assumed, and still does not abandon the one who thought it.

I don't mean the voice which is thought about in silence, and which is either Greek or Latin or any other language; but I mean when the matter itself, before any variety of expression in any language, is so to say naked to the intelligence in the bed-chamber of the mind, and which in order to come out from there is clothed in the voice of the speaker. Each of these, however, both what is being thought of by intelligence and what is sounding out loud in speech, is changeable and dissimilar; the first won't remain when you've forgotten it, nor will the second when you stop speaking. But *the Word of the Lord remains for ever* (Is 40:8), and abides unchanged and unchangeable.

Christ, God and man

4. And when from the world of time it took flesh, in order to come forth into our time-bound life, it did not in the flesh lose eternity, but rather on the flesh too bestowed immortality. Thus *he like a bridegroom coming forth from his chamber, exulted like a giant to run his course* (Ps 19:5). *Who, when he was in the form of God, did not think it robbery to be equal to God*; but in order for our sakes to become what he was not, *he emptied himself*, not losing the form of God, but *taking the form of a servant*; and through it *being made in the likeness of men*; not in his own proper substance either, but *being found in condition as a man* (Phil 2:6-7). All this, you see, that we are, whether in soul or in body, is our nature, but his condition; we, if we weren't this, wouldn't be at all; he, if he weren't this, would still of course be God.

And when he began to be this thing that he was not, he became man while remaining God, so that not just one of the following but each of them could be said with perfect truth: both *Since the Father is greater than I* (Jn 14:28), because he has become man; and *I and the Father are one* (Jn 10:30), because he remained God. Because if the Word had changed into flesh, that is God been converted into man, it's only *the Father is greater than I* that would be true; while *I and the Father are one* would be false, because God and man are not one thing. But perhaps he would be able to say, "I and the Father were one," not "are one." I mean, what he had been and has stopped being, obviously he isn't, but was. As it is, however, he could both truly say *The Father is greater than I* because of the form of a servant which he had taken, and also truly say *I and the Father are one* because of the true form of God in which he remained.

So he emptied himself among us, not by becoming what he was not in such a way that he would no longer be what he had been; but by concealing what he was and openly displaying what he had become. Accordingly, because the virgin conceived and bore a son, *a child is born for us*, on account of the manifest form of a servant. But because the Word of God which abides for ever became flesh, in order to dwell among us, on account of the form of God which is hidden but remains, we call his name, as Gabriel announced it, *Emmanuel.* He became man, you see, while remaining God, in order that the son of man too might rightly be called *God with us*; not one person being God, another being man.

And so let the world exult in the persons of all believers, for whose salvation the one through whom the world was made has come. The maker of Mary, born of Mary, the son of David, *David's Lord* (Mk 12:37), the seed of Abraham *who is before Abraham* (Jn 8:58), the maker of the earth, made on earth, the creator of heaven, created under heaven. He *is the day which the Lord has made*, and the Lord himself is the daylight of our minds. Let us walk in his light, *let us exult and be merry in it* (Ps 118:24).

Sermon 189

On Christmas Day

Kunzelmann and Fischer date this sermon to sometime before 410; Hill believes
that it was preached at a Christmas midnight Mass in Hippo and argues for a later
date based on the rhetorical style and the emphasis upon grace in section 2,
which Augustine would have stressed in his anti-Pelagian polemic. He employs
an engaging Socratic style of dialogue by proposing leading questions to the
congregation. The sermon reaches a peak in the memorable concluding para-
graphs, which lose none of their impact today.

Who can this day from day be?

1. This day has been sanctified for us by the day who made all days, about
whom the psalm sings, *Sing to the Lord a new song, sing to the Lord, all the earth.*
Sing to the Lord and bless his name; proclaim the good news of the day from day,
his salvation (Ps 96:1-2). Who can this day from day be, but the Son from the
Father, light from light? But that day who begot the day which would be born of
the virgin on this day; so that day has neither rising nor setting; the day I mean is
God the Father. Jesus, after all, would not be day from day, unless the Father were
day.

What is day but light? Not for eyes of flesh, not the light which is common to
human beings and animals, but the light which shines on angels, the light which
hearts are cleansed for seeing. This night, you see, is passing, the night in which
we are living now, in which the lamps of the scriptures are lit for us; and that is
coming, of which another psalm sings: *In the morning I will stand by and gaze*
upon you (Ps 5:3).

What justice can there be without faith?

2. So that day, the Word of God, the day which shines on the angels, the day
which shines in the home country we are in exile from, clothed himself with
flesh and was born of Mary the virgin. Born in a wonderful way; what could be
more wonderful than a virgin giving birth? She conceives, and is a virgin; she
gives birth, and is a virgin. The one who created her, you see, was created from
her, and he brought her fertility, he did not spoil her integrity.

Where did Mary come from? From Adam. Where did Adam come from?
From earth. If Adam's from earth, and Mary's from Adam, then Mary too is
earth. If Mary is earth, let us realize what we are singing: *Truth has sprung from*
the earth. What sort of benefit has this brought us? *Truth has sprung from the*

earth, and Justice has looked forth from heaven (Ps 85:11). The Jews, you see, as the apostle says, *not knowing the justice of God, and wishing to establish their own, did not submit to the justice of God* (Rom 10:3). From where can you or anyone get to be just? From yourself? Who is the poor man who can give himself bread? Who, if naked, can cover himself, unless he receives a garment? We didn't have any justice; the only things here were sins.

Where does justice come from? What justice can there be without faith, since *the just live by faith* (Rom 1:17)? Any who call themselves just without faith are lying. How can they not be lying, when there is no faith in them? If they want to speak the truth, let them turn to the truth. But it was so far away. *Truth has sprung from the earth.* You were asleep, it came to you; you were snoring, it woke you up. It made you a way along itself, in order not to lose you. So, because *truth has sprung from the earth*, our Lord Jesus Christ was born of the virgin; *Justice has looked down from heaven*, in order that people may have a justice which is not their own, but God's.

Christ was born that we might be reborn

3. What infinite consideration! Preceded by what fearful indignation! What was the indignation that preceded it? We were mortal, we were weighed down by sins, we were bearing our punishments. Every single human being, as soon as born, begins with misery. No need to look for a prophet; question the child as it's born, and see how it cries. So with this great indignation of God on the earth, what sort of consideration was suddenly shown? *Truth sprang from the earth.* He created all things, he was created among all things; he made the day, he came on the day; he was before all times, he set his seal on the times.

The Lord Christ is for ever, without beginning with the Father. And yet ask what today is; it's a birthday. Whose? The Lord's. Has he really got a birthday? He has. The Word in the beginning, God with God, has a birthday? Yes, he has. Unless he had a human birth, we would never attain to the divine rebirth; he was born that we might be reborn. Let nobody hesitate to be reborn; Christ has been born; born, with no need of being reborn. The only ones in need of rebirth are those who have been condemned in their first birth.

And so let his mercy come to be in our hearts. His mother bore him in her womb; let us bear him in our hearts. The virgin was big with the incarnation of Christ; let our bosoms grow big with the faith of Christ. She gave birth to the Savior; let us give birth to praise. We mustn't be barren; our souls must be fruitful with God.

The two births of Christ

4. The birth of Christ from the Father was without mother; the birth of Christ from his mother was without father; each birth was wonderful. The first was eternal, the second took place in time. When was he born of the Father? What do you mean, when? You're asking about "when" there, there where you won't find any time? Don't ask about "when" there. Ask about it here; it's a good question, when was he born of his mother. When was he born of the Father is not a good question. He was born, and he has no time; he was born eternal, from the eternal, coeternal. Why be astonished? He's God. Take divinity into consideration, and any reason for astonishment disappears.

And when we say he was born of a virgin, it's a great thing, you're astonished. He's God, don't be astonished; let astonishment give way to thanksgiving and praise. Let faith be present; believe that it happened. If you don't believe, it still happened, but you remain unbelieving. He agreed to become man; what more do you want? Hasn't God humbled himself enough for you? The one who was God has become man. The inn was crowded and cramped, so he was wrapped in rags, laid in a manger; you heard it when the gospel was read. Who wouldn't be astonished? The one who filled the universe could find no room in a lodging-house; laid in a feeding trough, he became our food.

Let the two animals approach the manger, the two peoples. *The ox*, you see, *recognizes its owner, and the donkey its master's manger* (Is 1:3). Be in attendance at the manger; don't be ashamed of being the Lord's donkey. You will be carrying Christ, you won't go astray, walking along the way; the way is sitting on you. Do you remember that young donkey that was brought to the Lord? Don't any of you feel ashamed — that's what we are. Let the Lord sit upon us, and take us wherever he wants. We're his mount, we're going to Jerusalem. With him seated on us we aren't weighed down, but lifted up; with him guiding us, we can't go wrong. We are going to him, we are going by him, we are not going off the rails.

Sermon 190

On Christmas Day

Augustine typically preaches a high Christology in his Christmas sermons, as evidenced here in his assertion that Jesus "chose not only the mother of whom he would be born, but also the day on which he would be born," an assertion that would be problematic for the typically lower Christologies which have prevailed in the past few decades. The bishop's treatment of gender equality, on the other hand, should resonate well with contemporary sensibilities: "He himself created both sexes; and that's why he wished to honor each sex in his birth, having come to liberate each of them.... The male sex is honored in the flesh of Christ; the female sex is honored in the mother of Christ." Hill suggests that the elaborate style demands an earlier date than that assigned by Kunzelmann and Fischer, namely about 395. Augustine is an early witness to Mary's virginity *ante partum, in partu* and *post partum*. He also sees Mary as the great model of the Church in so far as she is both mother and virgin.

Even the day of Christ's birth contains the mystery of his light

1. Our Lord Jesus Christ, who was with the Father before he was born of his mother, chose not only the mother of whom he would be born, but also the day on which he would be born. Fallible human beings often choose days, one for planting, another for building, another for setting out, and sometimes even for marrying a wife. When people do this, the reason they do it is in order that something already born, so to say, may grow up or turn out well. Nobody, however, can choose the day on which actually to be born. But he was able to choose both, because he was able to create both. Nor did he choose the day in the same way as people do, who vainly hang the fates of individuals on the dispositions of the stars. I mean, in this case the one who was born was not made lucky by the day, but he gave good luck to the day on which he was graciously pleased to be born.

Because even the day of his birth contains the mystery of his light. That, you see, is what the apostle says: *The night is far advanced, while the day has drawn near; let us throw off the works of darkness and put on the armor of light; let us walk decently as in the day* (Rom 13:12-13). Let us recognize the day, and let us be the day. We were night, you see, when we were living as unbelievers. And this unbelief, which had covered the whole world as a kind of night, was to be diminished by the growth of faith; that's why, on the day we celebrate the birth of our Lord Jesus Christ, the night begins to be encroached upon, and the day to grow longer.

So, brothers and sisters, let us keep this day as a festival; not, like the unbelievers, because of that sun up there in the sky, but because of the one who made that sun. That which was the Word, you see, became flesh, in order to be able for our sakes to be under the sun. Under the sun, indeed, in the flesh; but in divine greatness over the entire universe, in which he placed the sun. Now, though, he is also over that sun even in the flesh, the sun which people worship instead of God, because in their mental blindness they cannot see the true sun of justice.

Christ wished to honor each sex in his birth

2. So, Christians, let us celebrate on this day, not his divine, but his human birth, by which he adapted himself to us, in order that by means of the invisible one made visible we ourselves might pass over from visible things to invisible. Catholic faith, you see, obliges us to accept two births for the Lord, one divine, the other human; the first apart from time, the second in time; both, however, wonderful; the first without mother, the second without father. If we can't grasp this one, when will we ever tell the tale of that one?

Who can grasp this new, unheard of novelty, unique in the history of the world, something unbelievable that has become believable and is unbelievably believed throughout the whole world; that a virgin should conceive, a virgin should give birth, and a virgin she should remain in giving birth? Faith grasps what human reason cannot work out; and where reason falls back, faith marches on. Who's going to say, after all, that the Word of God *through whom all things were made* (Jn 1:3) could not make himself flesh even without a mother, just as he made the first man without either father or mother?

But the fact is, he himself created both sexes, male and female; and that's why he wished to honor each sex in his birth, having come to liberate each of them. You know, of course, about the first man's fall, how the serpent didn't dare speak to the man, but made use of the woman's services to bring him down. Through the weaker he gained a hold over the stronger; and by infiltrating through one of them he triumphed over both. In order, therefore, to make it impossible for us with a show of righteous, horrified indignation, to put all the blame for our death on the woman, and to believe that she is irredeemably damned; that's why the Lord, *who came to seek what was lost* (Lk 19:10), wished to do something for each sex by honoring them both, because both had got lost. In neither sex, then, should we wrong the Creator; the birth of the Lord encouraged each to hope for salvation. The male sex is honored in the flesh of Christ; the female is honored in the mother of Christ. The serpent's cunning has been defeated by the grace of Jesus Christ.

Both speechless infant and Word

3. So let each sex be born again in the one who was born today, and let each celebrate this day; not as the day on which the Lord Christ began to be, but on which the one who was always with the Father brought to light the flesh he had received from his mother; bringing his mother fertility, not depriving her of

integrity. He's conceived, he's born, he's an infant. Who is this infant? Infant, you see, means one who cannot *fari*, that is, cannot speak. So he's both speechless infant and Word. He says nothing through the flesh, he teaches through angels, by whom the prince and shepherd of shepherds is announced to the shepherds; and he lies in the manger, the feeding trough, as fodder for the faithful beasts. This had been foretold, you see, by the prophet: *The ox recognizes its owner, and the donkey its master's manger* (Is 1:3).

That's why he sat on the little donkey, when he entered Jerusalem to the plaudits of the crowd going ahead and following behind. Let us in our turn recognize him, let us approach the manger, eat the fodder, carry the Lord who directs us, so that under his guidance we may come to the heavenly Jerusalem. Christ's birth from his mother bears the stamp of weakness; but from the Father comes all-embracing greatness. Among the days of time he has a day of time; but he is himself eternal day from eternal day.

That weakness might become strong

4. Rightly are we stirred by the voice of his psalm, as of a heavenly trumpet, when we hear, *Sing to the Lord a new song, sing to the Lord, all the earth. Sing to the Lord and bless his name* (Ps 96:1-2). So let us recognize, and proclaim, *the day from day* who was born in the flesh on this day. Day the Son from day the Father, God from God, light from light. This, you see, is the salvation about which it says elsewhere, *May God have mercy on us and bless us; may he shed the light of his countenance upon us; that we may recognize your way on earth, among all the nations your salvation* (Ps 67:1-2). What he means by *on earth* he repeats by *among all the nations*; and what he means by *your way* he repeats by *your salvation*.

We remember that the Lord said himself, *I am the way* (Jn 14:6). And just now when the gospel was read, we heard how the old man, the blessed Simeon, had received a divine response that he would not taste death unless he had first seen the Christ of the Lord. When he took the infant Christ in his arms, and recognized how great this little one was, *Now, Lord*, he said, *you are letting your servant go, according to your word, in peace; since my eyes have seen your salvation* (Lk 2:29-30).

So let us proclaim the good news of *the day from day, his salvation*; let us proclaim *among the nations his glory, among all the peoples his wonders* (Ps 96:2-3). He lies in a manger, but he holds the whole world in his hands; he sucks his mother's breasts, but feeds the angels; he is swaddled in rags, but clothes us in immortality; he is suckled, but also worshiped; he could find no room in the inn, but makes a temple for himself in the hearts of believers. It was in order, you see, that weakness might become strong, that strength became weak. Let us therefore rather wonder at than make light of his birth in the flesh, and there recognize the lowliness on our behalf of such loftiness. From there let us kindle charity in ourselves, in order to attain to his eternity.

Sermon 199

On the Lord's Epiphany

The feast of the Epiphany started in the East with an emphasis on both the baptism of Christ and the arrival of the magi. It was introduced to Africa and the West sometime in the fourth century with an almost exclusive emphasis on the magi. Based on its elaborate rhetorical style, Hill suggests a date before 400 for this sermon, and perhaps even before Augustine's ordination as a bishop in 396. Augustine is distinctly opposed to any notion of astrology as supporting a fatalism which would limit human freedom and responsibility.

Christ the cornerstone

1. Recently we celebrated the day on which the Lord was born of the Jews; today we are celebrating the one on which he was worshiped by the Gentiles; because *salvation is from the Jews* (Jn 4:22); but this *salvation reaches to the ends of the earth* (Is 49:6). On that day the shepherds worshiped him, on this one the Magi. To those the message was brought by angels, to these by a star. Both learned about him from heaven, when they saw the king of heaven on earth, so that there might be *glory to God in the highest, and on earth peace to people of good will* (Lk 2:14).

For he is our peace, who made both into one (Eph 2:14). Already from this moment, by the way he was born and proclaimed, the infant is shown to be that cornerstone; already from the first moments of his birth he appeared as such. He began at once to tie together in himself two walls coming from different directions, bringing the shepherds from Judea, the Magi from the East; *so that he might establish the two in himself as one new man, making peace; peace for those who were far off, and peace for those who were near* (Eph 2:15.17). Thus it is that those hurrying up from nearby on the very day, and these arriving today from far away, marked two days to be celebrated by posterity, and yet both saw the one light of the world.

The Jews did not understand the time of Christ's coming

2. But today we must speak about these ones who were led to Christ by faith from far distant lands. They came, you see, and they asked for him, saying, *Where is the one who has been born as king of the Jews? For we saw his star in the East, and we have come to worship him* (Mt 2:2). They make an announcement and ask a question, they believe and they seek; representing, as it were, those who walk by faith and long for sight. Hadn't other kings of the Jews already been born so many times in Judea? How is it that this one is recognized by foreigners in the sky, sought by them on the earth; shines out on high, lies low in lowliness? In the East the Magi see a star, and in Judea they perceive the new-born king. Who is this king, so small, so great; not yet talking on earth, already promulgating edicts in the heavens?

He had given the Magi such a brilliant sign in the sky, and revealed to their minds that he was born in Judea; and yet for our sakes, because he wanted to become known to us from his holy scriptures, he wished them too to believe his prophets about him. In their search, you see, for the city in which the one had been born whom they longed to see and worship, they were under the necessity of interrogating the leading Jews; so that these would have to answer them from holy scripture, which they had at their fingertips but not in their hearts; unbelievers answering believers about the grace of faith, liars in themselves, truthful against themselves. What, after all, would it have cost them to become their companions in their quest for the Christ, when they heard from them that they had seen his star and had come eagerly to do him homage; to guide them to Bethlehem of Judah, which they had pointed out from the divine books, together with them to see, together to understand, together to do homage?

Now, however, having pointed out to others the fountain of life, they themselves died of thirst. They became for the Magi just so many milestones; they pointed the way to travellers walking along the road, but themselves remained inert and unmoving. The Magi were seeking in order to find; Herod was seeking in order to destroy; the Jews read about the city of his birth, but did not understand the time of his coming. Between the loyal love of the Magi and the cruel fear of Herod, they just faded away. They pointed to Bethlehem, but did not then seek Christ who was born there. When they did see him later, they would deny him; not then when he was a speechless infant, but later when he spoke to them, they would slay him. Blessed rather was the ignorance of the infants whom Herod persecuted in his panic, than the learning of these men whom he consulted in his anxiety. They were able to suffer for Christ, though not yet able to confess him; these others failed to follow the truth of his teaching, though they were able to know the city of his birth.

The Magi from among the Gentiles, the shepherds from among the Jews

3. That star, certainly, led the Magi to the very place where God the Word was to be found as an infant. Here now the sacrilegious nonsense and a kind of unlearned learning, if I may so put it, should blush for shame, which assumes that Christ was born under the control of the stars, just because it's written in the gospel that when he was born, the Magi saw his star in the East. This wouldn't be true, even if people were generally born under that sort of control; because they are not born, like the Son of God, according to their own will, but according to the condition of their mortal nature. But now, in fact, so abhorrent to the truth is the idea of Christ having been born under a star-governed fate, that nobody who has the right faith in Christ will believe that any human being is so born.

But fine; let empty-headed men speak their foolish opinions about the begettings of human beings, let them deny the free will by which they sin, let them fabricate the necessity by which they come to the defense of sins; let them strive to fix on the sky the blame for the abandoned morals they are detested for by people on earth, and stick to their lie that their depravity drips from the stars; then, however, let each one of them consider how he thinks, not his life but his household should be governed by any sort of authority. Because if he really has such ideas, he cannot allow himself to beat his slaves misbehaving in his house, without first blaspheming his gods shining so brightly in the sky.

Even so, they cannot suppose that Christ was born under the control of the stars, just because the Magi saw a star in the East when he was born, not even according to their own utterly groundless calculations and their books that certainly tell no fortunes but plainly tell falsehoods. What shows, you see, that Christ was not born under its control, but rather appeared as its controller, is the fact that it did not keep to the starry tracks in the heavens, but pointed out to the men who were looking for Christ the track to the very place where he had been born. So it wasn't the star that caused Christ wonderfully to live, but Christ that caused the star wonderfully to appear; nor was it the star that controlled Christ's miracles, but Christ that revealed the star as one of his miracles. He, you see, when born of his mother, presented the earth with a new star from the sky, just as when born of the Father he fashioned the earth and the sky.

When he was born a new light was revealed in the star, just as when he died the old light was veiled in the sun. When he was born the upper worlds were honored with a new brilliance, just as when he died the nether worlds trembled with a new fear, when he rose again the disciples were on fire with a new love, when he ascended the heavens were opened to a new form of homage. So let us celebrate as devoutly and solemnly as we can this day too, on which the Magi from among the Gentiles recognized and worshiped the Christ, just as we celebrated that other day on which the shepherds from among the Jews saw the Christ when he was born. The Lord our God himself, after all, chose the apostles from Jewry as the shepherds, by whose efforts he would gather together to be saved even the sinful sheep from among the Gentiles.

Sermon 205

On the Beginning of Lent

This sermon was likely preached on the first Sunday of Lent in Hippo sometime after 415. Augustine gives an extended meditation on the cross and calls fellow Christians to prayer and fasting from the pleasures of the flesh. Even married couples are recommended to abstain from carnal relations. The bishop is especially critical of those who abstain from eating certain meats or drinking wine but substitute other delicacies. Most importantly, Christians should fast from quarrels and discord.

If you don't want your footsteps to sink in the earthly quagmire,
don't come down from this cross

1. Today we enter upon the keeping of Lent, coming round again as it does every year; and every year too I owe you a solemn exhortation, so that the word of God, set before you by my service, may feed your minds as you set about fasting in the body; and in this way the inner self, nourished by its proper food, may undertake the chastisement of the outer, and sustain it all the more stoutly. It goes well with our devotion, after all, that as we are very soon going to celebrate the passion of the crucified Lord, we should also make a cross for ourselves out of the curbing of the pleasures of the flesh, as the apostle says: *But those who are Jesus Christ's have crucified their flesh with its passions and lusts* (Gal 5:24).

On this cross, indeed, the Christian ought to hang continually throughout the whole of this life, which is spent in the midst of trials and temptations. The time, you see, doesn't come in this life for pulling out the nails, of which it says in the psalm, *Let my flesh be transfixed with nails by the fear of you* (Ps 119:120). Flesh means the lusts of the flesh; the nails are the commandments of justice; with these the fear of the Lord transfixes those, and crucifies us as a sacrifice acceptable to him. That's why, again, the apostle says, *And so I beseech you, brothers, by the compassion of God, to present your bodies as a living sacrifice, holy, pleasing to God* (Rom 12:1).

So this cross, on which the servant of God is not only not put to confusion, but in fact glories in it, saying, *But far be it from me to glory except in the cross of our Lord Jesus Christ, by which the world has been crucified to me, and I to the world* (Gal 6:14); this cross, I repeat, is not just meant for forty days, but for the whole of this life, which is signified by the mystical number of these forty days. This may be because, as several authorities assert, the human being destined to live this life takes shape in the womb in forty days; or else because the four gospels agree with the tenfold law, and four times ten marks up this number, and indicates that in this life we need both parts of scripture; or for any other more probable reason which a better and brighter intelligence can find.

So it is that both Moses and Elijah and the Lord himself all fasted for forty days, to suggest to us that we are being worked upon in Moses and in Elijah and in Christ himself, that is in the law and the prophets and in the gospel itself, to ensure that we aren't conformed to this world and don't cling to it, but that instead we crucify the old self, behaving *not in gluttony and drunkenness, not in chambering and wantonness; but let us put on the Lord Jesus, and take no care for the flesh in its lusts* (Rom 13:13-14), Live here like that always, Christian; if you don't want your footsteps to sink in the earthly quagmire, don't come down from this cross.

But now, if that is what has to be done throughout the whole of this life, how much more during these days of Lent, in which this life is not only being spent, but in addition is also being mystically signified?

Works of penance

2. So on other days your hearts should never be weighed down with drugs and drunkenness; during these days, though, you should also fast. During the other days of the year you mustn't so much as touch upon adultery, fornication, and any other forms of unlawful depravity; during these days, though, you should also abstain from your marriage partners. What you deprive yourselves of by fasting, add by being generous to the alms you give. Let the time that was taken up with the payment of the marriage debt be spent in supplications; let the body, which was relaxing in demonstrations of carnal affection, prostrate itself in the purity of prayer; let the arms which were twined in embraces be raised and extended in orisons.

As for those of you who also fast on other days, add during these days to what you normally do. Those of you who throughout the other days of the year crucify the body by perpetual continence, cleave to your God during these days by more frequent and more earnest prayer. All of you, be of one mind and heart, all of you faithfully faithful, all of you, in this time of exile and wandering, full of heartfelt sighs and fervent love for the one, common home country. See to it that none of you envies, none of you mocks in another the gift of God which you don't have in yourself. In the matter of spiritual goods, regard as your own what you love and admire in your brother or sister; let them regard as their own what they love and admire in you.

None of us, under the pretense of self-denial, should make a point of changing, rather than cutting back on, our pleasures; looking out for special delicacies because we aren't eating meat, and for strange liquors because we aren't drinking wine; that way, under the cloak of taming the flesh we are conducting the business of pleasure. All kinds of food are indeed pure to the pure; but self-indulgent luxury is pure to nobody.

Fast from quarrels

3. Before everything else, brothers and sisters, fast from quarrels and discord. Remember how the prophet upbraided some people and cried out, *Your own wills are found on the days of your fast, because you dig your spurs into all who are under your yoke, and beat them with your fists; your voices are heard in shouting*; and more to that effect. After mentioning all this, he added, *That is not the fast I have chosen, says the Lord* (Is 58:3-5). If you want to shout, use the kind of shouting about which it says, *With my voice I shouted to the Lord* (Ps 142:1). That indeed is not a shout of quarreling, but of loving; not of the flesh, but the heart. Not such are those of whom it is said, *I waited for them to do justice, but they worked iniquity; and not justice, but a shout* (Is 5:7).

Forgive, and you will be forgiven; give, and it will be given you (Lk 6:37-38). These are the two wings of prayer, on which it flies to God; if you pardon the offender what has been committed, and give to the person in need.

Sermon 207

On the Beginning of Lent

This is a Lenten exhortation to prayer, fasting and almsgiving probably delivered in one of the outlying churches of Hippo between 400 and 405. Augustine recommends moderation even in marital relations. Lenten penitential practices should focus on repressing old pleasures rather than on finding ways around the law by substituting new delicacies.

Fasting without kindness and mercy is worth nothing to the one who's fasting

1. With the help of the mercy of the Lord our God, the temptations of this age, the crafty traps of the devil, the toils of this world, the allurements of the flesh, the swirl of turbulent times, and all bodily and spiritual adversity, are to be overcome by almsgiving and fasting and prayer. Christians ought to be fervently engaged in these things throughout their lives; much more so then at the approach of the great festival of Easter, which rouses our minds as it comes round again each year, renewing in them the salutary memory of what mercy our Lord, the only Son of God, has bestowed on us, of how he fasted and prayed for us.

"Alms," of course, comes from a Greek word meaning "mercy." What greater mercy, though, could there be toward the miserable, than that which pulled the creator down from heaven, and clothed the founder of the earth in an earthly body; which made the one who abides equal in eternity to the Father, equal to us in mortality, imposing the form of a servant on the Lord of the world; so that bread itself would be hungry, fullness be thirsty, strength become weak, health would be wounded, life would die? And all this to feed our hunger, water our drought, comfort our infirmity, extinguish our iniquity, kindle our charity. What greater mercy, than for the creator to be created, the master to serve the redeemer to be sold, the one who exalts to be humbled, the one who raises up to be slain? We, in the matter of giving alms, are instructed to give bread to the hungry; he, in order to give himself to us in our hunger, first surrendered himself for us to his enemies' anger. We are instructed to welcome the stranger; he, for our sakes, came to his own place, and his own people did not welcome him.

Let our soul, in a word, *bless him who shows himself gracious to all its iniquities, who heals all its infirmities, who redeems its life from corruption, who crowns it with compassion and mercy, who satisfies its desire with good things* (Ps 103:2-5). And so let us perform our alms and deeds of kindness all the more lavishly, all the more frequently, the nearer the day approaches on which is celebrated the alms, the kindness that has been done to us. Because fasting without kindness and mercy is worth nothing to the one who's fasting.

Let your fasting be accompanied by frugality

2. Let us also fast by humbling our souls, as the day approaches on which the master of humility humbled himself, *becoming obedient even to the death of the cross* (Phil 2:8). Let us imitate his cross, pacifying and nailing our lusts with the nails of abstinence. Let us chastise our bodies, and subject them to hard service; and to avoid slipping into unlawful pleasures because of the unruliness of the flesh, in breaking it in let us deprive it to some extent even of lawful ones. Drugs and drunkenness, of course, are to be avoided even at other times; but during these days even permissible meals should be cut. Adultery and fornication must always be abhorred and shunned; but during these days even marital relations should be moderated. The flesh will readily submit to you in not sticking to what belongs to others, if it has got used to being held back even from what is its own.

You must certainly beware of just revising, not reducing, your pleasures. I mean, you can see some people searching out unusual liquors as a substitute for the usual wine, and with the juices squeezed out of other fruits compensating themselves much more pleasantly for what they deny themselves from the grape; engaging in the quest for foods of the most delicious variety, other than meat; and concocting delicacies as suitable to this season, which at other times they are ashamed to bother with. The result is that the observance of Lent means, not the repression of old lusts, but the occasion for new enjoyments.

To avoid letting these persuasive suggestions creep up on you, brothers and sisters, be as watchful and prudent as you possibly can. Let your fasting be accompanied by frugality. Just as the cramming of the stomach is to be restrained, so the tickling of the palate is to be avoided. It isn't that some kinds of human food are to be regarded as unclean, but that the delights of the flesh are to be held in check. Esau wasn't rejected over Wiener schnitzel or pâté de foie gras, but for an inordinate longing for lentils. Holy David repented of having a greater desire for water than was just. So the body is to be refreshed, or rather supported in its fasting, not by elaborate and expensive dishes, but by any kind of cheaper food that is readily available.

Prayer must be chaste

3. During these days our prayer is lifted up to the heights with the support of kindhearted almsgiving and frugal fasting; because there is no impudence in asking for mercy from God, when it is not refused by one human being to another, and when the serene aim of the heart at prayer is not deflected by the cloudy, lowering images and fancies of the pleasures of the flesh. Prayer, though, must be chaste, so that we don't find ourselves expressing a wish for what greed, not love, is looking for; or calling down some evil on our enemies; or showing a savagery in prayer against people which we are unable to vent on them in actual harm or revenge. Undoubtedly, just as we are made fitter for praying by almsgiving and

fasting, so too our very prayer gives alms when it is directed to God and poured forth, not only for friends but also for enemies, and when it fasts from anger and hatred and all other such destructive vices. If we, after all, are fasting from food, how much more should our prayer be fasting from poison? Then again, we are sustained at the proper and convenient times by taking nourishment; let us never entice our prayer with such dishes as those. Let it undertake, rather, a perpetual fast; because it does have its proper food, which it is instructed to take without ceasing. So then, let it always fast from hatred, always feed on love.

Sermon 212

At the Handing Over of the Creed

The handing over of the Creed, or Symbol as it was called, has been restored in the Rite of Christian Initiation of Adults in the reform of the Roman Catholic liturgy. In the early days of the Church Christians were instructed to memorize it rather than write it down. This sermon was probably preached sometime between 410 and 415 on the fourth Sunday of Lent, when it was customary to hand over the Creed to those preparing for Baptism so that it could be memorized and given back the following Sunday, when they received the Lord's Prayer. Augustine only paraphrases sections of the Apostles' Creed before it was in fact "handed over."

Brief exposition of the Symbol

1. It's time for you to receive the Symbol in which is briefly contained everything that is believed for the sake of eternal salvation. It's called the Symbol because of a certain similarity; the word being transferred from commercial transactions, because merchants make agreements among themselves, called symbols, which guarantee their loyalty to the terms of their association. And your association is concerned with spiritual merchandise, so that you may be like *dealers looking for a good pearl* (Mt 13:45). This pearl is *the charity, which will be poured out in your hearts through the Holy Spirit, who will be given to you* (Rom 5:5).

One arrives at this as a result of the faith which is contained in this Symbol, as a result of your believing *in God the Father almighty*, invisible, immortal, king of the ages, creator of things visible and invisible, and whatever else genuine reason or the authority of holy scripture can fittingly say about him. Nor must you separate the Son of God from this absolute perfection and superiority. These things, you see, are not said about the Father in such a way as to be inapplicable to the one who said, *I and the Father are one* (Jn 10:30), and about whom the apostle said *who, since he was in the form of God, did not think it robbery to be equal to God* (Phil 2:6). Robbery, of course, means the seizing of what belongs to someone else, while that equality is his very nature; and thus, how will the Son not be almighty, *through whom all things were made* (Jn 1:3), since he is also *the power and the wisdom of God* (1 Cor 1:24), the wisdom about which it is written that *while she is one, she can do all things* (Wis 7:27)?

But that nature is also invisible, in the very form in which it is equal to the Father. By nature, of course, the Word of God is invisible, which *was in the beginning with God, and the Word was God* (Jn 1:1); and in that nature he also remains altogether immortal, that is totally unchangeable. I mean, the human soul is also after a fashion said to be immortal; but it can't be true immortality in something so changeable, which can fall away and make progress; so that its death is to be *estranged from the life of God by the ignorance that is in it* (Eph 4:18), while its life is to run to *the fountain of life* in order *in the light of God to see light* (Ps 36:9). It is to this life that you too by the grace of Christ are being revived from a kind of death which you are renouncing.

The Word of God, however, which is what the only-begotten Son is, always lives unchangeably with the Father; it neither falls away, because permanence cannot diminish, nor makes progress, because perfection cannot increase. He too is king of the ages, creator of things visible and invisible, because as the apostle says, *In him all things were established in heaven and on earth, visible and invisible, whether Thrones or Dominations or Principalities or Powers; all things were created in him and through him, and all hold together for him* (Col 1:16-17).

But since *he emptied himself*, not losing the form of God, but *taking the form of a servant* (Phil 2:7), through this form of a servant the invisible one was seen, because *he was born of the Holy Spirit and from Mary the virgin*. In this form of a servant the almighty became weak, because *he suffered under Pontius Pilate*; through this form of a servant the immortal one died, because *he was crucified and buried*; through this form of a servant the king of ages *on the third day rose again*; through this form of a servant the creator of things visible and invisible *ascended into heaven* from where he had never departed; through this form of a servant *he is seated at the right hand of the Father*, whose arm he is, of which the prophet says *And to whom has the arm of the Lord been revealed?* (Is 53:1). In this form of a servant *he is going to come to judge the living and the dead*, the form which he chose to share with the dead, though he is the life of the living.

Through him the Holy Spirit was sent to us from the Father and from himself, the Spirit of the Father and the Son, sent by both, begotten by neither, the unity of both, equal to both. This Trinity is one God, almighty, invisible, immortal, king of the ages, creator of things visible and invisible. Nor, you see, do we say that there are three Gods, or three almighties or three creators or anything else that can likewise be said about God's absolute supremacy, because they are not three Gods, but one God. Although in this Trinity the Father is not the Son, and the Son is not the Father, and the Holy Spirit is neither the Father nor the Son; but the first is the Father of the Son, the second the Son of the Father, the third the Spirit of the Father and of the Son. Believe, in order to understand, because *unless you believe, you will not understand* (Is 7:9).

From this faith you must hope for the grace by which all your sins will be forgiven. By this grace, you see, *you will be saved — not of yourselves, but it is God's gift — not by works, lest perhaps any one should preen himself.* The fact is, you will be *his workmanship, created in Christ Jesus in the good works which God has prepared, for you to walk in them* (Eph 2:8-10); so that laying aside all that is old and stale, and *putting on the new self* (Eph 4:24), you may be *a new creature* (1 Cor 5:17; Gal 6:15), singing *the new song* (Ps 144:9; Rv 5:9), ready to receive an eternal inheritance in terms of the new covenant. On the strength of this, you must also hope, after the death which has spread to all human beings, which was owed and actually paid to the stale old age of the first man, you must hope at the end for the resurrection of your bodies; not to suffer pain and grief, which is what the wicked are going to rise again to, nor to enjoy what the flesh desires, as silly people think, but as the apostle says, *it is sown embodying the soul, it will rise again embodying the spirit* (1 Cor 15:44). Then the body will be so subordinate to the spirit enjoying the beatific vision, so adapted with a marvelous felicity to enjoying every facility, that no longer will it *weigh down the soul* (Wis 9:15), nor require any sustenance because it will experience no wear and tear. But it will abide in eternal life, where eternity itself will be life for our spirit together with the body.

Keep the Symbol in your memory

2. So now, I have paid my debt to you with this short sermon on the whole Symbol. When you hear the whole of this Symbol, you will recognize this sermon of mine briefly summed up in it. And in no way are you to write it down, in order to retain the same words; but you are to learn it thoroughly by hearing it, and not write it down either when you have it by heart, but keep it always and go over it in your memory. After all, everything you are going to hear in the Symbol is already contained in the divine documents of the holy scriptures, from which you regularly hear extracts as the need arises.

But the fact that the Symbol, put together and reduced to a certain form in this way, may not be written down, is a reminder of God's promise, where he fore-told the new covenant through the prophet, and said, *This is the covenant which I will draw up for them after those days, says the Lord; putting my laws into their minds, I will write them also on their hearts* (Jer 31:33). It is to illustrate this truth that by the simple hearing of the Symbol it is written not on tables, or on any other material, but on people's hearts. The God who has called you to his kingdom and his glory will ensure that it is also written on your hearts by the

Holy Spirit, once you have been born again by his grace; so that you may love what you believe, and faith may work in you through love. In this way may you please the Lord God, the giver of all good things, not out of fear of punishment like slaves, but out of a love of justice like free people. So this is the Symbol which has already been imparted to you as catechumens through the scriptures and sermons in church, but which has to be confessed and practiced and made progress in by you as baptized believers.

Sermon 213

At the Handing Over of the Creed

Augustine defines the Creed (Symbol) as a "briefly compiled rule of faith, intended to instruct the mind without overburdening the memory." Hill suggests this sermon was preached several years before S. 212 and sometime before 410-412, based primarily on Augustine's scrupulosity in quoting the actual words of the Creed more extensively. The wording is substantially close to the language of the Apostle's Creed, which was the old baptismal Creed of the Roman Church. The sermons on the Creed were all preached in Hippo. S. 215, 1 specifies that the Creed was recited individually rather than given back by the group of catechumens as a whole. Some readers might be puzzled by Augustine's failure to recommend sacramental confession, but it must be remembered that frequent confession only became popular with the Irish penitentials in the sixth century. Augustine promotes the daily recitation of the Lord's Prayer for the forgiveness of everyday sins.

We are now hoping for what we are to receive

1. The apostle says, *It shall come to pass, everyone who calls upon the name of the Lord shall be saved* (Rom 10:13). It is to this salvation that you are hastening, all of you that have given in your names for baptism; a salvation, a welfare, not for a short time but for eternity; a salvation, a welfare, which is not shared by us and the animals, nor by good people and bad. You can see, of course, and it is plain to all of us, that present welfare or health, which people work so hard to obtain or restore, is something not only human beings have, but also animals, great and small; from dragons and elephants down to flies and worms does this kind of health extend. Furthermore, human beings enjoy this kind of health or welfare, both those who call upon God and those who blaspheme God.

That's why the holy psalm says, *Men and beasts will you save, Lord, as your mercy has been multiplied, O God; but the sons of men shall hope under the shelter of your wings.* So this salvation or welfare, by the multiple mercy of God, reaches to the least of animals; *but the sons of men,* who belong to the Son of man, *shall hope under the shelter of your wings.* That's what we are doing in this life; we are now hoping for what we are to receive afterward. And what does this very psalm promise us? *They shall get drunk on the richness of your house, and from the torrent of your pleasure you will give them to drink, since with you is the fountain of life* (Ps 36:7-9). The fountain of life is Christ; so that we might have some taste of it now, he became man; but its richness is being kept for us, which now more than satisfies the angels and all the heavenly ministries.

But this comes later; now though, so that we may be able to reach that, let us call upon God, so that we may be saved, according to the apostle who said, *Everyone who calls upon the name of the Lord shall be saved* (Rom 10:13). The prophet had said this before; but Paul the apostle was saying that the time had now passed for the fulfillment of what was written, *Everyone who calls upon the name of the Lord shall be saved.* I have already said with what kind of salvation or welfare, in case you should now say, "Why have those who call upon the name of the Lord not been saved?"; it says "shall be saved."

Then the apostle himself added, *But how shall they call upon one in whom they have not believed? Or how can they believe in one whom they have not heard of? Or how shall they hear without a preacher? Or how shall they preach if they are not sent? As it is written: How beautiful are the feet of those bringing the good news of peace, bringing good news* (Rom 10:14-15). So nobody can be saved who doesn't first call upon him; nobody can call upon him unless they first believe. So because that's the right order, that you should first believe, afterward call upon him, today you receive the Symbol of faith, in which to express your faith; while in eight days time it will be the Prayer, with which to call upon him.

I believe in God the Father Almighty

2. So the Symbol is a briefly compiled rule of faith, intended to instruct the mind without overburdening the memory; to be said in a few words, from which much is to be gained. So it's called a Symbol, because it's something by which Christians can recognize each other; that is what I shall first briefly recite to you. Then, as far as the Lord is good enough to grant, I will open it up for you, so that you may be able to understand what I want you to retain. This is the Symbol.

After the Symbol

It isn't very much, and it is very much; there's no need for you to count the words, but rather to weigh them. *I believe in God the Father almighty.* Notice how quickly it's said, and how much it's worth. He's God, and he's Father; God in power, Father in goodness. How lucky we are, to have discovered that our God is our Father! So let us believe in him, and promise ourselves everything from his kindness and mercy, because he is almighty. That's why we believe in God the Father almighty.

Nobody must say, "He can't forgive me my sins."

"How can't he, being almighty?"

"But," you say, "I've sinned so much."

And I say, "But he's almighty."

And you: "I've committed such sins as I can't possibly be cleansed and delivered from."

I reply, "But he's almighty."

Notice what you sing to him in the psalm: *Bless the Lord, my soul*, it says, *and do not forget all his recompenses, who shows himself gracious to all your iniquities, who heals all your weaknesses* (Ps 103:2-3). That's what we need him to be almighty for.

The whole of creation needs this, of course, in order to be created; he is almighty for making greater things and lesser things, almighty for making heavenly things and earthly things, almighty for making immortal things and mortal things, almighty for making spiritual things and material things, almighty for making visible things and invisible things; great in the great things, and not small in the least things; in a word, he is almighty for making whatever he has wished to make.

I mean, let me tell you how many things he can't do. He can't die, he can't sin, he can't lie, he can't be deceived or mistaken; so many things he can't do, and if he could do them he wouldn't be almighty. So believe in him and confess him; *For with the heart one believes unto justice, but with the mouth one makes confession unto salvation* (Rom 10:10). That's why, once you have believed, you must confess, when you give back the Symbol. So receive now what you are to retain, and afterward to give back, and never to forget.

Christ, the only Son of the Father, was made flesh

3. What's next? *And in Jesus Christ. I believe*, you say, *in God the Father almighty, and in Jesus Christ his only Son, our Lord*. If the only Son, then equal to the Father; if the only Son, then of the same substance as the Father; if the only Son, then almighty with the Father; if the only Son, then co-eternal with the Father. All this in himself, and with himself, and with the Father.

What for our sakes? What's in it for us? *Who was born of the Holy Spirit and the virgin Mary*. There you have how he came, and who, and to whom; by the virgin Mary, in whom not the man she was married to but the Holy Spirit acted; he made her fruitful while she remained chaste, and he preserved her intact. So that's the way in which the Lord Christ was clothed with flesh, the way the one who made man was made man; by taking on what he was not, not by losing what he was.

The Word, you see, *was made flesh, and dwelt among us* (Jn 1:14). Not "the Word was turned into flesh," but remaining the Word, by receiving flesh, though always invisible he became visible when he wished, *and dwelt among us*. What's "among us"? Among human beings; he became one of a number of human beings; one, and "only." "Only," for the Father; and for us, what? And for us the only savior; and for us the only redeemer; because nobody besides him is our redeemer; a redeemer, not with gold, not with silver, but with his own blood.

Crucified — buried in the flesh

4. So let us take a look at that commercial transaction of his by which we were bought. You see, after it says in the Symbol, *Born of the Holy Spirit and the virgin Mary*, what now did he suffer for us? It continues, *Under Pontius Pilate crucified and buried*. What? The only Son of God, our Lord, crucified? The only Son of God, our Lord, buried? The man was crucified, God wasn't changed, God wasn't killed; and yet, as man, God *was* killed. *For if they had known*, says the apostle, *they would never have crucified the Lord of glory* (1 Cor 2:8). He both showed that he was the Lord of glory, and confessed that he was crucified. Because if someone even tears your tunic without harming your skin, he does you an injury, and you don't shout on behalf of your clothes, "You've torn my tunic," but "You've torn me, you've ruined me, you've cut me to ribbons". You are undamaged as you say that, and yet you're telling the truth, and the one who injured you hasn't taken any skin off you.

That's the way, too, that the Lord Christ was crucified. He is the Lord, he is the only Son of the Father, he is our savior, he is the Lord of glory; yet he was crucified, but in the flesh, and buried in the flesh alone. I mean, where he was buried and when he was buried, then and there, there was no soul, but flesh alone was lying in the tomb; and yet you confess, *Jesus Christ his only Son, our Lord, who was born of the Holy Spirit and the virgin Mary*. Who was? Jesus Christ, the only Son of God, our Lord. *Under Pontius Pilate crucified*. Who was? Jesus Christ, the only Son of God, our Lord. *And buried*. Who was? Jesus Christ, the only Son of God, our Lord. "Flesh alone lies there, and you say 'Our Lord'?" I do say it, certainly I do; because I observe the clothes, and I worship the one clothed. That flesh was his clothes, because *since he was in the form of God, he did not think it robbery to be equal to God; but he emptied himself, taking the form of a servant*, not losing the form of God, *being made in the likeness of men, and found in habit as a man* (Phil 2:6-7).

He rose, he ascended into heaven, he sits at the right hand of God

5. Let us not think lightly, though, of that flesh alone; when it lay there, that is when he bought us. How is it that he bought us? Because he didn't lie there forever. *On the third day*, you see, *he rose again from the dead*. That's what

comes next in the creed; when we have confessed his passion, we also confess his resurrection. What did he do in his passion? Taught us what to endure. What did he do in his resurrection? Showed us what to hope for. Here the work, there the reward. The work in the passion, the reward in the resurrection.

Nor, because he rose again from the dead, did he stay here; but what comes next? *He ascended into heaven.* And where is he now? *He is seated at the right hand of the Father.* Understand the right hand properly, don't go looking there for a left hand. God's right hand means eternal felicity; God's right hand means inexpressible, incalculable, incomprehensible blessedness and well-being. That's the right hand of God, that's where he's seated. What does that mean, that's where he's seated? That's where he lives; one talks, after all, about where someone lives as his seat. I mean, when Saint Stephen saw him, anyone who said *He is seated at the right hand of the Father* wouldn't be lying. I mean, how did Stephen put it? *Behold, I see heaven opened, and the Son of man standing at the right hand of God* (Acts 7:56). Because he saw him standing, perhaps anyone would be lying, who said at that time, *he is seated at the right hand of the Father?* He's seated, so it means he stays, he lives there. How? The same way as you do. How does he stand? Who can say? Let us say what he taught, let us say what we know.

Christ, our judge and our advocate

6. And what's that? *From there to come to judge the living and the dead.* Let us confess him as savior, in order not to fear him as judge. Whoever believes in him now, you see, and carries out his commands, and loves him, won't be afraid when he comes to judge the living and the dead; not only won't be afraid, but will wish he would come. After all, what could be more fortunate for us than the coming of the one we desire, the coming of the one we love?

But we should be afraid, because he will be our judge. The one who will be our judge then is the one who is our advocate now. Listen to John: *If we say that we have no sin, we are deceiving ourselves, and the truth is not in us; but if we confess our sins,* he said, *he is faithful and just to forgive us our sins, and to purify us from all iniquity. I have written this to you, so that you should not sin; and if anyone does sin, we have an advocate with the Father, Jesus Christ, the just one; and he is the appeasement for our sins* (1 Jn 1:8-9; 2:1-2). If you had a case, to be tried by some judge, and you instructed counsel, you would be defended by the counselor, who would conduct your case as best he could; and if he didn't complete it, and you heard he was going to come as the judge, just imagine how overjoyed you would be, because the one who a short while before had been your advocate could now himself be your judge. And now he is praying for us himself, he himself is interceding for us. We have him as our advocate, and are we to fear him as judge? On the contrary, because we have sent him ahead as our advocate, we can hope without a qualm for his coming back as judge.

The Holy Spirit

7. That's the end in the creed of what concerns Jesus Christ, the only Son of God, our Lord. It goes on, *And in the Holy Spirit,* to complete the Trinity, Father, Son and Holy Spirit. But about the Son many things are said, because the Son took on a man; the Son, the Word, became flesh; not the Father, not the Holy Spirit. But the whole Trinity made the flesh of the Son; the Trinity, you see, works inseparably. So take the Holy Spirit in such a way that you don't believe him to be less than the Son, to be less than the Father. The Father, you see, and the Son and the Holy Spirit, the whole Trinity, are one God; there is no difference here, no variation, nothing defective, nothing contrary to another; eternal equality, invisibility, immutability of Father and Son and Holy Spirit. May the Trinity deliver us from the multitude of our sins.

The Church is like Mary because it is a virgin and gives birth

8. Now follows what concerns us: *In the holy Church.* The holy Church is what we are; but I don't mean "we" in the sense of just those of us who are here, you that are listening to me now; as many of us as are here by the grace of God Christian believers in this Church, that is in this city, as many as there are in this region, as many as there are in this province, as many as there are also across the sea, as many as there are in the whole wide world, since *from the rising of the sun to its setting the name of the Lord is praised* (Ps 113:3). Such is the Catholic Church, our true mother, the true consort of that bridegroom.

Let us honor her, because she is the bride of so great a Lord. And what am I to say? Great and unheard of is the bridegroom's gracious generosity; he found her a whore, he made her a virgin. She mustn't deny that she was once a whore, or she may forget the kindness and mercy of her liberator. How can she not have been a whore, when she used to go fornicating after idols and demons? Fornication of the heart was there in all her members, fornication of the flesh in some of them; of the heart in all. And he came, and made her a virgin; he made the Church a virgin. In faith she is a virgin; in the flesh she has a few virgins, the nuns; in faith she should have all of us virgins, both women and men. In that sphere, you see, there should be universal chastity and purity and sanctity.

Well, do you want to know how the Church is a virgin? Listen to the apostle Paul, listen to the friend of the bridegroom, jealous for the bridegroom, not for himself: *I have joined you,* he says, *to one husband.* He was speaking to the Church; and to which Church? Wherever his letter could reach. *I have joined you to one husband, to present you to Christ as a chaste virgin. But I am afraid,* he said, *that just as the serpent seduced Eve by his cunning, so your minds may be corrupted from the chastity which is in Christ* (2 Cor 11:2-3). If you are afraid of being corrupted, it means you are a virgin. *I am afraid,* he said, *that just as the serpent seduced Eve by his cunning.* Did that serpent lie with Eve physically?

And yet he extinguished the virginity of her heart. *This is what I am afraid of*, he said, *that your minds may be corrupted from the chastity which is in Christ*.

So the Church is virgin; let her be virgin; let her beware of being seduced, or she will find herself corrupted. The Church is a virgin. You're going to say to me, perhaps, "If she is a virgin, how does she give birth to children? Or if she doesn't bear children, how is it we gave in our names to be born of her womb?" I answer: she is both virgin, and she gives birth. She imitates Mary, who gave birth to the Lord. Didn't the virgin, Saint Mary, both give birth and remain a virgin? So too the Church both gives birth and is a virgin. And if you really think about it, she gives birth to Christ, because those who are baptized are his members, parts of his body. *You*, says the apostle, *are the body of Christ, and members of it* (1 Cor 12:27).

The forgiveness of sins by baptism and the Lord's prayer

9. *In the forgiveness of sins*. If this were not to be had in the Church, there would be no hope. If the forgiveness of sins were not to be had in the Church, there would be no hope of a future life and eternal liberation. We thank God, who gave his Church such a gift. Here you are; you are going to come to the holy font, you will be washed in saving baptism, you will be renewed in *the bath of rebirth* (Ti 3:5), you will be without any sin at all as you come up from that bath. All the things that were plaguing you in the past will there be blotted out. Your sins will be like the Egyptians, hard on the heels of the Israelites; pursuing them, but only as far as the Red Sea. What does it mean, as far as the Red Sea? As far as the font, consecrated by the cross and blood of Christ.

What's red, after all, reddens. Can't you see how part of Christ reddens? Ask the eye of your faith; if you can see the cross, observe the blood; if you can see what's hanging on it, observe what he shed. The side of Christ was pierced with a lance, and our price poured out. That's why baptism is signed with the sign of Christ — I mean the water in which you are dipped, and as it were pass over in the Red Sea. Your sins are your enemies; they follow, but as far as the sea. When you yourselves enter the sea, you escape them, they will be blotted out as the water overwhelmed the Egyptians, while the Israelites escaped dryshod. And what does scripture say? *Not one of them remained* (Ps 106:11). You have sinned much, you have sinned little; you've committed great sins, you've committed little sins; it makes no difference; *not one of them remained*.

But since we are going to go on living in this world, where nobody can live without sin, for that reason the forgiveness of sins is not confined only to the washing clean of sacred baptism, but is also to be had in the Lord's prayer which is also a daily prayer, and which you are going to receive in eight days' time. In it you will find, as it were, your daily baptism. So you must thank God for having granted his Church this gift, which we confess in the creed; so that when we say *in the holy Church*, we join onto it *in the forgiveness of sins*.

Resurrection of the flesh

10. After this, *the resurrection of the flesh*. That is now the end of it; but the resurrection of the flesh will be the end without end; but after it there will be no death of the flesh, no pain of the flesh, no distress of the flesh, no hunger and thirst of the flesh, no afflictions of the flesh, no old age and weariness of the flesh. So don't shudder at the prospect of the resurrection of the flesh; observe what's good about the flesh, forget its ills. Certainly, certainly, whatever fleshly complaints there may be now, there won't be any then. We shall be eternal, *the equals of the angels of God* (Mt 22:30), we will share one city with the holy angels.

We shall be possessed by the Lord; we shall be his inheritance, and he will be our inheritance; as we say to him now, *Lord, the share of my inheritance* (Ps 16:5); and about us it says to the Son, *Ask of me, and I will give you the nations for your inheritance* (Ps 2:8). We shall possess and be possessed, own and be owned. What am I to say? We worship and are worshiped; but we worship him as our God, we are worshiped, that is, cultivated, by him as his field.

To realize that we are cultivated, listen to the Lord: *I am the true vine, you are the branches, my Father the field worker* (Jn 15:1.5). If he is called the field worker, he works or cultivates the field. What field? He cultivates us. And the cultivator of this visible earth can plow, can dig, can plant, can irrigate, if he finds water — but can he rain? Cause growth, produce buds, cause trees to take root, push them up into the fresh air, put strength in their branches, load them with fruit, clothe them with leaves — can the cultivator do all that? But our cultivator, God the Father, can do all these things in us. Why? Because we believe *in God the Father almighty*. So hold on to what I have put before you and what, as God has been good enough to grant me, I have explained.

In eight days the repetition of the Symbol

11. In eight days time you are going to give back what today you have received. Let your parents, who support you, start teaching you, so that you may be found ready; teaching you how you should wake up at cockcrow for the prayers which you celebrate here. Now we begin by giving you the Symbol here, so that you may diligently learn it by heart; but none of you must get into a state, and because of such agitation fail to give it back. Don't worry, we are your fathers, we aren't carrying the canes and switches of schoolteachers. If any of you get the words wrong, at least don't get the faith wrong.

Sermon 215

At the Giving Back of the Creed

This sermon was preached on the Fifth Sunday of Lent (or the preceding Saturday). The year is not at all clear. Hill initially assigned the sermon a date between 391 and 395, based on its rhetorical style and due to its emphasis on the nonmaterial aspect of God in section 2, a clearly anti-Manichean concern associated with the earlier part of Augustine's ministry. Hill currently opts for a later date, based on the inclusion of the last article of the Creed, "we hope for life everlasting," which is not cited in his other sermons on the Creed. He believes the omission in other sermons is best explained by the fact that the earlier Creed used in Hippo more than likely wanted to come into line with the Creed used in other Churches. So he assigns a date of 425. But this argument of itself does not seem convincing, since Augustine also glosses the Apostles Creed with a phrase from the Nicene Creed, "true God from true God," which was not yet used regularly in the liturgy. Augustine stresses the mystery of the virgin birth and declares that Mary was a virgin *ante partum, in partum,* and *post partum.* He emphasizes the importance of belief not only on Mary's part but on that of all believers.

Always retain the Symbol in mind and heart

1. The Symbol of the most sacred mystery, which you received all together, and have given back today one by one, contains the words in which the faith of mother Church is solidly based on the firm foundation which is Christ the Lord. *For no other foundation can anybody lay, besides the one that has been laid, which is Christ Jesus* (1 Cor 3:11). So you have received and given back what you must always retain in mind and heart, what you should recite in bed, think about in the streets, and not forget over your meals; in which even when your bodies are asleep your hearts should be awake.

On renouncing the devil, you see, and withdrawing your minds and hearts from his parades and his angels, you must forget the past, reject as worthless the staleness of the old life, and join the new man in renewing life itself in holy behavior; and as the apostle says, *forgetting what lies behind, and stretching out to what lies ahead, follow on toward the palm of God's summons up above* (Phil 3:13-14); and you must believe what you cannot yet see, so that you may deservedly attain to what you have believed. *For why should one hope for what one can see? But if we hope for what we do not see, we wait for it with patience* (Rom 8:24-25).

We believe in God the Father Almighty

2. So this faith is also a rule for salvation, to *believe in God the Father almighty,* creator of all things, *king of the ages, immortal and invisible* (1 Tm 1:17). He is

indeed the almighty God who at the origin of the world made all things out of nothing, who is before the ages, and who made and governs the ages. He doesn't, after all, grow with time, or stretch out in space, nor is he shut in or bounded by any material; but he abides with and in himself as full and perfect eternity, which neither human thought can comprehend, nor tongue describe. I mean, if *neither eye has seen nor ear heard* the gift which he promises his saints, *nor has it come up into the heart of man* (1 Cor 2:9), how can either the mind conceive, or the heart consider, or the tongue describe the one who made the promise?

What cannot be suitably spoken can be faithfully believed

3. We believe also *in his Son Jesus Christ, our Lord*, true God from true God, God the Son of God the Father, but not two gods. He, after all, and the Father are one, and through Moses he instills the truth into the people, when he says, *Hear, Israel, the commandments of life; the Lord your God is one God* (Dt 6:4). But if you want to work out how the eternal Son was born of the eternal Father without time, the prophet Isaiah reproves you, when he says, *His birth who will explain?* (Is 53:8). And so you can neither work out nor explain the birth of God from God; all you are permitted to do is believe it, so that you may be saved, as the apostle says: *But it is necessary for the one who approaches God to believe that he is, and that he will be a rewarder of those who seek him* (Heb 11:6).

But if you desire to know about his birth according to the flesh, which he was pleased to take to himself for our salvation, listen, and believe that he was *born of the Holy Spirit and the virgin Mary*. Although, this birth of his too, who will explain? Who, after all, can put a proper value on the fact that God was willing to be born a human being for the sake of human beings, that a virgin conceived without male seed, that she gave birth without loss of virginity, and that after giving birth she retained her integrity? Our Lord Jesus Christ, you see, was pleased to enter the womb of a virgin, undefiled to lodge in the body of a woman, to make his mother fruitful without her losing her virginity, to be formed by himself and come out, opening the undamaged womb of her that bore him; all this in order to shed upon her from whom he was pleased to be born both the honor of being a mother, and the holiness of being a virgin. Who can work this out, who can explain it? So this birth too, *who will explain?*

Whose mind, after all, would be sufficient to ponder, whose tongue to express, not only that *in the beginning was the Word* who had no beginning to his being born, but also that *the Word became flesh* (Jn 1:1.14), choosing a virgin to make a mother for himself, making himself a mother whom he would also preserve as a virgin? The Son of God with no mother conceiving him, the Son of man with no man begetting him; bringing fruitfulness to a woman by his coming, not depriving her of her integrity by his being born. What is this? Who can tell it? Who can keep quiet about it? And wonderful to relate, what we are not capable of expressing we are not permitted to pass over in silence. We proclaim out loud in words what we cannot comprehend in the silence of our thoughts. Indeed we are unable to express this stupendous gift of God, because we are too little to explain his greatness; and yet we are obliged to praise him, lest by keeping silent we should remain ungrateful. But thank God, that what cannot be suitably spoken can be faithfully believed.

The blessed Mary conceived by believing the one whom she bore by believing

4. So let us believe *in Jesus Christ our Lord, born of the Holy Spirit and the virgin Mary.* You see, the blessed Mary herself conceived by believing the one whom she bore by believing. When she was promised a son, you see, and inquired how this might be, since she did not know a man, there was of course only one way known to her of conceiving and giving birth, which she hadn't indeed experienced herself, but had learned about in the natural way of things from other women; namely that a person is born of a man and a woman. Well, she received this answer from the angel: *The Holy Spirit will come upon you, and the power of the Most High will over-shadow you; for that reason the holy one to be born of you will be called the Son of God.* When the angel said this, she was so full of faith that she conceived Christ in her mind before doing so in her womb, and said, *Behold the maidservant of the Lord; may it happen to me according to your word* (Lk 1:34-38).

"May there be," she said, "one conceived in a virgin without the seed of man; may he be born of the Holy Spirit and a woman untainted, he in whom the Church may be born again untainted of the Holy Spirit. Let the holy one that will be born of a human mother without a human father be called the Son of God; since it was necessary that the one who was marvelously born of God the Father without any mother should become a son of man; and that as a tiny baby he should when born come out of a closed womb in the same flesh, as that in which as a grown man risen from the dead he would come in through closed doors." These things are wonderful, because they are divine; they are beyond our powers of expression, because they defy investigation; human lips falter in explaining them, because so do human minds in examining them. Mary believed, and what she believed came about in her. Let us too believe, so that we too may benefit from what came about.

So then, although this birth is also wonderful, just reflect, O man, what your God undertook for you, your creator for a creature; that God abiding in God, the eternal living with the eternal, the Son equal to the Father, did not disdain for the sake of the guilty and for the sake of sinful servants to put on the form of a servant. Nor, you see, was this something presented to humanity because it deserved it; I mean, what we deserved rather for our iniquities was punishment. But if he had noted iniquities, who would have borne it? For the ungodly, there-fore and for sinful servants the Lord saw fit to be born a servant and a man *of the Holy Spirit and the virgin Mary.*

Christ died for us while we were still sinners

5. Perhaps this may seem little enough, that he should come, clothed with human flesh, God for human beings, the just one for sinners, the innocent one for the guilty, the king for prisoners, the Lord for slaves; that he should be seen on earth and converse with men. So in addition *he was crucified, died and was buried.* Don't you believe it? You are saying perhaps, "When did this happen?" Listen to when: *Under Pontius Pilate.* Even the name of the judge is put there to tell you something, so that you needn't have any doubts even about the date. So believe that the Son of God *was crucified under Pontius Pilate and buried.*

But *greater love has nobody than this, that one should lay down one's life for one's friends* (Jn 15:13). Nobody, do you think? Absolutely nobody. It's true; Christ said it. Let's question the apostle, and let him answer us: *Christ*, he says, *died for the ungodly.* And again he says, *While we were enemies, we were reconciled with God through the death of his Son* (Rom 5:6.10). So there you are; in Christ we do find greater love, seeing that he gave up his life not for his friends but his enemies. How great must be God's love for humanity, and what extraordinary affection, so to love even sinners that he would die for love of them! *For God emphasizes his love toward us* — they are the apostle's words — *because while we were still sinners Christ died for us* (Rom 5:8).

You too, therefore, see that you believe this, and for your salvation's sake don't be ashamed to confess it. *For with the heart one believes unto justice, but with the mouth one makes confession unto salvation* (Rom 10:10). In any case, to help you not to doubt, not to be ashamed, when you first believed you received the sign of Christ on your forehead, as on the house of shame. Just remember your own forehead, and don't be afraid of someone else's tongue. *For whoever*, says the Lord himself, *is ashamed of me before men, the Son of man will be ashamed of him before the angels of God* (Mk 8:38). So don't be ashamed of the disgrace of the cross, which God himself did not hesitate to undergo for your sake. Say together with the apostle, *Far be it from me to boast, except in the cross of our Lord Jesus Christ* (Gal 6:14). And the same apostle will answer you himself, *I did not consider myself to know anything among you except Jesus Christ, and him crucified* (1 Cor 2:2). He, at that time crucified by one people, is now fixed in the hearts of all peoples.

The resurrection of the dead distinguishes our life of faith from the unbelieving dead

6. You though, whoever you are, who prefer to boast about power rather than about humility, here's something to console you, here's something for you to exult about. The one, you see, who *was crucified under Pontius Pilate and was buried, on the third day rose again from the dead.* Perhaps you also have your doubts about this, perhaps you hesitate. When you were told, "Believe that he was born, suffered, was crucified, dead and buried," you found that easy enough to believe about a man. Now, because you are told *on the third day he rose again from the dead,* do you hesitate, O man? Just to offer you one example out of many, look at

God, think about the Almighty, and stop hesitating. I mean, if he could make you out of nothing when you didn't exist, why could he not rouse from the dead his man whom he had already made?

So believe, brothers and sisters; where it's a matter of faith, there's no need for a long sermon. It is only this particular point of faith which distinguishes and separates Christians from all other people. I mean that he died and was buried, both the pagans now believe and the Jews then saw; but that *on the third day he rose again from the dead*, neither pagan nor Jew will admit. So it is the resurrection of the dead that distinguishes our life of faith from the unbelieving dead. The apostle Paul too, you see, when writing to Timothy, said, *Remember that Christ Jesus has risen from the dead* (2 Tm 2:8). So let us believe, brothers and sisters; we believe this happened in the case of Christ; let us hope for it's happening with us in the future. It is God, after all, who promised it; he cannot disappoint us or let us down.

Christ ascended into heaven

7. So after he rose again from the dead, *he ascended into heaven, is seated at the right hand of the Father.* You still don't believe, perhaps? Listen to the apostle: *The one who descended*, he says, *is himself the one who also ascended above all the heavens, in order to fill all things* (Eph 4:10). You are unwilling to believe in his rising again; just see you don't have to experience his judgment, because *whoever does not believe has already been judged* (Jn 3:18). You see, the one who is now seated at the right hand of the Father acting as advocate for us, *is going to come from there to judge the living and the dead.* Let us believe then, so that *whether we live, whether we die, we may be the Lord's* (Rom 14:8).

The Trinity

8. So let us believe also *in the Holy Spirit.* He is God, you see, because it is written *God is spirit* (Jn 4:24). Through him we have received *the forgiveness of sins*, through him we believe in *the resurrection of the flesh*, through him we hope for *life everlasting*. But take care you don't fall into error by counting, and imagine that I have said there are three gods, because I have given the one God a third name. There is one substance of godhead in the Trinity, one power, one might, one majesty, one name of divinity; just as he himself said to his disciples when he had risen from the dead: *Go, baptize the nations*, not in several names, but *in the one name of the Father and the Son and the Holy Spirit* (Mt 28:19). So believing then in the divine Trinity and the threefold unity, take care, dearly beloved, that no one seduces you from the faith and truth of the Catholic Church. Because, *Whoever preaches you another gospel, besides the one you have received, let him be anathema.* Listen to the apostle, not me, saying, *But even if we ourselves or an angel from heaven should preach you another gospel besides the one you have received, let him be anathema* (Gal 1:8-9).

Through the holy Church

9. You can certainly see, my dear friends, even in the very words of the holy Symbol, how at the conclusion of all the articles which belong to the sacrament of faith, a kind of supplement is added, which says, *through the holy Church.* So shun as best you can the many and various deceivers, the multitude of whose sects and names it would take far too long to explain now. You see, we have many things to say to you, but you cannot bear them now. One thing only I urge you to take to heart, and that is by every means possible to turn your minds and your ears away from the person who is not a Catholic, so that you may be able to lay hold of *the forgiveness of sins* and *the resurrection of the flesh* and *life everlasting* through the one, true, and holy Catholic Church, in which we learn of the Father and the Son and the Holy Spirit, one God, to whom is honor and glory for ever and ever.

Sermon 223

At the Easter Vigil

Augustine instructs the newly baptized Christians, who were commonly referred to as "infants" (*infantes*), not to be discouraged by the bad behavior of some of the faithful: "Stick close to those of the faithful who are good." Hill agrees with Suzanne Poque, who has done extensive work on the Easter homilies, that this was preached at an Easter Vigil (based on the reference to the white baptismal robes) and, more than likely, after 412, contrary to established opinion, which dated the sermon ten years earlier. There is a clear warning not to follow the example of the Donatist separatists. This allusion would support a date earlier than the great meeting between Donatist and Catholic bishops in 411.

The day which the Lord has made is the newly baptized

1. In the book called *Genesis* scripture says, *And God saw the light that it was good. And God divided between the light and the darkness; and God called the light day, and the darkness he called night* (Gn 1:4-5). So if God called the light day, then without a shadow of doubt those to whom the apostle Paul says, *You were once darkness, but now light in the Lord* (Eph 5:8), were day; since the one who *commanded light to shine out of the darkness* (2 Cor 4:6) had enlightened them.

These infants, whom you behold outwardly clothed in white, inwardly cleansed and purified, the brilliance of their garments representing the splendor of their minds, were once darkness, when the night of their sins was covering them. But now that they have been washed clean in the bath of amnesty, that they have been watered from the fountain of wisdom, that they have been bedewed with the light of justice, *this is the day which the Lord has made; let us exult and rejoice in it* (Ps 118:24). Let the day of the Lord listen to us; let the day made by the Lord listen to us; let it listen and obey, so that we may rejoice and exult in it; because, as the apostle says, this is our joy and our crown, if you stand fast in the Lord.

So listen to me, O you freshly born children of a chaste mother; or rather, listen to me, you children of a virgin mother. Because *you were once darkness, but now light in the Lord*, stick close to the children of light; and let me put it quite plainly: stick close to those of the faithful who are good. Because there are, you see, and this is a sad and sorry fact, a number of the faithful who are bad. They are the faithful who are called so, and are not really so. They are the faithful by whom the sacraments of Christ are misused; who live in such a way that they both perish themselves and ruin others. They perish themselves by living bad lives; while they ruin others by setting them the example of living bad lives. So you, then, dearly beloved, see you don't join such people. Seek out the good ones, stick close to the good ones, be good ones yourselves.

There are bad Christians in the Church of this present age

2. Don't be surprised, either, at how many bad Christians there are, who fill the church, who communicate at the altar, who loudly praise the bishop or the priest when he preaches about good morals; who fulfill what the one who gathers us together foretold in the psalm: *I announced, and I spoke; they have multiplied above number* (Ps 40:5). They can be with us in the Church of this time; but in that Church which will come into being after the resurrection, they will be unable to be gathered in with the saints.

The Church of this time, you see, is compared to a threshing-floor, having on it grain mixed with chaff, having bad members mixed with good; after the judgment it will have all the good members, without any bad ones. This threshing-floor holds the harvest sown by the apostles, watered by the teachers who followed them up till the present time, subjected to no little threshing under persecution by its enemies; but, the only stage remaining, not yet cleansed by the winnowing from above. However, the one is coming, about whom you have given back the article of the creed, *From there he is going to come to judge the living and the dead*; and, as the gospel states, *He will have a winnowing fan in his hand, and will cleanse his threshing-floor; and he will gather his wheat together into the granary, while the chaff he will burn with unquenchable fire* (Lk 3:17).

You older faithful, you listen too to what I'm saying. Any of you who are grain, rejoice with trembling, and stay where you are, and don't leave the threshing-floor. Don't attempt, on your own judgment, to shake yourselves free, as it were, from the chaff; because if you want to separate yourself now from the chaff, you won't be able to stay on the threshing-floor. And when that one comes who distinguishes infallibly between grain and chaff, he won't carry up to the granary anything he doesn't find on the threshing-floor. So it will be no good at that time for grains to boast about the ears of wheat they come from, if they have left the threshing-floor. That granary will be filled and closed. Anything left outside will be gutted by fire.

So then, dearly beloved, if you are good, you must put up with the bad; if you are bad, you must imitate the good. The fact is, on this threshing-floor grains can degenerate into chaff, and again grains can be resurrected from chaff. This sort of thing happens every day, my dear brothers and sisters; this life is full of both painful and pleasant surprises. Every day people who seemed to be good fall away and perish; and again, ones who seemed to be bad are converted and live. *God*, you see, *does not desire the death of the wicked, but only that they may turn back and live* (Ez 18:23).

Listen to me, grains; listen to me, those of you who are what I desire you to be. Don't let the mixture of husks depress you; they won't be with you forever. How much, anyway, is this pile of husks that is covering us? Thank God, it's very light. We only have to be grains, and however big it is, it won't crush us. *God*, after all, *is faithful, and he will not permit us to be tempted or tried beyond our capacity, but with the trial will also provide a way out, so that we can endure* (1 Cor 10:13).

Let the husks listen to me too; wherever they are, let them listen. I hope there aren't any here; but let me address them all the same, in case perhaps there are some here. So listen to me, you husks; though if you do listen, you won't be husks anymore. So listen. Let God's patience stand you in good stead. Let your association with the grains, and their advice and admonitions, make you too into grains. You are not denied the showers of God's word; don't let God's field in you be barren. So, grow green again, grow grain again, grow ripe again. The one who sowed you, after all, wishes to find full ears of corn, not empty husks.

Sermon 224

On the Octave of Easter

This sermon was preached to the newly baptized on the Sunday after Easter sometime between 412 and 416. It comes down to us in two distinct recensions: the Maurist and that of the *Revue Bénédictine* 179 (1969), which at times differ widely. Hill chose the text printed here from the latter although both are plausible. Augustine employs Neoplatonic categories to unpack his theology of the Word by illustrating the mechanics of human communication. An idea or thought is first conceived in the heart before it can be communicated through sound to the ears. Augustine is uncharacteristically blunt in his chastisement of husbands who regularly cheat on their wives while holding them to a higher standard. He dares to call women "whores" who participate in such arrangements, even if they themselves are faithful to the married men. The bishop admits the vast majority of Catholics may be lukewarm, and he mentions using sanctions such as anathemas and excommunication when necessary.

Choose for yourselves those in the people of God whom you would imitate

1. Today those who have been baptized in Christ and born again are to be mixed in with the people of God, now that the sacraments have been solidly celebrated. Let me address my remarks to them, and also to you in them and them in you. Here you are, you have become members of Christ. If you stop to think about what you have become, *all your bones will say, "Lord who is like you?"* (Ps 35:10). It is not, in fact, possible to think in a fitting way about what God has here seen fit to do to us. Doesn't all talk and perception quite fail to grasp or express how gratuitous grace has come your way, without any merits of yours preceding it? And that's why it's grace, because it has been given gratis, gratuitously, freely. What grace? That you should be the members of Christ the Son of God, that you too should be brothers and sisters of the only Son. If he is the only Son, how can you be his brothers and sisters, except that he is the only Son by nature, you are his brothers and sisters by grace?

So because you are members of Christ, I have some advice and suggestions for you. Those you are to be mixed in with should listen too. I really fear for you today, not so much from the pagans, not so much from the Jews, not so much from the heretics, as from bad Catholics. Choose for yourselves those in the people of God whom you would imitate. Because if you decide to imitate the majority, you will not find yourselves among the few who walk along the narrow road. Refrain from robbery, from fraud, from perjury. Turn your backs on the whirlpool of drunkenness. Dread all forms of fornication like death; not the death which releases the soul from the body, but the one in which the soul will burn for ever with the body.

*Against the whispered suggestions of the devil, we ought
to employ the enchantments of Christ*

2. My brothers, my sons, my daughters, my sisters, I'm well aware that the devil forms his own parties, and never stops talking in the hearts of those whom he seduces into joining his party. I know that the devil says to fornicating adulterers, who are not content with their own wives, that he says in their hearts, "Sins of the flesh aren't all that serious." Against this, against the whispered suggestions of the devil, we ought to employ the enchantments of Christ. Because the enemy is just deceiving Christians through the allurements of the flesh, when he makes what is a grave matter into a light one for them; but he does this by lying, not by really making it light. What's the good to you of Satan making light of what Christ has shown to be grave? What's the good to you of the colossal weight of infelicity weighing light in the scales of falsity? What good does it do you, the devil telling you it's only a light matter, when God tells you it's a grave one? Aren't you going to discover how grave indeed is what God told you, and how far away from you the devil will be with his promises?

Is the devil doing anything new, in telling the Christian faithful, "What you're doing is nothing, really; you're sinning in the flesh; after all, you're not sinning spiritually. It's something that's easily wiped off the slate, easily pardoned." What's so terrific about what he's doing? It's the same old ruse as he employed in paradise, when he said, "Eat, and you will be like gods; you certainly won't die." God had said, *The day you eat, you shall die the death* (Gn 2:17). Along comes the enemy and says, *You will not die, but your eyes will be opened, and you will be like gods* (Gn 3:4-5). God's injunction was slighted, and the devil's persuasion heeded. And then God's injunction was discovered to be true, and the devil's deception to be false. Did it do her any good, I ask you, that the woman said, *The serpent seduced me* (Gn 3:13)? Did the excuse carry any weight? If the excuse carried weight, why did the condemnation follow?

While God has promised forgiveness, he hasn't anywhere promised tomorrow

3. That's why I've got this to say to you, my brothers, my sons, those of you that have wives, don't go looking for anything else; those of you who haven't, and wish to marry, keep yourselves chaste for them, just as you want them to come chaste to you; those of you who have made a promise of continence, don't look back. There, I've had my say, I've absolved myself of guilt. God has placed me here to pay out, not to call in debts. And yet, where we can, where we are given the chance, when an opportunity occurs, when we know the facts, we correct, we reprove, we hurl anathemas, we excommunicate.

And yet it isn't we, really, who correct, because *neither the one who plants is anything, nor the one who waters, but only the one who gives the growth, God* (1 Cor 3:7). And now, the fact of my talking, of my warning you — what's the use of it, unless God listens to me on your behalf, and does something in you, that is in your hearts? I'll put it briefly, and draw this in particular to your attention; I am both scaring the faithful and building you up. You are members of Christ; listen, not to me, but to the apostle, *So shall I take the members of Christ, and make them members of a whore?* (1 Cor 6:15).

Someone or other's got to say, of course, "But she isn't a whore, she's my concubine."

Have you got a wife, you that said that?

"I have."

So she, whether you like it or not, is a whore. Go and tell her, "The bishop has insulted you." If you have a wife and another woman sleeps with you, whoever that one is, she's a whore. But perhaps she's faithful to you, and knows no other man but you alone, and is not disposed to know any other. So while she is chaste, why are you fornicating? If she does with one, why must you have two? You're not allowed to, not allowed to, not allowed to. At least from this place let me enjoy freedom of speech. At least from this place allow me to speak out. At least from this place allow me to say what is true.

People of this sort must put themselves right while they are still alive. Death only has to come suddenly, and there's no one there to be corrected. And we just don't know when the last hour may come, and yet you say, "I will put things right." When are you putting things right, when are you turning over a new leaf?

"Tomorrow," you say.

Look, as often as you say "Tomorrow, tomorrow, *Cras, cras*," you have become a crow. Look, I'm telling you, when you croak like a crow, ruin is staring you in the face. Because that crow, whose croaking you are imitating, went out from the ark, and *didn't come back* (Gn 8:7). As for you, though, brother, come back into the Church, which that ark then represented.

But you at least, you newly baptized, listen to me; listen to me, you that have been born again through the blood of Christ. I beg you, by the name that has been invoked over you, by that altar which you have approached, by the sacraments you have received, by the judgment that is to come of the living and the dead; I beg you, I bind you by the name of Christ, not to imitate those you know to be such, but to ensure that the sacrament abides in you of the one who did not wish to come down from the cross, but did wish to rise again from the grave.

Sermon 229

On Holy Easter Sunday, about the Sacraments of the Faithful

There is some controversy about the authenticity of this sermon, based primarily on the reference to the main celebrant as *sacerdos,* "priest," which is not at all common for Augustine. Nevertheless, it is not unusual for Augustine to preach on the Preface Dialogue, and the vivid eucharistic imagery is quintessentially his. In this discussion of the eucharist he explains the complex relationship between sacrament and word. The suggested dates for the sermon range between 405 and 411, although its relative brevity and engagingly direct style argue for a later date, when the bishop was a more seasoned preacher, conscious of the patience of his congregation's limited attention span.

The bread and wine on the altar become the body and blood
of the Word, which he made us into as well

1. What you can see here, dearly beloved, on the table of the Lord, is bread and wine; but this bread and wine, when the word is applied to it, becomes the body and blood of the Word. That Lord, you see, who *in the beginning was the Word, and the Word was with God, and the Word was God* (Jn 1:1), was so compassionate that he did not despise what he had created in his own image; and therefore *the Word became flesh and dwelt among us* (Jn 1:14), as you know. Because, yes, the very Word took to himself a man, that is the soul and flesh of a man, and became man, while remaining God. For that reason, because he also suffered for us, he also presented us in this sacrament with his body and blood, and this is what he even made us ourselves into as well.

Call to mind what this created object was, not so long ago, in the fields; how the earth produced it, the rain nourished it, ripened it into the full ear; then human labor carried it to the threshing floor, threshed it, winnowed it, stored it, brought it out, ground it, mixed it into dough, baked it, and hardly any time ago at all produced it finally as bread. Now call yourselves also to mind: you didn't exist, and you were created, you were carried to the Lord's threshing floor, you were threshed by the labor of oxen, that is of the preachers of the gospel. When, as catechumens, you were being held back, you were being stored in the barn. You gave in your names; then you began to be ground by fasts and exorcisms. Afterward you came to the water, and you were moistened into dough, and made into one lump. With the application of the heat of the Holy Spirit you were baked, and made into the Lord's loaf of bread.

Be one yourselves, in the same way as you
can see the bread and wine have been made one

2. There you have what you have received. So just as you can see that what has
been made is one, mind you are one yourselves too in the same way, by loving each
other, by holding one and the same faith, one and the same hope, an undivided
charity. When the heretics receive this sacrament, they receive what is a testimony
against themselves; because they insist on division, while this bread is a sign of
unity. So too the wine was there in many grapes, and has now been concentrated into
a unity; it is one in the pleasant taste of the cup, but only after the pressure of the
wine-press. And you, after those fasts, after the hard labors, after the humiliation and
the contrition, have now at last come, in the name of Christ, into the Lord's cup, so to
say; and there you are on the table, and there you are in the cup. You are this together
with us; we all take this together, all drink together, because we all live together.

Explanation of the rite of the Mass from the preface onward

3. You are about to hear what you also heard yesterday; but today what you
heard is being explained to you and also what you answered — or perhaps you
kept quiet when the answers were given, but you learned yesterday what you
should answer today. After the greeting that you know, that is, *The Lord be with
you*, you heard, *Lift up the heart*. That's the whole life of real Christians, *Up with
the heart*; not of Christians in name only, but of Christians in reality and truth; their
whole life is a matter of *Up with the heart*. What does *Up with the heart* mean?
Hoping in God, not in yourself; you, after all, are down below, God is up above; if
you put your hope in yourself, your heart is down below, it isn't up above. That's
why, when you hear *Lift up the heart* from the high priest, you answer, *We have it
lifted up to the Lord*. Try very hard to make your answer a true one, because you are
making it in the course of the activity of God; let it be just as you say; don't let the
tongue declare it, while the conscience denies it.

And because this very thing of your having the heart up above is something that
God, not your own capability, bestows on you, when you have said that you have
your heart up above, the high priest continues and says, *To the Lord our God let us
give thanks*. What should we give thanks for? Because we have our heart up above,
and unless he had lifted it up, we would be lying on the ground.

And from there we come now to what is done in the holy prayers which you are
going to hear, that with the application of the word we may have the body and
blood of Christ. Take away the word, I mean, it's just bread and wine; add the
word, and it's now something else. And what is that something else? The body of
Christ, and the blood of Christ. So take away the word, it's bread and wine; add the
word and it will become the sacrament. To this you say, *Amen*. To say *Amen* is to
add your signature. *Amen* means "True" in English. Then comes the Lord's prayer,
which you have already received and given back. Why is it said before we receive
the body and blood of Christ? Because if, as is the case with human frailty, our
thoughts have turned perhaps to something that they shouldn't have done, if our

tongues have poured out something they ought not to have done, if our eyes have looked at something they shouldn't have, if our ears have listened with more pleasure than was proper to something they shouldn't have; if by any chance we have contracted any of that sort of thing from this world's temptations and the frailty of human life, it's all wiped clean by the Lord's prayer, where it says, *Forgive us our debts* (Mt 6:12), so that we may approach without any anxiety; otherwise we may eat and drink what we receive to our own condemnation.

After that comes *Peace be with you*; a great sacrament, the kiss of peace. So kiss in such a way as really meaning that you love. Don't be Judas; Judas the traitor kissed Christ with his mouth, while setting a trap for him in his heart. But perhaps somebody has unfriendly feelings toward you, and you are unable to win him round, to show him he's wrong; you're obliged to tolerate him. Don't pay him back evil for evil in your heart. He hates; just you love, and you can kiss him without anxiety.

It's only a few things that you've heard, but they are important ones. Don't treat them as cheap because they are few, but as dear because they are weighty. Also it would be wrong to overload you, or you wouldn't remember what's been said.

Sermon 229N

Preached on the Saturday of the Easter Octave

This is the one of a series of sermons preached on the Octave of Easter, and it exhibits an unusual balance of power and authority between the leaders of the Church and the faithful. It was preached sometime after 410 on Saturday of the Easter Octave on the theme of Peter's threefold confession of love. Borrowing from Cyprian, Augustine insists that Peter represents the entire Church rather than the first pope, as was the view of later Catholic authors. The power to bind and to loose was not given simply to Peter alone but to the entire Church, including the laity.

Christ's questions to Peter about whether he loved him are addressed to us as well

1. Here is the Lord, again appearing to the disciples after the resurrection, and questioning the apostle Peter; and he obliges him three times to confess his love, because three times he had denied him through fear. Christ rose again in the flesh, and Peter in the spirit; because when Christ died in his passion, Peter died by his denial. Christ the Lord was raised from the dead; out of his love he raised Peter. He questioned him about the love he was confessing, and entrusted him with his sheep. After all, what benefit could Peter confer on Christ, by the mere fact of his loving Christ? If Christ loves you, it's to your advantage, not

Christ's; and if you love Christ, it's to your advantage, not Christ's. And yet Christ the Lord wanted to indicate in what way people ought to indicate that they love Christ, and he made it plain enough by entrusting him with his sheep. *Do you love me? I do. Feed my sheep* (Jn 21:15-17). All this once, all this a second time, all this a third time. Peter made no other reply than that he loved him; the Lord asked no other question but whether he loved him; when he answered, he did nothing else but entrust his sheep to him.

Let us love each other, and we love Christ. Christ, you see, while always God, was born a man in time. As a human being born of a human being, he appeared as a man to men; he performed many miracles, as God in man; he suffered many evils, as man from men; he rose again after death, as God in man. He conversed for forty days on earth as man with men; before their very eyes he ascended into heaven, as God in man, and is seated at the right hand of the Father. All this we believe, we can't see; and we are commanded to love Christ the Lord, whom we can't see; and we all shout and say, "I love Christ." *If you do not love the brother whom you can see, how can you love the God whom you cannot see?* (1 Jn 4:20). By loving the sheep, show the love you have for the shepherd; because the very sheep themselves are members of the shepherd. In order that the sheep might be his members, he was prepared to be a sheep; that the sheep might be his members, *like a sheep he was led to the slaughter* (Is 53:7); that the sheep might be his members, it was said of him, *Behold the lamb of God, behold the one who takes away the sins of the world* (Jn 1:29). But there's tremendous courage in this lamb. Do you want to know how much courage this lamb showed? The lamb was crucified, and the lion was conquered. Just observe and consider with what power Christ must govern the world, seeing that by his death he conquered the devil.

The keys entrusted to Peter are also held by all bishops, and even by all the faithful

2. So let us love him, let there be nothing dearer to us than he. So do you imagine that the Lord is not questioning us? Was Peter the only one who qualified to be questioned, and didn't we? When that reading is read, every single Christian is being questioned in his heart. So when you hear the Lord saying *Peter, do you love me?* think of it as a mirror, and observe yourself there. I mean, what else was Peter doing but standing for the Church? So when the Lord was questioning Peter, he was questioning us, he was questioning the Church.

I mean, to show you that Peter stood for the Church, call to mind that place in the gospel, *You are Peter, and upon this rock I will build my Church, and the gates of the underworld shall not conquer her; to you will I give the keys of the kingdom of heaven* (Mt 16:18-19). One man receives them; you see, he explained himself what the keys of the kingdom mean: *What you all bind on earth shall be bound in heaven; and what you all loose on earth shall be loosed in heaven* (Mt 18:18). If it was said to Peter alone, Peter alone did this; he passed away, and went away; so who binds, who looses? I make bold to say, we too have these keys. And what am I to say? That it is only we who bind, only we who loose? No, you also bind, you also loose. Anybody who's bound, you see, is barred from your society; and when he's barred from your society, he's bound by you; and when he's reconciled he's loosed by you, because you too plead with God for him.

May Christ's love lead us all to where there are no more tears

3. We all love Christ, you see, we are his members; and when he entrusts the sheep to the shepherds, the whole number of shepherds is reduced to the body of the one shepherd. Just to show you that the whole number of shepherds is reduced to the one body of the one shepherd, certainly Peter's a shepherd, undoubtedly a pastor; Paul's a shepherd, yes, clearly a pastor; John's a shepherd, James a shepherd, Andrew a shepherd, and the other apostles are shepherds. All holy bishops are shepherds, pastors, yes, clearly so. And how can this be true: *And there will be one flock and one shepherd* (Jn 10:16)? Then if *there will be one flock and one shepherd* is true, the innumerable number of shepherds or pastors must be reduced to the body of the one shepherd or pastor.

But that's where you are too; you are his members. These members, when the head cried out for his members, were being trampled on by that Saul who was previously a persecutor, afterward a preacher, breathing out slaughter, putting off faith. The whole force of his attack crumbled at a single utterance. What utterance? *Saul, Saul, why are you persecuting me?* (Acts 9:4) Could Saul so much as throw a stone at heaven, where Jesus is seated? Granted, for the sake of argument, that Saul was in the crowd when Jesus was hanging on the cross; granted that Saul too said with the crowd, *Crucify him, crucify him* (Lk 23:21); and that he was among those who were shaking their heads in mockery, and saying, *If he is the Son of God, let him come down from the cross* (Mt 27:40). But what could he do to him when he was seated in heaven? What harm could words do him, what harm yelling, what harm the cross, what harm the spear? Nothing could be done to him now, and yet he cried out "You are persecuting me."

When he cried out "You are persecuting me," he was indicating that we are his members. And so may the love of Christ, whom we love in you, the love of Christ, whom you love in us, lead us all, among our trials, our temptations, our toils, our sweat, our anxieties, our misfortunes, to where there's no toil, no misfortune, no groans, no sighs, no vexations; where nobody's born, nobody dies, nobody has to fear the wrath of the mighty man, all being protected by the countenance of the Almighty God.

Sermon 232

Preached During the Easter Octave

Hill believes this sermon was preached on Tuesday during the Octave of Easter between 412 and 413. In it we learn that Augustine's congregation was resistant to innovations in the liturgy, in particular the bishop's decision to have the four different Passion narratives read on successive years. He is particularly attentive to the different details in each of the synoptic versions. The first section contains invaluable liturgical information on the liturgies of Holy Week and Easter Sunday, including the order of the specific gospel selections on the resurrection: Matthew on Sunday, Mark on Monday, Luke on Wednesday. S. 239, 2 indicates there was some flexibility here, since Luke was read the day before Mark. Similarly, the order in S. 247 is Matthew, Mark and Luke, with John on the fourth day. The homily is decidedly pro-woman in its emphasis that women were the very first witnesses to the resurrection. Mary is depicted as the "new Eve." Section 8 is particularly important for its information on the penitential practices of Hippo, and the bishop acknowledges that he himself has resorted to excommunicating some members of the Church.

The Lord's resurrection recounted from all the gospels,
his passion only from Matthew

1. The resurrection of our Lord Jesus Christ was recounted today as well, but from a different book of the gospel, the one according to Luke. It was first read, you see, according to Matthew, while yesterday it was according to Mark, today according to Luke, the order of the evangelists as we have them; and his passion too was written up by all of them. But these seven or eight days give us space for the resurrection of the Lord to be recounted according to all the evangelists; while his passion, being read on one day only, is customarily read just according to Matthew. Once upon a time I wanted the passion too to be read according to all the evangelists on successive years. It happened; people didn't hear what they were used to, and were upset. Those, however, who love the divine literature, and are not willing always to remain uneducated, know all of them and diligently study them all. But, *as God has allotted each the measure of faith* (Rom 2:3), so each makes progress.

The women telling the truth about Christ's resurrection are not believed,
while Eve passing on the devil's lies had been believed

2. Now let us attend to what we heard today, when it was read. Today, you see, we heard more explicitly about what I also drew your graces' attention to yesterday, the unbelief of the disciples, to help us appreciate how much his good-

ness has bestowed on us, by enabling us to believe what we have not seen. He called them, he taught them, he lived with them on earth, he performed such stupendous miracles before their very eyes, to the very raising of the dead; he even raised the dead, and they didn't believe he could raise his own flesh.

The women came to the tomb; they didn't find the body in the tomb; they were told by angels that Christ had risen; women reported this to men. And what's written? What did you hear? *These things seemed in their eyes like stuff and nonsense* (Lk 24:11). How hugely unhappy is the human condition! When Eve reported what the serpent had said, she was listened to straightaway. A lying woman was believed, and so we all died; they didn't believe women telling the truth so that we might live. If women are not to be trusted, why did Adam trust Eve? If women are to be trusted, why did the disciples not trust the holy women?

And thus it is that in this fact we have to reflect on the goodness of the Lord's arrangements. Because this of course was the doing of the Lord Jesus Christ, that it should be the female sex which would be the first to report that he had risen again. Because mankind fell through the female sex, mankind was restored through the female sex; because a virgin gave birth to Christ, a woman proclaimed that he had risen again. Through a woman death, through a woman life. But the disciples didn't believe what the women had said; they thought they were raving, when in fact they were reporting the truth.

The two disciples going to Emmaus thought of Christ only as a prophet,
forgetting Peter's confession of him as the Christ, the Son of God

3. Here we are with two others, walking along the road, and talking to each other about the things that had been happening in Jerusalem, about the iniquity of the Jews, about the death of Christ. They were walking along, talking the matter over, grieving for him as if he were dead, not knowing he had risen again. He appeared and joined them as a third traveler, and entered into friendly conversation with them. Their eyes were held from recognizing him; their hearts, you see, needed more thorough instruction. Recognition is deferred; he inquires what they were talking about, so that they might confess what he already knew. And as you heard, they began by being astonished at being asked about a matter of such public knowledge by someone seemingly ignorant of it. *Are you the only stranger in Jerusalem and you do not know what has been done there? And he said, What? About Jesus of Nazareth, who was a prophet powerful in deeds and words* (Lk 24:16-19).

Is that it, you disciples? A prophet, was he, Christ the Lord of the prophets? You're giving your judge the title of herald. They had come down to what other people had said. What do I mean by what other people had said? Recall that when Jesus himself had said to his disciples, *Who do people say that the Son of man is?* they told him what others thought: *Some say*, they said, *that you are Elijah, others that you are John the Baptist, others Jeremiah, or one of the prophets.* These were the words of other people, not of the disciples. And here we are, these disciples have come down to the same words. *But you, now, who do you say that I am?* You have told me other people's opinions, I want to hear your faith. Then Peter said, one for all of them because unity among all of them, *You are the Christ, the Son of the living God.* Not just any one of the prophets, but the Son of the living God, the fulfiller of the prophets, the creator even of the angels.

You are the Christ, the Son of the living God. Peter then heard what it was fitting for him to hear after such words as these: *Blessed are you, Simon Bar-Jona, because flesh and blood did not reveal it to you, but my Father who is in heaven. And I say to you, You are Peter, and upon this rock I will build my Church, and the gates of the underworld will not conquer her. To you will I give the keys of the kingdom of heaven, and whatever you loose on earth shall be loosed in heaven, and whatever you bind on earth shall be bound in heaven* (Mt 6:13-19). It was faith that deserved to hear this, not the man; what was the man himself, after all, but what the psalm says: *Every man a liar* (Ps 116:11)?

How Peter was both blessed and Satan

4. Then immediately after these words he informed them about his passion and death. Peter was horrified, and said, *Far be it from you, Lord; this shall not happen. Then the Lord said, Get behind me, Satan.* Peter, Satan? Where now are those words, *Blessed are you, Simon Bar-Jona?* Surely Satan can't be blessed, can he? Well, blessed because of what is of God, Satan because of what is of man. In fact the Lord himself explained why he called him Satan: *For you do not savor of the things of God, but of the things of man* (Mt 16:21-23). What made you blessed just now? *Because flesh and blood did not reveal it to you, but my Father who is in heaven.* Why Satan so soon afterward? *You do not savor of the things of God* — when you did smack of them you were blessed — *but you smack of the things of man.*

Look how the souls of the disciples switched back and forth, as though from sunrise to sunset; one moment on their feet, the next flat on their backs; one moment enlightened, the next darkened. Enlightened how? *Approach him and be enlightened* (Ps 34:5). Darkened how? *The one who speaks a lie, speaks from what is his own* (Jn 8:44). The Son of God had said it, life had said it, and they were afraid that life might die, though it was absolutely impossible for life to die, and the Son of God had come precisely in order to die; if he hadn't come in order to die, what would ever have enabled us to live?

How we brought death to the Word, and he brought life to us

5. From where do we get life, from where does he get death? Just look at him: *In the beginning was the Word, and the Word was with God, and the Word was God*

(Jn 1:1). Look for death there. Where? Where from? What sort of Word? The Word with God, the Word that was God. If you can find flesh and blood there, you can find death. So where did death come from for that Word? On the other hand, where did life come from for us human beings, stuck on the earth, mortal, perishable, sinners? He had nothing where he could get death from; we had nothing where we could get life from. He accepted death from what was ours, in order to give us life from what was his. How did he get death from what was ours? *The Word became flesh, and dwelt among us* (Jn 1:14). He accepted from us here what he would offer for us. And where did life come from for us? *And the life was the light of men* (Jn 1:4). He was life for us, we were death for him.

But what sort of death? One due to his consideration, not his condition. Because he was courteously considerate, because he so willed it, because he took pity on us, he chose of his own authority to die. *I have the authority to lay down my life, and I have the authority to take it up again* (Jn 10:18). This was something Peter didn't know, when he was so horrified on hearing how the Lord would die.

But look now, the Lord had already said he was going to die and rise again on the third day. What he foretold had happened, and these two wouldn't believe what they had heard. *Why, it is now three days since these things happened, and we were thinking that he was the one who would redeem Israel* (Lk 24:21). You were hoping, now you're despairing? You have fallen from hope. The one who's walking along with you picks you up. They were disciples, they had heard him, they had lived with him, they had known him as their teacher, they had been instructed by him, and they couldn't even imitate and share the faith of the robber hanging on the cross.

Where the good thief found hope, the disciples lost it

6. But perhaps some of you don't understand what I have just said about the robber, as a result of not hearing the passion according to all the evangelists. It's this evangelist Luke, you see, who recounted what I am talking about. That two robbers were crucified with Christ Matthew also said; but that one of those robbers railed at the Lord, and that the other one believed in Christ, Matthew did not say, Luke said it. Let us bear in mind the faith of the robber, a faith Christ did not find after his resurrection in his disciples. Christ was hanging on the cross, and so was the robber; Christ in the middle, they on either side. One rails, the other believes, the one in the middle judges. The one who was railing at him, you see, said this: *If you are the Son of God, deliver yourself. And the other answered him: Do you not fear God? If we are deservedly suffering because of our deeds, what has this man done? And turning to him, he said: Remember me, Lord, when you come into your kingdom* (Lk 23:39-42). Great faith indeed; what could possibly be added to such faith, I really do not know. The ones who had seen

Christ waking the dead wavered; the one who could see him then and there hanging on the tree with him, believed him. When they wavered is precisely when he believed.

What wonderful fruit Christ picked from the dry wood! I mean, what did Christ say to him? Let's hear it: *Amen I tell you, today you shall be with me in paradise* (Lk 23:43). You are putting off what you are asking for; I am acknowledging you here and now. When would a robber ever hope to go from robbery to the judge, from the judge to the cross, from the cross straight to paradise? Anyway, he was paying attention to his deserts, and he didn't say, "Remember me so as to deliver me today"; but "*When you come into your kingdom,* then keep me in mind; so that if torments are my due, at least only until you come into your kingdom." *But Jesus said,* "Not so; you have invaded the kingdom of heaven, you have used force, you have believed, you have taken it by storm. *Today you shall be with me in paradise.* I am not putting you off for a single moment; I'm paying today, on the dot, what I owe to such great faith." The robber says, *Remember me when you come into your kingdom*; he not only believed he would rise again, but also that he would reign; to a man hanging there, crucified, covered in blood, stuck there, *when you come,* he says, *into your kingdom.* And these two — *We were hoping* (Lk 24:21); where the robber found hope, the disciple lost it.

It is worth much more having Christ in one's heart than in one's house

7. And now then, my dearest friends, we have recognized the great sacrament. Listen. He was walking with them, he is hospitably entertained, he breaks bread, and he's recognized. And we too must not say that we have not known Christ. We have known him if we believe. It's too little to say we have known him if we believe; we have him with us if we believe. They had Christ with them at a meal together; we have him inside in our spirits. It's a greater thing to have Christ in your heart than in your house. Our hearts, after all, are more inwardly attached to us than our houses. So now then, where ought the faithful to recognize him? The faithful know where; the catechumens, though, don't know; but nobody is shutting the door in their faces, to stop them knowing.

My riches are nothing else than your hope in Christ

8. Yesterday I warned you, and I'm warning your graces again that the resurrection of Christ is only in us if we live good lives; if our old bad life dies, and the new one makes progress every day. There are a great many penitents here; when hands are laid on them, there is an extremely long line. "Pray, penitents — and the penitents go out to pray." I examine the penitents, and I find people living bad lives. How can you be sorry for what you go on doing? If you're sorry, don't do it. If you go on doing it, though, the name's wrong, the crime remains. Some people have asked for a place among the penitents themselves; some have been excom-

municated by me and reduced to the penitents' place. And those who asked for it themselves want to go on doing what they were doing, and those who have been excommunicated by me and reduced to the penitents' corner don't want to rise from there, as though penitents' corner were a really choice spot. It ought to be a place for humility, and it becomes a place for iniquity.

It's you I'm talking to, you that are called penitents and are not so, it's you I'm talking to. *What am I to say to you? Can I praise you? On this point I cannot praise you* (1 Cor 11:22), I can only groan and moan. And what am I to do, having become a cheap song? Change your ways, I beg you, change your ways. The end of life is totally uncertain. Everyone of us is riding for a fall. You are all putting off living good lives, thinking that life will be long. You're thinking of a long life, and not afraid of a sudden death? But all right, let it be a long one; and I look for one real penitent, and I can't find one. How much better a long, good life will be, than a long, bad one! Nobody wants to put up with a long, bad dinner, practically everybody wants to have a long, bad life.

Surely, surely, if it's a great thing that we should be alive, this great thing should be a good one. I mean, is there anything that you want to be bad, tell me, in all your actions, thoughts, longings? On your land you don't want a bad crop — of course you don't want a bad one, but a good one, a good tree, good horse, good servant, good friend, good son, good wife. And why should I mention these important things, since you don't even want to have bad clothes? Finally, down to your very boots, you only want good ones. Or grant me that you want anything that's bad, and don't want anything good. I imagine you don't want a bad country place, but a good one. Your soul is the only thing you want to have bad. How have you offended yourself? How have you deserved so badly of yourself? Among all your good things, the only one you want to be bad is yourself.

I suppose I'm only saying what I'm in the habit of saying, and some people, perhaps, are only doing what they are in the habit of doing. I didn't say "certainly," but "perhaps." No one should accuse me of speaking fearfully rather than strongly. In the presence of God *I shake out my garments.* What I'm afraid of is being charged with being afraid. What do you want? I am carrying out my office, I am looking for profit from you. What I want to get from your good works is joy, not money. After all, your living a good life doesn't make me rich. And yet all the same, live a good life, and you do make me rich. My riches are nothing else than your hope in Christ. My joy, my consolation, and the breathing space from my dangers amid all these trials is purely and simply your good lives. I beg you, brothers and sisters, even if you forget yourselves, take pity on me.

Sermon 239

Preached During the Easter Octave

This homily based on Mark's resurrection account was clearly preached during the Octave of Easter. Several dates for it are proposed by various scholars: Kunzel and LaBonnardière say before 400; Poque suggests between 410-412 and Lambot before 417. Augustine appeals to ordinary people's attraction to making money by exhorting them to lend at exorbitant interest rates to God in expectation of a greater return on the investment. He finds it significant that two of the four evangelists came from "the Twelve": Matthew and John (*pace* modern biblical scholarship on the author of John). The Holy Spirit wanted to prevent people from thinking that the fountain of grace for evangelizing only extended as far as the apostles. There is a strong exhortation to extend hospitality to the stranger and to be generous toward the needy. God will return a hundredfold and eternal life. Christ's incarnation and willing embrace of human poverty and frailty should be the model for our generosity.

*Mark and Luke were chosen to be evangelists, though they were not apostles,
to signify that the task of evangelization continues in the Church to the end*

1. Today we have heard for yet a third time from the gospel about our Lord's resurrection. As you will remember that I've told you, this is the custom, for the Lord's resurrection to be recounted according to all the evangelists. It's Mark's gospel which we heard just now, when it was read. Mark, though, won this privilege, as did Luke too, though he had not been in the number of those twelve. While there are four evangelists, you see, Matthew, John, Mark, and Luke, only two of them come from those twelve, namely Matthew and John. Their precedence, however, was not so sterile that they couldn't have any companions to follow them. Mark and Luke were not the equals of the apostles, but their "sub-equals."

The reason, you see, why the Holy Spirit wished also to choose two men who were not among the twelve to write down a gospel, was to prevent people imagining that the grace of evangelizing got as far as the apostles, and that the fountain of grace then dried up with them. The Lord, after all, says about his Spirit and about his word, that if anybody receives and keeps it worthily, *it will become in him a fountain of water leaping up to eternal life* (Jn 4:14); a fountain, of course, reveals itself by welling up, not by remaining stagnant; through the apostles grace reached other people, and they too were sent to preach the gospel. Because the one who called the first preachers was the same one who also called the next ones; he went on calling them right up to the latest times of the body of his only-begotten Son, that is, the Church spread throughout the world.

At the breaking of bread the eyes of the disciples were opened,
not to see, but to know Christ

2. So what did we hear Mark saying? That the Lord appeared to two of them on the road, as Luke also said, whose gospel we heard yesterday: *He appeared,* he says, *to two of them on the road in another guise* (Mk 16:12). Luke, though, said the same thing in other words, but didn't deviate from the same meaning. Well, what did Luke say? *Their eyes were held, so that they would not recognize him* (Lk 24:16). And what did Mark say? *He appeared to them in another guise.* What the former said, *Their eyes were held, so that they would not recognize him,* is the same as what this one says, *in another guise.* Another guise was seen, I mean, because their eyes were held, weren't open.

So, brothers and sisters, what about the thing Luke said, as I imagine you remember from yesterday's reading, recent enough; that when he blessed the bread their eyes were opened? What are we to suppose: that if their eyes were opened then, it means they had been accompanying him on the road with closed eyes, and could still know where to put their feet, even if they had their eyes closed? So they were opened for purposes of recognition, not of straight sight. And so our Lord Jesus Christ is speaking with people, all unbeknown before the breaking of bread, he becomes known in the breaking of bread; because there, precisely, is he perceived, where eternal life is received. He is welcomed as guest, while himself preparing a home in heaven. He says, you remember, according to the evangelist John, *There are many lodgings at my Father's; otherwise I would have told you. I will go to prepare a place for you. But if I go and prepare it, I will come again and take you along* (Jn 14:2-3). The Lord of heaven chose to be a guest on earth, a stranger in the world though the world was made through him. He was prepared to be a guest, so that you might have the blessing of giving him welcome; not because he was in any need, when he came in as a guest.

Elijah is supported by the widow woman, for her good rather than for his

3. In a time of famine the Lord fed Saint Elijah through the services of a crow; persecuted by men, he was waited on by birds. The crow would bring the servant of God bread in the morning, meat in the evening. So he wasn't in any need, since God was feeding him by the ministrations of birds. And yet, although Elijah was not in any need, he is sent to a widow in Zarephath, and told, *Go to that widow, she will feed you.* Had God run out of resources, for Elijah to be sent to the widow? But if God were always to provide his servant with bread without human ministrations, where would the widow get her reward from? So, being in no need himself, he is sent to a woman in need; not starving himself, he is sent to a starving woman, and he says to her, *Go, and fetch me a little to eat.* She had a small amount, which she was going to eat, and die. She answered, she hinted to the prophet just how much she had; and the prophet said to her, *Go, first bring*

some to me. She didn't hesitate, but brought it. She offered refreshment, and earned a blessing. Saint Elijah blessed the jar of flour, and the flask of oil. That bit of flour was set there in the house, ready to be eaten up, and that oil was hanging from its peg, ready to be finished off; the blessing was attached, and those vessels became warehouses. The oil bottle became an oil well, the little bit of flour surpassed the most abundant crops.

The one welcomed is often better than the one who welcomes;
the one receiving richer than the one handing out

4. If Elijah was not in any need, can Christ have been? The reason, my brothers and sisters, so holy scripture is reminding us, the reason why God often makes his servants beggars of food, though he is perfectly capable of feeding them, is in order to find doers of good. Don't ever be proud because you give something to the poor; Christ was poor. Don't ever be proud because you welcome a stranger; Christ was a stranger. The one welcomed is better than the one providing the welcome; the one receiving is richer than the one handing out. The one who was receiving was the owner of everything; the one who was giving had received what he was giving from the one he was giving it to. So don't ever be proud, my brothers and sisters, when you give something to a poor person. Don't ever say in your heart, "I'm giving, he's receiving; I'm giving him a welcome, he's in need of shelter." Perhaps what you're in need of is rather more than that. Perhaps the one you are giving a welcome to is a just man; he's in need of bread, you of truth; he's in need of shelter, you of heaven; he's in need of money, you of justice.

Lend at extortionate rates of interest to God, not to another human being

5. Be a financier, lay out what you may get back with interest. Don't be afraid that God may judge you as a financier, and convict you of usury. Certainly, certainly, be a financier. But God says to you, "What do you want? To be a financier? What's being a financier? Giving less, and getting back more. Here then, give to me," God says to you; "I accept less and I give back more. How much? A hundredfold, and eternal life." The one you're looking for, to give something to, so that your capital may grow, the man you're looking for, rejoices when he receives it, weeps when he gives it back; comes bowing and scraping in order to receive it, blackens your name in order to avoid giving it back.

Yes, give to people too, and *do not turn away from the one who asks for a loan* (Mt 5:42). But only take back as much as you've given. Don't make the person you've given it to cry, because then you've lost all benefit from it. And if what was given, or what he received, is demanded, perhaps he hasn't yet got it to hand; you put up with him when he asked for it; wait for him when he hasn't got it. When he does have it, he'll pay you back. Don't make difficulties for one whose difficulties you relieved earlier on. All right, you gave the money, and you're demanding it back; but he hasn't got the means of paying back; he'll pay you back when he does have it. Don't start shouting and saying, "Am I requiring interest? All I'm asking for is what I gave; what I gave, that's what I'll accept."

You're doing good, but he hasn't got it yet. You aren't a financier or banker, and you want the person you favored with a loan to seek out a banker, in order to pay you back? If the reason you aren't demanding interest, is to spare him experiencing you as a financier, why do you want him, for your sake, to experience someone else as a financier? You're squeezing him, choking him, even if you are only demanding as much as you gave. Yet by choking him and making things hard for him, you haven't conferred any benefit on him at all, but rather have made things harder, more difficult for him than ever.

But perhaps you say, "He's got the means to pay; he's got a house, let him sell it; he's got a plot, let him sell it." When he asked you for a loan, the reason he asked for it was in order not to have to sell; don't make him do it because of you, since you came to his assistance to save him from doing it. Let that be how things are done between human beings; that's what God commands, that's what God wants.

God made his own Son poor for our sake

6. But you're grasping, are you? God says to you, "Be grasping, be as grasping as you can; but you must issue a summons against me to satisfy your grasping greed." God says to you, "Issue a summons against me; I made my rich Son poor for your sake." It was *because of us*, you see, that *Christ became poor, though he was rich* (2 Cor 8:9). Are you looking for gold? He made it. Looking for silver? He made it. Looking for a retinue? He made it. Looking for cattle? He made them. Looking for lands? He made them. Why look only for what he made? Accept the one himself who made them. Just think how much he loved you. *All things were made through him, and without him was made nothing* (Jn 1:3). All things through him, and himself among all things; having made all things, he was himself made among all things. Having made man, he himself was made man, became man; he became what he made, in case the one he made should perish. Having made all things, he himself was made among all things.

Consider his wealth; what could be wealthier than the one through whom all things were made? And yet he, though being rich, took flesh in the virgin's womb. He was born as a baby, wrapped up in baby clothes, laid in a manger; patiently he awaited the successive ages of life; patiently he endured the succession of times, the one through whom all times were made. He sucked the breast, he cried, he was manifestly a baby. But he lay there, and reigned; he was in the manger, and held the universe together; he was nursed by his mother, and worshiped by the nations; nursed by his mother, and announced by angels; nursed by his mother, and proclaimed by a shining star. Such his wealth, such his poverty; wealth, to get you created; poverty, to get you restored. So that poor man's being hospitably welcomed as a poor man, was doing the benefactor a favor, not relieving an unfortunate person's needs.

Christ is in need in his members

7. Perhaps you'll say to me, "Oh, how lucky they were, who were found worthy to welcome Christ! Oh, if only I had lived at that time! Oh, if only I had been one of those two, whom he found on the road!" You just be on the road, there will be no lack of Christ to be your guest. Do you really think, I mean, that you aren't now permitted to welcome Christ?

"How," you say, "am I permitted to do so? He had already risen when he appeared to his disciples, he ascended into heaven, that's where he is, at the right hand of the Father; he isn't going to come till the last age, to judge the living and the dead; but he will be coming in splendor, not in weakness; he will be giving a kingdom, not seeking hospitality."

Has it escaped you what he will be saying, when he gives out a kingdom? *When you did it to one of the least of mine, you did it to me* (Mt 25:40)? That rich man is in dire need until the end of the world. Without the slightest doubt he's in dire need, not in the head, but in his members. Where is he in need? In those in whom he suffered pain, when he said, *Saul, Saul, why are you persecuting me?* (Acts 9:4).

So let us take care of Christ. He's with us in those who are his, he's with us in ourselves; nor was it to no purpose that he said, *Behold, I am with you until the consummation of the world* (Mt 28:20). By doing this sort of thing, we recognize Christ in good works, with the heart, not the body; not with the eyes of the body, but with the eyes of faith. *Because you have seen, you have believed,* he said to a certain incredulous disciple of his, who had said, *I will not believe, unless I touch.* And the Lord said, *Come, touch, and stop being incredulous.* He touched, and he exclaimed, *My Lord and my God!* And the Lord said, *Because you have seen me, you have believed*; that's the whole of your faith, that you believe what you can see. I praise *those who do not see, and believe* (Jn 20:25-29); because when they see, they will rejoice.

Sermon 242A

During the Easter Season, on the Resurrection of the Body

Fischer and Kunzelmann both suggest Wednesday of Easter week for this sermon; Hill argues that it was preached later in the Easter season sometime after 411-412. Augustine addresses the difficulty people have in believing in their own future resurrection even if they dare not deny the resurrection of Jesus. The toil, weariness, sorrow, poverty and sickness experienced by the human body did not come about through our natural condition but are the result of inherited sin. The bishop counters disbelief in the resurrection with the daily miracles which occur abundantly in nature, in particular the miracle of birth itself.

Having raised up his own flesh, God will also raise up yours

1. That our Lord Jesus Christ rose from the dead on the third day is the testimony of the holy gospels, and the whole wide world now confesses this faith in the holy symbol or creed. The prophets didn't see such things, but they said they would happen; no, they didn't see them, but in the spirit they foresaw them. And I'm thinking now of some other people, and how ashamed they ought to be because, while they dare not deny the resurrection of Christ, they deny that ours is going to happen. They say, you see, "He rose again, as being the only one who had the right to rise again with the very flesh, which he so graciously took to himself. It doesn't follow from that though, does it, that our flesh too can rise again, just because his did? Clearly, his power and capacity is far and away above ours."

To which the answer is: "The divinity of Christ is far and away above you, but the infirmity of Christ has drawn close to you. In himself he's God, for your sake human; from what is properly his he made you, from what is properly yours he suffered for you. So if he made you from what is his own, he rose again from what is yours." The Word, certainly, had no flesh; *In the beginning was the Word, and the Word was with God, and the Word was God; this was in the beginning with God. All things were made through him* (Jn 1:1-3). Man too was made through him; but afterward he was made man himself, he through whom man was made; and so that man might not perish, Christ died.

But Christ rose again. What, in him, rose again? *The Word was made flesh, and dwelt among us* (Jn 1:14). The Word took to himself what he was not, but never lost what he was. So he remained the Word. What rose again? The Word. Why did he fall? In order to rise again. Why did the Word die? In order to come to life again. But we are saying that he died in the flesh which he took, not in the divinity in which he remained. So in the element in which Christ rose again, he did himself wrong, while providing a model for you; for him to rise again, you see, was a humiliation, it was a wrong. Go back to the Word, go back to *In the beginning was the Word, and the Word was with God, and the Word was God*, and consider what it means for that one to rise again; because having raised up his own flesh, he will also raise up yours. The reason, you see, he wished his own to rise again, was to preserve you from failing to believe that yours would rise again.

Bringing you alive from the tomb

2. But the people who are arguing against us say, " The flesh of Christ rose again because it was only three days in the tomb, and didn't *see corruption* (Ps 16:10; Acts 2:27), and neither decayed nor rotted nor crumbled to dust. Ours, on the other hand, whenever graves happen to be opened, well you can scarcely even find bones there, what's found is dust. Whatever was flesh is totally rotted away, totally crumbled into dust. So will it be able to rise again, seeing it hasn't been able to preserve its integrity?"

Just consider, friend, when you argue like that, just consider, I say, that there are bones in the grave; if nothing else, at least there are bones; in the grave there is also the dust of the body, in the place where it was received by the bosom of the earth. Go back now to your own origin, and inquire what you were, when you were begotten or seeded. He poured out our beginnings in the womb; think about it; compare a human being as buried, with a human being as seeded.

Of course we all know that we are mortal. So in the same way as we reflect on the womb of the earth, in which the body lies, seeded in order to rise again, let us also reflect on ourselves seeded in the wombs of our mothers, from which this complexity of limbs and organs arose. Where were these five senses of the body hiding? Where in that drop of moisture were eyes and tongue and ears and hands? Where did these various functions of different organs proceed from? Who created it all, who shaped it all? Wasn't it God? Very well then, the God who was able to thrust you out in proper shape from the womb, himself wishes you to judge what can be done from what has been done, and to believe that he can also bring you alive from the tomb.

That people are seeded here, that here, I repeat, human beings take shape in their mothers' wombs, is a daily miracle; but it's so excessively common it has lost its power to strike wonder, and by its very frequency has become common-place. But the thing that is only going to happen once, that is, the resurrection that is going to happen only once, is rehearsed over and over again by daily evidences. Nature cries it aloud, scripture insists on it; let us believe this thing is going to happen; let us believe, brothers and sisters, that this body of ours will rise again, to glory for the good, to pain and punishment for the wicked.

What you like comes to life again, what you don't like perishes

3. What, I mean to say, what, I ask you, is bothering you, unwilling as you are to believe that there will be a resurrection of the flesh? What is it about the body that you don't like? *Who ever hated his own flesh?* says the apostle (Eph 5:29). What is it about the body that you don't like? If the whole coordinated structure of the body is described, doesn't the one who hears it feel overwhelmed, and the one who describes it cannot do it justice? What is it about the body that you don't like? I will tell you; it's the body's liability to decay, its mortality. But the things you like will be there, the things you don't like won't. Listen to the apostle: *It is seeded as an embodiment of soul, it will rise as an embodiment of spirit; it is seeded in reproach, it will rise in glory; it is seeded in weakness, it will rise in strength.* Listen to a fuller statement: *This perishable thing must put on imperishability, and this mortal thing must put on immortality* (1 Cor 15:44.43.53). What you like comes to life again, what you don't like perishes.

So don't be ungrateful to your Redeemer, by not believing what he promised; but do what he commands, in order to receive what he promised. Your Redeemer, after all, can do everything, because he is God. If you don't like the body being resuscitated, then stop liking the body now. Why take such care of what you don't like? Why look after what you don't like? Why feed what you don't like? What do you prefer it to be safe and sound for? Or do you like it, in fact? Then be grateful, and believe in the resurrection.

So bodies will rise again, because Christ rose again; but they will have no needs or wants, because Christ too, when he rose again, ate some food because he was able to, not because he needed to. There will be no hunger there; we shall not stand there anxiously, and say, *Give us this day our daily bread* (Lk 11:3); we will always have eternal bread. But it's always to hand; we won't be hoping for rain because of it, we won't dread the cloudless skies of drought; because our bread will be the one who made the skies. And there will be no fear there, no toil, no sorrow, no decay, no poverty, no infirmity, no weariness, no clumsiness. None of these things will be there; but the body will be.

All these evils, you see, which we are aware of in the body, have been brought on by sin, they didn't come about through our natural condition. From the very beginning, after all, through the man who sinned, we have received this evil inheritance from our father the sinner. But there came to us another inheritance, that of the man who took on our inheritance and promised us his own. We were in possession of death through blame; he took death to himself without blame; though he wasn't a debtor, he was put to death, and so tore up the debtors' bills. So, all of you, let your minds be full of faith in the resurrection. What Christians are promised is not only everything that the scriptures proclaim has been done in Christ, but also what is going to be done in him.

Sermon 243

During Easter Week on the Lord's Resurrection according to John

This sermon is a careful yet bold reflection on the bodily dimension of the resurrection state, where body parts serve not only a functional but also an aesthetic
purpose: "So some parts of our bodies will be for show, not for use; for the display of beauty, not the service of necessity." The bishop manifests an impressive
respect for the bodily dimension of human beings that will strike many as vulgar, given the Neo-platonic tendency to spiritualize life after death. He specifies
such body parts as eyes, ears, nostrils, mouth, tongue, teeth, throat, stomach, intestines and even private parts, not to mention beards, breasts and nipples. Furthermore, Augustine seeks to unlock the meaning of Jesus' words to Mary in
John 20:17: *Do not touch me; for I have not yet ascended to my Father.* He
claims there will be mutual recognition in the resurrection state based not
merely on physical appearance but also on a greater kind of knowledge.

The problem of why Mary was told not to touch Jesus

1. The account of the resurrection of our Lord Jesus Christ according to the
evangelist John began to be read today. As you know, of course, and as I had
earlier reminded you, the Lord's resurrection is chanted during these days
according to all four evangelists. So in the account we have just heard, the one
thing that usually bothers people is why the Lord Jesus said to the woman who
was seeking his body, and now recognized him as being alive, *Do not touch me;
for I have not yet ascended to my Father* (Jn 20:17). But I've told you, and you
certainly ought to remember, that they don't all say everything; but things are
said by some which are passed over by others. Not, however, in such a way that
they must be thought to clash with each other — if there is no desire to pick
holes, but a devout desire to understand.

You see, as you can read in the evangelist Matthew, after he had risen he met
two women, one of them this one, and said to them, *Hail. But they approached,
and took hold of his feet, and worshiped him* (Mt 28:9). And of course he hadn't
yet ascended to the Father. So how can he now say to this one, *Do not touch me;
for I have not yet ascended to my Father?* I mean, these words seem to be saying,
rather, that Mary would be able to touch him when he had ascended into heaven.
If she can't touch him when he's located on earth, what mortal can touch him
when he's seated in heaven?

Touching Christ means believing in him

2. But this touching signifies faith; you touch Christ if you believe in Christ. I
mean, even that woman who was suffering from an issue of blood said to herself, *If*

I touch the hem of his garment, I shall be healed. She touched with faith, and the health she was so sure of resulted. Then, to show us what true touching really is, the Lord immediately said to his disciples, *Who touched me? And the disciples said, The crowds are crushing you, and you can say, Who touched me? And he said, Someone touched me* (Mk 5:28-31; Lk 8:46). As though to say, The crowd jostles, faith touches.

So it seems that this Mary, to whom the Lord said, *Do not touch me; for I have not yet ascended to my Father* (Jn 20:17), represents the Church, which precisely then came to believe in Christ when he had ascended into heaven. Look, I question all of you when you came to believe; I question the Church spread throughout the whole world, which is represented by this one woman, and with one voice it answers me, "The time I came to believe was when Jesus had ascended to the Father." What else is "the time I came to believe" but "the time I touched"? Many worldly minded, materialistic people thought Christ was only a man, they had no idea of the divinity hidden in him. They didn't touch him well, because they didn't believe well. Do you want to touch well? Understand Christ where he is co-eternal with the Father, and you've touched him. But if you just think he's a man, and think nothing further, then for you he has not yet ascended to the Father.

The functions of the various parts of the risen body

3. So the Lord Jesus presented the sight of his body to human senses, in order to confirm the resurrection of the flesh. The one thing he wished to teach us, by showing himself alive in the body after his resurrection, was that we should believe in the resurrection of the dead. So since all bodies are to be restored whole and entire, a difficult question about the use of their parts is often asked by people who are eager to know, and put as a challenge by people who are eager to pick a quarrel.

They say, you see, that our bodies have all their parts, and that it is apparent which parts are necessary for which functions. Who, I mean, wouldn't know, who can't see, that we have eyes for seeing, ears for hearing, tongues for talking, noses for smelling, teeth for chewing, hands for working, feet for walking; also those parts which are called private, or *pudenda*, for reproducing? Further, though, there are the bowels inside, which God wished to be covered up, in case their appearance should disgust us; for what functions our inner parts, and what are called intestines, are of use, many people, and doctors most of all, know very well.

So they argue and say to us, "If we'll have ears to hear with, eyes to see with, tongues to talk with; why will we have teeth, if we aren't going to eat, jaws, lungs, stomachs, intestines, through which food passes and is digested for the regulation of our health? Lastly, "why," they say, "will we have those parts that are called private, or shameful, where there will be no reproduction, no excretion?"

*On the beauty of the interconnection between the different parts
of the human body, and their functional design*

4. What are we to answer them? Can we possibly say to them that we will rise again without intestines, just like statues? I mean, about the teeth there is an easy answer. You see, teeth aren't only a help in chewing, but also in speaking; striking our tongues, like a plectrum the strings of a lyre, to produce syllables. So some other parts of our bodies will be for show, not for use; for the display of beauty, not the service of necessity. Just because they will be at leisure, does it mean they will be unsightly?

And indeed now, because we are ill-informed and ignorant of the causes of things, if our insides are ever seen, they inspire disgust rather than admiration. Which of us, after all, knows how these parts are linked with each other, and in what proportions they are fitted together? That's what harmony means, a word taken from music; where we can certainly see the sinews, the strings, stretched on the guitar. If all the strings make the same note, there is no tune; varied tension in the strings produces a variety of notes. But a variety of notes combined with intelligent art produces, not beauty for spectators, but sweetness for listeners. Anybody who has learned the intelligent art of this kind that is to be found in the parts of the human body is so amazed, so delighted, that this art, this harmony, this proportion is preferred by those who understand it to all visible beauty. Now we don't know about it; but then we shall. Not because our insides will be laid bare, but because even though covered up, they will not be able to remain hidden.

If the thoughts of our hearts will not be hidden, why should our entrails be?

5. Someone is going to answer me and say, "How will they be unable to remain hidden, if they are covered up?" Our hearts will not remain hidden, and will our entrails remain so? Those thoughts, my brothers and sisters, those thoughts which now only God sees, will all be visible to one another in that company of the saints. Nobody there wishes what they are thinking to be covered up, because nobody there is thinking bad thoughts. Which is why the apostle says, *Do not pass any judgment before the time*; that is, "Don't judge rashly, because you can't see with what sort of mind someone acts." If something is done which can be done even with a good intention, don't find fault; don't take to yourself any more right of judgment than humanity requires. To see the heart is God's privilege; human beings only have the right to pass judgment on what is out in the open. *So do not*, he says, *pass any judgment before the time.* What's *before the time*? He goes on to say: *until the Lord comes, and lights up the hidden things of darkness.* What darkness he means, he shows plainly in the following words. *And lights up,* he says, *the hidden things of darkness.* What does that mean? Listen to what follows: *And he will show up the thoughts of the heart* (1 Cor 4:5). Lighting up the hidden things of darkness is the same as showing up the thoughts of the heart.

So now our thoughts are in the light to each one of us, because we know our own. But they are in darkness to our neighbors, because they can't see them. Then, however, what you know you are thinking, the other person is going to know too. Why be afraid? Now you want to conceal your thoughts, now you are afraid to publish them; perhaps, I mean, you are sometimes thinking something bad, something dirty maybe, maybe something silly. Then, however, when you get there, you will think nothing but what is good, nothing but what is honorable, nothing but what is true, nothing but what is pure, nothing but what is sincere. Just as now you wish your face to be seen, so then you will want your conscience to be seen too.

After all, there's the matter of recognition, my dearest friends; won't we all recognize everybody else? Do you think you are going to recognize me, just because you have known me now, and are not going to recognize my father, whom you haven't known, or heaven knows what bishop who was over this Church many years ago? You will know them all. Those who are there won't recognize each other just because they see faces; mutual recognition will come from a greater kind of knowledge. They will all see each other, but much more perfectly, in the same way as prophets are accustomed to see things here. They will see in a divine manner, since they will be full of God. And there will be nothing to give offense, nothing to be hidden from people's knowledge.

Some parts of the body are for use, others for elegance

6. So then, there the parts will be entire that here are private or shameful, but won't be shameful or private there. There will be no concern for their complete seemliness, when there is no unseemliness of lust. And look, even here, where necessity is after a fashion the mother of all our activities — a necessity that won't exist then; we can still find some things that God has placed in our bodies, not for any use, but simply and solely to look nice.

I was running through the different parts a moment ago, and now let's unpick them a little more carefully. We've eyes for seeing, ears for hearing, nostrils for smelling, mouth and tongue for talking, teeth for chewing, throat for swallowing, stomach for receiving and cooking, intestines for passing the food down the line to the bottom, and the parts that are called private or shameful either for excretion or for reproduction; for working we've got hands, for walking, feet. Beards — what are they any use for, but beauty alone? Why did God create the beard in man? I see the look of it, I don't look for its use. It's obvious why women have breasts — to suckle babies, of course; why do men have nipples? Question their use, there isn't any; question the look of them, a chest with nipples suits men too. Take away the nipples from the manly breast, and see how much beauty you have spoiled, how much ugliness you have introduced.

If there's so much beauty in the human body now,
how much more so in the resurrection?

7. So then, dearly beloved, believe that that's how, firmly maintain that that's how a great many parts of the body won't have any use there, but none of them will

lack grace and elegance. There will be nothing graceless and inelegant there; there will be total peace, nothing discordant, nothing monstrous, nothing to offend the sight; God will be praised in everything. After all, if even now in this feeble state of the flesh and delicate functioning of the body's parts, its beauty can be so apparent as to entice the lustful, and excite either the studious or the curious to further research; and if the mathematical proportions discovered in the body show that there is not one craftsman of these, another of the heavens, but that it's the same creator of the lowest and the highest; how much more so there, where no lust, no corruption, no deformity or distortion, no painful necessity will be found, but only boundless eternity, true beauty, supreme felicity?

What are we going to do in the resurrection? Sing alleluia

8. But you'll say to me, "What am I going to do? There will be no functions for the parts of my body to perform; what am I going to do?" Doesn't it strike you as doing anything, just standing, seeing, loving, praising? Look here, these holy days which are being celebrated after the Lord's resurrection, stand for the life that will be ours after our resurrection. You see, just as the forty days of Lent before Easter stood for the difficulties of this mortal life and its troubles, so these happy days stand for the future life, where we will be reigning with the Lord. The life which is represented by the forty days before Easter is the one we now have; the life which is represented by the fifty days after the Lord's resurrection is not now being lived, but hoped for, and in being hoped for is loved. And by that very love God who promised all these things is being praised, and such praises are what *alleluia* is. After all, what is *alleluia*? It's a Hebrew word, *alleluia*, "Praise God"; *Allellu*, "Praise"; *Ia*, "God." So with *alleluia* we say "Praise God," and urge one another to praise God; with hearts in harmony we sing praises to God better than on the strings of the guitar; we sing *alleluia*.

And when we've sung it, because of our weakness we go away, in order to restore our bodies. Why do we need restoring, if not because we are constantly fading? Finally, such is the weakness of the flesh, such the irksome nature of this life, that everything, however wonderful, ends in boredom. How we have longed for these days to come again next year, when they were just ended! And how eagerly we come to them after an interval of time! If we were told, though, "Say *alleluia* without ever stopping," we would excuse ourselves. Why would we excuse ourselves? Because growing tired we would be unable to keep it up, because we would grow weary and get bored even with that good thing. There no fading away, no boredom will occur. Stand up, praise, *you who stand in the house of the Lord, in the courts of the house of our God* (Ps 134:1). Why do you ask what you are going to do there? *Blessed*, it says *are those who dwell in your house, Lord; they will praise you for ever and ever* (Ps 84:4).

Sermon 247

During Easter Week

Here Augustine shows himself the consummate teacher in his attempt to explain the differences in the appearence narratives that the congregation has heard during Easter week "because some of you are less quick on the uptake." Christians should not be surprised at how difficult it is to understand the bodily dimension of the resurrection, in particular the risen Christ's ability to pass through closed doors: "If you can understand it, it isn't a miracle." Augustine also calls his congregation's attention to the miraculous nature of the virgin birth, Christ's walking on the sea, and the countless everyday miracles found in nature. Lambot, Fischer and Kunzelmann date this sermon to Easter week of 400; Poque suggests about 410-412. Augustine specifies this is the second account from John's Gospel, so it is likely that the sermon was preached on Friday, since Matthew was read on the first day, followed by Luke on the next, Mark on the third and John on both the fourth day (the previous day) and the fifth.

All the resurrection narratives are read during Easter week

1. The story of our Lord Jesus Christ's resurrection, according to the truth told by the four evangelists, was completed yesterday, it seems. On the first day, you see, the account was read of the resurrection according to Matthew, on the next day according to Luke, on the third day according to Mark, on the fourth, that is yesterday, according to John. But because John and Luke wrote a great deal about the resurrection itself and what happened after it, which can't all be chanted in one reading, we heard something according to John both yesterday and today, and there are still more readings to come.

So what have we heard today? That on the very day on which he rose again, that is the Sunday, when it had got late, and *the disciples were in one place, and the doors were closed for fear of the Jews* (Jn 20:19), Jesus appeared among them. So on that very day, as the evangelist John bears witness, he appeared twice to his disciples, early in the morning, and late in the evening. The reading about his appearance in the morning has already been recited; that he appeared again late on the same day is what we heard when it was chanted just now. It wasn't really necessary for me to remind you of this, but it is necessary for you to take note of it. However, because some of you are less quick on the uptake, or more heedless, it was proper for me to remind you, so that you know not only what you heard, but also from what scripture the things you heard come from.

The problem of Christ's risen body appearing in a room through closed doors

2. So let's see what today's reading sets us to talk about. The reading itself, you see, makes its own suggestion to us, and tells us after a fashion to say something about how the Lord, who rose again in a body so solid that it could not only be seen

by the disciples but also touched, could appear to them when the doors were closed. Some people, you see, are so uneasy about this point that their faith is in real danger, as they bring the prejudices and assumptions of their own reasoning to bear against divine miracles. This, I mean, is how they argue: "If it was a body, if there were flesh and bones there, if it is what hung on the cross that rose again from the tomb, how could it enter through closed doors? If it couldn't," they say, "it didn't happen. If it could, how could it?"

If you can understand how, it isn't a miracle; and if it doesn't strike you as a miracle, you are on the verge of denying that he even rose from the tomb. Take a look back at the miracles of your Lord from the beginning, and give me a rational explanation of each of them. No man approached her, and the virgin conceived. Give a rational explanation of how a virgin conceived without male seed. Where reason falls down, that is where faith is being built up. There you have one miracle in the conception of the Lord; listen to one also in his birth. The virgin gave him birth, and a virgin she remained. Already at that time, before the Lord rose again, he was born through closed doors.

You put a question to me, and say, "If he entered through closed doors, where is the proper mode of a body?" And I answer, "If he walked on the sea, where is the proper weight of a body?" But the Lord did that as Lord. So did he cease, when he rose again, to be Lord? What about his also making Peter walk on the sea? What divinity could accomplish in the one, faith achieved in the other. But Christ did it because he had the power; Peter, because Christ helped him. So if you start looking for the rational explanation of miracles in human terms, I'm afraid you may lose your faith. Don't you know that nothing is impossible for God? So if anybody says to you, "If he entered through closed doors, he wasn't a body," answer him yourself with a counter argument: "On the other hand, if he was touched, he was a body; if he ate he was a body; and he did that miraculously, not naturally."

Isn't the daily course of nature itself a miracle, something to be wondered at? Everything is full of marvels and miracles, but they are so common that we regard them as cheap and of no account. Give me a rational explanation — I'm questioning you on something usual and everyday; give me an explanation of why the seed of such a big tree as the fig is so small that you can scarcely see it, while the humble pumpkin produces such an enormous seed. And yet in that tiny grain of seed, scarcely visible, there is, if you consider it with your mind, not your eyes; there is in that minuteness, in those infinitesimal limits, both a root hiding, and a trunk inserted, and the leaves to come are already tied on, and the fruit which is going to appear on the tree has already been programmed in the seed.

There's no need to run through many instances; nobody can give a rational explanation of everyday things, and you are demanding of me an explanation of miracles? So read the gospel then, and believe that the marvels there were really done. What God has done amounts to much more, and yet you don't marvel at what surpasses all his other works: there was nothing, and the universe is.

If God can thread a camel through the eye of a needle,
there's nothing to stop him putting a body through closed doors

3. But a bulky body, you say, couldn't pass through the doors, because they were closed.

How big was that bulk, I ask you?

As big, of course, as it is in everyone.

Not as big, surely, as it is in a camel?

Of course not as big as that.

Read the gospel, listen to Christ himself; when he wanted to illustrate the difficulty for a rich man of getting into the kingdom of heaven, he said, *It is easier for a camel to get in through the eye of a needle, than for a rich man to get into the kingdom of heaven.* When the disciples heard this, they reckoned that it is quite impossible for a camel to get in through the eye of a needle, and so they were disheartened, and said to each other, *If that's the case, who can ever save himself?* If it's easier for a camel to get in through the eye of a needle than for a rich man to get into the kingdom of heaven; in no way can a camel get in through the eye of a needle; so no rich man can be saved. The Lord answered, *Things that are impossible for men are easy for God* (Lk 18:25-27).

God can both thread a camel through the eye of a needle, and get a rich man into the kingdom of heaven. Why make difficulties with me about closed doors? Closed doors at least have chinks round the edges; compare the chink at the edge of a door with the eye of a needle, compare the bulk of a human body with the size of camels — and stop making difficulties about God working miracles.

Sermon 256

During Easter Week on Alleluia

Perler maintains this sermon can be precisely dated to Sunday, May 5, 418, the day before the feast of the martyrs Marianus and James, during the council which took place at Carthage from May 5 to 16, 418. It features the engaging technique, often employed by Augustine, of adopting a dialogue with an imaginary interlocutor, the bishop taking the part of both the apostle Paul and the congregation questioning him. We learn that it was customary in North Africa for the celebrant to recite the Lord's Prayer by himself, with the people responding in unison, "Deliver us from evil." The bishop insists on the continuity between our earthly body and the glorified body of the resurrection state.

The alleluia of the anxious and worrying

1. It is evidently the pleasure of the Lord our God that, finding myself present here in the flesh, I should also have been singing *alleluia* with your graces. In English that means "Praise the Lord." So let us praise the Lord, brothers and sisters, with our lives and our tongues, with hearts and mouths, with our voices and our behavior. That, surely, is how God wants *alleluia* to be sung to him, so that there is no discord in the singer. So first of all let there be harmony in ourselves between tongues and lives, between mouths and consciences. Let our voices, I repeat, be in harmony with our behavior, or else it may happen that good voices are witnesses against bad behavior.

Oh blissful *alleluia* in heaven, where the angels are God's temple! There, I mean, supreme harmony reigns among those who are praising, because there is no anxiety about their exultant singing. That's because there is no *law in the members fighting against the law of the mind* (Rom 7:23) there; no aggressive cupidity there, to endanger the victory of charity. So here let us sing *alleluia* while still anxious and worrying, so that there we may be able to sing it one day without any worry or care.

Why anxious and worrying here? Don't you want me to be anxious, when I read, *Is not human life on earth a trial and temptation* (Jb 7:1)? Don't you want me to worry, when I'm still being told, *Watch and pray, lest you enter into temptation* (Mk 14:38)? Don't you want me to worry when temptation is so plentiful that the Prayer itself prescribes worry, when we say, *Forgive us our debts, as we too forgive our debtors*? Every day we're petitioners, every day debtors. Do you want me to throw care to the winds, when every day I'm requesting pardon for sins, assistance against dangers? After all, when I've said, because of past sins, *Forgive us our debts as we too forgive our debtors*, I immediately go on to add, because of future dangers, *Do not bring us into temptation*. And how can the people be in a good way, when they cry out with me, *Deliver us from evil* (Mt 6:12-14)?

And yet, brothers and sisters, in this time that is still evil, let us sing *alleluia* to the good God, who does deliver us from evil. Why look all round yourself for what he is to deliver you from, when he delivers you from evil? Don't go a long way away, don't strain your mind's eye gazing all round. Come back to yourself, take a look at yourself. You, there, are still evil. So when God delivers you from yourself, that's when he delivers you from evil. Listen to the apostle, and understand there what evil you need to be delivered from. *I take delight*, he says, *in the law of God according to the inner self; but I see another law in my members fighting back against the law of my mind, and taking me prisoner under the law of sin, which is* — where? *Taking me prisoner*, he says, *under the law of sin, which is in my members* (Rom 7:22-23).

"Oh, I thought it had taken you prisoner under goodness knows what unheard of barbarians; I thought it had taken you prisoner under goodness knows what foreign nations, under goodness knows what human masters."

Which is, he says, *in my members*. So cry out with him, *Wretched man that I am, who will deliver me?* Who will deliver me from what? Tell us what from. One says from the press gang, another from prison, another from captivity among the barbarians, another from fever and illness; you tell us, apostle, not from somewhere we might be sent to, or led to; but from something we carry about with us, something we ourselves are: *from the body of this death* (Rom 7:24). From the body of this death? *From the body*, he says, *of this death*.

How we need to be delivered from ourselves

2. Another person will say, "The body of this death doesn't belong to me; it's my prison for a time, my chain for a time. I am in the body of death, I am not the body of death."

You're arguing, that's why you are not being delivered.

"I, after all," he says, "am spirit, I am not flesh, but I am in flesh; when I have been delivered from the flesh, what will I have to do with the flesh from then on?"

Do you want me, brothers and sisters, to reply to this line of reasoning, or the apostle? If I reply, it's possible the seriousness of the word may be treated lightly because of the worthlessness of the minister. I would rather keep quiet. Listen with me, my friend, to the teacher of the nations, listen with me to the *chosen vessel* (Acts 9:15), to deprive you of all grounds for argument or disagreement. Listen, but first say what you said earlier on. This, precisely, is what you said:

"I am not flesh, I'm spirit. I sigh and groan in my prison. When this chain, and this workhouse crumbles, I depart a free man. Earth is given back to earth, the spirit is welcomed in heaven. I go; I leave behind what I am not."

So this is what you were saying?

"Yes," he says.

I'm not the one to answer you. Answer, apostle, answer please. You preached, in order to be heard; you wrote, in order to be read. It was all done so that you might be believed. Speak.

Who will deliver me from the body of this death? The grace of God through Jesus Christ our Lord (Rom 7:24-25).

What will it deliver you from?

From the body of this death.

But aren't you yourself the body of this death?

He answers, *Therefore I myself serve the law of God with the mind, but with the flesh the law of sin* (Rom 7:25).

But that *I myself*, how can it be you yourself through different things?

With the mind, he says, because I love; *with the flesh*, because I covet. I'm the winner, indeed, if I don't consent; but still wrestling, with the opponent engaging me.

And how will it be, my dear apostle, when you have been delivered from this flesh; will you no longer be anything but spirit?

The apostle replies, death now imminent, the debt which no one can get out of: "I do not put off the flesh for ever, but I put it aside for a time."

So you are going to come back to the body of this death? But why? Let's listen rather to his own words. How can you return to the body, from which you cried out with such religious words that you need to be delivered?

He answers: "I return indeed to the body, but no longer of this death. Not because it will be another body, but because *this perishable thing must put on imperishability, and this mortal thing put on immortality.*"

My dear brothers and sisters, when the apostle said *this perishable thing, this mortal thing*, he was after a fashion touching his own flesh with the words. So it's not another one. "I do not," he says, "put off this earthy body, and receive a brazen body, or an ethereal body. I receive the same one, but not any longer of this death. Because *this*, not another, but *this perishable thing must put on imperishability, and this*, not another, but *this mortal thing put on immortality. Then will come about the word that is written: Death has been swallowed up in victory.* Let *alleluia* be sung. *Then will come about the word that is written*, a word no longer of people embattled, but of people triumphant: *Death has been swallowed up in victory.* Let *alleluia* be sung. *Where, death, is your sting?* Let *alleluia* be sung. *Now the sting of death is sin* (1 Cor 15:53-56). But *you will look for its place, and you will not find it* (Ps 37:10).

For the present, sing and keep on walking

3. But even here, among the dangers, among the trials and temptations of this life, both by others and by us let *alleluia* be sung. *God is faithful*, he says, *who will not permit you to be tempted beyond what you are able to endure.* So here too let us sing *allelluia*. We human beings are still in the dock, but God is faithful. He didn't say, "He will not permit you to be tempted," but *will not permit you to be tempted beyond what you are able to endure; but with the temptation he will also make a way out, so that you may be able to endure it* (1 Cor 10:13). You have entered into temptation; but God will also make a way out, so that you do not perish in the temptation; so that like a potter's jar, you may be shaped by the preaching, cooked by the tribulation. But when you enter the temptation, bear in mind the way out; because God is faithful, *God will watch over your going in and your coming out* (Ps 121:8).

Furthermore, when this body has become immortal and imperishable, when all temptation has been done away with; because *the body is dead* — why is it dead? *Because of sin. But the spirit is life* — they're the apostle's words; why? *Because of justice.* So do we leave the body dead? No, but listen: *But if the Spirit of him who raised Christ from the dead dwells in you, the one who raised Christ from the dead will give life also to your mortal bodies.* Now, you see, it's an embodiment of soul, then it will be an embodiment of spirit. *The first man*, you see, *became a living soul, the last man a life-giving spirit* (1 Cor 15:45). That's why *he will give life also to your mortal bodies, because of his Spirit dwelling in you* (Rom 8:10-11). Oh, what a happy *alleluia* there, how carefree, how safe from all opposition, where nobody will be an enemy, no one cease to be a friend!

God praised there, and God praised here; here, though, by the anxious, there by the carefree; here by those who are going to die, there by those who are going to live for ever; here in hope, there in hope realized; here on the way, there at home. So now, my dear brothers and sisters, let us sing, not to delight our leisure, but to ease our toil. In the way travelers are in the habit of singing; sing, but keep on walking. Ease your toil by singing, don't fall in love with laziness. Sing, and keep on walking. What's "keep on walking"? Make some progress, make progress in goodness. There are some people, you see, according to the apostle, who progress from bad to worse. You, if you're making progress, are walking; but make progress in goodness, progress in the right faith, progress in good habits and behavior. Sing and keep on walking. Don't stray off the road, don't go back, don't stay where you are.

Turning to the Lord etc.

And after the sermon

Tomorrow is the feast of the holy martyrs Marianus and James; but because I'm still rather busy on account of this big assembly of the holy council, I will, with the Lord's help, give the sermon I owe you for their birthday in two days' time.

Sermon 260

Preached on the Same Day in the Leontian Church: Advice to the Newly Baptized

This sermon is a model of brevity; it was most likely given during the octave of Easter in 409 to exhort the newly baptized (*infantes*) to live a Christian life consistent with their new state. These newborn Christians must now put their baptismal garments aside and mix in with the regular members of the congregation. The homily is a powerful moral exhortation to the virtue of chastity for both married persons and virgins.

To the newly baptized, not to stifle, by living bad lives,
what has just been reborn in them

We mustn't delay, we've got a great many things to do; to those who have been born again in baptism, and are today to be mixed in with the people at large, a short but serious sermon has to be given. You that have been baptized, and today complete the sacramental ritual of your octave, must understand, to put it in a nutshell, that the significance of the circumcision of the flesh has been transferred to the circumcision of the heart. According to the old law, infants are circumcised in the flesh on the eighth day, and this because of the Lord Christ, who rose again, after the seventh day of the sabbath, on the eighth, or Lord's day. There was an instruction to circumcise with knives of flint, or rock; *the rock was Christ* (1 Cor 10:4).

You are called infants, because you have been born again, and have entered upon a new life, and have been born again to eternal life, provided you don't stifle what has been reborn in you by leading bad lives. You are to be given back to the Christian people, you are to be mixed in with the people of the faithful; beware of imitating the bad faithful, or rather the false faithful; those who are faithful in their confession of faith, but unfaithful, unbelievers in the bad lives they lead.

I hereby give you notice that I am calling God and his angels to witness what I am telling you: keep yourselves chaste, whether in marriage, or in total continence. Each one of you, pay what you have vowed. If you haven't got wives, it is permissible for you to marry, but only women who haven't got husbands still alive. Women who haven't got husbands are permitted to marry, but only men who haven't got wives still alive. If you have got wives, don't do anything bad apart from your wives. Give them what you demand from them. They owe faithfulness to you, you owe faithfulness to them. The husband ought to be faithful to his wife, the wife to her husband, both of them to God. Any of you who have vowed total continence, pay what you have vowed; because it wouldn't be required of you, if you hadn't vowed it. What could have been lawful, is not lawful; not because marriage is condemned, but because the one who looks back is condemned.

Beware of fraud in your business dealings. Beware of telling lies and of perjury. Beware of being talkative and extravagant. Whatever you don't want done to you, don't do to others, whether to human beings or to God. Why should I burden you any further? *Do all this, and the God of peace will be with you* (Phil 4:9).

Sermon 267

On the Day of Pentecost

Augustine questions why the gift of the Holy Spirit no longer manifests itself in the gift of languages as on the first Pentecost. The Spirit manifests itself in the diverse gifts of the Church's members. Some saints work miracles, others proclaim truth, others preserve virginity or married chastity. The Holy Spirit does for the Church what the soul does for the body. Christians who cut themselves off from the body of the Church risk losing the Spirit. Fischer and Kunzelmann suggest Pentecost Sunday, June 2, 412 as the date of this sermon.

New wineskins were expecting new wine from heaven; and it came

1. Today's solemnity makes us remember the great Lord God and the great grace that has been poured out over us. That, after all, is why a solemnity is celebrated, to save something that only happened once, from being lost to the memory. A solemnity, you see, gets its name from what is "customary in the year." Just as we talk of a river being perennial because it doesn't dry up in the summer, but flows throughout the year; perennial, therefore, that is "through the year"; so too "solemn," something that is customarily celebrated every year. Today we are celebrating the coming of the Holy Spirit. The Lord, you see, sent the Holy Spirit from heaven, having promised him on earth. And because this is how he had promised he would send him from heaven: *He cannot come*, he had said, *unless I go away; but when I go away, I will send him to you* (Jn 16:7); he first suffered, died, rose again, ascended; it now remained for him to carry out his promise.

This is what his disciples were waiting for, a hundred and twenty souls, as it is written, ten times the number of the apostles; I mean, he chose twelve, and sent the Spirit on a hundred and twenty. So while awaiting this promised gift, they were together in one house, praying; because they were now awaiting in faith itself what they were expecting in their prayer and their spiritual desire. They were new wineskins, the new wine was expected from heaven; and it came. That great bunch of grapes, after all, had already been trodden and glorified. You see, we read in the gospel, *For the Spirit had not yet been given, because Jesus had not yet been glorified* (Jn 7:39).

The gift of tongues

2. You heard just now what the answer was; a great miracle. All the people present had learned one language. The Holy Spirit came, they were filled with it, they began to speak with the different languages of all nations which they didn't know, and hadn't learned. But the one who had come was teaching them; he entered, they were filled, he poured out from them. And then there was enacted this sign; whoever received the Holy Spirit, suddenly, filled with the Spirit, started speaking with the tongues of all; not only those hundred and twenty. The text itself teaches us this; when people believed, they were baptized, they received the Holy Spirit, they spoke with the tongues of all nations.

Those who were present were dumbfounded, some filled with wonder, others given to mockery, to the extent of saying, *These people are drunk, full of new wine* (Acts 2:13). They were jeering, and they were saying something true. Wineskins, you see, were filled with new wine. You heard about it when the gospel was read: *Nobody puts new wine into old wineskins* (Mk 2:22); the carnal person does not receive the things of the Spirit. Being carnal means being old, grace means newness. The more you are renewed for the better, the more you receive what smacks of the truth. The new wine was fermenting, and with the new wine fermenting, the languages of the nations were flowing freely.

Now is being fulfilled what was then being foreshadowed

3. Isn't the Holy Spirit being given nowadays, then, brothers and sisters? Anyone who thinks that, isn't worthy to receive it. It certainly is given nowadays. So why is nobody speaking with the tongues of all nations, as people spoke who were filled with the Holy Spirit at that time? Why? Because what that signified has been fulfilled. What was that? When we celebrated the fortieth day, remember, I drew your attention to how the Lord Jesus Christ drew a sketch of his Church and then ascended. His disciples were asking, "When will the end of the world be?" And he said, *It is not for you to know the times or moments, which the Father has placed under his own authority.* He had still to promise what he has carried out today: *You will receive the power of the Holy Spirit coming down upon you, and you will be witnesses to me in Jerusalem, and in the whole of Judea and Samaria, and as far as the ends of the earth* (Acts 1:7-8). The Church was then in one house, it received the Holy Spirit; it consisted of a few people, it consisted of the languages of the whole world.

There you have what it was pointing forward to now. The fact, I mean, that that small Church was speaking with the tongues of all nations, what else can it signify but that this great Church *from the rising of the sun to its setting* (Ps 113:3) is speaking with the tongues of all nations? Now is being fulfilled what was then being promised. We have heard, we can see. *Hear, daughter, and see* (Ps 45:11); the queen herself was being addressed. *Hear, daughter, and see*; hear the promise, see the fulfillment. Your God hasn't deceived you, your bridegroom has not deceived you, the one who gave his blood for your dowry hasn't deceived you. The one who found you ugly and made you beautiful, found you unclean and made you a virgin, has not deceived you. It's you that were promised to yourself; but promised in a few people, fulfilled in many.

The Holy Spirit is to the Church what the soul is to the human body

4. So none of you must say, "I have received the Holy Spirit; why aren't I speaking with the tongues of all nations?" If you want to have the Holy Spirit, consider this, my dear brothers and sisters: our spirit, by which every person lives, is called the soul; our spirit by which every single human being lives, is called the soul. And you can see what the soul does in the body. It quickens all its parts; it sees through the eyes, hears through the ears, smells through the nostrils, speaks with the tongue, works with the hands, walks with the feet. It's present simultaneously to all the body's parts, to make them alive; it gives life to all, their functions to each. The eye doesn't hear, the ear doesn't see, the tongue doesn't see, nor do ear and eye speak. But they're alive, all the same; the ear's alive, the tongue's alive; different functions, life in common.

That's what the Church of God is like; in some of the saints it works miracles, in other saints it proclaims the truth, in other saints it preserves virginity, in other saints it preserves married chastity; in some this, in others that. All doing their own thing, but living the same life together. In fact, what the soul is to the human body, the Holy Spirit is to the body of Christ, which is the Church. The Holy Spirit does in the whole Church what the soul does in all the parts of one body. But notice what you should beware of, see what you should notice, notice what you should be afraid of. It can happen in the human body — or rather from the body — that one part is cut off, a hand, a finger, a foot; does the soul follow the amputated part? When it was in the body, it was alive, cut off, it loses life. In the same way too Christian men and women are Catholics, while they are alive in the body; cut off, they have become heretics, the Spirit doesn't follow the amputated part. So if you wish to be alive with the Holy Spirit, hold on to loving-kindness, love truthfulness, long for oneness, that you may attain to everlastingness. Amen.

Sermon 272

On the Day of Pentecost to the *Infantes*, on the Sacrament

This is a classic example of Augustine's mystagogical preaching, or catechesis to the newly baptized, on the meaning of the Eucharist. As the bishop defines the term sacrament, "one thing is seen, another thing is to be understood." Christians were expected to keep secret what took place during the actual liturgy of the Eucharist. Since only the baptized were permitted to stay beyond the first part of the service, which concluded with the homily, the newly baptized needed help in understanding the rich mysteries which they were now experiencing for the first time. Augustine memorably draws a connection between the Eucharistic bread and wine and Christ's presence in the body of believers: "So if it's you that are the body of Christ and its members, it's the mystery meaning you that has been placed on the Lord's table; what you receive is the mystery that means you." Fischer, Kunzelmann, and Monceaux suggest this sermon was preached between 405 and 411. Several scholars assign the homily to Easter, although the Maurists accepted the consensus of manuscripts available to them that the homily was preached on Pentecost. Either is possible, given the strong eucharistic character of the homily and the specific allusion to the *disciplina arcani*, or maintaining the mysterious and hidden character of the eucharist, since Pentecost was the alternate date for the sacraments of initiation.

One thing is seen, another is to be understood

What you can see on the altar, you also saw last night; but what it was, what it meant, of what great reality it contained the sacrament, you had not yet heard. So what you can see, then, is bread and a cup; that's what even your eyes tell you; but as for what your faith asks to be instructed about, the bread is the body of Christ, the cup the blood of Christ. It took no time to say that indeed, and that, perhaps, may be enough for faith; but faith desires instruction. The prophet says, you see, *Unless you believe, you shall not understand* (Is 7:9). I mean, you can now say to me, "You've bidden us believe; now explain, so that we may understand."

Some such thought as this, after all, may cross somebody's mind: "We know where our Lord Jesus Christ took flesh from; from the Virgin Mary. He was suckled as a baby, was reared, grew up, came to man's estate, suffered persecution from the Jews, was hung on the tree, was slain on the tree, was taken down from the tree, was buried; rose again on the third day, on the day he wished ascended into heaven. That's where he lifted his body up to; that's where he's going to come from to judge the living and the dead; that's where he is now, seated on the Father's right. How can bread be his body? And the cup, or what the cup contains, how can it be his blood?"

The reason these things, brothers and sisters, are called sacraments is that in them one thing is seen, another is to be understood. What can be seen has a bodily appearance, what is to be understood provides spiritual fruit. So if you want to understand the body of Christ, listen to the apostle telling the faithful, *You, though, are the body of Christ and its members* (1 Cor 12:27). So if it's you that are the body of Christ and its members, it's the mystery meaning you that has been placed on the Lord's table; what you receive is the mystery that means you. It is to what you are that you reply *Amen*, and by so replying you express your assent. What you hear, you see, is *The body of Christ*, and you answer, *Amen*. So be a member of the body of Christ, in order to make that *Amen* true.

So why in bread? Let's not bring anything of our own to bear here, let's go on listening to the apostle himself, who said, when speaking of this sacrament, *One bread, one body, we being many are* (1 Cor 10:17). Understand and rejoice. Unity, truth, piety, love. *One bread*; what is this one bread? The one body which we, being many, are. Remember that bread is not made from one grain, but from many. When you were being exorcised, it's as though you were being ground. When you were baptized it's as though you were mixed into dough. When you received the fire of the Holy Spirit, it's as though you were baked. Be what you can see, and receive what you are.

That's what the apostle said about the bread. He has already shown clearly enough what we should understand about the cup, even if it wasn't said. After all, just as many grains are mixed into one loaf in order to produce the visible appearance of bread, as though what holy scripture says about the faithful were happening: *They had one soul and one heart in God* (Acts 4:32); so too with the wine. Brothers and sisters, just remind yourselves what wine is made from; many grapes hang in the bunch, but the juice of the grapes is poured together in one vessel. That too is how the Lord Christ signified us, how he wished us to belong to him, how he consecrated the sacrament of our peace and unity on his table. Any who receive the sacrament of unity, and do not hold the bond of peace, do not receive the sacrament for their benefit, but a testimony against themselves.

Turning to the Lord, God the Father almighty, with pure hearts let us give him sincere and abundant thanks, as much as we can in our littleness; beseeching him in his singular kindness with our whole soul, graciously to hearken to our prayers in his good pleasure; also by his power to drive out the enemy from our actions and thoughts, to increase our faith, to guide our minds, to grant us spiritual thoughts, and to lead us finally to his bliss; through Jesus Christ his Son. Amen.

Sermon 277A

On the Birthday of Saint Vincent

The general consensus of scholarship dates this homily to between 410 and 412, although Hombert suggests a later date, perhaps between 415 and 420. January 22nd is the feast day of the martyr Vincent, a deacon from Saragossa, Spain, who was killed in Valencia in 303 during the persecution launched by Diocletian. We possess five different homilies preached on this occasion. Augustine employs powerful and colorful language to contrast the justice of the martyr with the horrendous pain and suffering inflicted on him. The martyr is described as an athlete who has been equipped with grace to emerge victorious.

The martyr's justice makes beautiful the horrifying tortures he underwent

1. Christ commands us to celebrate with due solemnity the heroic and glorious sufferings of the holy martyr Vincent, and not to be slow in preaching about it. We have seen in spirit, and gazed in thought at all that he endured, that he heard, that he answered, and how a marvelous spectacle was staged before our very eyes: the wicked judge, the blood-thirsty torturer, the invincible martyr, a contest between cruelty and piety; on this side raving madness, on that a splendid victory. With the reading sounding in our ears, charity blazed up in our hearts; we would have loved to embrace and kiss, if it had been possible, those ravaged limbs; it amazed us that they could provide room for so many punishments, and with inexpressible feelings we yearned for them not to be tormented.

After all, who would want to see an executioner at his savage work, and a man, lost to all humanity, tearing furiously at a human body? Who would enjoy observing limbs wrenched apart by the machinery of the rack? Who would not oppose the natural shape of a man being violated by human technique, bones disjointed by being stretched, laid bare by the flesh being clawed off them? Who could fail to be horrified? And yet the justice of the martyr was making all this horror beautiful; and the stupendous courage he showed for the faith, for religion, for the hope of the age to come, for the love of Christ, was shedding over the hideous and ghastly aspect of his torments and his wounds a magnificent glory.

In a word, our interest in one and the same spectacle is quite different from that of the persecutor. He was enjoying the martyr's punishment, we its cause; he was taking pleasure in what he was suffering, we in why he was suffering; he in his torments, we in his strength; he in his wounds, we in his crown; he, because his pains were lasting such a long time; we, because he was not being broken by them in the least; he, because he was being ill-treated in the flesh; we, because he was abiding in the faith. And so at the very point where that man's monstrous inhumanity was being satisfied, he was himself being tormented by the martyr's superhuman fidelity; while we could scarcely endure the horrors he was imposing, but were still sharing Vincent's victory as he died.

The martyr's constancy and patience,
like everything else he and we have received, comes from God

2. All the same, it was not in himself or by himself that even this champion of ours emerged victorious, but in the one and by the one who being exalted above all others provides him with assistance, who having suffered above all others has left him an example. He it is who urges him on to the battle, who calls him to the prize; and who watches him in his contest in such a way that he helps him in his difficulties. He instructed his athlete what to do, and set before him what he would receive, while also supporting him to make sure he didn't fail. So then, pray with simplicity, if you wish to compete with simplicity, to win with agility, to reign in felicity.

We heard our fellow servant speaking, and with his steady and truthful answers silencing the tongue of the persecutor; but before that we heard the Lord saying, *For it is not you that are speaking, but the Spirit of my Father who is speaking in you* (Mt 10:20). And thus the reason this man overcame his adversaries is that he praised his utterances in the Lord. He knew how to say, *In God I shall praise the word, in the Lord I shall praise the utterance; in God I shall hope, I shall not fear what man may do to me* (Ps 56:10-11).

We saw the martyr so patiently enduring the most monstrous torments; but his soul was submitting itself to God, because it was from him that his patience came. And lest human frailty should fail through lack of patience, and deny Christ, and contribute to the enemy's joy, he knew to whom he should say, *My God, rescue me from the hand of the sinner, from the hand of the law-breaker and the wicked; since you are my patience* (Ps 71:4-5). In this way, you see, the person who sang these words signified how Christians should ask to be rescued from the hands of their enemies; not, certainly, by suffering nothing, but by enduring what they suffer with perfect patience. *Rescue me from the hand of the sinner, from the hand of the law-breaker and the wicked.* But if you ask how he wants to be rescued, look at what follows: *since you are my patience.* You will find a glorious passion, wherever there is this devout confession, so that *whoever boasts, may boast in the Lord* (1 Cor 1:31).

And so none of us should be proud of our intelligence, when we have made a good speech; none of us be proud of our strength of character when we suffer temptation; because, in order for us to speak good things, we have to get our wisdom from him; and in order, too, for us to suffer bad things, we have to get our patience from him. So it is ours to will, but we are required to will because we have been called; it's ours to ask, but we do not know what we should ask for. It is ours to receive, but what are we to receive if we don't have? Ours to have, but what do we have, if we haven't received? So there you are; *whoever boasts should boast in the Lord*.

And so the martyr Vincent was worthy to be crowned by the Lord, in whom he chose to boast through both his wisdom and his patience; worthy of his perennial renown, worthy of eternal bliss, to gain which, whatever the terrifying judge threatened him with, whatever the bloodthirsty executioner inflicted on him, is light indeed. What he endured, after all, is over and done with; what he received is not going to pass away. Certainly, I mean, that's how his limbs were ill-used, that's how his entrails were tormented; yes, yes, these things were done to him; and even if much more dreadful things were done, *the sufferings of this time are not worthy to be compared with the future glory that will be revealed in us* (Rom 8:18).

Sermon 278

On the Calling of the Apostle Paul, and on the Lord's Prayer

One of Augustine's favorite images for Christ was that of *Christus medicus*, the divine physician who knows how to diagnose the disease of sin skillfully and then apply the appropriate treatment to cure the human soul. All human beings are born broken and sick as a result of the fall of Adam and require a lifetime of treatment and recovery. The treatment can be bitter and painful medicine must be applied in a timely fashion before the infection or contagion spreads to the point of requiring radical surgery. Even venial sins (minor faults) are potentially life-threatening. Fischer and Kunzelmann suggest this homily was delivered between 412 and 416; Poque suggests between 400 and 410. It was probably preached during Easter time, when the Acts of the Apostles were routinely read, although there appears be an allusion to Lent in the final paragraph. Poque argues for the Saturday of Easter week.

Paul, from being a persecutor of Christ, was made into a preacher of Christ

1. Today this reading was recited from the Acts of the Apostles, in which the apostle Paul, from being a persecutor of Christians, was made into a preacher of Christ. Today in those regions the very places bear witness to what happened then; and now it is read out, and believed. The value, though, of this particular event is what the apostle himself mentions in his letters. He says, you see, that he was given pardon for all his sins, and for that raving madness which had him dragging Christians to the slaughter, as an agent of the fury of the Jews, whether in the stoning of the holy martyr Stephen, or in bringing and presenting others for punishment; that he was pardoned for precisely this reason: that none who may have been involved in great sins, and caught in the nets of great crimes, should despair of themselves, as though they would not receive pardon, if they turned to the one who prayed for his persecutors as he hung on the cross, saying, *Father, forgive them, because they do not know what they are doing* (Lk 23:34).

From being a persecutor he was changed into *a preacher and the teacher of the nations* (2 Tm 1:11). *Previously*, he says, *I was a blasphemer and persecutor and an insolent man. But the reason I obtained mercy was this, that Christ Jesus might demonstrate his total forbearance first of all in me, for the instruction of those who were going to trust him for eternal life* (1 Tm 1:13.16). It is by the grace of God, you see, that we are saved from our sins, which we are languishing in. His, his is the medicine which cures the soul. I mean, it was well able to injure itself, quite unable to cure itself.

To heal or restore us to life we need the doctor

2. In the body too, after all, people have it in their power to get sick, but not equally in their power to get better. I mean, if they exceed the proper limits, and live self-indulgent lives, and do all the things that undermine the constitution and are injurious to health, the day comes, if that's what they want, when they fall sick. When they've so fallen, though, they don't get better. In order to fall sick, you see, they apply themselves to self-indulgence; but in order to get better, they must apply the doctor's services to their health. As I said, they can't have it in their power to recover their health, as they have it in their power to lose it.

In the same way, as regards the soul, it was within the scope of man's free choice to fall into death by sinning, and so to change from being immortal to being mortal, and to be subjected to the devil who seduced him; with his freedom of choice he chose to turn aside to lower things and forsake the higher, to lend his ears to the serpent and close his ears to God, and set fairly and squarely between instructor and seducer, to comply rather with the seducer than with the instructor. He heard the devil, after all, with exactly the same ears as he heard God. So why didn't he rather trust the better of the two?

And so it was that he discovered what God had foretold was true, what the devil had promised was false. This was the first origin of all our ills, this the root of all miseries, this the seed of death, coming from the first man's very own free will. He had so been made, that if he obeyed God he would be blessed and immortal; while if he neglected and scorned the commandment of the one who wished to preserve perpetual health in him, he would tumble into the disease of mortality. So at that time the doctor was scorned by the healthy person, now at this time he cures the sick person. There are some things, you see, which medicine prescribes for the preservation of health; they are given to the healthy, to keep them from getting sick. While there are others that are prescribed for those who are already sick, to help them recover what they have lost.

It would have been good for the man to obey the doctor while he was in good health, so that he wouldn't ever need the doctor. After all, *it is not the healthy who need the doctor, but the sick* (Mk 2:17). By doctor, properly speaking, we mean one through whose services health is recovered. Because God is always needed as a doctor even by the healthy, to keep them in good health. So it would have been good for him to hold on to the perpetual health in which he had been created. He scorned it, abused it, fell by his self-indulgence into the ill health of this mortality; let him listen now, at least, to what the doctor prescribes, so that he may rise from the sickbed on which he was laid by sin.

Health is recovered only slowly by obeying the doctor's prescriptions

3. But now clearly, brothers and sisters, in the sphere of medicine a healthy person stays as he is by doing what the science of health dictates; but if he begins to get ill, he starts listening to certain prescriptions, and starts carrying them out, if he really cares about getting his good health back completely. However, when he starts doing that, he doesn't immediately get completely well again, but by regularly observing the prescriptions over a length of time, he eventually reaches that state of health which he had lost by being less than regular in his life. The advantage, though, he gets as he starts observing those prescriptions, is that his illness doesn't intensify, so that not only does he not get worse, but little by little he also gets better. There is, after all, some hope of complete health, when a person begins to get less and less sick.

In the same sort of way too, what else is living justly in this life, but listening to the prescriptions of the law, and carrying them out? So does that mean that those who carry out the prescriptions of the law are already healthy? Not yet; but it is in order to become healthy, that they carry them out. Don't let them flag in carrying them out, because what was lost in one go is recovered little by little. If man, after all, were to return at once to his original state of blessedness and bliss, it would just be a game for him to lapse into death by sinning.

What medicine prescribes is often painful

4. Someone has caught a disease of the body, for example, through self- indulgence; he has some growth in his body which needs to be lanced, or cut out. Undoubtedly he is going to suffer acute pains; but those pains won't be unprofitable for him. If he refuses to suffer the pains of being operated on, he will suffer the maggots of gangrene. So the doctor starts by saying, "Observe this and that prescription, don't touch this, don't take this or that food or drink, don't let that matter worry you." He starts doing it all, he's already observing the prescriptions; but he isn't yet healthy again.

So what's the value of his observance? To stop the infection he has caught getting worse, and even to get it to decrease. So what follows? He must brace himself to observe even the prescriptions of the doctor's hand as it wields the scalpel, and inflicts on him a salutary pain. So supposing he says, with his septic ulcer, "What's the use of my observing the prescriptions, if I have to suffer the pain of being cut?" He gets the answer, "But each will contribute to your cure; both observing the prescriptions, and enduring the pain. That, after all, is the measure of the damage you have done yourself, by not observing the prescriptions when you were in good health. So submit to the doctor until you are cured; after all, whatever inconvenience you suffer is only what your ulcer deserves."

The same rule applies to the healing Christ brings us

5. That's how Doctor Christ comes to the afflicted and those who labor, when he says, *It is not the healthy who need the doctor, but those who are sick. I did not come to call the just, but sinners* (Mk 2:17). He calls sinners to peace, he calls the sick to health. He prescribes faith, he prescribes self-control, self-discipline, sobriety; he restrains the cravings of greed; he tells us what to do, what to observe. Those who do observe all this may now be said to be living justly, according to the prescriptions of medicine. But they haven't yet received that health and that total well-being which God promises through the apostle, when he says, *For this perishable thing must put on imperishability, and this mortal thing put on immortality. Then the word will come true, which is written: Death has been swallowed up in victory. Where, Death, is your striving? Where, Death, is your sting?* (1 Cor 15:53-55).

That is when there will be complete health, and equality with the holy angels. But now, before that happens, my brothers and sisters, when we start observing the prescriptions which the doctor has prescribed, and find ourselves suffering some trials and tribulations, we mustn't think that we are observing the prescriptions to no purpose, because greater pain seems to follow your observance of them. You see, the fact that you are enduring tribulations indicates the hand of the doctor operating on you, not the sentence of the judge punishing you. This happens so that health may be complete; let us suffer, let us put up with the pains. Sin is sweet; so it is through the bitter taste of tribulation that this pernicious sweetness must be got out of the system. It gave you pleasure, when you did wrong; but by doing it you collapsed into infirmity. Medicine works in the opposite direction; for a time it causes you pain, so that you may receive health in perpetuity. Use it, don't push it away from you.

The antidote to all sins: Forgive us our debts, just as we too forgive our debtors; which, if said sincerely, contains the twin precepts, or prescriptions, of charity

6. Certainly, and above all, don't let that antidote be wanting, which avails against all festering sores, against the poison of all sins: your saying, and genuinely saying, to the Lord your God, *Forgive us our debts, as we too forgive our debtors* (Mt 6:12). This, you see, is the bargain which the doctor has struck, and sealed, with the sick. Since there are two sorts of sins: by one you sin against God, by the other against human beings. Thus there are also those two precepts, or prescriptions, on which depends the whole law, and the prophets as well: *You shall love the Lord your God with your whole heart, and your whole soul, and your whole mind; and you shall love your neighbor as yourself* (Mt 22:37-40). And these also contain the ten commandments of the law, where three commandments refer to the love of God, seven to the love of neighbor. This is something we have already dealt with enough at some time or other.

You sin against God when you wreck his temple in yourself by sins against yourself, even if they are not obviously against your neighbor

7. So just as there are two commandments, so also there are two kinds of sins. You either sin, I mean, against God, or against human beings. You also sin against God, though, by wrecking his temple in yourself. God redeemed you, after all, bought you back by the blood of his Son; although even before you were redeemed, whose slave were you, please, if not of the one who made all things? He wished, however, to have you in a special way as his own, when redeemed by the blood of his Son. *And you are not your own*, says the apostle; *for you have been bought at a great price; glorify and carry God in your body* (1 Cor 6:19-20).

So the one you have been redeemed by has made you into his house. Would you, for your part, want your house turned upside down? Well, neither does God want his, that is to say yourself, turned upside down. If you won't spare yourself for your own sake, spare yourself for God's, seeing that he has made you into his temple. *For the temple of God is holy*, he says, *which is what you are*; and, *Whoever ruins God's temple, God will ruin him* (1 Cor 3:17). When people commit that sort of sin, they imagine they are not sinning, because they are not harming anybody.

The evil done by those who sin against themselves

8. And so this is what I wish to propose to your holinesses, as far as the shortness of time permits: what evil and harm people do, who ruin themselves by glut-

tony, drunkenness, fornication; and who reply, when taken to task, "I've done it out of my own pocket, my own property. Whom have I robbed of anything? Whom have I filched anything from? Against whom have I done it? I want to have a good time with what God has given me." He seems to himself to be innocent, or harmless, because he's apparently doing nobody any harm.

But how can he be innocent, if he doesn't spare himself harm? Those people are innocent, you see, who don't do harm to anybody; because the standard of love of neighbor is taken from oneself. This, after all, is what God said: *You shall love your neighbor as yourself* (Mt 22:39; Lv 19:18). So how can love of neighbor be whole and entire in you, when your love of self has been wounded by self-indulgence? And anyway, God then says to you, "When you want to ruin yourself with drink, it isn't just anybody's house you're turning upside down, it's mine. Where am I going to live? In these ruins? In this filthy hovel? If you were receiving some servant of mine as a guest, you would repair and clean up the house my servant was to enter. Won't you clean up your heart, which is where I want to live?"

Do not turn God's gift to your own undoing

9. So I have mentioned this one thing, brothers and sisters, so that you may see how definitely those people sin who ruin themselves, though in their own opinion they are innocent, or harmless. But there's another point: in this life of mortal frailty it is difficult for us human beings not to go beyond due measure in those things which we make use of from necessity. So to meet that case, there is this remedy to be applied: *Forgive us our debts, as we too forgive our debtors* (Mt 6:12) — provided you say it, and say it sincerely. You are forbidden to commit adultery, and so wrong your neighbor. Just as you don't want anybody to touch your wife or husband, so you in your turn ought not to touch anyone else's.

If, however, you gratify yourself with yours to the point of self-indulgence, you don't think of yourself as harming anyone, do you, because after all you're doing it with one who is your own. But by the very fact of making rather immoderate use of something that is a concession to you, you are damaging in yourself God's temple. No outsider is accusing you; but what answer will your conscience give to God, when he says to you through the apostle, *that everyone of you should know how to possess his vessel in sanctification and honor; not in the disorder of desires, like the nations who are ignorant of God* (1 Thes 4:4-5). Are there any married people, though, who in their relations with their partners do not exceed the law of having children? That, after all, is why the concession was made; you are convicted by the contract drawn up in marriage. You are covenanted on how you should marry; the words of the covenant are ringing in your ears: *for the sake of having children*. So if you can manage it, you shouldn't touch your partner, except for the sake of having children. If you go beyond this limit, you will be acting against that contract and against the covenant. Isn't it obvious?

You will be a liar and covenant breaker; and God is looking for the integrity of his temple in you, and he can't find it; not because you have enjoyed your partner, but because you have done so immoderately. I mean you also drink wine from your own cellar, and yet if you drink it to the point of getting drunk, it doesn't mean that you haven't sinned, just because you have been enjoying what is your own. In fact, you have turned God's gift to your own undoing.

The petition for forgiveness in the Lord's prayer is the remedy for such sins of exceeding the limits

10. So what is to be done, brothers and sisters? It's as clear as day, and all of us are told so by our consciences, that it is difficult to make use of things allowed us, in such a way that we don't to some extent exceed due limits. But when you exceed due limits, you offend God, whose temple you are. *For the temple of God is holy, and it is what you are.* Don't deceive yourselves, any of you: *Whoever ruins the temple of God, God will ruin him* (1 Cor 3:17). Sentence has been passed, you are found guilty.

What are you going to say in your prayers, when you make your plea to God whom you are offending in his own temple, expelling from his own temple? How will you clean God's temple up again in yourself? How will you bring him back to you? How else, but by saying, with real sincerity of heart, both in words and in deeds, *Forgive us our debts, as we too forgive our debtors* (Mt 6:12)? Who, after all, is going to accuse you of indulging immoderately in your own food, your own drink, your own marriage partner? No human being is going to. And yet, because God takes you to task, since he requires of you the integrity of his temple, and his dwelling place unspoiled, he has given you a remedy, as though to say, "If you offend me by exceeding due limits — and I will hold you guilty, even when no human being is accusing you; forgive other human beings whatever sins they have committed against you, so that I may forgive whatever sins you commit against me."

If we ignore this remedy, no hope of salvation is left to us

11. Hold on to this very firmly, brothers and sisters. You see, should any of you turn down even this remedy, you will be left with no hope whatsoever of salvation. If you say to me, "I don't forgive the sins which people happen to commit against me," there are no grounds left on which I can promise you salvation. I, after all, can hardly promise what God doesn't promise. If I do, I mean to say, I will not be dispensing God's word, but dispensing the serpent's. The serpent, you see, promised them something good if they sinned, while God threatened them with death. And what else in fact happened to them, but what God had threatened them with? And something far different was done by him, from what that other one had promised.

So do you want me to tell you, brothers and sisters, "Even if you sin, even if you don't forgive other people their sins, you will all certainly be saved; when Christ Jesus comes, he will grant a pardon to everybody"? I don't say that, because I don't hear it. I don't say what isn't said to me. God indeed promises pardon to sinners — but forgiving all past sins to those who are converted, who believe and are baptized. I read this, I make so bold as to promise this, I do promise it, and what I promise is promised to me. And when it's read, we all hear it; we are all, you see, fellow students, there is just one master in this school.

The difference between grave sins, which require a stiffer work
of repentance, and light sins, which can sink us by their very numbers
unless they are forgiven by God

12. So all past sins are forgiven people on conversion; but for the rest of this life there are certain grave and deadly sins, which one can only be released from by the most vehement and distressing humbling of the heart and contrition of spirit and the pain of repentance. These are forgiven through the keys of the Church. If you start judging yourself, you see, if you start being displeased with yourself, God will come along to show you mercy. If you are willing to punish yourself, he will spare you. In fact all who repent and do penance well are punishing themselves. They have to be severe with themselves, so that God may be lenient with them. As David says, *Turn your face away from my sins, and blot out all my iniquities*. But on what terms? He says in the same psalm, *Since I acknowledge my iniquity, and my sin is always before me* (Ps 51:9.3). So if you acknowledge it, he overlooks it.

There are, however, light and tiny sins, which cannot entirely be avoided, which indeed seem to be of minor importance, but which weigh down by their very numbers. I mean, a pile of wheat is put together from the tiniest grains, and yet ships are loaded with it; and if they are overloaded, they sink. One bolt of lightning strikes someone and kills him; but if the rain too is excessive, it can still cause the death of many people with its tiny little drops. The first thing destroys at a stroke, the second drowns by its very numbers. Large wild animals can kill a man with one bite; but tiny ones, when swarming in sufficient numbers, frequently do people to death, and bring such destruction, that the proud people of Pharaoh earned the judgment of pains of that sort. So in the same way, although these sins are tiny, they are for all that so many, that collected together they can form a heap to overwhelm you; but God is good, and even forgives these sins without which this life cannot be lived. How, though, can he forgive them, if you won't forgive the sins committed against you?

By forgiving others, we pump out the bilges of our souls

13. This short sentence in the heart of a person is like the scoop with which a ship at sea is bailed out. It cannot avoid, you see, letting in water through the seams of its planking. Gradually, though, by this thin trickle coming in, a considerable quantity collects, enough to sink the ship if it isn't pumped out. In the same sort of way we have in this life too some seams and chinks in our frail mortality, through which sin trickles in from the waves of this world. Let us grab hold of this short sentence, like a bucket, and bail ourselves out, or we shall sink. Let us forgive our debtors their debts, so that God may forgive us our debts. With this short sentence (if it is put into practice, so that we say it genuinely) you pump out whatever has seeped into your bilges.

But be careful; you're still at sea. I mean, when you've done this once, that's not enough, until you have crossed this sea, and reached the *terra firma* of that home country, where you are not tossed about by any waves, and don't have to forgive what isn't committed against you, nor do you wish to be forgiven what you don't commit.

May you quickly forgive people the wrongs they do you

14. I think I have sufficiently urged this point upon your graces, and I do urge you, on account of the peril we are in from these waves: let us hold fast to this saving remedy. And just notice how much people must be sinning who are bent on harming the innocent, when even those who won't forgive anyone that harms them are not to be tolerated. So may our brothers consider carefully, and observe who the people are against whom they are nursing bitter feelings of hatred. If they haven't forgiven them, let them consider at least during these days what all this is doing to their hearts. Or else, if they think they're safe, let them put vinegar into jars in which they usually keep good wine. They don't put it there, and they are very careful to avoid tainting the earthenware; and yet they put hatred into their hearts, do they, and are not afraid of what damage it is doing there.

So, brothers and sisters, take good care not to harm anyone, as far as you can; and if the immoderate, self-indulgent use of things permitted has crept up on you, because of the weakness of our human life, keep firmly to this rule — because it is a matter of damaging the temple of God — that you quickly forgive people the wrongs they do you, so that your Father who is in heaven may forgive you your sins.

Sermon 283

On the Birthday of the Martyrs of Marseilles

Augustine uses the feast days of martyrs to encourage fellow Christians to follow their heroic example of courage and patience in the face of adversity. People are driven throughout life to maximize pleasure and avoid pain. Both can lead to sin. "Against pleasures continence is needed; against pains, patience." Augustine also extols the virtue of humility. Hill questions the authenticity and integrity of this sermon since there is a reference to a single unnamed martyr's being celebrated in the last section. Fischer and Kunzelmann believe that the sermon was delivered between 412 and 416. The link with the martyrs of Marseilles is based on the florilegia of Bede and Florus, but an old lectionary of the abbey of Saint Germain gives this as one of the sermons on Saint Vincent, and in fact there are several similarities to S. 276, which was delivered on his feast.

Against pleasure continence is needed; against pains, patience

1. Let us by all means admire the courage of the holy martyrs in their sufferings; but in such a way that we proclaim the grace of God. They themselves, after all, certainly did not wish to be praised in themselves, but in the one to whom it is said, *In the Lord shall my soul be praised.* Those who understand this are not proud; they ask shyly, they receive joyfully; they persevere, they don't lose any more what they have received. Because they are not proud, they are gentle; and that's why, after saying *In the Lord shall my soul be praised*, he added, *Let the gentle hear, and be glad* (Ps 34:2). Where would feeble flesh be, where would maggots and rottenness be, unless what we have been singing were true: *My soul will submit itself to God, since it is from him that my patience comes* (Ps 62:5)? Now the virtue the martyrs had, in order to endure all the ills inflicted on them, is called patience.

You see, there are two things by which people are either drawn or driven into sin — pleasure and pain; pleasure draws, pain drives. Against pleasures continence is needed; against pains, patience. This, after all, is how the suggestion is put to the human mind that it should sin: sometimes it's told, "Do it, and you will get this"; while sometimes it's, "Do it, or you will suffer this." A promise leads the way to pleasure, a threat the way to pain. So it's in order to get some pleasure, or to avoid suffering pain, that people sin. That's why against these two tempters, of which one works through smooth promises, the other through terrible threats, God too has been good enough both to make promises, and to inspire terror; promising the kingdom of heaven, terrifying with the punishments of hell.

Pleasure is sweet, but God is sweeter. Temporal pain is bad, but much worse is eternal fire. You have something to love instead of the world's loves, or rather of worthless loves; you have something to fear, in place of the world's terrors.

Continence and patience both gifts of God, and to be recognized as such

2. But it's not enough to be warned, unless you also obtain assistance. So this psalm here which we have been singing, has been teaching us that our patience in the face of pains certainly comes from God. Where can we find that our continence too, which we need against pleasures, also comes from him? You have the plainest proof here: *And since I knew*, he says, *that nobody can be continent unless God grants it; and this too was a matter of wisdom, to know whose gift this was* (Wis 8:21).

So if you have something from God, and don't know who you have it from, you won't be gifted, because you remain ungrateful. If you don't know who you get it from, you don't give thanks; by not giving thanks, you lose even what you have. *For the one who has, to him shall be given.* What is having, in the complete sense? Knowing where you have it from. *But the one who does not have*, that is, who doesn't know where he has it from, *even what he does have shall be taken away from him* (Mk 4:25). Finally, as the same author says, *this too was a matter of wisdom, to know whose gift this was.*

The difference between having the spirit of this world and the Spirit of God

3. In the same way the apostle Paul also said, when he was commending the grace of God to us in the Holy Spirit: *We, however, have not received the spirit of this world, but the Spirit which is from God.* And as though he were asked, "How do you tell the difference?" he went on to add, *that we may know what things have been bestowed on us by God* (1 Cor 2:12). So the Spirit of God is a Spirit of charity; the spirit of this world a spirit of self-esteem. Those who have the spirit of this world are proud, are ungrateful to God. Many people have his gifts, but do not worship him, though they have them from him; that's why they are unhappy. Sometimes one person has greater gifts, another has lesser ones, for example intelligence, memory. These are gifts of God. You will sometimes find a person of extremely sharp wits, with astonishing, incredible powers of memory; you will find another of little intelligence, and a poor memory, but endowed with both to a small degree. But the first is proud, the second humble; this one giving thanks to God for his small gifts, that one attributing the greater ones to himself.

The one who gives thanks to God for small gifts is incomparably better than the one who prides himself on great ones. You see, the one who gives thanks for little things is admitted by God to great things, whereas the one who doesn't give thanks for great things, loses even what he has. *For the one who has, to him shall be given; but the one who does not have, even what he has shall be taken away from him* (Mk 4:25). How can he not have, if he has? He has without having, if he doesn't know where he has it from. God, you see, takes back what is his, and the man is left with his own iniquity.

So: *Nobody is continent, unless God grants it.* You have a gift to protect you against pleasures; since *this was itself a matter of wisdom, to know whose gift this was; nobody is continent, unless God grants it* (Wis 8:21). You have a gift to help you against pains: since *it is from him,* he says, *my patience comes* (Ps 62:5). So *hope in him, every council of the people* (Ps 62:8). Hope in him, don't trust in your own powers. Confess your bad things to him, hope for your good things from him. Without his help you will be nothing, however proud you may be. So in order that you may be enabled to be humble, *pour out your hearts before him*; and to avoid remaining wrongly stuck in yourselves, say what comes next: *God is our helper* (Ps 62:8).

The difference between patience and obstinate insensitivity

4. The blessed martyr whom we are admiring, whose feast we are celebrating today, had this helper, in order to be victorious. Without him, he wouldn't be victorious. Even if he were victorious over pain, he wouldn't be victorious over the devil. Sometimes, you see, people conquered by the devil conquer pain; they don't have patience, what they have is obstinate insensitivity. So that helper was present, to give the martyr true faith, to make a good cause for him, to grant him patience for the sake of the good cause. Only then, you see, is it real patience, when it is preceded by a good cause. Faith itself, after all, is not given by anybody else but God.

The apostle insisted in a few words that each of them, both the cause for which we are to suffer and the patience with which we are to endure evils, comes to us from God. In encouraging us to be martyrs, he said, *Because to you it has been granted for Christ's sake.* There you have the good cause, *for Christ's sake*; if for the sake of some sacrilege, it's against Christ; if for heresy and schism, it's against Christ. Christ said himself, after all, *whoever does not gather with me, scatters* (Lk 11:23). So: *To you,* he says, *it has been granted for Christ's sake, not only to believe in him, but also to suffer for him* (Phil 1:29). That is true patience. So let us value this patience, let us hold on to it fast; and if we haven't got it yet, let us ask for it. And then we can honestly sing, *My soul will submit itself to God, since it is from him that my patience comes* (Ps 62:5).

Sermon 285

On the Birthday of the Martyrs Castus and Aemilius

Here Augustine corrects any notion that would glorify the suffering of the martyrs for suffering's sake: "What God takes delight in, after all, is our justice, not our torments." He rather creatively uses the example of the good thief who was crucified on one side of Jesus to make his point. The cross of Christ in the middle between the two thieves was a judge's bench from which one thief was condemned and the other set free. Christians need not pray *for* the martyrs but rather should pray *to* the martyrs as our advocates. Augustine repeats his constant anti-Donatist refrain: "It is not the punishment that makes God's martyr, but the cause." Possidius mentions this sermon along with others in his *Index* to Augustine's works. A range of dates is suggested by various scholars: Lambot and Perler propose 397; La Bonnardière suggests between 405 and 410; Kunzelmann dates the sermon to 416. All agree that the sermon was preached in Carthage where Castus and Aemilius were martyred about 250.

The courage of the martyrs did not come from themselves

1. I am urged to speak to your graces by the courage of the holy martyrs, courage that was not only heroic but also dutiful — that, after all, is the useful sort of courage, or rather the only true sort, properly to be called courage, when it serves in God's army, not in that of pride. So I am urged to speak to your graces, and urge you to celebrate the feasts of the martyrs in such a way that you also take delight in imitating them by following in their footsteps. The fact, after all, that they turned out so brave was not something that derived from themselves. That source, moreover, from which they drew their courage didn't only flow as far as them. The one who gave it to them is also powerful enough to give it to us, since one price was paid for all of us.

It is not the punishment that makes the martyr, but the cause

2. So the thing you have particularly to be reminded of, to remind yourselves of time and again, and to think about all the time, is that it is not the punishment that makes God's martyr, but the cause. What God takes delight in, after all, is our justice, not our torments; nor is inquiry made at the judgment of the Almighty and the True, what each one of us suffers, but why. You see, what has made us sign ourselves with the cross is not the punishment inflicted on the Lord, but the cause of it. I mean, if it had been the punishment, the similar punishment of the robbers would have had the same value. Three men crucified in the same place, the Lord in the middle, because *he was reckoned among the wicked* (Is 53:12). They placed the two robbers on either side, but they didn't have a similar cause. They were flanking Christ as he hung there, but they were far removed from him in reality. They were crucified by their crimes, he by ours.

And yet in one of them too it was made clear enough what the value was, not of his agony as he hung there, but of his piety as he confessed. The robber acquired in his pain what Peter lost in his fear; he admitted his villainy, he ascended his cross; he changed his cause, he purchased paradise. He thoroughly deserved to change his cause, because he did not dismiss Christ for suffering a similar punishment. The Jews dismissed him as he performed miracles, he believed in him as he hung on the cross. He acknowledged the Lord as his fellow sufferer on the cross, and by believing in him he took the kingdom of heaven by storm. The robber believed in Christ at the very moment when the apostle's faith was shaken with fear. Deservedly he deserved to hear, *Today you shall be with me in paradise* (Lk 23:43).

This is not indeed what he had promised himself; he was indeed commending himself to a great and generous mercy, but he was also thinking about his own deserts. *Lord*, he said, *remember me when you come into your kingdom* (Lk 23:42). Until the Lord came into his kingdom, he expected to be undergoing punishment, and he was begging for mercy to be shown him at least at his coming. In a word the robber, thinking of what he deserved, was putting his time off, while the Lord was putting the robber on to what he had had no hopes of. It's as if he were saying, "You are asking me to remember you when I come into my kingdom: *Amen, amen I tell you, today you shall be with me in paradise.* Recognize who it is you are commending yourself to. You believe I am going to come, but even before I come, I am everywhere. That's why, although I am about to descend into hell, I have you with me in paradise today; with me, not entrusted to someone else. You see, my humility has come down to mortal human beings, and to the dead themselves, but my divinity has never departed from paradise."

Thus three crosses were made, three causes. One of the robbers was scoffing at Christ; the other, confessing his evil deeds, was commending himself to Christ's mercy. The cross of Christ in the middle between them was not an instrument of punishment, but a judge's bench; from his cross, that is to say, he condemned the one who scoffed at him, set free the one who believed in him. Be afraid, scoffers; rejoice, believers. He will do the same in his glory, as he did in his humility.

The mysteries of grace and of judgment illustrated by the case of Peter

3. God's gifts come from the depths of the divine judgment; we can marvel at them, we cannot investigate and explain them. *For who has known the mind of the Lord?* and, *How inscrutable are his judgments, and unsearchable his ways!* (Rom 11:34.33). Peter, following in all Christ's footsteps, is dismayed and denies; he is looked round at, and weeps; his tears wipe away what his fear had smudged him with. That first stage did not mean deserting Peter, but educating him. Asked to love the Lord in his heart, he had been so sure he could also die for him; he had attributed this to his own powers. Unless he were left to himself for a little by his trainer, he would not be shown up to himself. He had the effrontery to say, *I will lay down my life for you* (Jn 13:37). This man for whom Christ had not yet laid down

his life to set him free, was usurping Christ's role, and boasting he would lay down his life for Christ.

To sum up, when he is overwhelmed with fear, as the Lord had predicted he three times denies the one for whom he had promised to die. As it says, *the Lord looked round at him*; he, for his part, *wept bitterly* (Lk 22:61-62). Recollection of his denial was necessarily bitter, so that the grace of redemption might be all the sweeter. If he hadn't been left to himself, he would not have denied; if he hadn't been looked round at, he would not have wept. God hates people relying presumptuously on their own powers, and like a doctor he lances this swollen tumor in those whom he loves. By lancing it, of course, he inflicts pain, but he also ensures health later on. And so when he rises again, the Lord entrusts his sheep to Peter, to that one who denied him; but he denied him because he relied on himself; later he would feed his flock as a pastor, because he loved him. After all why does he ask him three times about his love, if not to prick his conscience about his threefold denial?

Accordingly, Peter accomplished later on by the grace of God, what he had previously been unable to do by self-reliance. You see, after the Lord had entrusted him with his, not Peter's, sheep, to feed them, not for himself but for the Lord, he told him about his future martyrdom, which he had forfeited the first time, because he had been in much too much of a hurry. *When you are older*, he said, *someone else will gird you, and carry you where you do not wish to go. He said this, though, to signify by what death he was going to glorify the Lord* (Jn 21:18-19). It came about, Peter arrived at his martyrdom, having washed away his denial with his tears. What had been promised him by the Savior could not be taken away from him by the tempter.

(...)

The martyrs are our advocates, but again in Christ, not in themselves

5. The justice of the martyrs is perfect, because they have been perfected by their sufferings. That's why they aren't prayed for in the Church. The other faithful departed are prayed for, not the martyrs; they left the world, you see, so perfected that they are not our dependents, but our advocates. And this too, not in themselves, but in the one to whom as their head they have stuck close as his members. He, you see, is indeed the one advocate, *who intercedes for us, seated at the right hand of the Father* (Rom 8:34); but the one advocate in the same way as the one shepherd. Because *I must*, he said, *bring those sheep too, which are not of this fold* (Jn 10:16).

So Christ is a shepherd, Peter not a shepherd? Indeed Peter too is a shepherd, and all others like him are without the slightest doubt shepherds, pastors. I mean, if he isn't a shepherd, how can he be told, *Feed my sheep* (Jn 21:17)? But all the same, the real shepherd is the one who feeds his own sheep. Peter, you see, was not told "Feed your sheep," but "mine." So Peter is a shepherd, not in himself but in the body of the shepherd. I mean, if he were feeding his own sheep, what he was feeding would immediately turn into goats.

(...)

Sermon 286

On the Birthday of the Martyrs Protase and Gervase

This sermon was clearly preached on June 19th sometime between 425 and 430. Perler argues persuasively for a place very near Hippo, where a shrine, or *memoria*, had been dedicated to Protase and Gervase. Even though Peter was the first apostle, and very close to the Lord, he still lacked the courage of the martyrs to profess Christ openly. The martyrs' company even includes women who supposedly belong to the weaker sex. Augustine cites the case of two women, Agnes, a Roman girl martyr, and Crispina, an African of high rank. He identifies himself as a witness to the miracles that accompanied the discovery of the bodies of the martyrs Protase and Gervase while he was residing in Milan. He notes that God does not grant healing to all who invoke the martyrs, but to all who imitate the martyrs he promises eternal life. Neither does Christ always grant the requests of the martyrs, and many of the sick wracked with pain endure martyrdom on their sickbeds.

Martyrs are witnesses, who are prepared to testify to Christ even to the death

1. Martyrs — the word is Greek, but is now in common use in English — are called "witnesses" in English. So there are true martyrs and false ones, because there are true, and false, witnesses. But scripture says, *the false witness shall not go unpunished* (Prv 19:5.9). If the false witness will not escape punishment, neither will the true witness be denied a crown. And it was, indeed, easy to bear witness to the Lord Jesus Christ and the truth, because he is God; but to do so to the death, that was a great work.

There were some leaders of the Jews, mentioned by the gospel, who had believed in the Lord Jesus; but because of the Jews, it says, they did not dare confess him publicly. And straightaway a note is added to the chapter; the evangelist, you see, goes on to say, *For they loved glory with men more than with God* (Jn 12:42-43). So there were some people who would be ashamed to confess Christ before men; while there were others, already better, who would not be ashamed to confess Christ before men, but who could not confess him to the death. These things, you see, are in the gift of God; and sometimes they are nursed in the soul step by step.

First of all pay attention to a comparison of these three with each other; one who believes in Christ, and is so timid he can scarcely whisper the name of Christ; another who believes in Christ, and publicly confesses Christ; a third who confesses Christ, and is prepared in his confession to die for Christ. The first of these is so weak, that what defeats him is shame, not fear; the second already puts on a brave front, but not yet to the shedding of his blood; the third has everything, so that there is nothing left to be desired. He fulfills, you see, what is written: *Contend for truth's sake even to the death* (Sir 4:28).

The comparison illustrated in the case of Peter

2. What can we say about Peter? He preached Christ, he was sent, he proclaimed the gospel already before the Lord's passion. We know, after all, that the apostles were sent out to preach the gospel; Peter, then, was sent, and he preached. How much had he overcome those Jews, the man who was later on afraid to confess Christ publicly? But still, he wasn't yet the equal of Protase and Gervase. He was already an apostle, he was the first, he was very close to the Lord; he was told, *You are Peter* (Mt 16:18). But he still wasn't Protase and Gervase, still wasn't Stephen, still wasn't the boy Nemesianus; Peter still wasn't in that class. He wasn't yet what a number of women have been, what Agnes, what Crispina have been; Peter still wasn't in the class of these women, with all the weakness of their sex.

I will certainly praise Peter; but first I must blush for Peter. How ready his spirit! But without the slightest idea of how to take its own measure. Because of course, if it hadn't been ready, he wouldn't have said to the Savior, "I will die for you": *Even if I have to die with you, I will not deny you* (Mt 26:35). But the doctor, who knew how to take his pulse, foretold the dangerous climax of the fever. *You, he says, are laying down your life for me?* Recognize the correct order; I must first lay down mine. *You are laying down your life for me? Amen I tell you, before the cock crows, you will deny me three times* (Jn 13:38). The doctor foretold what the sick man didn't know. In this way the sick man discovered that his self-assurance had been totally misplaced, when he was questioned, *You are one of them, aren't you?* (Mk 14:67). The maid who questioned him was the fever. Look, the fever has reached its climax, it has taken hold. What am I to say? Look, Peter is in grave danger, look, Peter is dying.

What else is dying, after all, but denying life? He denied Christ, he denied life, he died. But the one who raises the dead, *the Lord, looked round at him, and he wept bitterly* (Lk 22:61-62). By denying he perished, by weeping he rose again. And the Lord died first for him, as was fitting; and later on Peter died for the Lord, as right order required; and the martyrs followed. The previously thorny track was paved, and worn smooth by the feet of the apostles, made easier for those who were going to follow.

The martyrs proclaimed Christ more effectively when dead than when alive

3. The earth has been filled with the blood of the martyrs as with seed, and from that seed have sprung the crops of the Church. They have asserted Christ's cause more effectively when dead than when they were alive. They assert it today, they preach him today; their tongues are silent, their deeds echo round the world. They were arrested, bound, imprisoned, brought to trial, tortured, burnt at the stake, stoned to death, run through, fed to wild beasts. In all their kinds of death they were jeered at as worthless; but *precious in the sight of the Lord is the death of his saints* (Ps 116:15).

Precious then in the Lord's sight only, now in our sight too. Then, you see, when being a Christian was a disgrace, the death of the saints was worthless in the sight of men. They were execrated, held to be an abomination, held up as accursed: "May you die like that, be crucified like that, be burnt to death like that." Now, though, is there any of the faithful who would not welcome such curses?

The discovery of the remains of Protase and Gervase in Milan in 387

4. So today, brothers and sisters, we are celebrating the memorial set up in this place in honor of Saints Protase and Gervase, the martyrs of Milan. Not the day when it was set up here, but the day we are celebrating today is the day of the discovery of the death of his saints, precious in the sight of the Lord, by bishop Ambrose, that man of God. Of that glorious occasion for the martyrs I was myself also a witness. I was in Milan, I know about the miracles that occurred, when God bore witness to the precious deaths of his saints, so that by means of those miracles that death might be precious not only in the sight of the Lord, but also in the sight of men.

A blind man, well known to the whole city, had his sight restored; he ran, he had himself led to the spot, he went home without a guide. I haven't heard that he died; perhaps he's still alive. He vowed that he was going to serve all the rest of his life in that basilica of theirs, where their bodies are. We all rejoiced at his being able to see, we left him there at his service.

God does not restore everyone to health through the martyrs, but to all who imitate the martyrs, he does promise immortality

5. God never stops bearing witness; and he knows the right way to bring his miracles to our notice. He knows how to act, so that they may be famous; he knows how to act, so that they don't become commonplace. He doesn't grant health to everyone through the martyrs; but to all who imitate the martyrs, he does promise immortality. What he doesn't give to everyone should not be sought by anyone he doesn't give it to; and those he doesn't give it to must take care not to grumble against him, so that he may give them what he does promise at the end. After all, even those people too who are now cured, die sooner or later; those who rise again at the end will live with Christ for ever.

The head has preceded us; he is waiting for the members to follow; then the whole body, Christ and the Church, will be complete. May he count us as inscribed there; and may he give us in this life what is best for us. He, you see, is the one who knows what is best for his children. *So if you*, he says, *though you are evil, know how to give good gifts to your children, how much more will your Father who is in heaven give good things to those who ask him?* (Mt 7:11). What good things? Not temporal ones, surely? He does give those too; but he also gives them to unbelievers. He does give those too; but he gives them also to the godless. We should be looking for the good things which we don't share with evil persons.

That Father knows how to give these good things to his children. Now a child of his asks for health of body; and he doesn't give it, he continues to chastise. But is the Father, when he chastises, not providing anything? He brandishes the rod, but just think what an inheritance he is getting ready. *He chastises*, it says, *every son whom he receives. For whom the Lord loves, he disciplines* (Heb 12:6). The reason I'm saying all this, my dear brothers and sisters, is that you shouldn't be disheartened when you ask and don't receive, and conclude that God hasn't got you in mind, if at the moment he doesn't pay attention to your wishes. The doctor, after all, doesn't always pay attention to the patient's wishes, although he is undoubtedly attending to his health and aiming at it. He doesn't give what the patient asks for; but he is attending to what he doesn't ask for. He asks for ice cream, he doesn't give it. Has he turned out cruel, the one who came to cure? It's his skill, not his cruelty. He doesn't give on the spot what gives the patient pleasure; some things are denied him while he's not yet well, so that when he does get well he may be able to take anything.

Comparison between the three boys in the fiery furnace,
and the seven Maccabee brothers

6. Think a bit about God's promises. What about these very martyrs? Do you suppose he gave them everything they requested? No. Many of them hoped they would be let off, and let off with some miracle, as the three boys were let out of the fiery furnace. What were the words of king Nebuchadnezzar? *Since they hoped in him*, he said, *and changed the word of the king* (Dn 3:28). What a testimonial, from the man who was trying to kill them! He wanted them burnt to death, and later came to believe through them. If they had died in the fire, they would have received the crown of martyrdom in secret, and it would have been no good to this king. That's why they were preserved for a time, so that the unbeliever might come to believe, the one who had condemned them might come to praise God.

The God of the three boys was the same as the God of the Maccabees. He delivered the first ones from the fire, he had the latter die in the fire. Did he chop and change? Did he love those more than these? A more splendid crown was given to the Maccabees. True, the others escaped the fire; but they were preserved for the perils of this world; these finished with all such perils in the fire. There remained no other trial or temptation, but only a victors' coronation. So the Maccabees received more.

Shake up your faith, bring the eyes of your hearts to bear, not your human eyes. You have other ones inside, after all, which God made for you. He opened the eyes of your hearts, when he gave you faith. Question those eyes: who got more, the Maccabees, or the three boys? I'm questioning your faith; if I were to question people who love this world — "I would rather be with the three boys" is what the weak soul says to me. Blush for shame in the presence of the mother of the Maccabees, who wanted her sons to die before herself, because she knew they weren't dying.

The martyrdom of the sickbed

7. I on occasion am reminded of the leaflets on the miracles of the martyrs, which are read in your presence. A few days ago a leaflet was read, in which a sick woman, wracked with the severest pains said, "I can't bear it." The martyr, to whom she had come to be healed, said, "What if you were enduring martyrdom?" So it is that many people endure martyrdom on their sickbeds, very many indeed. Satan has a certain method of persecution, more hidden and cunning than the ones he employed in those times. A believer is lying in bed, wracked with pain; he prays, he isn't listened to; or rather, he is listened to, but he is being tested, being put through his paces, being chastised in order to be received as a son.

So while he's being wracked with pain, along comes trial and temptation by tongue; either some female, or a man, if man he can be called, approaches the sickbed, and says to the sick man, "Tie on that *muti*, and you will get better; let them apply that charm, and you will get better. So-and-so, and So-and-so and So-and-so; ask, they all got better by using it." He doesn't yield, he doesn't agree, he doesn't give his consent; he has to struggle, all the same. He has no strength, and he conquers the devil. He becomes a martyr on his sickbed, and he is crowned by the one who hung for him on the tree.

Sermon 296

On the Birthday of the Holy Apostles Peter and Paul

This is a brilliant example of Augustine's preaching at its best. The bishop addresses Peter as if he were alive, present and engaged in conversation, which is a very powerful literary technique that he also uses with the congregation. This sermon was clearly preached on June 29, 411, on the feast of Saints Peter and Paul, in Carthage a few weeks after the famous conference presided over by Marcellinus, the imperial commissioner. The date is abundantly clear from specific references in sections 6-12. Augustine reminds his congregation that Christianity was not responsible for the recent sack of Rome, since Roman history indicates that this was actually the third time the city of Rome was ravaged, the first time under the Gauls and the second time when the emperor Nero set fire to the city. This is a theme that Augustine will develop at length in *The City of God*. The disaster is an opportunity for Christians to put their hope in everlasting goods rather than in temporal ones. Augustine asserts that Christians should be more concerned about interiorizing the memorials of the apostles than worrying about their burial sites. The real lesson to be learned from the events at Rome is how Christians should prepare themselves to deal with death and loss. The final section appeals to Catholics to allow repentant Donatists to return to Catholic unity and not presume to judge people's hearts and question their true motives.

The circumstances in which Peter was told by Christ to feed his sheep

1. This reading of the holy gospel, which sounded in our ears just now, is very apt for today's feast. If it also went down from our ears into our hearts, and there found a place of repose — God's word, you see, reposes in us, when we repose, and acquiesce, in the word of God — then it admonished all of us, who minister to you the Lord's word and sacrament, to feed his sheep. Blessed Peter, the first of the apostles, both lover and repudiator of the Lord Jesus Christ, as the gospel shows, followed the Lord as he was about to suffer; but at that time he wasn't able to follow him to the extent of suffering himself. He followed with his feet, he wasn't yet capable of following with his virtue.

He promised he would die *for* him, and he wasn't even able to die *with* him; he had staked more, you see, than his credit could stand. He had promised more than he could fulfill, because it was in fact unfitting that he should do what he had promised. *I will lay down my life*, he said, *for you* (Jn 13:37). But that is what the Lord was going to do for the servant, not the servant for the Lord. So as he had staked more than he was worth, he was then loving in a back-to-front sort of way; that's why he was afraid and denied Christ. Later on, though, the Lord, after he has risen, teaches Peter how to love. While he was loving in the wrong way, he collapsed under the weight of Christ's passion; but when he's loving in the right way, Christ promises him a passion of his own.

Peter is feeble, when he is presumptuously relying on himself

2. We remember Peter's weakness in being shocked at the idea that the Lord was going to die. That's what I'm reminding you of. Look, I'm reminding you; those of you who remember can tell themselves the story with me; those who have forgotten can call it to mind as I remind them of it. The Lord Jesus Christ himself foretold his imminent passion to the disciples. Then Peter, full of love for him, but still of a worldly sort, afraid of the slayer of death dying, said, *Far be this from you, Lord, far be it; do yourself a favor* (Mt 16:22). He wouldn't have said, *Do yourself a favor*, unless he acknowledged him to be God. So, Peter, if he's acknowledged by you to be God, why are you afraid of God dying? You're a man, he's God; and for man's sake God became man, taking upon him what he was not, without losing what he was. So the Lord was going to die in that respect in which he was going to rise again, as a man. So Peter was horrified at the prospect of a human death, and didn't want it to touch the Lord; unwittingly he wanted to close the purse from which our price would flow.

That's when he heard from the Lord, *Get back behind, Satan, for you do not share God's ideas, but men's* (Mt 16:23). A moment before he had said to him — when he had said, *You are the Christ, the Son of the living God — Blessed are you, Simon Bar-Jona, because it was not flesh and blood that revealed it to you, but my Father who is in heaven* (Mt 16:16-17). A moment before, blessed; next minute, Satan. But how and why blessed? Not for anything of his own: *It was not flesh and blood that revealed it to you, but my Father who is in heaven.* And how and why Satan? *For you do not share God's ideas, but men's.*

Such then was Peter; loving the Lord and wishing to die for the Lord, he followed; and it all turned out as the doctor had foretold, not as the sick patient had self-confidently presumed. Questioned by a maid, he denies once, twice, a third time. He's glanced at by the Lord, he weeps bitterly, with the tears of devoted love he wipes clean the dirt of denial.

The only question is "Do you love me?"; the only answer, "I do"

3. The Lord rises again, he appears to the disciples; now Peter sees him alive, whose death he had so feared; he sees, not the Lord slain, but death slain in the Lord. So now, encouraged by the example of the Lord's own flesh that death is not to be dreaded all that much, he is taught how to love. Now he really must love, now having seen the Lord alive after death, now he really can love, now he can love without anxiety; without anxiety, because he is going to follow.

So the Lord says, *Peter, do you love me?*

And he answers, *I do love you, Lord.*

And the Lord says, "I don't want you, because you love me, to die for me; that, after all, is what I have already done for you. But what? Do you love me? What are you going to give me in return because you love me? *Do you love me?*

I do love you.

Feed my sheep (Jn 21:15-17). And the same again, and the same a third time, so that love might declare itself three times, because fear had denied three times.

Notice, take it to heart, learn; the only question asked is *Do you love me?*; the only answer given, *I do.* When he gives that answer, he's told, *Feed my sheep.* And with his sheep entrusted to Peter, and Peter together with his sheep taken into his own care, he now goes on to foretell his death, and says, *When you were younger, you used to gird yourself and go where you wished; but when you are older, another will gird you, and carry you where you do not wish to go. But he said this,* adds the evangelist, *to signify by what sort of death he was going to glorify God* (Jn 21:18-19). You can see that what is involved in feeding the Lord's sheep is not refusing to die for the Lord's sheep.

*The shepherd equal to the responsibility is one who is capable
of paying for the sheep with his life*

4. *Feed my sheep* (Jn 21:17). Is he entrusting his sheep to a man equal, or less than equal, to the responsibility? First of all, what sort of sheep is he entrusting? Very valuable ones, bought not with gold, not with silver, but with blood. If a human master were entrusting his sheep to a slave, he would undoubtedly consider whether the savings of that slave are equal to the value of his sheep, and would say, "If he loses, or scatters, or eats any of them, he must have the wherewithal to pay for them."

So he would entrust his sheep to a slave equal to the responsibility, and would require the slave's means in money for the sheep he had bought with money.

In this case, however, the Lord Jesus Christ is entrusting the slave with sheep he bought with his blood, and so he requires of the slave the capacity to suffer to the point of shedding his blood. It's as though he were saying, *"Feed my sheep; I am entrusting my sheep to you."*

What sheep?

"Ones I bought with my blood. I died for them. *Do you love me?* Be ready to die for them." And as a matter of fact, while that human slave of a human master would pay money for sheep destroyed, Peter paid the price of his blood for sheep preserved.

Other shepherds, other ways of laying down one's life for the sheep

5. Here we go then, brothers and sisters, I would like to say something suitable for this particular time. It was not only Peter who heard what was entrusted to Peter, what was enjoined on Peter. The other apostles also heard, took it to heart, observed it; above all the one who shared Peter's sufferings, and this day with him, the apostle Paul. They heard all this, and transmitted it to us to be heard and listened to. We feed you, we are fed together with you; may the Lord grant us the strength so to love you that we are capable also of dying for you, either in fact or in fellow feeling.

Just because, you see, a martyr's death did not come the apostle John's way, it does not mean that he could be wanting in a spirit prepared for martyrdom. He didn't suffer, but he was able to suffer; God was aware of his readiness. It's like the three boys cast into the furnace in order to be burnt up, not in order to live; shall we deny they were martyrs, just because the flames couldn't burn them? Question the fire, they didn't suffer; question their willingness, they received the crown of martyrdom. *God is powerful enough*, they said, *to deliver us from your hands; but even if not —* there you have their steady hearts, their firm faith, their unshaken courage, their assurance of victory — *but even if not, be it known to you, O king, that we are not worshiping the statue which you have set up* (Dn 3:17-18). God had other plans; they were not burnt, but they extinguished the fires of idolatry in the spirit of the king.

Complaints about Rome being sacked during Christian times

6. So you can see, dearly beloved, what has been set before the servants of God during this age, on account of *the future glory that will be revealed in us*; a glory which no temporal tribulations of any kind or quantity can even begin to outweigh. *For the sufferings of this present time*, says the apostle, *are not to be compared with the future glory that will be revealed in us* (Rom 8:18). If that's the case, none of us should now be thinking in a worldly way, "This isn't the time." The world is being turned upside down, the old man is being shaken, the flesh hard pressed; let the spirit flow clear.

"Peter's body lies in Rome," people are saying, "Paul's body lies in Rome, Lawrence's body lies in Rome, the bodies of other holy martyrs lie in Rome; and Rome is griefstricken, and Rome is being devastated, afflicted, crushed, burnt; death stalking the streets in so many ways, by hunger, by pestilence, by the sword. Where are the memorials of the apostles?"

What's this you're saying?

"Here's what I'm saying; Rome is suffering such enormous evils; where are the memorials of the apostles?"

They are there, they are there, but they are not in you. If only they were in you, whoever you are that are saying these things, whoever you are, foolish enough to think these things, whoever you are, called in the spirit and savoring the flesh, whoever you may be of that sort! If only the memorials of the apostles were in you, if only you really gave a thought to the apostles! Then you would see whether they were promised an earthly felicity or an eternal.

Even if we don't know God's reasons, we must willingly accept his decisions

7. Listen to the apostle, if his memory, his memorial, is still alive in you: *For the temporary lightness of our tribulation works in us to an unbelievable degree, and beyond an unbelievable degree, an eternal weight of glory, if we do not fix our gaze on the things that are seen, but on the things that are not seen; for the things that are seen are temporary, but the things that are not seen are eternal* (2 Cor 4:17-18). In Peter himself the flesh was temporary, and aren't you willing for the stones of Rome to be temporary? The apostle Peter is reigning with the Lord, the body of the apostle Peter is lying in some place or other. His memorial is meant to stir you to love of eternal things, not so that you may stick to the earth, but so that with the apostle you may think about heaven.

Tell me, if you're one of the faithful, call to mind the memorials of the apostles, the memorial even of the Lord your God, who is certainly now seated in heaven. Listen to where the apostle is directing you: *If you have risen with Christ, savor the things that are above where Christ is, seated at the right hand of God; seek the things that are above, not the things that are on earth. For you have died, and your life is hidden with Christ in God. When Christ, your life, appears, then you too will appear with him in glory* (Col 3:1-4). What you've heard here is, in one word, "Lift up your hearts." So are you griefstricken, and crying, because timbers and stones have fallen down, and because people have died who were going to die anyway? Granted that someone who's dead is going to live for ever; are you grieving over the collapse of timbers and stones, and the fact that those who were going to die anyway have died? If you have lifted up your heart, where have you got your heart? Is there anything dead there, anything that has collapsed? If you have lifted up your heart, *where your treasure is, there is your heart* (Mt 6:21). Your flesh is down below, and if your flesh feels dread, don't let it shake your heart.

"But all the same," you say, "I didn't want it to happen."

What didn't you want to happen?

"I didn't want Rome to suffer such dreadful things."

We can pardon you for not wanting it. Don't you be angry with God because he did want it; you're only human, he's God. You're saying, "I don't want it," where he's saying, "I do." He doesn't condemn you for your "I don't want it," and are you going to reproach his "I do"?

"But why does God want this?"

Why does God want this? For the time being accommodate yourself to the will of the Lord your God; when you have become his friend, you will know the plans of the Lord your God. What slave when his master tells him to do something, would ever be so proud as to say "Why?" The Lord keeps his counsel and his plans to himself. They become clearer if he does his duty, if he does well, if from being a servant he becomes a friend, as the Lord himself said: *I will no longer call you servants, but friends* (Jn 15:15). Perhaps he will also learn his Lord's plans; meanwhile, before he knows the plans, let him willingly carry out the decisions.

Put up with what God wants, and he will give you what you want

8. The lesson I'm still teaching you, as a matter of fact, is patience, not yet wisdom. Be patient, it's the Lord's will. You ask why it's his will? Put off your eagerness for knowledge, prepare for the strenuous effort of obedience. He wants you to bear with what he wants; bear with what he wants, and he will give you what you want. And yet, my dear brothers and sisters, I make so bold as to say that you are going to listen to this gladly, if you already have the basic elements of obedience, if there is to be found in you the meek and mild patience of bearing with the Lord's will, not only when it is mild. When it's mild, of course, we don't bear with it, we love it; it's when it's hard and harsh that we tolerate it, when it's mild and easy we rejoice.

Observe your Lord, observe your head, observe the model of your life; pay attention to your redeemer, your shepherd. *Father, if it may be so, let this cup pass from me.* How perfectly he shows his human will, and straightaway turns his resistance into obedience! *However, not what I wish, but what you wish, Father* (Mt 26:39). And here, look, he also said this to Peter: *When you are old, another will gird you, and carry you where you do not wish* (Jn 21:18). He indicated in him too the human will, as it shrinks from death. Does it mean, because he didn't wish to die, that he didn't wish to receive the crown?

So with you too, what is it you didn't want? To lose your savings, perhaps, which you were going to leave behind here? Take care you don't remain behind with what should be left behind. You didn't want, perhaps, your son to die before you, you didn't want your wife to die before you. Well after all, even if Rome hadn't been captured, wasn't one of you going to be the first to die? You didn't want your wife to die before you; your wife didn't want her husband to die before her; was God going to accommodate both of you? Let the right order remain with him; he knows how to set in order what he has created. It's for you to accommodate yourself to his will.

How to answer those who blame the Christian times

9. I can already see what you are saying in your heart: "Look, it's during Christian times that Rome is being afflicted, or rather has been afflicted and burnt. Why in Christian times?"

Who are you, saying this?

"A Christian."

So you answer yourself, if you're a Christian: "It's because it was God's will."

"But what can I say to the pagan? He's insulting me."

What's he saying to you? How is he insulting you?

"Look, when we used to offer sacrifices to our gods, Rome continued to stand. Now, because the sacrifice of your God has won the day and been so frequently offered, and the sacrifices of our gods have been stopped and forbidden, look what Rome has to suffer."

For the time being, give him a very short answer, to get rid of him. You, however, should have quite other thoughts. You weren't called, after all, to embrace the earth, but to obtain heaven; you were not called to an earthly, but to a heavenly felicity; not to temporal success, and fleeting and fickle prosperity, but to eternal life with the angels. Still, for this lover of worldly felicity and grumbler against the living God, who prefers to serve demons and sticks and stones, there's a quick answer you can give. As their own histories tell us, this is the third time the city of Rome has been burnt. As their own history relates, their own literature relates, this burning of the city of Rome that has just happened is the third occasion. The city that was recently on fire amid the sacrifices of Christians had already been twice on fire amid the sacrifices of the pagans. It was once burnt like that by the Gauls, so that only the Capitol Hill was left. A second time Rome was set on fire by Nero, I don't know whether to say out of savagery or out of frivolity. Nero, the emperor of Rome, gave the order; the slave of idols, the slayer of the apostles, gave the order, and Rome was set on fire. Why, do you suppose, for what reason? A proud, conceited and frivolous man enjoyed the Roman blaze. "I want to see," he said, "how Troy was burnt." So it was burnt in this way once, a second time, and now a third time. Why do you like growling against God for a city that has been in the habit of being on fire?

While pagans may have something to wring their handsover in the sack of Rome, Christians haven't

10. "But," they say, "so many Christians suffered such dreadful evils in the sack of the city."

Has it escaped your notice that it is the prerogative of Christians to suffer temporal evils, and hope for everlasting goods? You pagan, whoever you are, have something to wring your hands over, because you have lost your temporal goods, and haven't yet discovered eternal goods. The Christian, though, has something to think about: *Reckon it every joy, my brothers, when you fall into various trials* (Jas 1:2). When this sort of thing was chanted to you in the temple: "The gods who protected Rome have not saved it now, because they no longer exist," you would say, "They did save it, when they existed."

We, though, can show that our God is truthful; he foretold all these things, you've all read them, you've heard them; but I'm not sure whether you've remembered them, you that are upset by such words. Haven't you heard the prophets, haven't you heard the apostles, haven't you heard the Lord Jesus Christ himself foretelling evils to come? When old age comes to the world, when the end draws near — you heard it, brothers and sisters, we all heard it together — *There will be wars, there will be tumults, there will be tribulations, there will be famines* (Mk 13:7-8; Lk 21:9-11). Why are we so contradictory to ourselves that when these things are read we believe them, when they are fulfilled we grumble?

The world is more to blame, after the gospel has been preached and ignored

11. "But more devastation," they say, "much more, is overtaking the human race now."

Well, I don't know about more, considering all past history; but for the time being, without prejudice to the truth on that point, suppose it is more; I think it is more. The Lord himself solves the problem. There's more devastation in the world now, much more devastation, he says. Why more devastation now, when the gospel is being preached everywhere? You observe how widespread is the preaching of the gospel; you don't observe in what a godless way it is being ignored. Right now, brothers and sisters, let's leave the pagans out of it for a moment or two, let's turn our eyes on ourselves. The gospel is being preached, the whole world is full of it. Before the gospel was preached, God's will was hidden; by the preaching of the gospel, God's will has become openly known. We have been told in the preaching of the gospel what we ought to love, what to think lightly of, what to do, what to avoid, what to hope for. We've heard it all, God's will is no longer hidden anywhere in the world.

Take the world as a servant, and pay attention to the gospel. Listen to the Lord's voice; this world is the servant: *The servant who does not know the will of his lord, and does not behave properly, will be beaten with a few lashes.* The servant, the world; it's the servant, because *the world was made through him, and the world did not know him* (Jn 1:10). *The servant who does not know the will of his lord*; there you have the world before; *the servant who does not know the will of his lord, and does not behave properly, will be beaten with a few lashes. But the servant who knows his lord's will*; there you have what the world is like now; now tell yourselves what follows, or rather let us all tell ourselves: *The servant who knows his lord's will and does not behave properly, will be beaten with many lashes* (Lk 12:48.47). And if only it may be beaten with many lashes, and not be once and for all condemned!

Why do you jib at being beaten with many lashes, you servant who know the wishes of your Lord, and do things deserving of lashes? You're told (here you have one wish of your Lord's), *Store up for yourselves treasure in heaven, where neither moth nor rust can spoil, and where thieves cannot dig through and steal* (Mt 6:20). You're on earth, he's in heaven, telling you, "Give to me, put your treasure where I can guard it, send it ahead of you; why save it?" What Christ is guarding for you, can the Goth take away from you? You, on the other hand, wiser and more farsighted, naturally, than your Lord, wish to store up treasure nowhere but here on earth. But you are well aware of your Lord's wishes; he wanted you to store it up above. So you, busy storing it up on earth, must be prepared to be beaten with many lashes. Look, you know your Lord's will, that he wants you to save it up in heaven; you, his servant on earth, are doing what thoroughly deserves lashes, and when you're beaten you blaspheme, you grumble, and you say that what your Lord is doing to you ought not to have been done. What you, a bad servant, are doing, that ought to have been done, I suppose?

God has only knocked pleasing toys out of the hands of undisciplined children

12. At least hold on to this position: don't speak ill of your God; praise him, rather, for correcting you; praise him for putting you right, so that he may give you consolation. *For whom the Lord loves he corrects, and he whips every son whom he receives* (Heb 12:6). You, self-indulgent son of the Master, would like both to be received and not to be whipped; so that you may be thoroughly spoiled and he may be proved a liar. So the memorial of the apostles, by which heaven is being made ready for you, really should have saved for you on earth the crazy follies of the theaters? That's why Peter died and was laid to rest in Rome, is it, in order that not a stone of the theater might fall? God is knocking the playthings of boys from the hands of ill-disciplined adults.

Brothers and sisters, let us decrease both our sins and our grumbles; let us be sworn enemies both to our iniquities and our grumbling; let us be angry with ourselves, not with God. *Be angry*, most certainly be angry; but for what purpose? *And do not sin* (Ps 4:4). That's why be angry, in order not to sin. Everyone, after all, who repents, is being angry with himself; being sorry for what he has done, he works off his anger on himself. So do you want God to spare you? Do not you spare yourself; because if you spare yourself, he won't spare you; because if he too does so, you are lost. Just as it's written, you see, *He whips every son whom he receives*, so also there's this other text to be afraid of: *The sinner has irritated the Lord*.

"How do you know" — it's as if he were asked — "How do you know that the sinner has irritated the Lord? I've seen the sinner prospering, every day I've seen him doing evil, and suffering no evil, and blaspheming against the Holy Spirit. I've been horrified and dismayed. *The sinner has irritated the Lord*; this sinner, who has done such evil things, and who suffers no evil has irritated the Lord, has he, provoked the Lord?"

For the greatness of his wrath, he will not search out (Ps 10:3-4). That's what comes next: *The sinner has irritated the Lord; for the greatness of his wrath, he will not search out.*

The reason he won't search out is that he is very angry; the one who withholds correction is preparing damnation. *He will not search out*, because if he did search out, he would do some whipping; if he did some whipping, he would put you right. Now, though, he's very angry, very angry with the wicked who prosper. Don't be jealous of them, don't wish to be like them. It's better to be whipped than damned.

You are God's sheep, we bishops are sheep with you, because we are Christians, but you too, with Peter, can feed Christ's sheep

13. So the Lord entrusted his sheep to us bishops, because he entrusted them to Peter; if, that is, we are worthy with any part of us, even with the tips of our toes, to tread the dust of Peter's footsteps, the Lord entrusted his sheep to us. You are his sheep, we are sheep along with you, because we are Christians. I have already said, we are fed and we feed.

Love God, so that God may love you; and you can only show you love God to the extent that you manifestly love God's profits. What have you got that you can offer God, you clever so-and-so? What can you offer God? What Peter also could offer him, all that: *Feed my sheep*. What can you do for God? Help him become greater, become better, become richer, become more honorable? Whatever you will be, he will just be what he always was. So just look next to you; in case perhaps what you should do for your neighbor is help him reach God. *When you have done it for one of these least of mine, you have done it for me* (Mt 25:40). So if you are bidden *to break your bread to the hungry* (Is 58:7), have you a duty to shut the Church in the face of someone who is knocking?

Augustine's grief that a Donatist who had come seeking admission to the Catholic Church, was objected to and driven away by some of the brethren

14. Why have I said this? I was saddened by what I heard, though I wasn't present myself, that when someone from the Donatists came to the Church, confessing the sin of rebaptism, and was being exhorted by the bishop to repentance, he was objected to by some of the brethren, and driven away. I confess to your graces, this really hurt my deepest feelings; I tell you frankly, this kind of diligence has pleased me not at all. I know they did it out of zeal, I don't doubt they did it out of zeal for God. But they should also turn their attention to that passage of the apostle Paul, where he laments even those who *have zeal for God, but not according to knowledge* (Rom 10:2).

Look here; he wasn't admitted today; he dies tomorrow; at whose hands will his death be demanded? You're going to say, "But he's pretending."

I answer, "But he's asking. Christian, I would now like you to teach me too; how do you know he's pretending?"

"Because he's afraid for his property."

We know of many who have been afraid for their property, and have become Catholics for that reason. When they have been absolved from their liability, some of them have returned to the Donatists, some though have stayed. As long as they didn't enter the Church, they were afraid for their property; and when they did enter, they learned the truth, and remained. So then, how do you know that this man who is afraid for his property will be among those who turned out to be insincere, especially when such a strong light of truth is shining as now, such an effective conviction of falsehood?

Why do you want to judge people's hearts, Mr. Man? Is that why we bishops have sweated away, that why we've toiled away, that why the truth should have been shown to be unconquered, that it should be made the enemy of those who seek it? We worked hard for the truth to be demonstrated, falsehood to be convicted. God helped us, it was done. Perhaps this man, for whose sake it was done, became a changed person by thinking about it carefully. Why do you want to pass judgment on his motives? I see him seeking admittance, and you accuse him of just pretending? Allow the truth, Christian, of what you can see, and leave judgment on what you can't see to God. Let me put the matter to your graces very briefly: we heard from the Lord himself that his sheep are to be fed; and we know what he says about the sheep through Ezekiel: that sheep must not push sheep around, sheep must not drive sheep away, the strong must not be a burden to the sick. Think of what the apostle says: *Correct the unruly, encourage the fainthearted, help the weak* (1 Thes 5:14). *Correct the unruly*; let this be done. *Encourage the fainthearted*; let this be done. *Help the weak*; let this be done. *Let nobody return evil for evil to anyone* (1 Thes 5:15); let that be done. He said so many things; do we pay none of them any attention, except *Correct the unruly*? Notice: *Correct the unruly*. Start counting: *Encourage the fainthearted, help the weak, let nobody return evil for evil to anyone.* You, though, only pay attention to *Correct the unruly*; take care you aren't unruly yourself, and what's worse, both want to be unruly, and don't want to be corrected.

I beg you through Christ, I implore you not to ruin all our work. Or are you thinking that the thing we have here to be pleased about is that we have defeated falsehood? It's always the truth that is victorious; as for us, what are we? Falsehood was defeated, it was defeated a long time ago. But thank God, it has now been openly defeated, and shown up to everybody. A lot of hard work has gone into the cultivation; why should it be prevented from yielding its crop?

All to be admitted, both those who had never been Catholics,
and those who had been; but on somewhat different terms

15. For the rest, brothers and sisters, these things must not happen. Nobody should love the Church in such a way as to grudge the Church its profits. It was the day before yesterday, or the day before that, that this thing I'm talking about happened; and the story went round loudly to everybody, that Donatists are not being admitted, when they come to the Church. Do you imagine that no harm was done when this story reached everybody's ears? I'm asking your help; let this voice of mine echo in your ears today in such a way that the thing that has sounded well may drown out the noise of the thing that sounded so badly. Get to work on it.

This is what we said, this is what we bishops proclaim: let them come, let them be admitted in the customary way, those who have never hitherto been Catholics. As for those who were once Catholics, and have been found to be shaky, found to be inconstant and weak, found to be faithless — am I to spare them? Yes, certainly faithless — well perhaps those who have been faithless, will turn out to be faithful. Let them too come, and be admitted to penance. Nor should they kid themselves, that when they went back to the Donatist party they did penance there. That penance was being sorry for a good thing; let there be true penance and genuine repentance for a bad thing. When they did penance in the Donatist party, they were being sorry for something good they had done. Now let them do it and be sorry for the bad thing they have done.

You're afraid that since they were found to be faithless, they may trample on that which is holy? But look, even here your fears are taken care of; they are admitted to penance; they will be in penance as long as they wish, with nobody forcing them, nobody terrifying them to be reconciled. Because a penitent Catholic is no longer subject to the threats of the laws; he begins to desire to be fully reconciled, with nobody now terrifying him; then at least, trust his sincerity. Let's grant, he was forced to be a Catholic; he will become a penitent. Who, apart from his own will, is forcing him to seek the place of reconciliation? So right now let us allow weakness to enter, so that later on we may test genuineness of will.

Sermon 299D

On the Birthday of the Holy Scillitan Martyrs

Augustine uses the occasion of the anniversary of the Scillitan Martyrs, the protomartyrs of Africa who died in Carthage in 180, to teach the importance of dying to self: "The holy martyrs, witnesses of God, preferred to live by dying in order not to die by living." Perler maintains this sermon was preached in 413, the year Augustine spent the entire summer in Carthage, at the New Market Basilica there. Augustine emphasizes the distinction between the necessities of life in this world and superfluities. Christ should never be denied for either. The necessities include health/well-being (*salus*) and friendship. To these must be added wisdom. Augustine also discusses friendship and mentions that it begins with one's spouse and then moves on to children and strangers.

We are to despise not only the superfluities but also the necessities of life for Christ's sake: well-being and friends

1. The holy martyrs, witnesses of God, preferred to live by dying, in order not to die by living; in order not to deny life by fearing death, they despised life by loving life. To get them to deny Christ, the enemy was promising them life, but not the kind Christ was. So as they believed the promises of the Savior, they laughed at the threats of the persecutor. Brothers and sisters, when we celebrate the festivals of the martyrs, we should know that examples are being set before us, which we should try to match by imitating them. After all, by getting together like this we don't increase the glory of the martyrs. The crowns they won are known to the congregations of angels. For our part, we could hear what they suffered when the account was read; but as for what they received, *neither has eye seen nor ear heard* (1 Cor 2:9).

Of the goods of this world some are superfluous, others necessary. Give your attention, please, as I speak about this for a few moments, so that we may distinguish, if we can, what the superfluous goods of this world are, and what the necessary ones; and so that you may see that Christ is not to be denied for the sake either of superfluous or of necessary things. Who could count the superfluous things of this world? If we wanted to make a list of them, it would take a very long time. So let's say what the necessities are; anything else will be superfluous. Necessities in this world amount to these two things: well-being and a friend. These are the things which we should value highly and not despise. Well-being and a friend are goods of nature. God made man to be and to live; that's well-being; but so that he shouldn't be alone, a system of friendship was worked out. So friendship begins with married partner and children, and from there moves on to strangers. But if we consider that we all have one father and one mother, who will be a stranger? Every human being is neighbor to every other human being. Ask nature; is he unknown? He's human. Is she an enemy? She's human. Is he a foe? He's human. Is she a friend? Let her stay a friend. Is he an enemy? Let him become a friend.

Wisdom comes, like a visitor, to join these two necessities, well-being and friends

2. So to these two things that are so necessary in this world, well-being and a friend, along came Wisdom as a visitor. She found everyone sunk in folly, going astray, cultivating the superfluous, in love with temporal things, ignorant of eternal things. This Wisdom was no friend to fools. So since she was no friend to fools and a long way away from fools, she took to herself a neighbor of ours, and became herself our neighbor. That's the mystery of Christ. What are so far from each other as folly and wisdom? What are so near, such neighbors to each other, as man and man? What such a long way away, I repeat, from folly as wisdom? So Wisdom took a man to herself, and thus became a neighbor to man through what was already a neighbor to him.

And lo and behold, since Wisdom herself said to man, *Behold, godliness is wisdom* (Jb 28:28); while it is the business of man's wisdom to worship God, because that's what godliness is; there were therefore given us two commandments: *You shall love the Lord your God with your whole heart, and with your whole soul, and with your whole mind*; the other, *You shall love your neighbor as yourself.* And the man who was told this said, *And who is my neighbor?* (Lk 10:27.29). He thought the Lord was going to say, "Your father and your mother, your wife, your children, your brothers, your sisters." That's not what he answered, but as he wished to impress on us that every human being is neighbor to every other human being, he undertook to tell a story.

Some man, he said, *or other.* Who? Someone or other, a human being all the same. *Some man or other.* So which man? Someone or other, but all the same a human being. *Went down from Jerusalem to Jericho, and fell among robbers.* Those too are called robbers, who keep on harrying us. Wounded, stripped, left half dead in the road, he was ignored by passers-by, by a priest, by a levite; but he was taken notice of by a passing Samaritan. He was approached, and after careful examination he was lifted onto the beast, brought to an inn; the order was given for him to be cared for, expenses were paid. The one who had asked the question is questioned himself; who was a neighbor to this man left half dead? Because two had ignored him, and it was neighbors that had ignored him, while a foreigner approached him. This man from Jerusalem, you see, regarded priests and levites as neighbors, Samaritans as foreigners. The neighbors passed by, and the foreigner became a neighbor. So who was a neighbor to this man? You there, tell us, you that asked the question, *Who is my neighbor?* Now answer what the truth is. It was pride that had asked; let nature now speak. So what did he say? *I suppose, the one who showed him kindness. And the Lord said to him, Go, and do likewise yourself* (Lk 10:36-37).

What is well-being for you must be well-being for your neighbor

3. Let's get back to the matter in hand. There are now three things we observe, well-being, a friend, wisdom. But well-being and a friend also come from this world; wisdom is from somewhere else. Well-being requires food and clothing, and if bad health comes along, medicine. The apostle who was well, speaking to people who were well, said, *But a great advantage is godliness with sufficiency. We brought nothing*, he said, *into this world, but neither can we take anything away. Having food and clothing, with these let us be content.* These are necessary for well-being; what's needed, though, for the superfluities? *For those who wish*, he says, *to get rich* — for the sake of superfluities, naturally — *fall into temptation and a snare, and many foolish and harmful desires, which plunge a person into destruction and ruin* (1 Tm 6:6-9). So where's the well-being? So for the sake of well-being, *having food and clothing, with these let us be content.*

What for the sake of a friend? What more could you be told than *You shall love your neighbor as yourself* (Lk 10:27; Mk 12:31)? So what is well-being for you must also be well-being for your friend. As regards the friend's clothing, *Whoever has two shirts, should share with the one who has none*; as regards the friend's food, *and whoever has food should do likewise* (Lk 3:11). You're fed, you feed; you're clothed, you clothe. All that from this world; from elsewhere though, which is where wisdom comes in, you learn, and you teach.

How the martyrs despised superfluities

4. Now set before your eyes the contest engaged in by the martyrs. Here comes the opponent, he's forcing them to deny Christ. But let's bring him on still coaxing, not yet raging. He promises riches and honors. They are superfluities; people tempted by such gifts to deny Christ haven't yet entered the contest, haven't yet experienced the struggle, haven't yet challenged the oldest enemy of them all to a real battle. The faithful man, though, who was promised such things, despised them, and said, "Shall I, just for the sake of riches, deny Christ? I, for the sake of riches, deny riches? I, for the sake of gold, deny the treasure? I mean to say, he is the one *who became poor for our sakes, though he was rich, so that we might be enriched by his poverty* (2 Cor 8:9). I mean to say, he's the one about whom again the apostle says, *in whom are all the treasures of wisdom and knowledge hidden away* (Col 2:30). Your mind is on what you are promising, because you can't see what you're trying to deprive me of. I, by faith, see what you want to take away from me; you, with the eyes of flesh, see what you want to give me. The things that the eye of the heart gazes on are better than what the eye of flesh can see. *For the things that can be seen are temporary, while the things that cannot be seen are eternal* (2 Cor 4:18). So I despise your gifts," said the faithful soul, " because they're temporary, they're superfluous, they rot, they fly away, they're full of dangers, full of temptations. We none of us have them when we want, or lose them when we want."

The maker of promises has been disdained, another figure comes on the scene, that is the persecutor; disdained in his coaxing, he starts raging; disdained as a snake, he has turned into a lion. "You don't want," he says, "to receive more ample riches from me? If you don't deny Christ, I will take away what you have."

"It's still against my superfluities that you're raging. *Like a sharp razor, you have practiced deceit* (Ps 52:2). You shave off the hairs, you don't cut the skin; take all that away from me too. Or rather, since you saw what I used to give from it to the poor, how I used to take in strangers, how I used to do what Paul advised: *Command*, he said, *the rich of this world, command them not to think proudly of themselves, nor to place their hopes in the uncertainty of riches, but in the living God, who provides us abundantly with everything for our enjoyment. Let them do good, let them be rich in good works, let them give easily, let them share, let them store up for themselves a good fund for the future, so that they may lay hold of true life* (1 Tm 6:17-19). When you take all this away from me, I'm not going to perform these good works; shall I be any the less in God's eyes, because I wish to, and am not able to? Or am I so deaf to the voice of the angels, *Peace on earth to men of good will* (Lk 2:14)? So deprive me of my superfluities; *we brought nothing into this world, but neither can we take anything away. Having food and clothing, with that let us be content* (1 Tm 6:7-8)."

How they even despised the necessities of life

5. But the persecutor says, "I can deprive you of food, I can deprive you of clothing." They have come now to the struggle, the opponent has started raging more hotly; superfluities are over and done with, they've got down to the necessities.

Do not withdraw from me, since affliction is very close (Ps 22:11).

There is nothing so close to your soul as your own flesh. Hunger and thirst and heat, these you feel in your flesh. That's where I want to see you, good martyr, witness of God.

See me, he says, see me. *Who shall separate us from the charity of Christ?* What is it you're threatening to do?

I can deprive you of food, I can deprive you of clothing.

Shall affliction, or distress, or hunger, or nakedness? (Rom 8:35).

Let the threat now come from the other side: I can deprive you of your friend, I can kill your nearest and dearest, I will butcher your wife and children before your eyes.

You can kill, you can kill? Let them only not deny Christ, and you can't kill them. What's this? Because you don't terrify me about me, can you terrify me about mine? If they don't deny Christ, you can't kill mine; if they do, you're killing strangers.

Let the persecutor go one step further still, let him rage, and say, "If you don't care about your own people, I will remove you yourself from this light of day."

From this light; surely not from the eternal light? From which light will you remove me? The light I have in common even with you. It can't be of great importance, the light even you can see. I, for the sake of this light, will not deny the light; *that was the true light* (Jn 1:9). I know to whom I can say, *Since with you is the fountain of life, and in your light we shall see light* (Ps 36:9). Take my life, take away the light; I will still have life, still have the light. I will have life where I will not have to endure you as a killer; I will have the light which, I won't say you, but not even any night will be able to deprive me of.

The martyr wins. Or is there any greater contest, anything anywhere else, we ought to be the spectators of? No. He threatens death, he savages bodily well-being, he plows with hooks, tortures with racks, burns with flames, brings on wild animals. Here too he is conquered. Why is he conquered? Because *in all these things we are more than conquerors through him who loved us* (Rom 8:37).

Nothing and nobody more necessary to us than Christ

6. So, my brothers and sisters, let Christ never be denied for the sake of super-fluities, never be denied for the sake of necessities; nobody is more necessary, more closely related to us, than he is. I was talking about necessities, well-being and a friend. You sin for the sake of well-being, and you deny Christ; by loving your well-being you ensure you won't have well-being. You sin for the sake of your friend, and in order not to offend him, you deny Christ. Woe is me! Some-times he's denied with a blush.

There's no persecutor raging, no plunderer despoiling, no torturer working on you; simply in order not to displease your friend, you deny your Lord. I can see what your friend has deprived you of; show me what he'll give you. What will he give? The very friendship by which you sin, by which you are made into an enemy of God. This man wouldn't be a friend to you, if you were one to your-self; but since you are your own enemy, you think your enemy is a friend. What makes you your own enemy, though? The fact that you love iniquity; *But whoever loves iniquity hates his own soul* (Ps 11:5). But Christ is not being denied to please a perverse and godless friend; he's not being denied, but he's being viciously attacked by the godless friend, accused by the godless friend, and not being defended by the shamefaced believer; he's being abandoned, kept quiet about, not being proclaimed. The blasphemer's tongue is tearing him to shreds, and there's no tongue singing his praises.

How many evil deeds are committed as if for the sake of necessities, for food, for clothing, for health, for a friend; and all these things which are being desired are in fact being lost. But if you make light of these things in the present, God will give you them for eternity. Make light of health, you will have immortality; make light of death, you will have life; make light of honor, you will have a crown; make light of the friendship of man, you will have the friendship of God. But there, where you have God as your friend, you won't be without the friend-ship of a neighbor; there as your friends these martyrs will be with you, whose confessions and deeds were being read to us a short while ago.

The courage of these martyrs, men and women;
what we will lose if we deny Christ

7. We heard about men acting bravely, confessing manfully; we heard about women being true to Christ, not like women, but forgetful of their sex. In that place we shall enjoy their friendship without any lusts of the flesh, and there will only be Wisdom to be enjoyed with friends. See what we lose, if we love these things here, and deny Christ! We won't be terrified there of a neighbor dying; there will be no grief there, where there's eternal life, nor will this be necessary anymore: *Having food and clothing, with these let us be content* (1 Tm 6:8).

Immortality will be our clothes, charity will be the food there, so will eternal life. Nor shall we be doing the good works there which are concerned with these things; but if we don't do them here, we won't get to them there.

You won't be told, *Break your bread for the hungry* (Is 58:7), where there is no famine. You won't be told, "Show hospitality," where you don't find any stranger or traveler. You won't be told, "Deliver the oppressed," where there is no enemy. You won't be told, "Pacify the quarrelsome," where there is eternal peace. Notice, my brothers and sisters, how much we put up with here in seeking peace; there, where we cannot perish, we shall just possess it. Do you seek well-being? Make light of it, and you shall have it. You deny Christ, being afraid of spoiling your friendship with men; confess Christ, and you will enjoy the friendship of the city of the angels, the city of the patriarchs, the city of the prophets, the city of the apostles, the city of all the martyrs, the city of all the good faithful. Christ himself *established it for ever* (Ps 48:8).

Sermon 302

On the Birthday of Saint Lawrence

Augustine takes advantage of the feast of St. Lawrence, who was probably martyred in 258 during the persecution launched by the Emperor Valerian, to express confidence in the powerful intercession of such heroes and friends of Jesus: "Did anyone ever pray there, and not obtain the favor asked for?" Fischer, Kunzelmann, and van der Meer all date this sermon to about 400. Hill, however, raises considerable doubts about whether we are dealing with a single sermon. Sections 10 to 21, with the appendix of 22, definitively seem to be from another sermon, the beginning of which we have lost. It is about an unpopular government official (*miles*) who was brutally lynched. This reference is helpful in dating the second part of the sermon, but the first part could have been preached at any time. Since both parts of the present single work make reference to St. Lawrence, it is likely that both were preached on his feast day but in different years, Augustine observes that good and bad things happen to Christians and non-believers alike. Christians should follow the martyrs' example and exercise more care in attaining eternal life than simply prolonging earthly life. Bishops have the burden of using their authority to appeal to government officials on behalf of the people even though at times they are scarcely admitted into the presence of such officials. The Church should continue to offer sanctuary to the good and bad alike.

Why God sometimes grants temporal benefits through the prayers of the martyrs

1. Today is the feast of the blessed martyr Lawrence. Readings suitable to this holy solemnity were heard. We have heard them and sung them, and followed the reading of the gospel with the greatest attention. So let us follow in the footsteps of the martyrs by imitating them, or else we will be celebrating their festivities to no purpose. Is there anyone who doesn't know about the powerful merits of this particular martyr? Did anybody ever pray there, and not obtain the favor asked for? To how many of the weaker brethren have his merits granted even the temporal benefits which he himself scorned! They were conceded, you see, not so that those who prayed for them might remain in their weakness, but so that by being granted inferior benefits, their love might be stimulated to seek the better ones.

A father, after all, often concedes trivial playthings to his small children, which they cry loudly about if they don't get them. A kindly and fatherly indulgence shares things, allows things, which he wouldn't like his children to remain attached to as they grow bigger, as they grow up. So he gives nuts to little boys for whom he is keeping an inheritance. Fatherly loving-kindness gives in to children at play and enjoying themselves with toys, in order not to demand too much from that tender age. This is to coax and wheedle and fondle, not to train and build up character. What the martyrs built up, what they were able to grasp, what with their great hearts they did grasp, what they shed their blood for, you heard in the gospel: *Your reward is great in heaven* (Mt 5:12).

Let us love eternal life in the same way as temporal life
is cherished by its lovers

2. However, my dearest friends, since there are two lives, one before death, the other after death, both sorts have had and have their lovers. What this short life is like, well is there any need to describe it? We all experience how distressing, how full of complaints it is; beset by trials and temptations, full of fears, feverish with all kinds of greed, subject to accidents; grieving when things go badly, smugly self-satisfied when they go well; cock-a-hoop over profits, in agony over losses. And even when cock-a-hoop over profits, it's in dread of losing what it has gained; the man dreading being investigated on their account, who before he had anything was never subjected to investigation. True unhappiness, false happiness. The person at the bottom of the heap longs to climb to the top, the person at the top dreads sliding down to the bottom. The have-nots envy the haves; the haves despise the have-nots. And who can find the words to unfold how extensively and conspicuously ugly this life is?

And yet this ugliness has its lovers; and how we long to find just a very, very few who love eternal life, which they cannot reach the end of, in the same way as lovers like that cherish this life, which we not only soon get to the end of, but which if it is at all protracted, we are terrified every day may come to an end any minute.

What can I do? What action am I to take? What am I to say? What sharp, well-aimed threats, what burning exhortations can I apply to hard and sluggish hearts, frozen in the ice of earthly numbness and dullness, to make them at last shake off the lethargy of the world, and catch fire at the prospect of eternity? What, I repeat, am I to do? What am I to say?

Well, there is something to hand, and it has just occurred to me that the affairs of every day have some advice for me, and suggest to me what I should say. From love of this temporal life advance, if you can manage it, to loving the eternal life which the martyrs loved, while they thought nothing of these temporal things. I beg, I beseech, I implore not only you, but together with you also myself and us clergy: let us cherish eternal life. I don't want us to love it more, though it is much more; let us just cherish it in the same way as temporal life is cherished by its lovers, not as temporal life was cherished by the martyrs. They, you see, cherished it either not at all or very little, and they found it easy to put eternal life before it. So I didn't have the martyrs in mind, when I said, "Let us cherish eternal life as temporal life is cherished"; I meant, as temporal life is cherished by its lovers, so let us cherish eternal life, love of which is what Christians profess.

It was not for the sake of this temporal life that we became Christians

3. That, after all, is why we became Christians; it wasn't for the sake of this temporal life. How many Christians, I mean to say, are snatched away before they have grown up, while sacrilegious people continue in this life until decrepit old age! But again, among them too there are many who die before they're grown up. Christians have many losses, the ungodly many gains; and again, the ungodly have many losses, Christians many gains. And the ungodly are frequently honored, while Christians are tossed aside; and again, Christians are frequently honored, while the ungodly are tossed aside. Since, then, these good and bad things are common to both sorts, can it be, brothers and sisters, that when we became Christians, we gave our name to Christ and submitted our foreheads to such a tremendous sign, simply in order to avoid these evils and obtain these good things?

You're a Christian, you carry on your forehead the cross of Christ. The mark stamped on you teaches you what you should profess. When he was hanging on the cross — the cross you carry on your forehead; don't delight in the sign of the wood, but in the sign of the one hanging on it — so when he was hanging on the cross, he was looking round at the people raving against him, putting up with their insults, praying for his enemies. Even while he was being killed, the doctor was curing the sick with his blood. He said, you see, *Father, forgive them, because they do not know what they are doing* (Lk 23:34). Nor were these words futile or without effect. And of those people, thousands later on believed in the one they had slain, so that they learned how to suffer for him who had suffered both for them and at their hands.

So here, brothers and sisters, is to be understood from this sign, from this stamp which Christians receive even when they become catechumens, here is to be understood why we are Christians; that it is not for the sake of temporal and passing things, whether good or bad; but for the sake of avoiding bad things that will not pass, and of acquiring good things that will have no limit and no end.

The things people do out of love for temporal life

4. However, as I had started to say, brothers and sisters, what I was reminding you of and proposing to you, please, please let us pay attention to the way this temporal life is cherished by its lovers. How filled with dread of dying people are, though bound to die anyway! You can see people tremble, take to their heels, look for hiding places, snatch at last-ditch defenses, beg, prostrate themselves; if it were possible, give whatever they have to be granted their lives, to live one day more, to extend just a little longer a life that is always uncertain.

So many things people do; who ever does anything like that for the sake of eternal life? Let me address the lover of this present life. What are you doing, why are you in such a hurry, why so full of dread, why taking to your heels, why looking for a hiding place?

In order to stay alive, he says.

Really to stay alive? To stay alive in such a way as to be alive always?

No.

Then you aren't going to all this trouble to destroy death, but only to delay it. If you go to such lengths just to die a little later, why not do something in order never to die at all?

You are prepared to be reduced to beggary in order to live a little longer, but not to give away your superfluities in order to reign for ever with Christ

5. How many people we find who will say, "Let the treasury take all my property, just so I may die a little later"! How rarely we find anybody who will say, "Let Christ take all my property, so that I may never die"! And yet, O lover of this temporal life, if the treasury takes it, it strips you of it in this world; if Christ takes it, he keeps it for you in heaven. For the sake of this life people want to have something to live on, and for the sake of this life they are ready to give up what they live on. What you are saving up in order to live on, you give away in order to live, only to collapse, maybe, from hunger. And yet you say, "Let them take it, what do I care? I'm prepared to beg." You give up what you live on, you're ready to beg in order to live. You're ready, after giving up even your necessities, to beg in this world; and you're not ready, after handing out your superfluities, to reign with Christ?

Please, I implore you, weigh them up carefully. If there are any just scales to be found in the drawers of your heart, bring them out, and place these two things on them, and balance them against each other: begging in this world, and reigning with Christ. There's simply nothing to balance; this thing, in comparison with that, has no weight at all. Even if I said reigning in this world, and reigning with Christ, there would be nothing to balance. I'm sorry I said weigh them up; there is absolutely nothing to weigh up. *What does it profit a man, if he gains the whole world, but suffers the loss of his own soul?* (Mk 8:36). Now it's the one who hasn't suffered the loss of his own soul that reigns with Christ. Who, though, can reign in this world securely? Suppose he does reign securely; does he reign eternally?

The folly of loving this life

6. Turn your attention to what I was proposing, the kind of lovers this present life has, this temporal life, short life, ugly life, what sort of lovers it has. Often enough for the sake of this life a man is reduced to rags, to being a beggar. You ask him why. He answers like this: "To keep alive." What have you fallen in love with, and what are you in love with? Where has it got you? What are you going to say, bad lover, wrong-headed lover? What are you going to say to this sweetheart of yours? Say it, talk to her, coax and court her, if you can. What are you going to say?

It is to these rags that your beauty has brought me.

She shouts at you, "I'm ugly, and you're in love with me?" She shouts, "I'm hard as nails, and you embrace me?" She shouts, "I'm flighty, and you strain yourself to follow me?" Here's how your sweetheart answers you: "I won't stay with you; even if I'm with you for a while, I won't remain with you. I have been able to reduce you to rags, I haven't been able to make you happy."

Eternal life is God himself; this life a mist that vanishes

7. So since we are Christians, let us implore the Lord our God to help us against the blandishments of this wrongly loved life, and let us love the beauty of that life, which *eye has not seen, nor has ear heard, nor has it come up into the heart of man.* This, you see, is the life *which God has prepared for those who love him* (1 Cor 2:9); and God himself is this very life. You cried out, you all sighed and groaned. Let us love this life with all our might. May God grant that we love it. Let us pour out our tears to him, not only to gain, but also to cherish this life.

How am I going to advise you, what am I going to demonstrate to you? Do I have to read books to you, to show you how uncertain this life is, how fleeting, how practically non-existent, how true it is, where it is written, *For what is your life? A mist appearing for a little while, and thereafter it will be dispersed* (Jas 4:14)? He was alive yesterday, he isn't today; he was to be seen a little while ago, now there isn't anyone there to see. A person is brought out to the grave; the mourners return home sad, they soon forget. People say, "Really, man is nothing at all," and a man says this himself, and a man doesn't correct himself, so that man may be, not nothing, but something.

So the martyrs were lovers of that other life, and the martyrs are the possessors of that other life. They have what they loved; they will have it more richly in the resurrection of the dead. So this is the road they paved for us with their terrible sufferings.

Saint Lawrence said of the poor,
"These are the treasures of the Church"

8. Saint Lawrence was an archdeacon. The treasures of the Church were demanded of him by the persecutor, as the tradition states. Which is why he suffered such dreadful torments, it is quite horrifying to hear about them. Placed on a gridiron, he was scorched all over his body, tortured with the most excruciating pain by fire. Yet he overcame all these bodily afflictions with the sturdy strength of his charity, helped by the one who had made him like that. *For we are his workmanship, created in Christ Jesus in good works, which God has prepared for us to walk in* (Eph 2:10).

Now this is what he did, to stoke up the fires of the persecutor's rage, not because he wanted him to be angry, but out of a desire to commend his own faith to posterity, and to show how he was dying without a care in the world: "Let some carts come with me," he said, "in which I can bring along the Church's treasures." Carts were sent, he loaded them with the poor, and ordered them to go back, saying, "These are the treasures of the Church." And it's true, brothers and sisters; the needs of the needy are the great wealth and treasure of Christians, if we really understand where we should be saving what we possess. The needy are there in front of us; if we deposit our savings with them, we won't lose them. We aren't afraid of anybody making off with them; the one who gave them to us, you see, is keeping them safe; nor could we find a better guardian, nor a more trustworthy maker and keeper of promises.

Let us always be on our toes to imitate the martyrs

9. So as we reflect on all this, let us be on our toes to imitate the martyrs, if we want the feast days we celebrate to be of any use to us. I have always admonished you about this, brothers and sisters, I have never stopped doing so, never kept quiet about it. Eternal life is to be cherished, this present life to be made light of. We must live good lives, must hope for the true good. People who are bad must change their ways; when they've changed, they must be instructed; when they've been instructed, they should persevere. *The one who perseveres to the end,* you see, *that is the one who will be saved* (Mt 24:13).

It is not lawful to rage against bad people

10. But many bad people say many bad things. And what would you have, yourself? Good things from bad people? Don't look for grapes on thorn bushes; you've been forbidden to do so; *it is from the abundance of the heart that the mouth speaks* (Lk 6:44-45). If you can manage anything, if you are no longer bad yourself, make an option for the bad person to become good. Why vent your rage on the bad?

"Because they're bad," you say.

By venting your rage on them, you are adding yourself to their number. I'll give you some advice; does the bad person displease you? Don't let there be two of them. You're objecting to him, and you're adding yourself on to him; you're increasing the number of the one you're condemning. Do you want to overcome the bad with the bad? To overcome evil with evil? There will be two evils, both needing to be overcome.

Can't you hear the advice of your Lord through the apostle: *Do not be overcome by evil, but overcome evil with good* (Rom 12:21)? Perhaps he's worse, though you too are bad; still, that makes two bad ones. I would like at least one of them to be good. Finally you vent your rage on him to the point of death. And what about after death, where none of your punishment now reaches that bad man, and only the malice of another bad man is finding expression? That's mindless madness, not avenging justice.

It's not enough not to have taken part in mob violence; there is
also the duty of forbidding subordinates to take part in it

11. What am I to say to you, my brothers and sisters, what am I to say to you? Don't give such people your approval. But am I really to think this of you, that you do approve of such people? Far be it from me to think that of you. But it isn't enough for you to disapprove of such people, not nearly enough; there is something more required of you. None of you should say, "God knows I didn't do it, God knows I didn't do it, and God also knows I didn't want it to happen." There you have two things you said: both "I didn't do it," and "I didn't want it to happen." It's still not enough.

No, it's certainly not enough, if you didn't want it to happen, if you didn't also forbid it. Bad men have judges to deal with them, they have the authorities to deal with them, about whom the apostle says, *For he does not carry the sword without reason. For he is the avenger in wrath, but against the one who does evil.* The avenger in wrath against the one who does evil. *But if you do evil,* he says, *be afraid. For he does not carry the sword without reason. But do you wish not to be afraid of the authorities? Do good, and you will have praise from them* (Rom 13:4.3).

How Saint Lawrence and other martyrs "have praise from the authorities"

12. "So what evil," someone says, "had Saint Lawrence done, that he should be put to death by the authorities? How was this fulfilled in his case, *Do good, and you will have praise from them* (Rom 13:3), seeing that precisely by doing good, he earned such terrible torments from them?"

If the holy martyr Lawrence didn't have praise from them, he wouldn't be honored today, he wouldn't be acclaimed by us, he wouldn't have his praises sung far and wide. So he does have praise from them, even though they don't want him to.

364 Saint Augustine — Essential Sermons

The apostle, after all, didn't say, "Do good, and the very authorities will praise you." I mean, all the apostles and martyrs did good, and the authorities didn't praise them, but in fact put them to death. So if he had said, "Do good, and they will praise you," he would have been deceiving you. But as it is, he tempered his words, he took a look round, he weighed them, measured them, circumcised them. Analyze what you heard: *Do good, and you will have praise from them.* You see, if the authorities are just, you will have praise from them, with them in fact praising you themselves. If, though, they are iniquitous, when you have died for the faith, for justice, for the truth, you will have praise from them, even while they are raging against you. It's from them, you see, you will have it, not because they are praising you, but because they are providing you with the occasion to be praised. So then, do good, and you will have it, and you will be sure of it.

Coming back to the case of the man who was lynched;
not everybody has the right to put evildoers to death

13. "But that bad man did so many things, oppressed so many people, reduced so many to beggary and penury."

There are judges to deal with him, there are the authorities to deal with him. The state is well ordered; *for the authorities that exist have been ordained by God* (Rom 13:1). What business is it of yours to vent your rage like that? What authority have you received — except that this isn't a case of public punishment, but of open brigandage? I mean, what's the position? Consider a man destined for the scaffold, and condemned, the sword already hanging over him; it is not permissible for him to be struck down by anyone among the various ranks of the authorities, but only by the one who is employed for this; the executioner is employed for this; it's by him that the condemned man is to be struck down. If the shorthand writer strikes the condemned man, already destined for the scaffold, isn't he both killing a condemned man, and also condemning himself as a murderer? Certainly the one he kills had already been condemned, already destined for the scaffold; but to strike him down in an unauthorized manner is murder.

So if it's murder to strike a condemned man in an unauthorized manner, what is it, I ask you, to wish to strike one who hasn't been tried, to wish to strike one who hasn't been judged, to want to strike a bad man without receiving any authority to do so? You see, I'm not defending bad men, or saying bad men aren't bad. Those who pass judgment on them will have to account for that. Why do you want to render a very difficult account for someone else's death, when you don't bear the burden of authority? God has saved you from being a judge; why grab someone else's responsibility? Give an account just of yourself.

The lesson driven home by the case of those
who brought the woman taken in adultery to Jesus

14. O Lord, how truly you pricked the consciences of men venting their rage, when you said, *Let the one who is without sin be the first to throw a stone at her* (Jn 8:7)! Cut to the quick by a sharp and weighty word, they examined their consciences, and blushed at the presence of justice in person; and departing one by one, they left the unhappy woman there alone. But the guilty woman wasn't alone, because the judge was with her, not yet passing judgment, but extending mercy. When those who were thirsting for blood withdrew, they left behind them a miserable woman and mercy. And the Lord said to her, *Has nobody condemned you? She answered, Nobody, Lord. Neither will I condemn you, he said. Go, from now on sin no more* (Jn 8:10-11).

Thoughts about the man who was lynched being a soldier

15. "But that soldier did such dreadful things to me." I would like to know, if you were a soldier, whether you wouldn't be doing the same sort of things yourself. Neither do I want such things to be done by soldiers that the poor are afflicted, I don't want it; I want them also to listen to the gospel. I mean it isn't being a soldier that prevents you doing good, but being evil-minded. After all, when soldiers came to be baptized by John, they said, *And what shall we do? John said to them, Do not ever rough anyone up, or bring false charges against anyone; let your pay be enough for you* (Lk 3:14).

And really, brothers and sisters, if soldiers and policemen really were like that, how fortunate a society we would have; but if it wasn't only the soldiers who were like that, but also if the customs men were like what is described there. Because the publicans too, that is the customs men, said, *And we, what shall we do? The reply was, Exact nothing more than what is laid down for you* (Lk 3:13). The soldier was put on the right lines, the customs man was put on the right lines; let the private citizen too be put on the right lines. You have some straightforward guidance for all kinds. *What shall we all do? Let the one who has two shirts share with the one who has none; and the one who has food, let him do likewise* (Lk 3:10-11). We want the soldiers to listen to what Christ commanded; let us also listen ourselves. I mean, he isn't Christ for them and not for us; or their God and not ours. Let us all listen, and live harmoniously in peace.

It's only bad people who vent their rage on bad people

16. "He oppressed me, when I was engaged in business."
What about you? Did you conduct your business honestly? Did you never cheat anyone in that business of yours, never swear a false oath in the course of that business? Did you never say, "By the one who carried me safely across the sea, I bought for so much" something you didn't buy for so much?

Brothers and sisters, I'll say it to you more bluntly, and as far as the Lord grants me, freely: It's only bad people who vent their rage on bad people. The obligations of authority are another matter. Because the judge is frequently compelled to unsheathe the sword, and he would prefer not to strike. As far as he is concerned, you see, he was willing to pass a sentence short of bloodshed; but perhaps he didn't want law and order to be undermined. It was the concern of his profession, of his authority, of his duty. What is your concern, but to beg God, *Deliver us from evil* (Mt 6:13)? O you who have said, *Deliver us from evil,* may God deliver you from yourself!

The duty of the bishop to intervene with the authorities

17. In a word, brothers and sisters, why are we carrying on so long? We are all Christians; I up here also bear the burden of a greater danger. It's often said about me, "Why does he go to that authority?" and "What's the bishop looking for with that authority?" And yet you all know that it's your needs which compel me to go where I would much rather not; to dance attendance, to stand outside the door, to wait while the worthy and the unworthy go in, to be announced, to be scarcely admitted sometimes, to put up with little humiliations, to beg, sometimes to obtain a favor, sometimes to depart in sadness. Who would want to endure such things, unless I was forced to? Let me be, let me not have to endure all that, don't let anybody force me to. Look, as a little concession to me, give me a holiday from this business. I beg you, I beseech you, don't let anybody force me to it; I don't want to have to deal with the authorities. He knows, I'm forced to do so.

And I behave with the authorities as I ought to behave with Christians, if I find Christians in that authority; and with pagans as I ought to behave with pagans; wishing them all well.

"But he should admonish the authorities," he says "to do good."

Am I to admonish them in your presence? Do you know if I've admonished them? You don't know whether I've done it, or whether I haven't. What I know is that you don't know, and that you are judging rashly.

All the same, my brothers and sisters, excuse me, but you can say to me about the authorities, "He could admonish him, and he would do good."

And I will answer, "I did admonish him, but he didn't listen to me." And I admonished him where you weren't there to hear. Who could ever take the people aside to admonish them? At least we have been able to admonish one man on the side, and say, "Act like this, or act like that," where no one else was present. Who could ever take the people aside, and admonish the people with nobody else knowing?

A bad man dead has to be mourned twice over

18. It is this emergency that compels me to speak to you like this, or I will have a bad account to render for you to God; or else he will say to me, "You should warn, you should hand out, I would exact repayment." So then distance yourselves, so

distance yourselves totally from these bloody deeds. Your only concern, when you see or hear about such things, should be to feel pity.

"But it was a bad man that died!"

He's to be mourned twice over, because he died twice over; both in time, and for eternity. I mean, if a good man had died, we would grieve out of human feelings, because he had left us, because we wanted him to go on living with us. Bad people are to be mourned much more, because after this life they are caught in the clutches of eternal pains. So let it be your business, my brothers and sisters, to grieve, let it be your concern to grieve, not to vent your rage.

It is up to householders and heads of families to forbid their dependents to take part in riotous behavior

19. But it's not enough, as I have already said, it's not enough for you not to do these things, for you to lament them, unless you do all in your power to prevent actions that do not fall within the rights and authority of the people. I am not saying, brothers and sisters, that any of you can go out and just tell the populace to stop; that's something not even I can do. But each one of you in his own house can prevent his son, his slave, his friend, his neighbor, his apprentice, his ward from taking part. Work on them so that they don't do these things. Persuade those you can; and be firm and severe with others, over whom you have authority.

One thing I do know, and everyone else knows it together with me, that you will find many households in this city in which there is not a single pagan; while there is no household to be found in which there are no Christians. And if you were to examine the matter carefully, there is no household to be found in which there aren't more Christians than pagans. It's true, you all agree. So you can see that these bad events wouldn't have occurred, if Christians hadn't wanted them to. You haven't got an answer to that. Bad things can be done secretly, but they cannot be done publicly if Christians forbid them and refuse to take part; because each one of you would restrain his slave, each one restrain his son; youth would be cowed by the severity of a father, the severity of an uncle, the severity of a teacher, the severity of a good neighbor, the severity of greater corporal punishment. If this sort of thing had been done, we wouldn't have been so saddened by these evil occurrences.

The wrath of God to be feared; the example of Sodom and Gomorrah

20. My dear brothers and sisters, I'm afraid of the wrath of God; God isn't afraid of mobs. How readily it's said, "What the people has done, it has done; who is there who can punish the people?" Really so, who is there? Not even God? Was God afraid of the whole world, when he brought about the flood? Was he afraid of those cities of Sodom and Gomorrah, when he destroyed them with fire from heaven? I don't wish now to speak of contemporary disasters, how many there have been, and where they have occurred, and I don't want to remind you of their

consequences, in case I should appear to be gloating. Did God in his wrath distinguish between those who did the bad deeds, and those who didn't? What he did, in fact, was to lump together those who did them and those who didn't prevent them.

Have nothing to do with those who take the law into their own hands

21. So let us at last wind up this sermon. My brothers and sisters, I urge you, I beseech you by the Lord and his gentleness, be gentle in your lives, be peaceful in your lives. Peacefully permit the authorities to do what pertains to them, of which they will have to render an account to God and to their superiors. As often as you have to petition them, make your petitions in an honorable and quiet manner. Don't mix with those who do evil and rampage in a rough and disorderly manner; don't desire to be present at such goings on even as spectators. But as far as you can, let each of you in his own house and his own neighborhood deal with the one with whom you have ties of kinship and charity, by warning, persuading, teaching, correcting; also by restraining him from such seriously evil activities by any kind of threats, so that God may eventually have mercy, and put an end to human evils, and *may not deal with us according to our sins, nor requite us according to our iniquities, but as far as the east is from the west may cast our sins far away from us* (Ps 103:10.12); and that he *may be gracious to our sins, lest the nations perchance should say, Where is their God?* (Ps 79:9-10).

After the sermon:

On the right of sanctuary

22. My brothers and sisters, on account of those who take refuge under the protection of mother Church, on account of its being the common refuge of all sorts, don't be careless and negligent about frequenting your mother, and not departing from the Church; she is anxious, you see, in case the undisciplined crowd should attempt something. For the rest, as far as those authorities are concerned, there are also laws enacted in the name of God by Christian emperors, which sufficiently and abundantly protect the Church; and the authorities seem to be the sort of men who wouldn't dream of acting against their mother, for which they would both be blamed by men and be liable to God's judgment. Far be it from them to do such a thing; we neither believe it of them, nor see any evidence of it.

But to ensure that the undisciplined crowd does not attempt anything, you should frequent your mother in considerable numbers, because, as I said, this is the refuge not merely of one or two people, but a general one. Even a person who has no cause to take refuge here, may be afraid he does have. I'm telling your graces:

Even the crooks take refuge in the Church from those who live upright lives, and those who live upright lives take refuge from the crooks; and sometimes the very crooks take refuge from crooks. There are three sorts of people who take refuge here. The good don't take refuge from the good, only the just don't flee from the just. But either the unjust flee from the just, or the just flee from the unjust, or the unjust from the unjust.

But if we wanted to sort them out, so that evildoers could be removed from the Church, there would be nowhere for those who do good to hide themselves; if we wished to allow noxious criminals to be removed from here, there would be nowhere for the innocent to flee to. So it's better that noxious criminals too should be protected by the Church, than that the innocent should be snatched from the Church. Bear these things in mind, so that, as I said, it is your presence in strength, not your savagery, that may inspire fear.

Sermon 311

On the Birthday of the Martyr Cyprian

Fischer, Kunzelmann, and Perler date this sermon to September 14, 405, the feast day of St. Cyprian. Section 5 indicates the sermon was preached in Carthage. Hill notes that Augustine was preaching not at "the Table of Cyprian," where the saint had been martyred, but in the Mappalia basilica, where he was buried. Martyrs are to be imitated because of their willingness to fight for the truth. Contemporary ears will find Augustine's admonition to despise the world troublesome. He praises the current bishop of Carthage, Aurelius, for successfully putting an end to the excessive drinking and partying that took place regularly at the martyr's tomb. Material things are not to be rejected outright as bad. Some good things (piety, faith, justice) are common to only good people; others (money, honor, power, office, health) are common to good and bad alike. God gives good things to bad people in order to teach us to desire better things.

The right way to celebrate the feasts of the martyrs
is by imitating their virtues

1. It is the passion of the most blessed martyr Cyprian that has made this day into a feast for us, and the celebration of his triumph that has brought us together in this place in such a spirit of devotion. But the right way to celebrate the festivals of the martyrs should be by imitating their virtues. It's easy enough to celebrate in honor of a martyr; the great thing is to imitate the martyr's faith and patience. Let us do the first thing in such a way that we commit ourselves to the second. Let us so celebrate the feast, that we prefer rather to imitate the virtues.

In this age there is an abundance of both errors and terrors; this most blessed martyr overcame the errors with his wisdom, the terrors with his patient endurance. It's a great thing that he did; by following the Lamb, he defeated the lion. When the persecutor was raging, the lion was roaring; but the lion was being trampled on here below, because the martyr's attention was fixed on the Lamb there above; the Lamb who destroyed death by his death, who hung on the cross, shed his blood, redeemed the world.

Would the apostles have been prepared to suffer what they did,
except out of a conviction of the truth and a love of Christ, the truth?

2. The first rams of the flock, the blessed apostles, saw the Lord Jesus himself hanging on the cross; they grieved at his death, were astounded at his resurrection, loved him in his power, and shed their own blood for what they had seen. Just think, brothers and sisters, what it meant for men to be sent throughout the wide world, to preach that a dead man had risen again and ascended into heaven; and for preaching this to suffer everything a raving, raging world could inflict: loss of goods, exile, chains, tortures, flames, wild beasts, crosses, painful deaths. All this for heaven knows what? I mean really, my brothers and sisters, was Peter dying for his own glory, or proclaiming himself? One man was dying that another might be honored, one being slain that another might be worshiped. Would he have done this, if he hadn't been on fire with love, and utterly convinced of the truth?

They had seen what they were proclaiming; I mean, when would they have been willing to die for something they had not seen? Should they have denied what they had seen? They did not deny it; they preached a dead man, whom they knew to be alive. They were well aware for what life they should be ready to scorn life, well aware for what fortune they should be ready to endure a transitory misfortune, for what rewards they should scorn these losses. Their faith would not be outweighed by the whole world. They had heard the words, *What does it profit a man if he gains the whole world, but suffers the loss of his own soul?* (Mk 8:36). The attractions of the world did not reduce their haste to be quit of things that pass away, nor did the prospect of any fortune, however brilliant and glorious, that had to be left behind here, and could not be transferred to another life, and sometimes had even here to be relinquished by the living.

So despise the world, Christians

3. So despise the world, Christians; despise the world, despise it. The martyrs despised it, the apostles despised it, the blessed Cyprian despised it, whose memory we are celebrating today. You all want to be rich, want to be held in honor, want to enjoy good health; the man in whose memory you have come together despised the lot. Why, I want to know, do you have so much love for what the man you honor like this had such contempt — the man whom you wouldn't be honoring like this if he hadn't held it all in contempt? Why do I find you to be a

lover of these very things whose scorner you venerate? Certainly, if he had loved these things, you wouldn't be venerating him.

So don't you love them either; after all, he didn't go in, and then shut the door in your face. See you despise them too, and go in after him. The way in lies open; Christ is the door. For you too the door was opened, when his side was pierced by the lance. Call to mind what flowed out from there, and choose the way you may enter. From the side of the Lord hanging and dying on the cross, after it had been pierced by the lance, water and blood flowed out. In one is to be found your purification, in the other your redemption.

Love of earthly things is the birdlime of the soul

4. Love, and don't love; in one connection love, and in another don't love. You see, there is something by your loving which you make progress, and something by your loving by which your way forward is blocked. Don't love the road block, if you don't want to find the execution block. What you love on earth is a blockage, a hindrance; it's the birdlime for spiritual wings, that is for the virtues on which one flies up to God. You don't want to be caught, and you love the birdlime? Just because you're caught nicely, does it mean you're not caught? I say this, and you applaud, and loudly approve, and love it. You get your answer, not from me but from Wisdom: "I want good deeds, not polite voices." Praise wisdom by the way you live; by producing, not just a noise, but a harmony.

We have sung for you, and you have not danced

5. The Lord says in the gospel, *We have sung for you, and you have not danced* (Mt 11:17). When would I, here, ever say such a thing, unless I read it there? Empty-headedness mocks me, but authority supports me. If I hadn't first stated who said this, could any of you have tolerated my saying, *We have sung to you, and you have not danced*? In this of all places, while psalms are to be sung, is anyone to be permitted to dance? Once, not so many years ago, even this place was invaded by the aggressive rowdiness of dancers. Such a holy place as this, where the body lies of such a holy martyr, even this holy place, I repeat, as many of you who are old enough will remember, had been invaded by the pestilential rowdiness of dancers. Throughout the night impious songs were sung, and people danced to the singing. When the Lord so willed, from the moment holy vigils began to be celebrated here on the initiative of our holy brother, your bishop, that abuse, after some resistance, later yielded to his diligence, and blushed for shame in the presence of his wisdom.

The song to which we should harmonize our lives and our habits

6. So such things, by God's favor, don't go on here now, because we are not celebrating games for demons, where things like this are habitually done to delight those being worshiped, and with their filth regularly deprave their worshipers; but what we celebrate here is the holy festival of martyrs. So there's no dancing here,

and yet, where there's no dancing, we hear it read out from the gospel, *We have sung for you, and you have not danced.* Those who didn't dance are being rebuked, reproved, accused. Heaven preserve us from the return, once more, of that abuse; listen rather to what was really intended by Wisdom.

The one who sings is giving a command; the one who dances is carrying it out. What is dancing, but moving the body to the rhythm of the song? What is our song? Don't let *me* play it, don't let it be mine. It's just as well that I am only the instrument, not the composer. I will recite our song for you: *Do not love the world, nor the things that are in the world. Whoever loves the world, the love of the Father is not in him; because all that is in the world is the lust of the flesh, and the lust of the eyes, and worldly ambition, which comes not from the Father, but from the world. And the world passes away, and the lust for it; but the one who does the will of God abides forever, just as God too abides forever* (1 Jn 2:15-17).

One dances in time to this song by charity, not by cupidity

7. What a song that is, my brothers and sisters! You've heard me singing it, let me hear you dancing to it; see that you all do, by keeping time with your morals, what dancers do by keeping time with their bodies and their feet. Do this inwardly; let your moral attitudes match that song. Let cupidity, greed, be uprooted, charity, love, planted. Anything that comes from this tree is good. Cupidity is unable to produce anything good, charity anything bad.

The thing is said, it's applauded — and there's no change in anybody. Surely not! It's not true, what I've just said. Some fishermen underwent a change, afterward even a great many senators were changed; Cyprian underwent a change, whose memory we are celebrating today. He writes himself, testifies himself to the sort of life he led once, how profane, how godless, how reprehensible and how detestable. He heard someone singing; he presented himself to dance, not with the body but the mind. He adapted himself to a good song, adapted himself to the *new song* (Ps 96:1); he adapted, he loved, he persevered, he fought, he won.

Bad times are only made by bad men

8. And you all say, "The times are troubled, the times are hard, the times are wretched." Live good lives, and you will change the times by living good lives; you will change the times, and then you'll have nothing to grumble about. What, after all, are times, my dear brothers and sisters? The spacing and unrolling of the ages. The sun has risen; having done its twelve hour stint, it sets on the other side of the world; next day it rises in the morning and again sets. Count how often; there you have the times. Who was ever harmed by the rising of the sun, who was ever harmed by its setting? So time, then, has never harmed anybody. It's people who are harmed, and it's people they are harmed by. What a painful thought! People are harmed, people are stripped of their possessions, people are oppressed. By whom? Not by lions, not by serpents, not by scorpions; but by human beings. Those who

are hurt make a fuss; if they had the chance, wouldn't they do themselves what they object to? Then, perhaps, we find a person who was complaining, when he could himself be doing what he was complaining about. I applaud him, yes, I applaud him, if he didn't do what he was accusing others of.

Like time, gold is good in itself; it's put to good use by good people, to bad use by the bad

9. Those people, though, beloved, who seem to have power and influence in the world, how they are praised when they do less than they are able to! The one scripture praised is the one *who was able to transgress and did not transgress; who did not go after gold* (Sir 31:10.8). Gold ought to go after you, not you after gold. Because gold is good; I mean, God did not create anything bad. Don't you be bad, and gold is good. Look here, I'm placing some gold between a good person and a bad one. Let the bad person take it; the needy are oppressed, judges bribed, the laws twisted, human affairs turned upside down. Why is this? Because a bad person has taken the gold. Let the good person take it; the poor are fed, the naked clothed, the oppressed delivered, captives redeemed. How much good effected by gold in the hands of a good man! How much evil effected by gold in the hands of a bad person!

So why say, when you're feeling disillusioned sometimes, "Oh, if only there were no such thing as gold!" You just see to it that you don't love gold. If you are bad, you go after gold; if you're good, it goes after you. What does that mean, it goes after you? You lead, you aren't led; because you possess it, you are not possessed by it.

There is really quite a large number of good people
among the Church's members, if you care to look for them

10. So let's get back to the words of sacred scripture, *Who did not go after gold. Who was able to transgress, and did not transgress. Who is this, and we shall praise him?* (Sir 31:8.10.9). Who is this, or who is there here? How many people are hearing, "And who is there here"! And yet God forbid I should despair of there being a single one here, or rather not a single one, but several. God forbid that I should despair of the threshing floor of such a great landowner. If you see the threshing floor from a distance, you think there is nothing there but chaff; you find the grain if you know how to look closely. The place where the chaff offends your eyes is where the heap of grain is lying hidden. The place where your eyes are offended by what is beaten in the threshing is where what is purged by the threshing is to be found. It's there, you can be sure, it's there. In any event, the one who sowed, who reaped, who brought it in to the threshing floor, is sure about it; he knows there's enough there to fill the granary, when it has been winnowed.

There was a kind of minor winnowing at the time of persecution; what grains emerged from that! From that came the flourishing White Mass of Utica; from that emerged such a great and choice grain as this most blessed Cyprian. How many rich people then scorned what they possessed! How many poor people then fell away when the test came! There you are; in that time of testing, as at a kind of winnowing, gold was no disadvantage to the rich, while it was no advantage to the poor, was it, not to possess any gold? The former overcame, while the latter fell away.

There is nothing wrong with things; it's the way they are used that is good or bad

11. It's only good loving that makes good living. Put gold aside when considering human dealings; or rather, let gold be present, to test the quality of human dealings. Cut out the human tongue because of the blasphemies uttered against God, and where will God's praises be found? What has the tongue done for you? Only let there be someone who sings well, and it is a good organ. Bring a good mind to the tongue; good things are said, disputes are amicably settled, mourners are consoled, the self-indulgent corrected, the irascible restrained; God is praised, Christ is proclaimed, the mind is kindled to love; but to a divine, not a human, a spiritual, not a carnal, love. These are the good things done by the tongue. Why? Because there's a good mind using the tongue. Bring a bad person to the tongue; you will get people blaspheming, going to law, telling tales, delating, and informing. All bad things from the tongue, because there's a bad person using the tongue.

Material things mustn't be eliminated from human dealings. Let them be there, and let there be a proper use of good things. There are some good things, you see, which are only to be found in good people, and there are other good things which are common to good people and bad alike. The good things only to be found in the good: piety, faith, justice, chastity, prudence, modesty, charity, and other things of that sort. The good things common to good and bad alike: money, honor, political power, office, the very health of the body. These things too are good, but they require good people.

Objections against the ways of God's providence

12. And now here comes that grumbler, who's always looking for something to find fault with, and that in God. If only he would go back to himself, really see himself, find fault with himself, correct himself! So that fault-finder and carping critic is shortly going to bring me this objection against God: "And why does God, who is in control of everything, give these good things to bad people? He should only give them to good people." Are you expecting to hear God's reasons and intentions from me? Who's expecting, from whom, and what? All the same, I will try to suggest to you, according to my understanding, as far as I can grasp it, as far as he sees fit to grant me, something that may not satisfy you perhaps, but there is somebody here whom it may satisfy. So let me sing; in such a big crowd as this, after all, it's impossible I should find no one to dance for me.

Here you are then; listen, wise guy; listen. That God gives these good things even to bad people is, if you would really like to understand, done for your education, not out of God's perversity. I know you still haven't understood what I've said; so listen then to what I was saying, you there whom I was saying it to, who are so ready to find fault with God and blame God, because he also gives these earthly and temporal goods to bad people, which according to your way of thinking you consider should only have been given to the good. It's from this idea, you see, that a deadly impiety has crept into some people's minds, so that they actually suppose that God takes no notice of human affairs. This, you see, is how they argue and what they say: "Surely, if God paid any attention to human affairs, that man wouldn't possess wealth, would he, that man wouldn't enjoy honors, that man wouldn't have such authority? God doesn't care about human affairs, because if he did, he would only give these things to good people."

Good things of this world are given to bad people,
in order to teach good people not to prize them highly

13. Go back to your heart, and from there to God. You're going back to God, you see, from the nearest possible place, if you have gone back to your heart. Because when you take offense at these things we've been talking about, it means you have gone out even from yourself; you've become an exile from your own bosom. You're upset by things outside you, and you lose sight of your own self. You yourself are inside, these things are to hand outside. There are good things outside, but outside is where they are. Gold, silver, money in all its forms, clothes, dependents, servants, flocks, honors, they are all outside. If goods of this lowest sort, earthly goods, temporal goods, transitory goods, were not also given to bad people, they would be prized highly by good people. So God, by giving these things to bad people, is teaching you to desire better things.

Look, this is what I'm saying: by this management of human affairs God is somehow addressing you as your father; and he's teaching you, like a silly boy, by means of these words which I am putting before you as best I can, and all the more confidently, the more he is prepared to abide in me. Imagine that God, who has made you into a new creature and adopted you, is saying to you, "Son, what's the meaning of your getting up every day, and praying, and kneeling, and banging your forehead on the ground, and sometimes even weeping, and saying to me, 'My Father, my God, give me wealth'? If I give it to you, you think you've acquired something really good and great.

"Because you have asked, you have received; there, do some good with it. Before you had it, you were humble; no sooner have you begun to possess wealth, than you have started despising the poor. What sort of good is it, by which you have been made worse? You've been made worse, because you were bad, and you had no idea of what could make you worse; that's why you were asking me for these things. I gave them to you, and I tested you; you found them, and were found out. When you didn't have them, your true self was hidden. Correct yourself; vomit out cupidity, drink in charity. What's so great about what you ask me for?" your God is saying to you. "Can't you see the people I've given it to? Can't you see the sort of people I've given it to? If what you are asking me for were a great good, would bandits have it, would cheats and breakers of their word have it, would people who blaspheme me have it, would disreputable clowns have it, would shameless harlots have it? Would all these types have gold, if gold were an excellent good?

"But you say to me, 'Isn't gold a good thing, then?' Certainly, gold is a good thing. But bad people do bad things with good gold; good people do good things with good gold. So because you can see the sort of people I've given it to, ask me for better things, ask me for more excellent things; ask me for spiritual things; ask me for myself."

The world still loved, in spite of the bitterness in it;
how much more would it be, if it were all sweetness!

14. "But," you say, "bad things are done in the world, harsh, vile, hateful things. It's a foul world, it shouldn't be loved." Yes, that's what it's like, and even so it's loved. The house is in ruins, and we are too lazy to move. When mothers or wet-nurses see their babies growing bigger, and when it's no longer right for them to go on being fed on milk, and yet they are still tiresomely demanding the breast, they smear their nipples with something bitter, to stop them sucking forever; this puts the infant off, so that it won't demand milk any more. So why do you go on sucking it with such pleasure, if the world has turned bitter for you? God has filled the world with all sorts of bitterness; and here are you, panting for it, here are you, clinging to it, here are you, sucking it; only from this and that in the world do you get any pleasure. How long for? Suppose it was all sweetness, think how it would be loved.

Do these things offend you? Choose another life. Love God, scorn all these things; look down on human affairs, seeing that some time or other you are going to be gone from here; I mean you are not going to be here forever. And yet even so, however bad the world is, however bitter the world is, however full the world is of disasters, if you were told by God that you would stay here forever, wouldn't you hug yourself for joy, exult, give thanks? And why? Because you would never be done with misery! The greatest unhappiness is the one that obliges you to love it; it would be less if it wasn't loved; it's all the worse, the more it is loved.

There is another life, much more worthwhile, which we should be preparing for

15. There is, after all, another life, my brothers and sisters; there is, believe me, after this life another life. Prepare yourselves for it; be indifferent to all the present life has to offer. If you are provided with it, do good with it; if you aren't, don't burn yourselves up with greedy longing. Transport it, transfer it ahead of you; let what you have here go on up there, where you are going to follow. Listen to the advice of your Lord: *Do not treasure up for yourselves treasure on earth, where moth and rust ruin things, and where thieves dig through and steal; but treasure up*

*for yourselves treasure in heaven, where a thief has no access, where moth does
not spoil things. For where your treasure is, there too is your heart* (Mt 6:19-21).
Every day, Christian believer, you hear, *Lift up your hearts*; and as though you
heard the opposite, you sink your heart into the earth. Transport it. Have you got
the means? Do good with it. You haven't got the means? Don't grumble against
God. Listen to me, you that are poor; what haven't you got, if you've got God?
Listen to me, you that are rich; what have you got, if you haven't got God?

Sermon 313A

Preached in Carthage, at the Table of the Blessed
Martyr Cyprian, on His Birthday, 14 September

The martyrs teach Christians two important truths: the rejection of pleasure
and the endurance of suffering. In Augustine's words: "Greedy cravings
should not be eliminated, but changed; fear should not be extinguished, but
transferred onto something else." This sermon is a powerful critique of pride,
ambition and self-importance. Christians are admonished to substitute their
love for shows and spectacles with a love of imitating the martyrs. Perler believes that this sermon was preached on the morning of September 14th, the day
after a particularly important meeting of a North African council.

*Two things which make the straight and narrow way for Christians:
the rejection of pleasure and the endurance of suffering*

1. The holy festival of this most blessed martyr, which has brought us here
together in the name of the Lord, requires something to be said about the merits
and glory of so great a martyr. But it is impossible to say anything really worthy of
him; perhaps, I suppose, a human tongue could have measured up to his virtues
and glory, if he had been willing to praise himself. Nonetheless, let me too praise
him, more by my devotion than by any ability I may have; or rather, let me praise
the Lord in him — the Lord in him, and him in the Lord. As to what he would be in
the Lord, the voice of martyrs was heard in the psalm when it was read: *Our help is
in the name of the Lord* (Ps 124:8). If the help of all of us is in the name of the Lord,
how much more the help of the martyrs! Where the battle is harder, there greater
help is needed.

You see, there are two things that make the way narrow for Christians: the
rejection of pleasure and the endurance of suffering. You win, any of you
engaged in the conflict, if you beat both what attracts and what repels. You win,
Christian, I repeat, any of you engaged in the conflict, if you beat what attracts
and what repels. We are dealing with the glory of the martyrs; it's easy to celebrate the feasts of the martyrs; it's difficult to imitate the martyrs' sufferings.

The doors of greed and of fear have to be shut,
if we would enter through the narrow gate

2. There are two things, as I had begun to say, which make the way of Christians straight and narrow: indifference to pleasure and endurance of suffering. So any of you engaged in the conflict should know that you are taking on the whole world; and in taking on the whole world, just beat these two things, and you beat the world. Just beat whatever is alluring, just beat whatever is threatening; because the pleasure is false, and the pain is passing. If you wish to enter by the narrow gate, shut the gates of greed and fear; it's by these, you see, that the tempter attempts to subvert the soul. Through the door of greed he tempts with promises; through the door of fear he tempts with threats.

There is something you should and may crave, in order not to crave these things; there's something you should fear, in order not to fear these things. Greedy cravings should not be eliminated, but changed; fear should not be extinguished, but transferred onto something else. What were you craving for, when you were giving in to the allurements of the world? What were you craving for? The pleasures of the flesh, the lust of the eyes, worldly ambition. This is What's-his-name, the three-headed dog of hell. But listen to the apostle John, who lay upon the Lord's breast, and belched forth in the gospel this that he had drunk in at Christ's banquet; listen to him saying, *Do not love the world, nor the things that are in the world. If anyone loves the world, the love of the Father is not in him; since everything that is in the world is the lust of the flesh, and the lust of the eyes, and worldly ambition* (1 Jn 2:15-16).

So this heaven and earth is called the world. In saying *Do not love the world*, he is not disparaging that world; whoever disparages that world, after all, is disparaging the maker of the world. Listen to the world mentioned twice in one place in different senses: it was said of the Lord Christ, *He was in this world, and the world was made through him, and the world did not know him* (Jn 1:10). The world was made through him: *Our help is in the name of the Lord, who made heaven and earth* (Ps 124:7). The world was made through him: *I lifted up my eyes to the mountains; from where will help come to me? My help is from the Lord, who made heaven and earth* (Ps 121:1-2). This world was made by God, and the world did not know him. Which world did not know him? The lover of the world, the lover of the work, the scorner of the workman.

Your love must migrate; cast off your moorings from creatures, moor yourself to the creator. Change your love, change your fear; the only things that make good or bad lives are good or bad loves. "That's a great man," someone will say, "he's good, he's great."

In what way, I'd like to know?

"He knows so much."

I'm asking what he loves, not what he knows.

So, *do not love the world, nor the things that are in the world. If anyone loves the world, the love of the Father is not in him; since everything that is in the world* — in the lovers of the world, of course — everything that is in the lovers of the world *is the lust of the flesh, and the lust of the eyes, and worldly ambition.*

The lust of the flesh involves pleasure, the lust of the eyes involves curiosity, worldly ambition involves pride. Whoever overcomes these three, well there isn't any craving left in him to overcome. Many branches, but just a threefold root. How many evils are contained in the appetite for the pleasures of the flesh, how many evils it perpetrates! From it come adulteries, fornications; from it come extravagance, drunkenness; from it comes anything that tickles the senses unlawfully, and penetrates the mind with poisonous sweetness, leaves the mind in bondage to the flesh, topples the ruler from its citadel, subjects the commander to the servant. And what can a man do uprightly when he's upside down in himself?

The effects of the vice of curiosity, the lust of the eyes

3. What evils vulgar, shameless curiosity is the cause of, the lust of the eyes, the avid craving for frivolous shows and spectacles, the madness of the stadiums, the fighting of contests for no reward! The charioteers compete for some prize; for what prize do the crowds fight over the charioteers? But the charioteer delights them, the hunter delights them, the player delights them. Is this the way it is, then, that vile baseness delights the decent man? You can also change your consuming addiction to shows and spectacles; the Church is offering your mind more honest and venerable spectacles. Just now the passion of the blessed Cyprian was being read. We were listening with our ears, observing it all with our minds; we could see him competing, somehow or other we felt afraid for him in his deadly peril, but we were hoping God would help him.

Anyway, do you want to know, in a word, what the difference is between our shows and spectacles and those of the theaters? We, to the extent that we are of sound and healthy mind, would love to imitate the martyrs whose contests we are watching; we, I repeat, would love to imitate the martyrs whose contests we are watching. Decent spectator, when you are watching a show in the theater, you're off your head if you have the audacity to imitate the performer you love. Look, here am I, watching Cyprian; I'm crazy about Cyprian. Imagine you are angry with me, curse me and say, "May you be like him!" I'm watching him, I'm delighted by him, as far as I can I embrace him with the arms of my mind; I see him competing, I rejoice when he wins. Be angry with me, as I said, and say to me, "May you be like him!" See if I don't jump at the idea, see if I don't choose to be so, see if I don't long to be so, see if I can't say I am unworthy, while to quail at the thought and to shrink from it is something I cannot do.

Now you watch your show, you be delighted with it, you be crazy about the performer. Don't be angry if I say, "May you be like him!" But I'll spare you, I shan't say it. Acknowledge me as your friend, together with me change the shows you attend. Let us be crazy about the sort of performers whom we don't have to blush about; let us love the sort of performers whom we would choose to imitate, so far as we were able.

"But the one whose performance is being watched is disreputable."

And is the one who watches it respectable? Eliminate your eagerness to buy, and there will be no indecency for sale. By watching it, you are establishing the whole disreputable business more firmly than ever. Why encourage something you find fault with? I would be very surprised if some of the disreputability of the person you're crazy about didn't brush off on you. But don't let it brush off, let decent respectability remain untarnished, if it can, while still being the spectator of lusts, the purchaser of vile pleasures!

Do I have the audacity to forbid shows and spectacles altogether? Yes, I do have the audacity to forbid them, I most certainly do. This place gives me the confidence to do so, and the one who set me up in this place. The holy martyr was able to endure the rage of the pagans, and shall I not be bold enough to instruct the ears of Christians? Shall I, here, dread unspoken criticisms, when he despised the shouts of open fury? I will say it straight out; I will certainly be refuted in the minds of my listeners, if what I say is untrue. It was an excellent act of the ancient Roman discipline, altogether an excellent act, to relegate every kind of showpeople to the place of infamy and shame. Not for them any post of honor in Senate or assembly, not even in one of the tribes of the common people; in every respect kept apart from the decent and respectable — and put up for sale to the decent and respectable! Why have you set them apart from yourself to preserve the dignity of your town council, and set them up in the theater to provide yourself with pleasure? Your pleasure should match your dignity. And these wretched unfortunates themselves have been put in bondage to the voices of the spectators, to the desires and preferences of the spectators, to the insane pleasures of the spectators. Eliminate all these things, these people are set free; when you refuse to be one of their spectators, you are doing them a kindness.

The evil consequences of worldly ambition

4. Let that do for the lust of the eyes. How much evil there is in worldly ambition! All pride is there; and what can be worse than pride? Listen to the judgment of the Lord: *God withstands the proud, while he gives grace to the humble* (Job 22:29; Jas 4:6; 1 Pt 5:5). So worldly ambition too is a malignant growth.

Someone's going to say, "The authorities of the world cannot be without it."

They most certainly can. One of their own authors — I can't remember which — said, "Agents infect their activities, each with their own faults." Of course they can. The ruler is set in a position of authority; let him rule himself, and he's become a ruler.

"But the human mind has a natural tendency to self-importance." Then self-importance should be checked. The one who sits in judgment on human beings must recognize he is only human himself. There's a disparity of rank, but a common share of human frailty. Anyone who thinks about this in a godfearing and religious way can both exercise authority and avoid lapsing into self- importance.

Cyprian overcame all these things. What, after all, did he not overcome, seeing that he held life itself to be of no account, riddled as it is with all these temptations? The judge threatened him with death; he confessed Christ, he was prepared to die for Christ's sake. When death comes, there will be no ambition left, no curiosity of the eyes, no appetite for sordid and carnal pleasures; one single life despised, and all these things are overcome.

Cyprian truly to be praised in the Lord

5. So, let the blessed Cyprian be praised in the Lord, because he has over-come all these things. When could he have done so, if the Lord had not come to his aid? When could he have been victorious, if the spectator, who was preparing a crown for him in his victory, had not provided him with the neces-sary strength in his toils? He too certainly rejoices, rejoices for us, not for himself, when he is praised in the Lord. He is very, very gentle, you see, and it is written, *In the Lord shall my soul be praised; let the gentle hear and be glad* (Ps 34:2). He was gentle; he wishes his soul to be praised in the Lord. Let his soul be praised in the Lord. Let his body be honored also, because *precious in the sight of the Lord is the death of his saints* (Ps 116:15). Let us celebrate in a holy way, let as celebrate as Christians. After all, we have not erected an altar to Cyprian as though he were God, but we have made an altar to the true God out of Cyprian.

Sermon 314

On the Birthday of the Martyr Stephen

There are two likely dates for this brief and powerful homily on the feast of the martyr Stephen, December 26th — either as early as 400, based on the eloquent and sophisticated rhetorical style which characterized Augustine's earlier preaching, or closer to 420, when the cult of Stephen was at its height after the discovery of his grave and the arrival of his relics in Africa. Augustine re-ceived relics for his church in Hippo in 424. The brevity of the homily cer-tainly points to a later date, when Augustine's sermons generally became shorter. He plays on the Greek meaning of the term *stephanos*, namely, the crown of laurel leaves awarded to winners in the games, which hints at a fairly sophisticated congregation with knowledge of Greek. Stephen was motivated to endure his suffering by thinking about the rewards to come. He was in a hurry to die for Christ in order to live with him.

Comparison between Christ's birthday on 25 December,
and Stephen's on 26 December

1. Yesterday we celebrated the Lord's birthday; today we are celebrating the birthday of his servant. But the birthday of the Lord which we celebrated was the one on which he was pleased to be born; the birthday we are celebrating of his servant is the one on which he was crowned. The Lord's birthday we celebrated was the one on which he received the garment of our flesh; his servant's birthday which we are celebrating is the one on which he threw aside the garment of his flesh. What we celebrated on the Lord's birthday was his becoming like us; what we are celebrating on his servant's birthday is his becoming as close as possible to Christ. Just as Christ, you see, by being born was joined to Stephen, so Stephen by dying was joined to Christ.

But the reason the Church marks the days of the birth and the passion of our Lord Jesus Christ with services of equal devotion, is that each of them is a salutary medicine for us, because he was born so that we might be born again, and he died so that we might live for ever. The martyrs, on the other hand, came to involvement in evil contests by being born, bringing with them the drag of original sin; while by dying they passed over to the most incontestable of goods, putting an end to all sin. After all, if the reward of bliss to come were not comforting them as they faced persecution, when would they ever have endured those various torments of martyrdom? If the blessed Stephen, facing that shower of stones, had not thought about the rewards to come, how could he have borne that terrible hailstorm? But he was bearing in mind the instruction of the one whose presence he could observe in heaven; and reaching out to him with the most ardent love, he longed to leave the flesh behind as soon as possible, and to fly off to him. Nor was he now afraid to die, because he could see that Christ was alive, though he knew he had been slain for his sake; and for that reason he was in a hurry to die for him, in order to live with him.

As to what the most blessed martyr saw as he engaged in that final, agonizing contest, you will no doubt recall his words, which you regularly hear from the book of the Acts of the Apostles; *Behold*, he said, *I see the heavens opened, and Christ standing at the right hand of God* (Acts 7:55). He could see Jesus standing; the reason he was standing, and not sitting, is that standing up above, and watching from above his soldier battling down below, he was supplying him with invincible strength, so that he shouldn't fall. *Behold*, he said, *I see the heavens opened.* Blessed indeed the man, to whom the heavens lay open! But who opened heaven up? The one about whom it says in the Apocalypse, *Who opens, and nobody shuts; shuts, and nobody opens* (Rv 3:7). When Adam was thrown out of paradise, after that first and abominable sin, heaven was shut against the human race; after the passion of Christ, the thief was the first to enter; then later on Stephen saw heaven opened. Why should we be surprised? What he saw in faith, he indicated in faith, and took violently by storm.

Exhortation to follow in Stephen's footsteps,
by praying for and forgiving our enemies

2. Come then, brothers and sisters, let us follow him; you see, if we follow Stephen, we shall be crowned with the victor's laurels. It is above all in the matter of loving our enemies that he is to be followed and imitated. You know, of course, that when he was surrounded by the surging throng of his enemies, and was being struck incessant blows by rocks hurled at him from this side and that, he remained calm and fearless, mild and gentle amid the stones that were killing him, and gazing upon the one for whose sake he was being killed, he did not say, "Lord, judge the manner of my death," but, *Receive my spirit*; he did not say, "Lord Jesus, avenge your servant, whom you see doomed to die by this form of execution," but, *Do not hold this sin against them* (Acts 7:59-60). So the most blessed martyr, standing firm in his witness to the truth, and on fire with the spirit of charity, came at last to his glorious end; and since, after being called, he persevered to the end, he acquired at the end what he was called; Stephen, by the glory of his name, was conducted to his crown.

So when the blessed Stephen shed his blood for Christ, being the first to do so, it's as though a crown came forth from heaven, so that by following him to the reward, those might receive it who had first imitated the example he set of courage in the combat. Innumerable martyrdoms later on filled the earth. All those who after him have shed their blood for confessing Christ, have placed that crown on their own heads, and preserved it intact for those who were to follow. And now, brothers and sisters, it's hanging down from heaven; whoever really longs for it, will swiftly fly up to it. And for me to encourage your holinesses briefly and clearly, I don't need many words: Follow in Stephen's footsteps, any of you that desires a crown.

Turning to the Lord, etc.

Sermon 330

On the Birthday of Some Martyrs

Augustine confronts the apparent contradiction between loving oneself and denying oneself implied in Jesus' invitation, *If anyone wishes to come after me, let him deny himself, and take up his cross and follow me.* Fischer, Kunzelmann, and Perler employ fairly complex arguments to date this sermon to 397. Perler, following Lambot, assumes that it was preached on the feast day of the *Massa Candida*, the so-called "White Mass" of martyrs, but there is no specific reference to them. The Maurists, based on a number of incoherences and *non-sequiturs*, were of the opinion that the sermon as it stands is incomplete and was probably extracted from Church lectionaries.

If anyone wishes to come after me, let him deny himself,
and take up his cross, and follow me

1. The feast of the blessed martyrs and the expectation of your holinesses is insisting on a sermon from me. I quite realize that this day calls for a discussion. This is what you want, this is what I want; may this be achieved by the one in whose hands are both ourselves and our words; may he who has granted us the will endow us with the capacity. It was in this respect, after all, that the martyrs were aglow with enthusiasm; on fire with love for invisible things, you see, they thought nothing of the visible. What has the person loved in himself, when he has thought nothing of himself in order not to lose himself? They were temples of God, you see, and experienced the true God dwelling in themselves; that's why they wouldn't worship false gods.

They had heard, they had thirstily gulped down and stored in the depths of their hearts, and after a fashion thoroughly digested what the Lord said: *If anyone wishes to come after me, let him deny himself. Let him deny himself,* he said, *and take up his cross, and follow me* (Mt 16:24). It's about this that I want to say something, and your eager attention frightens me, while your prayers assist me.

How to deny yourself when you love yourself

2. What, I ask you, is the meaning of *If anyone wishes to come after me, let him deny himself, and take up his cross, and follow me?* We can understand the meaning of *let him take up his cross;* let him bear with his troubles. "Take up," you see, means "bear," "endure." Let him patiently accept, he is saying, everything he suffers on my account. *And follow me.* Where to? Where we know he went after the resurrection. I mean, he ascended into heaven, and is seated at the right hand of the Father. That's where he has also placed us. Meanwhile, let hope go ahead, so that the reality may follow. In what way hope ought to go ahead, those of you know who really listen to the words, *Lift up your hearts.*

But it remains for me to inquire, as far as the Lord assists me, and to discuss, and if he opens to enter, and if he grants it to find, and to bring out to you whatever I manage to find — what he meant by saying, *Let him deny himself.* How can someone deny himself who loves himself? Well, that's a reasonable question, but humanly so; it's only a human being who says to me, "How can someone who loves himself deny himself?" God, though, says to such a person, "Let him deny himself, if he loves himself." By loving himself, you see, he loses himself; by denying himself, he finds himself. *Whoever loves his soul,* he says, *let him lose it* (Jn 12:25). This command was given by the one who knows what to command, because the one who knows what instructions to give knows what advice to give, and the one who was good enough to create knows how to restore. *Whoever loves, let him lose.* It is a painful thing to lose what you love. But from time to time even the farmer loses what he sows. He brings it out, scatters it, throws it away, buries it. Why be surprised? This despiser and loser is a greedy reaper. What has really been done is shown by winter and summer; the joy of the reaper shows you the wisdom of the advice of the sower. Therefore, *whoever loves his soul, let him lose it.*

Whoever is looking for fruit in it, let him sow it. So that's the meaning of "Let him deny himself"; let him not lose himself by crookedly loving himself.

The difference between the right and the wrong love of self

3. There isn't anyone, after all, who doesn't love himself; but we have to look for the right sort of love and avoid the wrong sort. You see, anyone who loves himself by leaving God out of his life, and leaves God out of his life by loving himself, doesn't even remain in himself, but goes away from himself. He goes away into exile from his own breast, by taking no notice of what's inside and loving what's outside. What's this I've said? Aren't all who do evil ignoring their own consciences, while anyone whose conscience shames him puts a limit on his iniquity? So because that person has ignored God in order to love himself, by loving outside himself what is not himself he has also ignored himself.

Notice, listen to the apostle giving his support to this understanding of the matter. *In the last times*, he says, *dangerous times will loom up.* What are the dangerous times? *There will be people loving themselves.* That's the core of the evil. So let's see if they remain in themselves by loving themselves; let's see, let's hear what comes next: *There will be people*, he says, *loving themselves, lovers of money* (2 Tm 3:1-2). Where are you now, you that were busy loving yourself? Obviously, you're outside. Are you, I'm asking you, are you money? Obviously, after loving yourself by neglecting God, by loving money you have even abandoned yourself. First you have abandoned, and then later on you have destroyed yourself. Love of money, you see, has caused you to destroy yourself. You tell lies on account of money; *The mouth which lies kills the soul* (Wis 1:11). There you are, while looking for money you have destroyed your soul.

Bring out the scales of truth, not of greed; bring out a balance, but of truth, not of greed. Bring it out, I beg you, and put on one side money, on the other the soul. Now it's you that are doing the weighing, and out of greed you're cheating with your fingers; you want the side that has money on it to sink. Put it there, but don't weigh it yourself; you want to cheat yourself; I can see what you're doing. You want to put money before your soul; to tell lies on account of the former, to destroy the latter. Put it on the scales, let God do the weighing; the one who doesn't know how to deceive or be deceived, let him do the weighing. There you are, he's weighing them; watch him weighing them, listen to him announcing the result: *What does it profit a man, if he gains the whole world.* It's the divine voice, it's the voice of the weigh-master who doesn't deceive, who is giving you a warning as he announces the result. You, on one side, were putting money, on the other the soul; notice where you put the money. What does the weigh-master reply? *What does it profit a man, if he gains the whole world, but suffers the loss of his own soul?* (Mt 16:26). But you were wishing to weigh the soul against gain; weigh it against the world. You were willing to lose it in order to acquire the earth; this thing outweighs heaven and earth together.

But you do this because by leaving God out of your life and loving yourself, you have also gone away from yourself; and you now value other things, which are outside you, more than yourself. Come back to yourself; but again, turn upward when you've come back to yourself, don't stay in yourself. First come back to yourself from the things outside you, and then give yourself back to the one who made you, and when you were lost sought you, and as a runaway found you, and when you had turned away turned you back to himself. So then, come back to yourself, and go on to the one who made you.

Imitate that younger son; because perhaps that's who you are. I'm speaking to the people, not to one person; even if they can't all hear me, I'm not speaking to one person only, but to the human race. So come back, be that younger son, who by living recklessly dissipated and lost his fortune, and found himself in want, fed pigs, being worn out with hunger took a deep breath, recalled his father to mind. And what does the gospel say about him? *And returning to himself.* He had even let go of himself, but returning to himself — let's see if he remained in himself. *Returning to himself, he said, I will arise.* So he had fallen. *I will arise*, he said, *and go to my father.* There you are, he's now denying himself after finding himself. How does he deny himself? Listen. *And I will say to him, I have sinned*, he said, *against heaven and before you.* He's denying himself: *I am now not worthy to be called your son* (Lk 15:17-19).

There you are, that's what the holy martyrs did. They thought nothing of things that are outside; all the allurements of this age, all the errors and the terrors, whatever could tickle the fancy, whatever could fill the heart with dread, they scorned it all, trampled on it all. They had also come to themselves, and observed themselves; they found themselves in themselves, and they didn't like themselves. They hurried off to the one by whom they could be refashioned, in whom they could come to life again, in whom they could remain, in whom what they had begun to be by themselves would perish, and only that would remain which he had established in them. That is what denying oneself means.

How Peter learned eventually to deny himself

4. This is something the apostle Peter could not yet grasp, when he replied to our Lord Jesus Christ's forecast of his passion, *Far be this from you, Lord; this will not happen* (Mt 16:22). He was afraid that life would die. Just now, when the holy gospel was read, you heard what answer the blessed Peter gave the savior when he was foretelling that he would suffer for us, and indeed after a fashion promising that he would. The captive was contradicting the redeemer.

What are you doing, apostle? How can you contradict? How can you say *This will not happen*? So is the Lord not going to suffer? Is the word of the cross a scandal to you? It's to those who are perishing that it's folly. You are to be bought back, and are you contradicting the trader paying for you? Allow him to suffer; he knows what he is doing, he knows why he came, he knows how to seek you, he knows how to find you. Don't try to teach your master; look for your price from his side. Listen to him yourself, rather, as he corrects you; don't you start wanting to do the correcting; that's perverse, it's getting things back to front. Listen to what he says: *Get behind me.* And because he said it, I can say it. I'm not keeping quiet about a word of the Lord, nor am I doing the apostle an injury. The Lord Christ said, *Get behind me, Satan* (Mt 16:23).

Why Satan?

Because you want to go in front of me. Get behind me. I mean, if you get behind me, you are following me; if you follow me, you will take up your cross, and you won't be my adviser, but my disciple.

Why were you scared, after all, when the Lord foretold his death? What made you scared, if not your fear of dying yourself? By being afraid to die, you failed to deny yourself; by loving yourself wrongly, you denied him.

But later on blessed Peter the apostle, after three times denying the Lord, wiped out his fault by weeping. When the Lord rose again he was strengthened, built up, he died for the one whom out of fear of death he had denied. By confessing him he encountered death, but by encountering death he laid hold of life. And lo and behold, Peter dies no more; all fear has passed away, no tears for him ever again, that has all faded away, he remains in bliss with Christ. He has trampled, you see, on all outside allurements, threats and terrors; he has denied himself, taken up his cross and followed the Lord. Listen to the apostle Paul also denying himself: *Far be it from me*, he says, *to glory except in the cross of our Lord Jesus Christ, through whom the world has been crucified to me, and I to the world* (Gal 6:14). Listen again to him denying himself: *I am alive*, he says, *not I*; an open denial of himself, but now follows a glorious acknowledgement of Christ: *but it is Christ who is alive in me* (Gal 2:20). So what's the meaning of "Deny yourself"? Don't you live in yourself. What's the meaning of "Don't you live in yourself"? Don't do your own will, but that of the one who is dwelling in you.

Sermon 339

On the Anniversary of His Ordination

This is a tour de force on the awesome responsibilities of a bishop and was preached on the occasion of Augustine's own anniversary of episcopal ordination. Augustine employs the term "burden" repeatedly. He regrets that he has so little time for leisure, study and contemplation because of the pressing demands of his ministry. We discover here that it was customary for the bishop to give a banquet for the poor on the occasion of his anniversary as a bishop. Hill is inclined to see this text as several sermons woven into one. The final part of it, sections 7-9, also appears as S. 40 in the enumeration of the Maurists, who no doubt discovered it in a separate manuscript. But Frangipane, based on the strength of a manuscript the Maurists were unaware of, treats it as one sermon. Hill suspects we have three sermons or pieces of sermons: first, the one printed as 339 by the Maurists, which consists of section 1, the first half of section 2, and then section 4, with an addition omitted from this text; second, the second half of sections 2 qnd 3 — clearly an incomplete sermon; third, sections 7-9, which appear as S. 40, dated early, 396-400. Hill is inclined to date this sermon later, based on the work of Lambot and Frangipane. If Lambot is correct and the original sermon consisted of section 1, the first part of section 2 and then section 4, the sermon should be dated to 425 or later. Indeed a comment by Augustine referring to "the arrival of his last days" in section 1 supports this. If Frangipane is correct and the entire text really is one sermon, this surely points to the later date and categorically excludes the earlier date.

The burden and the dangers of being a bishop

1. This particular day, brothers and sisters, is a serious warning to me to think very carefully about the burden I carry. Even if I have to think about the weight of it day and night, still this anniversary somehow or other thrusts it on my consciousness in such a way that I am absolutely unable to avoid reflecting on it. And the more the years increase, or rather decrease, and bring me nearer to my last day, which of course is undoubtedly going to come some time or other, the sharper my thoughts become, and ever more full of needles, about what sort of account I can give for you to the Lord our God. This, you see, is the difference between each one of you and me, that you, practically speaking, are only going to render an account for yourselves alone, while I shall be giving one both for myself and for you. That's why the burden is so much greater; but carried well it wins greater glory, while if it is handled unfaithfully, it hurls one down into the most appalling punishment.

So what am I to do above all else today, but present you with the danger I am in, so that you may be my joy? Now my danger is this: if I pay attention to how you praise me, and take no notice of the sort of lives you lead. But he knows, the one under whose gaze I speak, under whose gaze, indeed, I think, that I am not so much delighted by praise and popularity, as vexed and troubled about what sort of lives are led by those who praise me. As for being praised by those who lead bad lives, I don't want it, I shudder at it, detest it, it causes me pain, not pleasure. While as for being praised by those who lead good lives, if I say I don't want it, I will be lying; if I say I do want it, I'm afraid I may be more bent on vanity than on the solid good. So what am I to say? I don't completely want it, and I don't completely not want it. I don't completely want it, in case I should be imperiled by human praise; I don't completely not want it, in case it should mean that those to whom I preach are ungrateful.

The bishop is meant to be a watchman or lookout,
to warn his people of dangers to their salvation

2. My burden, though, is the one you heard about just now when the prophet Ezekiel was being read. It's little enough, after all, that the very day is a reminder to me to think about this burden; in addition, such a reading as that is chanted, to strike great fear into my heart, and make me think about what I am carrying; because unless the one who placed it on my shoulders carries it with me himself, I am bound to fail. Here's what you heard: *The land,* he says, *over which I will have brought the sword, and which has provided itself with a lookout, who is to see the sword coming down on it, and to speak and announce it; but if the sword comes, that lookout keeps quiet, and the sword coming down upon the sinner kills him; the sinner indeed will die for his iniquity, but his blood I will require from the hand of the lookout. But if he sees the sword coming down and blows the trumpet and announces it, and the one to whom he announces it pays no attention, he indeed will die in his iniquity, but the lookout will deliver his own soul. And as for you, son of man, I have set you as a lookout for the children of Israel* (Ez 33:2-7).

He explained what he meant by the sword, he explained what he meant by the lookout, he explained what sort of death he meant; he has not allowed us to make the obscurity of the passage an excuse for our negligence. *I have set you,* he says, *as a lookout. If I say to the sinner, "Dying you shall die," and you just keep quiet, and he dies in his sin, he indeed shall die in his sin rightly and justly, but his blood I will require at your hand. But if you tell the sinner, "Dying you shall die," and he pays no attention to himself, he shall die in his iniquity, but you have delivered your soul* (Ez 33:7-9).* And he added words which he wanted to have passed on to the people of Israel: *And so you shall say to the children of Israel, What is this that you are saying among yourselves: "Our iniquities overwhelm us, we are wasting away in our sins, how can we go on living?" Thus says the Lord: that I do not desire the death of the godless, so much as that the godless should turn back from his crooked way and live* (Ez 33:10-11).

That is what he has wished me to declare to you. If I don't declare it, I am going to have a bad account to render of my tour as lookout. But if I do declare it, I have done my part. It's over to you now; as for me, I'm reassured. But how can I be reassured, if you are in peril, and are going to die? I have no wish for my glory to be accompanied by your punishment. Yes indeed, I have been given my reassurance, but charity makes me anxious. Look, I'm saying it, and you know I've always said it, you know I've never kept quiet: *This is what God says: I do not desire the death of the godless, so much as that the godless should turn back from his very evil way and live.* What is it the godless were saying? He told us the words of the godless and the wicked: *Our iniquities overwhelm us, we are wasting away in our sins, how can we go on living?.* The sick are despairing, but the doctor is promising

---

* Here the Maurist text stops, resuming again at section 4.

hope. Mere man has said *How can we go on living?*; God says, "You can go on living." If *every man a liar*, let God *who alone is truthful* (Rom 3:4; Ps 116:11) delete what man has said and write what God has said. Don't despair, you can go on living, not on your evil deeds of the past, but on your good deeds of the future; you will delete the evil deeds, if you *depart from evil* (Ps 34:14). Everything, whether good or bad, is deleted by change. From a good life you turned aside to a bad one, you deleted the good one. Notice what you are directing your attention to, what you get for it; two deposit boxes have been prepared for you; what you put in is what you will find. God is a faithful bank manager, he will pay you back in your own coin what you have done.

Besides those who perish by despairing, there are others who perish by presuming

3. There are other people, though, who don't perish by despairing; they don't say to themselves, *Our iniquities overwhelm us, we are wasting away in our sins, how shall we be able to go on living?* (Ez 33:10). But they deceive themselves in another way; they beguile themselves with God's being exceedingly merciful, so that they never bother to correct themselves. This, you see, is the sort of thing they say: "Even if we do evil, even if we commit injustices, even if we lead lives of vicious self-indulgence, even if we ignore the poor, even if we conduct ourselves with pride and arrogance, even if we feel no prickings of conscience for our evil deeds, is God going to throw away such a vast multitude, and deliver only a few?"

So there are two dangers; one which we heard of just now from the prophet, the other about which the apostle does not keep silent. Because against those who die in despair, like gladiators who, being destined to the sword, have an insatiable appetite for vile pleasures, thinking nothing, it seems, of their souls as being already forfeit, the prophet tells us what they say to themselves: *Our iniquities overwhelm us, we are wasting away in our sins, how shall we be able to go on living?* While the other case is the one of which the apostle says, *Or do you make light of the riches of his goodness and mercy and forbearance?* Against those who say, "God is good, God is merciful, he won't throw away such a vast multitude of sinners and deliver only a few. Because of course, if he didn't want them to exist, they wouldn't even be alive. Seeing that they do such evil things and go on living, if this were displeasing to God, he would immediately remove them from the earth." Against them the apostle says, *Are you unaware that the patience of God is prompting you to repentance? You, however, according to the hardness of your heart, and your unrepentant heart are storing up wrath for yourself on the day of wrath and the revelation of the just judgment of God, who will repay each person according to his works* (Rom 2:4-6).

Who is he saying this to? To those who say, "God is good, he won't pay back." He most certainly will pay back each person according to his works. As for you, what are you doing? Storing up. What? Wrath. Add wrath upon wrath, increase the deposit; what you deposit will be paid back to you, the one you entrust it to doesn't cheat you. If on the other hand you put good works into the other deposit box, the fruits of justice, or continence, or virginity, or the chastity of marriage; if you are a stranger to fraud, to murder, to crime; if you remember the needy, because you yourself are also in need; if you remember the poor, because you yourself are also poor, whatever the abundance of your wealth, you are clothed in the rags of the flesh; if with such thoughts as these, and such actions as these you contribute to the good deposit box against the day of judgment, the one who cheats nobody, and will repay each person according to his works, will say to you, "Take what you have deposited, because there is plenty of it. When you were depositing it, you couldn't see it; but I was keeping it, just as I was going to repay it."

Because indeed, brothers and sisters, everyone who puts something into a savings box knows that he is putting it in, and cannot see it when he has done so. Suppose a savings chest buried in the earth, with one opening or small chink by which you put money into it. Little by little you put in what you have won, and you can't see it. If the earth is keeping for you what you have put in and can't see, will the one who made heaven and earth not keep it for you too?

To preach, to rebuke, to refute, to build up, to manage for everyone, is a labor he would gladly run away from; but the gospel terrifies him

4. So then, brothers and sisters, lighten my burden for me, lighten it, please, and carry it with me; lead good lives. We have our fellow poor to feed today, and we have to show them humanity and share with them; the rations I provide for you, though, are these words. I quite lack the means to feed everyone with visible, tangible bread. I feed you on what I am fed on myself. I am just a waiter, I am not the master of the house; I set food before you from the pantry which I too live on, from the Lord's storerooms, from the banquet of that householder who *for our sakes became poor, though he was rich, in order to enrich us from his poverty* (2 Cor 8:9). If I were to set bread before you, when the bread was broken you would each just carry away a scrap; even if I provided a great quantity, very little indeed would arrive in the hands of each one of you. Now, however, all of you get everything I say, and each and every one of you gets it all. You haven't, I mean to say, divided the syllables of my words among yourselves, have you? You haven't taken away, have you, one word each from my drawn-out sermon? Each of you has heard the whole of it.

But see to it how you have heard, because I am the one who pays out, not the one who collects the debts. If I didn't pay out, and kept the money, the gospel terrifies me. I could easily say, you see, "What business is it of mine to be wearisome to people; to say to the wicked, 'Don't act wickedly, act like this, stop acting like that'? What business is it of mine to be burdensome to people? I've received instructions how I should live; let me live as I've been told to, as I've been commanded. Let me sign for what I have received; why should I give an account for others?" The gospel terrifies me; because nobody could outdo me in enjoying such anxiety-free leisure. There's nothing better, nothing more pleasant than to search through the divine treasure chest with nobody making a commotion; it's pleasant, it's good. But to preach, to refute, to rebuke, to build up, to manage for everybody, that's a great burden, a great weight, a great labor. Who wouldn't run away from this labor? But the gospel terrifies me.

There was a servant, who stepped forward and said to his master, *I knew that you, a harsh man, reap where you have not sown*; I have kept your money, I did not wish to invest it. Take what is your own; judge if it is any less; if it is all there, do not be harsh with me.

But he said to him, *Wicked servant, out of your own mouth I condemn you.* Why so?

Since you have called me grasping, why did you neglect my profit?

But I was afraid to pay it out, in case I lost it.

Is that what you say? I'm frequently told, you see, "Why take him to task? What you say is lost on him; he doesn't listen to you."

And I, says that man, didn't want to pay out, in case I lost your money.

He answered him, *You should have laid out my money, and I, when I came, would have collected it with interest* (Lk 19:21-23). I gave you the post, he is saying, of an investor, not a collector; you should have done the job of investing, and left the collecting to me.

So with this debt collection to fear, we should all see to it how we receive. If I, engaged in investing the money, am afraid, should those who receive it be free from all anxiety? Let those who were bad yesterday be good today. That's my investment: let those who were bad yesterday be good today. They were bad yesterday, and are not dead; if they had died being bad, they would have gone where there's no returning from. They were bad yesterday, they are still alive today; let the fact of being alive turn to their advantage, let them stop leading bad lives. So why do they want to add a bad today to a bad yesterday? You want to have a long life, don't you want it to be a good one? Who could bear even a long, bad dinner? Has mental blindness grown so inveterate, is the inner man so utterly deaf, that he wants to have everything good, except himself?

Do you want to have a country cottage? I refuse to believe you want a bad one. You want to get a wife, but only a good one, a home, but only a good one. Why should I run through everything one by one? You don't want to have a bad shoe, and you want to have a bad life? As though a bad shoe can do you more harm than a bad life! When a bad, ill-fitting shoe starts hurting you, you sit down, take it off, throw it away or put it right or change it, in order not to damage a toe. A bad life, which can lose you your soul, you don't care to put right. But I can see clearly enough where you delude yourself; a hurtful shoe causes pain, a hurtful life causes pleasure. The first indeed hurts, the second pleases. But what pleases for a time, later on brings much worse pain, while what brings salutary pain for a time, later on brings endless pleasure and abundant, joyful happiness.

The servant's business is to lay out the money,
the master's to require an account

5. Notice the one having a good time, the one having a bad time; that rich man having a good time and that poor man having a bad time. The first was wining and dining, the second suffering agonies; the first being treated with respect in the midst of his household, the second being licked by dogs; the first getting indigestion from his banquet, the second not even getting his fill of the scraps. Pleasure came to an end, need came to an end; the rich man's good things passed away, and the poor man's bad things; there followed bad things for the rich man, good things for the poor man. The things that passed away could not be recalled; the things that followed could never be diminished. The rich man was burning in hell, the poor man was enjoying himself in Abraham's bosom. Earlier on the poor man had longed for a scrap from the rich man's table, later on the rich man longed for a drop from the poor man's finger. The want of the one terminated in final satisfaction, the pleasure of the other culminated in the endless pain that followed it. Thirst succeeded to surfeit, pain to pleasure, fire to the wearing of purple.

Here, on the other hand, is the dinner which Lazarus seems to have had in Abraham's bosom; this is what I wish all of you to enjoy, this is what I wish all of us to enjoy together. I mean to say, what would the dinner be like that I could provide for you, if I invited you all, and this church was filled with tables for people to feast at? Such things don't last, they're soon over. Think about what I am saying, so that you may come to the feast which you can never get to the end of. There, you see, nobody gets indigestion from feasting; nor are the very dishes such that they feed us by disappearing, and provide refreshment by being consumed. They will remain entire, and at the same time provide us with all the refreshment we want. If our eyes feed on light, and the light is not consumed, what will that banquet be like, which consists in the contemplation of the truth, in the vision of eternity, in the praises of God; with the assurance of happiness, with untroubled peace of mind, an immortal body, our flesh never withering with old age, our soul never fainting with hunger? There nobody grows bigger, nobody grows smaller. There nobody is born, because nobody dies; there you are not even compelled to do any of the good works which I am urging you to practice now.

The reward God has prepared for our doing good
here is nothing less than his own Son

6. Just now, you see, you heard the Lord saying, he said it to all of us: *When you make a feast, do not invite your friends* — he is showing you where you should be open-handed; don't bring your relations along, who have the means to recompense you — *but invite the poor, the disabled, the blind, the lame,* those in need, who have no means of paying you back. And will you lose by it? *You shall be recompensed in the recompensing of the just* (Lk 14:12-14). You just spend, he is saying, I'm the one who receives, makes a note of it, pays it back. God said that, and thereby urged us to do such things ourselves, so that he can pay us back. When he pays us back, who is going to take it away from us? *If God is for us, who is*

against us? (Rom 8:31). We were busy sinning, and he made a gift to us of Christ's death; we are now living justly, and will he disappoint us? Christ, after all, did not die for the just, but *for the ungodly* (Rom 5:6). If he made a gift to the wicked of the death of his Son, what can he be keeping for the just? What is he keeping for them? He has nothing better to keep for them than what he gave for them. What did he give for them? *He did not spare his own Son* (Rom 5:6). What is he keeping for them? The same Son, but now as God to be enjoyed, not as man to die.

There you have where God is inviting you to. But just as you pay close attention to where to, please also pay attention to which way, please also pay attention to how. But clearly, when you get there, you won't have this sort of thing said to you, will you: *Break your bread to the hungry; if you see someone naked, clothe him* (Is 58:7)? This passage is not going to be quoted to you, is it: *When you make a feast, invite the lame, the blind, the needy, the destitute*? There won't be anyone destitute there, any lame people there, any blind, any disabled, anyone needing hospitality, anyone naked; they will all be healthy, all robust, all well supplied, all clothed in everlasting light. Who can you see there as a stranger or foreigner? That's our home country, here we are all strangers and foreigners, we should be longing to get home. Let us carry out what we have been ordered to, so that we may demand what we have been promised, and take what is given us over and above that. If we demand it, I mean, as though God were unwilling to give ... ; of course he will give it, he won't cheat anyone.

Just consider this point, my brothers and sisters; notice how many good things the Lord our God gives to the bad: light, life, health, springs, the fruits of the earth, offspring; frequently also honors, high positions, places of authority. These are all good things which he gives to both good and bad alike. Are we to suppose that there is nothing which he keeps for the good, seeing that he gives so many good things even to the bad? None of us should entertain such a thought in our hearts. My brothers and sisters, God is keeping great goods for the good, but they are *what eye has not seen, nor ear heard, nor has it come up into the heart of man* (1 Cor 2:9). You can't conceive it before you receive it. You can see it when you receive it; to have some conception of it before you receive it, that you cannot do. What is it you want to see? ... It's not a guitar, not a flute, not a sound, which brings pleasure to the ears. What is it you wish to have some conception of? *It has not come up into the heart of man.*

And what am I to do? I can't see, can't hear, can't have any conception of it. What am I to do?

Believe. Faith is a great hold-all, a great jar in which you can receive a great gift. Get a jar ready for yourself, because you have to approach a great spring. What does that mean, get it ready? Let your faith grow, let it be enlarged, let it become strong; don't let your faith be slimy and muddy; let your faith be fired, not shattered, by the tribulations of this world.

But when you do this and have faith, like a suitable jar, capacious and strong, God will fill it. I mean, he won't say to you, as people say to someone who comes with a request, and says, "Please give me some wine, I beg you"; and the other says, "I'll give you some; come and I'll do it." He brings along a cask, and says, "I've come as you told me to." And the other answers, "I thought you would bring just one bottle; what's this you've brought, or where do you suppose you've come to? I haven't got enough to give so much. Take back the bigger receptacle you've brought, and bring something small; bring me something my poverty may be able to supply." That's not what God says; he's full, and you will be full when he has filled you up, and he will still have as much as he had before he filled you. God's gifts are lavish and plentiful, you can't find any such on earth. Believe, and you will prove the truth of this — but not now.

"And when?" you will ask.

Wait for the Lord, do manfully, and let your heart take courage (Ps 27:14); so that when you receive it, you can say, *You have given joy to my heart* (Ps 4:7).

Wait patiently

7. *Wait for the Lord, do manfully, and let your heart be strengthened, and wait for the Lord.* What does *Wait for the Lord* mean? Receive only when he gives, don't demand whenever you want. It's not yet the time for giving. He has waited for you, now wait for him. What's that I've just said, he has waited for you, now you wait for him? If you are now leading an upright life, if you have already turned back to him, if you are displeased with what you have done in the past, if you have now determined to choose a good new way of life — then don't be in a hurry to make demands of him. He waited patiently for you to change your bad way of life; now you just wait patiently for him to give you the prize for a good way of life. After all, if he hadn't waited patiently too, there wouldn't be anybody for him to give it to. So wait patiently, because you have been patiently waited for.

You though, who don't want to straighten yourself out, anyone there who still doesn't want to straighten yourself out — as though there were only one of you! I should rather have said, Whoever of you doesn't want to straighten himself out. You, though, standing there, having made no decision to put yourself right — let me speak like this as though to a single person. Whoever you are, you don't want to put yourself right; what are you promising yourself?

Are you perishing of despair or of hope? If you're perishing of despair, this is what you say to yourself: "My iniquity is overwhelming me, I'm wasting away in my sins. What hope have I got of living?" Listen to the prophet saying, *I have no wish for the death of the ungodly; only let the ungodly turn from his very evil way and live* (Ez 33:11). If you're perishing of hope, this is what you say to yourself: "God is good, God is merciful. God forgives everything, he doesn't pay back evil for evil." Listen to the apostle saying, *Do you not know that God's patience is drawing you to repentance?* (Rom 2:4).

So where are we? If I've made any impression on you, if what I've said has struck home, I see how you are going to answer me: "It's true, I'm not despairing, and so perishing of despair; nor am I hoping in a bad way so as to perish of hope. I don't say to myself, 'My iniquity is overwhelming me, I haven't any hope any more.' Nor do I say to myself, 'God is good, he doesn't pay back evil to anyone.' The prophet carries weight with me, so does the apostle."

So what do you say next? "I've still got a little time left to live how I like. These people are such a bore — so many of them, always pestering us. I've still got a little time to live as I like; later, when I've put myself straight, what the prophet said will of course be true: *I have no wish for the death of the ungodly, so much as that the ungodly may turn from his very evil way and live.* When I have been converted, he will wipe out all my evil deeds. Why shouldn't I add something to my pleasure, and live how I like as much as I like, and turn back to God later on?"

Why do you say this, brother?

"Why? Because God has promised me pardon if I change my ways."

I'm well aware, I know God has promised pardon. He promises this through the holy prophet, and he promises it through me, the least of his servants. It's perfectly true that he promises it, he has promised it through his only Son. But why do you want to pile evil days on evil days? *Sufficient unto the day be the evil thereof* (Mt 6:34). Yesterday a bad day, today as well a bad day, tomorrow too a bad day. Or do you think they are good days when you pander to your pleasures, when you pamper your heart with dissipation, when you set traps for another person's virtue, when you grieve your neighbor by cheating him, when you refuse to give back what has been entrusted to you, when you perjure yourself for cash? When you've indulged yourself in a good dinner, is that sufficient reason for thinking you've had a good day? Can the day possibly turn out good when the person spending it is bad? So you do want to pile bad days on bad days, don't you?

"I'm only asking," he says, "to be allowed a little more time."

Why?

"Because God has promised me pardon."

But no one has promised you that you are going to be alive tomorrow. Or else, just as you have read in the prophet, the gospel, the apostle that when you have turned back to him God will blot out all your iniquities, read out to me where a tomorrow is promised you, and then live in an evil way tomorrow.

Though of course, my brother or sister, I shouldn't really have said that to you. Perhaps you have a long life ahead of you. If it's a long one, let it be a good one. Why do you want to have a long, and bad, life? Either it won't be a long one, and you should be taking delight in that other long one which has no end; or else it will be a long one — and what harm will it do you to have lived a long life well? Do you really want to live a long life badly, don't you want to live it well? And for all that, nobody has promised you tomorrow.

Put yourself straight, listen to the scripture: *Do not be slow to turn to the Lord* (Sir 5:8). Those aren't my words — though yes, they are my words too. If I love they are mine. You try loving too, and they are yours. This sermon I'm now preaching comes from holy scripture. If you ignore it, it becomes your adversary. But now listen to the Lord saying, *Come to terms with your adversary quickly* (Mt 5:25).

What's the point of this terrifying sermon? You've come along to a joyful celebration, it's called the bishop's birthday today; should I be providing any fare to distress you? On the contrary, I'm providing something to give joy to the lover of God, and to annoy the one who ignores him; it's better for me to cause distress to the one who ignores God than to cheat the one who believes in him.

Be afraid with me, in order to rejoice with me

8. Let it be heard by all of you — I'm reciting the words of God's scripture. You in particular, you bad procrastinator with your bad longing for tomorrow, listen to the Lord speaking, listen to holy scripture preaching. I from this place of mine am only playing the part of a lookout. *Do not be slow to turn to the Lord, nor put it off from day to day.* See if he hasn't marked those people, see if he hasn't observed those people who say, "Tomorrow I'll live a good life, today let me live a bad one." And when tomorrow comes, you'll say the same thing again. *Do not be slow to turn to the Lord, nor put it off from day to day. For suddenly his wrath will come, and at the time for vengeance he will destroy you* (Sir 5:7).

Did I write that? Can I cross it out? If I cross it out, I'm afraid of being crossed out myself. I could keep quiet about it. I'm afraid of being kept quiet about! I'm compelled to preach it, in terror I aim to terrify. Be afraid with me, in order to rejoice with me. *Do not be slow to turn to the Lord.*

Lord, please note that I'm saying it. Lord, you know how you frightened me when your prophet was read. Here I am, saying it: *Do not be slow to turn to the Lord, nor put it off from day to day. For suddenly his wrath will come, and at the time for vengeance he will destroy you.* But I don't want him to destroy you. Nor do I want you to say to me, "I want to perish," because I, Augustine, don't want it. So my "I don't want it" is better than your "I do."

If your old father in your care had gone down with sleeping sickness, and you, a young man, were there with the sick old man, and the doctor said, "Your father's dangerously ill; this sleepiness is a mortal heaviness. Watch him, don't let him go to sleep. If you see him nodding off, shake him; if shaking's not enough, pinch him; and if even pinching's not enough, poke him, or your father may die." There you would be, a young man extremely troublesome to the old man. He would be relaxing and sinking into his pleasant disease; his eyes would be heavy with it, and he would close them. And you on the other hand would be shouting at your father, "Don't sleep!" But he would say, "Leave me alone. I want to sleep." And you would tell him, "But the doctor said, if he wants to sleep, don't let him." And he would say, "Please leave me alone; I want to die." "But I don't want it," says the son to his father. To whom? Clearly, to someone choosing to die. And still you want to postpone your father's death, and to live just a little longer with your old father, who is going to die soon anyway.

Well, the Lord is shouting at you, "Don't go to sleep, or you may sleep for ever. Wake up, to live with me, and to have a Father you will never have to carry to the grave." You hear — and you remain deaf.

Pray for the fulfillment of justice and the hallowing of God's name

9. So what have I been doing as a lookout? I'm free, I'm not really being a burden to you. I know what some of you are going to say: "What did he want to tell us? He scared us, coming down on us like a ton of bricks, making us guilty." On the contrary, I've been wanting to set you free from guilt. It's disgraceful, it's dishonorable — I won't say it's *wrong*, I won't say it's *dangerous*, I won't say it's *deadly* — it's dishonorable for me to deceive you, if God doesn't deceive me. It's the Lord who threatens the godless, the evildoers with death, cheats, rogues, scoundrels, adulterers, pleasure seekers, those who ignore him, who complain about the times and don't mend their ways; it's the Lord who threatens them with death, threatens them with hell, threatens them with everlasting destruction. What do they want? Me to promise them what he doesn't promise? Look here; an attorney gives you a guarantee; what use is it to you if his principal doesn't honor it? I'm just an attorney, just a servant. Do you want me to say to you, "Live how you like, the Lord won't destroy you"? The attorney has given you a guarantee; the attorney's guarantee is worthless. If only the Lord were giving it himself, and I were just trying to get you worried! After all, the Lord's guarantee would be worth something, even if I were against it; mine's worth nothing at all, if he's against it.

But what guarantee is there for any of us, brothers and sisters, for me or for you, except to listen seriously and carefully to the Lord's commands, and trustingly to wait for his promises? We grow tired of this, of course, being human; let us implore his help, let us send up our sighs to plead with him. We should not be praying for passing, worldly things, things that are come and gone and vanish like smoke. What we should be praying for is the fulfillment of justice, and the hallowing of God's name, not for getting the better of the person next door, but for getting the better of the lust and the greed inside; not for the healing of the flesh, but for the taming of avarice. That's what our prayers should be about; helping us in our inner struggles, till they crown us in our final victory.

Sermon 346A

On the Word of God as Leader of Christians on Their Pilgrimage

There is a dispute among scholars as to whether this is the transcript of a single homily or the recollection of a homily that was later reconstructed. Fischer, Kunzelmann, and Lambot agree on dating it to December of 399, based on a reference to the "games being staged" in section 7, presumably in conjunction with the *Saturnalia*. Augustine was rarely away from Hippo in the middle of winter. Hill is inclined to discount this, based on his sense that sections 7 and 8 are actually derived from another homily. Augustine discusses the hardships of following the narrow way and the necessity of staying on board the ark, the Church of Christ. Many of the rich will be saved because of their generosity while many of the poor will be condemned because of their greed. Augustine emphasizes human weakness and the need for Christ, the divine physician. Life's difficulties serve to remind us to stop loving earthly prosperity and to love and long for eternal life.

At a fork in the road on our journey through life stands a man, God made man, directing us to follow the hard rough road to the right, not the broad smooth road to the left

1. Brothers and sisters, we are Christians, and we all want to go on with the journey, and even if we don't want to, the journey is what in fact we have to go on with. Nobody is permitted to stay here; all who come into this life are compelled by the turning wheel of time to pass on. There must be no room for any kind of idleness; keep walking, or you will just be dragged along. As we travel on our journey we have been met at a fork in the road by a certain man; not just a man, in fact, but God who on man's account is man. And he has said to us, "Don't go to the left; that does indeed look an easy and delightful road to pass along, worn smooth by many, and broad; but at the end of that way lies ruin. But there's another way, which involves innumerable labors, difficulties, straitened circumstances, hardships; along which not only are there no delights to be found, but scarcely any humanity is shown either; a road you will have difficulty in walking along; but no sooner do you reach the end, than you come to the very pinnacle of joy, so that you avoid those traps and ambushes, which otherwise nobody can escape."

What the Word of God has foretold has always come true

2. Let us call past times to mind, and the holy scriptures. Isn't that man the Word of God? Didn't that very Word later on *become flesh, and dwell amongst us* (Jn 1:14)? Before he became flesh and dwelt amongst us, didn't that very Word speak through the prophets? God undoubtedly spoke by his Word to Abraham, that his stock was going to be wandering nomads; this though the man who was

told so was very old, and Sarah was an old and barren woman; he believed, it happened. That this stock, that is the people born from them according to the flesh, was going to endure slavery in Egypt for four hundred years; it happened. That it was to be delivered from that captivity; delivered it was. That it was going to receive the promised land; it received it. Things both far in the future and soon to occur were foretold, and they came about, and are now still being fulfilled.

The Word of God spoke through the prophets, that that nation would sin, to be delivered into the hands of their enemies because they offended against their God; it all happened. That it would go into captivity in Babylon; this too happened. That Christ the king would come from their stock; Christ came, Christ was born, because the Word himself declared that he would come himself. It was said that the Jews would crucify him; they did so. It was foretold that he would rise again and be glorified; it happened, he rose again, he ascended into heaven. It was foretold that the whole earth was going to believe in his name; foretold that kings would persecute his Church; this happened. It was foretold that kings were going to believe in him; we now have the faithfulness of kings before our eyes — and can we have doubts about the faithfulness of Christ? The lopping off of heresies was foretold; don't we see them too, and groan in the midst of the din they raise all round us? It was foretold that the very idols would be destroyed by means of the Church and the name of Christ; this too we can see being fulfilled. Scandals were foretold in the Church itself, tares too were foretold, chaff was foretold; all this we can also look on with our very own eyes, and we endure it with whatever fortitude we can muster, as granted us by the Lord.

In what respect has this man ever deceived you, the one who has told you, "Go this way"? Say yourself without the slightest hesitation, if you're a believer, with so much experience like that of the one who is speaking to you, "In all these things I find him true, because he has seen fit to be proved true in this way. If he is always telling me the truth, he never deceives me; all this that he says, I hold it all to be true, in no instance has he lied; that's what I know he's like. He is the Word of God; he has spoken through the mouths of his servants, and hasn't deceived me; can what he says from his own mouth be deceitful?" As for the one to whom he is not yet known, who still has his doubts about Christ, let him too say, "I will go this way, in case perhaps he's telling the truth, the one in whom the whole world has now come to believe."

We have to make sure of being in the ark, which is the Church,
if we are to be saved on the last day

3. My brothers and sisters, many who don't believe, or listen to the voice of the holy Fathers, will inevitably find themselves in the same case as that multitude found itself in during the days of Noah; the only ones to escape destruction were those who were in the ark. I mean, if they stopped to think, and changed their ways from their ungodliness and were converted to our Lord, they would make amends

for their crimes and misdemeanors, and begging with sighs and groans for his mercy they would most certainly not perish. God, after all, was not unmerciful toward Nineveh, which earned its salvation in three days. What a short period three days is! Yet for all that they didn't despair, with such little time available, of God's mercy, or of inclining him to clemency. So if such a great city as that had only the space of three days in which to incline God towards mercy, how much more could be done in the space of a hundred years, and two hundred, and three hundred, during which the ark was being constructed! From the moment Christ began to fell logs immune to decay from the forests of the nations, that is for constructing the Church, if those people would only change their ways and habits, if they would only appease God by offering him the sacrifice of a contrite heart, they would without the slightest doubt escape unharmed.

So then, people should all be afraid of finding themselves in such a case on that last day. But we too, brothers and sisters, should take steps to change our ways from ungodliness, and to mend our behavior while we have the time, so that that day may find us prepared; because he never lies, the one who says that it is going to come. Beware of doubting it, because it's true. That, after all, is how it was in the days of Noah: *They were eating, drinking, being married, marrying wives, buying, selling, until Noah entered the ark, the flood came and destroyed them all* (Lk 17:21), those who were placing their hopes in this world, and were eager to live in security, but not in the region of security, and none escaped except those who were in the ark.

So does this mean, if we wish to enter the kingdom of heaven,
we mustn't marry, or eat and drink, or buy and sell?

4. But now there are many people saying to themselves, "We are bidden to wait for that day, and not to be found like those who found themselves outside the ark and who perished in that flood. Most certainly, the trumpet call of the gospel terrifies us, the word of God frightens us out of our wits; what are we to do? So does it mean we shouldn't marry wives?" That's what a young man will say, or a growing lad. "So is there to be no eating, no drinking, just fasting all the time?" There are many who will be saying that. And those perhaps who were thinking of buying something will say to themselves, "So is nothing to be bought now, in case we should find ourselves numbered among those who perished in the flood?"

So what are we to do, brothers and sisters? If that's really the case, then it's a matter for lamentation, rather as the apostles felt shock for the human race, when they heard the Lord saying, *If you wish to be perfect, sell all your possessions and give to the poor, and you shall have treasure in heaven; and come, follow me* (Mt 19:21). The man who was told this was shocked, and went away; and while he had called the one, from whom he had sought advice about eternal life, *good master*, he only seemed to be a good master, while the man was able to give correct answers to what he was asked about. The Lord spoke, and the rich man was shattered. But as that man went sadly away, the Lord said, *With what difficulty does the rich man enter the kingdom of heaven!* (Mt 19:23) — as though the kingdom of heaven is shut in the face of the rich. What will happen? It's shut. But he also said, *Knock, and it will be opened to you* (Lk 11:9). And if only as few were to go into the fire as there are rich! But now as it is, many who are numbered among the rich are going to go into the kingdom of heaven, and of those counted among the poor many are going to go into eternal fire, not because they are rich in means, but because they are on fire with greed.

Nor should the rich despair because of what is said
about a camel and the eye of a needle

5. The disciples, though, were shattered. The Lord then said, "What is difficult for men is easy for God (Lk 18:27). You were upset by the difficulty, because I mentioned a camel; if it wishes, that enormous beast which is called a camel, can come in here through the eye of a needle." What can this mean? Let's see if it can be shown how. It's not without significance, you see, that John the Baptist too, the forerunner of the Lord himself, had a garment of camel's hair, as though he got his cloak from the judge who was coming after him, to whom he was bearing witness. Let us recognize in the camel mentioned a type of our Lord Jesus Christ; let us mark how great it is, and yet of so humble a neck, that nobody can put a load on it with his own hands, unless it lowers itself to the earth. In the same way Christ too *humbled himself to the death* (Phil 2:8), in order *to destroy the one who had the power of death, that is, the devil* (Heb 2:14). So let's see what the eye of the needle is, through which so great a one came in. Well, in the prick of a needle we can see the sufferings which he spontaneously endured, while in its eye we can see the straits he was reduced to. So now the camel has entered through the eye of a needle; the rich needn't despair; let them enter the kingdom of heaven without a worry in the world.

Poverty as such does not guarantee entry into the kingdom
just as wealth in itself does not result in exclusion

6. But let us realize what sort of rich people. Here comes heaven knows who across our path, wrapped in rags, and he has been jumping for joy and laughing on hearing it said that the rich man can't enter the kingdom of heaven; and he's been saying, "I, though, will enter; that's what these rags will earn me; those who treat us badly and insult us, those who bear down hard upon us won't enter; no, that sort certainly won't enter."

"But just a minute, Mr Poor Man; consider whether you can, in fact, enter. What if you're poor, and also happen to be greedy? What if you're sunk in destitution, and at the same time on fire with avarice? So if that's what you're like, whoever you are that are poor, it's not because you haven't wanted to be rich, but because you haven't been able to. So God doesn't inspect your means, but he observes your will. So if that's what you're like, leading a bad life, of bad morals, a blasphemer, an adulterer, a drunkard, proud, cross yourself off the list of God's poor; you won't be among those of whom it is said, *Blessed are the poor in spirit, since theirs is the kingdom of heaven* (Mt 5:3).

"And here I find a rich man like that — in comparison with whom you've flaunted yourself, and had the nerve to cast your eyes on the kingdom of heaven — I find him poor in spirit; that is, humble, godfearing, innocent, not a blasphemer, following God's will; and if by any chance he has lost in business failures any of this world's goods, he says at once, *The Lord has given, the Lord has taken away; as it pleased the Lord, so has it happened; may the Lord's name be blessed forever* (Jb 1:21). Here you have a rich man who's gentle, humble, doesn't resist, doesn't grumble, follows God's will, and finds his joy in that land of the living; *Blessed,* you see, *are the gentle, because they shall possess the land for their inheritance* (Mt 5:4).

"You, though, are perhaps poor, and proud. I praise the humble rich man; don't I also praise the humble poor man? The poor man has no reason to be conceited, while the rich man has, and he has to struggle against it. This man more than you, this rich man will enter, and against you the kingdom of heaven will be shut, because it will be shut in the face of the godless, of the proud, of the blasphemer, of the adulterer, of the drunkard, it will be shut in the face of the greedy and the grasping. The one who has trusted the promises made has acquired a trustworthy debtor."

But the rich man who is humble, humane, faithful, has this answer to make, and he says, "God is well aware I am not haughty in my ideas; and if I happen to shout sometimes, and say anything harsh, God knows my conscience, that I say these things out of the need to exercise authority; I never, for that reason, consider myself a cut above other people."

"God sees inside the works which follow; those, you see, who are rich in good works give things away easily, they share with the person who has nothing. That, after all, is where humility shows itself, if you are rich and humble. You maintain you are good and godfearing; let what you have be shared between you and the one who hasn't got anything, so that you may store up for yourself a good foundation for the future, in order to obtain the true and blessed life."

If they are like that, they need have no worries; when that last day comes, they find themselves in the ark. They will be part of its fabric, they won't be the prey of the flood. They shouldn't panic, just because they're rich. And if he's a young man, and cannot embrace celibacy, he is certainly allowed to marry a wife. But, because *the time is short, let those who have wives be as though they did not have them, and those who buy as though they did not, and those who weep as though they were not weeping, and those who rejoice as though they were not rejoicing, and those who make use of this world as though they were not doing so; for the form of this world is passing away* (1 Cor 7:29-31).

The judge is certainly going to come, so let us correct ourselves before he does

7. My brothers and sisters, someone will grumble against God and say, "The times are bad, the times are hard, the times are irksome."

And yet the games are being staged, and the times are called hard! How much harder are you, who fail to correct yourself in these hard times! All this crazy parade and ostentation still at full flood, all these superfluous luxuries and pleasures eagerly awaited, and there's no end or limit to greed. How sick our society becomes in the middle of all this! How much licentious self-indulgence has bubbled up everywhere because of the theatres, the organs, the flutes and the dancers! You want to make bad use of what you are aiming at; that's why you won't get it. Listen to the voice of an apostle; *You desire, and you do not have; you kill and you envy and cannot obtain; you quarrel, you ask, and you do not receive, because you ask badly, so that you are eaten up with your desires* (Jas 4:2-3).

Let us come to our senses, brothers and sisters, let us correct ourselves. The judge is going to come, and although he has come in one way, he is still being mocked; he is going to come, and then there will be no room for mockery. My dearest brothers and sisters, let us correct ourselves, because better times are going to come along, but not for those who lead bad lives. This age is already on the wane, and has declined toward old age. Are we going to come back to its youth, and ours? What have we here to hope for? We should already be looking for something else. Don't hope for other times, except for such as we can read of in the gospel. The times are not bad because Christ has come; but because they were bad and hard, one came who would bring us comfort.

Christ has come to heal us; but in this life the treatment is necessarily painful

8. Listen, my brothers and sisters; it was necessary, you see, for the times to be irksome, to be hard. How would we cope, if such a wonderful comforter were not present? The human race was gravely ill, from Adam right up to the end. From the moment we are born here, ever since we were turned out of paradise, life is clearly an illness; but at the end this was going to become more serious, with a possibility of taking a turn toward a recovery of health, and for some toward death. So since the human race was so ill, that great doctor takes over the care of the patient lying in a kind of huge bed, that is in the whole world — but just as any very skilled and experienced doctor observes the periods of an illness, and takes note and looks forward to what turns it is going to take; and first in the milder stages of the patient's illness he sends his assistants; in the same way our doctor too first sent the prophets to examine us. They spoke, they preached; through them he cured a certain number, and restored them to health. They foretold a future critical climax for the malady, and a severe agitation of

the patient, for whom the presence of the doctor himself would be needed, and his coming to him in person. And that's what happened.

He came, he was made man, sharing our mortality so that we might be given a share of his immortality. The sick man is still restlessly tossing about; and as he's panting and sweating copiously in his fever, he says to himself, "Ever since this doctor came, I've been suffering worse fevers, been more severely affected, been subject to frightful turmoil. What did he come to me for? I don't think it was for the best that he entered my house." That's what they all say, those who are still sick from the vanity of the world. Why does the vanity of the world make them ill? Because they won't accept from him the curative potion of moderation.

Seeing the poor wretches being tossed about with their anxieties, and preoccupied with the various concerns of this age, which are stifling their souls, God came as the doctor. And they're not afraid of saying, "Ever since Christ came, we have been suffering these times; ever since there have been Christians, the world has been falling entirely to pieces."

You stupid patient! It's not because the doctor has come that your illness has become graver; the doctor, good, considerate, just, merciful as he is, foresaw that; obviously, he didn't cause it. He came, after all, to bring you relief, so that you might really get better. I mean, what is he taking away from you, but what is simply superfluous? You see, you were panting after things that injure your health, and becoming addicted to them; the things you were gasping for were not good for your fever. Is the doctor being rough, when he snatches from the hands of his patient some fruits that are bad for him? What has he deprived you of, but a misguided sense of security which you were on the point of grasping? Rid yourself of your pernicious gut reactions; and then you will see that all this that you are groaning and grumbling about is part of your cure. Don't suffer torments against your will by being unwilling to be cured.

It's absolutely necessary that the times should be harsh. Why? To stop us loving earthly prosperity. It's vital, and it's good medicine, that this life should be troubled, and the other life loved. Look here; if human idleness can still be delighted by such earthly things as the race-course and the games, what would it be like if their activities were never blighted with misfortune? Here they are, mixed up with so many bitter elements, and still the world is so sweet!

Sermon 355

First Sermon on the Way of Life of His Clergy

This sermon is invaluable for the information it gives us about the life of a local church, in particular the expectations that Bishop Augustine had about the lifestyle of his own clergy. It was preached after Christmas, either at the end of December 425 or the beginning of January, shortly before Epiphany, 426 and is an excellent example of Augustine's transparency and sense of accountability to the people of God. He had asked as many as possible to attend in order to discuss a scandal involving the local clergy. He reviews the circumstances of his arrival in Hippo, when he was looking for a place to establish a monastery and to interview a potential recruit. He found himself pressed into service, ordained a priest in 391 and a bishop in 395 by Bishop Valerius, who provided land where Augustine could continue living in community. All the members of the community were expected to renounce private property and follow the ideal spelled out in Acts 4:32, *Nobody called anything their own, but they had all things in common.* Augustine naively expected the best from his fellow monks and failed to make sure that they had divested themselves of property. It came to the attention of all that one priest, Januarius, had not done so and that supposedly he was holding onto some assets for the sake of his daughter. As Januarius drew near to death he made out a will and bequeathed his assets to the church of Hippo. Augustine decided to refuse the inheritance and directed that the assets be returned to the children of Januarius as the rightful heirs. He accounts for all such legacies which were made under his stewardship. Bishops, he says, are held to higher standards than civil law. Augustine gives his fellow clerics in community a deadline to divest themselves of their properly; for the sake for those who are disinclined, he agrees to change his policy and allow them to remain as clerics, but they must leave the community rather than live as hypocrites. Here Augustine makes a vital distinction between the vocation to religious life (based on an inner prompting of the Holy Spirit to live a life of holiness) and the vocation to the priesthood (an outward call to service in the Church).

An important distinction between one's conscience and one's reputation

1. What I'm going to talk about is the matter for which I wanted your graces to come here today in greater numbers than usual, as I asked you to yesterday. We live here with you, and we live here for you; and my intention and wish is that we may live with you in Christ's presence forever. I think our way of life is plain for you to see; so that I too may perhaps make bold to say what the apostle said, though I can't of course be compared with him: *Be imitators of me, as I too am of Christ* (1 Cor 4:16). And that's why I don't want any of you to find an excuse for living badly. *For we aim at what is good*, says the same apostle, *not only in the sight of God, but also in the sight of men* (2 Cor 8:21).

As far as we are concerned, our consciences are all that matters; as far as you are concerned, our reputation among you ought not to be tarnished, but influential for good. Mark what I've said, and make the distinction. There are two things, conscience and reputation; conscience for yourself, reputation for your neighbor. Those who, being clear in their consciences, neglect their reputations, are being cruel; especially if they find themselves in this position, a position about which the apostle says, when he writes to his disciple, *Showing yourself to all around you as an example of good works* (Ti 2:7).

How Augustine established a monastery in the bishop's house

2. So then, in order not to detain you long, especially because I am sitting down as I talk, while you will soon get tired as you're standing: you all know, or almost all of you, that we live in the house which is called the bishop's house in such a way as to imitate, to the best of our ability, those holy people about whom the book of the Acts of the Apostles says, *Nobody called anything their own, but they had all things in common* (Acts 4:32). But some of you, perhaps, are not such keen examiners of the way we live that you know this in the way I would like you to know it; so let me spell out in more detail what I have just said in a few words.

I, whom by God's grace you see before you as your bishop, came to this city as a young man; many of you know that. I was looking for a place to establish a monastery, and live there with my brothers. I had in fact left behind all worldly hopes, and I did not wish to be what I could have been; nor, however, was I seeking to be what I am now. *I have chosen to be a nobody in the house of my God, rather than to dwell in the tents of sinners* (Ps 84:10). I separated myself from those who love the world; but I did not put myself on an equal footing with those who preside over Churches. Nor did I choose a higher place at the banquet of my Lord, but a lower, insignificant one; and he was pleased to say to me, *Go up higher* (Lk 14:10). So much, though, did I dread the episcopate, that since I had already begun to acquire a reputation of some weight among the servants of God, I wouldn't go near a place where I knew there was no bishop. I avoided this job, and I did everything I could to assure my salvation in a lowly position, and not to incur the grave risks of a high one. But, as I said, a servant ought not to oppose his Lord. I came to this city to see a friend, whom I thought I could gain for God, to join us in the monastery. It seemed safe enough, because the place had a bishop. I was caught, I was made a priest, and by this grade I eventually came to the episcopate.

I brought nothing with me; I came to this Church with only the clothes I was wearing at the time. And because what I was planning was to be in a monastery with the brothers, Father Valerius of blessed memory, having learned of my purpose and desire, gave me that plot where the monastery now is. I began to gather together brothers of good will, my companions in poverty, having nothing just like me, and imitating me. Just as I had sold my slender poor man's property and distributed the proceeds to the poor, those who wished to stay with me did the same, so that we might live on what we had in common. But what would be our really great and profitable common estate was God himself.

I arrived at the episcopate. I saw that the bishop is under the necessity of showing hospitable kindness to all visitors and travelers; indeed, if a bishop didn't do that he would be said to be lacking in humanity. But if this custom were transferred to the monastery it would not be fitting. And that's why I wanted to have a monastery of clergy in this bishops' residence. This then is how we live; nobody in our company is allowed to have any private property. But perhaps some do have some; nobody's allowed to; if any do have it, they are doing what is not allowed. But I have a good opinion of my brothers, and believing the best of them, I have always refrained from making any inquiries, because to make such inquiries would, so it seemed to me, indicate I had a low opinion of them. I knew, you see, and I still know, that all who were living with me knew about our purpose, knew about the law governing our life together.

The case of Januarius

3. We were also joined by the priest Januarius. He seemed to get rid of all he had by honestly distributing it, but he didn't get rid of it all. Some assets, that is, some money, remained with him, which he said was his daughter's. His daughter, by God's grace, is in a monastery of women, and we have good hopes for her. May the Lord direct her course, so that she may fulfill our hopes for her, by his mercy, not by her own merits. And because she was under age, and could do nothing with her own assets — while we could appreciate the splendid sincerity of her profession, we had some fears about the slipperiness of youth — it was arranged that that money should be kept, as if it were the girl's, so that when she came of age, she could do with it what befitted one of Christ's virgins, when she could do it finally to best advantage.

Before this time came, he himself drew near to death; and swearing consistently that it was his own, not his daughter's, he made a will about it. A priest, a companion of ours, staying together with us, living on the Church, professing the common life, made, I'm telling you, a will. He made a will, he said who would be his heirs. Oh, what a sad blow for that company of ours! What fruit, not produced by the tree which the Lord had planted! He made the Church his heir. I don't want these gifts, I don't like the taste of such bitter fruit. I myself had recruited him for God, he had made profession in our company: this is what he would keep to, this is what he would observe. He would have nothing? He shouldn't make a will. He had something? He shouldn't pretend to be our companion as one of God's poor.

This has been a great grief to me, brothers and sisters. I'm telling your graces, on account of this grief I have decided not to accept this inheritance for the Church. Let what he left belong to his children, let them do with it what they like. It seems to me, you see, that if I were to accept it, by that very fact I would be his partner in an action that displeases me and causes me real pain. This is what I did not wish to conceal from your graces. His daughter is in a monastery of women, his son in a monastery of men. He disinherited both of them; her, with words of praise, him with a clause in the will severely censuring him. Now I have recommended the

Church not to accept such legacies, which really belong to disinherited children, except when they have come of age. The Church keeps such property for them.

Then again, he has left his children an occasion for a quarrel which troubles me greatly. The girl says, "It's mine, you know that my father always said that." The boy says, "My father should be believed, because he couldn't possibly lie when he was dying." And what a really bad thing this wrangling is! But if these children are both servants of God, we can quickly put an end to this dispute between them. I will listen to them as a father, and perhaps better than their own father. I will see what the rights of the matter are, as God wills, together with a few of the faithful and respected brethren taken, by God's favor, from among your number, that is from this congregation. I will hear the case between them, and as the Lord grants us, I will settle it.

Augustine's policy about legacies left to the Church, and his answer to some critics

4. All the same, please, don't let any of you blame me because I don't want the Church to receive this legacy; first, because I detest his action; secondly, because it's my policy. Many of you will praise what I am going to say, but some too will criticize it. It's very hard to satisfy both parties. You heard just now when the gospel was read, *We have sung to you, and you did not dance; we have wailed for you, and you did not mourn. John came, neither eating nor drinking, and they say, He has a devil. The Son of man came, eating and drinking, and they say, Look, a greedy man, a toper of wine, a friend of taxmen* (Lk 7:31-34). So what am I to do in the face of those who are ready to find fault with me and bring their teeth to bear on me, if I accept legacies from those who are disinheriting their children in anger? Again, what am I going to do with those to whom I sing, and they refuse to dance? Those who say, "Look why nobody gives anything to the Church of Hippo; look why those who are dying don't make it their heir. It's because bishop Augustine in his goodness" — you see, they are biting me by their very praise, caressing with their lips, and digging their teeth in — "waives everything, accepts nothing."

I certainly do accept things, I assure you I accept good offerings, holy offerings. But if anyone is angry with his son, and disinherits him on his deathbed, if he lived, wouldn't I try to placate him? Wouldn't I have the duty to reconcile him with his son? So how can I wish him to be at peace with his son, when I have my eyes on his inheritance? But certainly, if he does what I have often urged people to do — he has one child, let him think of Christ as the second; he has two, let him think of Christ as the third; he has ten, let him make Christ the eleventh, and I will accept it. So because I have done this in a number of cases, they now wish to turn my goodness, or their estimate of my reputation, in another direction, to find fault with me in another way, that I refuse to accept the offerings of the devout. They should consider how many I have accepted. What's the point of listing them all? Here you are, I'll just mention one; I accepted the inheritance of Julian's son. Why? Because he died without children.

The case of Boniface's legacy

5. I refused to accept the legacy of Boniface, not out of softheartedness, but out of fear. I didn't want the Church of Christ to be a shipping company. There are indeed many people who make a fortune from ships. Yet should there be just one mishap, should a ship go aground and be wrecked, were we going to hand people over to the torture, at the customary marine inquest into the loss of a vessel, and have those who had been saved from the waves tortured by the judge? But we would not hand them over; no way, I mean, would it be proper for the Church to do that. So would it pay the resultant fine and damages? But what would it pay them from? It's not right for us to keep a reserve fund; it's not the bishop's business to save up gold, and repulse the beggar's outstretched hand. There are so many asking every day, so many groaning, so many needy people pleading, that we have to leave several of them unhappy, because we haven't got enough to give all of them something; and should we set up a fund to insure against shipwreck? So it was to avoid this that I did it, not out of generosity. Nobody need praise me for it, but nobody should blame me either.

Certainly, when I have granted a son what his father, dying in anger, took away from him, I have done well. Let those who wish praise me, those who don't want to praise me, at least spare me. What more, my brothers and sisters? Anyone who wants to make the Church his heir after disinheriting his son, should look for someone else to accept the legacy, not Augustine; or rather, by God's grace, may he not find anyone to take it. How that admirable action of the holy and venerable bishop Aurelius of Carthage filled the mouths of all who knew about it with the praises of God! Someone who had no children, and apparently no hope of any, gave all his property to the Church, keeping only the use of it to himself during his life. Children were in fact born to him, and the bishop gave back the endowment he had made, without his in the least expecting it. The bishop had the right not to give it back — but according to the civil law, not according to the law of heaven.

Augustine's change of policy about depriving of their clerical status those who do not keep his rules

6. Certainly your graces should also know this, that I have told my brothers, who stay with me that anyone who possesses anything should either sell it and distribute the proceeds, or donate it to the common fund; let the Church have it, through which God provides for us. And I have given them until Epiphany, for the sake of those who either haven't divided their property with their families, and have left what they have with their brothers, or who have not yet done anything about what is theirs, because they were waiting till they came of age. Let them do whatever they like with it, provided they are prepared to be poor together with me, and we all look together for support purely and simply to the mercy of God. But if they don't want to do this, as perhaps some don't — well certainly I'm the one, as you know, who determined to ordain no one a cleric unless he were willing to stay

with me; on such terms that if he chose to turn away from his purpose, I would have the right to deprive him of his clerical status, because he was throwing over his membership in a sacred association, which he had promised and begun.

Well here and now, in the presence of God and of yourselves, I am changing my policy: those who wish to keep some private property, for whom God and the Church are not enough, may stay where they like and where they can; I will not deprive them of their clerical status. I don't want to have any hypocrites. It's bad — who would deny it? — it's bad to fall away from one's commitment; but it's worse to pretend to have such a commitment. Look, this is what I am saying, listen: someone who deserts the fellowship of the common life which he has taken on, which is praised in the Acts of the Apostles, is falling away from his vow, falling away from his holy profession. He should watch out for a judge — but God, not me. I myself am not depriving him of his clerical status. I have set before his eyes what great danger he is in; let him do what he likes. You see, I know that if I decide to degrade someone who does this, he won't lack patrons, he won't lack supporters, both here and among bishops, to say, "What has he done wrong? He's unable to take this kind of life with you; he wants to stay outside the bishop's residence, he wants to live on his own income; should he forfeit his clerical status for that?"

I for my part know what an evil it is to make a holy commitment and not carry it through. *Make your vows*, it says, *and pay them to the Lord your God* (Ps 76:11); and, *It is better not to make a vow than to make one and not perform it* (Eccl 5:4). Take a virgin, for example; if she was never in a monastery, and is a dedicated virgin, it is not lawful for her to marry. She isn't compelled to be in a monastery; if however she has started off living in a monastery, and left it, and yet remains a virgin, half her life has collapsed. In the same way a cleric too has made a commitment to two things: both holiness of life and the clerical state. The holiness, meanwhile — as for the clerical state, God has placed it on his shoulders through the people; it's more of a burden than an honor, but *who is wise and understands these things?* (Ps 107:43) — so he has made a commitment to holiness; he has committed himself to live together in a community, he has professed *how good and pleasant it is, brothers dwelling in unity* (Ps 133:1). If he falls away from this commitment, and remains outside as a cleric, he too has fallen away from half his life. What's it got to do with me? I'm not judging him.

If he preserves sanctity of life outside, he has fallen away from half his life; if he stays inside and is just pretending, he has ruined the whole of it. I don't want him to have any need to pretend. I know how men love the clerical state; I won't deprive anyone of it who doesn't want to live in community with me. Those who wish to live with me have God. If they are prepared to be provided for by God through his Church, not to have any private property, but either to distribute it to the poor or put it in the common fund, let them stay with me. Those who don't want this may consider themselves free; but they should also consider whether they can have eternal felicity.

A further report on the situation promised after Epiphany

7. That must be enough for your graces for the time being. What I do with my brethren — I have good hopes, you see, that they will all obey me willingly, and that I am not going to find any of them possessing anything, except by necessity of religion, not out of sheer possessiveness — so what I do, I will inform your graces after Epiphany as God wills; and I won't conceal from you how I settle the dispute between the brother and sister, the two children of the priest Januarius. I have talked at length; please excuse the talkativeness of old age, that is also the timidity of ill-health. I, as you can see, have now grown old in years; ill-health made me an old man long ago. Still, if God is pleased with what I have said now, he will give me strength, I won't let you down. Pray for me, that as long as there is a soul in this body, and any kind of strength supplied to it, I may serve you in preaching the word of God.

Sermon 368

Sermon of Augustine the Bishop Preached on the Text,
Whoever Loves His Soul Will Lose It

All agree that this beautiful homily is an authentic sermon of Augustine even though it comes down to us through the works of Caesarius of Arles. Hill is inclined to date the sermon to Augustine's old age, between 424 and 430, when his approach had tended to soften and when his homilies became noticeably briefer. The bishop promotes a healthy love of self based on the seeming paradox of self-abnegation espoused by John 12: 25, *Whoever loves his soul will lose it.* Each and every person must begin by love of self, an innate instinct, before moving on to love of God and love of neighbor. This is seen in the universal tendency of all creatures toward self-preservation.

If nobody ever hated his own flesh, much less did anyone ever hate his own soul

1. Just now, brothers and sisters, while the divine reading was being read, we heard the Lord saying, *Whoever loves his soul will lose it* (Jn 12:25). This statement seems to be contradicted by what the apostle says: *Nobody ever hated his own flesh* (Eph 5:29). So if there's nobody who ever hated his own flesh, how much less anybody who ever hated his own soul? The soul, clearly, is much more important than the flesh, because it is the inhabitant, the flesh merely the dwelling; and the soul is the master, the flesh the servant; the soul the superior, the flesh the subject. So if nobody ever hated his own flesh, who can there ever have been to hate his own soul?

That being the case, the present reading from the gospel has landed us with no small problem; because in it we heard *Whoever loves his soul will lose it.* It's dangerous to love the soul, or it may perish. But if the reason it is dangerous for you to love your soul is that it may thereby perish, the reason why you ought not to love it is that you don't want it to perish. But if you don't want it to perish, that means you love it.

"But because I'm afraid of losing it, that's why I don't love it — and of course, what I'm afraid of losing, I love ... "

And the Lord says somewhere else, *What does it profit a man, if he gains the whole world, but suffers the loss of his own soul?* (Mt 16:26). There you have it, that the soul is to be so loved as to be preferred to gaining the whole world; and yet the one who loves his soul is to observe that if he loves it he will lose it. You don't want to lose it? Don't love it. But if you don't want to lose it, you cannot not love it.

The wrong kind of love of the soul which springs from hatred,
and the right kind of hatred of the soul which springs from love

2. So there are people who love their souls in the wrong way; and this is what the word of God means to correct — not that they should hate their souls, but that they should love them in the right way. It's by loving them badly, you see, that they lose them, and you're left with an enormous kind of back to front contradiction; still the fact remains, that if you love it in the wrong way you will lose it, if you hate it in the right way you will keep it safe. So there is a certain wrong way of loving the soul, and a certain right way of hating it; but the wrong way of loving springs from hatred, and the right way of hating springs from love.

What's the wrong way of loving the soul? When you love your soul in all kinds of iniquity. Listen to how this wrong kind of love springs from hatred: *But whoever loves iniquity, hates his own soul* (Ps 11:5). Observe on the other hand how the right kind of hatred springs from love: in the same place the Lord went on to say, *But whoever hates his soul in this age will find it for eternal life* (Jn 12:25). Obviously, you love very much what you wish to find for eternal life. What use, after all, is what you love for a time? Either you are removed from it, or it is removed from you; when it's you that are eliminated, what ceases to be is the actual lover; when that thing is eliminated, what vanishes is what you loved. So where either the lover ceases to be or the thing loved, it's not worth loving. But what is worth loving? What can be with us forever? If you want to have your soul safe forever, hate it for a time. So the right way of hating springs from love; the wrong way of loving springs from hatred.

The right kind of love must drive out the wrong kind

3. What, then, is the right way of loving the soul? Do you imagine the martyrs didn't love their souls? You can certainly see nowadays, if anyone is in peril of his life, life of this present age, how his friends rush around to save it; how they rush off to the church, how the bishop is begged to intervene; if there is anything he can

do, to be quick about it, to hurry up. Why all this? For the sake of a soul. And everyone is agitated, each one decides to drop every other business and get a move on; all haste is applauded, all delay complained of. Why? For the sake of a soul. What does that mean, for the sake of a soul? So that a man should not die. Didn't the martyrs know how to love their souls? And yet all this is for the sake of a soul, so that a man should not die.

A person's real death is iniquity. If you run a hundred miles for the sake of this life, how many miles should you run for the sake of eternal life? If you are in such a hurry to gain a few days, and those so uncertain — I mean, the man delivered from death today doesn't know whether he'll die tomorrow — still if there's all this rushing around to gain a few days, because even up to old age our days are few, how much rushing around should there be for the sake of eternal life? And yet people are so sluggish and slow about taking any steps toward it. You will have difficulty in finding even someone who has suffered making slow, hesitant moves for the sake of eternal life. So there's plenty of the wrong sort of love around; while very few people have the right sort of love. I mean, just as there's nobody who doesn't love his own soul, so too there's nobody who doesn't love his own flesh. So it can happen that both what the apostle said is true: *Nobody ever hated his own flesh* (Eph 5:29), and that the soul is not truly loved.

So let us learn then, brothers and sisters, how to love our own souls. Every pleasure provided by the world is going to pass away. There is a love that is useful and a love that does harm. Let love be hampered by love; let the love that does harm retire, and the love that is of use take its place. But it's because people don't want to retire from that sort, that this other sort can't gain entry to them. They are full up, so they can't hold anything else. They must pour something out, and then they can hold some more. They are full, you see, of the love of sensual pleasures, full of the love of this present life, full of the love of gold and silver, of the possessions of this world. So those who are full in this way are like jars. Do you want honey to gain entry into a jar from which you haven't yet emptied the vinegar? Empty out what you have, in order to take and hold what you don't yet have. That's why the first step is to renounce this world, and then the next is to turn back to God. When you renounce, you are emptying out; when you turn back to God, you are being filled — but only if it's done, not merely with the body, but also with the heart.

The right order of love, and progress in it

4. The question arises, brothers and sisters, how this love grows. You see, it has its beginnings, it has its increase, it has its perfection. And we clergy need to know who are just beginning, so that we may encourage them to increase; who haven't even begun, so that we may advise them where to begin; who have both begun and grown, so that we may urge them on toward perfection. The first thing for your graces to note is this: what people always love and value before anything else is themselves, and from there they go on to value other things. If you value gold, you first value yourself, and from there gold; because if you were to die, there wouldn't

be anyone to possess the gold. So with each and every one of us love begins with oneself, and cannot but begin with oneself. And nobody needs to be advised to love himself; this is innate, after all, not only in human beings but also in animals. After all, you can see, brothers and sisters, how not only huge wild beasts and large animals, like oxen and camels and elephants, but also flies, but also the tiniest little worms, how they don't want to die, and how they love themselves. All animals shrink from death. So they love themselves, they want to take care of themselves; some do it by speed, others by hiding, others by resisting and fighting back. All animals, nevertheless fight for their lives, they don't want to die, they want to take care of themselves. So they love themselves.

Something else also starts being loved. But what is this something else? Whatever it is you have loved, it is either the same as yourself, or it is inferior to you, or it is superior to you. If what you love is inferior to you, love it to console yourself with, love it as something to work at, love it as something to use, not as something to tie yourself to. For example, you love gold; don't tie yourself to gold. How much better are you than gold? Gold, after all, is shining earth; you though were made to the image of God in order to be illuminated by God. Since gold is one of God's creatures, yet it wasn't gold that God made to his image, but you; it follows that he placed gold under you. So this sort of love is to be treated lightly. Such things as these are to be acquired for use; one mustn't let oneself be stuck to them, as with glue, by the bonds of love. You shouldn't make extra limbs for yourself, which will cause you great pain and torment when they start being lopped of. So what, then? Rise up from this love by which you love things lower than you are; start loving things that are your equals, that, are the same as you are. But what need is there of many examples? If you want, you can do it very shortly.

A quick way to reach the perfection of love

5. In fact the Lord himself has told us in the gospel, and made it abundantly clear, what the proper order is for our obtaining true love and true charity. This is how he put it: *You shall love the Lord your God with your whole heart, and with your whole soul, and with all your strength; and your neighbor as yourself* (Mk 12:30-31). So first of all, love God, then yourself; after that love your neighbor as yourself. First learn, though, how to love yourself, and in this way love your neighbor as yourself; because if you don't know how to love yourself, how will you be able to love your neighbor in truth? Some people, you see, assume that they are appropriately and legitimately loving themselves, when they snatch other people's property, when they get drunk, when they make themselves the slaves of lust, when by a variety of false slurs they make unjust profits. Such people as these should listen to scripture saying, *Whoever loves iniquity, hates his own soul* (Ps 11:5). So if by loving iniquity you not only don't love yourself, but in fact hate yourself, how will you be able to love either God or your neighbor?

So if you want to keep the order of true charity, act justly, love mercy, shun self-indulgence; begin, according to the Lord's instruction to love not only friends but also enemies. And when you strive to maintain these standards faithfully with your whole heart, you will be able to climb up by these virtues, as by a flight of steps, to being worthy to love God with your whole mind and your whole strength. And when you reach this happy state of perfection, you will reckon all the desires of this world as nothing but dung, and with the prophet you will be able to say, *But for me to cling to God is good* (Ps 73:28).

Sermon 399

Sermon on the Christian Discipline

The bishop here emphasizes the discipline involved in living the Christian life and presents the Church as both a "house of discipline" and a "school of discipline." The consensus is that this sermon dates to around 398, but Hill prefers a slightly later date, when Augustine was at the height of his powers as a bishop. A number of points suggest that the sermon was preached with other bishops present, most likely in Carthage during a meeting of an all-African council. Yet there may be an allusion to the *refrigerium*, the partying at martyrs' tombs, which suggests an earlier date, before the bishop was successful in curtailing the practice. Augustine insists that Christians are called to love God and their neighbors (every single human being) more than they love their money, and he employs considerable irony and sarcasm to counter the skepticism that meets this challenge.

The Church is the house of discipline

1. The word of God has spoken to us, and it was uttered for our encouragement, with scripture saying, *Accept discipline in the house of discipline* (Sir 51:28.23). "Discipline" comes from *disco*, I learn; the house of discipline is the Church of Christ. So what is learned here, and why is it learned? Who are the ones who learn, and who do they learn from? What is learned is how to live a good life; how to live a good life is learned to enable you to live forever. The ones who learn this are Christians, the one who teaches it is Christ. So be good enough to listen to me saying a few things, as the Lord may grant me, first about what living a good life consists in; next about what the reward of a good life is; thirdly about who are true Christians; fourthly, about who is the true master.

We are all of us in the house of discipline, but there are many people who don't want to accept discipline, and what's even more perverse, they don't want to accept discipline even in the house of discipline. While the reason they ought to accept discipline in the house of discipline is so that they might keep it in their own homes; they, on the contrary, want not only to give way to indiscipline in their homes, but also to bring it with them even into the house of discipline.

So those of you among whom the word of God is not barren, who link your hearts to your ears, who are not the path, where the seed was eaten by the birds as soon as it fell, who are not the stony ground where the seed cannot have deep roots, and where it springs up for a moment and withers in the heat; who are not the thorny field, where as soon as the seed has sprouted and begun to grow up in the air, it is choked by the dense thorns; but who are the good soil, prepared to receive the seed, and to yield a crop of either a hundred, or sixty, or thirtyfold — you, of course, who have not entered the school of discipline in vain, will realize that I have brought these comparisons to your notice from the gospel; so those of you who are of that sort, please accept what the Lord thinks fit to tell you through me. What am I, after all, since he is doing the sowing? Not much more than the sower's basket; he is good enough to place in me what he wishes to broadcast to you. So don't pay any attention to the cheapness of the basket, but to the high value of the seed and the authority of the sower.

Living a good life means keeping God's commandments

2. So what is the lesson of living a good life that is learned here? There are many commandments in the law, in which this good life is contained, commanded, learned. Many commandments indeed, beyond counting. You could scarcely count the number of pages they take up, how much less the commandments themselves! However, there was something God was willing to do, for the sake of those who might be able to make excuses, such as that they haven't the time to read them all, or that they don't know how to read, or that they find it hard to understand them; he was willing, so that nobody should have any such excuse on the day of judgment, to sum up, as it is written, and to shorten the word on the earth, as the prophet had foretold about him: *A summary and a shortened word will the Lord make upon the earth* (Is 10:23). God didn't want this summary and shortened word to be obscure, either. The reason it's short is in case you haven't the time to read; the reason it's clear is so you can't say, "I wasn't capable of understanding."

The divine scriptures are a vast treasure, containing many wonderful commandments, like so many gems and precious jewels and huge chests, a real gold mine. But who can search through all this treasure, and make use of it, and reach everything to be found there? The Lord gave us this comparison in his gospel, and said, *The kingdom of heaven is like a treasure found in a field*; but in case anyone should say he was not up to searching through this treasure, he immediately gave another comparison: *The kingdom of heaven is like a trader looking for fine pearls, who found one precious pearl, and sold everything he had, and bought it* (Mt 13:44-46); so that if you were reluctant to search through a whole treasure-house, you shouldn't be reluctant to carry one pearl under your tongue, and walk around wherever you like without a worry in the world.

Love your neighbor as yourself; the question is, how do you love yourself?

3. So what is this summary and shortened word? *You shall love the Lord your God with your whole heart, and with your whole soul, and with your whole mind; and you shall love your neighbor as yourself. On these two commandments depends the whole law, and the prophets* (Mt 22:37.39-40). There you are, that's what's learned in the house of discipline; to love God, to love your neighbor; God as God, your neighbor as yourself. You won't find God's peer, after all, so that you could be told, "Love God as you love that one." About your neighbor a standard has been found for you, because you yourself are found to be your neighbor's peer. You ask how you are to love your neighbor? Look at yourself, and at how you love yourself, and love your neighbor like that. No room for any mistake there. So now I wish to commit your neighbor to you on those terms, that you love him as yourself; that's what I wish, but I still have my qualms about it.

I want to tell you, "Love your neighbor as you love yourself," and I have my qualms; I still wish, you see, to examine how you love yourself. So don't take it ill; you yourself are not to be lightly dismissed, since your neighbor is to be committed to your care; we mustn't deal with you in an offhand manner. You are one person, your neighbors are many. In the first place, you see, you shouldn't understand your neighbor as just being your brother, or relative, or one of your in-laws. Neighbor to every person is every single other person. Father and son, father-in-law and son-in-law are said to be neighbors. Nothing is so near, so much a neighbor, as one human being to another. But if we assume that only those born of the same parents are neighbors, let's turn our attention to Adam and Eve, and we are all brothers and sisters; brothers and sisters, indeed, insofar as we are human — how much more so in that we are Christians? As regards your being human, your one father was Adam, your one mother Eve; as regards your being a Christian, your one father is God, your one mother the Church.

If you love iniquity, you in fact hate yourself

4. So notice, then, how many neighbors one person has. All the people you come across, all those you can associate with, are your neighbors. So how important it is to examine whether you love yourself, since so many neighbors are to be entrusted to you, for you to love them as yourself. So don't be angry, any of you, if I examine how you love yourself. I, to be sure, am doing the examining, but it's you yourself who must do the finding. Why, after all, am I discussing the matter? Because I myself am going to find out? The reason I'm discussing it is so that you should question yourself, should become visible to yourself, should not escape your own notice, not hide from yourself, should place yourself squarely before your eyes, not behind your own back. May you do this while I'm speaking, do it without my knowing the result.

How do you love yourself? Whoever you are, listening to me, or rather whoever you are, listening to God through me in this house of discipline, consider yourself, and how you love yourself. Naturally, I mean, if I ask you whether you love yourself, you will reply that you do. Who, after all, ever hated himself? That's what you're going to say: "Who, after all, ever hated himself?" So you don't love iniquity, if you love yourself. Because if you do love iniquity, it's not me saying it, listen to the psalm: *Whoever loves iniquity hates his own soul* (Ps 11:5, LXX). So if you love iniquity, listen to the truth; the truth not flattering you, but plainly telling you, "You hate yourself." The more you say you love yourself, the more in fact you hate yourself, because *whoever loves iniquity hates his own soul.* What am I to say about the flesh, which is the less valuable part of a human being? If you hate the soul, how can you love the flesh? In any case, those who love iniquity and hate their own souls, perpetrate every kind of infamy through their flesh.

So now, you there who love iniquity, how were you wanting your neighbor to be entrusted to you, for you to love him as yourself? Man, why are you destroying yourself? I mean, if you yourself are loving yourself to your own destruction, that assuredly is how you are also going to be the destruction of the one you love as yourself. I don't want you to love anybody; at least be alone when you perish. Either correct your love, or eschew all company.

Lift up your hearts

5. You will be telling me next, "I do love my neighbor as myself." I hear you, certainly I hear you; you want to get drunk with this man whom you love as yourself. "Let's have a good time today, let's drink as much as we can." Notice that that's how you love yourself, and that you are drawing him to yourself, and inviting him to what you love. Loving him as you love yourself, you are bound to draw him there to what you also love. All too human man, or rather bestial man, by loving the same sort of things as the beasts! God, you see, made the beasts prone in form, with their faces to the ground, looking for their food from the ground; whereas you he set on your two feet, upright from the ground. He wanted your face to be looking upward. Don't let your heart contradict your face.

Don't have your face turned upward, and your heart turned downward. On the contrary, hear what is true and do what is true: "Lift up your hearts"; don't lie in the house of discipline. After all when your hear this, you answer; but let what you answer be true. Love yourself in that way, and you will really love your neighbor as yourself. What, after all, does it mean to have your heart lifted up, but what you were told first: *You shall love the Lord your God with all your heart, and with all your soul, and with all your mind* (Mt 22:37)?

So while there are two commandments, wouldn't it have been enough if he had just given one? Yes, even one is enough, if rightly understood. Because scripture sometimes speaks in this fashion, like the apostle Paul: *You shall not commit adultery, you shall not commit murder, you shall not lust, and any other commandment there may be, is summed up in this saying: You shall love your neighbor as yourself. Love of neighbor does not work any evil. So charity is the fulfillment of the law*

(Rom 13:9-10). What is charity? It's love. He appears to have said nothing about the love of God, but he said that love of neighbor alone was enough to fulfill the law. *Whatever other commandment there may be is summed up in this saying*, is fulfilled in this saying. In which one? *You shall love your neighbor as yourself* (Mt 22:39). There you have one. But certainly there are two commandments on which the whole law depends, and the prophets.

Notice how it has been shortened even more, and still we are so sluggish about doing it. Look, there were two, they have been reduced to one. Absolutely, love your neighbor, and it's enough. But love him as you love yourself, not as you hate yourself. Love your neighbor as yourself; but the first thing is to love yourself.

It is the Lord, not money, who confers true bliss

6. You're bound to ask how you are to love yourself; and you're bound to hear, *You shall love the Lord your God with your whole heart, and with your whole soul, and with your whole mind* (Mt 22:37). You see, just as man was unable to make himself, so he is unable to make himself blessed. It was another thing that made him man, which was not himself; it's another thing, which is not man himself, that is going to make him blessed. And then, when he's going astray he sees for himself that he cannot be blessed by his own means, and he loves something else by which to be blessed. He loves what he thinks will make him blessed. What, are we to suppose, does he love, which he thinks will make him blessed? Money, gold, silver, possessions; in a word, money, or chattels. Everything people possess on earth, you see, everything they are masters of, is called chattels. Be it slaves, utensils, fields, trees, cattle, whichever of these it is, it's called chattels. And why was it first called chattels? The reason we talk of chattels is that the ancients had all their wealth in cattle. The name "chattels" comes from "cattle." We read that the ancients were wealthy cattlemen.

So you love money, Mister, which you think can make you happy; it means plenty of goods and chattels, and you love it very much indeed. You were willing to love your neighbor as yourself; then share your money with him. I was discussing what you really were; you've been found out, been shown up to yourself; you've seen yourself, taken a look at yourself. You are not prepared to share your money with your neighbor. But what answer does kind, friendly avarice give me? How does it answer me? "If I share with him, there will be less both for me and for him. What I love will be diminished, and he won't have the whole of it, nor shall I have the whole of it; but because I love him as myself, my wish and hope for him is that he may have as much, so that what is mine won't grow less, and he is put on a level with me."

Envy and pride, diabolical vices

7. Your wish and hope is to have something you won't lose any of, and if only you were saying this, or wishing this truly and sincerely. You see, I'm afraid that in fact you are being envious. I mean, how can you be sociable and friendly in your

prosperity, when someone else's prosperity racks you with envy? Aren't you afraid, when your neighbor begins to grow rich, and begins as it were to rise, and to come after you, aren't you afraid he may follow you, afraid he may pass you? Oh sure, you love your neighbor as yourself. But of course, I'm not speaking to the envious. May God turn away this scourge from the souls of all men and women, not to mention Christians; it's a diabolical vice, the only one the devil is guilty of, and unatonably guilty. The devil, after all, isn't told, when he's condemned, "You committed adultery, you were guilty of theft, you grabbed someone else's estate," but "when you fell, you envied the human race standing firm."

Envy is a devilish vice, but it has its own proper mother. The mother of envy is called pride. Strangle the mother, and you won't be possessed by the daughter. That's why Christ taught us humility. So I'm not speaking to the envious, I'm speaking to those who entertain good wishes and hopes. I'm speaking to those who wish their friends well, who hope they will have as much as they have themselves. They wish the needy well, that they may have as much as they themselves; but they are unwilling to give them any of what they have themselves.

Is that what you pride yourself on, Christian man or woman, that you wish people well? The beggar is better than you are, because he wishes you many more things, and hasn't got anything. You are willing to wish him well, though he gets nothing from you; give something to him for wishing you well. If it's good to wish people well, give him his reward. The poor man wishes you well; why so alarmed? Let me add a point — you are in the house of discipline. Let me add to what I said, "Give to the one who is wishing you well"; it's Christ himself. He's asking you for what he has given you. You should blush for shame. He, though rich, was willing to be poor, so that you could have poor people to give something to. Give something to your brother, give something to your neighbor, give something to your companion. You, after all, are rich, he is poor. This life is a road, you are both walking along it together.

Lighten your load, by giving some of it to the poor to carry

8. But perhaps you'll say, "I'm rich, he's poor."

Are you walking along together, or not? What does it mean, your saying, "I'm rich, he's poor," but "I'm overloaded, he's traveling light." "I'm rich, he's poor." You're mentioning your burden, praising the weight you carry. And what's more serious still, you have strapped your burden to your shoulders; that's why you can't stretch out a hand. Overloaded, tightly strapped up, what are you being so proud of, why are you praising yourself? Undo your straps, decrease your burden. Give some of it to your companion, and you are helping him and giving relief to yourself. Among all these words of yours in praise of your burden, Christ is still asking, and not receiving anything; and you spread the name of family duty over cruel words, and say, "And what am I to keep for my children?" I play Christ against him, he counters by playing his children against me.

Is this, though, such wonderful justice, that your son should have the means of rolling in luxury, while your Lord is in want? *For when you did it for one of the least of mine, you did it for me.* Haven't you read that, haven't you taken any notice of it? *When you failed to do it for one of the least of mine, you failed to do it for me* (Mt 25:40.45). Haven't you read that, hasn't it frightened you? Look who's in want, and you're counting your children! Very well then, count your children, add one more to their number — your Lord. You have one child, let him be the second; you have two, let him be the third; you have three, let him be the fourth. But you don't want any of that. So there you are, that's how you love your neighbor, in such a way as to make him your companion in going to that perdition.

Bad conversations corrupt good morals

9. What am I to say to you? Do you really love your neighbor? What else are you whispering in his ears, you grasping fellow, but "Son, or brother, or father, it's good for us, while we are living here, that things should go well with us. As much as you have is as much as you will be. Break up the moon, make your fortune soon." These are the things you whisper to your neighbor, things you never learned in the house of discipline, and never heard here. I don't want you to love your neighbor like that. Oh, if only I could ensure that you associated with nobody at all! *Bad conversations*, you see, *corrupt good morals* (1 Cor 15:33). But I can't do it, I can't ensure that you don't associate with anyone, to whom you may whisper these bad things which you don't wish to unlearn, and which indeed you are not only unwilling to be untaught, but are even determined to teach. I don't wish, or rather I do wish, but am unable, to detach you from other people's ears. So let me warn those others, round whose ears you prowl, whose ears you strive to penetrate, into whose hearts you plan to force an entry through their ears.

O you that gladly receive sound doctrine in the house of discipline, *hedge your ears about with thorns* (Sir 28:24, Lat). *Bad conversations corrupt good morals. Hedge your ears about with thorns.* Hedge them about, and with a hedge of thorns, so that the one who presumes to enter inappropriately will be scratched and pricked as well as being driven off. Drive him away from you, and say, "You are a Christian, I am a Christian; this is not what we have received in the house of discipline, not what we have learned in that school where we were enrolled free; not what we learned under that master whose chair is in heaven. Don't say these things to me, and don't come near me again." That, you see, is hedging your ears about with thorns.

Money doesn't bring you bliss

10. Let me turn now to that man. You're greedy and grasping, you love money. Do you want to know bliss? Love your God. Money doesn't bring you bliss; you make it into handsome coins, it doesn't make you into a blissful person. But because you love money so much, and I can see that you go in whatever direction greed or cupidity bids you, go instead, idle fellow, in the direction love or charity

bids you. Look up, and observe what a difference there is between your money and your God. This sun in the sky is more beautiful than your money, and yet this sun is not your God. Accordingly, if this sunlight is more beautiful than your money, how much more beautiful must he be who made this sunlight? Or perhaps you are ready to compare your money to light? The sun sets, show me your money. It shines brightly, and at night I remove the lamp. Sure, you're rich; show me your riches. Now, if you're deprived of light, now if you haven't got the means of seeing what you have, where are your riches?

And that, all the same, is the way the horrid depths of avarice are hidden from our eyes, while they are seething in our souls. We have even seen blind people who are avaricious. Tell me, please, how blind people, who can't see, can be avaricious. He hasn't even got what he's got, this blind man, and yet he's greedy and grasping. Why? Because he believes he's got the stuff, he's greedy and grasping about it. It's faith that makes him rich; he's rich by believing, not by seeing. How much better it would be if he directed his faith to God! You can't see what you possess, and that is how I preach God to you. You can't yet see him; love him and you will see him. You love money, Mr. Blind Man, which you will never see. You possess it blind, you are going to die blind, you're going to leave behind here what you possess. You didn't really have it while you were alive, because you couldn't see what you had.

Let us at least love divine wisdom as much as we love money

11. What are you told about God? Here is what Wisdom herself says: *Love her like money* (Prv 2:4). It's unfitting, it's insulting, that wisdom should be compared to money, but love is being compared to love. What I see here, after all, is that you all love money in such a way that when love of money gives the order, you undertake hard labor, you put up with starving, you cross the sea, you commit yourselves to wind and wave. I have something to pick on in the matter of what you love, but I have nothing to add to the love with which you love. "Love like that, and I don't want to be loved any more than that," says God. "I'm talking to the riff-raff, I'm speaking to the greedy: You love money; love me just as much. Of course, I'm incomparably better; but I don't want more ample love from you; love me just as much as you love money."

At least let us be ashamed, and confess, and beat our breasts — but not just so as to tamp down a solid floor on top of our sins. I mean if you beat your breast without correcting your way of life, you are just tamping down your sins, not removing them. So let us beat our breasts, and beat ourselves, and be corrected by ourselves, or else the one who is the master here will beat us later on. So we've already said what is to be learned here; now it's time for why it is learned.

Why people go to school to learn their letters

12. Why did you go to school, and get beaten, and run away when taken there by your parents, and get looked for and found, and dragged back again, and laid

out on the floor when you were brought back? Why were you beaten? Why did you endure such ghastly evils in your boyhood? To make you learn. Learn what? Your letters. Why? So that you could earn money, or obtain honors, maintain a high social rank. Observe that while you are going to perish, for the sake of a perishable object, you learned this perishable object with such hard effort, driven by such severe punishments, and that the one who dragged you to these punishments did it because he loved you. Yes, it was the one who loved you that dragged you off to receive punishment. He had you beaten out of love for you — so that you would learn, what? Letters. Aren't letters a good thing? Yes, they are.

Yes, I know, you're going to say to me, "Why, what about you bishops? Didn't you study your letters? Why, haven't you used your education in order to study and expound the divine scriptures?" That's so, but that isn't why we learned our letters. I mean, when our parents sent us to school, they didn't say to us, "Learn your letters, so that you may be able to read and study the books of the Lord." Not even Christians say this to their children. But what do they say? "Learn your letters."

Why?

"In order to be a man."

What do you mean? Am I an animal?

"When I say, to be a man, I mean to be eminent among men. Hence the proverb, As much as you have is as much as you will be. In order to have as much as others, or as much as a few others; or more than the rest, or more than the few; as a result to acquire honor, rank, status."

And where will all that be when death comes along? How it disturbs us, this dread of death, how it interrupts and upsets our thoughts! How the very word, when I mentioned it, struck at your hearts! Your groans and sighs testified to your fear, and made it clear enough. I heard, yes, I heard. You sighed and groaned, you are afraid of death. If you're afraid, why don't you take precautions? You're afraid of death; why be afraid? It's going to come; fear it, or fear it not, it's got to come; sooner or later, it's going to come. Even if you're afraid, you will never manage to avert what you are afraid of.

Learn how to die a good death by learning how to live a good life

13. What you should fear instead is what won't happen if you don't want it to. What's that? Sinning. Be afraid of sinning, because if you love your sins, you will tumble into another death, which you would be able to avoid coming to, if you didn't love your sins. But as it is, you are so perverse, that you love death more than life.

"Nonsense," you say. "What human being would ever love death more than life?"

Perhaps I can convince you that you do love death more than life. Look, this is how I will convince you. You love your clothes, you want them to be good ones. You love your villa, you would like it to be a good one. You love your son, you want him to be a good one. You love your friend, you would like him to be a good one. You love your household, you want it to be a good one. What about your also wanting to have a good death? After all, you pray every day that since death is going to come anyway, God may grant you a good death; you say, "May God preserve me from a bad death." So there you are, you love your death more than your life; you're afraid of dying a bad death; you're not afraid of living a bad life. Put right your living a bad life, be afraid of dying a bad death. But no, don't be afraid of that; it's impossible to die a bad death, if you've lived a good life. I can most certainly confirm this, I have the audacity to say: *I have believed, therefore have I spoken* (Ps 116:10; 2 Cor 4:13); it is impossible to die a bad death if you have lived a good life.

Now you're saying to yourelf, "Haven't many just people perished in ship-wrecks? Oh sure, it's impossible to die a bad death, if you've lived a good life. Hasn't the enemy's sword slain many just people? Oh sure, it's impossible to die a bad death, if you've lived a good life. Haven't bandits killed many just people? Haven't wild beasts torn many just people to pieces? Oh sure, it's impossible to die a bad death, if you've lived a good life."

And I reply, "Is that what you think a bad death is? To perish in a shipwreck, to be struck with the sword, to be torn to pieces by wild beasts? Didn't the martyrs undergo such deaths as that, and here we are, celebrating their birthdays? What kind of death did they not undergo? And yet if we are Christians, if we remember that we are in the house of discipline, at least when we are here, at least when we are listening here, if we don't forget it all the moment we go out, if we remember what we hear in this place — don't we call the martyrs blessed? Inquire about the deaths of the martyrs; question the eyes in your head — they died a bad death; question the eyes of faith — *Precious in the eyes of the Lord is the death of his saints* (Ps 116:15). So whatever it is that horrifies you about their death, it won't horrify you at all, if you imitate them.

Take pains to lead a good life, and whatever the occasion is of your departing from this body, you depart to rest, you depart to bliss, which knows no fear and has no end. I mean, it was to all appearances a good death for the man clothed in purple and fine linen; but a bad death for the man so thirsty, and longing for a drop of water amid his torments. It was to all appearances a bad death for the poor man lying at the rich man's gate, among the tongues of dogs, a bad death for him, longing in his hunger and thirst for scraps from the table, a death to be avoided at all costs. But look at the end of it; you're a Christian, open the eye of faith: *It came about that that poor man died, and was carried away by angels into Abraham's bosom* (Lk 16:22). What good did his marble tomb do the rich man thirsty in hell? What harm did his rags, filthy with the pus from his sores, do the poor man at his ease in Abraham's bosom? The rich man, who had ignored him at his gate, saw him at his ease a long way off. Now choose your death; tell me, who died a good death, who a bad one? I rather think it's better for that poor man than for that rich man. Or would you rather be buried in fragrant spices, and thirst for ever in hell? You answer, "God preserve me from that!" Yes, I think that's what you'll say. So you will learn how to die a good death, if you have learned how to live a good life. The reward, after all, of a good life, is eternal life.

The sower sows, regardless of path, stones, and thorns

14. Those who learn this lesson are Christians; those who hear it and don't learn it — what are they to the sower? The hand of the sower is not deterred by the way, not deterred by the stones, not deterred by the thorns; he broadcasts what is his own. Whoever's afraid of the seed falling on bad soil never reaches the good soil. We too, in speaking, are casting the seed, scattering the seed. There are people who ignore us, people who find fault with us, people who mock us. If we are afraid of them, we are reduced to sowing nothing, we are reduced to going hungry at harvest time. So let the seed reach the good soil. I know that those who hear, and hear well, both fall away and make progress; they fall away from iniquity, make progress in the truth; fall away from the world, make progress in God.

It is Christ who is teaching; his school is his body

15. After all, who is the master that is doing the teaching? Not any sort of man, but the apostle. Clearly the apostle, and yet not the apostle. *Or do you wish*, he says, *to get proof of the one who is speaking in me, Christ?* (2 Cor 13:3). It is Christ who is doing the teaching; he has his chair in heaven, as I said a short while ago. His school is on earth, and his school is his own body. The head is teaching his members, the tongue talking to his feet. It is Christ who is doing the teaching; we hear; let us fear, let us act.

And don't despise Christ, just because for your sake he was born in the flesh, wrapped in the rags of mortality; for your sake felt hunger and thirst; for your sake was tired out and sat at the well; for your sake was weary and went to sleep in the boat; for your sake had unseemly abuse heaped on him, for your sake did not wipe people's spittle off his face; for your sake hung on the tree, for your sake breathed his last, for your sake was laid in the tomb. Perhaps you rather despise all this in Christ? Do you wish to know who he really is? Recall the gospel you just heard: *I and the Father are one* (Jn 10:30).

Concluding prayer

16. Turning to the Lord, let us implore him on our own behalf, and on behalf of all his people standing with us in the courts of his house, that he may be pleased to keep and protect it, through Jesus Christ his Son our Lord, who lives and reigns with him forever and ever. Amen.

Dolbeau 28
Sermon 20B

On the Response of the Psalm:
Give Us Help from Afflictions, and Vain Is the Salvation of Man

Augustine addresses the complex question of why God appears not to hear and heed the prayers of a faithful Christian when at other times he grants the prayers of a godless, crooked man. He shares with his congregation the toll of fatigue and suffering that age has imposed on him, which required a time for convalescence away from the local church. The first section refers to such a period of convalescence. There were two occasions in Augustine's life when he tells us he was seriously ill: the summer of 397 in Carthage, when he suffered from a painful attack of piles (Letter 38, 1), and the autumn and winter of 410-411, when he was stricken with a fever after returning to Hippo from the great conference with the Donatists in Carthage, at which he retired to a villa in the countryside for a long convalescence (Letter 118, 34; 122, 1). At the end of the sermon there is an allusion to a scar, which is evidently in connection with some sort of surgery. Given the number of sermons preached during this earlier period, Hill is inclined to assign a later date (about 427) to this sermon, due in particular to its rambling quality and the occasional inconsequential train of thought suggestive of an old man's discourse.

Augustine is glad to be back with his congregation
after a long absence due to illness; the value of such trials

1. I cannot thank the Lord God enough, nor your graces in his presence, for these joyful congratulations, which pour out, I can see very well, from the fountain of your love for me. It is this, you see, brothers and sisters, which revives me, which consoles me: your pure and genuine love, assisting me with the Lord, who has been good enough to restore me to you and my voice to your ears. Nor should you be surprised that we suffer such things in this body. It is fitting, after all, that we should suffer; nor can what the Lord wills ever in any instance be unjust; because on the one hand we are sinners and have to be scourged; and on the other, even if we were just, we would need to be tested.

In fact, if you opt for a healthy body in which the spirit which inhabits the body is not making any progress, you are opting for something futile and vain. God, however, does not consider your mistaken option, but his own merciful intention to set you free. The apostle, you see, says that *we do not know what to pray for as we ought; but the Spirit himself*, he says, *pleads on our behalf with inexpressible groanings* (Rom 8:26). Sometimes, after all, we opt for things for ourselves which God knows are against our best interests; and then he shows mercy if he doesn't listen to us; or rather, it is somehow truer to say: then he really listens to us if he appears not to do so.

How God treated Saint Paul

2. I mean to say, which of us, brothers and sisters, can claim to be the equals in merit of the apostle Paul, whose praises there is no need at all for me to sing? He is read every day, after all, so there's no point in anyone praising him. As a matter of fact, he didn't wish ever to be praised simply on his own account, considering what he said about his conversion; how the Churches which were in Christ from among the Jews (those, that is, who had believed in Christ) heard of it, and were astonished that he had been converted: he didn't say, "They glorified me," but *In me they glorified the Lord* (Gal 1:22-24). Again, when he had much to say about how effective he had been, *Not I*, he said, *but the grace of God with me* (1 Cor 15:10). So which of us can claim to be his equals either in humility or lovingkindness or doctrine or labors or afflictions or merits or finally in his glorious crown?

So he, then, twice pleaded with the Lord for the goad in his flesh to be removed from him, and it was not removed; and yet the Lord says to the soul that serves him well, *While you are still speaking, I will say, Lo, here I am* (Is 58:9), to grant what it was asking for. Would we have the nerve, any of us, to promise ourselves what was denied to Paul? So how can we say that God was not present, when the apostle says, *There was given me a goad in my flesh, an angel of Satan to knock me about*—to stop him getting conceited; *about which I asked the Lord three times to take it away from me, and he said to me: My grace is sufficient for you; because power is perfected in weakness* (2 Cor 12:7-9)? So wasn't he present? Didn't he say, *Lo, here I am*, when God explained why he wouldn't give what he was being asked for?

God always listens to us, even when he seems not to

3. God always listens, dearest brothers and sisters — you must be absolutely clear about this, so that you can pray with complete confidence; God listens, even when God doesn't give what we are praying for. God listens, and if ever in our ignorance we ask for heaven knows what unprofitable favor, he listens more effectively by not giving, while by giving he more effectively does not listen to some who need to be punished. This is what I'm saying: sometimes a faithful Christian asks God for something, praying in the genuinely religious manner, and doesn't receive what he is actually asking for, but does receive the benefit for the sake of which he is asking for it. Sometimes a godless man, a crooked man, a vicious man asks for something, and gets given it, because he deserves to be condemned, not to be heard.

So we have the example of the apostle Paul, that he asked for something and it wasn't given him, but he is shown that the thing for the sake of which he was asking for it was given him. Because whatever faithful Christians may ask for, they ought to ask for it for the sake of the kingdom of heaven, for the sake of eternal life, for the sake of what God has promised and is going to give us after this age; that's the reason why any who ask for anything ought to ask for it — for the sake of that perfect health which we will also have in the resurrection of the body. That, you see, is when our health will be perfect, when *death is swallowed up in victory* (1 Cor 15:44). So now, because I have mentioned the eternal health and salvation on account of which we ought to ask even for temporal benefits, when we do ask for them ... and let us take some everyday instances from this kind of doctor.

Examples from ordinary medicine

4. When a sick person asks the doctor to let him have something which he fancies at that moment — and the reason he sent for the doctor was to be restored to health through his services. The only point in sending for the doctor, after all, was in order to get better. And so it is, if he happens to fancy apples, if he fancies ice cream, he prefers to ask the doctor for them rather than his servant. He could, of course, to the detriment of his recovery, ask his servant for them and conceal this from the doctor. When the master commands, the servant complies, more responsive to the snap of the master's fingers than to the requirements of the master's health. But the prudent sick man, who values good health and looks forward to its restoration, prefers to ask the doctor for what he fancies at this moment, so that if the doctor refuses, he will forgo what would give him pleasure, but trust the doctor to give him back his health.

So you can see that even when the doctor does not give the sick man what he asks for, the reason he doesn't give is in order to give. The reason he does not gratify his immoderate will is to satisfy his more genuine desire for health. So by not giving to him he does in fact give, and more certainly gives what he was sent for to provide, which is health. So if he gives him this by not giving, by giving in to his importunate arm-twisting he in fact fails to give — though he will frequently give someone who is despaired of what he asks for. Sometimes, however, he will give the sick person what he asks for, so that the sharper pains that result may teach the patient some sense, teach him to trust the doctor; sometimes on the other hand, when he despairs of his recovery, doctors are in the habit of saying, "Give him now whatever he asks for; there is, after all, no hope of his recovery." So let us see if we can find examples in the scriptures to fit these three situations.

Again the example of Paul not being given, for his own good, what he asked for

5. Someone asks, and doesn't receive what he asks for. Let us turn to the example of the apostle Paul. Because the doctor actually told him why he was not giving it to him: *Power*, he said *is perfected in weakness.* Rest assured: the fact of his not giving it to you means he wants to heal you. Leave it to the doctor; he knows what to apply, what to remove, in order to restore you to health, and that's why he does this. The apostle begs the Lord three times; he was already being heard, but he didn't think he was, and he wouldn't have thought so, unless the doctor had come along actually to tell him, *Power is perfected in weakness*, so that he himself could also confidently say now, *When I become weak, then it is that I am strong* (2 Cor 12:8-10). So we have this person asking for heaven knows what unprofit-

able favor and not receiving it, in order for him to receive the thing for the sake of which he was asking for the other, which was for the sake of eternal salvation.

An example of receiving what you ask for, to your own detriment, as a warning

6. Let's now see if people ever receive something as a warning, so that they may suffer some affliction from it, and so go back to medical treatment, because they are sick. Thus the Lord said, *The doctor is not needed by the healthy, but by those who are ill* (Mk 2:17). So he came to a sick humanity, and he found people given over to their desires. Precisely to cause affliction, *God handed them over*, the apostle says, *to the desires of their hearts, to act indecently* (Rom 1:24.28). They had indecent desires, and were given the opportunity to satisfy them; thereby they fell into greater misery than ever, a prey to the pangs that all the unjust must unavoidably endure, all the wicked; pangs of fear, of lust, of error, of sorrow, of affliction, of anxiety. Never any reassurance, never any rest, never any friend to turn to.

There is no avoiding their suffering justly — and they're still alive. God is waiting for them; he allows these things to prod them into seeking medical treatment, so that when they suffer the painful consequences of their lusts, they may learn what they should really ask for. Because they are the ones who are told, *Do you not know that God's patience is leading you toward repentance?* (Rom 2:4). He was giving them over to the desires of their hearts, and they were doing what they liked; and yet he was sparing them, not removing them from this life in which there is still room for repentance; and he was all the time inviting them to repent, just as he still is doing, and he will never stop doing so with the human race until the final day of judgment.

The case of the devil; granted his request because he was despaired of

7. So let us next find an instance of the one who is allowed to do what he likes because he is now despaired of; and this too from the scriptures. Can anything or anyone be more despaired of than the devil? Yet he asked God to let him have Job to be tempted, and he was not refused. There are great mysteries here, great matters indeed, and worthy of careful consideration. The apostle asks for the goad in his flesh to be taken away, and is not granted his request; the devil asks for a just man to tempt, and his request is granted. But the just man's being granted to the devil for tempting did not do the just man any harm, nor the devil any good, because the former came through his trials with flying colors, and the latter suffered the torment of bitter disappointment.

God's reasons in allowing the just to be tempted and tried

8. Hold onto this firmly, brothers and sisters, what I have often told your holinesses, and don't let the worries of the world rub out from your minds what you have heard: when God either hands over the just to be tempted in order to test their mettle, or to be scourged if he wishes to correct them for their remaining sins, it is

for their own good. If, however, it is to show their true worth, because people didn't know about them, this is for the good of those who get to know about them, so that they may imitate them. Because God certainly knows his servants well, but sometimes they are not known to others, and can only be revealed to them in their true worth by undergoing various trials.

Sometimes, too, people are unknown to themselves, and quite unaware of what they may be capable of. They either think they can do more than in fact they can, and so they are shown that they can't do it yet; or else they despair of themselves, and think they cannot endure whatever it may be; and they are shown that in fact they can. When they have an immoderately good opinion of themselves, they are given a lesson in humility, and when they think they are broken reeds, they are rescued from despair.

The text of the response to the psalm, at last

9. Therefore, what we should understand in the psalm we were singing is that many people ask for good health, and sometimes it is not to their advantage. They are in good health, for instance, and they abuse it in order to sin. They would be better off sick and out of circulation, than in good health and gadding about. Sometimes, on the other hand, as a result of the scourge of tribulation, when something they hadn't bargained for happens to them, they are converted to God. They will emerge more careful, more chaste, more unassuming, altogether humbler, and can then rightly sing, *Give us help from affliction, and vain is the salvation of man* (Ps 60:13). He was looking for help, and help where from? He said to the Lord, "From affliction give us help, so that by being afflicted we may be corrected, may turn back to you through being humiliated, may no more stiffen our necks against you." Because when you give us help from tribulation, we will realize that *vain is the salvation* which foolish man frequently goes for, and when he gets it he doesn't use it for the joys of a quiet life, but as an opportunity for gadding about.

Often enough, for instance, a man was on the point of charging out, in a furious and quite unjustified temper, and aiming to do someone an injury who had probably done him no harm. He suddenly falls sick; what would be best for him — to charge out and commit an iniquitous assault or to be ill in bed and pray for health? It is not, you see, health from God or the salvation of God that is vain, but the health of man that is vain, which man thinks is so necessary for him, as if it were something to be highly valued. It's a false salvation, a false health, and rightly said to be "of man," if it is thought to come only from man. Because there, where it doesn't add "of man" and says, *Salvation is the Lord's* (Ps 3:9), what's the meaning of *Salvation is the Lord's*? It's the Lord who gives salvation, or health, who knows what to give, when and to whom to give.

As often as people, whose salvation seems to be despaired of, ask for salvation, it is God who gives it. It continues in that psalm, *And upon your people be your blessing* (Ps 3:9), that is, have mercy as much on your people, and give them the salvation which you give to those who do not belong to your people, even the salvation which this people of yours is ignorant of. You, after all, know what to give; this people doesn't know what to receive, except when this people of yours has received it. I mean, what sort of thing is this, brothers and sisters, to help you know what you are going to receive? *What eye has not seen nor ear heard, nor has it come up into the heart of man, the things that God has prepared for those who love him* (1 Cor 2:9). What do you think it is he has prepared? Eternal salvation, of course, everlasting health, which cannot come up into our hearts, which eye cannot see, and ear cannot hear; and yet he is preparing these things for those who love him, and when we have received them, we shall see what true health is, and how vain were the things that we thought were of such value.

The example of the martyrs

10. If the martyrs, after all, had opted for this health or salvation, that is, the salvation of man, and valued it highly, they wouldn't have said from the bottom of their hearts, *And the day of man I have not desired, you yourself know* (Jer 17:16 LXX). So if they had opted for this salvation and valued it highly, they would have lost that other eternal variety. As it is, however, they understand the meaning of *Give us help from affliction* (Ps 60:11), and they choose rather to be carried through to everlasting salvation, than on choosing this salvation of man to find it leading to their undoing and to their giving their consent to the persecutors. The persecutor, of course, would immediately grant them salvation. There was the martyr in chains, bound and confined in prison, even wasting away by himself from his wounds; had he yielded to the persecutor, he would immediately have had salvation; but *vain is the salvation of man.*

The persecutors, of course, were promising salvation, which they would give immediately. And what sort would they give? The sort the martyrs had known before those afflictions came upon them. But they were reaching out to that other sort which *eye has not seen nor ear heard, nor has it come up into the heart of man* (1 Cor 2:9). What the persecutor promises can be seen, and what he promises is unreliable, and short, and limited. If that greater salvation cannot be seen, but God promises that it will certainly follow (and he cannot deceive us), let us keep ourselves under his stern discipline, and not grumble under his rod; let us willingly endure his treatment and his cure, and then we will rejoice at God's presence in perfect health, fully aware at last of what he has given us, and saying, *Where, death, is your striving? Where, death, is your sting?* (1 Cor 15:55).

Augustine excuses himself for not continuing

11. I know your eagerness, brothers and sisters, but it is also necessary for you to spare my fragile state of health. No, I don't want to refuse your holinesses the ministry of my preaching, whatever it may be like, so that I may serve the Lord, who has restored me to health. However, we still have to deal gently with the more recent scar, which is not yet, perhaps, completely healed. May the Lord dispose of me as he will, adapting me to the salvation of us all and the service of his holy Church.

Turning to the Lord, let us pray. May he look upon us and perfect us by his saving word, and grant us to rejoice in accord with him and live in accord with him. May he put away from us *the prudence of the flesh* (Rom 8:6); may he throw down the enemy under our feet, not by our efforts, but by his holy name, in which we have been cleansed through Jesus Christ our Lord.

Dolbeau 9
Sermon 28A
Mainz 24

Sermon of Blessed Augustine on the Verse of the Psalm,
I Myself said in My Panic, Every Man a Liar
and on the Reading from Solomon where He Says,
If You Have Taken Your Seat at the Table of a Great Man,
to the Place where He Said, *He Goes to the House of His Chief*

This sermon displays the inventive connection that Augustine makes between Ps 116:12-13, *What shall I pay back to the Lord? The cup of salvation I will receive, and I will call upon the name of the Lord,* and the Eucharist: "What you are receiving is the very host who has invited you. You have taken your seat at the table of your shepherd; what you find there is the death of your host." Lambot maintains this was one of a series of sermons preached in 397 between May 24th, which was Pentecost Sunday that year, and the feast of John the Baptist on June 24th. Hombert, on the other hand, proposes the year 420, based on a parallel treatment of Proverbs 23 in Tractate 84 on John's Gospel, with its strong anti-Pelagian theme.

How can we repay God for all his benefits?

1. The apostle says, *But having the same spirit of faith, according to what is written:* "I believed; for which reason I spoke," we too believe; for which reason we also speak (2 Cor 4:13; Ps 116:10). If you want to speak when you don't believe, you are wanting to pour out from a jug you haven't filled. It has to be filled, for you to pour out. But it must be poured out for others in such a way that you are not left empty yourself. That's why the Lord, when promising believers an abundance of his Holy Spirit, said, *It will become in him a fountain of water leaping up to eternal life* (Jn 4:14). It's in the nature of fountains, you see, to pour out their water without getting empty. And if God grants us this, what shall we pay back to the Lord for all the things he has paid back to us?

And so the one who was speaking in the psalm as we heard, being full of the grace of God, and thinking about God's generous gift to him, looked around to see what he could give back in return, and didn't find any ready answer he could make. So he hesitated in his search, and said, *What shall I pay back to the Lord for all the things he has paid back to me?* (Ps 116:12). He didn't pay me, you see, but he paid me back, because what I deserved for the bad things I had done was bad things, and he paid me back good things for bad things. "What can I," he is saying, "pay the Lord — if, of course, I can pay the Lord back anything, since it says to him in another psalm, *I said to the Lord: you indeed are my God, because you have no need of my goods* (Ps 16:2)? So if the reason you are the Lord is that you have no need of my goods, *what shall I pay back to the Lord?*" And yet in his own opinion he had found something to pay back: *The cup of salvation shall I receive*, he said, *and I will call upon the name of the Lord* (Ps 116:13). This is paying back, is it? Surely, it's just receiving once again.

How to be truthful, when every man is a liar

2. He had said earlier on, however, *I myself said in my panic, Every man a liar* (Ps 116:11). In so saying, though, he seems to have presented people — but only those who don't understand properly and don't pay careful attention — not so much with a confession of sin as with a pretext for it. *Every man a liar*, said scripture. You can now say, "I will tell lies without a qualm, because *every man a liar*. So you see I'm not a man unless I'm a liar." You've had your relief from qualms; now take a dose of anxiety: *You will destroy all who utter lies* (Ps 5:7). So come back again anxiously and make further inquiries, because he didn't say "without a qualm," but *in my panic*. And so I could say to you, "He said it in panic, said it shaking in his shoes, he didn't know what he was saying, he said it in a disturbed state of mind." I could say this, if Paul the apostle hadn't confirmed the assertion, when he says, *God alone is truthful, but every man a liar, as it is written* (Rom 3:4).

So if God is truthful, and he alone is truthful, while *every man a liar*, how will man ever be truthful, unless he approaches the one who is not a liar? In any case, men are told, *You were once darkness* (Eph 5:8). There you have *every man a liar*. God on the other hand is told, *With you is the fountain of life, and in your light we shall see light* (Ps 36:9). And because God alone is truthful, *since God is light, and there is no darkness in him* (1 Jn 1:5), men are darkness, God is light; man a liar, God truthful. When will man ever be truthful? *Approach him and be enlightened* (Ps 34:5). So this is what scripture wished to demonstrate, that every human being, absolutely every single one, as regards being merely human, is a liar. It is precisely, you see, from what is our own that every one of us is a liar. Nor are we able, from what is our own, to be anything but liars — not that we cannot ever be truthful, but that we will never be truthful from what is our own.

Therefore, in order to be truthful, *I believed; for which reason I spoke* (Ps 116:10). Take away believing: *every man a liar*. When you pull away, after all, from God's truth, you will remain in your own falsehood, because *the one who speaks falsehood speaks from what is his own* (Jn 8:44). So then, if you have now become truthful, learn where you have got this from, or on this very point you will again be a liar. Yes, you see, truthful man, when you say, "I am truthful from what is my own," you are in those very words being a liar. So if you really are truthful, it's because you have been filled, because you have begun to participate in truth. You were empty, but you have been filled with truth from the heavenly fountain; that's why you will be able to say, *What shall I pay back to the Lord for all the things he has paid back to me?* (Ps 116:12). *I said in my panic*, and what I said was true, *Every man a liar* (Ps 116:11). But God pays me back, not punishment for lying, but good for evil, and by justifying the godless he turns me from being a liar into a truthful person.

Repay the Lord by taking the cup of salvation

3. So then, *What shall I pay back to the Lord? The cup of salvation shall I receive, and I will call upon the name of the Lord* (Ps 116:12-13). *The cup of salvation shall I receive*; the cup of Christ shall I receive. He, after all, is the salvation of God. I mean, it was about him that old Simeon said, *Now you are releasing your servant, Lord, in peace, since my eyes have seen your salvation* (Lk 2:29-30). So you then, if you are asking *What shall I pay back to the Lord?* for all the things he has paid back to you, receive *the cup of salvation*.

What cup?

The cup of salvation.

What salvation?

Christ. And which cup of Christ our salvation can it be, but the one he mentioned in his answer to the pair who had their sights set on the lofty heights and were ignoring the lowly depths: *Can you drink the cup which I am going to drink* (Mt 20:22)? Receive this cup, if you wish to pay the Lord back for all the things he has paid back to you. *For just as Christ laid down his life for us, so we too ought to lay down our lives for the brethren* (1 Jn 3:16). That is what paying him back means, accepting the cup of salvation.

But what are you afraid of, what do you dread in that sort of cup? He himself will be at your side to support you, just as he went ahead to set you an example. I mean, just look at this man who is inquiring what he can pay back, and who in his very inquiry, it seems, finds this cup, as though to say, "I have found what I can pay back; *the cup of salvation shall I receive*"; and being capable of drinking it, he boldly said, *and I will call upon the name of the Lord* (Ps 116:13). Accordingly when you are trying to pay back, you haven't in fact paid back what you have received, but have just received something more in addition. You have received once the grace to believe, and a second time the grace to drink the cup of salvation. So it is by him that all things have been given us; through him we have what we are, if we are anything good.

Returning Christ's hospitality by sharing his sufferings

4. So it is too that the reading which came before the psalm seems to suggest something of the same sort to us, provided we are capable of grasping the will of the one making the suggestion. He says, you see, *If you have taken your seat to dine at the table of a great man, observe shrewdly what is being set before you, and stretch out your hand, knowing that it will be your duty to prepare the same sort of food yourself* (Prv 23:1-2 LXX). If you have taken your seat at the table of a great man, you are being told to observe shrewdly what is being set before you; then you are next told to stretch out your hand, *knowing that it will be your duty to prepare the same sort of food yourself.* Is there any man greater than Christ? Take your seat to dine at his table: be humble as you approach his altar; sitting down, you see, is a mark of humility. So then, *observe shrewdly what is being set before you.* What you are receiving is the very host who has invited you. You have taken your seat at the table of your shepherd; what you find there, you see, is the death of your host.

Those who take their seats at this table know what I am saying; it isn't a trifling matter; the one who invited you is explaining himself to you. So then, *observe shrewdly what is being set before you, and stretch out your hand, knowing that it will be your duty to provide the same sort of food yourself.* What this means I told you a moment ago: *For just as Christ laid down his life for us, so we too ought to lay down our lives for the brethren* (1 Jn 3:16). This is the table of that great man; this is the dinner you have come to, if you have taken your seat in a humble frame of mind; or rather this is the dinner at which you have taken your seat, if you have come in a humble frame of mind. Notice what has been prepared for you: *Christ laid down his life for us.* This is what you are receiving, there you are, that's what you stretch out your hand to, *knowing that it will be your duty to prepare the same sort of food yourself.* So then, say what comes next: *So we too ought to lay down our lives for the brethren.*

So you're receiving the cup of salvation and calling upon the name of the Lord. You have received a precious death, you see; that's why you have drained the cup. What comes next? *Precious in the sight of the Lord is the death of his saints* (Ps 116:15). There you have how you eat such food, how you prepare such food.

Do not claim more credit than you are worth

5. But what's this that follows in the same reading? Let's attend to it and see; let's get to the bottom of it, if we can. *But if you are greedier*, he says, *do not set your heart on his banquets; for these things have a false life* (Prv 23:3). I see; the door's shut. And where's the knocker? Let's all knock together, so that it may be opened to us. He's a great man, it's a great man's table; you're seated at it, you have humbled yourself before it, stretching out your hand, knowing what sort of things it is your duty to prepare: to suffer for the name of the Lord who suffered for you. But *if you are greedier*, he says, *do not set your heart on his banquets.* What's the meaning of *If you are greedier*? Do you really want to know what *If you are greedier* means? If you give yourself more than you eat.

As I knock for all I'm worth in these obscure depths, this is what occurs to me at the moment, what he has been pleased to grant me; this for the moment is what he has opened the door upon. Look, it's a great man's table, it's the table of Christ, loaded with the grace of the Lord's passion. Take your seat at it; don't approach it in pride. *Stretch out your hand*; don't let the tongue hold forth, and the work keep quiet. That, you see, is what stretching out your hand means. Don't let there be words which are not solidly backed by deeds, faith which is not backed by works. *Stretch out your hand, knowing that you must prepare the same sort of things.* What with, you wretched pauper? From your own resources? Woe to you, if that's what you think! You will produce nothing, will have nothing. So, *if you are greedier* — giving yourself more than you are — *do not set your heart on his victuals.* Because if you give yourself more than you eat and still set your heart on his victuals, notice what follows: *for these things have a deceitful life.*

6. *These things,* he says, *have a deceitful life.* What things have a deceitful life? Your being greedier, giving yourself more, attributing more to yourself than you know you are worth, that's the deceitful life, that's hypocrisy, that's boastfulness, not obedience. It's a totally deceitful life. *For whoever thinks he is anything, when he is nothing, is deceiving himself* (Gal 6:3). Will you really pay back such a great man as that from your own means? Taking fare like that from such a great man as that, will you really prepare the same sort of things from your own resources? What loathsome greed, what a deceitful life! Finally, after he says *For these things have a deceitful life,* meaning if you give yourself more than you are, and are greedier in this way, and fail to perceive the grace when you approach the table of grace, notice what he adds, and the kind of advice he gives you. What is it you were saying, after all? "I'll pay back from my own resources, I'll give a return from my own means, I will prepare a meal from my own means, and I will prepare the same sort of meal as this rich man has provided."

Notice what follows: *Do not stretch yourself against the rich man, since you are poor* (Prv 23:4). Advice most salutary, if there's anyone to listen to it, if you hear it as a poor person, if you don't consider yourself rich in what is your own, if you don't stretch yourself against the rich man. By stretching yourself out, you see, you are more likely to be inflated than filled. You're saying all the time, "From what is mine, from what is mine"; against whom are you saying it? *For what do you have that you have not received* (1 Cor 4:7)? He is full, you are just inflated. *Do not stretch yourself against the rich man, since you are poor.* That is the deceitful life; you are remaining in the condition you stated in your panic: *Every man a liar* (Ps 116:11). *Do not stretch yourself against the rich man, since you are poor*; not against God, since you are merely human; not against the Just One, since you are a sinner; not against the one who had no sin, being yourself a human being who cannot live without sin. "*Do not stretch yourself against the rich man, since you are poor; but restrain yourself in your thoughts* (Prv 23:4). Take your own measure; do not go outside yourself and mock me, but enter into yourself and observe the real you."

If you fix your eye on him, he will nowhere appear

7. For *if you fix your eye,* he says, *on him, he will nowhere appear. For he has prepared wings for himself like an eagle's, and he is going away to the house of his*

chief (Prv 23:5). Who is this mighty man, whose table you were approaching, from whom you were receiving a meal and arranging to pay back the same sort of meal, apparently, from your own resources? Yes, you're stretching yourself, a pauper, against a rich man, and not rather restraining yourself in your thoughts, so that he may recognize you as needing assistance, and not find you deserving damnation. Who is this great man, whom you are seeking, it seems, to provide for from your own resources, and to provide for in the same style as he has in fact provided for you? Who is he — do you want to know? *If you fix your eye on him, he will nowhere appear.* What is this? He terrified us when he said, *he will nowhere appear.* But when will he nowhere appear? When you fix your eye on him, this squinting eye, with which you can't see straight, with which you can't understand rightly; if you fix this eye on him, *he will nowhere appear.* He will remain hidden, you see, he won't show himself; you won't grasp him, won't understand him. Acknowledge yourself as being less than he is, in order to be able to understand him as greater than you.

It can also be understood in this way: *If you fix your eye on him,* a human eye, seeking him as a mere man, *he will nowhere appear,* because he is not a mere man. *He will nowhere appear;* seek him in the east, seek him in the west, seek him among the patriarchs, seek him among the prophets, seek him among the apostles, he will nowhere appear to you; he is not, after all, only a man, but the God man. Accordingly, *if you fix your eye on him,* that is, a merely human eye, not the divinely given spirit, *he will nowhere appear.* If you seek him just as a man, you won't find him; if you seek the one who has been providing for you just as a man, you won't find him; *he will nowhere appear.*

8. *For he has prepared wings for himself like an eagle's* (Prv 23:5). Yes, he did this; he prepared himself wings like an eagle's — he was taken up, he flew away, since it was about him that scripture said, *His life shall be taken up from the earth* (Is 53:8). *And he will go away to the house of his chief* (Prv 23:5). He has returned to the Father; you, on the other hand, have remained among men. He, who made you, has gone beyond you. Yes, you don't think much of him, because he was also made, a creature for your sake. If you want to pay him back, accept from him the means to do it with. That's what poor people do, when they receive invitations from their rich patrons, and wish to invite them back in return; they beg from them something they can decently offer them.

The Father begot him equal to himself, begot him coeternal with himself, begot him of one and the same substance as himself; but for your sake he made him less, and became his chief, so that his Son could say about him, his Only-begotten, coeternal with him, equal to him: *The Father is greater than I* (Jn 14:28). What did he beget, do you want to know? Ask him, and listen to the answer: *I and the Father are one* (Jn 10:30). If you want to know what he was made for your sake, ask him, and listen to the answer: *Since the Father is greater than I.* Acknowledge his justice, cherish obedience, beware of pride; praise his power, admire his patience, obtain grace from him.

Appendix

The following information is intended as a brief overview for those interested in a highly condensed summary of the more important manuscripts. The largest collection of sermons was edited by Jacques-Paul Migne (1800-1875) and is found in volumes 38 and 39 (published in 1861) of the Latin section of *Patrologiae cursus completus*, commonly referred to as PL. Two authentic sermons (S. 395 and 396), later identified by the Maurists, are found in volume 46 along with 25 *Sermones* (23 of which are recognized as authentic) identified by Denis in 1792. Frangipane identified a further ten, four of which had previously been identified by the Maurists. Volume 47 of PL contains an overview of the *Sermones Caillu et Saint-Yves*, which resulted in an additional seven sermons being accepted as authentic. A detailed listing of all the significant manuscripts which contain authentic sermons of Augustine is found in Drobner's critical work, *Augustinus von Hippo: Sermones ad Populum*.

The most important manuscript discoveries of the twentieth century include the *Codex Guelferbytani* in 1917, edited by the Benedictine Morin, which brought to light an additional 34 sermons previously unknown; the *Codex Wilmart* (1921-1930), which published 21 new pieces, including one later deemed in-authentic and five which were found in better condition than the earlier Maurist edition; the *Codex Lambot* elaborated by Dom Cyrille Lambot added another 29 sermons, including five better versions than found in the Maurist edition as well as seven fragments. Specific mention should be made here of the important work of Adalbert Hamman, who edited the *Patrologia Latina Supplementum* (1958-1974), resulting in five supplemental volumes containing all of the newly discovered Latin texts and critical editions previously unpublished. The second of these five volumes contains the sermons which Migne had not included in PL 46: Callau et Saint-Yves, *Casinensis*, *Guelferbyanti*, Lambot, Liverani, Mai, Morin and Wilmart.

Pierre-Patrick Verbraken organized all of the previously known fragments of Augustine's preaching which had been lost over the centuries into one edition, providing a detailed analysis of dating and a history of the manuscript tradition. As new discoveries were made and published they were either identified by the scholar's name associated with the discovery (e.g. Sermon Lambot 10) or by the manuscript collection to which they belonged (e.g. Guelferbytanus 1). The present system of numbering the sermons is owed to Verbraken, who decided to incorporate the more recent manuscripts, named either for the discoverer or the collection, into the previous system of numbering adopted by the Maurists, by adding a letter to the number. Thus, Sermon Guelferbytanus 1 is now identified as Sermon 213 while Guelferbytanus 2 is now designated Sermon 218/B.

In summary, to the Maurists' claim of 396 sermons as genuinely authentic must be added an additional 175 sermons or fragments of sermons that scholars have identified as genuinely attributable to Augustine. The most recent discovery of sermons was made by François Dolbeau in 1990, who luckily came across 26 long-lost sermons from a 15th century Carthusian manuscript now preserved at a library in Mainz.[1] By far the most complete and accessible collection in Latin continues to be found in PL or the series *Corpus Christianorum*; the more recent work of Lambot and Verbraken was often published in *Revue Bénédictine*. A convenient table of the collections and the Latin editions is found in Fitzgerald's *Augustine through the Ages,* along with an excellent overview of the Sermons in Augustine's corpus.[2]

1. See François Dolbeau, *Vingt-six sermons au peuple d'Afrique* (Paris: Institut d'Études Augustiniennes, 1996) and the important collection of essays on the significance of the Dolbeau discovery in *Augustin prédicateur* (395-411). Actes du Colloque International de Chantilly (5-7 septembre 1966), édités par Goulven Madec (Paris: Études Augustiniennes, 1998). A convenient summary of the most important findings of this discovery is found in Henry Chadwick, "The New Sermons of St. Augustine," *Journal of Theological Studies* 47 (1996) 69-91.
2. See Éric Rebillard, "Sermones," *Augustine through the Ages: An Encyclopedia*, ed. by Allan D. Fitzgerald (Grand Rapids : William B. Eerdmans Publishing Company, 1999) 773-792.

THE COMPLETE WORKS OF ST. AUGUSTINE
A Translation for the 21st Century

Part I — Books

Autobiographical Works

The Confessions (I/1)
  cloth, 978-1-56548-468-9
  paper, 978-1-56548-445-0
  pocket, 978-1-56548-154-1
  Mobile App for iOS & Android available

Revisions (I/2)
  cloth, 978-1-56548-360-6

Dialogues I (I/3) forthcoming

Dialogues II (I/4) forthcoming.

Philosophical-Dogmatic Works

The Trinity (I/5)
  cloth, 978-1-56548-610-2
  paper, 978-1-56548-446-7

The City of God 1-10 (I/6)
  cloth, 978-1-56548-454-2
  paper, 978-1-56548-455-9

The City of God 11-22 (I/7)
  cloth, 978-1-56548-479-5
  paper, 978-1-56548-481-8

On Christian Belief
  cloth, 978-1-56548-233-3
  paper, 978-1-56548-234-0

Pastoral Works

Marriage and Virginity (I/9)
  cloth, 978-1-56548-104-6
  paper, 978-1-56548-222-7

Morality and Christian Asceticism (I/10)
  forthcoming

Exegetical Works

Teaching Christianity (I/11) (On Christian
  Doctrine)
  cloth, 978-1-56548-048-3
  paper, 978-1-56548-049-0

Responses to Miscellaneous Questions
  (I/12)
  cloth, 978-1-56548-277-7

On Genesis (I/13)
  cloth, 978-1-56548-175-6
  paper, 978-1-56548-201-2

The Old Testament (I/14) forthcoming.

New Testament I and II (I/15 and I/16)
  cloth, 978-1-56548-529-7
  paper, 978-1-56548-531-0

The New Testament III (I/17) forthcoming

Polemical Works

Arianism and Other Heresies (I/18)
  cloth, 978-1-56548-038-4

Manichean Debate (I/19)
  cloth, 978-1-56548-247-0

Answer to Faustus, a Manichean (I/20)
  cloth, 978-1-56548-264-7

Donatist Controversy I (I/21) forthcoming

Donatist Controversy II (I/22) forthcoming

Answer to the Pelagians (I/23)
  cloth, 978-1-56548-092-6

Answer to the Pelagians (I/24)
  cloth, 978-1-56548-107-7

Answer To The Pelagians (I/25)
  cloth, 978-1-56548-129-9

Answer to the Pelagians (I/26)
  cloth, 978-1-56548-136-7

Part II — Letters

Letters 1-99 (II/1)
  cloth, 978-1-56548-163-3

Letters 100-155 (II/2)
  cloth, 978-1-56548-186-2

Letters 156-210 (II/3)
  cloth, 978-1-56548-200-5

Letters 211-270 (II/4)
  cloth, 978-1-56548-209-8

Part III — Homilies

Sermons 1-19 (III/1)
  cloth, 978-0-911782-75-2

Sermons 20-50 (III/2)
  cloth, 978-0-911782-78-3

Sermons 51-94 (III/3)
  cloth, 978-0-911782-85-1

Sermons 94A-150 (III/4)
  cloth, 978-1-56548-000-1

Sermons 151-183 (III/5)
  cloth, 978-1-56548-007-0

Sermons 184-229 (III/6)
cloth, 978-1-56548-050-6

Sermons 230-272 (III/7)
cloth, 978-1-56548-059-9

Sermons 273-305A (III/8)
cloth, 978-1-56548-060-5

Sermons 306-340A (III/9)
cloth, 978-1-56548-068-1

Sermons 341-400 (III/10)
cloth, 978-1-56548-028-5

Sermons Newly Discovered Since 1990
(III/11)
cloth, 978-1-56548-103-9

Homilies on the Gospel of John 1-40
(III/12)
cloth, 978-1-56548-319-4
paper, 978-1-56548-318-7

Homilies on the Gospel of John (41-124)
(III/13) forthcoming

Homilies on the First Letter of John (III/14)
cloth, 978-1-56548-288-3
paper, 978-1-56548-289-0

Expositions of the Psalms 1-32 (III/15)
cloth, 978-1-56548-126-8
paper, 978-1-56548-140-4

Expositions of the Psalms 33-50 (III/16)
cloth, 978-1-56548-147-3
paper, 978-1-56548-146-6

Expositions of the Psalms 51-72 (III/17)
cloth, 978-1-56548-156-5
paper, 978-1-56548-155-8

Expositions of the Psalms 73-98 (III/18)
cloth, 978-1-56548-167-1
paper, 978-1-56548-166-4

Expositions of the Psalms 99-120 (III/19)
cloth, 978-1-56548-197-8
paper, 978-1-56548-196-1

Expositions of the Psalms 121-150 (III/20)
cloth, 978-1-56548-211-1
paper, 978-1-56548-210-4

Essential Texts Created for Classroom Use

Augustine Catechism: Enchiridion on
Faith Hope and Love
paper, 978-1-56548-298-2

Essential Expositions of the Psalms
paper, 978-1-56548-510-5

Essential Sermons
paper, 978-1-56548-276-0

Instructing Beginners in Faith
paper, 978-1-56548-239-5

Monastic Rules
paper, 978-1-56548-130-5

Prayers from The Confessions
paper, 978-1-56548-188-6

Selected Writings on Grace and
Pelagianism
paper, 978-1-56548-372-9

Soliloquies: Augustine's Inner Dialogue
paper, 978-1-56548-142-8

Trilogy on Faith and Happiness
paper, 978-1-56548-359-0

E-books Available

Essential Sermons, Homilies on the First Letter of John, Revisions,
The Confessions, Trilogy on Faith and Happiness, The Trinity,
The Augustine Catechism: The Enchiridion on Faith, Hope and Love.

Custom Syllabus

Universities that wish to create a resource that matches their specific needs using selections from any of the above titles should contact New City Press.

Free Index

A free PDF containing all of the **Indexes** from The Works of Saint Augustine, A Translation for the 21st Century published by NCP is available for download at www.newcitypress.com.

New City Press — The Works of Saint Augustine Catalog

For a complete interactive catalog of The Works of Saint Augustine, A Translation for the 21st Century go to New City Press website at: www.newcitypress.com

Electronic Editions

InteLex Corporation's Past Masters series encompasses the largest collection of full-text electronic editions in philosophy in the world. The Past Masters series, which includes *The Works of Saint Augustine, A Translation for the 21st Century*, published by New City Press, supports scholarly research around the world and is now being utilized at numerous research libraries and academic institutions. The Works of Saint Augustine (Fourth release), full-text electronic edition, is available for subscription from InteLex. The Fourth release includes all 41 of the published volumes as of May 2016. For more information, visit: http://www.nlx.com/home.

About the Augustinian Heritage Institute

In 1990, the Augustinian Heritage Institute was founded by John E. Rotelle, OSA to oversee the English translation of *The Works of Saint Augustine, A Translation for the 21st Century*. This project was started in conjunction with New City Press. At that time, English was the only major Western language into which the Works of Saint Augustine in their entirety had not yet been attempted. Existing translations were often archaic or faulty and the scholarship was outdated. These new translations offer detailed introductions, extensive critical notes, both a general index and scriptural index for each work as well as the best translations in the world.

The Works of Saint Augustine, A Translation for the 21st Century in its complete form will be published in 49 volumes. To date, 41 volumes have been published.

NEW CITY PRESS
of the Focolare

About New City Press of the Focolare

New City Press is one of more than 20 publishing houses sponsored by the Focolare, a movement founded by Chiara Lubich to help bring about the realization of Jesus' prayer: "That all may be one" (John 17:21). In view of that goal, New City Press publishes books and resources that enrich the lives of people and help all to strive toward the unity of the entire human family. We are a member of the Association of Catholic Publishers.

Free Index to *The Works of Saint Augustine*

Download a PDF file that provides the ability to search all of the available indexes from each volume published by New City Press.

Visit http://www.newcitypress.com/index-to-the-works-of-saint-augustine-a-translation-for-the-21st-century.html for more details.